THE GREEN TO GOLD BUSINESS PLAYBOOK

HOW TO IMPLEMENT SUSTAINABILITY PRACTICES FOR BOTTOM-LINE RESULTS IN EVERY BUSINESS FUNCTION

DANIEL C. ESTY
P. J. SIMMONS

WILEY

John Wiley & Sons, Inc.

Published by John Wiley & Sons, Inc., Hoboken, New Jersey.
Published simultaneously in Canada.

For general information on our other products and services or for technical support, please contact our Customer Care Department within the United States at (800) 762-2974, outside the United States at (317) 572-3993 or fax (317) 572-4002.

Wiley also publishes its books in a variety of electronic formats. Some content that appears in print may not be available in electronic books. For more information about Wiley products, visit our web site at www.wiley.com.

Library of Congress Cataloging-in-Publication Data:

Esty, Daniel, 1959–
   The green to gold business playbook : how to implement sustainability practices for bottom-line results in every business function / Daniel Esty, P.J. Simmons.
      p. cm.
   Includes index.
   ISBN 978-0-470-59075-1(cloth);   ISBN 978-1-118-01072-3 (ebk);
ISBN 978-1-118-01088-4 (ebk);   ISBN 978-1-118-01089-1 (ebk)
   1. Industrial management—Environmental aspects.   2. Corporations—Environmental aspects.   3. Business enterprises—Environmental aspects.   I. Simmons, P. J., 1967–   II. Title.
   HD30.255.E883 2011
   658.4′083—dc   222010042187

Printed in the United States of America.

10 9 8 7 6 5 4 3 2 1

To our parents

John and Katharine Esty

Patrica Bonin and E. Joseph Simmons, Jr.

Contents

Preface

When we set out to write *Green to Gold: How Smart Companies Use Environmental Strategy to Innovate, Create Value, and Build Competitive Advantage*, very few people in the business world were focused on environmental issues or broader sustainability concerns as a core element of strategy. But in the intervening years, in part spurred on by *Green to Gold*, many business leaders have come to recognize the importance of climate change, water, air pollution, waste management, land use, chemical exposures, food safety, and other environmental issues to marketplace success. Companies face evolving regulatory requirements, natural resource scarcities, shifting consumer expectations, rising demands from business customers who are "greening" their supply chains, and other sustainability pressures that shape the nature of competition.

Interest in green business has expanded considerably. Top executives in almost every large corporation now recognize that the environment and sustainability issues must be part of their business strategies. Leaders of mid-sized and even small companies increasingly find value in applying an environmental lens to their business activities. The number of entrepreneurs launching companies designed to sell environmental goods and services or traditional products with an environmental twist has expanded exponentially. Almost every city now offers green dry cleaners, green lawn care services, green printers, and green versions of many other day-to-day products and services.

Of course, interest in the environment generally and a focus on bringing green thinking into the business domain does not proceed in a linear fashion. Over the last several years, the significant worldwide economic downturn has caused some companies to pull back on their sustainability focus—and inspired Andrew to write *Green Recovery* (Harvard Business Press, 2009), which reformulated the green business case for tight times.

We were not surprised by this flow following the ebb of the green tide. But we were impressed by how many companies maintained, or even accelerated, their commitment to going green through the downturn, and how many others quickly reestablished sustainability as a priority as the recovery kicked in. The sustained interest in corporate environmental strategy should not, however, have come as a surprise. Eco-efficiency—the use of an environmental lens to look for opportunities to eliminate waste and inefficiency—has special value in a downturn. Lower energy consumption, reduced scrap, and more efficient use of every input in a production process cuts costs, and those savings drop straight to the bottom line.

Environmental activities are also a popular way to maintain employee morale during difficult times. Companies in many sectors and countries are ramping up their sustainability activities as a way to demonstrate to their workforce a commitment to corporate social responsibility and to being an attractive employer over the long term—even as layoffs and other cuts occur.

The quick reemergence of the environment and sustainability as central corporate strategy agenda items does not mean that interest in the environment and the societal commitment to respond to these challenges has been strengthened across all issues and in all places. Quite to the contrary, the United States seems to have broken down in its ability to address climate change in a thoughtful and serious manner. Moreover, significant uncertainties remain about the best path forward with regard to chemical exposures, waste, packaging, and many other concerns. And companies find themselves facing new challenges, evolving science, and changing public perceptions about what needs to be addressed and how.

The Green to Gold Business Playbook, which Dan wrote with P.J. Simmons, seeks to respond to these questions, building on the foundation laid in the original *Green to Gold*. This new book offers clear and pragmatic guidance on how to bring sustainability into each and every business function in a manner that delivers tangible results. *Green to Gold* reached many more people than we could ever have dreamed of, but many of the executives that have used it as a strategic template have asked us how to drive that kind of thinking into all aspects of the company. We are pleased to see the work that we started going in so many directions. We hope this new book will serve as a worthy companion to and extension of the strategies and tools we've already offered.

Dan Esty
New Haven, CT

Andrew Winston
Greenwich, CT

February 2011

Acknowledgments

Two names appear on the cover of this book as authors, but in fact, hundreds of people have contributed to its content. We are grateful for the ideas put forward by sustainability experts across the world, including the dozens of people whose stories are told in these pages. Indeed, *The Green to Gold Business Playbook* offers a distillation of best practices from many companies and individuals in corporations large and small who have been doing the hard work of bringing an environmental focus or a broader sustainability lens to their day-to-day operations—and in doing so, have helped clarify what works and what doesn't in the push to deliver "green to gold" results.

The *Playbook* builds on Dan Esty and Andrew Winston's pathbreaking book, *Green to Gold: How Smart Companies Use Environmental Strategy to Innovate, Create Value, and Build Competitive Advantage.* Thus, a great debt of gratitude goes to Andrew Winston whose many contributions to the original book provided the platform on which this volume is constructed. As a professor, it is a great joy to see a former student's career take off from the academic launch pad, and Dan therefore takes great pride in Andrew's emergence as a leading voice in the push to make sustainability a core element of business strategy.

We are also grateful for the important role played by Peter Price-Thomas, who led the research team during the project's first year. Peter's thinking about how best to present the green to gold story to a broad-based audience—building on his cutting-edge work with The Natural Step across Europe—helped shape the book in significant ways. We thank him (and his wife Annalise) for numerous contributions to the *Playbook*.

Clara Fang's role in the *Playbook*, beginning during her days as student at the Yale School of Forestry and Environmental Studies but continuing beyond, was both broad and deep. Her thoughts and ideas helped to shape every chapter. From chasing down important materials to drafting sections of the book, she played a critical role in pulling the final manuscript together. Clara is on her way to being a leading light in the field of sustainability, and we are deeply appreciative of all she did as a key part of our research team.

The intellectual content found in the *Playbook* draws from a great many sources above and beyond *Green to Gold*. A significant number of the frameworks and other analytic tools came out of the work of Esty Environmental Partners (EEP) (www.EstyEP.com), the sustainability strategy consulting firm that Dan launched in the wake of the considerable marketplace interest in *Green to Gold* and its introduction of the concept of Eco-Advantage. Dan's partners at EEP—George Favaloro, Amy Longsworth, and David Lubin—have made contributions both individually and collectively to substantial aspects of the content in this book. The rest of the EEP team, including Alicia Chin, Hannah Doran, Zeke Hart, Britt Harter, Sandra Lauterbach, John Masland, Lauren Sinatra, and Yamama Raza have all helped to refine the intellectual content and battle-test the frameworks and strategies that make this book an indispensible guide for anyone working on pollution control and natural resource management issues in a corporate setting.

The essence of the *Playbook* is its grounding in real-world business practice. Indeed, the seasoned executives at the companies with which EEP has worked and that comprise the Corporate Eco-Forum, which P.J. Simmons chairs, were an important source of inspiration for the ideas in this book and provided many of the case examples. We owe an enormous debt to this group for their commitment to sharing lessons learned and accelerating the spread of corporate sustainability best practices. In particular, we wish to thank the executive teams at: 3M, Abbott Laboratories, Alcoa, American Eagle, ArcelorMittal, AT&T, Aviva, Avon, Bayer, Bissell, BP, BT Group, Catterton Partners, Chevron, Clorox, Coca-Cola Enterprises, The Coca-Cola Company, Darden Restaurants, Dell, Delhaize Group, Deloitte, Deutsche Bank, Dimensional Fund Advisors, Disney, Dow, Duke Energy, Eastman Kodak, Ecolab, E.&J. Gallo, Ernst & Young, FedEx, Fidelity Investments, Ford Motor, Gamesa, General Electric, Hanesbrands, Hannaford, Harrah's Entertainment, Hewlett-Packard, IBM, Intuit, IKEA, Jones Apparel Group, Jones Lang LaSalle, Kaiser Permanente, Kimberly Clark, KPMG, LANXESS, Levi Strauss, Live Earth, Lockheed Martin, McKesson, Microsoft, Motorola, Naya Waters, Nestle Waters North America, NetJets, News Corp., NextEra Energy, Nokia, Northrop Grumman, Oracle, Peabody Energy, PG&E, Philips Electronics, Procter & Gamble, Sabre, Sanmina-SCI, SAP, S.C. Johnson, Scotts Miracle-Gro, Shaklee, Sony, Spectra Energy, Sprint Nextel, State Farm Insurance, SunGard, Swiss Re, Sybase, Symantec, Tata Consultancy Services, TechTurn, Tiffany & Co., Timex, TPG Capital, Transocean, U.S. Postal Service, United Launch Alliance, United Technologies, Veolia Water, Verizon, Walmart, Warner Bros. Entertainment Inc., Waste Management, Wells Fargo, Weyerhaeuser, Xerox, and Yahoo!.

We wish to extend special thanks to the individual leaders who have been particularly generous with their time and insights—either through the Corporate Eco Forum, EEP's Sustainability Innovators Working Group, or both: Kevin

Kramer and Jackie O'Brien at Alcoa, Jason Schmitt at ArcelorMittal, Toby Red-shaw at Aviva, Mary Armstrong at Boeing, J.P. Rangaswami at BT Group, Nancy Tuor and Joe Danko at CH2M HILL, Jeff Seabright, Ben Jordan, and Lisa Manley at The Coca-Cola Company, Megan Hellstedt at Delhaize, Jeff Baer and Andrew Stokes at Deutsche Bank, Beth Stevens and Aaron Frank at Disney, John Matthews and Moe Bechard at Diversey, Neil Hawkins and Anne Wallin at Dow, Roberta Bowman, Michelle Abbott, and Jenny Ward at Duke Energy, Rob Carter and Mitch Jackson at FedEx, Sue Cischke and John Viera at Ford Motor Company, Ann Klee and Kate Brass at GE, Jim Miller at Google, Wayne Balta and Jackie Jasiota at IBM, Paulette Frank at Johnson & Johnson, Lau-ralee Martin and Michael Jordan at Jones Lang LaSalle, Len Sauers at Procter & Gamble, Rob Bernard and Tony Scott at Microsoft, Jil Zilligen at Shaklee, Gavin Neath and Karen Hamilton at Unilever, Matt Kistler, Beth Keck, and Shannon Frederick at Walmart, and Patty Calkins at Xerox.

Much of the supporting research for this volume was done at Yale University, and Dan is grateful for the help provided by the University and a number of its leaders including President Richard Levin, and Deans Peter Crane, Harold Koh, Robert Post, and Gus Speth. For more than a decade, Dan's team at the Yale Cen-ter for Environmental Law and Policy (YCELP) (www.yale.edu/envirocenter) has played a key role in advancing thinking on the corporate sustainability agenda. Special thanks in this regard go to Ysella Edyvean, who managed the *Playbook* research project with great skill and energy over multiple years and many ups and downs. Thanks as well as to Bill Dornbos, Christine Kim, Rachel Easton, Susanne Stahl, and a long list of YCELP research assistants who have played roles in gathering the facts, building the case studies, and supporting the ef-fort to produce this book including Luke Bassett, Bryant Cannon, Anuj Desai, Patricia Devlin, Mary Fischer, Erin Burns Gill, George Haddad, David Henry, Maisah Khan, Ainsley Lloyd, Dustin Meyer, Anthony Moffa, Ian Sprague, Kristin Tracz, Dylan Walsh, and especially James Zhang, who was instrumental in helping us produce the buildings and facilities chapter.

Additional research and support for this book came from the Center for Busi-ness and the Environment at Yale (www.yale.edu/CBEY). The CBEY research team, led by Bryan Garcia and supported by Amy Badner, contributed signif-icantly to the ideas and case studies that unfold in the pages that follow and thanks go to Jesse Burkhardt, Raman Jha, Shazan Jiwa, Priyanka Juneja, and Igor Lukashov. Two research assistants in particular, Brent Peich and Kari Twaite, made heroic contributions. Brent worked with us tirelessly and cheerfully for over a year, adeptly handling every project tossed his way, and was pivotal in shaping the information technology chapter. Kari, too, made many outstanding contribu-tions, especially in the areas of impact assessment and supply chain management.

In recognizing that nothing concentrates the mind like having to teach a sub-ject, Dan would additionally like to thank all of the students who have taken his course, Environmental Management and Strategic Advantage, over the past decade at INSEAD as well as Yale. And special thanks go to Steve Ramsey who has co-taught this course with Dan for a number of years. Steve's perspective on the corporate sustainability challenges and opportunities—building on his career in the corporate sustainability realm, including 17 years as vice president for environment, health, and safety at General Electric—helped shape the flow of this book in numerous ways. The teaching assistants for the Esty-Ramsey course also provided insights, suggestions, and case studies that helped to clarify the critical concepts, frameworks, and strategies discussed in this book. Thanks in this regard go to Audrey Davenport, Stuart DeCew, Cat Manzo, and Anna Palazij.

The intellectual platform on which the *Playbook* stands owes its existence to a further set of academic colleagues. Professor Michael Porter at Harvard Business School, in particular, has been a source of inspiration and support for more than two decades. His competitiveness-based strategy model is foundational to the Eco-Advantage framework around which this book is built. The late C.K. Prahalad, one of the world's greatest management thinkers and a founding advisor to the Corporate Eco Forum, also leaves an extraordinary legacy of intellectual achievement on which we have tried to build—including his observation in 2009 that sustainability is becoming the "key driver of innovation."

Other scholars working on the corporate sustainability challenge whose ideas have contributed to the *Playbook* include: Tima Bansal, Lori Bennear, Marc Epstein, Tom Gladwin, Neil Gunningham, Stuart Hart, Andy Hoffman, Andy King, Mike Lennox, Tom Lyon, John Maxwell, David Orr, Eric Orts, Aseem Prakash, Forest Reinhardt, Rob Repetto, Ulrich Steger, Mike Toffel, and David Vogel.

The need to bring an environmental focus to the business world has been slow to develop but has now taken on great momentum due to the contributions of many other writers working in the environmental realm. In particular, we would like to thank: Ray Anderson, Alan AtKisson, Wendell Berry, Bill Blackburn, Craig Canine, Gregg Easterbrook, John Elkington, Chris Flavin, Hilary French, Gil Friend, Paul Hawken, Matthew Kiernan, Cary Krosinksy, Fred Krupp, Jonathan Lash, Amory Lovins, Hunter Lovins, Joel Makower, Bill McDonough, Bill McKibben, Ron Pernick, Carl Safina, Andy Savitz, Auden Schendler, Stephan Schmidheiny, Adam Werbach, Clint Wilder, and Pieter Winsemius. In addition, a number of journalists have shaped our thinking and helped to broaden understanding about how the environment and sustainability fold into corporate strategy, including: Natalie Angier, Jeff Ball, Felicity Barringer, Keith Bradsher, Frances Cairncross, Roger Cohn, Marla Cone, Tim Egan, Juliet Eilperin, Mark Gunther, Fiona Harvey, James Kantor, Verlyn Klinkenborg, Tom Knudson, Betsy Kolbert, Fred Pearce, Michael Pollan, David Quammen, Andy Revkin, Libby Rosenthal, Kit Seelye, Keith Schneider, Phil Shabecoff, Vijay Vaitheeswaran, Bryan Walsh, Mike Weiscoff, Ted Williams, and Carl Zimmer.

We also wish to thank several colleagues who have helped us over the years to refine our thinking and sharpen our understanding of the theory and practice of sustainability. Dan wishes to thank Paul Anastas, Mark Ashton, Gordon Binder, Ben Cashore, Marianne Chertow, Lisa Curran, Don Elliott, Bill Ellis, Landis Gabel, Brad Gentry, Tom Graedel, Hank Habicht, Ethan Kapstein, Matt Kotchen, Doug Kysar, Reid Lifset, Rob Mendelsohn, Dick Morgenstern, Bill Nordhaus, Bill Reilly, Carol Rose, and Anastasia O'Rourke. P.J. thanks Jessica Bailey, Boris Chen, Aimée Christensen, Kate Cook, Geoffrey Dabelko, Renaud des Rosiers, Tim Griffin, Ben Grant, Catherine Greener, Jeff Hittner, Heather Hurlburt, Priscilla Lewis, Michael Northrop, M.R. Rangaswami, Sonal Shah, Rachel Silverstein, Michael Terrell, David Sandalow, and Madhavan Vasudevan.

We have also received assistance in many forms from our publisher, John Wiley & Sons. We are especially grateful for the unswerving support and sage guidance of our editor Richard Narramore, editorial assistant Lydia Dimitriadis, and Production Manager Maureen Drexel.

No book of this kind could be produced without funding to support the research and writing. We are deeply grateful to Buddy Fletcher and the Fletcher Foundation, the GE Foundation, André Heinz and the Heinz Family Foundation, Jesse Johnson and the Johnson Family Foundation. Special appreciation also goes to Jesse and Betsy Fink whose support for the outreach effort for *Green to Gold*— produced a good bit of the material for *The Green to Gold Business Playbook*.

Special thanks to Marge Camera at the Yale Law School without whose help this book would never have come into being. And a particular note of appreciation to Joe Colonnese who helped Dan move from one project to the next over many years—and has just retired.

Deep gratitude also goes to our families and friends who put up with the long nights and weekends consumed by this project. Dan thanks his wife Elizabeth and children Sarah, Thomas, and Jonathan. P.J. owes the biggest thanks to Noah Aberlin, who has been his rock. Noah provided much-needed daily doses of encouragement, patience, perspective, kindness, and humor, and was a constant inspiration. P.J. is also grateful for the unswerving support of Robert and Mary Beth Aberlin, Kathryn Aberlin, Bruce Barney, Doug Bell and Danielle Briggs, Anisa Costa, Janelle Kellman, Laurie Kohn and Chris Murphy, Aidan and Caleb Kohn-Murphy, David Laudati, Priscilla Lewis, Christian Marsh and Amanda Monchamp, Dane Nichols, Jove Oliver, Biliana Pehlivanova, Jennifer Prediger, Juliet Sampson and Simon Mays-Smith, Marylene Smeets, Barbara and Ben Simmons, Miaoruo Simmons, and Stephen Thirolle. And P.J. is indebted to the following mentors, whose influence has been greater than they will ever know: Steve Dennis, John Harper, Stephen Heintz, Vida Johnson, Thomas E. Lovejoy, Walter Lubelczyk, Jessica T. Mathews, David Maxwell, M.R. Rangaswami, William K. Reilly, David Sandalow, E. Joseph Simmons Jr., and Sarah M. Terry.

Finally, we would like to thank our readers in advance. *The Green to Gold Business Playbook* is intended to be not simply a guide to corporate sustainability but also a constantly updated and refined resource for the thousands of companies and individuals working to build a sustainability focus into all corners of the corporate domain. We are committed to supporting their efforts with a website that provides a platform for keeping the material introduced here refreshed. So we invite you to make suggestions, provide feedback, and introduce your best practices at www.greentogoldplaybook.com.

Part One Introduction

Chapter 1 Why Every Business Needs an Eco-Strategy

CEO Jack Welch of General Electric (GE) seemingly could do no wrong in the 1990s. Named *Fortune* magazine's "Manager of the Century" in 1999, he presided over a company whose market value grew from $14 billion to over $400 billion in 20 years. While Welch pushed the company to manage environmental issues more rigorously, he didn't make everyone's Christmas card list. Critics saw GE as an environmental bad actor based on Welch's endless battles with the Environmental Protection Agency over whether and how to clean up the dioxin and other pollutants GE factories had dumped in the Hudson and Housatonic rivers decades earlier.

Welch's take-no-prisoners approach to the EPA left the company in a difficult strategic position. Regulators watched the company like hawks. Political leaders shied away from being seen as too friendly with the company. The GE human resources group began to notice that top recruits turned them down, citing doubts about the company's core values. Pitched legal battles cost the company tens of millions of dollars.

When Jeff Immelt took over as CEO of GE in 2001, he reversed course, working to make GE a world leader on corporate environmental matters. Today, many corporate sustainability experts cite GE's environmental management system as a model. The company's "digital cockpit" of performance metrics—scalable from a particular production line in a single factory to the entire company—wins praise for being top of the line. GE executives no longer see the environment as a burden with regulations to follow, costs to manage, and risks to mitigate. Indeed, they see environmental issues as opportunities for competitive advantage and marketplace success. As Immelt likes to say: "Green is green."

Jeff Immelt knows what he is talking about. Under his leadership, GE's "ecomagination" line of products and services has blossomed. With high-efficiency jet engines and locomotives, wind turbines, water purification technologies, solar power systems, and other clean energy equipment, GE has become a world-leading "environmental solutions" provider. Immelt's push to meet the government, business-to-business, and consumer demand for "green" does not mean that he is secretly a member of the Sierra Club or otherwise an "environmentalist."

No, his logic is pure business. Immelt sees the high-growth, high-margin eco-magination line as fundamental to GE's future ability to deliver value to its shareholders.[1] And while parts of the company have struggled in recent years, GE now earns over $20 billion per year from its ecomagination products and services with better than 20 percent annual growth in these lines of business.

REIMAGINING A BUSINESS THROUGH A GREEN LENS

GE's ecomagination success comes from the fact that it looks at environmental challenges through the eyes of the customer. All across the world, pollution control, energy efficiency, and careful stewardship of natural resources have become critical agenda items. Thus, GE's pitch of cutting-edge, efficiency-minded, less-polluting products grabs the customer's attention. The GEnx aircraft engine, for example, burns 15 percent less fuel, emits 30 percent less nitrous oxide, runs 30 percent quieter, and costs less to maintain than the prior generation of engines.[2] For an airline, replacing older jet engines with the GEnx model can mean fuel cost savings that run to the tens of millions of dollars.

GE's environmental commitment continues to grow with more than 80 product lines now bearing the ecomagination brand, up from 17 in 2005. And the company spends $1.5 billion each year on research and development aimed at generating additional eco-friendly technologies and services.[3]

You don't have to be a corporate giant to uncover the competitive differentiation that derives from bringing sustainability into strategy—what Dan Esty and Andrew Winston dubbed "Eco-Advantage" in *Green to Gold: How Smart Companies Use Environmental Strategy to Innovate, Create Value, and Build Competitive Advantage.* Smaller companies can also benefit from going green. Take Curtis Packaging Corporation, a 165-year-old Connecticut-based company with 188 employees that produces folding cardboard cartons for products such as cosmetics, pharmaceuticals, gourmet foods, and golf balls. In 2003, CEO Don Droppo decided to put sustainability at the heart of the company's business strategy. Rebranding itself as "luxuriously responsible," the company switched to renewable energy, reduced waste and emissions, and incorporated eco-friendly materials into its products. By 2007, annual sales had doubled to $47 million.[4] The Curtis management team attributes the gains to improved product quality and environmental goodwill, which secured customer loyalty and brought in new business partners.

The GE and Curtis Packaging stories are part of a much bigger drama playing out across the country and the world. Interest in environmental protection and sustainability is growing. In fact, sustainability has emerged as a business megatrend that promises to shift the foundations of competition in every industry in every marketplace. This Green Wave presents significant challenges for companies but also offers real opportunities for those who learn to ride it.

So let's be clear, you don't have to be an environmentalist to find this book valuable. *The Green to Gold Business Playbook* will be especially useful to those who are skeptical about the push to address climate change, perhaps see environmental fears as exaggerated, and don't share the enthusiasm for all things green. Our goal is not to get you to join Greenpeace. Rather, it is to position you to be a winner in a world where environmental factors shape competition and determine marketplace success.

WHAT DO WE MEAN BY SUSTAINABILITY?

"Sustainability" has a variety of meanings depending on the context. In the corporate realm, the term is often used to refer to a "triple bottom line" approach to business through which companies seek to deliver not just profits and solid economic results but also good performance from an environmental and social perspective. The environmental dimension of sustainability generally refers to the ability of a company to do business in a fashion that minimizes pollution and reflects careful management of natural resources. The social sustainability agenda encompasses a range of issues including labor conditions, diversity, workforce compensation, training, among others.

While in this book we generally focus on "environmental sustainability," we don't mean to underestimate the social dimension. On the contrary, an emphasis on people is critical to many companies' long-term success. In fact, much of the emphasis on the environment is a function of wanting to protect people—their health, economic opportunity, and development.

To be truly "sustainable," a company would have to eliminate all waste and emissions and only consume materials derived from renewable resources that were managed in a fashion that does not deplete the resource stock. Few companies are even close to this vision of true sustainability. The practical goal must therefore be to strive for *greater* sustainability while seeking to decouple business success from environmental impact.

How to Create Eco-Advantage

GE and Curtis Packaging didn't stumble into profits with their environmental efforts. They systematically pursued Eco-Advantage and the four strategic values identified in *Green to Gold*. Specifically, they looked to:

1. Identify and reduce environmental and regulatory risks, not only within their own operations but across their entire value chains, thereby reducing liabilities, avoiding costs, and increasing speed to market.
2. Cut operational costs and improve efficiency by reducing environmental expenses, including scrap, waste, disposal fees, regulatory paperwork, and energy spending.

3. Grow their revenues by designing and marketing environmentally superior products that meet their customers' needs for energy efficiency, improved resource productivity, and reduced pollution.

4. Create intangible value for their businesses by enhancing their brands, connecting with customers on an emotional level through environmental stewardship, raising workforce productivity, and attracting and retaining the best employees.

Let's examine each of these core elements of Eco-Advantage in a bit more detail.

Mitigating Risks

For many companies, the most immediate environmental challenges involve how to manage pollution and waste. For those who handle oil, heavy metals, or toxic chemicals, even a little mistake can lead to big problems in the form of costly accidents, legal liabilities, product recalls, regulatory violations, and government penalties. Inadequate risk management can lead to more than just higher costs. It can bring an abrupt end to an executive's career. Just ask Tony Hayward, ex-CEO of BP, who lost his job over the 2010 Gulf of Mexico oil spill.

Every business faces some eco-risks as a part of broader enterprise risks. Properly managed, this exposure need not present any real threat to the business. But if mismanaged or missed altogether, eco-risks can take a business down. Robert Eckert, the CEO of Mattel knows this reality all too well. In 2007, one of Mattel's suppliers in China was found to have painted its toys with lead paint in violation of U.S. law. The uproar that followed became a PR disaster for Mattel and a model of what happens when eco-risks are mismanaged.

The fact that the supplier had violated Mattel's explicit procurement guidelines offered no protection from the media and public onslaught. The company's reputation for quality, built up over generations, took a terrible battering. At the end of the day, Mattel had to recall over 21 million items—including Barbie dolls, Polly Pockets, and Fisher Price infant toys—at the cost of hundreds of millions of dollars. The CEO faced a congressional inquiry, Mattel stock fell over 20 percent in three months, and the company ended up paying a $2.3 million fine.[5]

If the Mattel story were unusual, we would not put so much stress on sound eco-risk management. But it is not. In recent years, stories of eco-risk management gone awry have become a staple of the media diet. Contaminated peanut butter, milk, chocolate, dog food, toothpaste, bottled water, eggs, chicken, spinach, and cough syrup have all hit the headlines. So in the chapters that follow, we'll show you how to look at your business through an environmental lens so as to reduce risk exposure and liability—which translate into cost. We'll walk through a number of strategies for digging out eco-risks, particularly in extended supply chains. This focus is especially important for big companies with consumer-facing brands who suffer the consequences and reputational loss if their suppliers misbehave. Simply put, we live in a world of "extended producer responsibility," meaning that companies can expect to be held accountable for anything that goes wrong anywhere in their value chain—from the extraction of raw materials to the end-of-life disposal of their products by their customers (or even their customers' customers).

ENVIRONMENT AS A STRATEGIC IMPERATIVE

At **Coca-Cola**, sustainability issues present clear challenges to business continuity—especially when it comes to water. As the company's top sustainability officer Jeff Seabright told us: "For us, water is essential—and a resource under growing stress around the world. Without healthy watersheds, we do not have a sustainable business."[6] The company is feeling increasing pressure in this regard all over the world—in Latin America, Asia, and Africa, where watersheds are under stress from poor management, overexploitation, deforestation, and climate change. Even in the company's home state of Georgia, a drought led to cutbacks in production for a number of months in 2009. With clarity about water as a strategic imperative, the company isn't trying to just manage its water use, but seeks to address the underlying problems as well: climate change, deforestation, and community-scale water needs.

The risks that need to be managed come in all sorts of shapes and sizes. Spills of toxic materials in the workplace, liability for improper disposal of hazardous waste, and exposure related to a product that later turns out to be environmentally harmful—they all need to be carefully managed. But less obvious risks also need to be addressed: Could regulatory changes disadvantage your company's products or service relative to the competition? Is the burden of paperwork related to chemicals in your production process adding costs that your competition does not bear? Will growing scarcity of a critical natural resource used as an input to one of your products make it much more costly to produce? Or limit the markets in which you can operate? Could shifting consumer tastes translate into reduced demand for your products? Or even expose you to activist boycotts?

Effective environmental risk management spots the full spectrum of possible threats to the business and maps out what sorts of liabilities might emerge. The best risk management systems look at scenarios and probabilities related to potential threats. And they explore exposure not just within the company's own operations but also upstream (across the supply chain) and downstream (involving a customer's use of the product).

EVEN HONEST MISTAKES CAN BE COSTLY

Known for its caffeinated beverage products, **Red Bull** came under fire in July 2009 for lax oversight of its recycling operations. It emerged that the company had not complied with its legal obligations for waste management in the UK for over eight years! The result: $450,000 in fines and a big PR black eye. Although an honest mistake, Red Bull paid dearly for its compliance failure.[7]

Cutting Costs

For many businesses, cutting costs is an ongoing imperative. Adding a sustainability focus to your corporate strategy can bring to light numerous ways to cut waste and inefficiency. Indeed, we've seen endless examples of companies that have achieved substantial cost reductions through "eco-efficiency." The biggest savings often come from better energy management. A well-designed eco-efficiency initiative explores ways to encourage energy conservation across all activities. Water consumption as well as production processes in which waste and scrap might be eliminated should also be viewed through the efficiency lens.

ADOBE GOES GREEN

Adobe Systems, a San Jose, California-based computer maker, decided in 2001 to renovate its headquarters with improvements in energy efficiency as a key focus. The design team identified a number of heating, ventilation, and air-conditioning upgrades that offered immediate payback. The company spent 1.4 million on the new systems but earned $390,000 in energy rebates and reduced its annual operating costs by $1.2 million for a 121 percent return on investment. This equates to a nine-month payback.[8] Not bad by anyone's standards.

Eco-efficiency depends on being structured (which is to say, data driven) in the search for waste. Firms that utilize the tools we offer in the chapters that follow, such as the AUDIO assessment (an issue spotting framework introduced in *Green to Gold* and discussed in Chapter 5), have cut their energy bills by 10 to 20 percent or more. The cost savings are available to big and small firms alike. For example, Town Sports, a New York-based company that manages fitness centers such as New York Sports Club, generated so much savings with a six-month eco-efficiency initiative that the company decided to expand the program to other locations. The company anticipates a payback of two years on its energy conservation investments.[9] Beyond efficiency gains, Town Sports obtained additional savings by working with World Energy, a Worcester, Massachusetts-based energy management company, to buy its electricity through competitive online auctions.[10] Maersk, the Danish shipping giant, launched its eco-efficiency campaign when the company's top executives realized that even a 10 percent reduction in the enterprise's $6 billion per year energy bill would yield hundreds of millions of dollars in savings.[11]

Other companies have focused their eco-efficiency efforts on reduced waste in production. Various "green manufacturing" tools have been developed to facilitate these operations-oriented initiatives. Diversified products giant 3M employs "Lean Six Sigma" (which others call "green Six Sigma") principles to reduce waste and improve efficiency. The company has achieved impressive results. By 2006, 55,000 employees had received Lean Six Sigma training, and 3M had reduced waste in operations by 30 percent over five years, 20 percent above its already ambitious target for efficiency gains.[12]

Optimizing the use of fixed assets in general (and buildings in particular) represents an area where many companies can make substantial improvements, which delivers both environmental and business benefits. By carefully reviewing facilities utilization, you can often identify excess space that you can eliminate or redeploy for savings in both energy costs and operational expenses. Investments in physical plant retrofits and automation upgrades can lead to speedy and substantial savings for you as well, especially in an era of high energy costs.

With oil prices down from their 2008 high of $140/barrel, many companies are breathing a sigh of relief. But remember this: even at $70/barrel, energy prices are double where they were in the early 2000s. This means that almost every business in America (and every household for that matter) can save money by investing in energy efficiency.

REDUCING WASTE, RESPONDING TO CUSTOMER DEMAND

Solon, Ohio-based **CardPak** makes "clamshell" packaging for a range of goods from cosmetic containers to MP3 players. In response to growing customer demand for environmentally sensitive materials, CardPak launched its EcoLogical packaging line, which eliminates up to 85 percent of the plastics used in regular packaging products and only utilizes 100 percent recycled cardboard. Two years after its launch in 2006, the EcoLogical line accounted for 35 percent of CardPak's revenue with sales rapidly growing.[13]

Driving Revenues

In the past few decades, there has been a marked shift in how business leaders think about the environment. Previously, the relationship consisted of pitched battles over regulations, ongoing disputes, and endless grumbling. Today, smart businesses treat environmental issues not as a burden but as an opportunity to advance their position in the marketplace. In a world of ever-greater environmental consciousness, many companies find that building environmental attributes into their portfolio of products and services helps them win customers and drive revenues. Not every customer will pay for improved environmental performance, but a growing number will. According to a 2008 survey conducted by the Hartman Group, more than 75 percent of Americans consider environmental and social aspects in purchasing decisions and about a third are willing to pay more for those benefits.[14]

Interest in greener products isn't limited to the United States or Europe. A 2009 survey found, for example, that 73 percent of Brazilian respondents planned to spend more on green products in the coming year, and that 38 percent of them would buy a green product even if the price were 30 percent higher than a comparable non-green product.[15]

As Professor Mike Porter at Harvard Business School has definitively demonstrated, innovation is the key to sustained competitive strength.[16] Porter has shown that a focus on environmental issues can spur innovation.[17] By looking at their market offerings through the environmental and sustainability lens, companies may find ways to add value to their goods and services. Redesigning a product or service to solve a customer's pollution control and natural resource management challenges can pay off handsomely. Business leaders at the front edge of the Green Wave seek not only to introduce new products and services that cater to the sustainability needs of existing customers, they also look for "green value innovation" opportunities that will allow them to capture an entirely new customer base.

Game-changing innovation can also be used to shift customer preferences and develop untapped markets. After recognizing an undeveloped niche market for natural cleaning products, Clorox launched its Green Works product line in 2007. The company's timing couldn't have been better. The market for natural, reduced-chemical cleaning products doubled within the first year of Green Works' launch.[18] Because Clorox had the right products in place to meet exploding demand, it now holds 42 percent of the $200 million natural cleaners market.[19] Even better, Green Works appealed to consumers' demands for less-hazardous household cleaning products and effectively set a new standard in the industry.

As we have seen, innovative companies can modify existing products and services to reduce wastes and costs while meeting consumer demand for healthy, environmentally friendly offerings. Systemic innovation within a company can also be used to break free from old ways of thinking—allowing a company to reposition itself to enter new sectors and markets.

For the growing ranks of environmentally conscious consumers, the most attractive products and services are those that help them save money and satisfy their environmental expectations. The domestic and international market for eco-friendly goods and services continues to grow, driven in part by greater public interest in and awareness of green offerings. The list of companies that

EMERGING GREEN MARKETS

Straus Communications, a public relations and marketing firm based in San Francisco, represents a prime example of how a small company can embrace green practices and reinvigorate its business model. In the wake of growing competitiveness within the dairy business, Michael Straus, founder of the Straus Family Creamery in northern California, shifted his business focus and sales effort to emphasize organic products as a market differentiator. Building on his success in "green marketing," Straus launched a new business selling sustainability-oriented PR and marketing services.[20]

have achieved market success based on eco-defined lines of revenue is long and growing: Club Med (travel), Whole Foods (groceries), Aveda (beauty products), Kashi (cereals and crackers), Patagonia (clothing), Interface (carpet and flooring), and Shaklee (household cleaning products) represent just a few.

Even in markets where environmental considerations might seem secondary, eco-based products and services have begun to get traction. For instance, in the hospitality industry, eco-friendly brands have emerged. Starwood has an entirely new hotel line called "Element," which offers LEED-certified buildings with Energy Star appliances, recycling bins, eco-friendly carpets, and compact fluorescent lightbulbs (CFLs) in every room.[21] Likewise, from El Nido Resorts off the island of Palawan in the Philippines to Hacienda Tres Rios in Mexico's Riviera Maya, companies have hit it big with high-end eco-resorts.

Once an industry reaches a tipping point, environmental sensitivity becomes an expectation.[22] In the travel industry, this point seems to have been reached. Indeed, the American Automobile Association (AAA) now includes in its *Tour-Book* guides an "eco" icon for hotels, motels, and other green-certified lodgings in addition to its traditional diamond ratings.[23] The commitment to providing eco-information caters to consumers' growing environmental awareness and creates a new dimension of competition across the hospitality industry. As traffic shifts to green-starred lodging options, traditional hotels and motels will come under increasing pressure to incorporate green practices.

Let's pause for a reality check. Going "green" is not a business panacea. And it can't be done willy-nilly. A green pitch rarely works as the sole focus of a marketing effort. Companies must also satisfy consumer expectations for price, quality, and service. Clorox's GreenWorks product line wouldn't sell if the soaps and detergents didn't clean well—or weren't priced competitively with standard cleaning products. We explore this point in more detail later, but from a marketing point of view, as Dan Esty and Andrew Winston observed, green generally only works as the "third button" to push, after you have convinced a customer with your product's price and performance.

GREEN ALTERNATIVES CAN DRIVE SALES

Clean Air Lawn Care's innovative approach to lawn and garden services shows how a small business can use sustainability to drive growth in a very staid market space. This privately held, Fort Collins, Colorado-based company mows lawns and provides landscaping services in a uniquely environmentally sustainable manner.[24] The company relies entirely on electric equipment powered exclusively by renewable energy. It recycles the grass clippings and all other organic waste. And it uses all-natural and organic products for fertilization and pest control. What started as a small local business now operates with franchises in nine U.S. states. By offering a green alternative to customers in a traditionally emissions-heavy sector, Clean Air Lawn Care has broken away from the pack using a sustainability theme.

Building Intangible Value

No one doubts that the market value of a company today goes beyond the numbers presented in financial statements. Many factors shape a company's value and its prospects for marketplace success, including intangible elements such as brand loyalty, corporate reputation, and workforce morale. Focusing your business strategy environmentally goes beyond short-term cost, risk effects, or even the ability to drive revenues. Some of the biggest payoffs in a sustainability strategy may come in the form of value gains that traditional accounting systems miss. As Muhtar Kent, CEO of Coca-Cola, has memorably said, "A brand is a promise made to your consumers and customers, your employees, your investors, communities, vendors, and suppliers. And trust is the glue that holds all these relationships together. Break a promise and you destroy a relationship. If a good brand is a promise, then a great brand is a promise kept."[25]

According to David Kaplan and Robert Norton, companies should systematically track a "balanced scorecard" of items critical to marketplace success—customer satisfaction, employee engagement, and corporate social responsibility.[26] With environmental concerns emerging as a major issue for various stakeholders, a company's credibility, authenticity, and transparency related to sustainability issues has become an additional item of importance to intangible value—requiring the same sort of structured management.

A reputation for environmental sustainability can help create brand "stickiness"—the ability to attract new customers as well as retain existing ones—in a world where a growing segment of the public wants to buy products with environmental attributes, but does not want to spend time researching who is green. Honda has played this card well. As one of the first automobile manufacturers to develop a line of fuel-efficient vehicles, Honda established itself as a company committed to drivers' budgets as well as environmental sustainability, benefiting financially in the process. In fact, during the recent economic downturn, while other carmakers saw sales slump, Honda reported not just growth in market share but absolute sales gains.[27] What explains the company's ability to buck the trend? It's hard to say definitively. But the public perception of Honda as an environmentally minded, trustworthy company selling cars that provide some relief from the burden of high prices at the pump certainly played a role.

In many industries, particularly those where "knowledge workers" are critical, a commitment to the environment has emerged as a highly valuable element of a company's corporate culture that contributes in a major way to the recruiting and retaining of top-quality employees. Businesses that have built environmental values into their corporate cultures not only find it easier to attract and retain the best workers, but they enjoy greater employee productivity as well. As Bob Willard details in his book, *The Sustainability Advantage*, people are more satisfied, more committed, and hence more productive at organizations that resonate with their ethics and values. He writes, "good leaders who align employees' efforts with inspired visions of sustainability leadership, who educate and empower their carefully recruited talent, and who provide the necessary support to make it happen, will see the difference in their bottom line."[28] Willard's observation rings especially true as public environmental appreciation and awareness grows.

DOING THE RIGHT THING RESONATES WITH EMPLOYEES

New Belgium Brewing Company, a craft brewery based in Colorado, experienced the people-related benefits of going green. It motivated its workforce by embracing sustainability in its core business strategy. The company's executive team points to their green initiatives as a source of increased employee satisfaction and a key reason for their employee retention rate of 95 percent. This motivated workforce has fuelled the firm's rapid growth. Between 2003 and 2007, New Belgium's compound annual growth rate of 13.4 percent surpassed the craft brewery industry average of 8.1 percent. On a national scale, it became the eighth largest brewery in terms of sales volume, up from thirteenth place only five years earlier.[29]

Sustainability efforts produce happy employees who bring the sort of motivation to their jobs that helps companies grow and prosper. An emphasis on environmental leadership can also shield a company from regulatory scrutiny, media inquiry, and NGO attention. As we noted earlier, Jack Welch's GE became an environmental whipping boy because of the company's perceived insensitivity to pollution clean-up. Today's GE, under the leadership of Jeff Immelt, could serve as the poster child for how to stay on the right side of the sustainability movement. GE's new reputation as a good corporate citizen creates a "green aura" that keeps hostile NGOs largely at bay and makes government officials want GE representatives in the room when there are policy decisions to be made. Media coverage of the Connecticut-based conglomerate has gone from largely hostile to highly favorable in just a few years—culminating in 2007, perhaps, with *Time* magazine naming Immelt a "hero of the planet." What is a turnaround in public attitudes like this worth? It is hard to pin down, but it's not small.

GOING GREEN IN TOUGH ECONOMIC TIMES

All well and good, you might say, to think about the environment when business is booming. But can a company afford to "go green" in a downturn?

Actually, many of the "green to gold" agenda items we highlight prove to be especially valuable during tough economic times. Squeezing out costs through eco-efficiency saves money that drops straight to the bottom line. So while the recent recession caused some companies to take their eyes off the environmental ball, others were using a "green lens" to achieve operational gains. They invested in more efficient production processes, rationalized space and fixed assets, cut their energy bills through improved heating and lighting, and squeezed waste out of their procurement and distribution systems. As one CEO told us, "during the downturn, it didn't make sense to put our capital into expanded production or new marketing campaigns, but energy efficiency proved to be a good bet."

Other companies have found that an environmental push kept employee morale up during the downturn, reminding the workforce that their company seeks to be a force for social good, even when marketplace constraints require hours to be cut and jobs to be shed. So while some companies pulled back on their environmental commitments, others used the slowdown as a moment to advance their sustainability efforts—adding to their capacity to differentiate themselves from others in the marketplace.

Reactive or Proactive?

Companies traditionally struggle against change—especially successful ones. As the old saying goes, "If it ain't broke, why fix it?" In this regard, some businesspeople see no reason to make sustainability or environmental thinking part of strategy. Others say, "we'll do whatever the government asks us to do." In fact, such a "compliance" approach to environmental protection dominated corporate attitudes for decades and remains the prevailing thinking in some companies today.

Being reactive won't fly in today's world. Environmental issues and concerns about sustainability have become core concerns of society—and must become central elements of business strategy. Companies that want to stay ahead of the pack have to view all aspects of their business through an environmental lens. In doing so, they can obtain significant and durable competitive advantages that reduce costs and risks and lead them to new revenue streams, better connections with customers, and stronger brands.

The Green Wave

Business interest in the environment as an element of strategy has grown slowly over the past several decades. In fact, we've seen companies go through—some are still going through it—a four-stage evolution:

1. **Eco-resistance:** Marked by hostility toward any regulations and the science behind topics such as climate change.
2. **Eco-compliance:** Indicated by acceptance of regulations and a commitment to meet the requirements of the law.
3. **Eco-efficiency:** Focused on lowering costs by cutting energy consumption and eliminating scrap and waste.
4. **Eco-Advantage:** Driven by efforts to innovate and to deliver processes, products, and services, which solve customer environmental problems.

In this book, we'll update you on the changing state of green business, putting a spotlight on the best (and worst) green practices. More important, we'll provide you with a practical guide to identify where your company lies on the "going green" spectrum and how you can incorporate green practices into your day-to-day business activities. The *Green to Gold Business Playbook* promises to help you understand critical environmental issues and build sustainability into your strategy. Drawing on real-world examples from hundreds of companies big and small, in manufacturing and services, in growing markets and shrinking industries, we'll show you how to create an enduring Eco-Advantage. We'll give you the tools you'll need to bring an environmental or sustainability lens to your operations, and in doing so, gain a marketplace edge that enables you to turn green into gold.

As we've suggested, society's expectations are changing. Companies and businesses must act responsibly to address environmental (and social) issues, and that is what makes sustainability a strategy imperative. While a number of multinational companies have led the sustainability charge, the need for change won't be confined to big corporations. Ultimately, the Green Wave will sweep over the whole business world, affecting all companies, from megaconglomerates to solo operators. We'll make an effort throughout the book to discuss how small and mid-sized companies can incorporate best environmental practices and contribute to addressing issues such as climate change, water quality, food safety, and land use. Likewise, we recognize that the sustainability pressures vary widely from industry to industry. We've therefore offered suggestions that apply across a spectrum of businesses—some more relevant to manufacturers and others aimed at companies in the services sector.

We don't promise that going green will be easy, quite the contrary. Unlike some "green" strategy advisors and eco-authors, we don't believe that every sustainable initiative will deliver win-win results that improve environmental *and* financial performance. Smart executives know that nothing comes that easily in the business world. The journey from green to gold requires vision and commitment, systematic analysis, careful strategizing, and real dedication to execution. Outcomes cannot be guaranteed, but for a growing number of companies, the results have been very rewarding—both economically and environmentally.

Finally, we want to emphasize that the world of corporate environmental strategy is very dynamic. We, therefore, work constantly to refine and deepen our understanding of what works (and what does not) in the green business realm. In this regard, we welcome your feedback, updates on your own experience bringing a sustainability lens to your business, or any stories or suggestions you're willing to share. Please visit *The Green to Gold Business Playbook* website—www.greentogoldplaybook.com—to email us.

Chapter 2 How to Use This Book

We have written this book so that companies of any size, in any industry, and with wide-ranging degrees of existing capacity to obtain an Eco-Advantage in the marketplace can profit from it. If you want an end-to-end sustainability game plan, read *The Green to Gold Business Playbook* from start to finish. We expect that "cleantech" entrepreneurs, small business owners with overarching management responsibilities, chief sustainability officers (CSOs), or those working with them, as well as any other executives with broad-gauge interest in environmental strategy or sustainability will find value in every chapter.

If you have more specialized responsibilities, it may make sense to skim Part II: "Gear Up: What Leaders Need to Know" and Part III: "Analyze: Identify Your Eco-Risks and Opportunities" and then to turn to the chapters in Part IV: "Strategize: How Each Business Function Can Benefit and Contribute" that address your specific business functions. In these chapters (8 through 17), we approach the corporate sustainability challenge in a job-specific fashion. We introduce basic concepts and analytic tools and then hone in quickly on the ideas and action items that apply directly to various areas of professional responsibility—from manufacturing to marketing and more. You can read each chapter independently. Of course, if you have very specific questions, you will find the index at the back of the book a useful reference guide—with entries related to dozens of key environmental and sustainability concepts and activities.

This volume builds on the foundation of Dan Esty and Andrew Winston's prize-winning book: *Green to Gold: How Smart Companies Use Environmental Strategy to Innovate, Create Value, and Build Competitive Advantage*. The *Playbook* updates the green business story and distills key messages in a highly practical and easy-to-use fashion. It seeks to reach not just c-suite executives but also line managers who increasingly face sustainability expectations associated with their roles. While it continues to draw lessons from the big businesses that led the corporate response to the first phase of the Green Wave, it provides a much greater focus on the needs and opportunities of small and midsized companies that have now taken on the environment and sustainability as part of their strategic direction.

Green to Gold focused largely on *what* companies needed to do to bring an environmental lens to strategy. *The Green to Gold Business Playbook* further chronicles best practices in the sustainability domain but also shifts the focus to *how* to deliver Eco-Advantage and win in the marketplace. To this end, we have structured each chapter around a series of basic, intermediate, and advanced "plays":

- **Basic plays:** Offer key concepts and strategies that are relatively easy to implement, offering quick returns on investment, without requiring significant sustainability-related training or existing capacity.
- **Intermediate plays:** Summarize what leading companies are doing to achieve an Eco-Advantage and introduce initiatives that involve more investment and effort.
- **Advanced plays:** Provide guidance on more involved and innovative ways to put your company at the front of the pack to become a sustainability leader.

In addition to laying out an action agenda, every chapter contains tools, case studies, and lots of real-world examples that spell out how companies have successfully implemented Eco-Advantage strategies—and the struggles that they have faced along the way. **Each chapter concludes with a summary list of the plays we have introduced and a set of Additional Resources** if you want to dig deeper on a particular topic.

Of course, given the unique nature of every business, you should plan to pick and choose among the plays, following the suggestions that match your specific circumstances and adjusting others as required. No doubt you will find items on which you wish we had provided more background, given more comprehensive guidance, or offered more detailed instructions. But in light of the huge scope of the sustainability agenda and space limitations in this book, we can only hope that the suggested readings, websites, and additional resources provided in each chapter (and more fully on the *Playbook* website: www.greentogoldplaybook.com) help to fill the gap.

We have structured the book sequentially—laying out in order the steps a CSO or other top-level executive would need to take to create and implement a comprehensive and cohesive sustainability strategy. **Part II: "Gear Up"** (Chapters 3 and 4) provides a starting point and an overview of what will be involved. We organized Chapter 3 around our list of the "Top 10 Action Items" essential for any company seeking to gain an Eco-Advantage. It introduces in an abbreviated form all of the key concepts, tools, and frameworks that you will need to construct a sustainability action agenda. Chapter 4 lays out the business logic for applying a "green lens" to strategy. It explains how to build an analytically rigorous business case for developing and executing a "green to gold" game plan. This discussion will be of special value to anyone who is skeptical about the value of going green—or who faces skeptics in his or her organization.

Part III: "Analyze" (Chapters 5 through 7) offers a series of checklists, matrices, and other diagnostic tools designed to help you make sense of the sustainability arena and provide a solid foundation on which to build your Eco-Advantage strategy. In Chapter 5, we systematically array the environmental and social issues that companies confront today and offer a set of frameworks that enables you to zero in on the concerns that are of strategic importance to your industry and company. Chapter 6 explains how to measure your company's "environmental footprint"—providing a structured way to gauge greenhouse gas emissions, water use, and waste and ecosystem impacts. We also demonstrate how and why it makes sense to look beyond your own factory gates and analyze eco-impacts across the entire "value chain"—from the procurement of inputs to product use (and disposal) by the end consumer. Chapter 7, "Benchmark Your Performance against Competitors and Best Practices," offers a rigorous approach to clarifying the choices that go into a corporate environmental or sustainability strategy. In highlighting the value of comparative analysis, it shows you how to identify sustainability "best practices" on an issue-by-issue basis.

> Achieving real Eco-Advantage requires fresh thinking and changed modes of operation in every business function.

Part IV: "Strategize" (Chapters 8 through 17) outlines how best to bring the sustainability lens to different aspects of corporate life. It spells out a series of specific actions that each division of a large company or functional activity in a small business can take to reduce eco-risks, cut costs, drive revenue growth, spur innovation, and enhance intangible market value related to brand loyalty, employee dedication, and other factors.

Chapter 8 shows you how to restructure day-to-day office activities to be more sustainable. Chapter 9 puts particular focus on how to manage buildings to optimize your use of space, consume less energy, reduce waste—and thereby cut expenses and improve employee health, motivation, and productivity. Chapter 10 explores opportunities to "green" information systems and use computer-based technologies to improve eco-efficiency and make your business more sustainable and effective. Chapter 11 offers guidance on "design for the environment" and how you can use concepts such as product stewardship, "cradle-to-cradle" thinking, and industrial ecology to deliver Eco-Advantage. Chapters 12 through 17 provide tools and recommendations for greening other business functions including: procurement, manufacturing, logistics and transport, marketing and sales, legal and regulatory affairs, as well as accounting and finance.

Part V: "Mobilize" (Chapters 18 through 21) delves into the key to a winning environment or sustainability strategy—execution. It provides guidance designed to ensure that your green strategy delivers on-the-ground results. Chapter 18 covers the plays you'll need to create a sustainability action plan. Because of the strategic significance of climate change and the importance of this issue to so many businesses and stakeholders, we devote Chapter 19 to the nuts and bolts of putting together your corporate climate strategy. Chapter 20 digs into the critical issue of employee engagement, provides tips on how best to mobilize your workforce in support of sustainability initiatives, and lays out a game plan for building a corporate culture that generates Eco-Advantage. Finally, Chapter 21 provides a road map for engaging external stakeholders and creating partnerships to enhance your sustainability strategy.

The scientific conclusions, public policies, societal attitudes, and technologies that frame our understanding of environmental issues and broader sustainability concerns constantly evolve. You cannot maintain an Eco-Advantage without updating your strategy from time to time. The final section of this book, **Part VI: "Optimize"** (Chapters 22 and 23) acknowledges this reality and spells out how to regularly review and renew your environmental or sustainability initiatives. It notes that we must assess progress and readjust goals based on what we've learned from systematic development assessments and the past efforts of others. Chapter 22 provides guidance on how to track progress, gauge results, and communicate about what your business has accomplished as well as what you have yet to accomplish. Chapter 23 offers concluding thoughts on celebrating your success and promoting continuous improvement.

> **Making the environment and sustainability an integral part of business thinking comes naturally to a few individuals and companies. For most of us, however, it takes real effort to put our strategies under the sustainability lens.**

Companies and their leaders must anticipate numerous challenges and setbacks on the path from green to gold. We are confident that this *Playbook* offers a useful road map if you want to position your company to achieve Eco-Advantage and marketplace success in the face of the Green Wave sweeping across society. Now is your time to dig in.

Part Two Gear Up: What Leaders Need to Know

Chapter 3 Building a Winning Eco-Advantage Strategy: Top 10 Action Items

Given the range of industries and business models as well as company structures and sizes represented by this *Playbook's* readership, we cannot offer a one-size-fits-all approach to creating competitive advantage based on the "green to gold" model. But this chapter does provide an action agenda—distilling all of the key elements that should be considered in bringing an environment or sustainability focus to business strategy. The remaining chapters of the book dig deeper into each of the elements introduced here. But for the time-pressed reader, this summary provides a good starting point.

Diving into sustainability can be done in several ways. One approach is to think about the key environmental **issues and impacts** your business faces. To do this, you need to analyze the full set of pollution and natural resource issues implicated by your operations and products or services, including:

- Waste, packaging, and recycling
- Air pollution
- Water pollution and availability
- Greenhouse gas emissions, energy use
- Chemicals, heavy metals, toxics in both waste streams and products
- Resource impacts, forests, minerals, oceans, and other water bodies
- Land use, open space, sprawl, habitat destruction, biodiversity

Some companies prefer to take a "triple bottom line" approach to sustainability and look beyond environmental issues at a broader set of "social" concerns at the same time, including:

- Worker wages and benefits
- Workplace diversity
- Poverty and community development
- Labor rights
- Child labor
- Human rights

- Workplace safety
- Ethics
- Health and nutrition

Another cut at sustainability centers on the **strategy risks and opportunities** presented by environmental or social concerns. In this regard, you should review each issue for its potential effect on competitive advantage. Specifically, you should assess whether better management of any of these issues would position your company to:

- Reduce business risks
- Cut costs (perhaps through improved "eco-efficiency")
- Drive revenue growth or spur innovation
- Build brand loyalty or corporate reputation

A final line into sustainability centers on how the issues and impacts as well as the strategy risks and opportunities play out across the various **business functions** of your enterprise. Applying a sustainability lens to each aspect of day-to-day business activities may offer you a way to reduce waste and inefficiency, spot opportunities to enhance customer value, and deliver top-line growth, and increase profitability in:

- Office activities
- Buildings and fixed asset management (rationalizing space and energy use)
- Information technology
- Product or service design
- Procurement and supply chain management
- Manufacturing and processing
- Logistics and transportation
- Sales and marketing
- Legal and regulatory affairs
- Accounting and finance
- Communications and corporate relations

We urge you to consider all three of these approaches as you develop your Eco-Advantage game plan. Each of these different ways of thinking about sustainability offers insights that can pay significant dividends. To get you started on building a winning "green to gold" strategy, next we present our Top 10 Action Items:

1. Issue Spotting

Understanding which environmental issues (or broader social concerns) might affect your company is the first step in a structured approach to folding sustainability thinking into your business strategy. With regard to each of the issues identified earlier, you should ask:

- Does my business create impacts for which I will be held accountable?
- Could any of these issues impinge on how I conduct my business?

The first question is what we call the *inside out* perspective. Sustainability-minded executives need to be very clear on which issues their industry in general and their own business model in particular affect others through pollution or other impacts. The second question turns the issue around with an *outside in* perspective—recognizing that many businesses depend on access to natural resources as well as clarity about regulatory expectations for marketplace success. Changes in these factors could shift competitive advantage both within an industry and across industries.

There are lots of ways the sustainability agenda could become a matter of strategic importance. New regulations could require the purchase of additional pollution control equipment or limit access to inputs needed for a manufacturing process. Price changes in natural resources, most notably oil or other fossil fuels, could realign the competitive landscape favoring those who have invested in efficiency and penalizing those with resource-intensive business models. New scientific discoveries could change what is considered safe or appropriate in the way of materials. Who would have guessed, for example, that chlorofluorocarbons (CFCs), the family of miracle chemicals developed in the 1950s and used in everything from hairspray to refrigerators to foam cups, would be banned in the 1990s for breaking down the planet's protective ozone layer?

Likewise, new technologies may emerge in response to sustainability pressures—launching new industries and killing off others. As we discuss in more detail in the chapters that follow, dozens of new automobile makers (focused largely on electric motors or hybrid engines) have emerged in the last five years while Chrysler and GM have gone broke. Consumer preferences may also change in ways that shift marketplace strength. Interest in organic food, for instance, has boomed, making Whole Foods America's fastest growing grocery store chain. Issue spotting requires careful thought about the factors that could shift the fundamentals of competition in your industry.

With sustainability pressures coming from all directions, executives must be systematic in assessing the issues their companies face. To ensure that your issue scan is comprehensive, we suggest the use of the AUDIO framework (explained in detail in Chapter 5, "Spot the Eco-Issues that Could Impact Your Bottom Line"), which emphasizes that companies must analyze not only their own environmental **impacts,** but also those impacts that occur **upstream** as a result of the production processes of their suppliers and **downstream** as a result of customer use of their products. In a world of "extended producer responsibility," companies, particularly those with big brand names, must expect to be held accountable for any and all environmental impacts across their entire value chain. The **issues** identified must be addressed. But recognize that problems can be turned into **opportunities** any time a company figures out how to manage an issue better than the competition.

A company's actual impacts matter a great deal, but so do perceptions. In establishing their sustainability issue agenda, executives must understand who their key stakeholders are and how their company and industry is perceived by these individuals or groups. Stakeholder mapping (details in Chapter 5) helps companies get a clear fix on the government officials and agencies, environmental groups and other NGOs, community leaders, suppliers, customers, and others who wield influence that can affect company operations, corporate reputations, or conditions in the marketplace.

The issues that matter may change over time, so it pays to look for future trends that could redefine the sustainability agenda. Are there significant scientific uncertainties regarding materials that your business uses that might bring new risks? Are there ramped-up regulatory requirements under consideration? Important technology developments on the horizon? Resource scarcities emerging? The dynamism of the sustainability arena makes systematic trend tracking an essential component of sound issue spotting (again, details in Chapter 5).

Companies also need to refine their sustainability issue scan and deepen their analysis of the risks and opportunities presented over time. We've provided some potentially useful tools—such as guidance on how to do a carbon footprint—that highlight the major sources of greenhouse gas emissions for which companies are increasingly held accountable. And we introduce the concept of Life Cycle Analysis, which can help facilitate your thinking about the upstream and downstream impacts that you need to address.

2. Benchmarking and Prioritization

After identifying a wide range of issues, a second critical action item comes to the forefront—figuring out what you should do and in what order. Of course, it makes sense to take on the most significant issues and sustainability initiatives first. Prioritization requires a sense of scale and context.

One way to get a fix on priorities is through benchmarking—or comparative analysis. Knowing the issues that others have focused on and what they are doing in response to those issues can give you a big shortcut when it comes to establishing your sustainability action plan. We suggest that you compare your company's environmental management practices and results against several benchmarks: other companies in the same industry, sustainability leaders, and our template of best practices (details provided in Chapter 7 "Benchmark Your Performance"). Knowing what others who are similarly situated are doing in response to sustainability pressures (particularly industry peers) is especially helpful because it will reveal what others find important, and perhaps even what is possible, in the way of sustainability actions. We urge companies to examine not only the issues that their competitors are focused on but also their targets and timetables for improved results. To be clear: tracking the sustainability goals and implementation efforts of your competitors is essential—and any failure to do so can lead to unforeseen marketplace challenges and competitive disadvantage.

In industries where the Green Wave has not yet surged, tracking industry peers is useful but insufficient. To get a sense of what is possible and perhaps even advisable in the sustainability realm requires benchmarking against a set of companies that have taken a leadership position on environmental or social issues—or against an established set of sustainability best practices.

Prioritization requires more than comparative analysis. Each company's circumstances will be different, which means that you must tailor your company's sustainability strategy to its own market realities, strengths, and capacities. As a top executive, you need to know not just which issues require attention but what the options are for responding to them. With a full set of potential sustainability initiatives in hand, you can then evaluate the costs and benefits of the various options and assess which interventions your company is best positioned to carry out.

3. Vision and Alignment

To ensure that sustainability initiatives deliver on their promise, frame them in a fashion that is clear to everyone in the company and carefully aligned with the management team's broader business strategy. Articulate a "sustainability vision" that puts the entire company on notice that environmental issues (and perhaps social concerns as well) have been elevated to a core element of strategy. Supplement this vision with a more detailed statement that highlights the priority actions that will come out of the commitment to sustainability. Many companies start with a focus on risk reduction and eco-efficiency-based cost savings—and develop strategies for revenue growth and other aspects of sustainability-driven value over time.

The sustainability thrust must be consistent with and reinforce the company's broader strategic priorities. For instance, a promise to undertake expensive new environmental activities (such as a clothing maker announcing plans to buy only organic cotton and to use environmentally benign dyes—both of which will add expense) will create dissonance if launched alongside a management plan that focuses on cutting costs. In contrast, CEO Andrew Liveris's 2015 sustainability goals for Dow have energized the company because their emphasis on innovation aligns perfectly with the company's growth strategy that aims to provide solutions to societal problems.

SETTING THE RIGHT GOALS

Xerox's top environmental executive Patty Calkins knows that setting stretch goals is tough for big organizations. Most people want targets that are achievable. But she's witnessed the power of bold goals to prompt innovation and drive business results. Calkins told us that when Xerox announced it's "energy challenge" goal in 2003 to reduce greenhouse gas emissions 10 percent by 2012, the company had some idea of how it could reach half that target. "For the rest," she says, "we had no clue—none whatsoever—so people were very nervous." But she and her peers put together a powerful cross-functional Steering Committee chaired by the President of Xerox's Global Business and Services Group, with key representatives from every part of the business. Together, the team built effective working teams to tackle the challenge in areas with the biggest emissions—manufacturing, fleet, real estate, supply chain, and more. By 2006, the company had far exceeded its goal 2010 and achieved an 18 percent reduction. The lesson for Calkins: "Rally people around clearly defined target, focus where it matters, make the right people accountable, and you can accomplish far more than you thought you could."[1]

In developing a sustainability vision, some companies focus on an ambitious overarching goal—a North Star—as a way to motivate fresh thinking and dramatic action. DuPont, for instance, committed more than a decade ago to "zero waste" as a way to raise the sights of employees across the company. This audacious target has not been reached, but striving in the direction of zero waste has generated substantial results. Other companies have taken a more operational approach—setting targets such as a 10 percent reduction in energy consumption. We recommend a mix of longer-term, aspirational goals, and more concrete, day-to-day targets for which managers will actually be held accountable.

4. Eco-Advantage Strategy

Clarity on the vision as well as the set of sustainability issues and response options provides the starting point for creating a sustainability game plan. The next step is to screen the potential action items for their strategic value. Give priority to those initiatives that offer the potential for enduring Eco-Advantage—a sustainability-derived differentiation from your competition.

In recent years, some future-minded executives have come to realize that environmental issues (and social concerns) are not just a burden that involves regulations to follow, costs to control, and risks to manage. They know that these issues can be a significant competitive differentiator in the marketplace. Moreover, they have come to recognize that real potential exists for companies to go beyond playing "defense" on sustainability. Companies that can solve their customers' environmental problems will see revenues rise. Businesses that position themselves as solution providers may well build goodwill, add to their brand luster, and experience a rise in market value based on intangibles that go beyond growth in sales or profits.

When applying your sustainability lens to strategy, pay careful attention to the points of competitive leverage that we identified in the opening paragraphs of this chapter:

- Risks
- Costs
- Revenues
- Brand (including reputation and other aspects of intangible value)

You can reduce the risks and costs related to environmental issues in many ways. For instance, eliminating toxic substances from a product or production process can cut down on cumbersome regulatory paperwork and reduce the risk of costly accidents, which in turn, lowers insurance costs, simplifies worker training, and may make access to capital easier. Likewise, careful issue management can help companies get out in front of new regulations, avoid costly retrofits of pollution control equipment, and even avoid NGO-led protests or boycotts that might create a consumer backlash.

From a cost perspective, investing in more eco-efficient buildings, manufacturing processes, distribution systems, and communications may yield quick dividends, especially in a world where energy is much more expensive than in the past. And rising populations and growing wealth in the developing world have triggered competition for natural resources from minerals to farmland to water—further rewarding those who focus on "resource productivity" and other elements of eco-efficiency.

Given rising public interest and societal investment in a range of problems including climate change, food safety, air pollution, and water quality as well as availability, companies that deliver sustainability solutions stand to profit. Real competitive advantage will go to companies that innovate and develop breakthrough technologies or services. With these payoffs in mind, many top executives have launched sustainability innovation efforts. At Alcoa, for example, CEO Klaus Kleinfeld has pushed his leadership team to innovate using sustainability as a driver of the process.

Being seen as a leader in the push for a more sustainable future and as a good corporate citizen can enhance a company's market position by deflecting regulatory focus, strengthening customer loyalty, building brand recognition, and helping to recruit and retain top talent, particularly the critical "knowledge workers" who care a great deal about the values of the companies to which they devote their lives. The direct payoff from these "intangible" rewards for a successful sustainability initiative may be hard to gauge, but many top executives are convinced of the value. Indeed, Muhtar Kent of Coca-Cola, Paul Polman of Unilever, and many other CEOs of public-facing companies have embraced sustainability with these strategic elements in mind.

A systematic review of the wide-ranging sustainability initiatives for their potential to deliver competitive advantage—and thus profitability—lies at the heart of a successful "green to gold" strategy. In deciding exactly which options to pursue, company leaders must utilize a disciplined, value-oriented, and hard-nosed analysis. They must make calculations regarding how much each initiative would cost to implement and what its potential payoff would be in terms of risk reduction, cost savings, revenue growth, or intangible value gains. Smart companies construct their Eco-Advantage strategies with the same commitment that they routinely apply to careful projections, business modeling, scenario planning, sensitivity analysis, core capability assessments, and all of their other strategic planning management tools.

5. Ownership and Accountability

While the chief sustainability officer or a "green team," in consultation with the CEO and a few top managers, might develop the initial sustainability vision, a broader buy-in is essential. Any manager who will have a role in implementing the sustainability or environmental strategy (and in most companies this would encompass almost all managers) needs to have a chance to be part of the strategy development process. A collaboratively built game plan that is based on a diversity of views about the company's sustainability risks and available opportunities will most certainly be stronger than one created by a small group in isolation. The "co-creation" model draws on a wider range of perspectives and experiences—and establishes a broader base of "ownership," which is critical to successful implementation.

Ultimately, the CEO (backed by the board of directors in public companies) must make clear the strategic importance of the agreed-upon sustainability agenda. Absent leadership from the very top of the company, middle managers, and lower-level employees are likely to be uncertain as to how seriously to take the green strategy. Doubt about the seriousness of this commitment leads skeptics to drag their feet and underperform. You'll hear them say things like: "this too shall pass," or "but climate change isn't real," or "going green is going to cost us money," or "we don't have the capacity to manage this additional agenda."[2]

Some of these complaints may have an element of validity, but most reflect a lack of understanding about the upside that comes from bringing a sustainability focus to strategy. Successful execution depends on cascading the game plan throughout the organization. And it falls to the senior management team to explain the logic, walk middle managers through the new expectations, and show them how to square the sustainability thrust with existing performance goals such as trimming costs, improving operational efficiency, growing revenues, and increasing profit margins.

To ensure that sustainability roles and responsibilities are clear, fold this agenda into the company's existing management and accountability structure. In companies where leadership is serious about Eco-Advantage, all of the top executives will have "key performance indicators" (KPIs) related to sustainability results. Bonuses and promotions will also be linked to success in delivering against clear (quantitatively defined) targets. All of this requires an environmental management system (EMS), which tracks results on the high-priority issues. Most companies find it useful to set both short- and long-term targets for improved performance.

6. Employee Mobilization

Making a "green to gold" strategy pay off requires that everyone in the company play a role. In many companies we've worked with, the line workers step up as the most enthusiastic participants in a sustainability initiative. It turns out that almost everyone wants to work for a company that is seen to be a good corporate citizen. Few issues signal a company's values and sense of social obligation as clearly as good environmental stewardship. In fact, during the recent downturn, we know of a number of companies that expanded their green commitments as a way to remind the workforce of the company's dedication to corporate social responsibility even while pink slips were being distributed.

There are many ways to engage employees in the push toward a sustainable future. 3M invites workers from the c-suite to the factory floor to submit ideas that might fit into its "Pollution Prevention Pays" initiative—and thousands of these efficiency-enhancing suggestions have been implemented over the past 35 years adding up to billions of pounds of pollution avoided and billions of dollars saved. Walmart asks each of its associates to sign up for a "personal sustainability project" and to make a commitment to some concrete action—from replacing incandescent lightbulbs to increased recycling—that makes a difference. When summed across Walmart's million-person-plus workforce, the impact of these individual acts really adds up.

Companies that have made a commitment to sustainability, fold environmental modules into their training and human resources development programs. Every executive in Nokia's senior leadership course, for example, participates in a sustainability module. To build consciousness about the sustainability agenda, informal discussions can also be helpful. Big companies often invite speakers to spur conversation about the Green Wave and the risks and opportunities it presents. Small businesses may simply want to put sustainability on the agenda for a staff meeting. Dow's Evergreen website provides a platform for an ongoing sustainability "conversation," through which employees share ideas, suggestions, and information.

Corporate leaders who want to drive home the point that the environment or sustainability needs to be a priority for everyone should consider handing out awards for distinguished performance. At Northeast Utilities, the CEO hosts an annual Environmental Awards Ceremony and personally congratulates the individuals and teams being honored (giving each winner not just a plaque but also $500 in company stock).

7. Stakeholder Engagement

As we made clear in the issue-spotting discussion previously, no company can define its sustainability agenda in isolation from the communities in which it operates or from the broader environmental agenda of society. This reality makes stakeholder engagement an essential element of any "green to gold" strategy. Smart executives know that they must be on good terms with the mayors, city councilors, and civil society activists in every community in which they operate. Companies must also stay on the good side of regulators and work to ensure that political leaders at every level understand their commitment to being good corporate citizens.

Executives who want to become sustainability leaders should systematize their stakeholder outreach through regular meetings with environmental groups and other NGOs. Invite critics and well as supporters to these dialogues. While listening to people vent about all that the company is doing wrong can be painful, it turns out to be far better to hear from those who are unhappy directly rather than waiting for them to lodge complaints in the newspaper or online. A growing number of companies stay on top of emerging issues and get feedback on their sustainability efforts through an outside advisory board that meets regularly—sharing perspectives from the environmental community, consumers, academics, and other stakeholders.

For many businesses, the most important stakeholders are those in their value chain—their suppliers and customers. Sustainability leaders, such as Coca-Cola and Unilever, have "co-created" their sustainability programs in conjunction with key outside constituencies including suppliers, customers, and NGOs. Any business selling to Walmart (and there are 70,000 of them) knows that it must take part in an ongoing dialogue with the Bentonville, Arkansas–based retailer on the topic of sustainability performance. To focus this conversation, Walmart requires each supplier to submit a sustainability assessment—and the retail giant is developing a "scorecard" to make its environmental expectations clear.

8. Reporting and Communications

We live in an increasingly transparent world. In the sustainability arena, this reality translates into an expectation that companies will report regularly on their environmental results. Some disclosure is now mandatory. Large companies operating in Europe must report on their greenhouse gas emissions. And the U.S. Environmental Protection Agency has also issued greenhouse gas reporting regulations for large emitters. Other reporting pressures come from the marketplace. As mentioned earlier, many companies are now demanding that their suppliers provide them with environmental performance data. Some are even making certification under an environmental management scheme, such as ISO 14000, a requirement. Still other data demands emerge from the capital markets in the form of shareholder resolutions or investment analyst surveys.

For many companies, these requests seem to be multiplying beyond control not to mention offering redundant and inconsistent methodologies and requirements. Complaining generally provides little relief, and the penalty for nonresponsiveness—low scores—is high. The best game plan is to invest in a structured and systematic environmental data collection and reporting system covering all of the key issues highlighted previously. You should take special care to be sure that the data reported is accurate. Companies must be clear about what reporting methodologies they plan to follow (details on the options are in Chapter 22, "Communicate and Report Results"), including what baseline year to use, how the data are to be normalized to ensure that appropriate comparisons can be done, and whether numbers are absolute or intensity based.

In recent years, many big companies have published annual sustainability or environmental reports. The trend seems to be moving away from printed documents toward a regularly, up-to-date, website that permits a degree of "drill down" for those who are interested in underlying details. Many companies, particularly those of some scale, will still find it useful to undertake more targeted communications related to their sustainability performance, perhaps through highlighting information on their websites for each of the geographic locales in which they operate.

Internal sustainability communications remain very important as a way to keep employees in the know about the company's environmental and social initiatives and results. Whether this takes the form of newsletters, online web resources, or "blast" emails, companies can gain much by disseminating sustainability information so that everyone in the enterprise can move toward the identified best practices. Likewise, when things go wrong—from a chemical spill to the identification of a product flaw or the occurrence of an environmental violation—it is important to share the lessons learned with all employees.

9. Execution

Building a sustainability strategy is only half the battle. Execution is the key to getting results from a "green to gold" initiative. We have already touched on many of the elements critical to success: a clear fix on the issues, a compelling vision, alignment with the company's broader business strategy, CEO leadership, broad ownership of the sustainability agenda, carefully drawn lines of accountability, and quantitative goals linked to executive performance evaluation. Companies that are committed to establishing an Eco-Advantage also know that they must properly resource a sustainability effort. There will be certain investments that must be made—and a chief sustainability officer (or some executive

designated with sustainability responsibilities) will have to drive the agenda forward. In bigger companies, we see the CSO emerging as a critical player in the
c-suite with a staff that professionalizes the sustainability effort over time. In
smaller companies that cannot afford a full-time CSO, someone still needs to
hold this title (alongside other roles) to ensure systematic follow-through on the
sustainability game plan.

Of course, everything cannot be done at once. Priorities must be set. For
most companies, it makes sense to break a sustainability strategy down into
one-year, two-year, and five-year action plans. Go after the low-hanging fruit
first—invest in energy efficiency, which often delivers quick payoffs; reduce major
environmental risks that create serious exposure; launch a pilot project or two;
and find ways to engage employees. On a longer-term basis, look for ways
to bring new products or services to the marketplace that help others address
their sustainability challenges. And seek opportunities to enhance the company's
brand and reputation through environmental or community leadership.

To put the execution challenge another way, start by doing old things in new
ways that address sustainability pressures. Then turn to doing new things such
as delivering green products and services that generate added value. And finally,
think about new business models that will position your business to thrive in a
resource-competitive world.[3]

10. Continuous Improvement

Sustainability must be understood not as an endpoint but as journey. Issue
spotting isn't something you do once and then move on. Every company needs
to regularly update its impact analysis and rethink the risks and opportunities
presented by the evolving set of sustainability pressures. The pursuit of Eco-
Advantage must be done iteratively. The action items we have highlighted in this
discussion should be undertaken on a basic level and then redone on intermediate
and advanced levels—as each of the chapters that follow will explain in detail.

Because the environmental arena is highly dynamic, circumstances will
change—and the sustainability strategy must be updated accordingly. Scientific discoveries regularly lead to the identification of previously unrecognized
environmental threats and revised risk assessments. Technological developments
constantly shift the "possibility frontier" that defines how we address environmental challenges. Likewise, public expectations evolve—particularly in societies
that are developing rapidly and achieving new levels of prosperity. Companies
must be committed to embedding a sustainability lens into their strategy development system.

What might have counted as a leading-edge position in sustainability last
year, will often be a baseline requirement for the next year. So targets must be
constantly revisited and reset. A company must recalibrate its overarching vision
at regular intervals. The effort required may seem substantial—and it is. But the

companies that do the necessary work will find rewards in a world where the sustainability megatrend becomes even more deeply rooted.

ADDITIONAL RESOURCES

"Ceres Roadmap for Sustainability" (Ceres). Outlines 20 sustainability criteria Ceres believes companies must meet to stay competitive in the twenty-first century. www.ceres.org/ceresroadmap.

Confessions of a Radical Industrialist: Profits, People, Purpose—Doing Business by Respecting the Earth by Ray Anderson (St. Martin's Press, 2009).

Getting Green Done: Hard Truths from the Front Lines of the Sustainability Revolution by Auden Schendler (PublicAffairs, 2009).

Green Recovery: Get Lean, Get Smart, and Emerge from the Downturn on Top by Andrew Winston (Harvard Business Press, 2009).

"Leadership in the Age of Transparency," by Christopher Meyer and Julia Kirby (Harvard Business Review, 2010).

Natural Capitalism: Creating the Next Industrial Revolution by Paul Hawken, Amory Lovins, and L. Hunter Lovins (Little, Brown and Company, 1999).

The Responsibility Revolution: How the Next Generation of Businesses Will Win by Jeffrey Hollender and Bill Breen (Jossey-Bass, 2010).

The Step-by-Step Guide to Sustainability Planning: How to Create and Implement Sustainability Plans in Any Business or Organization by Darcy Hitchcock and Marsha Willard (Earthscan, 2008).

Strategies for the Green Economy: Opportunities and Challenges in the New World of Business by Joel Makower (McGraw-Hill, 2009).

Strategy for Sustainability: A Business Manifesto by Adam Werbach (Harvard Business Press, 2009).

The Sustainability Handbook: The Complete Management Guide to Achieving Social, Economic, and Environmental Responsibility by William R. Blackburn (Environmental Law Institute, 2007).

"The Sustainability Imperative," by David A. Lubin and Daniel C. Esty (Harvard Business Review, 2010).

Sustainable Value: How the World's Leading Companies Are Doing Well by Doing Good by Chris Laszlo (Stanford University Press, 2008).

The Triple Bottom Line: How Today's Best-Run Companies Are Achieving Economic, Social, and Environmental Success—And How You Can Too by Andrew Savitz (John Wiley & Sons, 2006).

The Truth about Green Business by Gil Friend (FT Press, 2009).

"Why Sustainability Is Now the Key Driver of Innovation," by Ram Nidumolu, C. K. Prahalad, and M. R. Rangaswami (Harvard Business Review, 2009).

Chapter 4 Making the Internal Business Case for Going Greener

"I've been looking over your 'green' proposal. It's fine, just fine—I'm sure it'll make people feel real good about the company . . . should go over big with the tree huggers too. . . . But see, the folks that I report to—they don't eat granola. So let me ask you: Why would I sign this?"

—Skeptical executive in 2009 IBM TV commercial

Whether trying to broaden internal support for a sustainability strategy or pushing a particular environmental project, you should anticipate skepticism. Every company faces limits in terms of management time and attention as well as money. Eco-Advantage initiatives always face competition from other potential uses of scarce corporate resources. Top management will expect details on how a "green" proposal advances core business objectives. CFOs and others who control the purse strings will want to see hard, dollars-and-cents justifications before lending support to any new investments. Short-staffed line managers will resist eco-efforts that further stretch their departments if they don't see what's in it for them.

Getting clear on the business case for bringing an environment or sustainability lens to strategy is critical. Making your case will be easier when the numbers are straightforward and your proposal promises a big return on investment (ROI). But what about action items with less obvious bottom-line benefits? How, for example, do you make the financial case for phasing out a chemical that regulators may not ban for years to come—if ever? How do you justify the investment in an employee eco-training effort that *could* create a more innovative culture? How do you calculate the potential ROI of a brand-enhancing leadership play, such as being the first company in your industry to pledge carbon neutrality?

Building a business case is both an art and a science, with entire books devoted to the subject. This chapter provides recommendations and tools specific to the unique challenges of making a business case involving eco-related costs and benefits. Building on the Risk-Cost-Growth-Brand framework outlined in Chapter 1, it will help you:

- Spell out the four core elements of Eco-Advantage that you should look to establish.

- Argue more effectively for making the environment or sustainability a higher strategic priority within your company or unit.

- Strengthen the case for specific projects or initiatives with green attributes.

BASIC PLAYS: OUTLINE YOUR CASE

1. Identify the Ways Your Proposal Could Generate Business Value

It's important to frame proposed green efforts in terms of business value—not as philanthropy or corporate social responsibility. How will your proposal advance core business objectives? By reducing risk? Cutting costs? Improving productivity? Bolstering brand loyalty? Improving customer satisfaction? Enhancing profit margins? Reducing time to market? Pushing up market share? Boosting the company's reputation—and softening the attitude of regulators? Helping the company recruit or retain talented people? To get started, consider four big "buckets" of Eco-Advantage opportunity as shown in Figure 4.1.

As you build your case, always try to anticipate what decision makers will be looking for. Consider the person or people you are trying to influence: What are their goals, interests, and motivations? In what format will they want information? How does your proposal align with the company's overall strategy?

2. List All Possible Financial Impacts, Including Intangible Costs and Benefits

List the ways you believe your green initiative could affect sales and cost factors that directly or indirectly help the bottom line. In each case, outline a clear cause-and-effect rationale. For instance, eliminating a hazardous substance in manufacturing might generate cost savings by cutting regulatory paperwork, reducing legal exposure, eliminating the need for protective equipment for plant operations, and reducing the costs of hazmat training.[1] A new packaging design might lower shipping expenses by making it possible to fit more units in a truck, requiring fewer trips, or by avoiding take-back requirements imposed by some B2B customers (e.g., Walmart) or political jurisdictions (e.g., Germany).

Brainstorm all potential costs and benefits:

- **Across the entire life cycle of your product or service:** Consider how your proposed effort will shape costs and benefits in the following phases: (1) *Initial*

Figure 4.1 **Business Benefits of Eco-Efforts**

1. Reduce Risks

Regulatory, marketplace, and economic pressures on companies due to environmental issues need careful scrutiny. Companies that anticipate and manage risks can avoid potentially crippling surprises, share expenses, and gain competitive advantage.

Stay ahead of regulatory developments that could limit product or production choices.

Avoid potential legal liabilities by taking actions today that head off future regulatory requirements, shareholder lawsuits, civil and criminal fines and penalties, property damage costs, clean-up costs from an accident, or ecosystem restoration costs.

Avoid damage to corporate reputation and brand by avoiding spills, accidents, product recalls, or other performance issues that could induce the ire of NGOs, regulators, or the buying public.

Avoid supply chain disruptions and shocks by managing exposure to scarce natural resources, extreme weather events, and energy price volatility.

2. Cut Costs

Green is the new lean. Eco-efficiency efforts can lead to higher margins by slashing direct costs and operating expenses.

Cut operating expenses by slashing energy, water, and waste-related costs in buildings and facilities, data centers, and fleet.

Cut product and process costs by increasing resource productivity, reducing materials and energy intensity, extending the life of products or equipment, and enabling recyclability.

Reduce supply chain and distribution costs by lowering or eliminating expenses upstream and downstream.

Reduce or avoid regulatory and compliance costs by reducing or eliminating pollution or toxics that otherwise would lead to regulatory paperwork, fees, and clean-up obligations.

3. Grow Revenue

The market for sustainable products and services will only continue to grow.

Win sales through more desirable goods and services. Companies can grow their revenues by designing and marketing environmentally superior products that meet their customers' needs for energy efficiency, improved resource productivity, and reduced pollution.

Improve sales by driving down costs through eco-efficiency or "design for the environment" differentiation.

Gain market share or access to new markets by meeting the growing demand for cleaner/greener/healthier products.

(continued)

Figure 4.1   (*Continued*)

4. Build Brand and Intangible Value

Green efforts can create significant business benefits that are significant drivers of future earnings and shareholder value, even if they are not easily measured or accounted for on financial statements.

Enhance reputation and brand equity: In our brand-conscious world, the "goodwill" embedded in a company's name or product line can be the source of a hard-to-measure but critical bond with customers. Some studies have found that 50 to 90 percent of a company's market value is connected to brand and other intangibles—and up to one-third of a company's public reputation can be based on sustainability performance (which includes social as well as environmental responsibility). Reputation can affect a company's stock price and its ability to generate sales, charge premium prices, close deals, attract partners, and retain talent.

Reduce operational burden and interference: Improved sustainability reputation can pay off in the form of lighter regulatory scrutiny, less pressure from environmental groups and other NGOs, and less risk of boycotts or bad publicity that could damage sales.

Protect social license to operate: Failing to attend to environmental and social concerns of the local communities on which a company operates or the broader society can—in extreme cases—make it impossible to continue operation.

Strengthen consumer acceptance, loyalty, and emotional connection: Shoppers want to buy brands that they trust. A company's performance on environmental and social issues can help shape customer perceptions.

Lower cost of capital: Investors and lenders are increasingly factoring companies' social and environmental performance into their decisions. Sustainability leaders pose fewer risks and may therefore enjoy greater access to capital at a lower cost.

Attract and retain top talent: A growing number of employees, particularly high-end knowledge workers, want to be part of a company with a culture and values they share. Workplace practices and environmental commitment can translate directly into positive associations in the labor market, easier recruitment of top talent, and increased retention rates.

Boost employee satisfaction and productivity: Our research shows that corporate eco-efforts can boost employee productivity by inspiring people around a shared mission and a corporate purpose that goes beyond profits. Green buildings, for example, can create a more pleasant and healthier work environment, which in turn can reduce health costs, improve employee satisfaction, and raise productivity.

Drive innovation, smart business models, and technological leadership: The sustainability mindset can drive the creation of products and services that anticipate and better address customer needs, tap into new markets, and support a culture of innovation.

Sources: William R. Blackburn, *The Sustainability Handbook: The Complete Management Guide to Achieving Social, Economic, and Environmental Responsibility* (2007). Sonali Rammohan, "Business Benefits to Hewlett-Packard Suppliers from Socially and Environmentally Responsible Practices in China—A Case Study" (2008).

or up-front phase (prior to operating a process, product, system, or facility), including costs relating to licensing, capital, siting, design, raw materials, installation, etc.; (2) *Operational or use phase*, defined as costs connected to operations and maintenance incurred during the operating lives of processes, products, systems, or facilities—such as energy, water, cleaning, and regulatory costs; (3) *Product use*, including risks from customer use (and misuse) and changing expectations about who bears responsibility for environmental harms arising from product use; (4) *Back-end, disposal or end-of-life phase*, which are costs that follow the useful life of products or processes—such as the disposing, recycling, or reprocessing of materials; decommissioning a facility; or complying with future regulations.

- **Across the value chain:** Consider impacts in the following areas: (1) acquisition of raw materials; (2) inbound distribution or logistics; (3) manufacturing operations or production; (4) outbound distribution or logistics; (5) marketing and sales; (6) after-sales service or maintenance; and (7) end-of-life product disposal.

Think about costs and benefits holistically. For instance, eco-friendly integrated building systems may entail higher up-front costs than traditional systems but be easier and faster to install—thereby offering an immediate cost advantage through savings in labor cost and construction schedule. To help you brainstorm impacts, consider the types of eco-costs and benefits in Figure 4.2.

After identifying possible costs and benefits, determine which factors could be decisive to making your case given the particular circumstances and decisionmakers involved. How do the costs and benefits relate to what the decisionmakers care about the most? How could your proposal help alleviate their pain points? Which of your assertions might they be skeptical about? Focus on the most important factors, then set out to assemble the "proof" that will undergird your business case. In some cases, qualitative or anecdotal data may be all that is available, especially for intangible benefits. In most instances, however, you will want to assign dollar values to your claims about potential costs and benefits. The "Intermediate" plays and Additional Resources at the end of the chapter will help you in both circumstances.

3. List Potential Risks Related to Your Proposal, along with Risks of *Not* Pursuing It

Your business case should catalog all of the possible risks that might undermine the project's success or cost/benefit structure. Clarify the assumptions on which your analysis is based. In some cases, it may be appropriate to evaluate outcomes under a range of circumstances or scenarios. For example, do your projections of savings depend on shaky cost estimates from suppliers? Are there risks of a new technology not working exactly as expected? What if some workers resist your proposed measures—will that slow down productivity? Does your project's

Figure 4.2   Eco-Related Costs and Benefits (A Guide to Commonly Used Terms)

Easier to Quantify	Harder to Quantify
Cash. Costs or benefits that directly affect bottom-line financial profit or loss (e.g., capital costs, labor, materials, transportation). **Internal/Private.** Costs or benefits that directly affect a firm's bottom line. Also can refer to costs for which a business can be held legally responsible. Can be direct or indirect. **Conventional.** Refers to costs associated with a capital or revenue project. Can be direct or indirect. **Direct.** Costs clearly and exclusively associated with a particular product or service (e.g., direct cost of capital investment, operations, labor, raw materials, site, and waste disposal not allocated to overhead). May be recurring or non-recurring costs. Includes capital and operations and maintenance (O&M) costs. **Overhead/Indirect/Administrative/Hidden.** Costs for activities or services that may benefit multiple projects/products/processes and are not easily allocated to specific projects. Can be fixed or variable, recurring or non-recurring, capital and O&M, or outsourced. (e.g., costs from facilities, rent, administrative staff, security, reporting, regulatory affairs, insurance, monitoring, energy use, and waste disposal not overhead tracked to individual products or processes). **Regulatory/Compliance.** Costs incurred to comply with federal, state, or local laws (e.g., notification, monitoring, reporting, training, labeling, etc.). Can be direct or indirect. Often treated as overhead.	**NonCash/NonFinancial/Less Tangible/Intangible.** Umbrella terms often used interchangeably to cover a range of internal and external costs or benefits that can directly or indirectly impact shareholder value. **Internal Intangible.** Hard-to-measure but nonetheless real costs or benefits to the company. (e.g., costs to maintain customer acceptance and loyalty, worker morale and wellness, union relations, corporate image, community relations). Sometimes used to refer to avoided costs (e.g., fines, capital). **Image and Relationship.** A subset of "Internal Intangible." Costs or benefits from improved or impaired perception of stakeholders (e.g., costs from prolonged licensing process or tougher monitoring). **Future/Prospective.** Costs certain to be incurred at some point, but exact timing is unknown (e.g., an asset retirement obligation (ARO) liability for future disposal of an asset or some other future clean-up obligation). **Contingent/Contingent Liability.** Costs that may be incurred in the future (e.g., fines and penalties, property damage costs, lawsuits, accident clean-up costs, personal injury claims, ecosystem restoration costs).

(continued)

Figure 4.2 *(Continued)*

Easier to Quantify	Harder to Quantify
Voluntary. Costs incurred for going beyond compliance. Could be direct or indirect. Often treated as overhead.	**External/Societal/Externalities.** Costs or benefits to external stakeholders that do not directly affect the firm's bottom line and for which the firm is not (yet) financially responsible (e.g., damage to an ecosystem, long-term pollution effects). Business is not legally responsible today but could be in the future due to stricter environmental regulation, taxes, or fees. Often divided into environmental or social costs or benefits, though "social" is sometimes used as an umbrella term to include environmental. May be expressed qualitatively or in physical terms (e.g., tons of releases) or in dollars and cents.

Source: Adapted from EPA, *An Introduction to Environmental Accounting as a Business Management Tool: Key Concepts and Terms* (1995), and Table 1-2: "Costs Typically Included in Environmental Accounting" (1995).

ROI hinge on certain market conditions that could change overnight? Be comprehensive about possible downsides both in terms of what might go wrong and what has been done to mitigate each risk identified. Such "clear-eyed" analysis is critical to business credibility—and to overcoming a presumption (held by some executives) that green proposals tend to be "soft" or lacking in analytic rigor.

Be sure to factor the potential risks and costs of inaction into the analysis. Business decisions are never made in a vacuum. In many cases, taking action will have a cost, but the failure to take action imposes even higher costs. Likewise, you should consider what economists call the opportunity cost—what other initiatives won't accomplish if the activity you propose goes forward. A green initiative isn't justified simply because it has a positive ROI. It must compete successfully against alternative plans of action that might better utilize the limited resources, including management time as well as money.

DRIVING THE CASE HOME

When green-minded executives at the Canadian logistics company **Purolator** proposed converting the company's in-city delivery fleet to hybrid-electric vehicles (HEVs), it wasn't just the CFO who was skeptical. While the numbers looked good at senior management meetings, many employees feared the vehicles wouldn't work well or be comfortable. The key to winning support was the decision to give employees a chance to test-drive the HEVs. Once they did and gave good reviews, the deal was sealed.[2]

4. Provide Real-World Examples and ROI Success Stories

If you provide examples of how others have already generated bottom-line benefits from doing what you propose, you can defuse objections. The more concrete and quantitative your "case studies," the better. Keep in mind the following cautionary words of John O'Keefe, former managing director of Limehouse Studios: "Citing what competitors are doing can be seen as disloyal, unless you keep it positive—'we can do better.'"[3] See the "Real-World ROI Success Stories" chart on page 52 for scores of examples.

FOUR TIPS FOR GETTING STARTED

David Bent, head of Business Strategies at the UK-based NGO Forum for the Future, offers the following sound advice for those looking to build the business case for a sustainability investment:

1. **View the business case as part of a wider change program**. That means knowing who the internal stakeholders are that you need to influence, especially in the finance function. Is there someone who could be a champion among the accountants?

2. **Go to the finance department with a safe pilot**. Identify something—an initiative, project, decision, or process—where the business case can be investigated without becoming too resource intensive.

3. **Use the pilot to build credibility and awareness**. If possible, get the finance department to do the business case analysis themselves. Finance types always find their own results more persuasive than those of outsiders, especially those perceived to have a stake in the outcome of the analysis.

4. **Keep creating a "permission and results" cycle**. Throughout the process, work to create a logic for extending the analysis so that you will get permission to take the business case to the next level. Along the way, you will be strengthening the capacity of individuals and groups within the firm to understand and act on sustainability.

Source: Drawn from David Bent, "How to Build a Business Case for Sustainability: Four Tips on Getting Buy-In from Finance," *Greenbiz.com*, November 23, 2009. http://www.greenbiz.com (accessed August 18, 2010).

INTERMEDIATE PLAYS: SUPPORT THE CASE WITH NONFINANCIAL DATA

5. Use Weighted Criteria to Evaluate Tradeoffs

While dollars and cents analysis is very important, in some cases the promise of an eco-project will not be fully captured by traditional financial accounting systems. Many companies have therefore developed analytic tools designed to integrate hard-to-quantify or nonfinancial criteria into their decision processes.

THE EVOLUTION OF NORTHROP GRUMMAN'S WEIGHTED CRITERIA MODEL

Northrop Grumman Corporate Program Director David Hitchings and his team set out to build a new cost-benefit analytical model that could accommodate eco-criteria alongside traditional ROI calculations.[4] The company had already adjusted its financial model to include true cash benefits typical to eco-projects that are often excluded from calculations—third-party incentives, government grants, tax credits, and so forth. It had also developed a way to estimate potential project cost savings associated with CO_2 reductions. The goal was to create an expanded, credible framework to evaluate and communicate additional nonfinancial benefits of proposed environmental projects and initiatives.

Hitchings, a 21-year Northrop veteran, knew his efforts would be facilitated in part by the company's "balanced scorecard" culture. Senior executives were already accustomed to looking beyond pure financial measures when making decisions about budgets, projects, and capital expenditures. And they understood how "soft" factors—like the ability to recruit and retain top talent—mattered to shareholder value. Still, Hitchings recognized that many of his defense and aerospace industry peers might be skeptical.

The most effective approach, Hitchings concluded, would be to involve peers in the analytical process—to enlist them in the work to evaluate how environmental issues could positively or negatively affect business value. He invited an influential group of cross-functional executives (from business development, marketing, human resources, supply chain, and more) to weigh in. First, he shared a draft checklist of the various eco-costs and benefits that might be added to the traditional ROI model and cost-benefit analyses. Then he asked the team members to help refine the checklist and devise a weighted-points system based on their judgments about what mattered most.

The resulting "Eco-model" offers a credible, standardized way for decision makers to compare different projects' potential to add value beyond what existing financial models can capture. A cross-functional team assigns scores to projects based on their ability to advance key business objectives, including: employee attraction and retention; business development; customer satisfaction; corporate image and reputation; and voluntary corporate social responsibility (CSR) commitments.

Today, if two projects with similar projected returns are competing for limited investment capital, Northrop Grumman executives generally select the one with more eco-points. And any proposed investment that scores zero eco-points gets subjected to added scrutiny.

The secret to success in this case lies in the participatory approach Hitchings designed. The model got traction quickly because of the credibility and diversity of the individuals who created it. Project evaluation scores, though based heavily on qualitative judgments, are trusted because they rely on multiple perspectives and the assessment of many experts within the company and not just on one office's opinion. More important, the results are rigorous—not torqued by those with a sustainability axe to grind.

6. Use Performance Indicators to Highlight Opportunities

Using performance indicators to reinforce the potential value of eco-efficiency proposals can add to the business logic of an investment under review. Metrics that evaluate critical resource inputs, such as energy, water, or raw materials are particularly useful. In particular, they can underpin efforts to improve "resource productivity." These measures can also help to underscore a proposal's potential to deliver real bottom-line value:

- **Return on resources (ROR)** is the ratio of *profit, revenue, or intended result to critical resource inputs*, showing how much money your organization makes—or how much output you produce—per unit of critical resources used. Gil Friend, CEO of Natural Logic, a California-based eco-consulting firm, suggests that companies explore many kinds of ratios (e.g., profit per ton of raw material or units of product per pound of hazardous waste) to see which ones disclose meaningful patterns that help drive better decisions. Friend suggests putting the intended result in the numerator. This way, "the resulting ratio has the same 'up is good' directionality of most financial indicators like revenue, profit, and market share, rather than the 'down is good' vector of most environmental indicators."[5]

- **Productive to non-productive ratio (P2NP)** is the ratio of productive output (the intended result you want to produce) to "non-productive output" or NPO (the unintended or unwanted pollutants, scrap, or waste you can't sell or reuse), which provides a window into how wasteful a particular production process is. It is calculated as follows:

$$\text{Finished product}/(\text{Finished Product} + \text{NPO})^6$$

This single metric, Gil Friend observes, can be "one of the most powerful change drivers" available. The result of the P2NP analysis, he notes, always looks "far worse than companies estimate." This reality helps managers see that "producing NPO makes no business sense at all."[7]

7. Bring Credible External Voices into the Mix

Sometimes a fresh voice from the outside can make all the difference. Who from outside your company could help persuade your audience? Would a world-renowned scientist or subject matter expert lend credibility to your arguments? Would it impress your colleagues if a senior executive from another respected company shared a case study on how they benefited from actions similar to what you propose? What if a top customer outlined its environmental priorities and expectations for your company and your competitors?

ADVANCED PLAYS: SHARPEN THE PENCIL

8. Assign a Monetary Value to Each Key Factor, and Calculate Net Present Value

Translating eco-related costs and benefits into a traditional accounting framework isn't easy. No simple, one-size-fits-all method can meet the diverse requirements of every executive reading this report. In working to make the business case for an environmental or sustainability project, a net present value calculation is often the Holy Grail.

Carefully and systematically consider which factors, if measured and monetized, produce the most convincing analysis and business case. If you believe an employee engagement initiative will help retain talent, you should focus on metrics such as the average cost of losing a good employee and the average cost of recruiting and on-boarding a new hire along with a credible way to estimate the percentage of your workforce that might stay with the company longer because of your proposed program.

Be selective. The process of generating financial numbers—especially hard-to-quantify ones—can be costly and time-consuming. And you won't have the time or resources to gather data on everything. Moreover, your credibility could suffer if your approach is overly complex. Focus on getting the picture right.

GOING THE EXTRA MILE

Steve Yucknut, Vice President of Sustainability at **Kraft Foods**, counsels approaching sustainability projects and investments with the same hard business lens as usual—but with a commitment to do a little more homework. "Everyone would love me to say that I've lowered the hurdle rate for sustainability-related projects and investments because it shows our genuine commitment to the planet. That is just not pragmatic. We are a 'for-profit' business and we shouldn't be ashamed of that. We are accountable to our shareholders and have to be consistent with our fiscal approach. The business case—the internal rate of return, the top and bottom-line benefits—that needs to be the motivation. But if, like us, your company really wants to seize sustainability business opportunities, you *will* need to work a little harder when analyzing projects because our systems aren't used to doing financial analysis with a sustainability lens. You'll need to run different sensitivity analyses with new assumptions, sometimes trying a little longer before you give up. We've accepted that we have to absorb some degree of incremental effort until we get better at it. But the results have been worth it."[8]

Finally, remember that numbers are only as good as the assumptions on which they are based. Make sure calculations can withstand scrutiny so your reputation remains solid. Test and refine your assumptions. Carefully assess the potential for downside risks (technical, cost, operational, market, circumstantial) and be prepared to explain their probability and how they can be mitigated or controlled. Think about which of your assumptions might be challenged. Have a compelling explanation for each of your assumptions ready to go. You might even want to run sensitivity analyses to demonstrate which assumptions drive the anticipated outcomes.[9]

To develop and refine your game plan, consult the sample sustainability ROI model from HDR, Inc., shown in Figure 4.3, as well as the Additional Resources at the end of this chapter. The tools listed can help you identify and choose relevant parameters, obtain data, and translate data into dollars and cents for inclusion in your ROI calculations and other financial analyses.

9. Try a Portfolio Approach

As Dan Esty and Andrew Winston discovered in their research for *Green to Gold*, some companies have found it useful to "pair" or "bundle" sustainability-oriented projects that don't meet existing hurdle rates for investment. By combining a high eco-value project with others that have a high ROI, a high value overall portfolio can be created. GE, for instance, calculated one overall rate of return for a portfolio of 60 energy efficiency retrofit projects across a number of facilities. While some individual investments wouldn't have met GE's usual two-year payback hurdle, the portfolio approach enabled executives to justify the full effort and meet their objective of division-wide sustainability progress. By creating some flexibility within the overall parameters of business logic, the GE managers also were able to claim some of the intangible benefits—bragging rights with shareholders, enhanced brand value, and happier employees—at an acceptable cost.[10]

10. Push Back on Others' Numbers When Appropriate

Financial forecasts and projections are only as good as the assumptions behind them. Don't assume others' numbers are any better than yours. Dig into the underlying assumptions. Ask about the sensitivity of the analysis to these assumptions. Remember that strict adherence to traditional financial accounting can lead to shortsighted decisions when sustainability variables are in play. If your company refuses to make exceptions, consider pointing to the benefits accruing to other companies (particularly competitors) that have undertaken farsighted projects with long-term benefits.

Many leaders of the world's most successful companies have found that it makes sense to adjust their financial models to accommodate commonly overlooked environmental and social factors. For instance, Unilever's capital investment process "requires an environmental profile of an investment, which may trigger a lower hurdle rate."[11] 3M has cut its standard 30 percent hurdle rate

Figure 4.3   HDR, Inc.'s Sustainability ROI (SROI) Model

HDR, Inc., a large international architectural, engineering, and consulting organization, developed the "SROI" model to measure the financial value of social, environmental, and economic impacts of projects or programs aimed at the sustainability triple bottom line. The model helps both public and private sector decision makers evaluate projects competing for limited funding. Its approach draws heavily on stakeholder input, which lends credibility to the controversial process of assigning monetary values and assessing probability associated with key variables. The approach consists of the following steps:

1. **Identify all potential cash benefits** using life cycle costing, then calculate a financial return on investment (FROI).

2. **Identify all potential non-cash benefits to a company and external benefits to society** using structure and logic maps to reveal all variables.

3. **Quantify inputs and assign a monetary value** to each, using the best-available third-party research, contingent valuation, and other means.

4. **Assess statistical probability** of various outcomes and assign a probability distribution for each variable.

5. **Validate assumptions** with stakeholder groups and build consensus.

6. **Calculate the ROI** for a range of possible alternatives, using a Monte Carlo simulation to account for the various values and variables.

This example shows how a standard financial ROI valuation would not reflect full impacts and benefits. The difference between the values shown for the financial ROI (the black curve) and the sustainable ROI (the lightest gray curve far right) is the value of "sustainability." More information available at: www.hdrinc.com.

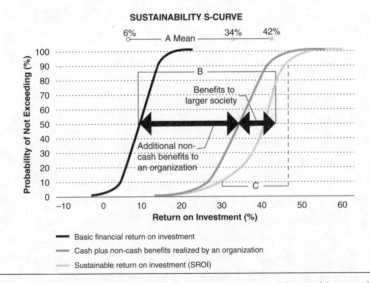

(A) Compare FROI (black curve) to SROI (lightest gray curve far right). In this example, the mean SROI (at 50% probability) is over six times greater than the traditional ROI; (B) Evaluate non-cash internal benefits (such as improvements in employee health and productivity) and external benefits to society; (C) Assess statistical likelihood that return will fall within an 80% confidence interval. In this example, the SROI ranges from 30–48%.

Source: HDR, Sustainable Return on Investment. www.hdrinc.com (accessed November 2010). Reprinted with permission.

to 10 percent for its highly successful Pollution Prevention Pays projects.[12] The business logic of these choices is sound. It's the traditional business tools that ignore key costs and benefits.[13]

When opponents say, "We can't afford to make this investment," consider countering with the argument that "we can't afford *not* to make the investment"—if you believe that to be true. According to Harvard professor Clayton Christensen, "discounted cash flow and net present value, as commonly used, underestimate the real returns and benefits of proceeding with an investment." Look out for faulty straight-line projections based on static assumptions. Analysis of an energy efficiency investment, for instance, should probably reflect rising prices from both long-term supply/demand imbalances and emerging carbon pricing. As Christensen writes: "In most situations . . . competitors' sustaining and disruptive investments over time result in price and margin pressure, technology changes, market share losses, sales volume decreases, and a declining stock price. The most likely stream of cash for the company in the do-nothing scenario is not a continuation of the status quo. It is a nonlinear decline in performance."[14]

SUMMARY

Key Plays

1. Identify the ways your proposal could generate business value.
2. Consider all financial impacts, including intangible costs and benefits.
3. List potential risks related to your proposal, along with the risks of *not* pursuing it.
4. Provide real-world examples and ROI success stories.
5. Use weighted criteria approach to cost-benefit analyses.
6. Use performance indicators to highlight opportunities.
7. Bring credible external voices into the mix.
8. Assign a monetary value to each key factor, and calculate net present value.
9. Try a portfolio approach.
10. Push back on others' numbers when appropriate.

ADDITIONAL RESOURCES

GENERAL GUIDANCE ON BUILDING A STRONG BUSINESS CASE

"How to Build a Business Case" by Jack Molisani and Bonni Graham (2008). 3-page article outlining essential elements of a strong business case. www.prospringstaffing.com

Business Case Essentials: A Guide to Structure and Content by Marty J. Schmidt (2009). Practical, 100-page introduction to business case analysis that assumes no prior background in finance. www.solutionmatrix.com

The Next Sustainability Wave: Building Boardroom Buy-In by Bob Willard (New Society Publishers, 2005). Sound, practical advice from a 35-year veteran of IBM on building the internal case for sustainability action. www.newsociety.com

Buy-In: Saving Your Good Idea from Getting Shot Down by John P. Kotter and Lorner A. Whitehead (Harvard Business Review Press, 2010). www.hbr.org

"Show Me the Money: Demonstrating Green Business Value to Skeptics" by P.J. Simmons and M.R. Rangaswami (Corporate Eco Forum, 2009). www.corporateecoforum.com

BUILDING THE CASE IN SPECIFIC AREAS

The Sustainability Advantage: Seven Business Case Benefits of a Triple Bottom Line by Bob Willard (New Society Publishers, 2002). How to identify and monetize internal costs and benefits of proposed sustainability efforts, including easier hiring and retention of top talent, increased employee productivity, lowered expenses at commercial sites, increased revenues and market share, reduced risk, and easier financing. www.sustainabilityadvantage.com

"Making the Business Case for a Carbon Reduction Project: How to Win over the Board and Influence People" (Carbon Trust, 2009). Practical recommendations for building the case for carbon (including considerations of finance and risk), anticipating what decision makers will be looking for, gathering data and evidence, drafting and presenting the proposal, and keeping momentum. www.carbontrust.co.uk

"Guide to the Business Case and Benefits of Sustainability Purchasing" (Sustainability Purchasing Network, 2007). Outlines the financial, social, and environmental costs and benefits of sustainability purchasing. www.buysmartbc.com

"The Lean and Green Supply Chain: A Practical Guide for Material Managers and Supply Chain Managers to Reduce Costs and Improve Environmental Performance" (EPA, 2000). Introductory guidance on how to identify environmental costs and benefits in mainstream materials and supply chain management decision making. www.epa.gov

Forging New Links: Enhancing Supply Chain Value through Environmental Excellence (Global Environmental Management Initiative, 2004). Outlines ways in which environmental initiatives can boost overall supply chain performance and enhance shareholder value. www.gemi.org

"Corporate Ecosystem Valuation: Making the Business Case" (World Business Council for Sustainable Development, 2009) 20-page article outlining the importance of factoring ecosystem costs and benefits into corporate decisions. www.wbcsd.org

Greening Our Built World: Costs, Benefits and Strategies by Greg Kats (Island Press, 2009). Outlines findings from extensive financial analyses of over 150 green buildings in the United States and 10 other countries. www.islandpress.org

"The Business Case: What Is the Cost and Value of Green Building?" (Canadian Green Business Council, 2007). A chapter from the CaGBC Municipal Green Building Toolkit that offers universally applicable guidance for evaluating the costs and benefits of green buildings. www.cagbc.org

"The Business Case for Environmental and Sustainability Employee Education" (National Environmental Education Foundation, 2010). Outlines the business benefits of educating employees on environmental and sustainability practices. www.neefusa.org

"The Effects of Employee Satisfaction on Company Financial Performance" (Marketing Innovators International, 2005). Summarizes research on the correlation between corporate financial performance and employee satisfaction. www.marketinginnovators.com

SUSTAINABILITY ROI MODELS AND SOFTWARE

HDR Inc.'s Sustainability ROI (SROI) Model (see Figure 4.3). A methodology that helps companies evaluate the full economic, social, and environmental value of projects by assigning monetary values to all costs and benefits. www.hdrinc.com

True Impact Web-Based ROI Calculator and Other Software Tools. True Impact developed a web-based software that helps companies measure and monetize social, financial, and environmental impacts of current or prospective programs. www.trueimpact.com

ORC Worldwide's Return on Health, Safety and Environmental Investments (ROHSEI) Method/Software. An analytical process with supporting software designed to help environmental, health, and safety professionals develop business cases and make capital and expense investment decisions involving competing safety, health, and environmental scenarios. www.orc-dc.com

ENVIRONMENTAL ACCOUNTING AND COST-ASSESSMENT TOOLS
See Chapter 17 ("Accounting and Finance") for related guidance and recommended resources, including:

- Introduction to key concepts and tools in environmental accounting.
- Cost assessment methods to include eco-factors in decision making on product design, costing, supply chain management, logistics, and more.
- Monetizing potential liability costs and risks.
- Monetizing value to brand.
- Updating traditional financial statements to include environmental factors.

REAL-WORLD ROI SUCCESS STORIES

Buildings and Facilities

- **Dell** expects to save about $5.8 million a year as a result of energy-saving initiatives and building upgrades, cutting its global power use by about 48 million kilowatt hours per year.[15]

- **Mack Molding** invested $450,000 in a new fluorescent lighting system for its custom plastics manufacturing facility, a move that is expected to increase productivity and pay for itself in energy savings within two years.[16]

- The **Energy Star** rating earned by 3,300 commercial buildings in 2008 translated to $1 billion in utility bill cost savings.[17]

- **Adobe Systems** recently earned $390,000 in energy rebates and reduced its annual operating costs by $1.2 million for a 121 percent return on an investment in heating, ventilation, and air-conditioning efficiency upgrades in San Jose, California.[18]

- **Northrop Grumman** saved $2 million in energy costs at a single facility by installing reflective roofs and fluorescent lighting, replacing old equipment, and making minor temperature and humidity-level adjustments.[19]

- **Walmart:** An employee suggestion to simply turn off the lights in break room vending machines is saving the company about $1 million a year.[20]

Information Technology

- **Toyota Motor Sales USA** expects to reduce energy costs by 10 percent through a program with **IBM** and **Southern California Edison** to pinpoint power and cooling inefficiencies in its data center.[21]

- **IBM** saved $49 million by investing $1 million in a green overhaul of one of its data centers in Kentucky; it also boosted the center's IT capacity eight times without raising the energy footprint through energy efficiency improvements.[22]

- **Citi**'s newly completed data center was the first to earn LEED Platinum certification from the US Green Building Council (USGBC) and uses about 70 percent less power than conventional data centers.[23]

- **Intel** estimates saving $2.87 million in a 10 MW data center by using an air economizer to cool servers more efficiently.[24]

Telecommuting

- **IBM** saves at least $700 million a year in real estate costs alone by allowing approximately 25 percent of its 320,000 employees to telecommute.[25]

- **McKesson Corporation** reports that the group that has the highest job satisfaction, outside of executives, is composed of over 1,000 nurses who work from home.[26]

Energy

- **Agilent** will save $3.5 million in energy costs over the first 10 years of its solar array system operations at its headquarters.[27]

- Agricultural company **Verdegaal Bros.** will save $60,000 per year as a result of its fixed-mount solar installation. The system will offset 99 percent of the company's energy bills and provide 82 percent of its energy needs.[28]

- The **Climate Corps** of students enlisted by the Environmental Defense Fund in 2009 saved participating companies $54 million in lifetime energy, information technology and heating and cooling costs through energy efficiency projects.[29]

- **Holiday Inn** expects to save $4 million annually by replacing its neon signage with LED lighting as part of its global brand relaunch.[30]

- **Staples** saved $6.5 million in energy costs and $1.5 million in fuel costs through green initiatives in 2008.[31]

- **Pepsico**'s Chicago headquarters reduced energy usage by 22 percent and paper usage by 37 percent last year thanks to the efforts of the company's "Green Team."[32]

Manufacturing and Process

- **3M**'s "3P" (Pollution Prevention Pays) program has saved the company nearly $1.4 billion and eliminated 3 billion pounds of pollution since its inception in 1975 by drawing on the ingenuity of employees to prevent pollution at the source, in products and manufacturing.[33]

- **Dow**'s 1995–2005 sustainability goals enabled the company to earn a return of $5 billion on an investment of $1 billion in processes and technologies.[34]

- **Baxter International** over the past decade has received an average return of approximately $3 for every $1 invested in its environmental initiatives, which it has documented on its annual Environmental Financial Statement of environmental costs and benefits.[35]

- **Lockheed Martin** reduced its year-to-year water usage in 2008 by 275 million gallons—an 11 percent decrease. The company is working toward a 25 percent reduction of carbon emissions, waste, and water by 2012.[36]

- **Trojan Battery Company**, a battery manufacturer in California, used value and energy stream mapping plus kaizen events to cut $100,000 in annual energy costs.[37]

- **Mission Rubber**, using a five-day value stream mapping event and two kaizen events, simultaneously reduced energy use by 473,076 kWh, saved $40,000 per year, and increased productivity and sales.[38]

- **Canyon Creek Cabinet Company**, manufacturer of fine cabinetry, used the EPA's Lean and Environment program combined with stream mapping and kaizen events to realize savings of $1 million per year.[39]

Carbon Reduction Activities

- **General Electric** achieved $100 million in energy savings (between 2004 and 2008) from its internal greenhouse gas reduction program.[40]

- **Jones Lang LaSalle** generated $95 million in energy savings for real estate clients in 2008 by helping clients reduce their carbon footprints by over 438,000 tons.[41]

- **Johnson & Johnson** saved $30 million between 1995 and 2005 by reducing greenhouse gas emissions via energy efficiency measures—while still driving up revenues.[42]

- The **Walt Disney Company** saved $2.3 million annually as a result of a simple "Building Tune-Up Program" that saved 46 million kWh of electricity and reduced energy use by 5 to 20 percent.[43]
- A single **General Electric** facility in Ohio saved $1 million by cutting fuel consumption from 20,000 gallons to 10,000 gallons and eliminated 5,000 metric tons of greenhouse gas emissions in 2007.[44]

Packaging

- **Sprint**'s eco-friendly packaging for mobile phones and accessories is expected to save the company $2.1 million annually and produce 647 fewer tons of waste each year.[45]
- **Cadbury** has cut shipping costs by replacing customary metal tins with cardboard, reducing a product's weight by 45 percent.[46]
- **Walmart** expects to save an estimated $3 billion in transportation costs by reducing packaging 5 percent by 2015.[47] It also saved $3.5 million in transportation expenses by trimming toy packaging during the 2008 holiday season.[48]
- **Earthbound Farms** has moved to 100 percent post-consumer PET packaging, a move expected to save the company about 425,000 million BTUs of energy and avoid 16,000 tons of CO_2 emissions annually.[49]

Waste Reduction, Materials Reuse and Recycling

- **ArcelorMittal**'s specialty rolling mill plant in Pennsylvania has saved $200,000 in annual energy bills through efficiency improvements including automated systems that idle electrical machinery during production delays.[50]
- Flooring manufacturer **Shaw Industries** saved $623,000 in energy costs during 2008 by converting 9.5 million pounds of carpet and 12 million pounds of wood waste into energy and using it to run a manufacturing plant in Georgia.[51]
- **Sonoco** opened up a revenue stream of $770,000 after finding more than 70,000 tons of recyclable scrap while conducting waste audits in 34 North American plants in 2008.[52]
- **Coca-Cola**: System-wide packaging efficiency efforts in 2009 avoided the use of approximately 85,000 metric tons of primary packaging, resulting in an estimated cost savings of over $100 million.[53]
- **Hospitals** saved $138 million and diverted 4.3 million pounds of waste from landfills in 2008 by working with a company that reprocesses single-use medical equipment.[54]

Logistics and Fleet

- **UPS** has saved about $10 million a year in gas costs just by having drivers avoid taking left turns so they aren't stuck waiting at red lights.[55] The company expects its Smart Pickup program (innovative software that coordinates efficient scheduling) to save another 793,000 gallons of fuel by reducing 8 million driving miles.[56]
- **Boeing Corporation** cut fuel use 3 percent on 737 airplanes by adding "winglets" to reduce air resistance, which were inspired by the biomechanics of bat and dragonfly wings.[57]

- **McKesson Corp.** expects the use of more fuel-efficient vehicles in its pharmaceutical sales fleet will save the company $300,000 in 2010.[58]

- **Macy's** reduced annualized transportation costs by $25,000 by participating in the Empty Miles Service, a program that fills one company's empty trucks with another company's cargo.[59]

- **AT&T**'s fleet of 105 renewable-energy vehicles saved the company more than 34,000 gallons of fuel and cut emissions by more than 300 metric tons in 2008.[60]

- In North America, **Procter & Gamble**'s use of intermodal transport (combining trucks and trains) has saved the company 11 million liters of diesel fuel annually.[61]

- **Cisco System**'s environmentally sound packaging program, which eliminates millions of pounds of unnecessary packaging, is forecasted to save $24 million annually increasing transportation load utilization.[62]

- **Dell**, simply by rearranging how it packs and delivers electronics, has increased the average per truckload weight from 18,000 pounds to 22,000 pounds. Although each trip uses more fuel, the net result is savings due to fewer trips.[63]

- **3M** saved $111,000 per year by reducing truckloads by 40 percent. It eliminated the use of truck cabs with lighter sleeping berths and used packing pallets on two levels, enabling all necessary trips to be made in one day.[64]

- **SC Johnson** saved about $1.6 million through a truckload-utilization project that balanced maximum capacity with maximum weight to reduce total number of truckloads.[65]

- **Novo Nordisk** implemented a driver-training program that, in six months, increased fuel efficiency by 2.6 percent while simultaneously eliminating 700 metric tons of CO2 emissions.[66]

- **Carrier** achieved $1 million in fuel savings and 30 percent less emissions by right-sizing vehicles, reducing vehicle weight, and using telematics technology.[67]

- **Poland Spring** has saved $20,000 a year by reducing truck idling.[68]

- **Abbott Laboratories**, along with many other environmentally conscious companies, has started using fuel-efficiency vehicles to achieve a self-imposed greenhouse gas baseline target.[69]

- **Infinity Insurance** expects to reduce operation costs by 10 percent, improving fuel efficiency by 25 percent, and reduce greenhouse gas emissions by 16 percent by simply using fuel-efficient vehicles.[70]

Supply Chain Management

- **GM** cut $12 million from disposal costs by sharing reusable packaging with its suppliers.[71]

- **Texas Instruments**, through efficient supply chain practices, including reducing and reusing packing and source material reduction, saves $8 million each year.[72]

- **Walmart** has improved customer relations, saved 100,000 gallons of fuel, and cut 672,000 miles traveled annually by purchasing peaches from farmers in 18 states rather than from a few large suppliers.[73]

- **Kodak** has a take-back program in which 70 percent of customers have returned their used cameras allowing Kodak to manufacture new cameras with 85 percent recycled materials. This has also reduced Kodak's manufacturing costs.[74]

Greener Products and Services

- **Procter & Gamble's Tide Coldwater,** a detergent designed to function in cold water, saves 3 to 4 percent and $60 in home energy use and has realized profits of $13.1 billion. Procter & Gamble estimates $50 billion in sales of "sustainable innovation products" by 2012.[75]

- **Clorox** announced in early 2009 that its **Green Works** line of plant-based cleaning materials, launched in early 2008, captured 42 percent of the natural cleaning products market in its first year.[76]

- **Chemical suppliers** experienced 30 percent revenue growth per year from 2006–2008 by helping customers manage chemicals over life cycles and reduce chemical use and waste. The global market for chemical management services is expected to triple in the next 5 to 10 years.[77]

- **Boeing**'s customized landing-path program for airliners saved more than 1 million pounds of jet fuel over a yearlong testing period at one airport.[78]

- **DuPont** set a goal of generating an additional $6 billion in annual revenues by 2015 through product innovation based on sustainability. Of this growth, $2 billion is targeted annually from products that increase energy efficiency or reduce GHG emissions.[79]

- **GE** is now aiming for $25 billion in revenue from its Ecomagination line by 2010, after sales jumped 21 percent in 2008 to $17 billion.[80]

- **Mitsubishi** plans to achieve sales of about $13.3 billion by 2016 from clean technologies such as solar systems, heat pumps, and other energy efficient power devices.[81]

- **Henkel** (the German company behind major consumer brands including Dial and Right Guard) credits sustainability thinking for driving profitable innovations—including creating Purex Natural Elements laundry detergent, now the bestseller in its category in the United States.[82]

- **Philips** announced that its green products rose to 25 percent of overall sales (up from 20 percent in 2007), putting the company on track to hit its 30 percent goal by 2012.[83]

- **Xerox**'s decision to lease machines and provide document services has raised customer satisfaction, lowered energy use, and led to a 91 percent recycling of printers. Xerox is aiming for waste-free products in waste-free facilities to promote waste-free offices for customers.[84]

- **CardPak**, a packaging company, created the EcoLogical line of packaging that eliminates up to 85 percent of the plastics used in regular products and utilizes only 100 percent recycled cardboard. Two years after its launch in 2006, EcoLogical accounted for 35 percent of CardPak's product sales and is rapidly growing.[85]

- **Curtis Packaging Corporation** rebranded itself as "luxuriously responsible" by switching to renewable energy, which reduced waste and emissions and incorporated eco-friendly materials into its products. By 2007, annual sales had doubled to $47 million. The Curtis management team attributes the gains to improved product quality and environmental goodwill, which secured customer loyalty and brought in new business partners.[86]

- **Anderson Corporation** uses manufacturing waste to create a material that can be used in some of its saleable products, windows, and doors. The company expects 50 percent ROI and has decreased solid lumber purchases by 750,000 board feet.[87]

Part Three Analyze: Identify Your Eco-Risks and Opportunities

Given the swirl of media attention on climate change, chemical exposures, rainforest loss, water availability, air pollution, and other challenges, most corporate leaders have come to recognize that environmental issues and concerns about sustainability could affect their business prospects. But recognizing the need to pay attention to these issues and actually bringing them into business strategy in a systematic and carefully defined way that works to the company's advantage are two different things.

While some environmental advocates promise that every environmental initiative will pay off—enhancing competitiveness and profitability—such claims make no sense. Not every R&D project produces a breakthrough. Nor does every marketing campaign deliver the desired results. So we want to be clear: Bringing an environmental focus to strategy is not easy. It requires discipline and the same attention to costs and benefits, trade-offs, risks, and opportunities that undergird any other element of strategy. The key to good environmental strategy is to be *businesslike*—which starts with sound analysis.

The chapters that follow offer a structure for folding an environment or sustainability element into strategy. They provide a set of frameworks and tools drawn from our research with hundreds of companies over the past several decades that will clarify the critical issues and establish priorities. This process has been battle tested in dozens of strategy development exercises. So while every company must tailor its "green" strategy to its own circumstances and corporate culture, we have provided an analytically rigorous way to think through which environmental issues will matter to your business—and which will not.

Some agenda items are easy to spot. For example, the prospect of climate change (and regulations to address greenhouse gas emissions) looms large across the economy—and will soon have an impact on every sector and every company. But other threats are less obvious. Some issues are defined by the nature of your business. Others demand attention because the law requires it, critical stakeholders expect it, or changing circumstance in the marketplace make it a competitive necessity. To help you be systematic in your analysis, in Part III, we offer a step-by-step approach required for cutting-edge sustainability strategy.

ISSUE SPOTTING

We begin with "Issue Spotting." At the outset, company leaders must understand the scope of the environment or sustainability challenges they need to address. In fact, they must decide whether their focus will be on environmental issues or a broader "triple bottom line" agenda that encompasses economic and social issues. We believe every company faces an array of such concerns—many of which will merit at least some management attention. Some companies manage all these issues together as a package. Others think it works best to have a team that does the environment-related work and separate groups that cover community relations, ethics and governance, diversity, and workforce engagement. We don't believe there is an easy or "right" approach to these issues. The method you choose depends on the type and scale of your operations. Bigger companies have more flexibility and can have multiple groups to manage the various dimensions of sustainability. In a small business, the entire agenda will likely fall to one person.

In Chapter 5 ("Spot the Eco-Issues that Could Impact Your Bottom Line"), we provide lists of both environmental issues and social concerns. We argue that being comprehensive in addressing these matters is often necessary because the NGO community can be unforgiving about when it believes a company has overlooked certain issues. You must *set priorities* as well. So we offer a way to identify issues and to assess which ones matter both from an internal company perspective (driven by the nature of the business and "on the ground" reality as the company sees it) and from an external perspective that derives from legal requirements, the agendas of critical stakeholders, and changing circumstances in the marketplace. In addition, we'll introduce you to a tool for *tracking trends* so that your prioritization does not only take care of today's issues but also tomorrow's.

We turn next to measuring your *environmental footprint*. Before launching a green strategy, company leaders need to be clear on the sources of their eco-impacts—and where they originate. This process needs to be done in a methodologically rigorous way with metrics that can be tracked over time. Such a quantitative approach allows you to identify the biggest problems to go after first, figure out whether your efforts to reduce risks are paying off, and compare results across facilities to determine the action items with the highest payoff.

There has been a great deal of talk in recent years about "carbon footprints." Knowing the scope of your greenhouse gas emissions is critical. But it is also important to track water use and the consumption of other natural resources, air and water pollution, land use, and waste disposal including both solid and toxic wastes. Some of this may seem difficult to do, but there are many tools available to help. More and more frequently, governments, capital market analysts, and even customers are asking companies to report their environmental impacts. So get used to filling out pollution control and natural resource management "scorecards." To be blunt, impact assessment is increasingly no longer optional.

Companies must, of course, measure the harms that arise from their own facilities as a result of production processes. This now includes going beyond the factory gates to analyze the company's entire "value chain"—from the procurement of inputs to the use (and disposal) of the product by the ultimate consumer. In fact, in our world of "extended producer responsibility," companies with big brand names will find that they are assumed to be able to shape the behavior of their suppliers and customers—and thus are held accountable for environmental results both upstream and downstream. Chapter 6 ("Assess and Measure Your Environmental Impacts") provides a set of tools and approaches to help you pin down the full spectrum of impacts and to establish where your biggest harms are coming from.

BENCHMARKING

When it comes to reducing harms, it helps to have a clear picture of what you can do about each issue. *Benchmarking* offers a good way to establish what others are doing in response to the same set of challenges—and a mechanism for identifying "best practices" on an issue-by-issue basis. Chapter 7 ("Benchmark Your Performance against Competitors and Best Practices") lays out a set of tools to establish a comparative context for action. The proper framework for analysis should begin with a gauge of how your own results and practices stack up against industry peers. From a competitiveness point of view, it is important for you to know what others in the same line of business are up to. For many companies, especially any that aspire to be sustainability leaders, benchmarking cannot stop there. Use the tools we provide to assess your company's performance against the practices of established sustainability leaders. We also offer a template of "best practices" drawn from our research and the consulting experience of Esty Environmental Partners.

LAYING THE PROPER FOUNDATION FOR STRATEGY

The process of developing an environment or sustainability strategy should always begin with analysis. We've seen company leaders try to cut out or limit this foundational work. In fact, we sometimes hear executives say: "We know our challenges. We've got a clear fix on the issues we face and what our stakeholders are saying." Even so, you should be aware that any shortcut on analysis presents real risks. In fact, we have never worked with a company that had a clear enough picture of its own strengths and weaknesses, issues and opportunities, present challenges, and future trends that it could afford to jump straight to strategy development. Simply put, there is no substitute for supporting your sustainability strategy with a structured program of issue spotting, stakeholder mapping, benchmarking, trend tracking, and action item prioritization.

Our goal, please remember, is not just to help you "go green." It is to provide you with a structured and analytically rigorous way of applying an environment or sustainability lens to your business strategy. We want to make you more profitable and more competitive—as well as a better steward of the planet.

Chapter 5 Spot the Eco-Issues that Could Impact Your Bottom Line

There was a day when most companies saw environmental issues as peripheral to their marketplace success. Small businesses paid virtually no attention to the harms they might be causing. Big companies knew that there were air and water pollution laws to obey and waste management regulations to follow. They largely thought of the environment as a "compliance" matter—best left to the general counsel's office, with top management making it clear that the less they needed to discuss these issues, the better. Today, no company can afford to ignore environmental challenges or broader sustainability concerns. These items have become significant elements of strategy.

Pollution control and natural resource management affect competitiveness and profitability in a variety of ways. Compliance, of course, still matters. Those who fail to pay attention to the legal rules end up paying a high price—as we spell out in Chapter 16 ("Legal and Regulatory Affairs"). In fact, there are ever more laws to follow and standards to meet—from the local level to the global scale. Europe, for example, now regulates carbon dioxide and other greenhouse gas emissions. While federal greenhouse gas controls have not yet been adopted in the United States, both the Securities and Exchange Commission and the EPA have initiated emissions reporting requirements. And the EPA has begun to explore regulation of carbon dioxide under the 1990 Clean Air Act. Moreover, 32 states have adopted rules designed to reduce greenhouse gas emissions using policy tools including "renewable portfolio standards" that mandate that some percentage of electricity sold in the state be from non-fossil fuel sources, energy efficiency requirements for buildings, and other means.

Beyond climate change, more stringent regulations on a variety of other issues have been adopted in the United States and around the world. The EU's REACH Directive imposes tough new regulatory requirements on any business that uses chemicals in production processes or products anywhere in Europe. New rules concerning water quality, food safety, and chemicals have just been implemented or are under debate in the United States. Companies that track these laws and regulations efficiently and fulfill their legal obligations effectively can gain a leg up on others who bear higher compliance *costs*.

Environmental issues can impose costs in other ways. Rising energy prices, for instance, can fundamentally change the business landscape. Every business felt the pain when oil prices reached $140/barrel in mid-2008. The high prices created a relative advantage for some companies—those who had worked to improve their energy efficiency—as well as those who had energy-efficient products to sell to an ever more conservation-minded public. Other companies suffered competitive disadvantages when their costs skyrocketed or the public shunned their fuel-guzzling products.

Beyond the obvious energy price impacts, companies face the risk of what the World Resources Institute and A.T. Kearney call "ecoflation" as climate change, water scarcity, deforestation, and other environmental effects on land use threaten to reduce the availability of some critical inputs to manufacturing, driving up prices.[1] Broader sustainability issues, including population growth and rising demand, especially in the emerging economies of the developing world, seem likely to reshape all commodity markets. These price pressures will strike those who have not attended to their "resource productivity," but could create opportunities for those able to reuse, recapture, or recycle the metals and other materials that are in demand.

Environmental issues can also pose *risks* that profoundly affect corporate success and must be carefully tracked and managed. These risks come in many forms:

- Accidents or spills of fuel, chemicals, or hazardous materials.
- Liability for products linked to environmental harms.
- Changed prices or availability of inputs.
- Shifts in the availability of natural capital (water, arable farm land, etc.).
- Tougher regulations.
- Political disfavor and new laws.
- Changed community attitudes and willingness to work with a company.
- Shifts in consumer buying habits.
- Public backlash.
- Withdrawal of the "social license to operate."

Risks can quickly translate into costs. No one understands this more than BP. The oil giant faces tens of billions of dollars in cleanup costs, fines, payouts, and diminished market value as a result of its 2010 Gulf of Mexico oil spill and the mishandling of the risks related to deepwater oil drilling. Likewise, California-based Natural Selection Foods was nearly wiped out when it had to recall spinach contaminated with E. coli bacteria in 2006.

In case you thought these were isolated incidents, eco-related risks have hit many other companies and industries in recent years including: ski areas (diminished supplies of natural snow), chocolate makers (contaminated milk products), gasoline additive producers (ban on MMT to enhance octane), soft drink companies (backlash against pesticide residues), plastic bottle makers (bans on the chemical BPA), and the list goes on.

Some companies never saw the risks coming. Apple couldn't believe that its cutting-edge Macs, iPods, and other iconic products would come under attack for being laced with toxics and otherwise environmentally unacceptable materials. But Greenpeace's "Green my Apple" campaign forced the company to address a set of eco-related risks. Others should have been well aware of their eco-exposure. Companies with sophisticated risk management systems stay ahead of their issues. Unilever, for instance, recently cut off several of its palm oil suppliers for failing to meet its rainforest protection standards, but only after numerous warnings.

The same environmental issues that create risks and costs for some companies produce opportunities for others. Tracking eco-issues is no longer an "optional activity." For many companies, it will be a matter of survival. Those that manage their exposure well and use a focus on sustainability as a spur to innovation will thrive. Others will find their markets shrinking and their brand names tarnished as the public shifts allegiances.

You don't have to look farther than the auto industry to see how profound the realignment driven by the "sustainability megatrend" can be. In a world of high gasoline prices and concern about carbon footprints, the public demand for fuel efficiency has transformed the car market. GM and Chrysler have gone broke. New competitors have launched vehicles sporting super-lightweight materials, advanced hybrid engines, electric motors, and even the capacity to run on alternative fuels.

NEW ECO-CAR COMPANIES

Aptera Motors (California)	Hybrid Technologies (Nevada)
Ariel Motor Company (Britain)	Koenigsegg (Sweden)
Better Place (California)	Lightning Car Company (Britain)
BYD Auto (China)	Noble Automotive (Britain)
Carbon Motors (Indiana)	Shelby Supercars (Washington)
Coda (California)	Tesla Motors (California)
Fisker Automotive (California)	Think (Norway)

Source: Popular Mechanics (October 2009) supplemented with author Internet research.

Sustainability concerns have become a core element of strategy in almost every industry. Where top executives once saw the environment as simply about regulations to follow and pollution control costs to bear, today they recognize that superior management of eco-related costs and risks can translate into significant marketplace advantage. Farsighted CEOs track environmental issues not just as a defense mechanism to keep their companies out of the gaze of government enforcement officials and watchful NGOs, but as an offensive strategy designed to strengthen their competitive position and growth potential. As Mark Parker, president and CEO of Nike says, "Sustainability is key to Nike's growth and innovation. Making our business more sustainable benefits our consumers who expect products and experiences with low environmental impact, our contract factory workers who will gain from more sustainable manufacturing, and our employees and shareholders who will be rewarded by a company that is prepared for the future."[2]

In this chapter, we provide you with tools that you can use to identify your environmental issues and sustainability concerns. Once they have been identified, you need to track them to avoid eco-surprises in the form of costs or risk, but also to discover the potential "upside" opportunities that you can use to drive revenues by bringing new goods or services to the marketplace and building brand loyalty. In particular, we show you how to:

- Spot issues.
- Map stakeholders.
- Evaluate your environmental exposure.
- Track emerging trends.
- Assess the materiality of issues.
- Prioritize the environmental and broader sustainability issues you face.

BASIC PLAYS: KNOW WHAT ISSUES MATTER TO YOU

1. Scan for the Big Issues That Could Affect Your Bottom Line

Every business needs to be aware of a range of environmental issues and broader sustainability concerns. So much is going on in the world today that it is hard to stay on top of all the developments. So here is our list of the top dozen environmental issues that deserve your attention.

For anyone who wants to go beyond an environmental perspective to a broader "triple bottom line" approach that encompasses social aspects of sustainability, consider the following additional issues.

Not every company will be affected by all of these issues, but it makes sense for most companies to be aware of them at least in a general way. We'd suggest that you analyze these issues in two ways: inside out and outside in. By *inside out*, we mean that you should analyze how your company's activities affect the

TOP 12 ENVIRONMENTAL ISSUES

Climate change: The buildup of greenhouse gases in the atmosphere contributes to global warming and the accompanying rising sea levels, changed rainfall patterns, droughts, floods, and increased intensity of storms.

Energy: The way we produce and consume energy dramatically affects our environment. Fossil fuels, in particular, are a major source of greenhouse gases, local air pollution—and their extraction poses real risk to ecosystems. Higher fossil fuel prices and a carbon-constrained future will require a shift toward greater energy efficiency and cleaner modes of power generation, which inevitably raises new concerns and tradeoffs.

Air pollution: Smog, particulates, carbon monoxide, and other airborne pollutants pose a risk to public health, especially in the developing world where air quality is worsening. In addition, indoor air pollution, caused by burning wood, coal, or dung for heating and cooking, has emerged as a critical public health threat in developing countries.

Ozone layer depletion: The phaseout of chlorofluorocarbons (CFCs) has substantially reduced the thinning of Earth's protective ozone layer, but some CFC substitutes continue to cause damage, and ongoing use of CFCs in violation of the Montreal Protocol ban has been detected in some places such as Russia.

Chemicals, toxics, and heavy metals: These contaminants create risks of cancer, reproductive harm, and other health issues in humans, plants, and animals.

Waste: Many communities still struggle with the disposal of both solid and toxic waste. Disposal concerns are especially serious in rapidly urbanizing and industrializing countries that have not yet developed an adequate waste management infrastructure.

Fresh water: Issues of water quality and availability plague many communities around the world—constraining business activities and putting the "social license to operate" of water-intensive companies at risk.

Oceans and fisheries: Due to overfishing, oil spills, climate change, and other pollution, fish stocks and marine ecosystems have vastly declined over the last century.

Land use: From suburban sprawl in the developed world to unplanned agricultural expansion in developing nations, changing patterns of land use generate concerns over harm to critical ecosystem services (such as natural barriers against fires, windstorms, and floods), altered hydrological flows, loss of open space, and habitat destruction.

Deforestation: Driven by agriculture, logging, and urban development, deforestation leads to soil erosion, water pollution, loss of biodiversity, and is the number one contributor to climate change.

Biodiversity: The loss of the rich diversity of life on earth and the terrestrial and aquatic ecosystems on which they depend is a major deprivation for scientific advancement, economic growth, and cultural preservation.

Food safety: From pesticide exposure to chemical contaminants, the health and safety of food and beverages has emerged as a major concern all around the world, driving interest in products that are organic and more natural.

Source: Updated from Esty and Winston, *Green to Gold* list.

environment. Do you use toxic materials? Does your facility pollute? Do you consume fossil fuels? If so, from what sources?

By *outside in*, we mean that you should try to understand your company's dependence on "natural capital" such as water or other natural resources. Do your products require specialized inputs? Perhaps rare elements or minerals? Many companies are dependent on hard-to-get elements without even being fully aware of that fact. Cell phones, for example, contain 77 different elements from the periodic table.[3] Do you depend on agricultural products as an input to your goods or services? Have you thought about how your access to critical inputs might be affected by environmental stresses such as climate change?

SOCIAL ISSUES

Community development	Employee safety and well-being
Corporate governance	Workforce pay scale and benefits
Transparency and political activity	Labor rights
Ethics	Human rights
Diversity	Child labor
Health and nutrition	Poverty
Education and training	Responsible marketing

2. Conduct an AUDIO Analysis to Clarify Your Issue Exposure

Beyond basic issue identification, companies need to analyze their environment or sustainability exposure and opportunities in more depth. In particular, companies need to go beyond their own immediate impacts to examine their entire supply chain. They must understand the issues that might be implicated by their suppliers and their customers—and any ultimate consumer beyond that. In addition, when you have identified various environmental aspects as possible problems, you should also examine them as possible opportunities. As we noted previously, sustainability leaders want to understand the potential for playing "offense" on the environment as well as defense.

To help business leaders think systematically about the issues they need to consider, Dan Esty developed the following framework. Refined and published as the AUDIO matrix in *Green to Gold*, it provides a structured way to analyze environment or sustainability issues across the value chain, including:

- **Aspects:** Highlight environmental issues that might affect the company.
- **Upstream:** Ensure that the analysis extends to suppliers (and their suppliers as well).

- **Downstream:** Assess impacts that occur as a result of consumer use or disposal of the product.
- **Issues:** Explore which impacts might have implications that must be managed.
- **Opportunities:** Turn the analysis around to see if the issues presented provide a way to differentiate your offerings to the market, and thus, step ahead of your competition.

As this structure makes clear, every problem or issue has a flip side of opportunity—such that managing the issue better than the competition provides a platform for comparative advantage.

The AUDIO analysis requires all of a company's business functions to collaborate on identifying environmental issues. Energy consumption, greenhouse gas emissions, and water use should be the first priority. Next, look at other possible sustainability concerns. Don't just focus on what goes on inside the factory gates. Sourcing of materials, distribution, and the impacts of products in consumption all need to be factored in. So analyzing impacts upstream and downstream on the value chain will bring to the fore similar dependency or exposure for your suppliers and consumers. Remember that even if an issue is not central to your business, one that is critical to your suppliers or consumers becomes an important issue for you. Harms they cause will be linked to you.

Once you know your vulnerabilities, look at how these issues might be turned around—and made into opportunities for competitive advantage. Would reducing your water or energy use allow reduced exposure and greater profit? Can you sell greener products and create a better business? (See Figure 5.1.)

INTERMEDIATE PLAYS: PRIORITIZE ISSUES

Knowing that there are environmental (and perhaps social) issues that need attention is not enough for a serious sustainability strategy. Companies need to know which issues matter and how much. The frameworks introduced in this section will clarify the materiality of the potential issues and provide a basis for prioritizing some concerns over others. With so many issues on the sustainability agenda, figuring out which issues require a strategic focus becomes critical. Top executives need a structure that allows them to prioritize. They must understand both the constraints and the opportunities presented by environmental issues and the broader set of sustainability concerns.

Two separate "screens" are needed. First, companies need to look at the issues through an "internal" lens to gain a clear understanding of which items have the potential to significantly affect their business prospects and competitive position. Play 3 ("Assess Business Materiality") offers a framework for this process.

Figure 5.1 Simplified Sample AUDIO Analysis for a Big-Box Retailer

Challenge	Aspects	Upstream	Downstream	Issues	Opportunities
1. Climate change	Emissions from energy use	Distribution system emissions; Supplier emissions from operations	Emissions from customers driving to store; Energy use from products sold in stores	Possible carbon constraints or charges	Launch eco-efficiency effort targeted at energy use and related greenhouse gas emissions
2. Energy	Energy consumption and rising costs	Supplier choice of energy and sensitivity to changes in energy costs	Energy use from products sold in stores	Energy sourcing and cost burden; Reliance on grid	Reduce energy use through store retrofit; Negotiate favorable rates; Sell energy-efficient products
3. Air pollution	Air emissions from facilities	Emissions at supplier factories and energy sources	Emissions from products	Tightening controls on air emissions	Increase efficiency to reduce emissions and costs
4. Ozone layer depletion	Residual CFC use in refrigeration	CFC releases by suppliers	CFC leaks from products	Legal constraints on use of CFCs	Partner to develop non-CFC products
5. Chemicals, toxins, and heavy metals	Use of chemicals in store operations	Fertilizer runoff from farms for food sold	Chemicals in products sold	Possible liability for chemicals in environment or humans	Sell organic food and other green products
6. Waste	Quantity of garbage generated	Solid and toxic waste from supplier production	Disposal of packaging by customers	Rising cost of waste disposal and increased "take-back" legislation	Reduce packaging and offer take-back and recycling options

Issue					
7. Fresh water	Contaminated runoff from buildings and parking lots	Water use in agriculture for food sold in store	Toxic products (such as lawn and garden supplies) ending up in waterways	Rising pressure for improved water quality	Redesign parking lots and runoff flows
8. Oceans and fisheries		Declining global fish stocks and rising prices		Rising costs and growing pressures to track seafood sources	Sell sustainably caught seafood
9. Land use	Suburban sprawl; Unplanned agricultural expansion	Needs for sustainable agriculture		Sprawl	Lead their on smart growth
10. Deforestation	Land clearing for facilities	Wood supplier reliance on unsustainable timber sources		Risk of consumer protest or even boycotts	Set sourcing criteria for suppliers
11. Biodiversity	Habitat fragmentation	Products that rely or reduce biodiversity	Customer product use (or misuse) that causes ecological damage	Local development constraints and concern about "sprawl"	Invest in land conservation and build corporate reputation
12. Food safety	Pesticide exposure or chemical contaminants	Chemical use in farming		Health and safety of food and beverages	Producing organic or more natural foods

[1] *Source: Esty and Winston, Green to Gold pp. 62–63.*

Second, they must assess the issue portfolio based on "external" pressures to understand the priorities of the key stakeholders who shape their business landscape: regulators, NGOs, the communities in which they operate, employees, customers, and in some cases, capital markets. Simply put, companies operate within societies that shape the issue agenda and thus determine, in part, which issues must be given attention. To put it bluntly, companies do not get to choose their own sustainability priorities. Play 4 ("Map Your Stakeholders") shows how to keep abreast of this broader agenda.

Even smart companies sometimes take a bit of time to learn this lesson. Dan Esty has worked with the Coca-Cola Company for many years, serving on its external advisory board since 2001. As the company began to develop its "stewardship" strategy, top executives did an exhaustive issue analysis (using the AUDIO framework)—and came up with three priorities: water, agricultural sustainability, and packaging/waste. From an internal point of view, these were clearly the right places to focus. But Dan and other external advisors pointed out that climate change needed to be on the priority list as well—given the attention that the world's political leaders and NGOs were giving the issue. After initially balking (and worrying about adding another priority to his already overburdened team), then-CEO Neville Isdell reversed course, concluding that because climate change mattered to key Coca-Cola stakeholders, it needed to matter to the company. Of course he was right. And the Coca-Cola Company today has four priority issues.

3. Assess Business Materiality

Company leaders can find plenty of guidance to help them flesh out the sustainability issues that they need to turn to first. We like the approach developed by AccountAbility,[4] which focuses on design criteria highlighting the value that each issue can bring to the company. Every company and every industry will be a bit different in terms of what matters. But, in designing, a "business materiality" screen, the principles shown in Figure 5.2 offer a good starting point.

Our own materiality framework builds on the forces that shape competitive advantage as identified by strategy guru Mike Porter.[5] In our view, you should assess the materiality of each potential sustainability issue at the business level with an eye toward its potential to drive changes in:

- Operating costs and risks.
- Supplier relationships—including access to and price of inputs.
- Customer loyalty—incorporating brand value and corporate reputation and emerging public expectations and social values.
- Product differentiation—reflecting price, quality/performance, and perceived value.

- Barriers to entry—affecting the number and sophistication of competitors.
- Innovation opportunities.
- Industry growth rate.
- Stakeholder priorities.
- Government policies and regulatory stringency.

Any issue that could shift one of these factors has the potential to realign the competitive landscape. Consider those carefully. Give issues with high potential impact the greatest focus. And remember that this process needs to be thought of in an iterative fashion, with prioritization being revisited on a regular basis.

Figure 5.2   Design Principles for Business Materiality Determination

Approaches will differ and develop but any successful methodology to determine materiality must address a set of common issues and challenges:

It needs to be able to:

Identify and prioritize issues for action
according to the degree of significance to the business.

Determine what information is useful and meaningful to different stakeholders.

It should be based on:

Broad-based and inclusive research and engagement with stakeholders.

Strong alignment with business strategy and value drivers.

Clear and transparent criteria to help decide what is material.

Integration and embeddedness into governance processes.

It needs to be:

Rigorous
Replicable, defensible, assurable, and credible.

Practical
Simple enough to be widely used and communicated, sophisticated enough for the needs of complex organizations.

Purposeful
Able to trigger action, not just defend it.

Source: AccountAbility, "The Materiality Report: Aligning Strategy, Performance, and Reporting" (2006). Reprinted with permission.

We have generated "materiality scorecards" for a number of industries highlighting critical issues that companies might want to address. The matrix shown in Figure 5.3 offers a sense of how this sort of ranking works.

Figure 5.3   **Material Issues across Six Subsectors**

Material Sustainability Issues	Industry Classification Benchmark Subsector					
	AUTOMOBILES	AIRLINES	PAPER	ELECTRICITY	DIVERSIFIED REIT'S	BANKING
BIODIVERSITY	0	0	5	4	4	0
BUSINESS MODEL	0	0	2	0	5	10
CHILD AND FORCED LABOR	0	0	2	0	0	0
CLIMATE CHANGE MANAGEMENT	12	13	10	15	14	15
COMPETITIVE AND ETHICAL BEHAVIOR	0	7	2	5	0	7
CORPORATE CITIZENSHIP/PHILANTHROPY	0	4	3	0	5	0
CUSTOMER PRIVACY	0	0	0	0	0	10
CUSTOMER SATISFACTION	13	12	3	12	10	7
DIVERSITY AND EQUAL OPPORTUNITY	0	3	0	1	0	7
ENERGY	0	14	10	13	12	0
ENVIRONMENTAL MANAGEMENT	0	0	12	0	8	3
EXECUTIVE COMPENSATION POLICIES	5	0	0	0	0	5
EXTERNAL COMMUNICATION/STAKEHOLDER ENGAGEMENT	1	4	7	5	5	8
IMPACTS ON COMMUNITIES	8	12	0	10	0	15
LABOR RIGHTS AND COMPENSATION	8	7	5	0	0	1
LOBBYING & POLITICAL CONTRIBUTIONS	0	5	2	7	3	7
MARKETING AND COMMUNICATIONS	0	2	4	10	5	12
MATERIALS AND WASTE	0	0	14	0	12	0
OCCUPATIONAL HEALTH & SAFETY	5	4	0	7	3	0
POLITICAL RISK AND CONFLICT	0	0	2	0	0	7
POLLUTANTS AND EMISSIONS	9	12	14	14	4	7
PRODUCT AND OPERATIONAL EFFICIENCY	14	10	4	8	12	0
PRODUCT ENVIRONMENTAL IMPACT	15	8	5	14	14	12
PRODUCT IMPACTS ON HEALTH	0	4	0	9	13	0
PRODUCT QUALITY AND INNOVATION	13	0	12	12	10	0
PRODUCT SAFETY	15	13	0	0	7	0
RECRUITMENT AND SUCCESSION PLANNING	3	1	0	2	2	2
RESEARCH AND DEVELOPMENT	10	5	0	10	3	0
SOURCING PRACTICES	8	7	14	4	5	5
STAFF ENGAGEMENT	5	4	3	4	1	3
STANDARDS AND CODES OF CONDUCT	0	0	0	3	10	0
SUPPLY CHAIN IMPACTS	4	0	0	4	4	0
TRAINNING AND DEVELOPMENT	3	3	5	1	1	2
TRANSPORT	1	0	2	0	0	3
WATER	0	5	14	11	8	3

| 19 | – Top 10 issues for each sector are shaded, based on the strength of the meteriality score, indicated in the center of the box. |

Source: Steve Lydenberg, Jean Rogers, and David Wood, "From Transparency to Performance: Industry-Based Sustainability Reporting on Key Issues" (Cambridge, MA: The Hauser Center and Initiative for Responsible Investment, June 2010). http//hausercenter.org. Reprinted with permission.

4. Map Your Stakeholders—And Their Issues

As we noted earlier, society, in part, defines priorities, so companies preparing sustainability strategies must "map" the critical stakeholders that affect their industry. Employees, banks, and investors ensure the success of the company.

Figure 5.4   **The Stakeholder Wheel**

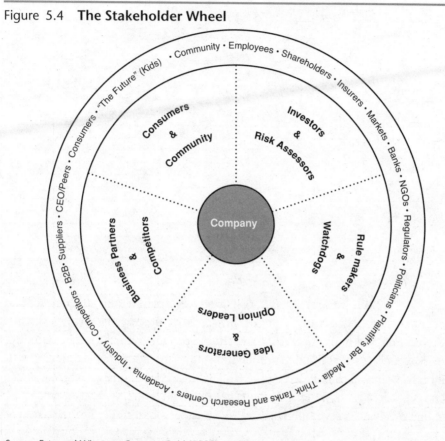

Source: Esty and Winston, *Green to Gold* (2009), p. 97.

Communities and governments give companies the goodwill to operate. NGOs, media, and rule makers keep the public informed about company misdeeds and exert pressure on them to do better. Industry peers and competitors keep track of each other's activities. Think tanks and academia generate new research and technologies to help companies progress. No company can afford to be without a strategy for managing stakeholder concerns or taking advantage of opportunities to advance their business with the help of stakeholders. Knowing which stakeholders care about your industry or company and which ones really matter because they have the capacity to shape the competitive landscape is essential. *Green to Gold* offered a very useful tool for this purpose—the Stakeholder Wheel (see Figure 5.4).

We urge you to do a comprehensive review of all the stakeholder groups that you identified. In each category, the critical questions are: Which groups are active? Are there particular individuals who drive the debate? What are the issues that they care about? What are their priorities for the coming year? Whose interests align with your own? Who will stake out a position in opposition? How hard will they push? What happens if they prevail? How much is it worth investing in any particular issue or battle?

Figure 5.5   **Stakeholder Impact Assessment**

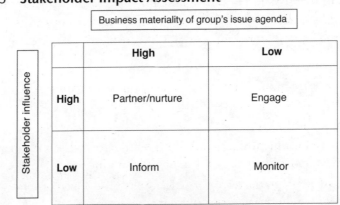

Source: Builds on the "Players Influence Map" from Esty and Winston, *Green to Gold* (2009), p. 265.

Stakeholder clout varies widely. So it is important not only to identify the players but also to assess their strength. Just because stakeholders have influence on your company doesn't mean that you should engage with all of them equally. Are there some who are taking too much time and effort? Are there some that you should pay attention to but have ignored? The matrix in Figure 5.5 shows where your stakeholders can fall in the stakeholder spectrum and how you engage them depending on their level of influence and the business materiality of their group's issue agenda.

It is often useful to group the relevant players into four categories to analyze their influence and business materiality. Groups with high stakeholder influence and high business materiality, found in the upper left square, need to be nurtured and receive ongoing attention from the company. They make the best potential NGO partners. Inversely, groups that are not very influential and lack materiality, such as those in the lower right square, should not receive much consideration and should simply be monitored. Groups in the upper right with high stakeholder influence yet low business materiality should be engaged, as they may influence policymaking far beyond their direct materiality to the business. The group in the lower left should be kept informed, since their high business materiality puts them at risk of becoming a problem if they are ignored. For each group, always ask why they are or are not getting as much attention as they should and what can be done to improve relations with those stakeholders.

5. Track the Trends

In assessing materiality and setting priorities, companies must evaluate not just the circumstances that they face today but also those that are likely to emerge in coming years. You should supplement any issue spotting exercise with a commitment to looking at future trends that might reshape your analysis. Your critical point of focus should be on what might change. Thinking carefully about issues marked by a degree of uncertainty or other elements of flux is essential.

These are the main factors that you should consider:

- Evolving science.
- Realignment in economic structures and production patterns—including the effects of industrialization and globalization.
- Demographic shifts.
- Changing social norms, values, and attitudes toward risk—with rising wealth among other factors likely to reshape public thinking.
- Divergence of views on the topic across generations—which promises changing social mores as a younger perspective gains majority status.
- Pressure from nature—changing rainfall patterns, exposure to windstorms, and so on.
- Prospect for technology breakthroughs—gauged in part by how much venture capital and other innovation investment is going into the issue or related sectors.
- Intensity of political interest and debate.
- Presence of critical "thresholds"—which, if reached, could change issue perceptions.
- Degree to which the issue is fully "internalized" by current regulations—harms that are currently "externalized" and not strictly regulated or fully paid for are likely to be increasingly internalized over time, leading to added costs.

In thinking about the future, some company leaders find that it makes sense not to try to forecast specific trends but rather to build alternative future scenarios that help to highlight critical issues and variables. Shell has used scenario planning famously to strengthen its preparation for future developments in the oil and gas world.[6] If you want help thinking about the range of future challenges that might emerge and dilemmas that your company might have to face, check out www.gemi.org/sustainabilitymap where the Global Environment and Management Institute has developed a richly detailed "Map of Future Forces Affecting Sustainability" that allows the viewer to dig deeper on particular issues.

6. Prioritize the Issues

Base how much attention you give to a particular issue on a calculus that reflects the internal business materiality and the sum of the external pressures from key stakeholders—adjusted for likely future trends. If you put all the issues that you've identified into the matrix shown in Figure 5.6 (drawn from work done by Ford Motor Company's sustainability team) it can help you identify priorities.

Figure 5.6   Ford Motor Company's Materiality Matrix

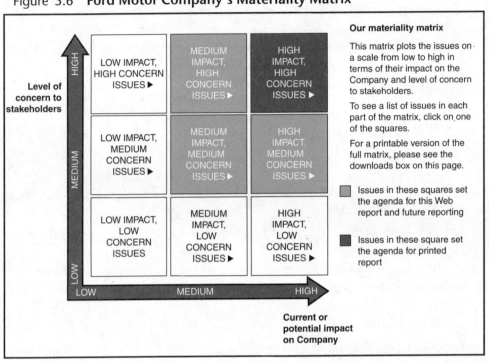

Source: Ford Motor Company, from AccountAbility, "The Materiality Report," written and developed by Maya Forstater, Simon Zadek, Deborah Evans, et al. (November 2006). Reprinted with permission.

It should be obvious that you must constantly review and revise the priorities you establish. Things will change. New issues will emerge. What seemed critical last year may well not be a top concern next year. Plan to regularly revisit the entire exercise of issue spotting, stakeholder mapping, trend tracking, and priority setting. Most companies need to plan to do some degree of updating every year with more thorough reassessments undertaken every three to four years.

ADVANCED PLAYS: REFINE AND REVISIT

7. Dig Deeper

You can take issue spotting to greater and greater levels of refinement. If your company has already done a "quick and dirty" first pass to establish your issue agendas, then we suggest that your first "advanced" play should be to go back through all the frameworks and exercises outlined earlier in this chapter on a more granular basis. If you want to dig deeper, we identify some other advanced tools in the Recommended Resources section that follows, which can be useful as you seek to refine your issue understanding and take your sustainability analysis to an even deeper level.

SUMMARY

Key Plays

1. Scan for the big issues that could affect your bottom line.
2. Conduct an AUDIO analysis to clarify your issue exposure.
3. Assess business materiality.
4. Map your stakeholders—and their issues.
5. Track the trends.
6. Prioritize the issues.
7. Dig deeper.

ADDITIONAL RESOURCES

IDENTIFYING ECO-RELATED RISKS AND OPPORTUNITIES

"Green Returns Implementation Workbook" (Environmental Defense Fund). Basic framework to help identify strategic environmental opportunities that add business value. www.edf.org/

"The SIGMA Guidelines—Toolkit: SIGMA Opportunity and Risk Guide" (SIGMA Project). Simple guidance and tools to help organizations improve their understanding and management of sustainability risks and opportunities. www.projectsigma.co.uk

"Rattling Supply Chains: The Effect of Environmental Trends on Input Costs for the Fast-Moving Consumer Goods Industry" by A.T. Kearney (World Resources Institute, 2008). A scenario-driven analysis of how future environmental policies and rising natural resource constraints will affect supply chains and raise the cost of doing business. www.wri.org

"How to Undertake a Climate Risk Assessment" by John Sterlicchi (Business-Green, 17 Feb. 2010). Recommended steps and tools for assessing a company's risks related to climate change. www.businessgreen.com

"Investing in Climate Change: An Asset Management Perspective" (Deutsche Bank, 2007). Analysis of sector-specific risks and opportunities associated with climate change. www.dws.com

Corporate Water Strategies by William Sarni (Earthscan Press, 2011). Roadmap for corporate water management strategies featuring best-practice recommendations and case studies.

"At the Crest of a Wave: A Proactive Approach to Corporate Water Strategy" by Linda Hwang, Sissel Waage, and Emma Stewart, of BSR and Jason Morrison, Peter H. Gleick, and Mari Morikawa of the Pacific Institute (Business for Social Responsibility and Pacific Institute, 2007). Guidance for measuring water footprint, assessing risks, and developing and implementing corporate water strategy. www.bsr.org/reports

Global Water Tool (World Business Council for Sustainable Development, March 2009). The Global Water Tool is a free and easy-to-use tool for companies and organizations to map their water use and assess risks relative to their global operations and supply chains. www.wbcsd.org

"TEEB—The Economics of Ecosystems and Biodiversity Report for Business" (UNEP, 2010). Findings from a major global study on how ecosystem decline and biodiversity loss pose business risks and opportunities. Includes tools for assessing and managing related risks. www.teebweb.org

Corporate Ecosystem Services Review (World Resources Institute, 2007). Provides methodology and tools that guide managers through questions to help pinpoint priority risks and opportunities and direct them to more specialized tools to further assess and manage impacts. www.wri.org/ecosystems/esr

Map of Future Forces Affecting Sustainability (Institute for the Future & GEMI, 2007). A tool to encourage thoughtful discussions that help companies formulate business strategies based on sustainability trends. www.gemi.org/sustainabilitymap

KEEPING UP WITH TRENDS

"CEF Weekly Briefing" A short Monday morning briefing for busy executives summarizing top corporate sustainability news, research and tools. www.corporateecoforum.com

Environmental Leader Comprehensive site for business energy and environmental news. www.environmentalleader.com

Greenbiz.com A leading source for green business news, opinion, and resources.

Chapter 6 Assess and Measure Your Environmental Impacts

A decade ago, you could probably count on two hands the number of companies that had calculated and reported their carbon footprints. Today, the landscape had changed dramatically. Any Fortune 500 company that has not calculated its CO_2 emissions data seems behind the times. Many companies now voluntarily report their carbon emissions *publicly*, and services like Google Finance and Bloomberg make their filings easy to find.[1] And it's not just the big companies that are doing the measuring. From neighborhood small businesses to high-powered clean technology start-ups, companies are tracking and reporting their "climate impacts" to differentiate themselves in the marketplace. Even the hit television show 24 declared itself to be "carbon neutral" in March 2009.[2]

The pressure to disclose data on carbon impacts represents the mere tip of a transparency iceberg, indicative of a larger trend, which some have called the "age of transparency." In this new era, companies are increasingly expected to account (figuratively and literally) for the impacts they have on the world. As companies are taken to task for a range of harms for which they previously were not held liable,[3] we might also say we've entered a new "age of accountability."

But how do companies know which impacts need measuring? How far should an analysis go before it gets too deep into the weeds? The answers depend on which of the following goals a company hopes to advance through impact assessment:

- **Comply with legal reporting requirements.** Examples include the U.S. Toxic Release Inventory or the 2010 EPA greenhouse gas reporting requirements.

- **Identify priority risks and opportunities.** Companies have much to gain by tracking risky activities and liability exposure—and pinpointing costly inefficiencies.

- **Benchmark current performance relative to peers.** Knowing the right impact-related data makes it possible to do "apples-to-apples" comparisons of your results versus competitors who publish similar data.

- **Set goals and manage them.** Impact analyses can generate the baseline data you need to help set the right goals, whether "safe" or "stretch" goals, as well as to evaluate and manage performance toward those goals.

- **Motivate internal change.** Collecting and disseminating data on a company's environmental impacts can engage and motivate employees and unlock creative ideas for improving eco-performance.

- **Rethink existing products and spur new product innovation.** Understanding the details behind a product's ecological impacts can lead to better choices about materials, processes, and design.

- **Improve supply chain and logistics.** Finding more eco-friendly and cost-efficient transportation modes or methods of packaging can pay real dividends.

- **Respond to customer inquiries.** More big companies—Walmart, McDonald's, Tesco, HP, Phillips, Procter & Gamble, and Sprint, just to name a few, now require environmental impact data from their existing (and potential) suppliers.

- **Satisfy investors and shareholders.** Shareholders are pushing companies harder every year to disclose more detail about environmental risks and impacts—especially on carbon emissions.

- **Prepare external reports.** Environmental sustainability reporting has quickly moved from the "nice to do" to the "must have" category in a matter of a few short years.

- **Engage stakeholders.** Collecting and reporting impact data can help establish credibility with external stakeholders, appease critics, and win *support* for proposed actions that require regulatory or community approval.

- **Apply for funding.** Environmental impact data is often a requirement for state or federal grants.

- **Substantiate claims for sales and marketing.** Any company wishing to use "green" to boost its brand or market a product or service needs impact data to back up their claims.

We consider it a "basic" good practice today for every company to evaluate its carbon footprint, even if only roughly. You should also consider tracking air and water pollution, waste, and compliance with existing regulations obligatory. As companies advance up the eco-maturity ladder, they will want a more detailed accounting of their carbon footprint and waste streams, plus assessments of their air and water pollution, and other ecological impacts. This chapter is meant to be a reference tool you can return to again and again as you grapple with different challenges along the way. It's designed to complement Chapter 7 ("Benchmark Your Performance against Competitors and Best Practices") and Chapter 22 ("Communicate and Report Results").

You can execute this chapter's plays at varying degrees of depth from quick, back-of-the-napkin assessments that produce rough estimates to comprehensive analyses according to rigorous methodologies that generate much more granular data. For some companies, a blunt, largely qualitative analysis is sufficient. For others, a deep dive may make sense—or be necessary for external reporting or to substantiate marketing claims. So while we have broken the plays into Basic, Intermediate, and Advanced, what really matters is the depth with which the analyses are undertaken. At the end of the chapter, we provide a detailed list of additional resources to help with the execution of any of the plays, at whatever stage is appropriate for your company.

BASIC PLAYS: UNDERSTAND YOUR METRICS AND ASSESSMENT TOOLS

1. Get Familiar with Common Indicators of Business Environmental Impact Metrics

When it comes to evaluating a company's environmental impacts, businesses draw from a vast universe of indicators and metrics—as do the watchdog groups and experts that evaluate them. From the purely quantitative and easily measurable ("total annual electricity used") to the totally subjective ("positive influence on consumer attitudes"), indicators exist for just about anything—which makes sense given the range of issues and interests at play. But this diversity of metrics and associated standards can frustrate assessment efforts and overwhelm executives who are trying to figure out which impacts are most important to track.

As we explain in more depth in Chapter 18 ("Create an Action Plan") and Chapter 22 ("Communicate and Report Results"), there are some commonly accepted guidelines, such as the Global Reporting Initiative, that provide a useful starting point. But in reality, there's no simple answer. The right choice of indicators and metrics to use depends entirely on the nature of your business and your goals. Are you trying to get a rough cut on how much solid waste your facilities produce for benchmarking purposes? Or do you need a precise measurement of a certain type of waste to know how to improve a particular manufacturing process? Do you simply need to get a sense of whether your company is generally improving its performance on, say, water use? Or are your stakeholders expecting detailed accounting based on a publicly stated goal?

In Figure 6.1, you'll see some of the most common quantitative measures used by sustainably focused businesses and NGOs. Most companies using these indicators would report on them annually using absolute units of measurement (tons, cubic meters, kilowatts/gigajoules, and so on).

In addition to "absolute data" metrics, smart businesses also evaluate and measure environmental impacts using *trend data* (annual data presented over a number of years to evaluate performance over time, such as total CO_2 emissions for each of the last five years) and *normalized data* or *intensity-based* metrics (relating two absolute figures to each other, such as proportion of recycled waste to total waste or total CO_2 emissions per unit of output).[4]

When it comes to measuring performance, context is critical. It doesn't help to know that you reduced 2,000 tons of waste unless you know whether that

Figure 6.1   **Common Metrics Used to Assess Business Environmental Impacts**

Categories	Inputs and Outputs
Energy and climate change	*Inputs* • Total energy/electricity use from fossil fuels • Percentage of power from renewable sources • Total fleet fuel consumption *Outputs* • Total direct greenhouse gas (GHG) emissions • Total indirect GHG emissions from purchased electricity, steam, or heat
Pollution, hazardous/ toxic materials and releases	*Inputs* • Total toxic/hazardous material inputs used (according to lists such as www.epa.gov/epawaste/hazard/wastemin.htm) *Outputs* • Total air emissions of sulfur oxides (SO_x) that cause acid rain, ozone-depleting substances, volatile organic compounds (VOCs), nitrogen dioxide (NO_2) and other nitrogen oxides (NO_x), carbon monoxide (CO), ozone (O_3), and fine particles (soot) • Total reportable toxic/hazardous materials released (e.g., as reported to the Toxic Release Inventory [TRI]) • Total hazardous waste treated and/or released • Total number of spills (over 10,000 gallons or 10,000 pounds) • Total environmental fines and penalties • Total wastewater discharge (and mass or concentration of regulated pollutants within water discharged)
Materials use and solid waste	*Inputs* • Total materials used (by type) • Percentage of input materials that were recycled or recovered (versus virgin materials) *Outputs* • Total solid waste disposed • Total e-waste
Freshwater use	*Inputs* • Total volume of water used (in cubic meters including direct, purchased, and cooling) *Outputs* • Total volume of water discharged
Ecosystems and biodiversity impacts	*Inputs* • Amount of land used, cleared, or negatively affected by operations or facilities • Percentage of sustainably certified products/inputs (raw materials, wood, paper, agricultural products, food, fish, etc.) *Outputs* • Amount of land restored or protected

Source: Draws on EPA's "Basic Environmental Measures for Lean Enterprises," www.epa.gov/lean/toolkit (accessed August 4, 2010), and a review of many third-party rating and ranking systems.

represents 1 percent or 90 percent of your total waste stream. Exactly what you should track depends on the nature of your industry and your company's issue sensitivity (see Chapter 5 where we provide a tool for assessing the "materiality" of issues to your business).

Finally, third-party evaluators and stakeholders often look at *comparative results* and other performance indicators including safety, health, and equity indicators when making judgments about a company's environmental performance. For example, Sustainable Asset Management, which produces the Dow Jones Sustainability Index, only includes the top 10 percent of any industry globally or the top 20 percent in North America, so being ranked is entirely a function of cumulative comparative results. Some of those rankings rely on survey data or qualitative measures of performance (such as the *strength* of a company's climate change strategy). The subjectivity of this type of indicator can be quite high—alarmingly so for companies that do not feel that they've been fairly ranked.

A WINDOW INTO THE VAST UNIVERSE OF ENVIRONMENTAL METRICS

Here are some examples that illustrate the broad spectrum of possibilities:

"Trend" Data

- Total water use by year from 2006–2011
- CO_2 emissions trends from 2006–2011

Normalized and Intensity-Based Data

- Energy productivity (sales/total direct and indirect energy consumption in gigajoules)
- Waste productivity (sales/total amount of waste produced in tons; percentage of total waste recycled)
- Water productivity (sales/total water use in cubic meters; total water used per unit of output)
- Carbon productivity (sales/total CO_2-equivalent emissions in tons; total CO_2 emissions per unit of output)
- Amount of toxic/hazardous materials per unit of production

Other Performance Indicators

- Total GHG offsets purchased, source of offsets
- Percentage of emissions reductions from offsets
- Efforts to support/oppose bipartisan environmental legislation
- Money spent on a public eco-education campaign
- Net return on investment (ROI) on energy efficiency investments
- Revenue from sales of "greener" products

If your company is just starting out, you should simply become familiar with the range of available metrics, which will help you evaluate options for your own data tracking. We explore these issues further in Chapter 7 ("Benchmark Your Performance against Competitors and Best Practices") and Chapter 22 ("Communicate and Report Results").

2. Plot Your Company's Carbon Footprint

Measuring a company's carbon footprint—the total amount of greenhouse gases it emits into the atmosphere—can be a time-consuming, labor-intensive, and sometimes expensive process. So why do so many companies bother? One of the top reasons is because the process often generates insights that lead to bottom-line savings.

When it comes to carbon footprinting, information is power. Greenhouse gas emissions are intimately tied to energy use, so measuring emissions forces management to pay serious attention to their energy spending. That scrutiny often reveals a treasure trove of opportunities to save money. The consulting firm Groom Energy says that carbon footprinting led one of its customers to discover they were paying over $100 million annually for electricity, making it the second-fastest growing cost center (after health care) in the business. The data collection process revealed myriad opportunities to control those costs—addressing billing errors including double billing and payments being made for offices no longer occupied led to opportunities to rationalize the company's fixed assets and shed excess space.[5]

Carbon footprinting also puts a spotlight on where the emissions come from. Analyzing these sources—buildings, manufacturing, logistics, and so on—can smoke out the best opportunities to reduce emissions and bring down energy spending.

Here are the top five things you need to know before undertaking any carbon footprinting effort:

1. **The term "carbon footprint" covers all heat-trapping "greenhouse gases" (GHGs), not just carbon.** Carbon dioxide (CO_2) is the most commonly discussed greenhouse gas—but it is only one of six major greenhouse gases arising from human activities. Other notable GHGs include methane, nitrous oxide, chlorofluorocarbons, and hydrochlorofluorocarbons. Not all greenhouse gases are created equal. Some gases break down relatively quickly in the atmosphere while others, such as CO_2, persist for centuries. Greenhouse gases also vary in their "radiative forcing" or heat-trapping strength. Methane, for instance, is about 23 times more powerful than CO_2, while sulfur hexafluoride (SF_6) is a whopping 22,200 times more powerful (see Figure 6.2). These differences mean that you need to be aware of the "global warming potential" of your emissions and prioritize action on those with the biggest impacts as well as the most cost effective intervention opportunities. At the end of the chapter, we offer a variety of additional resources to help you with the "carbon accounting" you'll need to do.

Figure 6.2   **Greenhouse Gases**

Greenhouse Gas	Activities Associated with It	Atmospheric Lifetime	Global Warming Potential
Carbon dioxide (CO_2)	Fossil fuel combustion	5–200 years	1
Methane (CH_4)	Livestock digestion and landfills	12 years	23
Nitrous oxide (N_2O)	Manure and sewage management	114 years	296
CFC-12 (CCl_2F_2)	Liquid coolants, foams	100 years	10,600
HCFC-22 (CCl_2F_2)	Refrigerants	11.9 years	1,700
Perfluoroethane (C_2F_6)	Aluminum smelting, semiconductor manufacturing	10,000 years	11,900
Sulfur hexafluoride (SF_6)	Dielectric fluid	3,200 years	22,200

Source: Pew Center for Climate Change, "1B. The Main Greenhouse Gases," www.pewclimate.org/ (accessed August 21, 2010). Reprinted with permission.

2. **It is common practice to convert all of the greenhouse gases into a common metric called "carbon dioxide equivalents"** (CO_2e), typically measured in metric tons. For example, a ton of released methane counts as 23 tons of CO_2e because it is equivalent to releasing 23 tons of CO_2.

3. **You can measure a carbon footprint at many "levels."**[6]

  • *For the entire organization or business:* Used mainly for voluntary reporting in corporate sustainability reports and to carbon registries, such as the EPA Climate Leaders, Carbon Disclosure Project (CDP), and the Climate Registry.

  • *For a facility:* Used for mandatory reporting under greenhouse gas (GHG) regulations, including the U.S. Environmental Protection Agency (EPA) reporting requirements.

  • *For a project:* Used either to: (1) measure emissions *caused by* a particular project (e.g., to help evaluate options) and gauge future "carbon exposure"; or (2) to calculate the emissions *reduced or avoided* due to a particular project, which can be useful in assessing whether a particular energy efficiency investment makes sense or as a way to gauge the amount of carbon offsets or credits a project might produce.

  • *For an individual product or service:* Used mainly to evaluate options and trade-offs in product design and sometimes for marketing. A properly constructed product-level footprint impact assessment measures emissions over the full life of a product from the extraction of raw materials and manufacturing right through to its customer use and disposal.

4. **The "Greenhouse Gas Protocol" is the internationally accepted standard for measuring and reporting carbon footprints at the corporate entity level.**[7] Developed through a joint project of the World Business Council for Sustainable Development and the World Resources Institute, the Greenhouse Gas Protocol offers a methodologically consistent way of accounting for emissions. As such, it provides a useful basis for comparison across companies.

5. **A credible carbon footprint analysis must be clear on the boundary and scope of what's included.**[8] Debate remains over exactly what emissions a company should be held accountable for. Thus, you will see reporting at different scopes. Many companies choose to measure only scope 1 (direct emissions from its own facilities and activities) and scope 2 (emissions associated with purchased electricity). Others will also report on scope 3 emissions (covering emissions generated by suppliers and employees). Figure 6.3 gives examples of scope 1, 2, and 3 emissions.

For a quick, back-of-the-napkin estimate of your organization's carbon footprint, try using one of the online calculators listed at the end of this chapter. Though blunt instruments, these can help focus your company on the big-ticket items that are easily measured—and can generate ideas for low-cost, high-return actions that cut emissions and save money. The process of doing rough emissions estimates can help to raise internal awareness and help generate momentum and enthusiasm for digging deeper.

For a more rigorous analysis, you'll need to follow a few key steps: (1) set the boundaries for what will get measured—and what won't; (2) build your data-gathering strategy; (3) convert the raw data into CO_2e emissions figures. If this is your first footprint analysis, keep your eyes on the prize: Your top priority should be to produce good *insights* and to improve *capacity* for carbon data collection and analysis. Don't worry about perfection or gathering every bit of data on every possible impact. But *do* try to be clear about your assumptions and keep careful records every step of the way. By doing so, you'll build a solid foundation for a better, more efficient data collection system that enables progressively more rigorous analyses.

Step 1: Set the boundaries for what will get included—and what won't—over what time period. (See Figure 6.4.) First determine the *organizational boundary:* for instance, will you include all branches, subsidiaries, partnerships, and franchises?[9] Next, define the *operational boundary* (i.e., scope 1, 2, and/or 3 emissions). To follow GHG Protocol requirements for an organizational footprint, you will need to include all scope 1 and 2 emissions. The emerging norm, however, also factors in major scope 3 emissions. For example, Salt Spring Coffee Company, operating in the Gulf Islands off Canada's west coast,

Figure 6.3   What Exactly Are Scope 1, 2, and 3 Emissions?

Scope	Description
1	**"Direct" emissions** from sources your company owns or controls, including: • On-site fuel combustion including the generation of heat, steam, and electricity in company-owned equipment (e.g., boilers, furnaces, or generators) • Fuel combustion in company-owned vehicles/airplanes/ships/heavy machinery • "Fugitive emissions" from company-owned facilities or equipment due to leaks, spills, or evaporation (e.g., methane from on-site landfills, SF_6 from electrical equipment, and HFCs from chillers and air conditioning) • Agricultural activities and land use changes (e.g., fertilizer use, forest clearing)
2	**"Indirect emissions"** from purchased electricity, steam, or heat used to run offices, factories, and other facilities
3	**"Other indirect value chain" emissions** triggered by your company's activities but from sources not owned or directly controlled, including: • Fuel combustion in vehicles/airplanes/ships/rail owned by others (including emissions from business travel, freight transportation, shipping and courier services) • Employee commuting • Customers' use of the products or services sold • Recycling and disposal of the product • Extraction and production of all goods purchased (e.g., emissions produced to make the paper or product packaging your office uses) • Waste disposal and wastewater treatment that is contracted out • Any other supply chain or outsourced activities Note: *The accounting procedures for measuring Scope 3 emissions are highly controversial given the inherent complexity and potential for double-counting. Businesses are working with NGOs, academics, and governments to create standards that everyone can agree on—but progress has been in fits and starts.*

Source: Clean Air-Cool Planet and Forum for the Future, "Getting to Zero: Defining Corporate Carbon Neutrality" (2008), www.cleanair-coolplanet.org/. Reprinted with permission.

Figure 6.4   **Setting Boundaries**

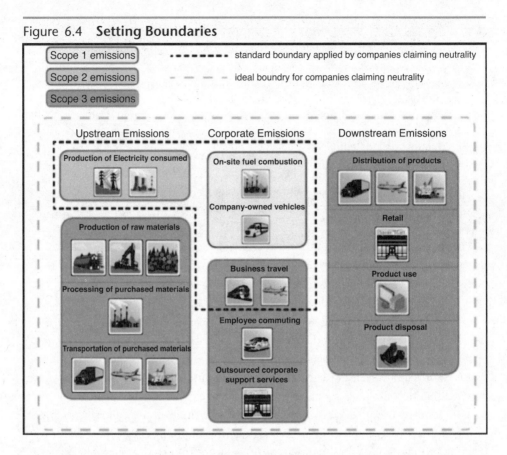

Source: Clean Air-Cool Planet and Forum for the Future, "Getting to Zero: Defining Corporate Carbon Neutrality" (2008), www.cleanair-coolplanet.org/. Reprinted with permission.

suspected that scope 3 emissions due to air travel (shipping beans from the point of origin) and ferry travel were significant. And when they measured them, they found that these scope 3 emissions caused about one-third of the company's carbon footprint.[10] DHL Express Nordic analyzed scope 3 emissions from outsourced transportation companies and found them to account for 94 percent of their carbon footprint.[11] PG&E launched an industry-first initiative to measure the scope 3 emissions in its supply chain. The project will survey 50 PG&E suppliers and select three to five candidates for comprehensive life cycle assessment (LCA) case studies and the development of greenhouse gas reduction strategies.[12]

Don't bite off more than you can chew. If you haven't done a carbon footprint previously, focus first on scope 1 and 2 emissions. Finally, choose the *time boundary* and set the baseline for future comparison. Over what period will you assess emissions? For what year(s) will you be able to get meaningful data? You need to choose some set period (usually a fiscal or calendar year) as a baseline for comparison.

CARBON NEUTRALITY?

A number of environmentally conscious companies have set out to be "carbon neutral"—reducing their greenhouse gas emissions and buying carbon offsets to cover what they cannot eliminate. The baseline for this calculation can be controversial. A study by Clean Air-Cool Planet, a New England-based advocacy group committed to solving the climate change problem, found that most companies claiming to be "carbon neutral" define neutrality based solely on their scope 1 and scope 2 emissions. Some add in their business travel, reflecting a sliver of their scope 3 emissions. But the Clean Air-Cool Planet team argues that the boundary for companies claiming full neutrality would be all scope 1, 2, and 3 emissions—a huge feat that few companies even contemplate.

Step 2: Build your data-gathering strategy. The toughest part of doing a carbon footprint is finding the data you need—especially the first time you do it. One of the most important things you'll need is information on energy and fuel use, which can take time to hunt down. Identify who has the data you need or knows how to get it, and make specific individuals accountable for getting particular types of information. Figure 6.5 offers a list of some commonly used data sources you might start with. As business sustainability expert Gil Friend counsels, "it's not the end of the world" if some pieces of information are missing, such as a utility bill or fuel invoice for a given month: "You can extrapolate from data available (make sure you document your assumptions) and plan to eliminate the gaps next year."[13] Most important, view your first data-gathering effort as an opportunity to create and road test systems that will help you streamline the process in the future.

As you plan your data-collection process, keep in mind the following recommendations that build on best practices in carbon information management identified in a joint report by IBM and the Carbon Disclosure Project, a London-based NGO:[14]

- **Use templates** to simplify data collection and make it more consistent. Develop templates with business units to ensure buy-in.
- **Split the task** of data gathering and data management across business units.
- **Piggyback on existing data streams** where possible.
- **Automate whatever you can,** moving over time from manual spreadsheet entry to more sophisticated software systems. Over 70 vendors offer "enterprise carbon accounting" software, which can streamline the process of calculating, managing, and reporting emissions.[15]
- **Create a reminder system** to prompt employees to submit data on time.
- **Document everything.** "Establish a carbon data 'archive,' which can support the ever-increasing range of inquiries and reporting requirements."

Figure 6.5   **Commonly Used Data Sources**

Scope	Description
1	• Fuel purchase records and invoices (fuel type and units such as gallons/liters or cubic feet/meters) • Fuel tank logs (fuel type and units) • Records to help estimate miles/km traveled if actual fuel consumption records are unavailable (e.g., trip records, odometer readings, and/or maintenance records with vehicle make/model) • Equipment specs and industry or government publications to estimate fugitive emissions
2	• Utility bills and/or meter reading records (kWh data, BTUs, pounds of steam)
3	• Expense reports for business travel (miles/km traveled, mode of transportation) • Survey data from employees on commuting habits • Shipping and delivery invoices (weight shipped, mode of transport) • Amount of space leased (square feet/meters and number of days) to estimate portion of electricity/heat/cooling • Receipts from purchases (e.g., total amount of paper purchased and type of paper) • Product and service life cycle analysis calculators and estimates (see recommendation #6)

Source: Adapted from Paul Lingl, Deborah Carlson, and the David Suzuki Foundation, *Doing Business in a New Climate.* A *Guide to Measuring, Reducing and Offsetting Greenhouse Gas Emissions*, 2010. Reprinted with permission.

- **Consider seeking help** from non-profit organizations such as the Carbon Disclosure Project or the Carbon Trust, industry organizations, and specialized consultancies.
- **Consider using a third-party auditor** to validate your approach and to help guide your future steps.

Step 3: Convert the data into standard CO_2e units. To do this, you can use any number of existing tools (spreadsheets, online calculators, software) that do calculations for you using pre-determined "conversion factors," which translate data such as "liters of gasoline" or "kilowatt hours of grid electricity" into tons/kilograms of CO_2e. Or you can use standard conversion factors to create your own tool. See the Additional Resources at the end of the chapter.

As you forge ahead, be patient. It will take considerable time to get all the data you need to produce accurate findings. Missed elements and miscalculations are inevitable. Be prepared to make adjustments along the way. Be transparent about recalculating if serious flaws emerge that make a "redo" of the entire exercise necessary.[16]

3. Measure Your Company's Waste

As we argue in Chapter 3, companies that are serious about obtaining an Eco-Advantage know that "waste" in any form—whether solid, liquid, or gaseous, hazardous or not—means lost profit. When the resources a company buys (raw materials, consumables, energy, water) don't fully convert into something of value that can be sold, the result is waste that translates into cost in the form of treatment, recycling, or disposal—and paperwork.

Just as carbon footprinting helps reveal waste in the form of unnecessary energy use, businesses large and small can also benefit enormously from getting a handle on how much other kinds of waste they produce and where it comes from. The very process of measuring waste inevitably leads to "a-ha" moments that can improve the bottom line and lays the foundation for waste reduction that will improve efficiency and resource productivity over time.

What needs measurement, of course, depends entirely on the type of waste your business produces. An office-based service company might focus on all the paper or toner cartridges tossed into the trash or recycling bin. A toy manufacturer would benefit from knowing how much paint doesn't actually make it onto products and ends up going to a landfill or into the sewer. A furniture maker should know how much extra wood or metal ends up as scrap, or how much packaging waste results from what they buy or sell. Companies that handle toxic or hazardous waste may not have a choice but to measure and report. Indeed, the U.S. Toxic Release Inventory (TRI) requires companies that treat, recycle, handle, or dispose of more than 500 pounds of toxic chemicals to follow "cradle to grave" waste tracking rules.

The first step in measuring waste is an audit to identify the type of waste you're producing, approximately how much of it you generate, and where it comes from (see Figure 6.6). Common methods for collecting information include:

- **Asking for hauler records:** Waste and recycling haulers are becoming increasingly sophisticated about tracking data on what they pick up—amount, type (even commodity-specific), and source—because companies are demanding it. Ask your hauler if they are equipped to provide records, and if not, consider contracting with one that can. Alternatively, you can get a rough approximation by determining the capacity of your dumpster and multiplying that by how often it gets emptied.

- **Conducting a waste audit:** Physically collecting, sorting, and weighing waste is one of the most effective ways that an organization can get a handle on its waste streams. The more audits that are done across the enterprise (i.e., the larger the data sample), the more accurate the results will be.

Figure 6.6   **Sample Waste Audit Worksheet**

Date and time: Location:	Weight	Volume	Notes
RECYCLABLES:			
Paper			
Cardboard			
E-waste			
Total Recyclable			
TRASH			
Organics			
Non-organics			
Total Trash			
TOTAL WASTE			

- **Reviewing purchasing records:** Invoices and other purchasing records from your company or suppliers can be a useful supplementary data point, helping to pinpoint the amount and quantities purchased of particular goods that end up as waste.
- **Surveying and talking to employees:** While the information generated may be anecdotal, asking employees can yield helpful data—particularly in identifying what to look for and where to look for it.
- **Walking through facilities:** Walk-throughs can also be a valuable tool in helping you focus on what needs measurement, even if data is qualitative and incomplete.

When starting out, estimates based on good judgment will usually be enough to pinpoint major problems and opportunities. After that, you'll be better equipped to determine where to invest in efforts that produce a more detailed accounting—particularly so that you can measure the financial return on targeted waste-reduction efforts. We recommend several excellent resources and tools at the end of this chapter, whether you are designing a simple rough waste audit or working to produce more granular data. Chapter 22, "Communicate and Report Results," includes additional recommendations for tracking your progress in reducing waste over time.

4. Assess Your Company's Water Footprint and Related Impacts

While experts have been sounding red alerts for years about freshwater scarcity, the warnings largely fell on deaf ears in the business community—until recently. With 47 percent of the world's population predicted to face severe water shortages by 2030,[17] business leaders are now waking up to the reality that worldwide water trends threaten to seriously raise the cost of doing business in some markets. Companies with a strategic dependence on water, such as Nestle, Coca-Cola, and Pepsi, have thus stepped up to the global water challenge in a big way.[18] They know that public scrutiny is growing. Indeed, in 2010, the Carbon Disclosure Project launched with great fanfare its "Water Disclosure Project"—a harbinger of rising stakeholder expectations with regard to reporting on water-related impacts.

Other water assessment tools are also emerging. The Water Footprint Network (working closely with Coca-Cola) and the Water Risk Index (created through a partnership between Goldman Sachs, GE, and the World Resources Institute) both provide powerful tools to identify and mitigate water-related corporate risk.

HOW MANY GALLONS OF WATER DOES IT TAKE TO MAKE . . .

One bottle of water:	1.85	One pair of jeans:	505
One pint of beer:	20	One hamburger:	630
One cup of coffee:	35	One ton of cement:	1,360
Two liters of soda:	85–130	One pound of beef:	2,113
One cotton t-shirt:	400	One car:	39,090
		One ton of steel:	62,000[19]

For businesses there are two main categories of water impacts to consider:

1. How much water your business and products *use*—and whether the amount you use is reasonable given *where* the water comes from. There will be a big difference if the water is sourced from a freshwater-abundant place like Seattle or Stockholm versus a water-stressed area such as Phoenix or Chennai, India. How much water a business uses in direct operations including in buildings and manufacturing, plus how much water is used indirectly (called "virtual" or "embedded water") throughout the value chain to make its products or services determines a company's water footprint.[20]

2. How much your business and products *pollute water bodies* directly or indirectly through effluent or other activities that threaten freshwater ecosystems.

Does your company discharge wastewater into rivers or streams? Does it pave over wetlands or cut down trees that help purify water? Does it apply fertilizers or pesticides to the land that run off into waterways and disrupt ecosystems? Companies need to look at not only their own water impact but also the impact of their suppliers. As Veolia Water Americas' CEO and president Laurent Auguste pointed out, "looking at the water content of a product doesn't give information on water stress."[21] To go beyond the obvious, the Carbon Disclosure Project (CDP) Water Disclosure Project asks companies not only to report total volumes of water *consumed* (its footprint), but also information on their discharges, water recycling and reuse, and water intensity.[22]

As with the hunt for carbon emissions and waste data, some numbers on water impacts are easier to come by than others. It's pretty easy, for instance, to estimate a facility's water footprint by adding the gallons or liters on water bills. It's another matter to try to get data from all facilities worldwide, assess that data in light of the particulars of local ecosystems, get suppliers' information on their water use relating to what they do for you, and so on.

Here is a list of the basic steps companies should take to get a sense of their water-related impacts, followed by specific resources at the end of the chapter to help you execute each one:

- **Map out and measure total water directly used in your operations.** Walmart tells its suppliers that the "first step in improving water efficiency is to gain an understanding of where water is being used" including appliances, cooling/heating systems, landscaping, sanitation, kitchens, manufacturing, and so on.[23] By adding up the numbers, you'll get an important baseline against which you can evaluate future progress.

- **Assess indirect use of water.** Here's where it gets tougher (and more controversial). Tracking indirect water use is akin to measuring scope 3 carbon emissions: What are the indirect uses of water in your company's operations or products? How much water do your suppliers consume or pollute? What are the water impacts created by the farmers who grow the crops that are inputs to your business? How much water is used to make packaging? How much water went into growing trees for your lumber or paper? What is the water footprint of the mining company that produces the metal you use to make your product?

Some companies like Intel and Dell, for instance, are measuring even the water that goes into all the electricity needed to make their products (it takes 520 gallons of water to produce one megawatt hour of electricity in a coal-fired power plant, versus 20 gallons to produce one megawatt hour from solar power).[24] But tools for assessing data are getting more sophisticated—especially in sectors like food and beverages, forestry, or mining where the "embedded water" can be the bulk of the footprint.[25]

SABMILLER'S WATER FOOTPRINTING EXPERIENCE

London-based beer maker **SABMiller**, whose entire business is based on water, partnered with the World Wildlife Fund to measure the water footprint of its operations in South Africa and the Czech Republic. The company looked at water used in:

- **Crop cultivation:** Including irrigation, crop transport, and water related to energy use of farm machinery.

- **Crop processing:** Such as water related to raw materials (including crop importation), energy used in crop processing and transportation to the brewery; excludes water used to manufacture any machinery.

- **Brewing and bottling:** Water in the beer, water used in the manufacture of bottles and cans, water use related to recycling and labeling.

- **Distribution:** Water use related to energy used in transport.

- **Consumer use:** Water used in relation to consumer recycling and disposal.

The company found that 90 percent of its water footprint came from growing the crops necessary for brewing beer. It also found that about three times the amount of water was needed to produce a liter of beer in South Africa versus the Czech Republic, because South Africa relies more heavily on irrigated crops and has to import more agricultural raw materials.[26]

- **Evaluate water use in context.** Do you operate facilities in places with serious water shortages or stress? Do your suppliers? Do various steps or inputs for your products require water from stressed areas—say, growing crops in hot, dry regions that require heavy irrigation? What's the percentage of what you're using relative to others in your same industry?

- **Assess and measure any harm your company may be doing to water ecosystems.** Pollution discharges to water systems are the big ticket item in this category. But companies need to consider things beyond that as well, based on their type of business: Could certain waste disposal practices contaminate groundwater? Is water being used for industrial cooling—perhaps raising the temperature of the rivers into which this "clean" water is discharged? Will the construction of a new facility create construction runoff that harms a sensitive watershed? Do chemical or bacterial by products of a production process end up in water systems? These are illustrative of the tough questions companies need to ask and around which business tools are being built and refined.

5. Evaluate Your Company's Impacts on Ecosystems and Biodiversity

When most people think of "the environment," they think of the issues most prominent in the media: climate change, toxic pollution, and more recently, fresh water. It is easy to overlook business impacts to the natural ecosystems on which we depend for our health, well being, and economic activities. The "natural capital" coming from the earth's forests, oceans, land, and atmospheric systems delivers an estimated $33 trillion per year in goods and services in the form of breathable air, drinkable water, farmable (fertile) land, edible fish, valuable raw materials, barriers to the spread of disease and invasive species, protection from floods and wildfires, and much more.[27]

As a society we do very little to manage these "ecosystem services" or conserve nature's endowments. We don't even put a value on much of what we take from nature. We also tend to overlook the damage we inflict and fail to account for the natural resources we consume. But some businesses are beginning to feel the pinch. A 2010 study by PricewaterhouseCoopers and the UN Environment Program showed that the annual economic cost of damage to natural ecosystems around the world—through contamination of water supplies, the loss of fertile land through soil erosion and drought, and supply chain disruptions due to deforestation and overfishing—stands between $2 and $4.5 trillion, which is about 7.5 percent of global gross domestic product.

The practice of ignoring the natural capital that forms the foundation of our economy is starting to change. Smart businesses have begun to plan for the day when they will have to pay for natural inputs—and for the pollution harms their businesses cause (which economists call "externalities"). Companies serious about Eco-Advantage need to look beyond their obvious issues (climate, water, and waste) and consider their direct and indirect impacts on "everything else" in the natural environment. What goes into that bucket for analysis depends entirely on the nature of your business, what goes into your products, who uses them, and where you're physically based. A North American company that makes wood furniture from a nearby, sustainably managed forest likely has a far smaller negative impact than an Chinese manufacturer that makes the same amount of furniture using wood obtained from virgin Indonesian rainforest—and that ships the finished product to customers thousands of miles away.

The best place to begin your big-picture assessment is the "Corporate Ecosystem Services Review" methodology and tools from the World Resource Institute (www.wri.org/ecosystems/esr), which guides managers through a series of questions to help companies pinpoint priority risks and opportunities and direct them to more specialized tools to further assess and manage impacts. We list additional resources at the end of the chapter to help you track developments and new tools in this dynamic, rapidly evolving field.

INTERMEDIATE PLAY: CONDUCTING LIFE CYCLE ASSESSMENTS

6. Undertake a Life Cycle Assessment of Your Products and Services

Assessing environmental impacts of individual products or services (we'll call them "products" for short) is one of the most important things you can do in creating the diagnostic foundation that your company needs to pursue

Eco-Advantage. Product-level impact analyses can help fine-tune your understanding of eco-related risks and opportunities, pinpoint specific areas for you to target for improvement, and help you evaluate complex options and trade-offs in product and process design. But conducting product impact assessments is tricky. There are many competing methodologies and tools available for product "life cycle analysis/assessment" (LCA)—from "LCA Light" rapid assessment tools to costly software tools that can intimidate PhDs. It's an inherently messy affair because of the extraordinarily complex nature of the challenge. You are trying to account for and quantify every possible environmental impact of every input and output at every stage of a product's life cycle—from raw material extraction to use to end of life. With such exercises, it's easy not only to lose sight of the forest for the trees, but also to get lost deep in the forest and spend a huge amount of time and money trying to find your way out.

LEARNING FROM LCAs

- **Timberland** found that the biggest cause of greenhouse gas (GHG) emissions from making shoes was from the leather—and not because of electricity or fuel used to feed the cows and process the hides, but rather from the heat-trapping methane gas generated by the cows themselves during digestion.[28]
- **Stonyfield Farm**'s LCA on yogurt containers showed that the *size* of the containers affected the environment even more than the type of material or manufacturing process: creating and shipping all those single-use 8-ounce containers required 27 percent more energy than for 32-ounce containers.[29]
- **Levi Strauss** realized that about 60 percent of the climate emissions from its signature product, denim jeans, comes during the consumer phase—and nearly 80 percent of that because people dry their clothes in electric dryers.[30]
- **Tropicana** found that about a third of the carbon emissions from making a carton of orange juice came from using fertilizer, which produced large quantities of nitrous oxide.[31]

Fortunately, most companies don't need to—and shouldn't—aim for perfection or full-fledged LCA studies when it comes to analyzing product impacts. What usually matters most is getting a good enough *sense* of what a product's main impacts are (and which elements are the chief culprits) to steer you on the right path to reducing them. In those cases, simple tools that produce rough estimates will likely suffice. If, however, a business wants to share results with external audiences—especially to make marketing claims about how "green" a product is—they will need to plan to invest in rigorous analytical efforts and be ready to share the methodologies behind them.

Below are the top seven things we believe every business should know in order to undertake product life cycle analysis:

1. **LCA is a generic term used to cover many different types of studies.**

   The basic idea behind the LCA method is to assess various environmental impacts across different stages of a product's life—from extracting and processing raw materials to manufacturing, use/reuse/maintenance, and disposal/recycling. Coca-Cola conducted the first LCA in 1969 to assess the relative impacts of glass versus plastic bottles.[32] Today, LCAs are used for a wide variety of purposes and, as such, can differ sharply in breadth and depth. The biggest differences stem from choices about the life cycle stage and types of impact:

   - *Life cycle stage:* Most LCAs set out to assess, even if only roughly, the environmental impacts of products from "cradle to grave"—that is, from resource extraction to final disposal. But LCAs sometimes use different boundaries, including: "cradle-to-gate" (resource extraction to factory gate just before transport to the customer—often used for "environmental product declarations" to support marketing claims); "gate-to-gate" (from the gate through which materials enter the production process to the gate through which they leave—used to study the impacts of a specific *process* in the value chain); and "cradle-to-cradle" (resource extraction to *recycling* as opposed to disposal). Industry-specific LCA jargon exists for all of these, too: the automobile industry, for instance, has conducted studies in terms of "well-to-wheel," "well-to-station," "well-to-tank," "tank-to-wheel," and so on.[33]

   - *Type(s) of impact:* To make things more manageable, some LCA studies limit their scope to assess impacts on just one environmental issue, such as climate change; in fact, a "product carbon footprint analysis" is actually a type of LCA—and is a monumental undertaking in and of itself, given the complexity of assessing energy use and emissions from cradle-to-grave. Other LCAs strive to assess impacts more comprehensively, including threats to human health or ecosystems from toxic chemicals, depletion of natural resources, freshwater use, degradation of critical ecosystems, destruction of habitat, and more. Other LCAs focus on social impacts of particular products and processes or workers and communities.

2. **It's critical to know *why* you want to do a product LCA so you can choose the right tool.**

   Before embarking on a potentially time-consuming and expensive LCA, get clear on the following: What question(s) are you trying to answer? What problem(s) are you trying to solve? What decision(s) do you need help with? In other words, what's your company's goal for the analysis? Being explicit about this up front is a crucial prerequisite to choosing the right tools for the task. You don't want to use a sledgehammer for a nail: In some cases, getting what you need can simply be a matter of organizing a good discussion with the right people in the room.

3. **Most studies build off an international standard approach for LCAs.**

   A set of international standards have been painstakingly built over decades to establish a unifying framework on which most LCAs build: ISO 14040 and ISO 14044 (see Figure 6.7).

4. **An LCA is only as good as the data and assumptions behind it—and no LCA is perfect.**

   Xerox Vice President of Environment, Health and Safety Patty Calkins summed up the LCA challenge by telling us a joke circulating in sustainability circles: "How many people does it take to do an LCA? One to do it, and one to change it when you get more data." With so many potential variables at play, the reality is that even the most meticulously crafted LCAs can produce findings that are uncertain, incomplete, or controversial. The challenge with LCAs is only partially described by the age-old problem of "garbage in,

Figure 6.7   The Four Phases of a Life Cycle Analysis

Define the Goal and Scope →	Assemble the "Life Cycle Inventory" (LCI) →	Assess the Impacts	Interpret the Results
Get clear on *why* the analysis is needed, and what it will be used for **Define the "functional unit,"** the basis for analysis and comparison (e.g, for a plastic bottle or aluminum soda can it would be something like the "delivery of 12 ounces of soda") **Define scope and boundaries** (e.g., cradle-to-grave or cradle-to-gate? Only climate impacts or environmental impacts?) **Specify the approach** for the study	Map out the product's life cycle system to identify all its component parts and all the flows among them (see the example in the "Life Cycle of a paper cup" box) **Identify and collect data on the major "inputs"** (e.g., energy, extracted raw materials, land use) required for every life cycle stage **Identify and collect data on the major "outputs"** (including air and water emissions, materials, waste) at every stage *Note: The inputs and outputs are sometimes referred to as "elementary flows"*	Use a process called "Life Cycle Impact Assessment (LCIA)" to put the input/output data into the context of actual environmental impact (e.g., CO_2 data gets translated into "Global Warming Potential," while data on Volatile Organic Compounds (VOC) emissions gets converted to "Photo-Oxidant Creation Potential"	Analyze the results in light of original goals to reach conclusions and recommendations

Sources: Based on the International Standards Organization's ISO 14040 and 14044, which lays out four major phases of the LCA method. International Organization for Standardization, ISO 14040 and ISO 14044, www.iso.org/iso/home.html (accessed August 4, 2010); Timothy Allan, "Life Cycle Tools and Approaches—Implementing Change," *Life Cycle Thinking*, http://lifecyclethinking.locusresearch .com/2008 (accessed August 4, 2010).

garbage out." To understand why, consider the following hypothetical example of two competitors conducting separate LCAs on their nearly identical products:

Company A spends tens of thousands of dollars to generate its own primary data, while Company B uses publicly available data based on sector averages. Company A inadvertently omits a few seemingly insignificant manufacturing-related inputs from the study, but Company B meticulously includes every single one. Company A assumes that consumers will use the product about 8 hours a week for 32 weeks, while Company B assumes 7 hours a day for 40 weeks. Company A weights impacts on local watersheds 33 percent more than Company B. Now imagine the difficulty in deciding whose final numbers are "better" when they end up being different—yet this type of scenario happens all the time in real life.

THE LIFE CYCLE OF A PAPER CUP

A full life cycle analysis of a disposable paper drinking cup would need to factor in the following:[34]

- Forestry practices to grow and harvest trees.
- Steel to make the machines that turn trees into pulp, and energy to run those machines.
- Water and dyes to turn pulp into paper.
- Glue to put the cup together.
- Electricity or natural gas for operating the machinery to form the cup.
- Production waste (e.g., wastewater, scrap paper material, waste glue, rejected low-quality cups).
- All the packaging- and transportation-related inputs and outputs involved in shipping the cup to the retailer or customer.
- The consumer's trip to the store to purchase the cups.
- The trash that results from disposing of the cup and original packaging.

Similarly, when it comes to numbers in LCAs, keep in mind the old adage that "it's all relative." Unless two companies' products are verified by the same third-party certification agency, there is little meaning in comparing environmental impacts across competitors. As Deloitte has pointed out in a white paper on the subject: "Small differences in assumptions related to system boundaries or valuation techniques can lead to radically disparate results."[35] The natural tendency with LCAs is to try to distill complexity down into single numbers or "scores"—but doing so when nature is involved inevitably requires subjective judgments, which means numbers can only be trusted to a point. In this way, LCA is as much an art as it is a science.

5. **When it comes to LCA tools, it's the Wild West.**

As Locus Research's Managing Director Timothy Allan puts it, "LCA is a method, not a tool."[36] There are more tools than you can imagine out there—from simple Excel spreadsheets and free "rapid LCA" calculators to complex, customizable software packages. And as you read this, you can be sure that countless PhDs, consultants, and developers are hard at work picking apart existing tools and creating new ones.

The good news is that LCA methodologies are rapidly advancing, building on years of accumulated sweat equity. Three of the leading (albeit costly) LCA software packages are PRé's SimaPro, PE International's GaBi, and Ecobilan's TEAM. There are also countless specialized LCA tools and consultancies focused on carbon footprinting, joining some of the more established firms including Carbon Impact at SAP, Planet Metrics, and Clear Carbon. One of the more promising developments in 2010 was the launch of a new open-source initiative called Earthster (www.earthster.org), which is working to make the LCA process simpler and more affordable to businesses of all shapes and sizes.

TWO BASIC CATEGORIES OF LCAs, HUNDREDS OF VARIATIONS

"Simplified" or "Screening" LCA

This is the most common approach to LCA because it is relatively quick and cheap—even for small and medium-sized businesses. Large companies like GE make tools based on these approaches available to product designers, engineers, and others who need to make daily decisions involving trade-offs in products and processes (e.g., which materials or chemicals are preferred under which circumstances).

There are scores of competing approaches and tools with fancy names, such as: Basic/Partial LCA, LCA Light, Qualitative or semi-qualitative LCA, Eco-Indicator LCA, Environmental Effects Analysis (EEA), Basic Material(s) Assessment, Economic Input-Output LCA (EIO-LCA), Basic Materials Assessment, Material Input Per Service Unit (MIPS), Flaesche Input Per Unit Service (FIPS), Weighted Criteria Product Evaluation Spreadsheets, and many more. Though they differ in form, all versions of simplified LCAs essentially boil down to fewer variables under analysis, smaller data sets (sometimes just guesses based on professional judgment), and rough but helpful results.

"Full" or "Extensive" LCA

Extensive LCAs are costly, resource-intensive exercises usually undertaken only by large companies and/or businesses that plan to market environmentally friendly aspects of their products. They require high degrees of environmental domain knowledge and previous experience with LCAs. Companies that do perform them either rely on specialized staff experts, external consultants, specialized commercial software, or a combination. As with their simplified counterparts, myriad competing approaches and tools exist.

6. **The search is on to standardize approaches.**

   Recognizing the high costs and challenges of going it alone, many companies are pooling resources to develop cheaper, better, and faster ways of doing LCAs. Most notably, the Sustainability Consortium—backed by Walmart and about 50 other major companies—is working to develop "transparent methodologies, tools, and strategies" for assessing the life cycle sustainability attributes of a wide array of consumer products—including a database of product LCA information. The hope is that companies one day will be able to use a common methodology to evaluate suppliers' products and convey green product attributes to consumers in stores. Green business expert Joel Makower describes the effort as a "man-on-the-moon-caliber undertaking," while skeptics insist it's essentially a wild goose chase. Without placing any bets on any specific outcomes, we believe the effort will advance the state of the field—in useful ways.

7. **It's never too early for companies to start building their assessment capacity.**

   While LCAs may be difficult, they aren't going away—and the pressure on companies to understand and disclose their products' environmental impacts will only grow in the years ahead. By performing even a simple LCA, a company will not just get to know its products better; it will also build internal capacity to think and innovate along life cycle lines and ask the right questions when the time comes to consider hiring a consultant, investing in a software package, or building your own tools. One of the best initial investments we recommend is to spend $10 to download Rita Schenck's quick guide, "LCA for Mere Mortals" (www.iere.org/mortals.html)—an outstanding primer that can be skimmed in an hour. We list other resources and "LCA Light" tools to get your feet wet at the end of this chapter.

ADVANCED PLAY: EXTEND THE ANALYSIS

7. Redo Each of the Analyses at a More Advanced Level

As we noted at the outset of this chapter, each of the plays can be carried out at a basic, intermediate, or advanced level. For companies that have completed all of the exercises in the plays listed earlier, it is time to dig deeper. For those who have only done a rough-cut carbon footprint, it makes sense to undertake a more detailed data-rich analysis. If you have calculated your scope 1 and 2 emissions, it is time to look at the challenging scope 3 emissions. And if you have fully assessed your company's own GHG impacts, it would likely be illuminating for you to do a "value chain" carbon footprint. Indeed, when the consumer products giant Unilever did such an analysis of impacts upstream and downstream as well as within its own operations, it discovered that 90 percent or more of the emissions from its food products occurred upstream as a result of the activities of the farmers from whom it purchased crops. With regard to its consumer products, the vast bulk of the emissions occurred downstream as a result of customer energy use associated with washing clothes or showering.

SUMMARY

Key Plays

1. Get familiar with common indicators of business environmental impact metrics.

2. Plot your company's carbon footprint.

3. Measure your company's waste.

4. Assess your company's water footprint and related impacts.

5. Evaluate your company's other impacts on ecosystems and biodiversity.

6. Undertake a life cycle assessment of your products and services.

7. Redo each of the analyses at a more advanced level.

ADDITIONAL RESOURCES

CALCULATING ORGANIZATIONAL AND PRODUCT CARBON FOOTPRINTS

"How to Calculate a Carbon Footprint" (Clear Carbon, 2010). Step-by-step guide to defining corporate greenhouse gas inventory parameters, quantifying emissions, and reporting an organization's footprint. www.clear carboninc.com

"Carbon Footprinting: The Next Step to Reducing Your Emissions" (Carbon Trust, 2010) Guidance for footprint analyses at the organization-wide level and the product or service level. Particularly helpful to small and mid-sized companies. www.carbontrust.co.uk

Office Carbon Footprint Tool (EPA). Free tool to assist offices in assessing and making decisions to reduce the greenhouse gas emissions associated with their activities. www.epa.gov/solidwaste

GHG Protocol. The leading international accounting tool for both businesses and governments to calculate and manage their greenhouse gas emissions. www.ghgprotocol.org

GHG Protocol Sector Toolsets. Sector-specific GHG calculation tools. www.ghgprotocol.org/calculation-tools/sector-toolsets

Carbon Express Track. Low-cost, online software program that helps businesses simplify carbon accounting and manage and reduce their climate impact. www.carbonfund.org/cet

"Designing a Customized Greenhouse Gas Calculation Tool" (World Resources Institute, 2006). Tool for advanced users of the GHG Protocol that provides guidance on defining scope and boundaries, emissions factors, and the major methodologies of emissions calculations. www.wri.org/publication/designing-customized-greenhouse-gas-calculation-tool

The Climate Registry Information System. Online greenhouse gas calculation, reporting, and verification tool that builds on the standards set by the Climate Registry, a nonprofit membership organization working to harmonize greenhouse gas monitoring and reporting in North America. www.theclimateregistry.org

BSI PAS 2050. The British Standards Institution's (BSI) method for calculating greenhouse gas emissions from products across their life cycle. www.bsigroup.com/Standards-and-Publications/How-we-can-help-you/Professional-Standards-Service/PAS-2050

MEASURING WASTE

Green Business Guide to Waste Audits (NRDC). Overview of recommendations and tools for conducting waste audits that reveal opportunities to save resources and cut costs. www.nrdc.org/enterprise/greeningadvisor/wm-audits.asp

ReduceYourWaste.org. Interactive tool that generates sector-specific, customized recommendations to help businesses cut waste.

WasteWise (EPA). Free, voluntary EPA program to help organizations eliminate costly municipal solid waste and select industrial wastes. www.epa.gov/epawaste

WasteWise Re-TRAC System (EPA). Data management and reporting system to help companies collect, organize, analyze, and report their municipal solid waste information. www.epa.gov/epawaste

Hazardous Waste Information Site (EPA). Recommendations and tools for identifying, reducing, disposing of, and recycling hazardous or toxic waste. www.epa.gov/osw/hazard/index.htm

MEASURING WATER IMPACTS

"At the Crest of a Wave: A Proactive Approach to Corporate Water Strategy" (Business for Social Responsibility and Pacific Institute, 2007) Guidance for measuring water footprint, assessing risks, and developing and implementing corporate water strategy. www.bsr.org/reports/BSR_Water-Trends.pdf

Global Water Tool (World Business Council for Sustainable Development). Free, easy-to-use tool for companies and organizations to map their water use and assess risks relative to their global operations and supply chains. www.wbcsd.org

"Water Footprint Manual: State of the Art 2009" (Water Footprint Network). How to conduct a detailed assessment of direct and indirect water consumption. www.waterfootprint.org/downloads/WaterFootprintManual2009.pdf

Water Impact Index (Veolia Water). A framework that helps companies comprehensively assess their impacts on water ecosystems factoring in consumption, resource stress, and water quality. www.veoliawaterna.com/sustainable/water-impact-index

Collecting the Drops: A Water Sustainability Planner (Global Environmental Management Initiative, 2007). Helps companies assess a facility's water-related needs, impacts, and business risks. www.gemi.org/waterplanner

"GE's Solutions for Sustainable Water Savings." How manufacturers can calculate water footprints, identify opportunities, and create an optimization plan. www.gewater.com/water_efficiency/index.jsp

Alliance for Water Efficiency. Resources and tools for a variety of commercial, institutional, and industrial water users. www.allianceforwaterefficiency.org

"Product Water Footprint Assessments: Practical Application in Corporate Water Stewardship" (Coca-Cola, The Nature Conservancy, 2010). www.waterfootprint.org

MEASURING IMPACTS ON ECOSYSTEMS AND BIODIVERSITY

"TEEB—The Economics of Ecosystems and Biodiversity Report for Business" (UNEP, 2010). Findings from a major global study on how ecosystem decline and biodiversity loss pose business risks and opportunities. Includes tools for assessing and managing related risks. www.teebweb.org

"Corporate Ecosystem Services Review" (World Resources Institute, 2007). Methodology and tools to help businesses pinpoint priority risks and opportunities and find specialized tools to further assess and manage impacts. www.wri.org/ecosystems/esr

Forest Footprint Disclosure Project (Global Canopy Foundation, 2009). Aims to improve understanding of companies' "forest footprints" caused by using forest risk commodities, such as soy, palm oil, timber, cattle products, and biofuels. www.forestdisclosure.com/docs/FFD_Annual_Review_WEB.pdf

"Measuring Corporate Impact on Ecosystems: A Comprehensive Review of New Tools" (Business for Social Responsibility, 2008). An overview of ecosystem impact assessment tools. www.bsr.org

LIFE CYCLE ASSESSMENT (LCA)

Background

"LCA for Mere Mortals" by Rita Schenck (Institute for Environmental Research and Education). Excellent primer that you can skim in an hour. www.iere.org

Life Cycle Assessment Research (EPA). Extensive online resource including a "101" LCA introduction; a detailed online handbook on the concepts behind and application of LCA techniques; and links to LCA software tools, standards, and databases. www.epa.gov/nrmrl/lcaccess/index.html

Life-Cycle.Org. A clearinghouse pointing to various LCA-related resources on the Web. www.life-cycle.org

Life Cycle Thinking (European Commission). Extensive directory of Web links related to LCAs, including links to software tool providers, consultants, and other service providers, and data sources for LCA and footprint analyses. http://lct.jrc.ec.europa.eu

United Nations Environment Programme and Society of Environmental Toxicology & Chemistry Life Cycle Initiative. Seeks to compile and share life cycle data from companies and industries around the world. Website contains links to LCI databases, forms for submitting data, and project publications. http://lcinitiative.unep.fr

Basic LCA Tools

Life Cycle Assessment Calculator (Industrial Design Consultancy). Free tool that estimates product environmental impacts by calculating energy input and carbon output from cradle to grave. www.lcacalculator.com/index.html

Intermediate-Advanced Tools

OpenIO (Sustainability Consortium and University of Arkansas). Open-source tools and resources to help companies estimate the sustainability of products and services. http://openio.walton.uark.edu

Earthster. Open-source tool for monitoring different types of data in supply chains. Data then used in preparing footprints or life cycle assessments, which can be distributed across supply chains. www.earthster.org

Greenfly. Web-based program that incorporates life cycle modeling to show environmental impacts of potential product design choices. www.greenflyonline.org.

"Calculating Materials Input Per Service Unit (MIPS): Resource Productivity of Products and Services" (Wuppertal Institute for Climate, Environment and Energy, 2002). Manual for using the MIPS methodology to estimate environmental impacts of products or services. www.wupperinst.org

Economic Input-Output Life Cycle Assessment (EIO-LCA). Method and data sets estimating the materials and energy resources required for, and emissions resulting from, economic activities. www.eiolca.net

"Guidelines for Social Life Cycle Assessment of Products" (UNEP, 2009). Methods for assessing not only a product's potential eco-impacts, but also social and socioeconomic impacts on workers, local communities, consumers, and society. www.unep.org/publications

LISA (LCA in Sustainable Architecture) Software. Streamlined LCA decision support tool to help designers make informed choices based on whole-of-life environmental considerations. www.lisa.au.com

Case Studies

Science in the Box (Procter & Gamble). P&G's overview and case studies of how it has used LCA in products including cleaning supplies and laundry detergents. www.scienceinthebox.com

University of Michigan Center for Sustainable Systems. Case studies on LCAs to understand all aspects of industry and the consumer products. www.css.snre.umich.edu/publications

CHOOSING METRICS FOR EVALUATION AND REPORTING

From Transparency to Performance: Industry-Based Sustainability Reporting on Key Issues (Steve Lydenberg, Jean Rogers, and David Wood, Hauser Center and Initiative for Responsible Investment, 2010). Outlines a materiality-based approach to corporate reporting, with recommendations for choosing key performance indicators on sustainability impacts of US corporations in specific industries. www.hausercenter.org/

The Metrics Navigator (GEMI). Web-based tool that helps organizations develop and implement the "critical few" metrics that provide insight into complex issues and contribute to business success. http://www.gemi.org/metricsnavigator/

Chapter 7 Benchmark Your Performance against Competitors and Best Practices

One of the most important diagnostic tools for any company developing an environmental or sustainability strategy is comparative performance analysis—often known in the business as "benchmarking." Assessing your company's pollution control and natural resource management results and programs relative to others in your industry—or against a template of best practices—gives you a way to clarify your strengths, weaknesses, and priorities for improvement. While there is no established corporate sustainability benchmarking methodology or even an agreed upon list of key elements to consider, we offer in this chapter a starting point for this sort of comparative analysis. Given, however, the diversity of eco-issues and business circumstances, you will need to tailor our list to the particular needs of your business.

This chapter provides tools to:

- Gauge your environmental performance and systems.
- Assess the overall status of your corporate eco-strategy relative to peers and best practice.
- Identify key strengths and, more important, weaknesses or gaps that merit focus.

BASIC PLAY: CONDUCT A RAPID ASSESSMENT

1. Do a Quick Assessment of Your Company's Current Eco-Performance Relative to Best Practice

Before diving into any particular area, we recommend stepping back to evaluate your organization's relative strengths and weaknesses in four areas vital to seizing an Eco-Advantage: (1) **Eco-Strategy**; (2) **Commitment, Culture, & Capacity**; (3) **Execution and Eco-Achievements**; and (4) **Communications and Engagement**. Grab a pencil and take the four tests presented in Figures 7.1 through 7.4, which draw on a framework developed by Esty Environmental Partners. Circle the statements that most closely match your organization's current status. Doing so will help you identify areas for priority action. At the end of the tests, we list relevant *Playbook* chapters to help you expand on particular strengths or address specific gaps you've circled (see Figure 7.5).

Figure 7.1   Benchmarking Test #1: ECO-STRATEGY

BASIC *Needs Improvement*	INTERMEDIATE *Keeping Up*	ADVANCED *Leading*
Analytics • Basic understanding of eco-impacts based on first-cut assessments • No system to analyze value chain impacts upstream (suppliers) or downstream (distributors and customers) • No company-wide system to track Eco-Advantage challenges and opportunities • Limited understanding of external stakeholders' eco-priorities • Tracking environmental policy/regulatory landscape in a general way *Overall Eco-Strategy* • Focused on compliance with existing laws and regulations *Climate Change Strategy* • No comprehensive strategy—perhaps some eco-initiatives under way	*Analytics* • Big-picture understanding of priority eco-impacts and risks • Some effort to analyze and quantify value chain impacts • Familiar with major external stakeholders' eco-priorities *Overall Eco-Strategy* • Focus on addressing top impacts and risks, but strategy may not deal comprehensively with company's eco-impacts • Focus is mainly on reducing impacts and becoming "less bad" • Strategy centers on managing risks and cutting costs (eco-efficiency) • Focuses mainly on short-term considerations *Climate Change Strategy* • Includes broad goals, some hard targets, and specific action steps	*Analytics* • Comprehensive, ongoing assessment of priority eco-impacts and risks • Comprehensive approach to analyzing value chain impacts • Actively solicits external opinion and expertise (e.g., active stakeholder dialogues or regular input from an external advisory board) *Overall Eco-Strategy* • Comprehensive and actionable, addresses all the company's major environmental issues with specific goals and metrics • Accounts for long-term considerations • Aspires not just to address but to solve eco-problems • Focus includes "upside" Eco-Advantage (revenue growth, innovation, etc.) as well as brand building elements *Climate Change Strategy* • Includes hard targets for absolute reduction of greenhouse gases and specific actions to meet those goals • Offsets emissions that cannot be eliminated

Figure 7.2 Benchmarking Test #2: COMMITMENT, CULTURE, & CAPACITY

BASIC *Needs Improvement*	INTERMEDIATE *Keeping Up*	ADVANCED *Leading*
Culture • Sustainability largely seen as a philanthropic issue, not connected to core business objectives • Commitment to corporate social responsibility (avoid bad behavior) *Management & Accountability* • Limited CEO engagement • No senior executive dedicated to corporate-wide environment or sustainability strategy • No environmental management system (EMS) in place • Management-level employees are not expected to take environmental considerations into account *Employee Engagement & Training* • Limited education or training on eco-issues • No systematic internal communication on sustainability issues	*Culture* • Some influential executives see business value of sustainability efforts, but others remain skeptical • Employee understanding and engagement on eco-issues is growing but not comprehensive *Management & Accountability* • CEO shows support • Executive in place responsible for corporate-wide environmental sustainability strategy, though relatively less senior or influential than c-suite counterparts • Environmental Management System (EMS) in place but may not cover all key issues of business units • Management-level employees expected to take environmental considerations into account, but no formal link between compensation or career advancement and environmental performance *Employee Engagement & Training* • Occasional educational or training events of limited scope or reach • Programs to encourage recycling and other eco-behavior within company	*Culture* • Environment reflected in company's mission and vision • Entire top leadership team embraces eco-commitment, as do most employees • Eco-thinking/principles deeply embedded in day-to-day strategy *Management & Accountability* • CEO deeply committed, takes personal responsibility for the company's environmental performance, and strives for industry leadership • High-level, influential executive (VP or higher) is focused on corporate-wide environmental performance and positioned for impact • Company has enterprise-wide environmental management system (EMS) in place • Accountability for eco-performance is shared across company • Compensation or career advancement is explicitly linked to environmental performance for management-level employees *Employee Engagement & Training* • Comprehensive programs to engage and build capacity of employees—from senior executives to line workers • Mature system to share tools and lessons learned across the company

Figure 7.3 Benchmarking Test #3: EXECUTION & ECO-ACHIEVEMENTS

BASIC *Needs Improvement*	INTERMEDIATE *Keeping Up*	ADVANCED *Leading*
Eco-Efficiency • Little/no progress on reducing energy use or improving eco-efficiency	*Eco-Efficiency* • Scattered energy, waste, water, carbon, recycling, and/or packaging reduction efforts, not systematic; early, incomplete or intensity-only results	*Eco-Efficiency* • Systematic focus on eco-efficiency gains in all areas on an enterprise-wide basis in ways that encourage investment (e.g., easier ROI hurdle, pool of funds, etc.) • Committed to LEED (or similar) standards for new buildings and renovations
Eco-Impacts • Complying with existing laws and regulations, with some voluntary efforts to reduce impacts	*Eco-Impacts* • Incremental progress on some eco-issues—about average relative to competitors	*Eco-Impacts* • Recognized industry eco-leader with sustained absolute reductions in two or more key impacts; uses precautionary principle
Products & Services • No products or services with green features or attributes	*Products & Services* • Updating or developing some products and services with eco-attributes • No company-wide approach to green design	*Products & Services* • Measurable goals toward enterprise-wide eco-innovation; offers market-leading, third-party certified green products or services that are clearly "a step ahead" of the competition • Uses "Design for the Environment" (DfE) protocol in core design process
Upstream (supplier) Impacts • No policies or system to address supplier eco-impacts	*Upstream (supplier) Impacts* • Has supplier code of conduct with broadly defined or "suggested" eco-management goals and practices • Taking some steps to require direct suppliers (Tier 1) to meet eco-standards, beginning to expand focus to indirect suppliers (Tier 2)	*Upstream (supplier) Impacts* • Rigorous, performance-oriented code of conduct for suppliers, with regular auditing and appropriate response for at least all Tier 1 suppliers • Comprehensive procedures to require indirect suppliers to meet environmental standards
Downstream (distributor and customer) Impacts • No steps to address customer impacts • No focus on product "end of life" impacts	*Downstream (distributor and customer) Impacts* • Minor steps to address	*Downstream (distributor and customer) Impacts* • Meaningful progress in minimizing downstream impacts, with consumer recycling and voluntary take-back programs
Global Certifications • No standards	*Global Certifications* • Management focus on sustainability standards	*Global Certifications* • Broad adherence to established standards related to company's key impacts; helping to develop, define, and promote new standards

Figure 7.4 Benchmarking Test #4: COMMUNICATIONS & ENGAGEMENT

BASIC *Needs Improvement*	INTERMEDIATE *Keeping Up*	ADVANCED *Leading*
Reporting • No environmental report • Little to no information shared on website about company's eco-footprint or performance *Customer & Consumer Engagement* • No environmental marketing • Making implausible, irrelevant or misleading "green" claims • Does not invite consumer feedback on eco-issues *Broader External Stakeholder Engagement* • Largely defensive position vis-à-vis stakeholders • No partnerships in place	*Reporting* • Has issued environmental report or sustainability report with substantial environmental section • Data posted on website *Customer & Consumer Engagement* • Uses tools of marketing and corporate communications to make its customers aware of its sustainability commitments and/or products • Has programs that inform consumers and/or customers about relevant environmental issues • Has a mechanism for consumer feedback on environmental issues *Broader External Stakeholder Engagement* • Engaged in projects with NGOs or participates in government sustainability programs • Ad hoc dialogue with key stakeholders • Membership in external stakeholder groups such as USCAP, Carbon Mitigation Initiative, or EPA Climate Leaders	*Reporting* • Issues a regular formal environmental report whether stand-alone or part of broader sustainability report • Key environmental metrics regularly updated on website • Uses absolute as well as normalized (efficiency-gain) metrics • Discloses major eco-related risks and liabilities • Reports goals missed as well as goals achieved. Metrics in report include those in which the company has not excelled • Independent verification • Report shows how company tracks GRI standards *Customer & Consumer Engagement* • Showcases company's solutions to issues • Educates consumers and/or customers about environment issues • Leads the way by helping consumers or customers change behavior • Explicitly solicits and uses consumer feedback to improve company's sustainability *Broader External Stakeholder Engagement* • Systematic outreach to NGOs and other critical stakeholders • Company has created and/or led outside organizations, and engaged peers on eco-issues • Company plays constructive role in shaping policy (state, federal, international)

Figure 7.5 below lists chapters in this Playbook that can help you expand on particular strengths or address specific gaps you identified in the Benchmarking Tests #1–4.

Figure 7.5   **Support for Raising Your Game by Chapter**

Area	Relevant Playbook Chapters
Analytics	5–7, 22
Overall Eco-Strategy	All chapters, especially 3
Climate Change Strategy	5–14, 19
Commitment and Culture	3, 4, 20
Management & Accountability	3, 18
Employee Engagement & Training	3, 20
Eco-Efficiency	8–14
Eco-Impacts	5, 6, 8–14
Products & Services	11
Upstream Supply Chain Impacts	5, 6, 12
Downstream Customer Impacts	5, 6, 11
Reporting & Communications	22
Consumer & Customer Engagement	15
Broader External Engagement	21

INTERMEDIATE PLAY: BENCHMARK AGAINST PEERS

2. Compare Your Performance to Industry Peers

One of the most valuable aspects of benchmarking is the window it opens on what others facing similar circumstances are doing to respond to the issues you need to address. The actions and results of industry peers provide context to help you understand what you can do and how to do it. To deepen your understanding of what sustainability targets to set and which issues to prioritize, it makes sense to undertake some comparative analysis relative to your peer companies. For this exercise, we recommend the following process:

Step 1: Put together a list of the most important key performance indicators (KPIs) for your sector. To identify the indicators, start by drawing on the list of "Common Metrics Used to Assess Business Environmental Impacts" in Chapter 6. Circle the KPIs that seem most relevant to your business, jotting down others that are missing given your company's or industry's impacts. Then scan the websites and published environmental sustainability reports of a cross-section of peers in your sector to see which KPIs they are externally reporting on. Consult the websites of key stakeholder groups, including major corporate "watchdog" NGOs that are actively tracking business performance in your sector (See Chapter 5 recommendation 4, "Map Your Stakeholders—And Their Issues.") Scan the metrics used by third-party assessment schemes by consulting the "Major Corporate Sustainability Rating and Ranking Systems" listed at the end of this chapter in the "Additional Resources." Be selective. Choose only the metrics you think matter most. For instance, an electric utility might choose indicators such as carbon reductions achieved, publicly stated carbon reduction goals, waste metrics, percent of renewables in total energy portfolio, renewables targets, membership in credible stakeholder groups, Carbon Disclosure Project Leadership Index score, and so on. Run your draft list of KPIs by both internal experts at your company and external stakeholders (NGO contacts, key customers, board members, etc.) for comment.

Step 2: Identify 4 to 8 companies in your industry that provide a good basis for comparison. Choose a representative cross-section of companies that range from perceived stragglers on environmental issues to recognized leaders.

Step 3: Create a matrix listing KPIs on the vertical axis and your business and the comparison companies on the horizontal axis. Collect the internal data you need and use publicly available information from other companies' websites to fill in the matrix shown in Figure 7.6. Include explanatory notes whenever they provide valuable context. You may find it challenging to standardize the metrics to make the comparisons work. For instance, companies often report carbon emissions statistics using different baseline years or boundaries on what and what not to include in their emissions inventory. You may need to adjust the KPIs on the vertical axis. It is also useful to track the leaders in each category. Highlight the areas where your company or others are leading or lagging.

Figure 7.6 Hypothetical Comparison of Utilities

Key: Light gray box = LEADING ahead of competitors
Dark gray box = LAGGING behind competitors

	Your Company	Competitor A	Competitor B	Competitor C
Greenhouse Gas (GHG) Reductions	Cut 25 million metric tons since 2005 (Note: need % reduction figure)	Cut 42 million metric tons since 2000	Cut emissions by 8% between 2001–2010	Cut emissions 15% between 2000–2010
GHG Goals	Cut 25 million metric tons over 2010 (Note: need % reduction figure)	5% reduction over 2010 levels by 2020	50% reduction over 2010 levels by 2050 (no clear short-term goal)	25% reduction over 2010 levels by 2020
% Renewables in Electricity Mix	5%	<1%	9%	15%
Commitments to Alternative Energy	600 MW new solar and 12,000 MW new wind (Note: calculate % of mix)	None	10% by 2030 (Note: find out MW equivalent)	20% by 2020 in MA + 30% in VT by 2030 (Note: find out MW equivalent)
Engagement with NGOs and Other Stakeholder Groups	None	EPA Climate Leaders	EPA Climate Leaders, USCAP, Pew Center Business Environmental Leadership Council	EPA Climate Leaders, USCAP
Carbon Disclosure Project Score (2008)	70	No CDP reporting	79	85

ADVANCED PLAYS: DEEPEN THE ANALYSIS

3. Focus the Lens on Priority Areas

Once you are armed with a general understanding of where your company stands relative to best practice and competitors, you can dive more deeply into areas of special importance, ramp up performance on issues where you currently lag, and identify opportunities for leadership. Before looking, however, for ways to differentiate your products or services on the basis of sustainability, be sure that "your ducks are in a row." Gaps in basic pollution control or natural resource management must be addressed before you draw attention to your company with claims of industry leadership. As we stressed in Chapter 5 ("Spot the Eco-Issues"), you need to focus not only on internal concerns but also on issues that key stakeholders are watching closely. See Chapter 2 ("How to Use This Book") and Figure 7.5 presented earlier for issue-specific *Playbook* chapters that spell out best practices across a range of business functions and in a number of specialized areas.

4. Benchmark outside the Box and into the Future

If your company stands ahead of industry peers, we urge you to look beyond your direct competitors and today's definitions of "best practice" as you benchmark. Corporate sustainability expectations are rising. As the goalposts move, you have to raise your game. You must demonstrate ongoing commitment and innovation to stay ahead of the pack.

Business practices that get an "A" rating or leadership award today might only merit a "C" a few years down the line. To anticipate future standards of excellence, you will need to track emerging regulatory requirements, technology developments, and evolving public attitudes.

We urge you to develop a strategy for continuous improvement—and mechanisms for ongoing "peer review" of your sustainability goals and performance. Invite trusted NGO experts and thought leaders to weigh in on what best practices will look like in your industry in 5 or 10 years. Find out what leaders in other sectors are doing to be more sustainable. Engage in environmental information "arbitrage." Look at the issues emerging and solutions being deployed in other sectors and in other parts of the world as a potential early signal of changes that may be coming to your industry.

SUMMARY

Key Plays

1. Do a quick assessment of your company's current eco-performance relative to best practice.

2. Compare your performance to that of industry peers.

3. Focus the lens on priority areas.

4. Benchmark outside the box and into the future.

ADDITIONAL RESOURCES

MAJOR CORPORATE SUSTAINABILITY RATING AND RANKING SYSTEMS

Global 100 Most Sustainable Corporations in the World (Corporate Knights). An annual project that highlights the global corporations judged to be "most proactive in managing environmental, social, and governance (ESG) issues." Focuses almost exclusively on midcap-sized and larger firms. www.global100.org

The 100 Best Corporate Citizens List (*Corporate Responsibility* magazine). Compares performance of large-cap companies in the Russell 1000® in environment, climate change, human rights, employee relations, philanthropy, financial performance and governance. Rankings are based solely on publicly available information. www.thecro.com

***Newsweek* Green Rankings** (*Newsweek*). Works with environmental researchers KLD Research & Analytics, Trucost, and CorporateRegister.com to rank the 500 largest U.S. companies based on their environmental performance, policies, and reputation. http://greenrankings.newsweek.com

Greenopia Green Brands List. Rates eco-friendly U.S. brands based on green building design, supply chain, recycling programs, green power, and sustainability reporting. Uses a scorecard that weights various inputs based on publicly available information. Ratings criteria and metrics are sector-specific. www.greenopia.com

AccountAbility's Tomorrow's Value Rating. Sector-specific ratings of large companies' records in managing social and environmental issues. Based on companies' performance in five key areas: strategy, governance, engagement, value chain, and innovation. www.tomorrowsvaluerating.com

Climate Change

Climate Counts Company Scorecard (ClimateCounts.org). Annual scorecard that rates large companies' self-reported efforts on climate change on a 100-point scale. www.climatecounts.org

The Carbon Disclosure Project's Leadership Index (CDLI). Assesses the quality and depth of a company's response to an annual questionnaire, not on its actual emissions. www.cdproject.net

MAJOR INVESTMENT INDICES AND REPORTS

Dow Jones Sustainability Index (DJSI). A series of indices that identify and track the financial performance of sustainability-driven companies worldwide. The DJSI World Index sets the highest bar. www.sustainability-indexes.com

Goldman Sachs GS SUSTAIN. Uses publicly disclosed data to identify companies that will sustain competitive advantage and superior returns over the long term. Analyzes company performance relative to peers in three areas: Abatement Leaders in carbon intensive industries, Adjustment Leaders in less intensive industries, and Solutions Providers exposed to growth opportunities. www2.goldmansachs.com

FTSE4Good Index Series (EIRIS Survey Research). Global and regional indices that classify companies as high, medium, or low impact based on the environmental footprint of their activities. The higher the environmental impact of the company's operations, the more stringent the inclusion criteria used. Uses publicly available information for the initial assessment, then invites companies to verify and contribute additional information. www.ftse.com

MSCI Index Series (Intangible Value Assessment Ratings, FTSE KLD Indices, KLD/Jantzi Indices). MSCI acquired Risk Metrics in 2010, which had previously acquired Innovest and KLD. MSCI has three categories of environmental, social, and governance (ESG) indices: (1) *ESG Best-of-Class indices* that include companies with high ESG ratings relative to sector peers; (2) *Values-based indices* that include companies compatible with certain values, norms, or ethical standards and those with high ESG ratings relative to sector peers; (3) *Environmental indices* that include businesses providing products and services that focus on particular environmental issues such as clean energy or renewable fuels. www.mscibarra.com

Ethibel Sustainability Index Series. Evaluates companies in six areas: human rights, human resources, environment, business behavior, corporate governance, and community involvement. Analysis conducted by Standard & Poor's, which uses publicly available information and enables companies to comment on initial results. Series features two global indices (ESI Pioneer

Global and ESI Excellence Global) as well as two Europe-based indices (ESI Pioneer Europe and ESI Excellence Europe). www.ethibel.org

Calvert Social Index. A broad-based stock market index created by the Calvert Group that includes a subset of the 1,000 largest U.S. companies that meet a range of criteria related to workplace and community relations, product safety and impact, and environmental responsibility. www.calvert.com

Part Four

Strategize: How Each Business Function Can Benefit and Contribute

Chapter 8 Office Activities

For most companies, day-to-day office activities don't generate big environmental impacts. But symbolically they are very important. Getting employees to see the environment as a serious element of corporate strategy will be a challenge if they don't perceive a sustainability commitment within their own surroundings. Likewise, companies gain credibility when they practice what they preach. What's more, office sustainability efforts can produce cost savings and productivity gains.

Greening the office requires attention on many fronts to a number of issues and activities. One priority focus should be improving the energy efficiency of the office building itself: We offer detailed recommendations for buildings and facilities managers on everything from lighting and HVAC systems to grounds and landscaping in Chapter 9. A second priority should be tackling eco-impacts associated with computers and information technology: We cover these issues extensively for IT professionals in Chapter 10. This chapter also outlines several general plays that almost everyone in an office can help to execute.

Bringing the sustainability agenda to life in the office setting isn't always easy. We've all seen offices with mountains of paper waste, unused recycling bins, and lights and computers left running in empty rooms. Success requires changing mind-sets and habits, adopting new systems, and making sustainability practices the norm rather than the exception practiced by a handful of "do-gooder" individuals. For some companies, the push for a greener workplace has come from bottom-up employee initiative. In other cases, it emerges from an environmental "champion" in the executive ranks. Once in a while, initiatives from outside the company (such as a government program or an industry association commitment) can motivate action.

No matter what the origin of the interest in sustainability, it makes sense to establish a "green team" charged with examining office procedures, exploring opportunities, making action recommendations, and helping to lead change in ways that bring everyone on board. We've seen such teams lead the charge toward sustainability in companies of all shapes and sizes—in services as well as manufacturing businesses, and in every imaginable industry. The exact contour of the group need not conform to any particular structure, but broad representation from across the company is useful. What matters most is empowering a core group to think about the problems at hand and how to solve them—and to take leadership in putting forward solutions that mesh well with the organization's culture and existing practices.

In this chapter, we:

- Highlight office sustainability opportunities that make business sense and that most everyone in an office can help execute.
- Provide a list of "Key Steps to a Greener Office" to fuel brainstorming in light of a company's unique circumstances.

BASIC PLAYS

1. Use a "Reduce, Reuse, Recycle" Lens to Spot the Opportunities

The old environmental adage "reduce, reuse, and recycle" didn't become venerable for nothing. And the sequence of the "3Rs" is quite deliberate: Too often, our habit is to think of "recycling" as the answer—whereas the top priority should be to cut back on unnecessary purchases and resource use in the first place.

Work to build a culture where employees are mindful of eco-impacts and waste—and vigilant about cracking down on them. Once employees start paying attention, the possibilities for improvements are endless. The biggest areas of office eco-impacts and waste are:

- **Paper** (paper, envelopes, boxes, packaging)
- **Trash** (plastic, foam, food)
- **Electricity** (lights, computers and monitors, other peripherals, even stuff plugged in sucking vampire energy)
- **Water** (bathrooms, kitchens, cafeterias)
- **Travel** (commuting, planes, individual cars, taxis, deliveries)
- **E-waste and other toxic waste** (electronics, cables, toner cartridges, paint)

Think first about opportunities to *reduce* the purchase and use of resources by cutting back wherever there is excess. For instance, does your office have more personal printers than necessary? Does the company buy hundreds of individual bottles of water or water cooler jugs when a filter on the kitchen tap would suffice? Does the company keep buying foam or plastic cups when they could instead provide reusable coffee mugs or water bottles? Are lights left on in rooms where daylight from windows is adequate? Is the air conditioning on so high that people are wearing sweaters? Do employees routinely print unnecessary drafts of presentations?

Usually it just takes a few such examples to elicit great ideas from the people who know their offices best—some entirely unexpected. One employee, for instance, told us how a sustainability lens helped her notice that the soap in her company's bathrooms left such a "slimy" residue that she needed about 30 seconds of running water to rinse it off—which prompted her office to find an alternative that rinses clean in a few seconds, substantially reducing bathroom water use.

Next, consider broadly all the possibilities to *reuse* what otherwise might get tossed in the wastebasket or recycling bin. An opened envelope can be used over and over for routing purposes or as scrap paper. Paper printed on one side can replenish the fax machine. When you have something you can't reuse, consider donating or selling it—someone else might want it. Entire business models are being developed today around the old adage that "one man's trash

---

ENGAGE EMPLOYEES IN THE EFFORT TO GREEN THE OFFICE

Eco-initiatives will not succeed without the broad support and participation of employees. Here are a few tips for engaging employees:

Set an example at the top. Employees are likely to become greener at the office if the company's top executives set a strong example. At Sun Light & Power in Berkeley, California, founder and CEO Gary Gerber established a net energy consumption goal of zero. He allows no *new* furniture in the office (the conference rug is made of recycled soda bottles) and drives an electric car to work.[1]

Recruit a "green team." Getting your most committed employees to lead the charge can be critical. Tapping the passion of employees is the best way to spot opportunities and come up with action plans. The green team should, of course, run an open process, giving other employees opportunities to make suggestions and weigh in. The team should meet periodically to evaluate progress and adjust the strategy.

Make it visible, easy, and routine. A key to success is keeping it simple and making it "the norm." For instance, make it common practice not to bring handouts of their slide decks at meetings and to use projectors instead. Distribute short lists of preferred greener vendors. Work with IT to install software that facilitates greener choices. Post creative signs that remind people to do the right thing. Use staff meetings to reinforce key "asks." Consider giving employees hand-held video cameras to document progress and help inspire others in the company to follow suit.

Offer incentives and celebrate success. Honor great green ideas and performance with rewards that resonate in your culture—whether cash awards, prizes, or even just "shout outs" in meetings or newsletters. Post periodic results to show progress and inspire employees to keep up the great work. Provide incentives for employees that take public transport, carpool, bike, or walk to work. Consider using cost reductions from green initiatives to pay green bonuses, which will stimulate more innovation. Google gives "points" to employees who get to work without consuming gas—which employees can use to make donations to the charity of their choice.

Start a competition. Getting the competitive juices flowing in support of efforts to green the office can pay big dividends. Create friendly rivalry between employees or departments to see who can achieve the most energy savings. Yale University launched an energy savings competition pitting its 12 "colleges" (dormitories) against each other. For $300 worth of pizza for the winning students, the University found more than a million dollars worth of energy savings.

is another man's treasure," such as Recycle Match (www.recyclematch.com). Consider buying used products whenever this option makes sense.

Finally, set up a comprehensive *recycling* program that makes it easy for everyone to participate. Put recycling bins next to wastebaskets—and have them both emptied by the custodial staff. Don't make people who want to recycle carry their paper to a bin at the end of the hall. If your company leases space, ask the property management company for details on the building's recycling strategy and, if necessary, offer to help them improve it.

Remember that results depend on actual practice. More than once we've heard stories about employees who saw janitors dumping recyclables and trash in the same container. In some instances, this means that the janitor is not onboard the recycling program. But in other cases, it may be okay—if the building's waste management company sorts the trash for recyclables after collection. If there is doubt in such instances, you might ask for a site visit to see how the recycling program works in practice and communicate findings back to your office.

Be careful about introducing big changes without getting buy-in. If what you are asking people to do seems burdensome or the requirements irritate large numbers of them, the chances of a successful initiative will plummet. But being careful doesn't mean you can't be ambitious. Several companies at the leading edge of the sustainability wave have set zero waste targets. The effort to divert all waste from the landfill itself forces fresh thinking about office systems and procedures. In 2007, for example, the Miller-Coors Brewing Company facility in Trenton, New Jersey, set a goal of having zero waste in five years, which was no small feat since the company produced 1.6 million pounds of trash.[2] The company established a 40-person "green team" devoted solely to cutting waste. Today, the brewery recycles 99.8 percent of its waste, including 100,000 pounds of grain sent to cattle farmers for feed, 5 million pounds of crushed and recycled glass, 4 million pounds of shredded cardboard, and 500,000 pounds of crushed aluminum sent to a recycling center. The remaining 0.2 percent of waste ends up in a waste-to-energy facility in Indiana.

Inspire your team to stay on top of cutting-edge eco-strategies and tools across each area of office life. For example, best-practice landscapers know that it makes no sense to collect and bag grass clippings while mowing a lawn. Rather, the clippings should be left to decompose, which returns nutrients to the soil and protects against weeds. As Tony Nardella of Connecticut-based Nardella's Turf Care says: "The old way of doing things just doesn't make sense today . . . green is what is in, especially for lawns."

2. Promote Smarter Printing and Paper Use

But taking the most basic step—switching from paper-based systems to electronic ones—can be surprisingly difficult. Existing paper flows have inertia behind them, and people are often comfortable with the status quo no matter how inefficient. But change is coming. Companies in all fields from distribution to banking to hospitals are moving to all-electronic communications and record keeping.

By shifting to electronic invoices, Cox Communications, an Atlanta-based cable and broadband services company, reduced its paper consumption by more than 3 tons per year. In doing so, the company eliminated more than 10 tons of CO_2 emissions—all while saving money.[3] Similarly, by introducing Adobe Live-Cycle and Adobe Acrobat to generate, authenticate, and disseminate documents electronically, the United States Government Printing Office saved more than 20 tons of paper and $1 million over five years.[4]

The financial services industry has likewise moved rapidly toward a paperless world. One leader in this revolution, Bank of America, has expanded its online banking options and begun to charge a fee to those who still rely on bank tellers. It estimates that the emphasis on electronic banking has cut paper use by 25 percent overall and dramatically improved the efficiency of its operations.[5]

> **Our Information Age provides an endless number of ways to improve environmental results and enhance efficiency.**

Every company has documents that don't *need* to be printed. And unnecessary paper use means unnecessary expense. Research by Xerox found that over 40 percent of printouts are discarded within 24 hours.[6] Work toward building a culture where people think twice before printing or copying.

Paper use can be significantly reduced with smarter printing practices, such as setting all printers and copiers to print "double-sided" as a default. Encourage employees to fit more words on the printed page by changing document margins and using smaller fonts. Post creative recommendations and reminders at the point of printing. For examples, see the Environmental Defense Fund's "Educational Signs to Encourage Double-Sided Printing and Copying" at www.edf.org. Use software tools like PrintWhatYouLike.com, GreenPrint (www.printgreener.com) and HP's Smart Web Printing that make it simple for employees to choose paper-saving options and print only exactly what they need—in some cases even tallying up the avoided costs. Consider using a security system for shared printers that requires employees to enter a PIN or swipe a card to collect a print job—otherwise the job will eventually be cancelled. These systems also protect confidentiality and eliminate the need for energy-wasting stand-alone printers.

The payoff for these simple interventions can be significant from both an environmental and efficiency perspective. If a firm with 5,000 employees moves to double-sided printing and cuts paper use by just 10 percent, the savings could be as much as $250,000. In addition, the move to double-sided printing would eliminate 28 tons of waste and reduce water and wood consumption by 500,000 gallons and 87 tons respectively.[7] Green and Save, an online environmental resource center, estimates that simple paper reduction measures often generate up to $1,250 per employee per year with a return on investment (ROI) of over 300 percent.[8] Barclays Capital in the UK requires employees to use swipe cards to pick up print jobs at shared devices, which has helped the company cut in-house paper use by almost 50 percent and save £200,000.[9]

In addition, work toward optimizing the equipment. Consider replacing older, inefficient printers, copiers, scanners, and fax machines with fewer, more efficient devices that use less energy and produce less waste. According to Xerox's top environmental officer Patty Calkins, the average utilization rate of office printers is only 1 to 2 percent—meaning that most printers are idle (but still drawing power) about 98 percent of the time.[10] By investing in multifunction printers, offices can reduce environmental impacts while boosting productivity and cutting bills for energy, supplies and maintenance. Explore eco-friendly solid ink printers that can cut waste-to-landfill by 90 percent over laser counterparts.[11] When considering new investments, look beyond the initial hardware costs and consider other factors including cost of supplies, maintenance, and potential productivity gains. Use Xerox's free "Sustainability Calculator" to estimate the benefits of an optimized scenario versus the status quo.

Measure paper flow and set targets to reduce paper use and increase re-use and recycling. Establish key performance indicators and task individuals with tracking and reporting on progress. Ask vendors about the tools they offer to help. Printer manufacturer Ricoh Americas, for instance, introduced @Remote GreenReports in 2010 to help companies monitor the number of pages printed, percentage of jobs that are printed two-sided or using other paper saving modes, and the resulting paper, energy, and carbon savings.[12] Xerox, too, offers a wealth of workflow management software and collaboration tools to companies trying to go green.

See "Key Steps to a Greener Office" at the end of this chapter for additional recommendations.

3. Clean Green

The choice of cleaning supplies may not seem like a big issue, but for some employees it represents another test of whether a company that is committed to going "green" is walking the walk as well as talking the talk. Maximize the use of all-purpose cleaners to cut down the number of chemicals used and to minimize potential danger of mixing. Purchase cleaners in concentrated form that allows for different strengths for different purposes. This reduces total volume of package, which reduces packaging material and transportation costs.

The cleaning world is changing fast, with more and more companies offering new ways to meet marketplace demands for effective products that are also greener. For instance, Activeion unveiled in 2010 its "Ionator EXP" cleaning device that turns tap water into a chemical-free green cleaning solution and kills over 99.9 percent of harmful germs—a solution that Forbes.com hailed as one of the 10 best "disruptive technologies that could change the world."[13] Likewise, Ed Lonergan, CEO of industrial cleaning giant Diversey, told us: "We've got to run out in front of our customers—and be there with solutions that meet their multiple desires, which these days include reduced chemical exposures without reduced efficacy."[14]

So for those who thought the custodians would be the last ones to go green, it isn't so. In fact, there are lots of "go green" workshops, programs, and support now available for those with building cleaning and maintenance responsibilities. The Additional Resources section at the end of this chapter provides some starting points.

INTERMEDIATE PLAYS

4. Green the Kitchen and Cafeteria

Office kitchens and cafeterias offer myriad opportunities to reduce impacts and educate and engage employees. One of the first steps greener companies take is to get rid of an iconic symbol of environmental negligence: foam cups and containers, which crowd landfills and survive for about 500 years.[15] It may make sense to move away from throw-away paper plates, cups, and utensils if high-efficiency dishwashers are available. And exploring ways to boost energy efficiency—particularly in lighting and appliances—should be high on the agenda.

Companies can also make a difference by focusing on the food itself. Conventional agriculture uses vast amounts of petrochemical, water, and energy inputs. Unsustainable farming practices harm both people and the planet. And the transportation of food across vast distances—on average 1,300 to 2,000 miles from farm to consumer—causes significant emissions.[16] Look to offer healthy, seasonal, local, and more sustainable food options when possible. Information on what counts as "sustainable" is increasingly available. For instance, when buying fish, look for species on the Monterey Bay Aquarium Seafood Watch Guide "approved" list or fish certified by the Marine Stewardship Council.

If changing the menu isn't an option, or you don't have a cafeteria, consider following in the footsteps of Clif Bar: Their headquarters offers an Amy's Kitchen vending machine with organic frozen entrees.[17] And you might try to help your employees eat right at home. Austin's Sustainable Food Center sets up lunchtime farmers' markets that allow downtown workers to buy locally grown food. See the Additional Resources section at the end of this chapter for tools to help evaluate the sustainable food options.

Once the cafeteria is under the sustainability microscope, many companies find that the agenda grows. More and more employees want healthier and more natural food options as well as a lower environmental footprint. So the greening of the cafeteria might extend to nutrition and health as well as waste and pollution. In this regard, some companies have taken to subsidizing fruits and vegetables in the cafeteria or put in company-sponsored fitness centers. Others, like Google, give away snacks—and always make fruit and nuts and other healthy items available.

Spread the word about the sustainability program (and why various changes are being made) with posters, table tents, menu notes, and other means. One firm offers a monthly "Lunch with the Chef," where people can talk directly with dining staff about sustainability and other issues.

TAKING SUSTAINABLE FOOD TO NEW HEIGHTS

Saatchi & Saatchi's employees took the initiative to create a community rooftop vegetable garden in Spring 2010 at the company's 375 Hudson Street headquarters in New York City. The purpose of the garden, named "RTG:375," was to give employees a deeper connection to the land and a greater understanding of the seasonal growing cycle of the food they consume. It's a space where co-op members can take a break from their work day to relax, garden, and socialize within view of the unparalleled New York City skyline. The garden is fully local and organic, featuring transplants from the Brooklyn Rooftop Farm in Greenpoint and soil from McEnroe Organic Farm in the Hudson Valley. The plants are housed in SmartPots: a fully compostable planter pot made from recycled fibers. The wide range of vegetables grown by the co-op members include kale, carrots, chard, tomatoes, peppers, basil, chives, eggplant, and edible marigolds.

The garden was the "icing on the cake" in 375 Hudson's 2010 LEED Gold certification; it is the first existing building in New York City to be awarded the LEED Gold certification due to building retrofit improvements. RTG:375 will expand in 2011 to include additional plant varieties, seating, and a new, dynamic online interface, rtg375.com, which will allow users to interact with their plants (and gardeners) via webcams, YouTube, and Twitter.[18]

---

5. Trim Business Travel

For many companies in the services sector, business travel turns out to be one of the most significant aspects of their environmental footprint. There is no substitute for face-to-face meetings in some contexts, such as when new groups are getting organized and relationships being forged. But new technologies provide more and more opportunities to replace "live" meetings with effective "virtual" ones—especially among those who have been collaborating for a long time.

Videoconferencing is one of the most attractive alternatives because it can simulate the "feel" of an actual meeting at a fraction of the cost (and environmental impact). Cisco's TelePresence and HP Halo's telepresence, for example, produce high-end results that provide a way to connect that closely resembles an in-person meeting. As the costs for advanced videoconferencing solutions continue to decline, the payback for these systems can be fast. See the Additional Resources at the end of the chapter for resources to help you evaluate options for virtual meetings.

For small businesses, there are a growing number of free and low-cost video-conferencing solutions—from well-established offerings like Cisco's WebEx to newer options including Megameeting, Skype Group Chat, and Paltalk, which allows free video chats for up to 10 people. In addition, software packages such as "Go to Meeting" enable all of the participants in a telephonic discussion at remote locations to see the same PowerPoint deck. Even "old-fashioned" tele-conferences can be useful in some contexts.

Companies are finding dramatic cost savings—amounting to hundreds of millions of dollars for some multinational corporations—by systematically moving to virtual meetings rather than actual travel.[19] And the savings tabulated don't even include the reduced wear and tear on the executives—never mind the greenhouse gas emissions avoided.

6. Green Your Meetings and Events

As we just noted, the most sustainable meeting is one that does not involve the physical presence of the participants in the same place. Of course, no one can eliminate sales events and conferences entirely. So the next best option is to make your events "green." While there are many elements to consider in running a green workshop, meeting, or conference, lots of resources are now available to help. Greenhome.com, an online environmental store, offers a comprehensive listing of issues and ideas for those who want to ensure that they have covered all the bases for a greener meeting. They offer advice on food and beverages, cleaning supplies and practices, and space utilization, among other things.

Meegan Jones walks her readers through a range of ways they can make their events "model examples of a harmonious balance between human activity, resource use, and environmental impact" in her book, *Sustainable Event Management: A Practical Guide*. In a similar vein, Greenyourevent.com offers a six-step checklist, summarized below, for those who want to run a green event.

One of the most important factors in the environmental footprint of a conference is the travel of those attending. In this regard, finding a location that is central to the participants can go a long way toward reducing impacts—although optimizing on this variable might be at odds with other values such as going to a location (Florida in February rather than Kansas City?) that excites the participants. Make it easy for employees to pick the lowest carbon-footprint options for their travel. Lots of travel sites now make this quite a simple exercise. And remember to provide guidance on public transportation options to and from airports or train stations. Routerank.com enables door-to-door planning for many

GREEN EVENTS CHECKLIST

1. Make "green" a factor in the event-planning process—alongside price, convenience, quality, and style.

2. Focus on the green opportunities in three stages:
   - Advance purchase products and services (invitations, decorations, food service)
   - Event itself
   - Aftermath (what is left over after everyone has gone home)

3. Green your shopping list—choose the more sustainable options when cost and convenience don't demand another choice.

4. Ask vendors about their focus on sustainability—and factor their answers into your purchasing decisions.

5. Consider green in selecting event locations.

6. Let the meeting participants or event guests know about the role they can play in making the event more sustainable. For example, direct them to recycling bins and thank them for participating.

7. Figure out how to divert as much of the leftover materials from the waste stream: donate, gift, reuse, compost, and recycle.

Source: Adapted from Greenyourevent.com. Reprinted with permission.

cities in Europe and North America, and calculates the amount of carbon dioxide your travel will produce, even providing you the option to offset that amount.[20]

Another way to green an event is to make it "carbon neutral" by buying offsets for the emissions related to the gathering. As we explain in more detail in Chapter 19 ("Build Your Climate Change Plan"), there are a variety of ways to obtain carbon offsets. And there are a growing number of companies willing to sell offsets for an event or for corporate travel more generally.

7. Promote Greener Employee Commuting

Companies are increasingly being asked to measure not just their direct greenhouse gas emissions but also their indirect contributions to climate change—as Chapter 6 ("Assess and Measure Your Environmental Impacts") made clear. For many companies, employee commuting turns out to be a big deal. But changing commuting practices can be tough. You have the potential for big gains when making the choice of an office location. The key is to pick a site that has good access to public transportation. To focus employees on how they might minimize their own personal commuting footprints, it makes sense to consider subsidizing bus or subway passes where this option is available. *Not* subsidizing parking will also shape behavior. Likewise, providing free parking or preferential spaces for those who are carpooling or involved in van pools adds to the incentive for employees to minimize their own commute-related emissions. Yahoo! and Google offer employees convenient, attractive home-to-work shuttle vans with wireless so employees can get a jump on their day or finish last-minute emails on the way home.

Having employees work from their homes offers another way to cut down emissions. Telecommuting eliminates the pollution that would otherwise be associated with travel to and from work. And it further reduces the environmental footprint of the office because those at home don't consume office space, electricity, heating, and lighting. Work-at-home employees will not be right in every circumstance. But if your company has a job that could be done at home, even just some of the time, it makes sense to look at that opportunity.

Fortune magazine's 2010 rankings of the 100 Best Companies found that 84 permitted telecommuting, an option that contributes significantly to workforce morale.[21] Studies have also shown that telecommuting increases productivity and bumps up (not down!) the number of hours that employees put into their work.[22] The sustainability benefits go beyond emissions reductions to include reduced traffic, fewer weather-related work disruptions,[23] more flexibility with child care, and better work options for people with disabilities.[24] At Deloitte, 93 percent of employees regularly telecommute.[25] Intel, Accenture, and PricewaterhouseCoopers all have 70 percent of their workforce working from home at least some of the time.

ADVANCED PLAYS

8. Go Digital Wherever Possible

Many companies are working to eliminate the need for paper wherever they can. Lockheed Martin, for example, eliminated 8 million pages of printed material and saved $250,000 by putting a standard 100-page workplace manual on the Internet—rather than printing thousands of copies each year.[26] GE estimates that its digitization efforts have saved the company $1.6 billion over the course of the past decade.[27] Indeed, paper flow reduction represents a prime opportunity for companies of every size in every industry, everywhere in the world.

Inspire employees to brainstorm opportunities to convert from paper to digital—for billing, procurement, internal information exchange, presentations, and more. Work with the IT department to introduce software to boost collaboration that helps employees share computer-based documents and other information without sending physical copies or requiring people to work in close physical proximity. Google Docs, Dropbox, PBworks, EditMe, and Xerox's DocuShare and Virtual Filing System are only a few of the many examples.

For many businesses, the biggest advantage of going paperless is improved performance—with cost savings from reduced paper purchases and filing space simply gravy. Productivity gains from reduced document processing time alone can be enormous: Turnaround time to process a digital document averages 10 seconds, compared with two days for a paper document.

PAPERLESS CAN BOOST THE BOTTOM LINE

- **Cox Communications**, an Atlanta-based cable and broadband services company, reduced its paper consumption by more than 3 tons per year by shifting to electronic invoices. In doing so, the company eliminated more than 10 tons of CO_2 emissions—all while saving money.[28]

- **NTUC Income Insurance Co-Operative Limited**, Singapore's leading insurance company, converted its 40 million pages of insurance policies and related documents into digital images and expects to save $6 million a year printing and filing expenses when all the processes are in place.[29]

- **Western Forest Products** in British Columbia uses Xerox's CDIT-DocuShare AP solution to enable remote offices and over 2,500 suppliers to email, scan, or fax invoices directly to the accounts payable office. The system quickly paid for itself by saving $20,000 a month in hard costs while improving turnaround times and reducing errors.[30]

- **The United States Government Printing Office** saved more than 20 tons of paper and $1 million over five years by introducing Adobe LiveCycle and Adobe Acrobat to generate, authenticate, and disseminate documents electronically.[31]

With efficiency in mind, PBD Worldwide Fulfillment Services asked UPS to clear its shipments through customs using electronic data instead of paper forms. This small shift in standard operating procedures greatly sped up the processing time while reducing data entry errors and lost documentation. As Steve Hochradel, assistant VP of distribution observed, "Now when a package comes in, we just scan the barcode. What was taking 20 seconds is now down to less than five. With a peak volume of over 3,000 pieces (per day), saving 15 seconds on each—that's a lot of time and money."[32]

The new Children's Hospital of Pittsburgh's choice to go paperless has helped improve the delivery of services. Wait times fell by 24 percent and the error rate dropped as well. For example, doctors and nurses were 33 percent more likely to vaccinate at-risk patients.[33]

9. Keep Up with the Latest Greener Product and Services

Choose products and services that help you reduce impacts by delivering the same performance with less materials, energy, or waste. Products made with high percentages of recycled content put less stress on natural ecosystems and generally require less energy (and emissions) to manufacture. Energy-efficient lighting, electronics, and appliances help trim energy bills and have lower lifetime impacts. Nontoxic products reduce harm to the environment and can create a healthier workplace. Products with minimal packaging prevent needless waste while lowering disposal costs. Water-efficient faucets, showerheads, and low-flow toilets reduce pressure on local watersheds and lower water bills.

Eco-innovations are booming to meet the growing business need for cost-effective, sustainable solutions. For instance, companies can avoid buying boxes they only need temporarily through any number of companies like "RentaGreenBox.com" that rent moving and storage containers with free delivery and pickup—which conserves resources and saves businesses the hassle of disposal and recycling unneeded boxes.

EcoNation car service, now operating in a dozen cities across the United States, chauffeurs its customers to the airport or their other appointments in hybrid vehicles. Likewise, Enterprise Rent-A-Car features a fleet of 4,000 hybrid vehicles and a carbon offset program, which allows their customers to minimize their CO_2 emissions and offset any that remain while they are on the road.[34]

Colorado-based ECOvention has revolutionized the office pizza party. They've come up with a 100 percent recycled cardboard pizza box that can break down into plates on which to serve the slices as well as a small container to store leftovers without wrap or foil—all of which fit into standard-sized recycling bins. In 2010, the company launched a partnership with Whole Foods in support of the effort to transform the pizza delivery business everywhere.[35]

Thegreenoffice.com is a good place to start finding providers, but we urge you to review the "key steps to a greener office" (Figure 8.1), the Additional Resources featured at the end of this chapter as well as the suggestions put forward in Chapter 12 ("Sourcing and Procurement").

SUMMARY

Key Plays

1. Use a "Reduce, Reuse, Recycle" lens to spot the opportunities.
2. Promote smarter printing and paper use.
3. Clean green.
4. Green the kitchen and cafeteria.
5. Trim business travel.
6. Green your meetings and events.
7. Promote greener employee commuting.
8. Go digital wherever possible.
9. Keep looking for greener products and services.

Figure 8.1   **Key Steps to a Greener Office**

Lighting, HVAC, Water *(See also Chapter 9, "Buildings and Facilities")*	<ul><li>Encourage everyone to **turn off lights** when they leave a room.</li><li>**Alert management to energy-saving and water-saving opportunities**—such as leaky water faucets, excessively hot water temperature, or overheating or overcooling of certain office areas.</li><li>**Point your building manager or landlord** to relevant recommendations in Chapter 9 ("Buildings and Facilities").</li></ul>
Printing, Copying, and Faxing	<ul><li>**Go digital/paperless when possible.**</li><li>**Create a print-on-demand system** that enables the printing of up-to-date forms, brochures and corporate literature where and when they're actually needed.</li><li>**Encourage everyone to share documents online** versus in hard copy.</li><li>**Make double-sided copying/printing** the default setting.</li><li>**Post creative recommendations and reminders** at the point of printing.</li><li>**Put scrap and recycling piles next to printers** to encourage paper re-use.</li><li>**Replenish fax machines** with scrap paper (printed on one side).</li><li>**Encourage employees to fit more words on the printed page** by, for example, setting document margins and using smaller fonts.</li><li>**Use software tools** like PrintWhatYouLike.com, GreenPrint (www.printgreener.com), and HP's Smart Web Printing that make it simple for everyone to print only what they need.</li><li>**Eliminate nonessential printing/copying devices,** which encourage unnecessary paper use.</li><li>**Replace multiple printers/copiers/scanners high-efficiency multi-function devices.** Look for Energy Star devices.</li><li>**Use a security system for shared printers** requiring employees to enter a PIN or swipe a card to collect a print job.</li></ul>
Computers and Electronics *(See also Chapter 10, "Information Technology")*	<ul><li>**Urge people to disable screen savers and turn off computers and monitors** when not in use and at night.</li><li>**Use smart power strips** that cut off power to computers and peripherals when not in use.</li><li>**Enable power management** for office equipment (e.g., low-power sleep mode).</li><li>**Install supplemental computer power management software.**</li><li>**Purchase Energy Star-certified electronics**—PCs, printers, copiers, and monitors.</li></ul>

(continued)

Figure 8.1   (*Continued*)

Cleaning	• Use nontoxic cleaning compounds. • Maximize the use of all-purpose cleaners to cut down the number of chemicals used. • Purchase cleaners in concentrated form that allows for different strengths for different purposes.
Waste Reduction and Recycling	• Promote reducing and reusing first, then recycling, with disposal as an option of last resort. • Re-use everything you can—envelopes, boxes, cups, and so forth. • Set up a recycling program that makes it easy for everyone to participate. • Contact product manufacturers to see if they have a "take back" program for electronics and other toxic items like toner cartridges. • Consult 1800recycling.com to find local options for proper recycling or disposal.
Kitchen/Food/ Cafeteria	• Buy ENERGY STAR-certified appliances, most of which offer payback through energy savings within 3 years. • Require energy savings devices on vending machines or ask vendor to provide more efficient machines. • Encourage the use of tap water, providing filters on faucets instead of bottled water or jugs. • Stock the kitchen with reusable mugs, glasses, plates, and silverware—and eliminate foam and plastic cups. • Offer local, sustainable, healthy food options when possible.
Office Supplies, Furniture, Paint, Carpeting	• Look for products with high recycled content. • Select paper suppliers that can provide post-consumer content recycled paper at a competitive cost—and look for Forest Stewardship Council (FSC) certified paper. • Use materials with zero or low emissions of "volatile organic compounds" (VOCs) to enhance indoor air quality and help control the growth of microbial contamination. • Seek out low-impact paint—paint with light and moderate tints (almost always low-VOC), water-based over oil-based, and recycled context latex paint for exteriors. Avoid aerosol paint. • Install low-impact carpeting—low-VOC carpets made from recycled content, carpet "tiles" that make it easy for selective replacements in heavily trafficked areas. Look for Carpet and Rug Institute (CRI) Green Label Plus designation. Ask suppliers to identify recycling options.

(*continued*)

Figure 8.1   *(Continued)*

Employee Commuting	• Reward pedestrians, mass-transit riders, carpoolers, and cyclists and discourage single-passenger car driving (e.g., preferential parking spots for carpoolers, subsidized bus or subway passes, ample bicycle racks). • Make telecommuting options available when appropriate.
Business Travel and Transportation	• Use videoconferencing to eliminate unnecessary business travel (see Chapter 10, "Information Technology"). • Create a no-idling policy for company vehicles or vehicles on company property. • Look for greener taxi companies, car services, and rental car companies that use fuel-efficient vehicles including hybrids.

Sources: European Environmental Paper Network, "Tips and Tools: Saving Paper in the Office," www.shrinkpaper.org/pages/tips-and-tools/saving-paper-in-the-office.shtml (accessed November 11, 2010); CalRecycle, "Measuring the Success of Office Paper Reduction Efforts," www.calrecycle. ca.gov/ReduceWaste/Business (accessed November 11, 2010); Heather Sarantis, Business Guide to Paper Reduction, ForestEthics, 2002, www.forestethics.org/downloads/reduce.pdf; "How to Green Your Office" NRDC video, www.youtube.com (accessed November 11, 2010); Daniel Lyons, "The Paper Chasers," November 21, 2008, www.newsweek.com/2008/11/20/the-paper-chasers.print.html (accessed November 10, 2010).

ADDITIONAL RESOURCES

GENERAL

"How to Green Your Office" (NRDC). A 6-minute video with basic recommendations that could help kickstart a brownbag lunch discussion within your office. www.youtube.com

"Seven Steps to Green an Office" (Xerox) www.xerox.com

"Green Office Guide: A Guide to Greening Your Bottom Line through a Resource-Efficient Office Environment" (Sustainable Development Office of Portland). Overview of opportunities to save energy, resources, and costs through choices about office lighting, water, paper, equipment, HVAC, transportation and parking. Written for Oregon businesses but broadly applicable. www.oregon.gov

OFFICE EQUIPMENT AND SUPPLIES

The Green Office. Comprehensive selection of greener office products, including technology, lighting, paper, furniture, cleaning supplies, and more. www.thegreenoffice.com

For a more comprehensive list, see **"Finding Greener Products and Services"** *under Additional Resources at the end of Chapter 12 ("Sourcing and Procurement").*

Paper

Cutting Paper (Lawrence Berkeley National Laboratory). Department of Energy-sponsored website with practical recommendations and tools for reducing office paper use. http://eetd.lbl.gov

"Simple Ways to Reduce Office Paper Waste and Make Better Use of the Paper You Need" (Natural Resources Defense Council). Guidance on how to develop an effective office paper policy that reduces paper use and increases recycling. www.nrdc.org

Paper Calculator v2.0 (Environmental Defense Fund). Helps users quantify the benefits of eco-friendly paper choices. Shows the environmental impacts, including greenhouse gas emissions and waste, of different papers across their life cycle. www.environmentaldefense.org

Environmental Papers (Conservatree). A one-stop source for information on environmental papers. Includes lists of products and where to buy. www.conservatree.org

WASTE REDUCTION AND RECYCLING

"How to Start a Recycling Program" (Earth911.com). Practical steps for improving office recycling. www.earth911.com

Waste Prevention and Recycling at the Office (CalRecycle). How to set up recycling programs and implement paper reduction strategies, with multiple case examples. www.calrecycle.ca.gov

ReduceYourWaste.org. Interactive tool that generates sector-specific, customized recommendations to help businesses cut waste. www.reduceyourwaste.org

Green Business Guide to Waste Audits (NRDC). Overview of recommendations and tools for conducting waste audits that reveal opportunities to save resources and cut costs. www.nrdc.org

Northeast Recycling Council's Environmental Benefits Calculator. Estimates environmental benefits of office waste recycling (including computers) and reuse. www.nerc.org

Recycle Match. Matches companies that have waste with companies that can use the materials productively. www.recyclematch.com

1-800-RECYCLING. Easy-to-use, one-stop site that makes recycling easy. www.1800recycling.com

See also "Finding Greener Products and Services" under Additional Resources at the end of Chapter 12 ("Sourcing and Procurement").

FOOD AND CAFETERIA

"Sustainability in the Food Service Environment" (IMFA Foundation, 2009). Overview of key sustainability issues in the food service environment with practical guidance for managers. www.ifmafoundation.org

Sustainable Food Policy Guide. Outlines options and recommendations for making sustainable food purchases. Includes sample purchasing policies along with RFP and contract language. www.sustainablefoodpolicy.org

TRAVEL AND COMMUTING

Green Commuting/Telecommuting (Business.gov). U.S. government guide on how companies can encourage greener commuting options and take advantage of government incentives and programs. www.business.gov

National Business Travel Association Corporate Social Responsibility Toolkit 2010 Toolkit update includes guides on Responsible Groups and Meetings and Technology Solutions. www.nbta.org

"Select and Deploy a Videoconferencing Solution" (InfoTech Research Group). PPT deck that helps IT leaders to evaluate the strengths and weaknesses of leading videoconferencing vendors relative to specific business requirements. www.infotech.com

EVENTS

Green Your Event.com. Checklist for greening business events. www.greenyourevent.com

Sustainable Event Management: A Practical Guide by Meegan Jones (London: Earthscan, 2009). Book provides step-by-step approach to planning and managing sustainable events, including case studies to illustrate common mistakes

LIGHTING, HVAC, AND OTHER BUILDINGS ISSUES

See Additional Resources in Chapter 9 ("Buildings and Facilities").

REDUCING OFFICE CARBON EMISSIONS

Office Carbon Footprint Tool (EPA). Free tool developed to assist offices in assessing and making decisions to reduce the greenhouse gas emissions associated with their activities. www.epa.gov/solidwaste

See also Additional Resources at the end of Chapter 6 ("Assess and Measure Your Environmental Impacts") and 19 ("Build Your Climate Change Plan")

Chapter 9 Buildings and Facilities

Bragging rights used to go to the tallest buildings. Now it's the greenest. Bank of America announced in 2010 that the U.S. Green Building Council had given its new 55-story, 2.1-million-square-foot office building in New York City a "platinum" score, making it the first high-rise commercial office tower to be awarded the top green building rating available in the United States. The building's sustainable features include a glass curtain wall that permits maximum sunlight while blocking unwanted heat, an under-floor air delivery system that filters outside air and heats and cools it to local settings, and an ice-storage system that reduces the building's peak energy demand during the summer. An on-site 4.6 megawatt cogeneration plant provides power, and the building has a rainwater collection and graywater recycling system. In addition, almost all of the construction materials used came from recycled or local sources.[1]

GREEN BUILDING PAYBACKS

- **IBM** performed recommissioning projects at 30 locations over two years, optimizing building and central utility plant control systems to minimize energy use and establish metrics to maintain optimal performance, saving $6.7 million in energy costs.[2]

- **Mack Molding**, a custom plastics molder and manufacturer, invested $450,000 in a new fluorescent lighting system for its manufacturing facility that is expected to increase productivity and pay for itself in energy savings alone within two years.[3]

- **Dow** saved $1M in its Michigan lab and office facilities in 2009 by turning off lights, using night time temperature setbacks, closing chemical fume hood sashes, and utilizing occupancy sensors to turn off lights and reduce lab air change rates when personnel were not in the area.[4]

- **Northrop Grumman** saved $2 million in energy costs by installing reflective roofs and fluorescent lighting, replacing old equipment, and making minor temperature and humidity-level adjustments at a single California facility.[5]

Until recently, many green building opportunities remained untapped due to perceived cost barriers, a lack of awareness about eco-efficiency possibilities, and misaligned incentives between owners and builders—and those who paid the utility bills. But this pattern is changing fast. A recent explosion of green building activity around the world has sped up the exchange of best-practice information and the dissemination of practical tools to aid green design and construction. Moreover, the cost of making a facility environmentally cutting edge is coming down. The upfront cost premium for a commercial green building today is only about 2 percent compared to a traditional building. And with lower operating costs, the time to recoup the green premium has dropped to an average of three to four years. Over a 20-year period, the return on investment (ROI) on a green building now stands at about four to six times the upfront cost.[6]

By applying best environmental practices to existing buildings or new construction, businesses can save money *and* the environment. Companies that take their green building initiatives seriously can also anticipate collateral benefits including higher worker productivity, enhanced corporate reputation, and improved asset value for their properties.[7] If your company lacks a comprehensive sustainability strategy aimed at facilities, then you're most likely missing out on some big Eco-Advantage opportunities, particularly to reduce your energy spending (see Figure 9.1). This chapter will help you:

- Identify low- or no-cost opportunities to improve your bottom line by "greening" existing buildings.
- Create a systematic green buildings strategy to seize the full range of business benefits on all new construction.
- Analyze potential costs, benefits, and ROI associated with green building options.
- Prepare for changes in buildings standards, technologies, programs, and policies.

BASIC PLAYS: HARVEST LOW-HANGING FRUIT

1. Start by Tackling the Obvious Inefficiencies

To get started, let's review a list of simple, low-cost actions that can quickly translate into big savings on your energy bills. The box that follows provides our "Top Dozen" quick fixes. This list of action items is pretty simple. But you'll want to assemble a team of people who know your facilities well to ensure that you capture all potential benefits and prioritize the easy-to-implement action steps that make financial sense to pursue immediately.

12 EASY WAYS TO STOP WASTING MONEY ON ENERGY

Get the most out of available lighting

- Clean lighting fixtures to maximize available light.
- Look for spaces where you can reduce or turn off lighting without sacrificing performance or employee comfort.
- Calibrate light controls to employee needs and avoid over-lighting.
- Use timers to avoid lighting unoccupied spaces.

Plug the holes

- Check for obvious air leaks in doors, walls, and windows; and seal with appropriate materials/techniques—all of which can save on heating, ventilation, and air-conditioning (HVAC) costs.
- Encourage the use of existing revolving doors and calibrate automatic doors to minimize air loss.

Tune up heating, ventilation, cooling, and air/water distribution systems

- Make sure settings for indoor temperatures and humidity don't over-do heating and air-conditioning—set thermostats to heat to 67 F degrees in winter and cool to 75 F degrees in the summer.
- Review occupancy schedules and adjust HVAC control schedules according to when the building areas are actually being used.
- Tune sensors (e.g., room and duct thermostats, humidistats, pressure sensors) and other systems (e.g., ventilation dampers and value controls) to optimize performance and fulfill potentials established in original design specs.
- Seal ducts, which can reduce leakage by about 80 percent and heating and cooling energy needs by up to 35 percent.

Encourage smart energy use

- Use posters, email, and other outreach efforts to remind your employees that everyone can (and should) play a part in reducing energy consumption.
- Look for "self-help overrides" of building systems (e.g., windows open during winter heating or summer air-conditioning) as a signal that you need to make adjustments.

2. Benchmark Your Building's Current Performance

The first challenge in "greening" a building is to understand what energy savings are possible. To get started, we suggest that you assess how your buildings stack up to comparable facilities and best practices. EPA's Energy Star program offers an interactive energy management tool, Portfolio Manager (www.energystar.govi/star/pmpam), to gauge a building's energy and water consumption and to compare the results with a portfolio of similarly situated

Figure 9.1 Benefits of Making Buildings Eco-Smarter

Cut Costs and Risks	Build Revenues and Intangible Value
Cut energy and water bills. By paying an extra 2 percent up front for efficient green features, you can save as much as 30 percent on energy and water bills. Efficient buildings are also easier to operate and maintain.	**Increase rent and occupancy.** According to a 2008 CoStar study, LEED buildings command rent premiums of $11.33 per square foot over non-LEED buildings and have 4.1 percent higher occupancy rate.
Receive government incentives, tax credits, tax deductions, and property and sales tax abatements. Governments have recognized the benefits to society provided by high-performance green buildings and have offered numerous incentives to developers and owners of such buildings.	**Increase building resale price.** LEED buildings are selling for $171 more per square foot over non-LEED buildings while Energy Star buildings sell for an average of $61 more.
Reduce exposure to energy price volatility by buying renewable energy. By entering into fixed-rate renewable energy contracts, your company can reduce its exposure to volatile prices in the energy market.	**Improve work productivity.** Daylighting has been shown to increase worker productivity. A 1 percent productivity increase can nearly offset a company's entire annual energy cost, and a 10 percent increase in productivity would pay for the entire building.
Secure lower costs for commercial insurance. Insurers are offering discounts and special programs for energy efficient and sustainable buildings.	**Attract and retain the best employees.** With a building that backs your reputation as a good corporate citizen, your company will have an edge in recruiting and retaining employees.
Obtain faster permitting and planning approval. In Chicago, Illinois, and Los Angeles, California, the city governments have allowed green projects to receive priority processing.	**Distinguish yourself in the marketplace.** By instituting green building strategy into your real estate portfolio, your company will be more attractive to a growing group of environmentally conscious corporate, public, and individual consumers.
Stay ahead of environmental regulations and insurance requirements. By instituting green building policies today, companies can avoid costly future retrofits to meet increasingly strict building requirements from governments and insurance companies.	**Boost your brand image as a good corporate citizen.** High-performance buildings and their companies are often welcomed as good neighbors due to their community-conscious design.
Achieve more predictable results. Holistic green design techniques minimize surprises that can lead to costly errors and delays while ensuring the delivery of buildings that perform as promised.	**Gain access to green financing.** There are many funds that are specifically targeting investments in green buildings and retrofits. Higher net operating income resulting from lower energy bills may allow you to secure bigger loans.

Sources: Natural Resource Defense Council, "Lower Your Operating and Maintenance Costs." www.nrdc/org/ (accessed August 21, 2010); Jerry Yudelson, "The Business Case for Green Buildings," Yudelson Associates. www.greenbuildconsult. com/ (accessed August 21, 2010); U.S. Green Building Council, "Making the Business Case for High Performance Green Buildings." www. buildsagreen.org/ (accessed August 21, 2010); Norm Miller, Jay Spivey, and Andy Florance, "Does Green Pay Off?" CoStar; Natural Resource Defense Council, "Command Higher Rents." www.nrdc.org/ (accessed August 21, 2010); CoStar, "CoStar Study Finds Energy Star, LEED Bldgs. Outperform Peers." www.costar.com/ (accessed November 8, 2010).

buildings (www.energystar.gov/benchmark). We also recommend the EPA's Energy Program Assessment Matrix, which can help you evaluate your current energy management practices (www.energystar.gov).

3. Do a Systematic Building Audit

As straightforward as it sounds, the first step in any green building strategy should simply be to make sure all of the building's systems are functioning properly. One approach to this analysis is through "recommissioning"—a comprehensive review of the heating, lighting, ventilation, and other building systems aimed at identifying design flaws, construction defects, substandard equipment performance, and other problems that might lead to unnecessary operating costs.

ESTIMATING FINANCIAL IMPACTS OF BUILDING UPGRADES

Use the **EPA Building Upgrade Value Calculator** to help estimate the business value of potential upgrades and prioritize among all the possible options. Go to energystar.gov and search for "Building Upgrade Value Calculator" on the home page.

Whether you do it internally or by enlisting a third party, the recommissioning process should help you spot opportunities to save energy and money. Tuning up a building's systems improves equipment life spans, reduces maintenance, necessitates fewer contractor callbacks, and creates other non-energy benefits. Investigators found that recommissioning for existing buildings typically costs $0.27/square foot up front but yields an average 15 percent in energy savings, with the expense usually recouped in under a year.[8] The National Institute of Building Sciences provides resources on building recommissioning in its Whole Building Design Guide, available at www.wbdg.org/project/buildingcomm.php.

INTERMEDIATE PLAYS: GET STRATEGIC

Once you've identified all the "no-brainer" action steps, you'll be in a strong position to make solid judgments about which medium- and long-term opportunities to pursue. This section outlines key strategic action areas and concludes with a comprehensive list of recommendations. Consult the chart at the end of the chapter for a list of the best available tools to help you with everything from developing a business plan to fine-tuning an air compressor.

4. Upgrade Insulation and Strengthen the Building "Envelope"

To maximize energy-efficiency savings, you'll want to do all you can to prevent money from flying out the windows or seeping through the walls or roof in the form of lost heating or cooling. Taking steps to make a typical building more airtight can cut HVAC costs up to 40 percent.[9] Installing high-performing windows with low-emission coatings, triple or quadruple panes, and aerogels can save up to 39 percent of heating and 32 percent of cooling energy.[10] Using shades, deflectors, and light shelves to reduce summer sun can also make a dramatic difference on cooling bills and worker comfort. Installing radiant barriers—materials that reflect heat radiated by hot surfaces and keep heat out or in—can save up to 10 percent in cooling energy.[11]

Better roof design can help insulate buildings against temperature extremes. As a result, "green roofs" have become increasingly popular all over the world. The New York–based utility Con Edison installed a green roof and a white roof at its Manhattan headquarters. The green roof, consisting of 21,000 plants, cuts summer heat absorption by up to 84 percent and winter heat losses by up to 37 percent compared to a traditional black roof. The white roof—just painted white—reduces summer heat gains by up to 67 percent.[12]

5. Upgrade Lighting

Lighting consumes close to 35 percent of electricity used in U.S. commercial buildings. According to the EPA, we waste at least 50 percent of the energy used in lighting because of inefficient design, poor maintenance, or inappropriate use. Because lighting significantly affects other key building systems, including heating and cooling loads, it should be a central focus of your green building strategy. Upgrading lighting—installing new light sources, fixtures, and controls—can deliver some of the highest and fastest returns on investment in the form of lower energy bills, improved worker productivity, and a reduced burden on HVAC and electrical systems.

EFFICIENT DAY LIGHTING BOOSTS EMPLOYEE PRODUCTIVITY

The cost of staff salaries and business operations in a building over a 20-year period can be up to 200 times greater than the initial design and construction costs.[13] Reports have shown that good lighting increases employee productivity—so, investments in labor productivity can quickly translate to significant bottom-line savings for an employer.

LED lighting has quickly emerged as *the* light source of choice. The new Ecosmart LED bulb uses about 80 percent less energy than a 40-watt incandescent bulb, contains no mercury, and lasts up to 17 years.[14] Tests suggest the bulb will save about $150 dollars in electricity costs over its life and pay for itself in less than two years. Fresh and Easy Neighborhood Market, the U.S. subsidiary of Tesco, uses LED lighting in all its freezer and medium temperature cases in its 159 U.S. stores.

In some cases fluorescent lamps and electronic ballast technologies may be your best option. A compact fluorescent bulb (CFC), which lasts about 10 times longer and uses 75 percent less energy than incandescent bulbs, can save $40 in electricity costs over its lifetime.[15] Occupancy sensors that automatically switch lights on and off have low up-front costs but can reduce energy consumption 35 to 45 percent.[16] Photo-sensor devices that adjust lighting output based on available daylight require an up-front investment but can trim energy consumption by 30 percent.[17]

Lighting retrofits may not seem glamorous, but they offer real financial gains. A U.S. Department of Energy (DOE) survey found that of the more than 2.7 million office and commercial buildings built before 1980, fewer than 500,000 had undertaken lighting upgrades. A rough estimate would be that the remaining 2.2 million buildings could easily cut their 900 billion or so kilowatt hours of annual electricity consumption in half and save a cumulative $60 billion per year.[18]

Some facilities managers have decided to cash in on the lighting opportunity. San Jose State University reports savings of $300,000 per year from a lighting retrofit that cut energy use by 25 percent overall.[19] Pittsburgh International Airport switched to LED lighting, cutting the lighting element of the airport's electric bill by 80 percent—which saves about $160,000 per year.[20] Westwood Gateway Towers, an 800,000-square-foot high-rise in Los Angeles, undertook a similar retrofit and cut its electric bill by 35 percent, amounting to more than $160,000 per year in savings.[21]

6. Upgrade Heating, Ventilation, and Air-Conditioning Systems

HVAC systems account for a large share of most buildings' and facilities' energy bills—and more than half of the energy consumed in U.S. office buildings overall.[22] As with lighting, businesses often waste enormous amounts of energy because their systems are inefficient due to improper sizing, inadequate maintenance, or outdated technology. Start with simple adjustments and retrofits in fan, heating, and cooling components. Fine-tune automatic controls in light of actual building usage and occupancy. Replace inappropriate and outdated equipment with modern alternatives, which are more energy efficient, operate more quietly, reduce maintenance costs, and boast longer equipment life. As your strategy matures, explore options to capture and use excess waste heat from production processes, furnaces, air compressors, boilers, and exhaust ducts to preheat boiler feed water, to warm offices (e.g., by using heat exchangers), and more.

7. Reduce Energy Demands from Equipment

Building equipment—whether mechanical, electrical, or electronic—can substantially drive up energy costs directly through power consumed and indirectly, by emitting heat that requires additional cooling. Start by focusing on better power management to prevent energy waste—from software to employee education. Then look for opportunities to upgrade to more energy-efficient equipment, such as appliances that have the Energy Star label.

Many businesses now use smart meters to monitor their energy use and reduce inefficiencies. A number of vendors provide systems to support such efforts. For instance, SiteSMART, an energy demand program offered by EnerNOC Inc., uses technology to monitor a customer's energy use in real time. It identifies inefficiencies, problems, and periods of peak usage so that companies can address issues before they get billed for them.[23] Small and medium businesses can use energy monitors to track their energy use and address demand peaks. The eMonitor, provided by Powerhouse Dynamics, sends out email alerts when there's a usage spike and users can go online for details and tips of where to cut inefficiencies. Many utility companies now also offer smart meters to help customers track their energy use in real time.[24]

8. Cut Water-Related Costs

Buildings use—and waste—large quantities of water. This inefficiency translates into big water bills as well as unnecessary impacts on the surrounding community. Heating water, moreover, adds to energy bills and is often done inefficiently. In fact, just reducing the water temperature setting from the default of 140 degrees to 120 degrees Fahrenheit can save 6 to 10 percent of water-heating energy without affecting performance.[25] Other sensible measures include increasing insulation around tanks and pipes and installing timers on electric heaters to heat water at night using cheaper, off-peak electricity.

To reduce a building's overall water usage, start by plugging leaky pipes, which can account for 10,000 gallons of water wasted in a typical U.S. home every year, enough to fill a backyard swimming pool.[26] Perform regular maintenance to prevent future leaks. Install water-conserving fixtures such as low-flow toilets, showers, and faucets. Install smart water meters, which can track water flows and alert you to leaks and inefficiencies.[27] Solar hot water heaters use the energy of the sun to heat water and can lower energy costs by 50 to 80 percent compared to conventional water heaters.[28] Using native plants and installing smart irrigation control systems in landscaping also reduces water demand.

Explore options for recycling graywater or collecting rainwater. In dry climates and during droughts, a rainwater collection system relieves pressure from municipal water systems and ensures a backup supply of water. The Minnesota Twins baseball team, for instance, uses a rainwater recycling system in their stadium that reduces the need for municipal water by 50 percent or 2 million gallons a year.[29] The Hilton Hotel in Houston, Texas, reduced carbon emissions by 260 metric tons by using a water recycling system for its laundry facility. The AquaRecycle system reuses water to help the laundry maintain its ideal operating temperature, reducing use of natural gas for heating, and cutting water usage from 630,000 gallons to 157,000 gallons, a 74 percent decrease.[30]

9. Explore Energy Performance Contracting through Energy Service Companies

Energy service companies (ESCOs) are now offering energy performance contracts that make it easy to move toward cutting-edge building efficiency. ESCOs allow companies to "outsource" their conservation efforts to experts who keep up with the rapid improvements in green building best practices and technologies. Consider hiring an ESCO to identify, evaluate, and possibly even implement energy-saving retrofits that you can repay through increased efficiency and cost savings. In return, the ESCO will demand a portion of the savings—but will guarantee that realized savings meet or exceed annual payments to cover all project costs over the course of the contract. The ESCO will also provide staff training and long-term maintenance services in addition to paying the cost difference if savings do not materialize. In effect, the ESCO contract offers you a way to finance and manage energy-related projects while minimizing the associated technical and performance risks. Be aware, however, that ESCOs will rarely offer "breakthrough" technologies. Instead, they'll rely on proven approaches to minimize their own risk. For more details on ESCOs, see EPA's "Introduction to Energy Performance Contracting" available at EPA's Energy Star website (www.energystar.gov).

10. Green Grounds and Landscapes

Greening grounds and landscapes generates many benefits for people and the environment in addition to cutting costs. For businesses that depend on the outdoors, such as golf courses, resorts, ecotourism operations, and real estate, a green landscaping strategy can seriously reduce your environmental footprint and increase the value of your business. Habitat protection requires careful attention to how parking spaces, paved roads, and other aspects of the "built environment" connect with the surrounding ecosystem. Many traditional elements of design don't work well from a sustainability point of view. The old model of surrounding an office or factory with acres of paved parking spaces, for instance, has given way to new "best practices" that use more-porous surfaces to absorb storm water and replenish groundwater. Using native plants in your landscaping reduces the amount of labor, pesticides, and water needed to maintain green spaces. In some cases, using native plants and xeriscape principles can eliminate the need to water altogether, even in the driest climate. If you do need to water, a smart irrigation system and graywater recovery can dramatically reduce the amount of water you'll need. Instead of bagging lawn clippings, spreading them on the lawn is healthier for the grass and less energy intensive. Avoid overusing fertilizers because they usually run off the land and pollute rivers and streams.

After finding ways to do less damage while caring for your lawn, think of ways to do even more. Use your facility's grounds to develop a green space that employees, clients, and wildlife will enjoy all year. Planting trees cools temperatures, beautifies the landscape, sequesters carbon, and creates wildlife habitat. Restoring areas of native vegetation and creating nature trails can enhance the ecosystem as well as nearby property values. Digging artificial ponds retains water from the landscape and creates wildlife habitat.

Some companies even plant vegetables in their green spaces. Corporate gardens have been on the rise. Google, Yahoo!, *Sunset* magazine, and even Pepsi have started organic corporate vegetable gardens, where employees are encouraged to participate in growing and enjoying the food. At Kohl's headquarters in Milwaukee, the organic garden supplies a local food bank, and children at the company day care can come to play there as well. Employee-run gardens can work to bring people together and to diminish the divisions of corporate cultures.[31]

11. Reduce Building-Related Waste

Reducing waste is a strategy that companies should employ in every aspect of business, from buildings and facilities to manufacturing and product design. Reducing waste is not just about more recycling and less garbage, but also about eliminating inefficiencies in building materials use and facilities operations. On the building materials front, reducing construction-related waste has become a major area of focus for many entities. As part of Abu Dhabi's model eco-city, the new Masdar Institute of Science and Technology, a graduate research university launched in collaboration with MIT, set a lofty goal for its campus to reuse or recycle all of its construction waste. Now that the gleaming new, glass-reinforced concrete building with its glued-laminated timber and zinc-clad roof is in place and the last bits of wood scaffolding have been chipped into mulch, the Masdar team claims a 99 percent rate of success in diverting construction waste from landfill disposal.

ADVANCED PLAYS: INTEGRATE SYSTEMS AND BUILD GREEN

12. Consider LEED or Energy Star Certification

Building certifications can inspire new goals and demonstrate your sustainability commitment to customers, clients, and employees. Leadership in Energy and Environmental Design, commonly known as LEED, is a nationally recognized benchmarking system developed by the U.S. Green Building Council (USGBC) that sets the standard for environmentally sustainable construction. A building project can be "LEED certified" based on points awarded for environmental attributes according to a standardized system that covers siting, water efficiency, energy use, materials, indoor environmental quality, and eco-innovation in the design process. Studies show that LEED certified buildings have higher occupancy rates, rental prices, and sales prices than non-LEED certified peers.[32] (see Figure 9.2). Jim Lampman, president and founder of Lake Champlain Chocolates, comments that "Our customers appreciate Lake Champlain Chocolates being environmentally responsible, and LEED certification makes sense for many additional reasons. It creates a healthier workplace for our employees, reduces our environmental impact, and produces operational efficiencies for the lifetime of the building."[33]

Energy Star certification is more straightforward. It requires that a building's energy efficiency be gauged using the EPA's Portfolio Manager software, with certification available to those who fall into the upper twenty-fifth percentile. Pursuing LEED or Energy Star certification can raise up-front costs for design and construction due to higher standards for materials and greater architectural complexity—but payback can be quick and the ROI significant. Not only do green buildings have lower operational costs, they often generate higher productivity, tax benefits, and intangible gains including improved employee morale and reputational gains for the brand.

There are many facets to a "green" or "eco-smart" building. Figure 9.3 offers a checklist of items to consider.

Figure 9.2 **Value of Green Certification**

Building Type	Occupancy Rate	Rental Rate per ft²	Sale Price per ft²
ENERGY STAR Certified	91.5%	$30.55	$288
Non-ENERGY STAR peers	87.9%	$28.15	$227
LEED certified	92%	$42.38	$438
Non-LEED Peers	87.9%	$31.05	$257

Source: CoStar Group, "Commercial Real Estate and the Environment"; data based on 2008 building costs. Reprinted with permission.

13. Buy Clean Energy

A commitment to renewable energy offers not only a way to be greener, but also a hedge against fossil fuel price volatility and rising electricity prices. Payback times for alternative energy systems continue to shorten as the costs associated with solar arrays, wind turbines, and other renewable energy technologies decline. And most jurisdictions make it possible to sell any "excess" power generated back to the local electricity distribution company. The Tennessee Valley Authority, for example, will purchase 100% of electricity generated by qualifing renewable energy systems at a rate higher than the retail rate.[34]

Note that you no longer need a big capital investment to get into the alternative energy game. Any number of "green power" companies, such as Sun Edison, will install and maintain their equipment and sell you a set amount of renewable energy at a fixed price. Adventist HealthCare, a Rockville, Maryland-based network of health-care providers, for instance, signed renewable energy purchasing contracts in 2010 that are expected to save the company $1.25 million by locking in electricity rates through mid-2013.[35] Likewise, BJ's Wholesale Club, after entering into a power purchase agreement with Tioga Energy, was able to install solar photovoltaic panels on four of its large outlets at no cost. Under the agreement, Tioga Energy pays for the installation, monitoring, and maintenance of the systems and BJ's pays for the electricity generated at a price lower than standard utility rates.[36]

For many manufacturing companies, an investment in cogeneration—combined heat and power production—may make sense. Some companies have even found ways to use waste materials from their manufacturing processes as fuel. The Budd Inlet Treatment Plant in Washington, for example, burns methane and other sewage treatment byproducts in its cogeneration facility. Combined with an aeration blower retrofit currently under way, the cogeneration system is expected to save Budd Inlet about $200,000 per year in power costs.[37] In a similar vein, the Huisha Farm in Shenyang, China, has an adjacent biogas power plant that burns dried manure from 250,000 cows at a nearby dairy farm to generate 38,000 megawatts per hour of power annually.[38] Using locally produced organic waste products as fuel cuts waste management costs as well as the cost of fuel.

For large companies another alternative is to use an energy broker to buy power on the wholesale market—and insist that a certain portion be from renewable energy sources. Companies such as Worcester, Massachusetts-based World Energy will even run an online auction to ensure low prices, delivering whatever percentage of "green" power a purchaser chooses.

14. Integrate Systems with Advanced Measurement Metrics and Services

Because of recent advances in integrated software technology, facility managers now have powerful tools with which to manage their buildings. These new building management systems not only measure energy use, they also support regulatory compliance and maximize space utilization. A number of software companies have developed programs that track energy use, costs, and environmental impacts and help companies increase efficiency and lower costs. For example, Energy Expert compares daily energy consumption against a norm generated over time. Mextrix4, another utility tracking software, can normalize extreme weather events so that you can see your energy usage without the distorting effects of extremely hot or cold weather. See the resources at the end of this chapter for a list of suggested software.

15. Build Green

There are inherent limits to efficiency upgrades in existing buildings as some original design inefficiencies are either cost prohibitive or impossible to fix. So if the need arises to construct a new facility, seize the opportunity to do it right. An integrated design process that folds environmental thinking into other building attributes is the key to success. Open communication between the designer, owner, architect, and tenants can raise the odds that the building will be both operationally and environmentally efficient—and retain its value in the long run. Engage designers who are familiar with the latest technologies in energy, water, and carbon management and understand how to connect the dots between various systems. Involve builders with a track record of efficiently using raw materials, minimizing transportation costs, and maximizing the use of renewable or recycled materials.

Buildings don't exist in isolation. A building's location and relation to surrounding buildings and landscapes define its environmental footprint more than any other feature. A building located far from an urban center, where most of your customers and employees are going to be, will have a huge transportation footprint. Locating buildings close to public transportation encourages less driving. Building on brownfields or otherwise already developed land often means that some infrastructure (water, sewers, roads, and power lines) will already be in place, cutting costs and reducing environmental impacts in comparison to a project sited on undeveloped land. Buildings situated to take advantage of natural energy flows will greatly reduce their energy demand when in operation. Take advantage of the sun for heat and daylight. Avoid windy spots or plant trees as windbreakers to reduce energy loss. Study road patterns and the orientation of nearby buildings to ease the flow of traffic in and out of the building. Let local geography and climate determine what constitutes "best practice."

Finally, it is critical that any push toward a greener building does not run contrary to the operational requirements of the intended space. In planning for its new green building, the Los Angeles Westside YMCA realized that waterless urinals did not make sense in a facility that serves hundreds of "aim challenged" boys each day.[39] Any gain in reduced water use would be overwhelmed by added bathroom cleaning costs. Simply put, a green building that isn't functional

BASIC PRINCIPLES FOR NEW "GREEN" CONSTRUCTION

- Take a holistic approach; always consider the interactions among all system components.
- Design to minimize impact on the local environment.
- Design to maximize use of local and regional resources in a sustainable way.
- Minimize or design away extra space.
- Design for durability and longevity.
- Integrate design aspects for multiplicity of function.
- Use software systems and IT to enable collaborative design.
- Utilize permeable surfaces when possible to minimize storm water runoff.
- Locate near existing infrastructure.
- Locate/orient the building to utilize shading and natural lighting.
- Use outside air for cooling and ventilation. If used in combination with efficient HVAC, energy bills can be cut up to 10 percent.
- Use thermal mass (brick, concrete, stone) to moderate swings in buildings' indoor temperatures and take advantage of outdoor temperature differentials between day and night.
- Design pumping systems by laying out pipes first (to minimize distance and elbows), followed by motors and other equipment. Favor big pipes and small motors.
- Keep air intakes away from exhaust areas.
- Design HVAC systems for long-term flexibility and efficiency (e.g. under floor delivery, personal control).
- Maximize the use of renewable or recycled materials.
- Use the least toxic materials and manufacturing processes.
- Use integrated planning of demolition and construction programs to minimize the generation of waste.

Sources: Anderson, Ray C., *Mid-course Correction: Toward a Sustainable Enterprise: The Interface Model* (2005); WBCSD, *Energy Efficiency in Buildings: Business Realities and Opportunities*, 2007. www.wbcsd.org/web/eeb.

isn't sustainable. You must always balance energy efficiency and environmental attributes against other goals.

16. Green Your Lease

For companies in leased space, a green facilities initiative requires a different strategy. The easiest "play" is to look for a green building when it comes time to rent an office or other space. Many landlords now tout the sustainability elements of their buildings and offer "green leases."

If you have an ongoing lease or need to stay in your existing building, then some negotiation will be required to achieve sustainability advances. Andrea Carruthers, a leading real estate lawyer at Minneapolis-based Faegre & Benson, highlights some of the issues to look into:

- Specify sustainability standards and programs that you want.
- Manage uncertainty about sustainability performance.
- Get operating costs broken out to create incentives for waste reduction and efficiency.
- Seek an option to opt out of building services (e.g., cleaning) if you're not satisfied with the sustainability of the standard offering.
- Ask for an annual environmental performance report.[40]

It may not be possible to get every aspect of leased space up to "best practice" standards, but any step toward a greener building is positive. And landlords increasingly recognize the value of improving the sustainability of their properties. So, it never hurts to ask.

SUMMARY

Key Plays

1. Start by tackling the obvious inefficiencies.
2. Benchmark your building's current performance.
3. Do a systematic building audit.
4. Upgrade insulation and strengthen the building "envelope."
5. Upgrade lighting.
6. Upgrade heating, ventilation, and air-conditioning systems.
7. Reduce energy demands from equipment.
8. Cut water-related costs.
9. Explore energy performance contracting through energy service companies.
10. Green grounds and landscapes.
11. Reduce building-related waste.
12. Consider LEED or Energy Star certification.
13. Buy clean energy.
14. Integrate systems with advanced measurement metrics and services.
15. Build green.
16. Green your lease.

Figure 9.3   Eco-Smart Buildings Checklist

	• **Invest in high-quality, ongoing maintenance and optimization** to extend life and maximize efficiency of systems and equipment • **Make building envelopes air tight** and stop unwanted transfer of heat through thermal bridges • **Maximize *system* efficiency,** not just component efficiency • **Replace old inefficient equipment** with new high-efficiency equipment that will deliver payback and ROI in energy savings over its life span • **Constantly look for unnecessary uses of energy or resources** (excessive lighting or HVAC, fans and motors that are too large or never turn off, wasted water, etc.).
Plug Air Leaks and Strengthen the Building Envelope	• **Check for obvious air leaks** in doors, walls, and windows and insulate/seal with appropriate materials/techniques—all of which can save 10–40% in HVAC costs • **Encourage use of revolving doors and calibrate automatic doors** to minimize air loss • **Install radiant barriers**—materials that reflect heat radiated by hot surfaces and keep heat out or in, which can save up to 10% in cooling energy • **Use shades, deflectors, and light shelves** to reduce summer sun • **Upgrade roof insulation and use cool roofing**—roofs coated with reflective paints or materials to deflect heat from building. Visit www.coolroofs.org. • **Explore the option of high-insulating technology windows and window films,** which can save up to 39% of heating and 32% of cooling energy • **Install fast-acting doors** in factory and warehouse exits to minimize time the door is open to outside • **Plant trees to shade** eastern, western, and southern windows • **Consider switchable glaze (electrochromic) windows,** which can save up to 26% of cooling loads and 65% of lighting energy
Use Smart, Efficient Lighting	• **Train employees to turn off lights** when not in use • **Use daylight whenever possible,** installing controls that reduce electric lights in response to daylight • **Switch to LED lights** • **Follow a strategic lighting maintenance plan** of scheduled group re-lamping and fixture cleaning • **Look for areas where you can reduce lighting** without sacrificing performance or employee comfort • **Calibrate light controls** according to design specs • **Consider task-specific lighting** when lighting a whole room is unnecessary • **Replace incandescent lighting with compact fluorescents,** which last about 10 times longer than conventional incandescent lamps and can cut lighting costs by up to 80%.

(continued)

Figure 9.3 (*Continued*)

	• **Install motion detectors or automatic controls** to turn indoor and outdoor lights off when not needed, which can save up to 90% of lighting energy for individual spaces
	• **Switch to LED and Energy Star exit signs,** which consume only 2 watts each
	• **Install high-efficiency fluorescent or metal halide bulbs, electronic ballasts, and reflectors**
	• **Replace T12 with T8 linear fluorescent lamps**
	• **Favor low-mercury fluorescents**
	• **Install dimmable ballasts, photo-sensors, and dimming controls** in indoor daylit zones
	• **Upgrade outdoor lighting** to high-pressure sodium fixtures or metal halide fixtures
Repair and Upgrade Heating, Ventilation and Cooling (HVAC)	*Maintain & Fine-Tune Existing Equipment* • **Set up regular inspection and maintenance schedules** for all heating and cooling equipment—including filters, ducts, and intake and exhaust fans • **Correct excessive settings** for indoor humidity and temperature • **Maximize use of natural ventilation,** heating, and cooling • **Review occupancy schedules and fine-tune HVAC** control schedules according to when the building areas are actually being used • **Calibrate indoor and outdoor sensors** according to original design specs (room thermostats, duct thermostats, humidistats, and pressure and temperature sensors) • **Use improved controls** to implement temperature or pressure reset, economizer cooling, and demand-controlled ventilation • **Seal ducts,** which can reduce leakage by about 80% and heating and cooling energy needs by up to 35% • **Check damper and valve controls** to ensure they are functioning properly • **Tune up water chiller systems** by cleaning water chiller tubes, treating water, unloading reciprocating compressors, and performing a "chilled-water reset" • **Monitor boiler steam traps** frequently for stuck traps and leaks • **Fine-tune combustion airflow** in fossil-fueled boilers to ensure minimum safe use of air and prevent excess air use, which wastes fuel • **Clean boiler tubes** and treat water to improve efficiency *Upgrades* • **Replace old HVAC components and systems with modern high-efficiency equipment** as necessary

Figure 9.3 *(Continued)*

	<ul><li>**Install programmable thermostats**</li><li>**Correctly size and retrofit HVAC fan systems** and heating and chilling components</li><li>**Install adjustable/variable speed devices** wherever practical</li><li>**Convert Constant Volume (CV) to Variable Air Volume (VAV) systems,** which have lower life-cycle costs</li><li>**Harness nature with outside air economizers**—systems that cool a building or data center using air from outside the building</li><li>**Replace old boilers with new high-efficiency units** that have Annual Fuel Utilization Efficiency of at least 85%</li><li>**Explore options to capture and use excess waste heat** from processes, furnaces, air compressors, boilers, exhaust ducts to heat boiler feed water, offices (e.g., using heat exchangers), and more</li><li>For buildings in moderate climates, **consider an air-source heat pump** that uses differences between outdoor and indoor air temperatures to provide heating and cooling and can save up to 60% of heating energy</li><li>**Explore feasibility of other best-available energy-saving technologies** such as:<ul><li>–Condensing water heaters</li><li>–Condensing boilers and furnaces</li><li>–Dedicated outdoor air systems (DOAS)</li><li>–Displacement ventilation (DV) cooling technology</li><li>–Electric heat-pump water heaters (HPWH)</li><li>–Heat and energy recovery ventilation (ERV)</li><li>–Soft-starting/control motor technologies</li></ul></li></ul>
Repair and Upgrade Mechanical Systems	<ul><li>**Fine-tune settings of all electric motor-driven systems** (air compressors, pumps, fans) to minimize installed horsepower and maximize motor efficiency</li><li>**Make sure that all fans and motors are right-sized, high-efficiency, and adjustable-speed**</li><li>**Install multiple small motors** to handle varying volumes rather than one big motor</li><li>**Run equipment during non-peak hours** when possible to save money and reduce demand on utilities</li><li>**Move to energy-efficient flat and conveyer belts** (e.g., replace standard V-belts with cogged or synchronous belt drives)</li><li>**See this book's Chapter 13, "Manufacturing and Processing,"** for more detailed recommendations</li></ul>
Stop Wasting Water and Cut Water-Related Costs	<ul><li>**Repair leaks**</li><li>**Reduce water flows wherever possible to meet actual load requirements**</li></ul>

Figure 9.3 (*Continued*)

	• **Install low-flow fixtures** in restrooms and kitchen areas
	• **Install low-flow toilets or toilet displacement devices** and high-efficiency urinals
	• **Reuse water,** including boiler water, whenever possible
	• **Adjust water heater temperatures**—changing from default 140°F setting to 120°F doesn't affect performance and can save 18% of water heating energy
	• **Set timers to heat water in electric heaters at night** using off-peak electricity
	• **Replace old water heaters with high-thermal-efficiency versions** with an energy factor of at least 62%
Reduce Energy Demand from Office Equipment, Appliances, and Supplies	• **Buy Energy Star–certified appliances,** most of which offer payback through energy savings within three years
	• **Purchase Energy Star-certified electronics**—PCs, printers, copiers, and monitors
	• **Use servers with 80 plus-certified power supplies** (converter cords) for PCs and servers
	• **Enable power management** for office equipment (e.g., low-power sleep mode), which can cut equipment energy costs up to 36%
	• **Install supplemental computer power management software**
	• **Require energy saving devices on vending machines** or ask vendor to provide more efficient machines
	• **Run equipment and processes during non-peak hours** when possible to save money and reduce demand on utilities
	• **For more ideas, see**
	• Chapter 10, "Information Technology"
	• Chapter 13: "Checklist for Reducing Waste"
Use Healthier Eco-Friendly Materials	• **Minimize finishes,** such as paints and coatings
	• **Use finishes and materials with zero or low emissions of "volatile organic compounds"** (VOCs) to enhance indoor air quality and help control the growth of microbial contamination
	• **Seek out low-impact paint**—paint with light and moderate tints (which almost always are low-VOC), water-based over oil-based, and recycled content latex paint for exteriors. Avoid aerosol paint.
	• **Install low-impact carpeting**—low-VOC carpets made from recycled content, or carpet "tiles" that make it easy for selective replacements in heavily trafficked areas. Look for Carpet & Rug Institute (CRI) Green Label Plus designation. Ask suppliers to identify recycling options.
	• **Use nontoxic cleaning compounds**

(*continued*)

Figure 9.3 *(Continued)*

	• **Maximize the use of all-purpose cleaners** to cut down on the number of chemicals used and to minimize the potential danger of chemicals mixing • **Review the Green Seal Environmental Standard for Cleaning Services** (GS-42) • **Buy cleaners in concentrated form** that can be mixed at different strengths for different purposes, reducing packaging and transportation
Green Your Landscape and Grounds	• **Landscape to help protect** or even enhance local habitat and biological diversity • **Compost organic matter** and plant debris • **Mulch lawn clippings,** which saves water, promotes plant growth, improves appearance, and suppresses weed growth • **Use native plants** adapted to the local environment that don't require much maintenance and **xeriscape** (landscaping and gardening in ways to reduce supplemental irrigation) by using plants adapted to local rainfall conditions • **Recycle graywater for landscaping** • **Avoid using cleaning chemicals outdoors** • **Install high-efficiency watering systems** and smart irrigation controllers • **Install permeable surfaces** for walkways and common areas so they help control storm water and retain less heat • **Employ Integrated Pest Management** to minimize use of chemical pesticides • **Build storm water retention ponds** to minimize volume and temperature spikes on local waterways from rain • **Create eco- and employee-friendly spaces**—bird boxes, butterfly gardens, employee-run vegetable gardens, nature trails, etc.
Make Buildings Friendly to Green Transport	• **Find ways to reward pedestrians, mass-transit riders, and cyclists** and discourage single-passenger car driving (e.g., make employees pay for parking, subsidize bus or subway passes, and provide bicycle racks) • **Consider locating new facilities adjacent to mass transit**

Sources: Environmental Defense Fund, *Climate Corps Handbook,* 2008. www.edf.org/ (accessed August 5, 2010); Anderson, Ray C., *Mid-Course Correction: Toward a Sustainable Enterprise: The Interface Model* (White River Junction, VT: Chelsea Green, 2005); WBCSD, Energy Efficiency in Buildings: Business real, July 2008. www.wbcsd.org/ (accessed August 5, 2010); Energy Star, *Building Upgrade Manual,* revised October 2007. www.energystar.gov (accessed August 5, 2010); StopWaste, *A Guide to Green Maintenance and Operations,* 2009. www.stopwaste.org (accessed August 5, 2010).

ADDITIONAL RESOURCES

FINDING LOW-HANGING FRUIT

"Sustainability 'How-to Guide' Series: No-Cost/Low-Cost Energy Savings Guide" (IFMA Foundation, 2010). A guide to no-cost/low-cost energy efficiency measures in buildings for facility operations personnel. www.ifmafoundation.org

Flex Your Power Best Practice Guides and Case Studies (California's Efficiency Partnership). A comprehensive website outlining best-practice building strategies for hotels, restaurants, food growers, and commercial office buildings. www.fypower.org

"Climate Corps Handbook: Energy Efficiency Investment Opportunities in Office Buildings and Data Centers" Second edition (Environmental Defense Fund, 2009). A practical guide to help users identify and prioritize cost-effective investments in commercial office buildings that save energy and cut GHG emissions. www.edf.org

"A Guide to Green Maintenance and Operations" (Stop Waste, 2009). 20-page basic guide with recommendations on lighting, paint, flooring, furniture, appliances, water efficiency, mechanical, janitorial supplies, and landscaping. www.stopwaste.org

MAKING THE BUSINESS CASE

Greening Our Built World: Costs, Benefits and Strategies by Greg Kats (Island Press, 2009). Outlines findings from extensive financial and technical analyses of over 150 green buildings in the United States and 10 other countries. www.islandpress.org

"The Business Case: What Is the Cost and Value of Green Building?" (Canadian Green Business Council, 2007). A chapter from the CaGBC Municipal Green Building Toolkit that offers universally applicable guidance for evaluating the costs and benefits of green buildings. www.cagbc.org

"The Post-Carbon Economy: 5 Secrets for Corporate Leadership When Carbon is Priced" by Amit Chatterjee and Jay Whitehead (SOFICO books, 2009).

See also Chapter 4 ("Making the Internal Business Case for Going Greener").

GREEN AND ENERGY-EFFICIENT BUILDING PRODUCTS

Oikos. Online directory of sustainable and energy-efficient building products. oikos.com/green_products

GreenSpec® Directory. Product descriptions for over 2,000 environmentally preferable products. www.buildinggreen.com

BENCHMARKING AND AUDITING

Green Business Guide to Energy Audits (NRDC). An energy audit format that analyzes and evaluates your company's existing energy-use practices with an eye toward cost savings. www.nrdc.org

Energy Program Assessment Matrix (EPA). Helps organizations assess their energy management practices relative to those outlined in the ENERGY STAR Guidelines for Energy Management. www.energystar.gov

How to Conduct Your Own Energy Audit (Nicor). A simple step-by-step guide to conducting an initial commercial energy audit. www.nicor.com

Portfolio Manager (ENERGY STAR). Free, online energy management tool to help organizations benchmark and track energy consumption, water consumption, and greenhouse gas emissions within a single building or across a portfolio of buildings. Helps identify underperforming facilities, track energy savings from efficiency measures, and evaluate potential energy-saving measures. www.energystar.gov

"Sustainability 'How-To Guide' Series: EPA's ENERGY STAR Portfolio Manager" by Maureen K. Roskoski, Laurie Gilmer, and Greg Hughel (IFMA Foundation, 2009). A guide to using ENERGY STAR's Portfolio Manager effectively. www.ifmafoundation.org

Building Upgrade Value Calculator for Office Buildings (EPA). Estimates the financial impact of proposed investments in energy efficiency in office properties, calculating net investment, reduction in operating expense, energy savings, return on investment (ROI), internal rate of return (IRR), net present value (NPV), net operating income (NOI), and impact on asset value. www.energystar.gov

Facility Energy Decision System (FEDS) (DOE). Software that performs energy efficiency assessments and energy retrofit project analyses for buildings of all sizes, including multi-building sites. www.pnl.gov/feds

Rapid Energy Modeling (Autodesk). Workflow software specially designed for rapid assessments with limited data for modeling energy use and building auditing. www.autodesk.com

INSULATION, BUILDING ENVELOPE: INSULATION, WINDOWS, AND ROOFS

Whole Building Design Guide: Building Commissioning Guide (National Institute of Building Sciences). Thorough guide to commissioning process, including determining project performance requirements and documenting compliance and acceptance. www.wbdg.org

Whole Building Design Guide: Building Envelope (National Institute of Building Sciences). Comprehensive guide to exterior envelope design and construction. www.wbdg.org

Insulation Thickness Computer Program (3E Plus®). An energy management computer program that determines the amount of insulation necessary for a variety of industrial sites and operations. www.pipeinsulation.org

Cool Roof Calculator (DOE). Estimates cooling and heating savings for flat roofs with non-black surfaces. www.roofcalc.com

ENERGY STAR Building Upgrade Manual (EPA, 2008). A guide to help prepare and install profitable energy-saving modifications. www.energystar.gov

LIGHTING

Green Lighting: How Energy-Efficient Lighting Can Save You Energy and Money and Reduce Your Carbon Footprint by Brian Clark Howard, William J. Brinsky, and Seth Leitman (McGraw-Hill, 2010).

Efficient Lighting Strategies (DOE, 2002). Six-page document outlining best practices for building lighting. www.eere.energy.gov

Sustainability "How-to Guide" Series: Lighting Guide (IFMA Foundation, 2009). Reviews options for saving energy while maintaining performance and enhancing indoor quality. www.ifmafoundation.org

The MIT Design Advisor. Web-based energy simulators that model a building's energy performance and give long-term cost estimates for different design options. designadvisor.mit.edu/design/

DIAL Light Building Software. Planning program for calculating and visualizing indoor and outdoor lighting systems. www.dial.de

HEATING, VENTILATION, AND AIR-CONDITIONING SYSTEMS

Room Air Conditioner Cost Estimator (DOE). Online calculator that compares life cycle costs of high-efficiency rooftop and room air-conditioners versus standard equipment. www.pnl.gov

Whole Building Design Guide: HVAC and Refrigerating Engineering by Charles E. Gulledge and Dennis Knight (National Institute of Building Sciences, 2010). Thorough guide to refrigerating and HVAC systems and providers. www.wbdg.org

Process Heating Tip Sheets (DOE). Multiple pdfs on various topics that provide technical advice to improve process heating systems. www.eere.energy.gov

WATER

WATERGY Software (EPA). Software that uses utility and facility data to analyze relationship between water and energy and determine potential savings. www.eere.energy.gov

GROUNDS AND LANDSCAPES

EPAGreenScapesProgram. A website that provides cost efficient solutions for large- and small-scale landscaping. Also includes tips, potential benefits, and case studies. www.epa.gov/greenscapes

LEED AND ENERGY STAR CERTIFICATION

LEED Certification Information (Natural Resources Defense Council). Introduction to LEED with tips for getting certified. www.nrdc.org

U.S. Green Building Council. Comprehensive background on LEED certification with reference guides and information on becoming a LEED AP or Green Associate. www.usgbc.org

LEED 2009 for Existing Buildings: O&M Resources & Tools (U.S. Green Building Council). Guide to getting existing buildings LEED certified. www.usgbc.org

ENERGY STAR. Includes resources and tools for measuring current energy performance, setting goals, tracking savings, rewarding improvements, and gaining ENERGY STAR certification. www.energystar.gov

ENERGY MANAGEMENT AND OPTIMIZATION

Building Energy Software Tools Directory (DOE). A comprehensive directory of software tools for calculating energy use as well as many other resource flows in buildings. www.eere.energy.gov

Free Software Tools for Energy System Management at Plants and Industrial Facilities (DOE). Comprehensive guide to software tools that help managers analyze energy-system savings opportunities at plants and industrial facilities. www.eere.energy.gov

EnergyPlus Energy Simulation Software (DOE). A whole building simulation program that models heating, cooling, lighting, ventilating, and other energy flows as well as water in buildings. www.eere.energy.gov

Superior Energy Performance Certification Program. A program of the U.S. Council for Energy-Efficient Manufacturing (U.S. CEEM) working to give industrial facilities a road map for continuous improvement in energy efficiency while maintaining competitiveness. www.superiorenergyperformance.net

ENERGY PERFORMANCE CONTRACTING

Introduction to Energy Performance Contracting prepared by ICF International National Association of Energy Services Companies (EPA, October 2007). An overview of energy performance contracting in the context of overall energy efficiency programs. www.energystar.gov

CLEAN AND RENEWABLE ENERGY

Database of State Incentives for Renewables and Efficiency (DOE). Comprehensive guide to federal, state, local, and utility level incentives and policies to promote renewable energy and energy efficiency. www.dsireusa.org

Solar-Estimate.org. Clearinghouse site for national and region-specific solar program and utility information, including solar energy calculators that assess costs and benefits based on location and individual building needs. www.solar-estimate.org

PVWatts Calculator (National Renewable Energy Laboratory). Online tool that determines production and cost savings of grid-connected photovoltaic energy systems. www.nrel.gov/rredc/pvwatts

Find Solar. Guide to local solar energy providers, manufacturers, installers, and retailers. www.findsolar.com

American Wind Energy Association. Clearinghouse for wind energy information, including resources for installing individual wind turbines. www.awea.org

Merit Software. Supply and demand matching software for renewable energy systems. www.esru.strath.ac.uk

DESIGN AND NEW CONSTRUCTION

Whole Building Design Guide (National Institute of Building Sciences). Comprehensive clearinghouse site offering up-to-date information on a wide range of building-related guidance, criteria, and technology from a whole buildings perspective. www.wbdg.org

Checklist for Building Design Guidance (EPA). Guidance for the following steps in building design: setting goals, assembling a design team, pre-design, schematic design, design development, construction and bid documents, commissioning the building, tracking, measurement and verification, and ENERGY STAR. www.energystar.gov

Los Alamos National Laboratory Sustainable Design Guide (DOE). Examines the process for designing energy-efficient buildings and estimates the added value created by sustainable architecture and facility construction. www.eere.energy.gov

"Asset Lifecycle Model for Total Cost of Ownership Management: Framework, Glossary & Definitions." Framework to enable effective communication among key decisionmakers involved with facilities and physical infrastructure investment and management, including building managers, operators and technicians. www.ifma.org

BEES (Building for Environmental and Economic Sustainability) Software (National Institute of Standards and Technology). Free software to help builders select cost-effective, environmentally preferable building products by evaluating building products' performance using a life cycle assessment approach. www.bfrl.nist.gov

LISA (LCA in Sustainable Architecture) Software. Streamlined LCA decision-support tool to help designers make informed choices based whole-of-life environmental considerations. www.lisa.au.com

Building Life-Cycle Cost Program (DOE). Analyzes the relative cost effectiveness of alternative buildings and building-related systems or components. www.eere.energy.gov

The Law of Green Buildings: Regulatory and Legal Issues in Design, Construction, Operations, and Financing by J. Cullen Howe, Michael Gerrard, and Frederick R. Fucci (American Bar Association, 2010).

GREEN BUILDING NEWS

Greenerbuildings.com. Daily news, opinion pieces, and tools on green buildings from Greenbiz.com. www.greenerbuildings.com

Chapter 10 Information Technology

When Georgia-based AtlantaNAP incorporated in 1994 to provide data center services and disaster recovery data backup systems, nobody was thinking much about energy efficiency or environmental impact. Today, with a 65,000-square-foot facility deploying over 6,000 servers and requiring four megawatts of power, the company is a green data center pioneer. What happened?

In keeping with "green IT" best practices, AtlantaNAP's data center has aggressively pursued "virtualization" (optimizing server utilization) and regular equipment updates to deliver the most energy efficient computational power. To meet the heating needs of its adjacent office building, AtlantaNAP installed heat pumps in the data center that transfer waste heat from the computers to the offices. As a result, the offices do not have to utilize an outside source of heat, resulting in a 50 percent energy savings for the AtlantaNAP offices. The facility's cooling system draws air from the outside into the data center and out of the facility via one large outtake fan, effectively reducing cooling needs. The company also dug its own well on the property to take advantage of the groundwater's year-round 50-degree temperature for heating and cooling needs. In addition, AtlantaNAP worked vigilantly to reduce its e-waste. A local computer recycling company picks up all old server equipment, and all scrap metals are recycled. The company insists on reduced packaging for its new equipment and asks vendors to ship equipment in bulk whenever possible. The logistics department has cut packaging waste by nearly two-thirds. Because IT is always changing, AtlantaNAP's leadership team remains focused on "continuous improvement" and is constantly on the lookout for ways to become more energy efficient and to improve operations.[1]

The role of the CIO and IT professionals in driving companies' Eco-Advantage cannot be underestimated. First, most companies spend a lot of money on energy bills because of IT—so green IT efforts focused on energy efficiency can generate serious bottom-line savings. IBM, for instance, says its clients routinely get 15 to 70 percent reductions in operating costs through IT eco-efficiency initiatives, with full payback on investments within 1 to 2 years. IBM itself saved $49 million by investing $1 million in a green overhaul of one of its data centers in Kentucky: By boosting the center's IT capacity eight times, the company avoided the need to build a new data center.[2]

Second, companies will face mounting pressure to address the rising eco-related impacts of IT—especially in the areas of greenhouse gas emissions and toxics. Consulting giant McKinsey predicts that by 2020 the biggest source of greenhouse gas emissions worldwide could come from information and communications products and technologies including laptops, PCs, mobile phones, data centers, and telecommunications networks.[3] And the issues of toxics and e-waste in connection with manufacturing and disposal of IT equipment are increasingly demanding center stage.

Finally, the potential for IT to be a sustainability solutions driver—within companies and more broadly in the global economy—presents a wealth of opportunities for businesses to create new revenue streams. Just ask C3, SAP, and Oracle, three of the many companies developing software innovations to tap into growing customer demand for high-powered analytics involving a slew of sustainability metrics. Or GE, which is betting on substantial revenue growth from sales of IT-related ecomagination products like its WattStation charging station for electric vehicles.

In this chapter, we show you how to pursue a "green IT" strategy that will:

- Cut costs, improve information systems efficiency, and reduce your company's carbon footprint.
- Reduce and manage e-waste.
- Optimize the energy efficiency and performance of data centers.
- Promote efficiency across your entire business.
- Help drive eco-innovation.
- Seize opportunities for revenue growth.

BASIC PLAYS: FIND LOW-HANGING FRUIT

1. Do a Basic IT Audit and Assessment

Start by charting your current IT utilization and comparing it to best-in-class IT systems. If you don't have significant in-house technical IT capacity, consider engaging an experienced independent auditor who is familiar with green IT issues and guidelines of the Information Systems Audit and Control Association (ISACA). For example, HP offers services and tools aimed at data centers under 5,000 square feet to measure their power and cooling capacity, infrastructure condition, and energy efficiency. Collect information about the following key areas, adding any others that are important to your business:

- An accurate inventory of office and end-user hardware, including desktop computers, monitors, laptops, printers, scanners, copiers, smart phones, voice over internet protocol (VOIP) phones, and so on.

- A careful review of IT data center hardware, including servers, IP and SAN communications switches, storage arrays, tape libraries, and so on.

- A list of all software, including all company-wide platforms and any systems being used by individual employees.

- Paper consumption statistics from your paper handling devices (faxes, printers, scanners, copiers, etc.). *Hint:* These devices often have an "odometer" on the back showing page counts, or you can print out management information that includes these counts. Then you can estimate pages per month based on the date of purchase or serial records from your manufacturers.

- A list of people involved with your day-to-day IT operations, including employees on your payroll, contract workers, and external vendors.

- Energy consumption for each IT hardware and software component as well as per-person consumption.

- Energy consumption of data center mechanical and electrical overheads, such as air-conditioning, humidification, uninterruptible power supplies (UPS), transformers, and distribution losses.

The goal is to get a clear fix on how much energy the IT infrastructure and facilities consume. Use the 15-minute "Aberdeen/IBM Green IT Assessment and Net Return on Investment (ROI) Calculator," a web-based diagnostic tool to help you benchmark your current state in light of best-in-class green IT implementation. The tool provides a basic evaluation of your company's current state in three key areas—energy efficiency, virtualization, and collaboration—then it produces a customized report outlining options and potential ROI for each. It is available for free at http://greenit.aberdeen.com/.

2. Hunt for Glaring Inefficiencies Using a Green Lens

Assemble a team to review current IT assets and policies in light of the following:

- *Redundancies and waste:* Some forms of redundancies and waste are easy to recognize. For example, do many of your employees use individual printers, when a few shared network printers would suffice? Do you have significantly different numbers of pages printed by some teams compared to others? Do employees fail to power down their computers at night? Do you see a high percentage of employees with high-energy consumption PCs instead of 90 percent low-energy consumption laptops?

- *Low-utilization PCs and servers:* Do any of your company's enterprise-wide applications suffer from an unusual amount of downtime? Can you identify any areas in IT that generate an unusually large number of help desk calls? Looking at indicators such as these can help you identify underperforming IT assets, which often lead to sources of waste. At the very least, you might spot

IT gaps or problems that cause a decrease in employee productivity. If you look deeper, you may find aged IT resources that are ready for an efficiency upgrade that will lower energy use and shrink your environmental footprint—such as using Virtual Desktop Infrastructure (VDI) solutions for PCs or virtualization and technology refresh for servers.

- *Inconsistencies between your IT policies and your company's overall sustainability goals:* Review your company's overall sustainability priorities. Are they fully reflected in your IT policies? Spell out the links and cross-check the alignment.

TRACKING PRINTER EFFICIENCY AND ECO IMPACTS

Xerox offers a free Sustainability Calculator to help companies evaluate existing printers, copiers, and multifunction devices and measure potential savings in energy and paper use, solid waste, water, air and greenhouse gas emissions from optimized scenarios. **Ricoh Americas** created @Remote GreenReports in 2010 to help companies monitor the number of pages printed, percentage of jobs that are printed two-sided or using other paper saving modes, and the resulting paper, energy, and carbon savings.[4]

---

3. Foster Collaboration between IT and Facilities Managers

In most companies IT managers optimize the operational value delivered by their systems while an entirely separate facilities management team supervises the company's electricity budgets and manages power purchases. This disconnect can be costly for many companies. Bringing IT and facilities management colleagues together can generate win-win results. In *The Greening of IT: How Companies Can Make a Difference for the Environment*, John Lamb argues that companies should appoint an "Energy Czar"—someone tasked with closing the gap between IT and facilities management on electricity use.[5] This person should:

- Put tools in place to estimate and manage IT power consumption.
- Track IT's percentage of overall company electric usage (which becomes particularly important if you adopt some of the recommendations we make later in the chapter).
- Track overall IT "Power Usage Effectiveness" (PUE) trends and compare various facilities internally and with external examples.
- Work with facilities management to negotiate rebates with electric companies to take advantage of government programs related to IT power consumption and to source power from renewable sources where available. For example, one major financial services firm systematically replaced its power contracts with renewable energy contracts as part of their company's commitment to achieve CO_2 neutrality within the next several years. eBay now assigns electric bills for data centers directly to their corresponding IT departments'

budgets, which motivated the IT team to implement a number of cost-saving techniques, including increased use of virtualization for noncritical applications and upgrading servers to achieve better efficiency.[6]

- Communicate energy-saving IT tips and power consumption progress throughout the company. IBM has accomplished this by fostering cross-organizational collaboration by empowering a team of employees from the IT and Facilities divisions to implement and continually update cooling best practices in data centers. IBM has found that eliminating transient cooling air flow through cable penetrations and open rack slots, directing cooling delivery to the hotter racks, and idling unneeded air conditioning units can reduce data center energy use by up to 10 percent. (Material used with permission from Pearson).

4. Change Employee Computer and Peripheral Use Behavior

Simple changes in everyday work habits can make a big difference. The Alliance to Save Energy and the technology company 1E estimated that 50 percent of all office workers using computers don't switch them off at night. For a company managing 10,000 PCs, this amounts to $260,000 in unnecessary annual electricity costs—not to mention avoidable pollution. Marty Poniatowski, in his book, *Foundations of Green IT: Consolidation, Virtualization, Efficiency, and ROI in the Data Center*, notes that leaving a computer on 24 hours a day results in annual carbon dioxide emissions of 1,500 pounds. Imagine the impact you could make if you only kept computers on in your company for an average of eight hours a day.

A few basic practices will vastly reduce IT's environmental footprint:[7]

- *Hibernate or turn off computers when not in use weekends.* If you fear losing productivity time during startup and shutdown, setting PCs to hibernate is the next best thing—sometimes as good, as some modern PCs consume zero energy in hibernation mode. To get a sense of how much energy and money you can save from reducing the amount of time a computer is left on, visit www.pcremoteshutdown.com/pc-energy-saving-calculator/.
- *Enable standby mode and other power management settings on computers.* According to Alan Meier at Lawrence Berkeley National Laboratory, standby energy accounts for 1 percent of total worldwide carbon emissions alone.
- *Eliminate screen savers.* Modern monitors don't need them and they use as much energy as keeping your computer fully running. Better to power off your monitor when you aren't using it.
- *Use smart power strips to tackle energy "vampires."* Devices like the "EcoStrip 2.0" have automatic sensors that stop drawing power when devices are off.
- *Encourage Voluntary Adoption of Power Management.* IBM has established a function within its software update and patch process to identify workstations which have not implemented power management and offer employees a one-click power management implementation.

- *Install a centralized power management system.* For example, Faronics Power Save automatically gets computers to sleep, hibernate, or shut down depending on the detected amount of Central Processing Unit (CPU), application, and keyboard and mouse activity. Faronics Power Save enabled Chaffey Joint Union High School District in San Ramon, California to save $350,000 a year on IT energy costs.[8]

- *Switch to a low-ink font.* The University of Wisconsin-Green Bay switched to Century Gothic as its default font for emails and printed documents, which they estimate will save them up to $10,000 a year in toner costs. Century Gothic uses less ink than Times New Roman and 30 percent less ink than Arial. Microsoft switched its default Outlook and Word screen fonts from Arial and Times New Roman to Calibri and Cambria. They reasoned that these fonts are easier to read on screen, which means that readers will be less likely to print what they see.[9]

Everyone in the company should be asked to do his or her bit. Make it a practice to review drafts of documents and emails onscreen rather than printing them, turn off printers and other peripherals when not in use, print double-sided, and use shared network printers whenever possible.

2010 GUIDE TO GREENER ELECTRONICS

Greenpeace publishes a regularly updated environmental performance scorecard on the major electronics makers, including all of the major PC and laptop manufacturers, called "Guide to Greener Electronics." Its 2010 ranking from best to worst includes:

1. Nokia	8. Acer
2. Sony Eriksson	9. LGE, Samsung
3. Phillips	10. Toshiba
4. Motorola	11. Fujitsu
5. Apple, Panasonic, HP, Sony	12. Microsoft
6. Sharp	13. Lenovo
7. Dell	14. Nintendo

Source: Reprinted with permission.

---

5. Streamline and Upgrade IT Equipment

First and foremost, get rid of underperforming assets and unnecessary personal devices. Next, consider replacing old inefficient equipment with new high-efficiency equipment that will deliver payback and ROI in energy savings over its lifespan.

Anyone managing the procurement process should buy energy-saving certified equipment, including monitors, printers, scanners, and other peripherals. Energy Star–certified electronics really do cut down on energy usage, reduce your carbon footprint, and lower your energy costs. In fact, if all the computers sold in the United States met Energy Star standards, we could cut electricity bills by $1.5 billion per year and reduce greenhouse gas (GHG) emissions by the equivalent of taking 2 million cars off the road.[10]

If your company still uses bulky old cathode ray tube (CRT) monitors, switch to flat-screen LCD monitors that reduce electricity consumed by about 60 percent—especially super-efficient ones with LED backlighting.[11] Consider switching from desktop computers to laptop computers. In a migration of 1,200 users from desktops to laptops in a financial firm in London, the firm was able to show per-user IT energy savings of 90 percent, simply by moving from always-on PCs (for overnight patching, etc.) to energy-efficient, modern, high-performance laptops used just when the business users needed them. One IT executive we heard from in a different firm mentioned that his company holds "Laptop Tune Up Days." Employees bring in laptops for performance enhancements such as disk reimaging, or swapping out and replacing faulty keyboards. These events prolong laptop lives by six to nine months, saving the company money and reducing e-waste.

Evaluate your electronic purchases with the following criteria:[12]

- *How energy efficient is the equipment?* Look for energy-efficient certifications, such as the U.S. EPA's Energy Star label. Newer software has better energy management than older versions. For example, Microsoft's Windows 7 operating system handles idle time and computer device management much more efficiently than preceding Windows operating systems. It also optimizes application processing and allows for remote power optimization by network administrators.

- *What is the vendor/manufacturer's policy regarding toxic substances?* Computers contain toxic substances such as arsenic, brominated flame retardants, polyvinyl chloride, and phthalates. European countries have been enacting regulations to phase out the use of these toxics in electronics, but many companies still use them. You can find out about a product's toxic or chemical materials by looking up specifications on company websites or by looking at Greenpeace's "Guide to Greener Electronics," which rates electronic brands by environmental performance on toxics, recycling, and energy efficiency.

- *Is the equipment designed with recycling or remanufacturing in mind?* Xerox, for instance, has been a pioneer in designing products with reuse in mind, using fewer parts and facilitating disassembly. The company also makes it easy for customers to return spent equipment and toner for reuse and recycling.

- *What are the vendor/manufacturer's take-back and recycling policies?* European Union regulations require electronics companies to take back their products from consumers at the end of the product's useful life. In the United States many computer manufacturers have implemented voluntary take-back policies. Some companies take this product stewardship responsibility more seriously than others. So pay attention to companies that make it easy to return the old equipment and those that do not.

6. Manage E-Waste

E-waste (or electronic waste) is a global problem. Businesses are facing mounting social and regulatory pressure to deal with the heavy metals and toxics in this waste stream. An e-waste recycling law passed in Wisconsin requires manufacturers to recycle 80 percent of the electronics they sell, while New York law now requires that manufacturers take back consumers' used electronics for recycling.[13] According to the U.S. EPA, in 2007 Americans alone produced over 3.1 million tons of e-waste, of which only 13.6 percent got recycled.[14] The rest ended up in landfills. Market research firm TechNavio estimates that 53 million tons of e-waste will be generated by 2012, with about 60 percent containing environmentally dangerous heavy metals such as cadmium, lead, and mercury.[15]

Here are some ways to start reducing your company's e-waste—and potentially save some money in the process:

- *Cash in your old computers.* Companies that "refresh" their computers regularly (every three to four years) will often be able to sell the machines they are retiring to a computer refurbisher. Be sure to use a reputable company. For example, Texas-based TechTurn not only pays for the opportunity to collect laptops and other electronic equipment, but will wipe clean the hard drive, certify that resold machines will be loaded with properly licensed software, and guarantee that any equipment that can't be refurbished will be properly recycled.[16]

- *Donate usable old equipment.* If an old computer is still functional consider donating it to a local school or nonprofit organization. Make sure that all data is fully erased and operating systems are reset to factory settings. For example, Seventh Generation, maker of green household and personal care products, gives its old IT equipment to Vermont Business Materials Exchange, a web-based marketplace that takes reusable items from businesses, municipalities, and nonprofit organizations and makes them available to the general public. Citigroup leverages its clout with software vendors so that software licenses transfer along with the equipment being donated.[17]

- *Recycle or dispose of used electronic devices with manufacturers.* Some computer manufacturers—Apple, Dell, HP, Lenovo, to name a few—will accept used equipment from original buyers. And 20 U.S. states now have e-recycling laws. Minnesota, for instance, requires manufacturers to recycle 60 percent of their nationwide sales from the previous year. Oregon, Washington, and Rhode Island require manufacturers to provide convenient drop-offs in every county. Through a partnership with Goodwill, and a well-publicized recycling campaign, Dell recovered nearly 85 percent of all computers (not just those manufactured by Dell) sold in Texas.[18]

- *Consider buying or leasing refurbished equipment.* Using refurbished equipment can often meet your company's needs at a lower cost than buying new equipment straight from the manufacturer. Better yet, by using refurbished equipment you save it from going into landfills and delay the consumption of resources required to produce new equipment. See, for example, the wide range of rebuilt technology options at TechTurn's online store: www.techturn.com.

- *Exercise proper product stewardship.* Ensure that the company or organization that receives your used equipment commits to recycle or dispose of it in a responsible manner when they "retire" the asset. This attention to proper environmental stewardship reflects not just good corporate citizenship, but also avoids the exposure that might arise if the entity receiving the equipment mishandles its disposal. Remember that in our litigious world, there is no "passing the buck."

INTERMEDIATE PLAYS: TACKLE BIG COSTS AND FIND BIG SAVINGS

Up to this point, we've presented easy-to-implement plays with relatively short payback times. Most of our action items center on behavioral changes that make computing by individual employees more energy efficient. We turn now to enterprise-wide green IT efforts, which have the potential to generate bigger cost savings and environmental footprint reductions. But they take a bit more effort and investment.

7. Use Videoconferencing and Other Cutting-Edge Technologies to Reduce Corporate Travel

For many companies, especially service businesses, corporate travel represents a significant source of greenhouse gas emissions. Motorola, for example, estimated that emissions caused by business travel represented 20 percent (almost 115,000 tons of carbon dioxide equivalents) of its total 2009 carbon footprint.[19] While some travel is unavoidable, not every trip is truly necessary. Cutting unnecessary trips saves money and reduces your corporate environmental footprint. Consider the following opportunities for emissions and travel cost savings:

- *Use videoconferencing technology.* A growing number of free and low-cost videoconferencing solutions are available to businesses of any size—from well-established offerings like Cisco's WebEx to newer options including Megameeting, Skype Group Chat, and Paltalk, which allows free video chats for up to 10 people. In addition, advanced options such as HP Halo telepresence and videoconferencing produce high-end results that simulate in-person meetings. And mid-range, portable options are on the rise. The costs for advanced videoconferencing solutions continue to decline, and the payback can be fast. We've seen estimates that effective use of videoconferencing could reduce travel-related costs by up to 75 percent.[20] Researchers from the Aberdeen Group found that employers using videoconferencing technology reduced corporate travel by 24 percent.[21] A Verdantix and Carbon Disclosure Project study, "The Telepresence Revolution," found that the equipment will pay for itself in 15 months or less by reducing travel costs. Of course, the associated emissions go down as well. In fact, the study estimates that if all U.S. and UK companies with over $1 billion in revenue adopted videoconference technology, they could achieve a total of $19 billion in financial benefits by 2020.[22]

- *Use collaboration and shared productivity applications.* Companies such as Google (Google Docs), Dropbox, PBworks, EditMe, and Microsoft (certain features in Office) offer applications that allow employees to easily share computer-based documents and other information without sending physical copies or requiring people to work in close physical proximity.

- *Increase remote access to important enterprise-wide applications for telecommuters.* Make full use of today's technology to access documents, networks, and communication tools remotely to enable telecommuting. Authors Kate Lister and Tom Harnish estimate that if all U.S. employees eligible to telecommute worked half of their time from home, it would reduce annual emissions of carbon dioxide from commuting by nearly 53 million metric tons—equivalent to taking over 9.6 million cars off the road.[23] They also report that IBM's telecommuting program saved the company $50 million in real estate costs. In addition, flexible work schedules such as working four days a week, 10 hours a day, saves travel time and carbon emissions.[24] Web conferencing tools are used widely across IBM, further reducing travel, with over 140,000 meetings (2,700 per week), 953,000 participants (average 7 participants per meeting), and 74 million connect minutes during 2009.[25]

8. Green Your Data Center

Data centers consume an enormous amount of energy. According to the U.S. Environmental Protection Agency and Department of Energy, data centers represent about 1.5 percent of all energy use in the United States—a figure that will most likely double over the next five years.[26] Smarter IT offers a huge potential to reduce energy spending and emissions. Here are a few tips on where to start:

- *Metrics: Understand what you're looking for.* Most servers operate much less than they could. Dr. Jonathan Koomey, an expert on green IT, told us that most servers only operate at 5 to 15 percent of their maximum load. In addition, it takes a great deal of energy to cool servers. When looking for inefficiencies, your first step is to measure the electricity draw of your servers. There are lots of ways to gauge data center energy efficiency. The box that follows spells out two commonly used metrics.

- *Employ server virtualization technology.* Most companies try to maintain enough server capacity to handle large, unexpected spikes in usage. This practice often results in lower *average* server utilization. The Alliance to Save Energy and tech firm 1E estimate that companies waste $24.8 billion every year simply by operating unused servers.[27] Virtualization technology allows companies to run multiple different server "instances" on a single machine—creating the capacity of multiple servers without maintaining a correspondingly large number of actual servers. Virtual servers can be shifted relatively easily from machine to machine, depending on IT needs. This flexibility allows consolidation of physical servers and energy savings. The savings from virtualization can be significant. According to a Forrester Research report commissioned by virtualization software provider VMware, companies utilizing virtualization software find they can consolidate as many as 10 physical servers into one and improve server utilization by as much as 85 percent.[28]

DATA CENTER ENERGY METRICS

Power Usage Effectiveness (PUE) provides a basic measure of data center energy efficiency using a simple ratio: Total Facility Power/Total IT Equipment Power. The goal is to achieve a ratio of 1.0—the point at which total power consumed by data center operations exactly equals or is less than the total power consumed by the servers in the data center. Or simply put, the data center does not consume any additional energy for cooling, lighting, or other components. Petroleum Geo-Services' (PGS) data center in Weybridge, UK, has achieved a PUE of 1.17, and Google boasts a PUE of 1.2 compared to typical data centers that routinely maintain PUE ratios greater than 2.0.[29] PGS's data center reduced power consumption by 6.7 million kilowatt hours and saved approximately $957,000 in the first year of operation.[30]

In some cases, companies can achieve PUE below 1.0. Industry experts now contend that if you use waste heat generated by the servers, it can offset electricity used by other equipment in the data center. Equally, if you offset your load with onsite renewable generation such as solar or geothermal heat pumps, then you could also approach or beat a 1.0 PUE.

Corporate Average Data Center Efficiency (CADE), developed by the Uptime Institute and McKinsey, multiplies the PUE by the amount of time servers actually perform computing operations.[31] CADE tells you not only whether your data center is being run efficiently, but also whether or not you need all of the servers you're running. If you score well on the part of CADE related to PUE but still receive a low overall CADE score, chances are you're operating too many servers at low utilization—which leads to unnecessary energy expenditures and unnecessary carbon emissions.

- *Optimize storage capacity.* The problem with electronic storage space is similar to the problem with excess servers; normal utilization rates are often extremely low, resulting in an excess of power-hungry hardware. Forrester Research estimates that the amount of storage capacity actually utilized hovers at about 40 percent.[32] Moreover, in many companies, data storage is extremely redundant, meaning that many more copies of documents than necessary are stored.[33] Solutions to this problem, known as storage virtualization, thin provisioning, and data deduplicating technologies, allow IT managers to reserve storage space only as needed and to delete redundant files automatically. Such storage optimization efforts translate into reduced hardware, lower electricity consumption, and a smaller overall company environmental footprint.

- *Use efficient power supplies and servers.* Switching from 110V AC to 220 V AC or switching to 48V DC power supplies reduces losses from electricity conversion. Newer servers often have higher-efficiency processors with better cooling systems and more efficient power supplies. Therefore, it is worthwhile to invest in new servers every few years. Intel refreshes its server environment every four years in order to improve energy efficiency.[34]

- *Improve data center cooling.* Cooling a data center can consume as much energy as it takes to power the server itself. An analyst from market research firm IDC noted that "ten years ago, around 17 cents out of every dollar spent on a new server went to power and cooling. Today, that's up to 48 cents, and if things don't change, that number will eventually grow to 78 cents."[35] You can employ a number of strategies to enhance data center cooling and avoid the need to install more power-hungry air-conditioners:[36]

  - Design your data center to improve natural air flow between server racks.

  - Install containment solutions to improve isolation of colder supply air from warmer return air. This reduces the Computer Room Air Conditioner (CRAC) unit power consumption quite dramatically if well implemented.

  - Raise thermostats in data center "cold aisles" from the older 68 to 72 degrees Fahrenheit (20 to 22 degrees Celsius) to 77 to 80 degrees Fahrenheit (25 to 27 degrees Celsius), which may also permit the water coils (if used) to run at a higher temperature. Note that this has to be done carefully, with a view to the reduced temperature safety margin in case of cooling failure, but if planned correctly, can usually be achieved in most data centers.

  - Swap the old "on or off" fan motors in CRAC units with modern energy-conserving motors, ideally with temperature-sensor feedback loops.

  - Widen the humidity bands to minimize unnecessary humidification and de-humidification. For example—most modern equipment today will permit a 20 percent to 80 percent Relative Humidity ratio, so you may wish to consider 30 to 70 percent or 25 to 75 percent limits for your data center, depending of course on what your equipment vendors recommend.

  - Use a water economizer to bypass or partly bypass the main chillers if the outside air conditions are cool enough.

  - Optimize the fans that bring fresh air into the facility so that they can serve double duty to provide cooling when the outside air temperature and humidity are appropriate.

  - Install an air economizer, which will cycle outside air through the data center instead of cooling and recirculating the same air.

HP's Wynyard data center in Newcastle, UK, channels cold North Sea winds to cool the data center, resulting in 40 percent reduction in energy costs. The data center also collects rainwater from the roof and uses it for dehumidification.[37] Yahoo!'s green data center in upstate New York has also cut average costs by 40 percent by relying almost exclusively on outdoor air for cooling: The center's innovative "Chicken Coop" design depends on long, narrow building that facilitates air circulation.[38]

IBM has taken to using a liquid-cooling system to reduce energy at its data centers. A network of conduits attached to the back of processors and connected to pipes on the rack circulates water through the data center. The heat from the computers is transferred directly into the water coils, instead of being blown out as hot air. The warmer water can then be passed through heat exchangers to allow the heat to be used for other purposes (e.g., warming office space), or to feed directly to the central cooling systems. Compared with air-cooled servers, IBM estimates that its liquid-cooled system reduces energy use by 40 percent and lowers the carbon footprint by an estimated 85 percent.[39]

- *Plan for green when building new data center facilities.* Building a new, green data center facility requires a careful consideration of trade-offs. On one hand, you want to build a data center that can accommodate future growth, but you don't want to build a cavernous facility that requires enormous amounts of energy and may not be fully utilized for 10 years. Some companies we've heard from build modular data centers, some using shipping containers. This allows for piece-by-piece construction of data centers, accommodates present needs, but also allows for future growth. Some companies, especially ones that have been hard-hit by natural disasters, such as Hurricane Katrina, have even contemplated building mobile data centers that can be moved out of harm's way.

GREEN DATA CENTER ROI CASE STUDY

Verizon Communications Inc. operates more than 200 data centers in 23 countries. In 2008, the company participated in an energy assessment, conducted by the U.S. Department of Energy (DOE) Industrial Technologies Program, to examine the energy performance of one of its data centers. The assessment helped Verizon implement several energy saving changes. They:

- Raised chiller water set point from 42°F to 48°F to save chiller energy.
- Repaired water-side economizer to reduce the chilled water plant power consumption.
- Shifted the data center temperature set point to a range of 68°F to 78°F.
- Broadened humidity set point to result in more efficient cooling coil and chilled water system operation.
- Shut down three computer room air handling units because they could still provide sufficient cooling without them.
- Installed lighting controls to reduce power use in rooms with no occupants (which happens most of the time).
- Reduced engine generator heater temperature set point to 80°F (from 140°F).

The total cost for all measures added to $235,000 but generated savings of 1,540,700 kilowatt hours and $181,500 per year. The total payback time was 1.3 years.

Source: U.S. Department of Energy, "Energy Efficiency and Renewable Energy," *DOE Assessment Identifies 30 percent Energy Savings for Broadband and Wireless Communication Company,* www.eere.energy.gov/industry/saveenergynow.

Where you locate your data center can also have huge implications for your company's carbon footprint and your electric bill. Locating a data center in Washington state, where heating and cooling requirements are minimized and where the majority of electricity comes from hydropower, is much less carbon intensive than operating a data center in Kentucky, where most of the electricity is produced from coal. Other companies consider generating their own electricity at their data centers. Consulting giant KPMG runs a micro combined heat and power (CHP) turbine at its data center, taking care of both its electricity and cooling (the heat is used to operate chilling towers), lowering its purchasing costs, and running its turbines more cleanly than the local power company.

To encourage companies to improve their data centers, EPA launched an Energy Star label for top-performing stand-alone data centers in June 2010. In order to earn the label, data centers must be in the top 25 percent of their peers in energy efficiency measured by power usage effectiveness. The EPA claims that improving the energy efficiency of U.S. data centers by just 10 percent would save more than 6 billion kilowatt hours annually, enough to power more than 350,000 homes, while saving more than $450 million every year.[40]

9. Embrace Cloud Computing

Cloud computing, which puts computing services on the Internet, offers another eco-efficiency opportunity. While the concept of "cloud computing" covers many ideas and applications, the potential for efficiency gains comes from moving IT systems out of the office onto shared computing infrastructure in cyberspace.[41] This shift in the locus of computing power offers benefits similar to server and storage virtualization. In particular, it reduces the dependence on physical IT equipment, which translates into lower energy consumption, reduced costs, and a smaller environmental footprint. A 2010 study by Microsoft and Accenture argued that large organizations could cut 30–90% of their energy consumption and carbon emissions by using cloud computing.[42] Consider the following strategies:

- *Deploy software as a service.* Software as a Service (SaaS) allows computer users to use software, whether word processing applications or complex enterprise-level applications, on demand over the Internet. In a report prepared by cloud computing software vendor NetSuite and GreenSpace, analysts estimated that each adopter of NetSuite's enterprise-level cloud software applications saved, on average, $10,300 per year in avoided server operations costs and prevented 7.55 metric tons of carbon dioxide per year from entering the atmosphere.[43]

- *Deploy data centers and storage as a service.* Not every company needs to operate its own data center. "Renting" server time eliminates the need for physical data centers and storage, lowering cost burdens and in many cases improving reliability and uptime. It takes advantage of the provider's scale and efficiency. A company utilizing these services must do a considerable amount of due diligence, however, and not just to ensure the fairest price. Make sure that any provider maintains high privacy standards, can always provide you with copies of data you own (and takes exceptional measures to protect it), guarantees performance and uptime, and shares appropriate environmental metrics. To be very clear, outsourcing is *not* a way to dodge environmental burdens. Even if your company uses an outside data center operation, it doesn't mean that you can ignore the environmental impacts, costs, and benefits of these vendor services. Unfortunately, as we learned from a leading services company that outsources its extensive data center operations, many data center providers have yet to develop effective methods of metering their individual clients' energy use (and by extension, carbon footprint). As service providers become more sophisticated, they are certain to overcome this reporting limitation.

ADVANCED PLAYS: USE INFORMATION TECHNOLOGY TO DRIVE ECO-ADVANTAGE

The basic and intermediate green IT plays we've covered to this point have focused on reducing costs and impacts from IT equipment and its use. The advanced plays below focus on the enormous opportunity of IT as a solutions driver at every level of the enterprise: to optimize end-to-end business processes, drive greater eco-efficiencies and resource productivity, and spur sustainability innovation that leads to new growth and revenue potential. The territory remains largely uncharted and ripe for exploration.

10. Deploy IT to Improve Your Company's Eco-Strategy and Performance

As companies advance towards greater Eco-Advantage, their information needs multiply. Advanced companies, for instance, find it useful to:

- Perform complex, real-time analytics to further optimize the efficient use of energy, water, and other resources.
- Eliminate the manual compilation of environmental data from multiple spreadsheets.
- Put complex sustainability data into easy-to-use, practical tools—such as "dashboards" or customized reports that help employees track performance and spot opportunities for improved efficiency.
- Streamline the process of responding to external demands for data, disclosure, and reporting—both for voluntary efforts such as the Carbon Disclosure Project (CDP) and the Global Reporting Initiative (GRI), as well as government-mandated efforts such as the permitting program and new greenhouse gas emissions reporting rules from U.S. EPA's National Pollution Discharge Elimination System (NPDES).

EXAMPLES OF GREEN IT 2.0 PLAYS

- **UPS uses GPS technology to plan routes, reduce fuel use, and cut carbon dioxide emissions.** UPS' IT-enabled Package Flow system tracks packages as they're loaded onto trucks and plans delivery routes to avoid heavy traffic and minimize left turns. In 2008, the company said that Package Flow allowed it to cut fuel use by 3 million gallons, reducing its carbon dioxide emissions by 32,000 tons.[44]

- **Metro Cash & Carry's Star Farm provides a data exchange for suppliers and customers.** German grocer Star Farm asks suppliers to enter information about their products into a database that customers can access using either in-store bar code readers/terminals or a web site. Star Farm then data mines customer queries to get a better sense of what customers value in the products it offers.[45]

- **Moore Recycling Associates manages a business-to-business plastics exchange.** Moore, a California-based recycling consulting company, established a web site in 2000 to facilitate connections between buyers and sellers of plastic scrap.[46]

- **Nike uses IT to help designers build environmentally friendly shoes.** Nike created a system called the Considered Index, based on a software application that provides its designers with weighted scores based on environmental criteria for each type of material used in the shoe manufacturing process. The system has helped drive product innovations, reduce toxic liabilities and risks, mobilize employees, and generate useful environmental data for marketing.[47]

- **Seventh Generation integrates environmental data into its ERP system.** The green consumer products leader uses this data to create greener products using attributes such as ingredient sources and the recyclability of packaging components.[48]

- **Sun World uses IBM analytics technology for energy efficient harvesting.** By switching from manual to automated tracking processes the company has reduced per unit water use by almost 9 percent and equipment fuel consumption by 20 percent.

The ever-growing needs of businesses in this realm are inspiring a wealth of innovative IT solutions, which Forrester Research analyst Doug Washburn has labeled "Green IT 2.0"—the innovative use of IT to advance environmental problem-solving across the enterprise and value chain, not just within the IT department.[49] For instance, Tesco—one of the largest retailers in the world—uses CA Technologies' EcoSoftware to help analyze its sustainability performance. Previously, Tesco had collected sustainability data from thousands of locations around the world on spreadsheets that it would pass around by email, which made it difficult to ensure the quality, accuracy, and security of the data. CA Ecosoftware enabled Tesco to collect data accurately and securely in a centralized system. The interactive software prompts users on how to input data and can be used in different languages. Simon Palinkas of Tesco's ITGroup says that gathering data is now quicker and there are fewer issues.[50] Coca-Cola, Intuit, News Corp., and Safeway use Hara's environmental and energy management software to identify cost-saving carbon reduction opportunities.[51] Countless other enterprise software examples exist, with new products constantly being released.

11. Use IT to Engage Customers on Sustainability

In the age of social networking and connectivity, companies are using IT in innovative ways to engage customers and improve their environmental performance. According to data from Anderson Analytics, an estimated 110 million Americans, more than a third of the population, regularly use online social networks.[52] Engaging customers through social media can help companies highlight their sustainability efforts and build customer loyalty. Celestial Seasonings, a U.S. tea company, is using Facebook to engage customers in its "PossibiliTEAS" campaign. For every user that answers a few thought-provoking questions on Facebook, the answers of which align with one of nine symbolic Asian characters found on boxes of Celestial Seasoning's new green tea, Celestial Seasonings will donate $1, up to $50,000, to Conservation International's "Protect an Acre" campaign. When participants enlist the support of 14 of their friends on Facebook they can protect one acre of tropical forest.[53]

Travelocity, the online travel booking company, has created a fan page on Facebook where it offers to offset any fan's holiday travel for free. Its Facebook friends can also search for "green" hotels and volunteer opportunities though Travelocity's green directory.[54] Whole Foods uses Twitter to conduct cheap promotions. Followers of Whole Foods on Twitter can enter a contest for a chance to win a $50 gift card.[55] As David Raycroft, vice president of product strategy at Milyoni, says, "if you are not engaging in these member communities, you've already lost control of the conversation."[56]

12. Seize Revenue Opportunities by Tapping into Demand for IT Sustainability Solutions

IT has the potential to transform how we do business in entire industries. The most ambitious business leaders see the revenue potential of IT as a sustainability solutions driver—not just for their own businesses, but for other companies, cities, regions, and even countries.

We have already seen a revolution in farming, for instance, by putting computers and GPS systems on board tractors. Ramped-up IT allows for greater precision in the application of fertilizers, pesticides, and irrigation. "Digital farming" produces efficiencies that reduce chemical use, and thus pollution runoff, leading to lower costs as well as better environmental results. Technology also exists to use artificial intelligence, GPS coordinates, and soil-specific data to enable farmers to optimize crop choice, nutrients, water, and pesticides—reducing inputs and lowering costs.[57]

But that is just the tip of the iceberg when considering the potential for IT to solve sustainability challenges. Computing and consulting giant IBM is seizing the opportunity with a far-reaching plan, called "Smarter Planet," to combine its IT expertise with environmental initiatives and create what it calls "smart ecosystems."[58] The company aims to bring networks of sensors, communication lines and devices, and computing power to environmental services, resulting in system efficiencies (and cost savings), environmental benefits, and community engagement. Its efforts in traffic management, called "smart traffic," focus on reducing congestion to save time, fuel, and money while simultaneously reducing carbon dioxide emissions and smog. In collaboration with the Swedish Royal Institute of Technology, the company built a comprehensive system of networked traffic sensors, fed the collected data into its servers and analytics software, and used the results to better direct traffic, particularly during rush hours. As a result, the city of Stockholm was able to reduce total traffic flow by 20 percent, average travel times by nearly 50 percent, and carbon dioxide emissions by 10 percent.[59] IBM plans to extend its network by connecting with the GPS systems of the city's 15,000 taxicabs, building weather and pollution sensors, and connecting with delivery trucks. It then will analyze the data and make it directly available to Stockholm residents so they can better plan travel around the city.

The opportunities in this sphere are as limitless as one's imagination. Advanced companies will anticipate customer and societal needs based on sustainability trends and pursue IT hardware and software innovations to meet them.

SUMMARY

Key Plays

1. Do a basic IT audit and assessment.
2. Hunt for glaring inefficiencies using a green lens.
3. Foster collaboration between IT and facilities managers.
4. Change employee computer and peripheral use behavior.
5. Streamline and upgrade IT equipment.
6. Manage e-waste.
7. Use videoconferencing and other cutting-edge technologies to reduce corporate travel.
8. Green your data center.
9. Embrace cloud computing.
10. Deploy IT to enhance your company's eco-performance.
11. Engage customers.
12. Seize revenue opportunities by tapping into demand for IT sustainability solutions.

ADDITIONAL RESOURCES

GENERAL/GREEN IT STRATEGY DEVELOPMENT

The Greening of IT: How Companies Can Make a Difference for the Environment by John Lamb (IBM Press/Pearson, 2009). Covers benefits and roadblocks of moving to greener IT, with step-by-step guidance and case studies on measuring energy usage and optimizing data center cooling equipment, leveraging virtualization, and more.

Network World/Computerworld 2010 List of Top 12 Green IT Products www.networkworld.com

ASSESSMENT AND BENCHMARKING

Green IT Assessment and ROI Calculator (Aberdeen/IBM). Helps users conduct a rapid analysis of a company's current green IT performance against best-in-class practices, then provides an actionable road map with estimated ROI for recommended investments. http://greenit.aberdeen.com

Green Maturity Assessment Tool (Accenture). 15-minute diagnostic tool to evaluate a company's green IT performance. www.accenture.com

ComputerWorld List of "The Top Green-IT Organizations www.computerworld.com

Uptime Institute "Global Green 100 for Corporate Leadership in IT Energy Efficiency" http://uptimeinstitute.org

ELECTRONICS AND COMPUTER POWER MANAGEMENT

PC Energy Savings and Power Management Tool List (Climate Savers Computing) Guide to free applications including energy savings calculators and power management tools. www.climatesaverscomputing.org

The Green Electronics Council's EPAT (Electronic Product Environmental Assessment Tool) Criteria, Registry and Rankings. Helps purchasers evaluate, compare, and select electronics based on environmental attributes. www.epeat.net

ENERGY STAR Computer Power Management Savings Spreadsheet (EPA). Estimates typical savings from ENERGY STAR qualified computers and/or power management features. www.energystar.gov

ENERGY STAR Savings Calculator for Computers (EPA). Estimates life cycle costs for ENERGY STAR qualified desktops/side computers. www.energystar.gov

ENERGY STAR Savings Calculator for Displays (EPA). Estimates the life cycle costs for ENERGY STAR qualified monitors. www.energystar.gov

TELECOMMUTING AND TELEPRESENCE

Green Commuting/Telecommuting (Business.gov). U.S. government guide on how companies can encourage greener commuting options and take advantage of government incentives and programs. www.business.gov

National Business Travel Association Corporate Social Responsibility Toolkit. 2010 Toolkit update includes guides on Responsible Groups and Meetings and Technology Solutions. www.nbta.org

"Select and Deploy a Videoconferencing Solution" (InfoTech Research Group). PPT deck that helps IT leaders to evaluate the strengths and weaknesses of leading videoconferencing vendors relative to specific business requirements. www.infotech.com

Cisco TelePresence Calculator. Shows both greenhouse gas emissions avoided and how quickly an investment in a telepresence system will pay off. www.cisco.com

E-WASTE

eCycling (EPA). Resources for electronics recycling. www.epa.gov

ecyclingtools.com. Outlines cost-saving and other benefits of electronics recycling. www.ecyclingtools.com

Responsible Recycling Practices for Electronics Recyclers (R2) (EPA). Outlines responsible recycling ("R2") practices for use in accredited certification programs that assess electronics recyclers' environmental, health and safety, and security practices. www.epa.gov/waste

Northeast Recycling Council's Environmental Benefits Calculator. Estimates environmental benefits of office waste recycling (including computers) and reuse. www.nerc.org

WEEE Forum. Association of e-waste collection and recovery systems for cooperation and exchange of best practice. www.weee-forum.org

GREENING THE DATA CENTER

Checklist: 12 Steps to a Greener Data Center (IT Management.com). Six-page introductory guide to greening data centers. www.itmanagement.com

The Green Data Center: Steps for the Journey (IBM). Outlines recommendations to help organizations move quickly to an optimized green data center with sustainability designed into both the IT and facilities infrastructures. www.ibm.com

Climate Corps Handbook: Energy Efficiency Investment Opportunities in Office Buildings and Data Centers (Environmental Defense Fund). A practical guide to help users identify and prioritize cost-effective investments in commercial office buildings that save energy and cut GHG emissions. www.edf.org

ENERGY STAR Program for Data Centers (EPA). Guidance for establishing an energy management program, benchmarking data center performance, along with ENERGY STAR data center product specifications. www.energystar.gov

Saving Energy in Data Centers (DOE). Tools and resources to help data center owners and operators benchmark data energy use, identify opportunities to reduce energy, and adopt energy efficient practices with best-in-class case studies. www.eere.energy.gov

DC Pro Online Diagnostic Tool (DOE). Profiling Tool and System Assessment Tools to perform energy assessments on specific aspects of a data center. www.eere.energy.gov

"The Shortcut Guide to Data Center Efficiency" by David Chernicoff (Real-time Publishers, 2010). Insight on building a data center infrastructure that optimizes efficiency and cuts operating costs. www.realtimepublishers.com

Data Center Efficiency Calculator (42U). Estimates short and long-term savings that can be achieved through energy efficiency enhancements. www.42u.com

Free Cooling Tools for North America and Europe (The Green Grid). Estimates potential savings from utilizing "free-air cooling." www.thegreengrid.org

Chapter 11 Product Design

"Design a better mousetrap, and the world will beat a path to your door," suggests one of the oldest known business maxims. And it is true: Design innovation has long been a key to marketplace success. In the era of the sustainability megatrend, new lines of design opportunity have emerged.

An up-and-coming Vermont-based compounds and coatings company, Sto Corp, offers a good example of this potential. Across Asian cultures, the lotus is a symbol of purity because of its ability to remain clean while growing in a dirty environment. Tiny peaks and valleys on the surface of the lotus leaf cause water to pearl and roll off the leaves carrying dirt with it. Sto Corp has managed to replicate the surface microstructure of the lotus leaf in paint. Buildings coated with Lotusan paint, the Sto Corp product inspired by nature, never have to be washed. Rainwater removes any dirt and grime. Lotusan also protects buildings from fungus and algae that thrive in dirty moist conditions better than conventional paints.[1] As a water-based product with low VOCs, it represents a superior product from the perspective of human health—and the environment as well.

Research shows that a product's eco-footprint—natural resources consumed; pollution, including carbon emissions, energy, and water use; and waste—is largely fixed during the design process.[2] By factoring in sustainability considerations up front, through a structured Design for the Environment process (sometimes abbreviated "DfE"), companies can realize cost savings, efficiencies, and environmental benefits that accrue throughout a product's life cycle. For many companies, the potential cost savings in production have motivated a DfE push. But the real DfE gains come from driving revenue growth and profits through greener products and services that solve a customer's environmental problems. But remember, when building in environmental attributes, you must do it with an eye on customer value. Improving environmental performance at the price of reduced quality or higher costs rarely works.

GREEN BY DESIGN

- **Procter & Gamble** plans at least $50 billion in cumulative sales of "sustainable innovation products" by 2012.[3]
- **DuPont** expects an additional $6 billion in annual revenues by 2015 through product innovation based on sustainability.[4]
- **Clorox**'s Green Works line of plant-based cleaning materials, launched in early 2008, captured 42 percent of the natural cleaning products market in its first year.[5]
- **GE** earns more than $18 billion a year from its "ecomagination" product lines each of which contributes to solving global sustainability challenges.[6]
- **Chemical suppliers** experienced 30 percent revenue growth per year from 2006–2008 by helping customers manage chemicals over life cycles and reduce chemical use and waste.[7] The global market for chemical management services will most likely triple in the next 5 to 10 years.
- **Mitsubishi** expects $13.3 billion in annual sales by 2016 from clean technologies, including solar systems, heat pumps, and other energy efficient power devices.[8] **Philips'** expects its "Green Products" to represent at least 30 percent of its overall sales by 2012.[9]
- **Green toy sales** will probably exceed $1 billion, or 5 percent of toy sales, by 2015.[10]
- **Sprint** is saving about $2.1 million a year through greener packaging for its entire wireless accessory line introduced in 2009.[11]

This chapter will help you:

- Analyze the environmental impact of your current products and services.
- Redesign existing products and services to minimize environmental impacts (without harming the bottom line).
- Better meet customer needs and grow revenues.

BASIC PLAYS: BUILD CAPACITY INTO DESIGN FOR THE ENVIRONMENT

There are many possible paths to success in developing greener products and services. In the case of Interface, a leading carpet manufacturer, founder Ray Anderson announced a stunning goal—for the company to be "zero-impact" by 2020.[12] Anderson's sustainability-driven vision galvanized the entire organization and led to breakthrough products such as recycled (and recyclable) Interface FLOR modular carpet tiles.

Others look for design breakthroughs on a more modest scale. Nike, for instance, focused for years on a series of small sustainability projects before setting bold goals and "selling" the environmental attributes of their products. Terracycle co-founder Tom Szaky built his company around a single green product idea (plant food made by worms sold in used plastic bottles) that ended up inspiring a multimillion dollar (and growing) business with an ever-expanding number of product lines made from waste.[13]

Our research suggests that eco-pioneering companies have certain traits in common: (1) a corporate *culture* that makes sustainability a core value, and (2) a capacity for innovation as well as systemic thinking. In their 2008 research report, "Aligned for Sustainable Design," the design firm IDEO and Business for Social Responsibility (BSR), building upon previous work that IDEO had done with The Natural Step, argue that building an organization's capacity for eco-design—its "sustainable design intelligence"—offers the key to long-term success.[14] This intelligence requires evolving thinking, a focus on continuous improvement, and a commitment to innovation. In addition, because of the complexities and interconnections involved in meeting sustainability challenges, companies need to work across traditional silos. That calls for management structures, analytic frameworks, information systems, and reward structures that foster cross-cutting thinking and reward collaboration.

1. Work Across Issues, Functions, and Traditional Divisions

A successful DfE requires a cross-functional team that draws on the knowledge and experience of people in the operations *and* customer-facing sides of the business. Make sure you have technical experts, creative thinkers who relish the opportunity to solve design problems, marketing and branding professionals who are deeply familiar with market trends, and supply chain professionals who know the ins and outs of sourcing and logistics. As green business expert Gil Friend puts it, the key is to "mix it up" to make sure that "innovation isn't thwarted by decisions that were 'already made' in some other silo."[15]

Another critical part of the process involves uncovering potential problems with any new design and asking critics to be forthright. Setting up a robust internal review program can avoid costly mistakes and unwelcome trade-offs down the line. As we noted earlier, DfE does not deliver good results if a customer perceives a loss in value through lower quality, deteriorated service, or a higher price (that isn't fully justified by better results). "Staff new projects with people resilient in the face of adversity. Compose a team that is passionate, but not overzealous, about the project. If their approach is pragmatic, their passion will be infectious," concluded BSR and IDEO from their in-depth case study of Clorox's "re-design" success with Green Works.[16]

2. Offer Frameworks to Spur Fresh Thinking

Sometimes a new way to think about an old problem helps to get the creative juices flowing. We've seen a number of frameworks that can help in this reconceptualization process. The "closed loop" thinking behind "industrial ecology"[17] or eco-architect Bill McDonough's "cradle-to-cradle" vision[18] can help a DfE team focus on reducing waste and designing for efficiency. Real-world examples of businesses that are thriving by putting eco-concepts into practice can also provide inspiration. The "Real-World ROI Success Stories" chart at the end of Chapter 4 may be useful in this regard.

Nike offers a powerful lesson with regard to the value of fresh thinking and new frameworks. Sarah Severn, who was at the table from the start in Nike's journey to more sustainable product design, says that the key move was to frame the issue in terms of "innovation and abundance" instead of "restriction and reaction." With this upside opportunity in mind, people got "very, very excited." Eyes would roll at the mention of "environmental management systems" and "eco-efficiency," says Severn. But designers got fired up when the conversation turned to how to create positive solutions at the front end of the design process that made sense for nature *and* commerce.[19] And keep in mind IDEO's good counsel: "traditional designers generally dislike following checklists or manuals. They want to imagine prototype, build, and iterate on projects. Conditions that facilitate creativity are fundamental to inspiring innovations that lead to a product breakthrough."[20]

See the recommendations and Additional Resources in Chapter 20 ("Engage Employees and Build an Eco-Innovation Culture") to prompt creative ideas for inspiring colleagues to take a fresh look at challenges and think big.

VALIDATING ENVIRONMENTAL CLAIMS

In 2009, **Johnson & Johnson** launched EARTHWARDS™, an internal process to better understand products' environmental footprints and identify opportunities for improvements. Product teams use an EARTHWARDS™ Product Scorecard to evaluate how product changes lead to quantifiable improvements in materials, packaging, energy, waste, and water use. If the product shows results in at least three priority eco-areas, teams can submit the scorecard to the EARTHWARDS™ board, which includes external evaluators, for review and validation. The process better equips marketing and communications teams to make responsible environmental claims to retailers, customers, and key procurement groups. According to Paulette Frank, the company's Vice President of Sustainability for its consumer products division, EARTHWARDS™ "enables us to drive eco-innovation to the product level at J&J."[21]

---

3. Learn by Doing

Getting started on a redesign initiative depends on your company's goals, culture, and capabilities. In many situations, a project with a modest goal, small investment, and quick payback works best as a starting point. In companies more open to risk and experimentation, a more ambitious project might make sense.

Examine your eco-impacts to look for possibilities for greener design. If your company has high rates of scrap as waste, that represents big potential payoffs for redesign. Likewise, the presence of toxics in one of your product creates possible exposure—and thus a DfE opportunity. Any reliance on scarce natural resources or materials from threatened habitats also needs scrutiny. From a design perspective, big issues equal big opportunities.

The key to successful design is meeting the full array of customer expectations: quality, price, and environmental impact. Herman Miller's Mirra Chair, launched in 2003, was born of a pilot project to better meet customer needs while employing DfE techniques.[22] Ninety-six percent of the chair's components can be easily recycled, and the chair can be disassembled using basic tools in 15 minutes or less. Herman Miller used the experience to build a blueprint for redesigning 27 percent of its product line, based in no small part on positive customer feedback. The company aims to have 100 percent of sales from DfE approved products by 2020.[23]

In prioritizing among various redesign options, consider the following questions: What issues matter most to your customers? How much value could the redesign add to your product? At what cost? What's within your control? Do breakout innovation opportunities exist? From which projects could the design team learn the most? Where do you have existing technical capacity to address an identified problem? Which results could be scalable? As with any project, you'll want to set goals, establish metrics to evaluate progress, and set up systems to document lessons learned that can be applied down the road.

INTERMEDIATE PLAYS: GET CREATIVE

The following plays provide a sampling of techniques used by companies to design greener products and services.

4. Set "Dematerialization" and Reduced Energy Use Goals

Eco-Advantage companies make reducing materials and energy use a centerpiece of their green design strategies. They often set quantitative targets for reduced product impacts. Nike, for instance, designed its eco-friendly "Considered Boot" to use 61 percent less material, 35 percent less energy, and 89 percent less in the way of industrial solvents than its average boot.[24] The key to success often turns on identifying where materials and energy use are greatest in the product's life cycle, then giving designers the space to problem solve. Procter & Gamble, for example, discovered through life cycle environmental assessment that the top eco-impact of its Tide laundry detergent stemmed from the energy used when washing clothes in hot water. That revelation led its product team down the innovation path to create Tide Coldwater. This redesigned product dramatically reduced this flagship product's eco-footprint, generated cost savings for customers, and became the first detergent to win the Green Good Housekeeping Seal.[25]

Leading-edge companies also focus on opportunities to rethink packaging design. Lightweighting containers and redesigning the shape and size of packaging can significantly cut back on material inputs, reduce waste, and save energy both in manufacturing and distribution (see Chapter 14 "Logistics and Transport" for more on packaging). HP designers won Walmart's 2008 Home Entertainment Design Challenge by redesigning the packaging for the company's HP Pavilion laptop. HP replaced conventional shipping materials and boxes with a stylish protective bag made from 100 percent recycled materials. This alteration was equivalent to removing the CO_2 emissions of one out of every four trucks previously used to deliver the notebooks to Walmart and Sam's Club stores around the United States.[26]

In a similar vein, Nestlé Waters redesigned its bottles to use 30 percent less plastic—reducing greenhouse gas emissions as well as waste. The 2007 Eco-Shape bottle shows the company's responsiveness to concerns about its environmental impacts.[27] But keep the reality of tradeoffs in mind. For example, optimal packaging design addresses the unsustainability of overpackaging, yet still prevents product damage caused by underpackaging.

5. Use Green Chemistry

Chemicals have improved human lives as well as opened a Pandora's box of ecological and human health challenges. See Chapter 5, "Spot the Eco-Issues that Could Impact Your Bottom Line" for more on these issues. Green chemistry attempts to rethink how chemicals are used so as to limit the harm to the environment or human health.

Chemists Paul Anastas and John Warner summarized green chemistry in 12 principles, including preventing waste, designing safer chemicals, using renewable chemical feedstocks, designing chemicals for natural degradation, and preventing chemical accidents.[28] Some techniques for employing green chemistry techniques in product and service design include:

- **Utilize green and black lists.** Some companies, such as SC Johnson, created a "greenlist" of environmentally preferred chemicals for product designers and manufacturers.[29] And some companies urge designers to steer clear of chemicals on *black* lists in favor of greener alternatives wherever possible. Developing these lists takes some effort, but many resources are available to assist in the process. The U.S. EPA's Design for Environment (DfE) certification program offers a great starting point. This program focuses largely on consumer cleaning products and chemical ingredients, and companies that follow strict guidelines get to carry the EPA's DfE label.[30]

- **Substitute toxic ingredients for nontoxic ones.** Anytime toxics can be removed from a product or a production process without compromising quality, cost savings will emerge. Handling toxic substances generates regulatory requirements (and costs) as well as disposal, insurance, and training burdens. Clorox, best known for its harsh but effective bleach, launched a new line of redesigned cleaning products in 2008. The Green Works line derives 99 percent of its material from plants and has dramatically reshaped the company's image and generated booming sales.[31]

- **Design ahead of regulation.** The European Union's 2006 Directive on the Registration, Evaluation, Authorisation, and Restriction of Chemical substances (REACH), forced thousands of companies to reformulate their products—or prove the safety of the ingredients in those products. Some companies moved quickly to reformulate their products—thus minimizing disruption of the new Directive. Others waited until REACH rules took effect and faced added costs and supply disruptions as a result. A similar shift in the "burden of proof" concerning the safety of chemicals is coming to the United States as reform of the Toxic Substances Control Act (TSCA) moves forward. Once again, smart companies are applying a "green chemistry" lens to their products before the regulatory hammer falls.

6. Separate Design for the Environment Options

If you separate Design for the Environment (DfE) into several well-established strategies you can minimize impacts on public health and ecosystems:

- **Design for recycling.** Create products that can be easily recycled at the end of the product's life. For example, designers using plastics in a product might aim to use only plastic components that are commonly recyclable in most markets. A common tactic to improve recyclability is to use as few components as possible. Hitachi famously simplified its washing machines so that they could be taken apart by removing as few as six screws.[32] And when the EU mandated in 2005 that cars be 85 percent (95 percent by mass) recyclable,[33] Volkswagen had a big jump on the competition because they had focused on recycling and product end-of-life problems since the late 1990s.[34]

- **Design for reconditioning.** Make products that can be refurbished efficiently extends the life of those products. L.L. Bean, for example, has long been willing to resole its iconic Maine Woodsmen's boots at a fraction of the cost to the consumer of a new pair.[35] Likewise, Interface Carpet's "Flor" line of carpet tiles are designed to be easily put together and taken apart, so that customers are able to cost-effectively replace carpet tiles in heavily trafficked areas rather than tearing up the entire carpet when one small area looks worn.[36]

- **Design for longer life.** Create durable products that will not need to be replaced for long periods of time. Compact fluorescent lamp (CFL) and light emitting diode (LED) bulbs consume less energy and produce less heat than traditional incandescent bulbs. But even more important, they last much longer. This long life reduces maintenance costs (fewer bulbs need to be changed)—and cuts down on the materials consumed in lighting and waste that needs to be disposed.

7. Promote Product Stewardship

Manufacturers—and especially those with big brand names—are starting to be held accountable for the environmental impacts of their products over the good's entire life cycle and across its full value chain. This "extended producer responsibility" requires companies to supervise their supply chain and ensure that their customer's use of a product does not result in avoidable environmental impacts. These rising expectations shift the principles of Design for the Environment from optional to increasingly mandatory. Since the producer must take full product responsibility, efficient and cost-effective end-of-life product disposal must be thought through in advance—and designed into the product.

Careful product stewardship can be a critical competitive factor, particularly in low-margin markets. In some contexts, legal regimes mandate extended producer responsibility. In Europe, the Waste Electrical and Electronic Equipment Directive (WEEE) requires electronics manufacturers to take back their products from the public free of charge at the end of product life.[37] In the United States, the Electronic Waste Recycling Act (EWRA) in California requires that electronic devices be disposed of by authorized recycling or disposal agents after consumers deposit the devices. Companies must pay for the cost of disposal.[38]

In addition to having companies shoulder the cost of the recycling or disposal of their products, product stewardship directives ultimately seek to motivate companies to think about the design of their products so that products generate less waste at the end of use period. The best way to do this is to use waste generated in the course of production or use one product as feedstock for another product. Bill McDonough and Michael Braungart made the case for continuous cycle design in their pathbreaking book, *Cradle-to-Cradle*. Their central theme, "waste equals food," describes two distinct cycles, the technical and biological cycles, and draws on the Japanese concept of waste (*muda*) use in lean manufacturing. In nature, they argue, waste produced by living organisms returns to ecosystems as food for other organisms—a logic that should inform effective processes in industrial design.

NEVER FORGET THE REALITY OF TRADEOFFS: SUNCHIPS SAGA

Remember that average consumers have multiple virtues in mind with each buying decision. Eco-designs fail if environmental gains come at an unacceptable cost in terms of other product attributes. **Frito-Lay's** compostable SunChips bag crinkled in such a deafeningly loud way it had to be withdrawn from the market in 2010.

Byproducts of chemical processes should therefore be recovered and used again in other processes. Water contaminated by one process should be safely recycled for use in others, ideally returned to the natural world in a cleaner state than when it entered industry. Examples of the "waste is food" product design concept listed on McDonough's website include a form of nylon, called Nylon 6, which can be de-polymerized and re-polymerized with a 99 percent energy and material recovery rate, as chemicals firm BASF has done.[39]

INNOVATION PAYS OFF FOR AKZONOBEL

AkzoNobel, a Dutch multinational that produces paints, performance coatings, and specialty chemicals, focuses 2.5 percent of its R&D spending on "big breakthrough" programs—about 60 percent (about 300 million Euros) of which is "completely sustainability-driven," according to the company's top sustainability executive Andre Veneman. The goal is to produce what the company calls "eco-premium solutions" for its customers—high-end, competitively priced products that offer greater environmental benefits than their mainstream alternatives. One of the first such innovations is nontoxic anti-fouling hull coatings for container ships. Smooth as nonstick cookware, the paint boosts a ship's fuel efficiency by about 10 percent. Another is an asphalt additive that enables roadworkers to reduce temperatures needed to pave roads, which also eliminates the need for some heavy equipment, exposes workers to fewer solvents, and shortens the time needed for paved roads to dry. "These may not be sexy products," says Veneman, "but they have a higher growth rate and higher contribution margin because they deliver a greater value proposition to customers." Moreover, the products link AkzoNobel to new customers like Steelcase, Herman Miller, Ikea, and Walmart, all of whom have set the sustainability bar very high. In 2007, 17 percent of Akzo's total turnover was in eco-premium solutions. In 2010, it was 22 percent, and it is projected to be 30 percent by 2015.[40]

The *Cradle-to-Cradle* authors created a four-level (basic, silver, gold, and platinum) certification program based on the following green design criteria:[41]

- **Materials used:** Whether all materials can be identified down to the 100 part-per-million level, material impact on human and environmental health, and forest source and wood harvesting standards;
- **Material reutilization strategies and rates:** Whether a company has a well-defined plan for reutilization; whether materials can be reutilized into a product of equal or higher value; and whether materials are reutilized at 50 percent or greater, 65 percent or greater, or 80 percent or greater rates;
- **Energy:** Whether a company has characterized the energy sources used in its products and processes, the percentage of solar energy greater than 50 percent used for product assembly, and the percentage of solar energy greater than 50 percent used in the entire production process;
- **Water:** A plan for water use and the implementation of water conservation and quality measures;

- **Social responsibility:** Whether a company has posted ethics and "fair labor" statements, has developed metrics to measure social responsibility, and has received third-party social responsibility assessment and certification.

For more details, consult the nonprofit Cradle to Cradle Products Innovation Institute in California (www.c2ccertified.org).

ADVANCED PLAYS: CREATE NEW PRODUCTS AND SERVICES EMPLOYING ADVANCED GREEN DESIGN

Advanced green design plays have the power to transform a product and even an industry—leading to new business models and substantial bottom-line benefits. If done right, they advance environmental goals as well as economic results.

8. Go Outside Your Company for Ideas

Sun Microsystems co-founder Bill Joy coined a phrase that became known in management circles as Joy's Law: "No matter who you are, most of the smartest people work for someone else."[42] Green innovation companies have taken this to heart, and have looked outside their own offices to draw in innovation and redesign options. Some have turned to green design competitions or "crowd sourcing" to solve eco-problems.

NEW MINDSETS ON INTELLECTUAL PROPERTY

According to **Nike's** Green Xchange lead Charlie Brown, "transitioning to a corporate culture where intellectual property is used as a tool for collaboration versus exclusion takes time—but the payoff to innovation can be enormous." At Nike, the shift has taken years to unfold. "It's been challenging," Brown told us, "because not only did we need to forge new partnerships with outside organizations like universities or competitors...we also needed new partnerships *internally*, with IP and product managers, chemists, and corporate responsibility staff coming together for the very first time." A key success factor to getting buy-in, says Brown, has been to "focus on where sustainability, business opportunity, and capacity align the most."[43]

Starbucks, for instance, launched a contest in 2010 offering a $10,000 prize for the winning design for a recyclable coffee cup.[44] The Green Xchange takes this concept to a whole new level, providing a platform that allows companies to access the green technologies of other companies, including patented research. Many green innovations are "public goods," which can be transferred or adapted by other companies without posing a competitive threat to the original company.

Author Agnes Mazur notes, "If a company like Nike, for example, has performed extensive research on maximizing the efficiency of air pressure in sneaker design, a company that manufactures truck tires may apply the patent in a way that saves materials and money, creates a more eco-friendly product, and does not harm Nike's sales."[45] Nike submitted 400 patents to the Xchange and expects to contribute many more in the years to come.[46]

9. Look to Nature for Inspiration

Biomimicry introduces a simple idea—that nature often operates efficiently and solves eco-related problems—to the design calculation. Popularized by Janine Benyus in her 1997 book, *Biomimicry: Innovation Inspired by Nature*, this concept suggests that designers might use nature as an inspiration when trying to solve sustainability challenges. Benyus argues that "life's principles" are the key to sustainable design.[47] She seeks to "build from the bottom up, self-assemble, optimize rather than maximize, use free energy, cross-pollinate, embrace diversity, adapt and evolve, use life-friendly materials and processes, engage in symbiotic relationships, and enhance the bio-sphere." More generally, biomimicry principles suggest designers should:[48]

- Break design issues into core components.
- Seek the most efficient solutions.
- Emulate natural processes.
- Use non-toxic materials derived from nature.
- Use renewable energy.
- Build for evolution, not perfection.

Calera, a building materials company, turned the idea of cement on its head after being inspired by nature. Cement ranks high on the list of biggest industrial polluters, especially in terms of greenhouse gas emissions. Calera developed a carbon capture and storage technology that promises to extract carbon dioxide from industrial emissions and embed them into cement. The inspiration? A process used by ocean creatures to make shells and reefs.[49] Similarly, Boeing was inspired by the biomechanics of the wings of bats and dragonflies to put "winglets" on thousands of its 737 airplanes to reduce air resistance—cutting each plane's fuel use by three percent.[50]

10. "Servicize" Your Product

Anyone who has rented rather than purchased a product has participated in a form of "servicization." Yet only recently have companies and designers viewed the concept as a green business model. FedEx has servicized its products to the benefit of its customers, the environment, and the company's bottom line. In particular, FedEx's Print Online service takes advantage of the Internet to speed up delivery. It allows, for example, a New York lawyer to upload documents online for a client in Boulder, Colorado—which a FedEx employee in Boulder will print, copy, bind, and deliver locally the next morning. The documents' physical journey drops from thousands of miles to a few. And the customer gets added value: more time to prepare the document instead of rushing to meet a FedEx delivery deadline and possibly better format and presentation options than if handled internally.[51]

Other successful servicizing business models include:

Zipcar gives its customers access to a car when—and only when—they need it. The company has popularized car sharing—allowing its customers to avoid owning a car. The company claims large environmental benefits as well. It says that each of its shared cars takes 15 to 20 fully owned vehicles off the road. Zipcar also says that shared car drivers drive far less than drivers who own cars, saving 32 million gallons of crude oil per year.[52]

Chegg.com offers college textbook rentals. College textbooks can cost hundreds of dollars, eating up a significant portion of the budget of cash-strapped college students. Several websites now rent textbooks to students instead of selling them. For about half the price of buying a textbook, students can rent them for a quarter or a semester and return them free of charge. Chegg claims to have saved more than $60 million for students at more than 6,400 colleges. The company also plants a tree every time someone rents a book on Chegg, and they have planted more than 2.5 million trees so far.[53]

11. Dematerialize Your Product or Service

By now even the most casual music aficionado appreciates the dramatic changes that have taken place over the past few years in the recorded music industry. Major brick-and-mortar retailers no longer exist thanks to the spread of e-commerce. Digital music players like Apple's iPod, supported by services such as iTunes, have revolutionized how we buy, store, and listen to music. An entire industry has been upended by *dematerialization*. Companies like Apple that embraced this change—and helped to accelerate it—have profited handsomely. The same can be said for Amazon, which is riding the wave of a similar transformation in the book industry with its pioneering Kindle.

Intuitively, it should come as no surprise that reducing material intensity in an industry results in positive environmental impacts. Researchers Christopher Weber, Jonathan Koomey, and Scott Matthews estimated recorded music energy use and carbon emissions, starting with final recorded album masters and ending in a range of scenarios from CDs delivered to brick-and-mortar stores to digital files delivered over the Internet to computers. They found that purchasing music online and accessing it via digital download reduces energy consumption and carbon dioxide emissions by 40 to 80 percent over the traditional in-store retail.[54]

Their research shows how dramatically a new business model can change behavior and transform technology, and also how such a model can shrink a product's eco-footprint.

SUMMARY

Key Plays

1. Work across issues, functions, and traditional divisions.
2. Offer frameworks to spur fresh thinking.
3. Learn by doing.
4. Set dematerialization and reduced energy use goals.
5. Use green chemistry.
6. Separate Design for the Environment options.
7. Promote product stewardship.
8. Go outside your company for ideas.
9. Look to nature for inspiration.
10. "Servicize" your product.
11. Dematerialize your product or service.

ADDITIONAL RESOURCES

GENERAL

"Aligned for Sustainable Design: An A-B-C-D Approach to Making Better Products" by Chad White with Emma Stewart of BSR's Environmental R&D team and Ted Howes with Bob Adams of IDEO (Business for Social Responsibility, May 2008). Outlines how companies can assess, bridge, create, and diffuse sustainable-design capabilities into a more integrative design process within their organizations. Includes in-depth case studies. www.bsr.org/reports

"Green Product Development" (Small Business Administration). Outlines options and resources for businesses to use environmental problems as catalysts for innovative new products and services. www.business.gov

"Remaking the Way We Make Things: Creating a New Definition of Quality with Cradle to Cradle Design" by William McDonough & Michael Braungart (2005). Short article synthesizing key insights from authors' classic work, *Cradle to Cradle: Remaking the Way We Make Things.* www.mcdonough.com

"**Growing Green: Three Smart Paths to Developing Sustainable Products**" by Gregory Unruh and Richard Ettenson (*Harvard Business Review*, June 2010). Describes the strategies that companies use in order to align their capabilities with their green goals. Broadly grouped as *accentuate, acquire, and architect* these strategies are central to executive MBA course offerings in sustainable business strategy. http://hbr.org

"**Better By Design—An Innovation Guide: Using Natural Design Solutions**" by Fran Kurk and Curt McNamara (Minnesota Pollution Control Agency, 2006). Outlines simple recommendations for weaving environmental considerations into product design and building the business case for change. www.pca.state.mn.us

"**CPG Innovation & Growth: Developing the Right Innovation & Product Lifecycle Management Strategies for Today and Tomorrow**" (Grocery Manufacturers Assoc., Accenture, and Information Resources, 2009). How consumer packaged goods (CPG) companies can improve Product Lifecycle Management. www.gmaonline.org

GreenBlue. Nonprofit focused solely on guiding business and industry toward sustainable design and production. www.greenblue.org

Cradle to Cradle Products Innovation Institute. Nonprofit organization that administers a Cradle to Cradle certification standard and provides training and resources. www.c2ccertified.org

CHEMICALS AND MATERIALS SELECTION

Cleangredients. An easily searchable and constantly updated list of approved DfE chemicals. www.cleangredients.org

Chemicals and Materials Selection (Minnesota Pollution Control Agency). Two-page article listing materials cited by eco-label programs as chemicals to avoid and possible alternatives. www.pca.state.mn.us

Green Chemical Alternatives Purchasing Wizard. Web-based tool that allows the user to search from a select list of solvents commonly used in the laboratory and associated processes. http://ehs.mit.edu

NATURE-INSPIRED DESIGN

The Biomimicry Institute/ "Ask Nature" Database. Promotes sustainable designs and technology innovation modeled after biological systems. Sponsors an extensive database (www.asknature.org) on possible design applications from examples in nature. www.biomimicryinstitute.org

GREEN PRODUCT CERTIFICATIONS

Design for the Environment (DfE) (EPA). A certification program that recognizes safer consumer, industrial and institutional products. Defines best practices in areas ranging from auto refinishing to nail salon safety. www.epa.gov/dfe/index.htm

Cradle to Cradle® Certification. A multi-attribute eco-label offered by McDonough Braungart Design Chemistry (MBDC) that assesses a product's safety to humans and the environment and design for future life cycles. www.mbdc.com

Ecolabel Index and "Global Ecolabel Monitor." Definitive, searchable online guide to ecolabels across all industry sectors. www.ecolabelindex.com

"Global Ecolabel Monitor" (Ecolabel Index and World Resources Institute, 2010). A report on the performance and organizational structure of ecolabels around the world. www.wri.org

GOVERNMENT INCENTIVES FOR GREEN PRODUCT INNOVATION

Environmental Grants, Loans, and Incentives (Business.gov). List of financial and technical assistance for developers of greener technologies. www.business.gov

The Tax Incentives Assistance Project. Information on federal income tax incentives for energy efficient products and technologies. www.energytaxincentives.org

Chapter 12 Sourcing and Procurement

Home Depot knows more than most how important the sustainability of suppliers can be. Forest Ethics, a San Francisco-based NGO, targeted Home Depot in the early 2000s for sourcing lumber from old growth forests. After protest banners got hung from the rafters in a number of stores, Home Depot realized that it would have to take action. The company moved quickly to find suppliers that could provide sustainably sourced wood—and in doing so, transformed the market for lumber. Home Depot CEO Frank Blake tells this story with relish—explaining that the Forest Ethics experience has helped to ensure his company's focus on sustainability as a critical priority in procurement.[1]

Home Depot has now issued a comprehensive supplier Code of Conduct that sets out standards, including sustainability requirements, for anyone doing business with the company. The issues covered include worker safety, air and water emissions, disposal of chemicals and hazardous wastes, bribes, fraud, and conflicts of interest. The company conducts annual audits of suppliers' social and environmental responsibility programs, including unannounced visits to their forests and facilities. For suppliers who do not have a sustainability or corporate responsibility program, Home Depot will work with them to build their internal capabilities to meet the requirements. This rigorous supply chain management takes real management time and involves substantial costs, but the value of brand protection far outweighs the burden.[2]

> In our world of "extended producer responsibility," companies, particularly those with big brand names, will be held accountable for the shortcomings of their suppliers.

While price, quality, and service remain key considerations in the procurement process, purchasing today is a more complicated business.

Simply put, sustainability cannot be ignored. Although supply chain management has much to do with risk exposure, it has upsides as well. Many companies—particularly retailers, and most famously, Walmart—collaborate on efficiency initiatives with suppliers, often finding these efforts more rewarding than further focus on operation gains within their own facilities.

SUSTAINABLE SOURCING PAYS OFF

- **Texas Instruments** saves $8 million each year through its supply chain management practices, particularly by reducing and reusing packaging and source material reduction.[3]

- **Walmart** gave up purchasing peaches from a few national suppliers and started buying more fruit locally from farms in 18 states. This switch saves the company 100,000 gallons of diesel while cutting down on food transport by 672,000 miles each year—and meets the growing demand for fresher produce.[4]

- **Duke Energy** has developed a storage technology that eliminates the wooden reels on which electrical lines used to be wrapped, reducing costs by $500,000 each year.[5]

- **Mars**, the candy giant, plans to source all of its chocolate from sustainable suppliers by 2020. It will deepen its relationship with a select set of cocoa suppliers that meet its environmental, labor, and production standards. This purchasing switch will help Mars meet its sustainability commitments by securing a steady supply of a key ingredient that is otherwise subject to volatile production and price swings.[6]

The logic for "greening" the supply chain has many elements including:[7]

- **Raising product quality** by sourcing higher performance raw materials and other inputs.
- **Facilitating production processes** by finding materials and semi-finished goods that enhance efficiency.
- **Reducing costs** by looking at supply-chain-wide opportunities to trim expenses not only in procurement but through the optimization of transportation and logistics.
- **Improving inventory management** to avoid shortages that could impede business continuity or even halt production because of inputs that fail to meet legal requirements, production standards, or customer expectations.
- **Protecting corporate reputation** by making choices about suppliers, products, and practices that avoid nasty surprises and scandals.
- **Enhancing customer value** through products that contribute to a more sustainable world and make purchasers feel good about the products they are buying.

Applying a green lens to sourcing and procurement can advance all of those objectives. This chapter covers plays to help sourcing and procurement leaders:

- Identify and head off supply chain eco-risks.
- Manage costs by rooting out waste and inefficiency across the value chain.
- Engage suppliers in improving their environmental and social performance.
- Create policies to advance the sustainability of their supply chain.
- Improve relationships with customers and gain new ones.

BASIC PLAYS: IDENTIFY ISSUES AND SUPPLIERS

As we have argued in earlier chapters, there is no magic formula for reaching Eco-Advantage. Given the rapid pace of innovation and ever-rising expectations of customers, regulators, and stakeholders, the first step must be to make sustainability a part of the procurement process. Changing the mindset of buyers will take some work. Some companies may well complain that adding a sustainability screen to their process will be too cumbersome or detract from their ability to maximize cost savings. And for companies that purchase thousands of items, this concern has some validity. The key, as with many other things, lies with building a system that embeds sustainability in the acquisition process.

For small businesses with simple procurement procedures, the challenge will not come from the complexity of the supplier network, but from a lack of easy access to more sustainable products and services. The market for green alternatives is growing but still limited in many categories. Usually, small businesses are not in a position to pay a price premium for greener products—and most lack the market power to push suppliers to provide more sustainable options.

Larger companies with more complex supply chains to master will first need to focus on big risks and opportunities. The basic plays in this chapter offer some sensible first steps to get you going on your way toward a more comprehensive green procurement action plan.

1. Identify Your Critical Suppliers

The first step toward a greener supply chain is to figure out what you are buying and from whom. Big companies with procurement departments probably have buyers who have a handle on all of their company's purchases—and a good list of suppliers. Small businesses may not be so systematic; so getting the supplier list together may take some work.

Retailers should identify the manufacturers of each product they sell. Manufacturing companies should list all the materials that go into their products as well as inputs that go into the manufacturing process (such as energy, water, chemicals). All companies, including service companies, then need to add into the mix the materials and services required to administer the business, such as office supplies, IT equipment, furniture, and vehicles.

Obviously some suppliers are more important than others. Identifying which suppliers pose the greatest eco-related risks to your company—and which bring the greatest potential for solving problems—is step two. We suggest you single out the suppliers that:[8]

- **Supply components that comprise a large part of the value of your final product.** For example, restaurants and food processors should pay special attention to who they buy their ingredients from. A communications company should focus on their IT equipment.

- **Focus on the eco-issues you identified as most relevant to your company or industry (as identified in Chapter 5).** For example, you should note suppliers that have a huge impact on climate change or deal with issues specific to your company, such as a forests or land use.

- **Provide essential inputs for your operations.** For example, fuel or chemicals needed during the manufacturing process.

- **Work on your site as subcontractors.** Their environmental safety record can affect your record directly—especially if they manage your hazardous waste.

- **Encounter environmental challenges in their own operations.** Their issues could become supply interruptions, increased costs, or legal liability for you.

- **Can improve your performance with their expertise.**

- **Are opinion leaders or which the public would expect your company to be able to influence.** This facet implicates them as part of your extended producer responsibility.

Finally, review your competitors' websites or published sustainability reports to determine what they are doing to bring a higher degree of eco-sensitivity to their procurement process. Which issues or inputs do they focus on? Do they have procurement policies or supplier codes of conduct in place? What do they require of suppliers? What benefits have they publicly reported?

2. Determine Which Issues to Address

Every company's supply chain is unique. So you'll want to concentrate on figuring out which of your company's issues to prioritize. In every case, think about costs and risks as well as opportunities to enhance customer value and build brand loyalty and corporate reputation. The box that follows provides a quick review of the issues to consider.

3. Implement a Green Procurement Policy

After you have identified the suppliers and issues that matter the most, you need to spell out your sustainability expectations. If your company already has a procurement policy, environmental (and social) requirements can simply be added to the existing standards. If your company has procurement rules that relate to sustainability concerns, you need to determine whether they are sufficiently comprehensive and rigorous. To do this, we suggest using one of the following green purchasing self-assessment tools:

- **GEMI New Paths to Business Value:** This guide located at www.gemi.org/resources/newpath.pdf shows how "green" procurement can enhance business value. It encourages a selective approach that you can tailor to your individual company needs and provides practical advice for procurement officials.

- **Eco-S.A.T. A Green Purchasing Self Assessment Tool:** This 66-page guide to green sourcing and procurement located at www.cec.org/Storage/52/4498_Eco-SAT-draft-Winter2003-2004_EN.pdf includes a useful self-assessment tool, guidance on implementing a green purchasing policy, green office practices, and sourcing and bid solicitation.

SPOTTING TOP RISKS AND OPPORTUNITIES IN PROCUREMENT

- **Product attributes and inputs:** Is the product made from materials or chemicals that could be harmful to human health? Does the production product's use create environmental harms? How energy efficient is it? Is it made of any reused or recycled materials?

- **Risks connected to production processes:** Where did the product come from? How was it produced?

- **Inefficiency and waste in packaging:** Are there ways to cut down on packaging used by suppliers? Walmart, for instance, evaluates suppliers' packaging based on (1) material type, (2) material weight, (3) material distance (how far packaging components travel before being filled), and (4) packaging efficiency (how efficiently available space is utilized and packaged to product ratio).

- **Inefficiency and pollution in transportation:** How are products delivered? What mode of transportation is used? And how frequently? Is there a way to reduce carbon emissions and cost from suppliers' shipping operations?

- **Supplier sustainability performance:** Does the supplier comply with all environmental regulations? What are its air, water, and waste emissions? What is its carbon footprint? Are human rights met and worker conditions healthy? Is the supplier working to reduce its environmental impact?

Source: GEMI, *New Paths to Business Value,* 2001. http://www.gemi.org/resources/newpath.pdf (accessed August 22, 2010); Walmart, *Supplier Sustainability Assessment,* walmartstores.com/download/4055.pdf (accessed August 22, 2010).

To begin greening your procurement system, you may find it useful to introduce a simple policy commitment that demonstrates the company's plans to build sustainability factors into procurement. For some companies, this could be a decision to go "green" for commonly purchased items when there is an obvious sustainable choice. A sample green procurement policy might include directives to buy recycled paper; use paper rather than Styrofoam cups; and switch to green cleaning products, Energy Star computers, and IT equipment.

For example, the city of Santa Monica, California, requires as part of its procurement policy that in addition to performance and cost criteria, vendors must include environmental and health specifications in their bids. General Motors of Canada worked with suppliers and dealers to purchase 6,650 reusable crates and pallets to deliver plastic parts to dealers, eliminating the need for roughly 266,000 cardboard crates per year.[9]

Fortunately many resources exist to help procurement professionals find environmentally preferable products. For example, eco-labels and certifications help companies and consumers distinguish environmentally preferable products from the pack. The USDA organic label and Energy Star label for energy efficient appliances are some of the most common. In July 2010, Carbonfund.org launched a CarbonFree Certified Product label that companies can utilize to promote their climate-neutral products.[10] Other labels include:

- **Forest Stewardship Council:** A strict code for sustainably harvested wood and forest products.
- **Marine Stewardship Council:** Certification for seafood from sustainable fisheries.
- **Green Seal:** Certification for a wide variety of environmentally preferred products—from personal care items to building materials.
- **Green-e:** Certification for renewable energy.

Of course, not all green labels are created equal. When choosing a certified product, it is important to know what entity is doing the certifying (and, in particular, whether it is a "neutral body"), what standards are being applied, and how the requirements are enforced. The definitive online guide to ecolabels around the world is available at www.ecolabelindex.com.

For products that are not certified, companies will have to do the legwork themselves to establish the product's environmental footprint. The Responsible Purchasing Network provides sample procurement policies and purchasing guidelines for a wide variety of products. And other screening mechanisms are emerging. For instance, Big Room Inc. (www.bigroom.ca) has applied to create a global eco-label based on a system of .eco domain names that will provide detailed eco-information on any product sold by a registered .eco company.

The resources at the end of this chapter offer additional recommendations on how to set up the supporting criteria for a green procurement policy.

Green procurement initiatives are often hard to implement. Old habits die hard. Some environmentally preferable products are not readily available.

Others may not meet performance specifications. And still others may not be cost competitive. Making the relevant information readily available and easy to access is critical. Catalog retailer Norm Thompson created a simple scoring system with sustainability criteria to help its buyers evaluate purchasing options. To create an incentive to take the criteria seriously, the company tied 10 percent of the buyers' commission to improvements in their sustainability score over time.[11] Along the same lines, Staples created an online "Green Guide" catalog to help its customers more easily find sustainably produced and eco-conscious office products.

For small businesses, the trick may be to aggregate purchases with others to achieve economies of scale—and better prices on sustainable products. For example, a company with an office in a larger building can join with those in the other offices to purchase larger quantities of recycled paper or IT equipment.[12]

4. Draft a Supplier Code of Conduct

Very often a green procurement policy is not enough. Companies also need to draft a code of conduct for suppliers. A code of conduct specifies practices and requirements that a supplier must meet to do business with your company. Codes often contain stipulations regarding supplier ethics, labor practices, environmental management, permitting and compliance, and even human rights. Walmart prepared a crisp, practical slide deck that outlines its expectations for information disclosure and recommends specific tools for suppliers. Apple requires that its suppliers pass a strict code of conduct that includes proper management of hazardous materials, monitoring and control of air and water emissions, safe worker conditions and adequate compensation, and periodic audits to ensure compliance with these rules.[13] Tesco asks its suppliers to match its own company's goals: Cut carbon 30 percent by 2020 and be carbon neutral by 2050. To maintain transparency and encourage customers to cut their emissions, Tesco has started to carbon label its products. The company released carbon footprints for 114 Tesco products in 2009 with the goal of labeling 500 products over the next several years.[14]

Simply having a code of conduct doesn't get the job done. Companies must also find ways to ensure *compliance* with their supplier codes of conduct. Home Depot provides a hotline where anyone, including a supplier's employee, can call to report violations of the code of conduct. The company also requires that suppliers report any changes in their operations to Home Depot, which triggers greater compliance scrutiny. To maintain vigorous enforcement, you can try routine announced and unannounced audits of your suppliers' facilities. Play 7 provides more details on how to undertake such audits.

INTERMEDIATE PLAYS: ENGAGE SUPPLIERS

5. Engage Suppliers in an Ongoing Dialogue

Not all suppliers are able to immediately meet the requirements of new procurement policies or codes of conduct. Some need guidance and time. Engaging suppliers in a conversation and working mutually to solve problems is crucial to successful supply chain management. As a Corporate EcoForum study found, best-in-class companies "foster long-term relationships so that companies can work on issues that require long-term investment . . . [which] provides stability and time to realize bottom-line value and work out kinks."[15] They treat suppliers as partners—listening to them, sharing knowledge with them, and learning with them over time.

We suggest that companies begin a dialogue with their top-tier suppliers. Offer your assessment of their environmental performance. Invite them to respond. If you can't find publicly available information on their sustainability performance, ask them for it. And have them tell you about their environmental initiatives. Share your company's interests, needs, and policies with suppliers and take the time to understand what challenges they face in meeting your sustainability expectations.

You might also consider hosting a "supplier summit." Intel, for instance, holds Supplier Days where it discusses its company's directions and expectations with more than 700 equipment suppliers. Walmart reaches out to its huge network of suppliers through in-person meetings and web-based platforms, including webinars that outline the company's priorities, goals, and expectations. When meeting with suppliers, be sure to emphasize the benefits they can get from eco-initiatives—including cost savings, increased process efficiencies and product quality, and better customer relationships—as well as the risks of inaction. You may even consider creating an arrangement that incentivizes performance through shared cost savings: for example, a manufacturer might say, "We think you can save five cents' worth of plastic for every part you make. We want a three-cent per piece price reduction, but you can keep the additional two cents per part."

6. Consider an Industry-Wide Collaboration

In some cases, it may be difficult to get traction with suppliers on an individual company basis. It may make sense to engage suppliers through an industry association or group. If your company has little market power over suppliers, a collaborative effort may be your only option. For example, when Disney, 20th Century Fox, Warner Brothers, and other players in the home entertainment industry (selling videos and DVDs) came under pressure in 2008 from retailers such as Walmart to improve their environmental performance, these entertainment companies concluded that each company individually would have a hard time convincing the handful of production companies that were stamping out videos and DVDs in Asia to change their ways. But working together, they developed an "agenda for sustainable entertainment" and launched a shared initiative to green their suppliers and "save the planet one disk at a time."[16]

Similarly, Duke Energy, PG&E, and Northeast Utilities are among the many members of the Electric Utility Industry Sustainable Supply Chain Alliance, which seeks to advance sustainable business practices in the utilities sector.[17] Working together, the group can press for improved products and services that no individual company could demand on its own.

From a strategic point of view, the question of where to pursue a collaborative green supply chain initiative versus a go-it-alone effort turns on several questions. First, can your company induce change in suppliers on its own? Big companies are often able to; small ones are not. Second, if you have to pay a premium for a greener input, can you turn around and sell your product for a price premium that justifies the added expense? Third, will you be able to differentiate your product as the greener option in the marketplace in a manner that makes up for the added expense? Fourth, are there scale economies in carrying out a supply chain initiative that argue for collaboration? Fundamentally, the answer to these core questions will determine whether you want to seek competitive advantage by striking out on your own and positioning your company as the greener alternative—or whether you'd do better to transform the entire industry (getting everyone to go along so that your commitment to higher sustainability standards does not impose a cost burden on your business that your competitors don't bear).

7. Undertake Formal Audits

As suppliers sign and comply with company codes of conduct, ensuring compliance with the established standards is a necessity. There are many options for companies to assess and verify that suppliers are submitting accurate information, meeting expectations, and carrying through on commitments. Ultimately, there is no substitute for on-site audits, including unannounced factory visits. Your success depends heavily on identifying the right performance metrics, creating systems that do not overly burden suppliers, and being crystal clear about expectations.

The number of surveys sent to companies regarding sustainability performance is exploding. These demands are overwhelming many businesses—particularly straining the limited resources of small and medium-sized businesses. To minimize the burden, we recommend that companies adopt the following principles that draw on guidance developed by GEMI:[18]

1. **Research a supplier's environmental performance.** Suppliers often have their own system in place for evaluating and advancing sustainability. They may

provide reports that companies can use to determine if they want to buy from them. Use information that is available rather than have suppliers generate new reports just for you.

2. **Build on existing frameworks.** For instance, rather than creating your own questions about greenhouse gas emissions, consider asking suppliers if they have reported to the Carbon Disclosure Project. Use third-party certification as a means of getting information and verification at the same time. Piggyback on standardized industry association frameworks so suppliers only have to complete one form that many companies can use.

3. **Request additional information.** If the information you are seeking cannot be found in a supplier's own reports or existing frameworks, request that information through surveys, meetings, or memos. But don't ask for information that your own company hasn't produced or information that you won't use. Ask detailed questions about management systems, corrective actions, and other qualitative measures of performance in "live" meetings, not on a form. Create a framework so that suppliers can easily monitor and update their information on a year-to-year basis.

4. **Be selective about who you audit.** Audit first those suppliers whose issues "directly impact operating costs, threaten continuity of supply, or threaten reputation or product quality"[19]

5. **Use on-site audits or supervision for critical suppliers.** To ensure that supply companies are following company guidelines, it may be necessary to visit key suppliers from time to time. Apple stipulates that it be allowed to visit suppliers and audit their operations with or without notice in its supplier code of conduct. It also requires self-audits and reports from suppliers. You must supervise subcontractors, hazardous waste disposal providers, and contract manufacturers to ensure that their actions do not have a negative impact on your company's environmental performance.[20]

No one has taken supplier sustainability further than Walmart. The Bentonville, Arkansas-based retailing behemoth has created Sustainable Value Networks (SVNs)—composed of suppliers from specific sectors and Walmart representatives along with a sprinkling of NGOs, experts, academics, and government officials—that are developing new ways to make their shared value chain more eco-efficient and sustainable. This sustainability consortium is also helping Walmart refine its supplier sustainability scorecard. See Figure 12.1.

Not all supply chain initiatives will be successful, and some suppliers will inevitably do worse than others. However, a company that is honest about its supply chain and reports the good, bad, and the ugly will have more credibility with customers, investors, and other stakeholders and will not be accused of "greenwashing." HP, for example, has committed to providing GHG emissions from at least 75 percent of its suppliers in 2009. Patagonia has an interactive website, "The Footprint Chronicles," that allows customers to track the entire supply chain of Patagonia's products.[21]

Figure 12.1   **What Does Walmart Ask Its Suppliers?**

Sustainability Supplier Assessment Questions

Energy and Climate *Reduce energy costs and green-house gas emissions*	• 1. Have you measured and taken steps to reduce your corporate greenhouse gas emissions (Y/N) • 2. Have you opted to report your greenhouse gas emissions and climate change strategy to the Carbon Disclosure Project (CDP)? (Y/N) • 3. What are your total annual greenhouse gas emissions in the most recent year measured? (Enter total metric tons CO2e, e.g. CDP 2009 Questionnaire, Questions 7-11, Scope 1 and 2 emissions) • 4. Have you set publicly available greenhouse gas reduction targets? If yes, what are those targets? (Enter total metric tons and target date, e.g. CDP 2009 Questionnaire, Question 23)
Material Efficiency *Reduce waste and enhance quality*	• Scores will be automatically calculated based on participation in the Packaging Scorecard in addition to the following: • 5. If measured, please report total amount of solid waste generated from the facilities that produce your product(s) for Walmart for the most recent year measured. (Enter total lbs) • 6. Have you set publicly available solid waste reduction targets? If yes, what are those targets? (Enter total lbs and target date) • 7. If measured, please report total water use from the facilities that produce your product(s) for Walmart for the most recent year measured. (Enter total gallons) • 8. Have you set publically available water use reduction targets? If yes, what are those targets? (Enter total gallons and target date)
Nature and Resources *High quality, responsibly sourced raw materials*	• 9. Have you established publicly available sustainability purchasing guidelines for your direct suppliers that address issues such as environmental compliance, employment practices, and product/ingredient safety? (Y/N) • 10. Have you obtained 3rd party certifications for any of the products that you sell to Walmart? If so, from the list of certifications below, please select those for which any of your products are, or utilize materials that are, currently certified.
People and Community *Vibrant, productive workplaces and communities*	• 11. Do you know the location of 100% of the facilities that produce your product(s)? (Y/N) • 12. Before beginning a business relationship with a manufacturing facility, do you evaluate their quality of production and capacity for production? (Y/N) • 13. Do you have a process for managing social compliance at the manufacturing level? (Y/N) • 14. Do you work with your supply base to resolve issues found during social compliance evaluations and also document specific corrections and improvements? (Y/N) • 15. Do you invest in community development activities in the markets you source from and/or operate within? (Y/N)

Source: Walmart, Supplier Sustainability Assessment, walmartstores.com/download/4055.pdf (accessed August 22, 2010). Reprinted with permission.

8. Develop a Supplier Mentoring Program

Some suppliers do not meet company codes for suppliers but they supply an essential input or are difficult to replace. Rather than cutting them out or lowering expectations for their performance, leading companies work with them to raise their environmental game.

IKEA uses a "staircase model" where suppliers work with the company to identify achievable targets. When the lagging supplier reaches those targets, IKEA helps them set new ones. The model establishes four levels of achievement. Level 1 is basically unacceptable and means the supplier needs to develop an immediate action plan for reaching Level 2, the company's minimum standard. Level 3 is yet a higher standard, and Level 4 suppliers meet even stricter third-party standards such as the Forest Stewardship Council's certification, widely considered the toughest standard in sustainable forestry. IKEA actively provides guidance and support (including financial backing) to its suppliers to help them improve their performance. One Romanian furniture supplier, with loans from IKEA, invested in modern equipment including a new boiler, ventilation, and air filters, and installed a machine to turn briquettes from waste to energy and profit.[22]

ADVANCED PLAYS: EXPAND SCOPE AND REACH

9. Reach Deeper into the Supply Chain

Companies with advanced supplier management programs care about the sustainability of their own suppliers *and* their supplier's suppliers, or "tier 2" suppliers. Companies can influence tier 2 or tier 3 suppliers by including them in the requirements of their direct (tier 1) supplier's standards. Or they can insist that all suppliers hold their suppliers to the company's supplier code of conduct. Herman Miller, for example, expects its tier 3 suppliers to follow its strict requirements regarding any materials or chemicals that will wind up in Herman Miller products. As Paul Murray, Director of Environmental Affairs and Safety at Herman Miller, reports, "We reach down to 4th and 5th tiers at times to find the chemical formulas."[23]

10. Optimize with Technology

New supply chain technologies are enabling companies to have an integrated view of supply chain impacts. Now, companies can use sophisticated software to gather information about suppliers and compare performance over time or across value chains. Life cycle analysis software allows companies to find out the impact of products and processes without needing to collect information directly from a supplier. Aberdeen Group's 2008 "Building a Green Supply Chain" identified four areas of technology enablement:[24]

1. Role-based green dashboards
2. Sustainable/efficient assets
3. Waste disposal/tracking/analytics
4. Sustainable transport/logistics

As more companies mature their sustainable supply chain initiatives in the coming years, more firms will take advantage of these tools and have the in-house expertise to do it effectively.

11. Form Cross-Industry Partnerships to Raise Standards

Leading companies know that some challenges are too big for any one company and are better tackled in a team. For example, Nike and Patagonia teamed up with other cotton purchasers to create a more robust market for organic cotton. Each company individually purchased quantities too small to induce growers to invest in the organic product, but as a group they had sufficient buying power to drive change.[25] The Electronics Industry Citizenship Coalition (EICC) created a uniform code of conduct for the entire electronics and computer industry supply chain with unified standards for social and environmental practices. The EICC code requires that suppliers: obtain all necessary permits, approvals, and registrations, reduce or eliminate all wastes including water and energy, identify and manage hazardous substances, and characterize, monitor, control, and treat air emissions.

General Mills, Nestle, Kraft Foods, Coca-Cola, Unilever, Kellogg's, Diageo, and a dozen others have launched AIM-PROGRESS, a consortium of fast-moving consumer goods companies working to advance sustainability through a shared responsible sourcing initiative. The group has committed to using their market presence to improve the efficiency and effectiveness of the supply chain.[26]

SUMMARY

Key Plays

1. Identify your critical suppliers.
2. Determine which issues to address.
3. Implement a green procurement policy.
4. Draft a supplier code of conduct.
5. Engage suppliers in conversation.
6. Consider an industry-wide collaboration.
7. Undertake formal audits.
8. Develop a supplier mentoring program.
9. Reach deeper into the supply chain.
10. Optimize with technology.
11. Form cross-industry partnerships to raise industry standards.

ADDITIONAL RESOURCES

SELF-ASSESSMENT

Eco-Eval (North American Green Purchasing Initiative). Helps professional purchasers identify opportunities to improve their organizations' environmental procurement practices. Includes best practice case studies and specialized resources. www.cec.org/eco-eval

"Eco-S.A.T.: A Green Purchasing Self-Assessment Tool" (North American Green Purchasing Initiative). 66-page guide with benchmarking guidance and tools to implement green purchasing practices. www.cec.org

DEVELOPING AND IMPLEMENTING GREEN PURCHASING STRATEGY

"Forging New Links: Enhancing Supply Chain Value through Environmental Excellence" (Global Environmental Management Initiative, 2004). Outlines strategies for using supply chain initiatives to boost overall supply chain performance and enhance shareholder value. www.gemi.org

"New Paths to Business Value: Strategic Sourcing—Environment, Health and Safety" (GEMI). Outlines how green procurement can enhance business value. Encourages a selective approach tailored to individual company needs and provides practical recommendations for procurement professionals. www.gemi.org

"Guide to the Business Case and Benefits of Sustainability Purchasing" (Sustainability Purchasing Network, 2007). Outlines the financial, social, and environmental costs and benefits of sustainability purchasing. www.buysmartbc.com

Green Supplier Network. U.S. government-sponsored effort to help companies find customized solutions to manufacturing challenges, save money and increase capacity, achieve additional savings and efficiencies beyond traditional lean techniques, and improve supply chain relationships. A joint effort of the U.S. Environmental Protection Agency, Department of Commerce, National Institute of Standards and Technology, and Manufacturing Extension Partnership Program. www.greensuppliers.gov

Responsible Purchasing Network (RPN). An international, membership-based network of buyers dedicated to socially responsible and environmentally sustainable purchasing. www.responsiblepurchasing.org

The Green Purchasing and Green Public Procurement Starter Kit (International Green Purchasing Network). Interactive web- and CD-ROM-based package with interactive modules to help businesses implement green purchasing programs. www.igpn.org

Sustainable Food Policy Guide. Outlines options and recommendations for making sustainable food purchases. Includes sample purchasing policies along with RFP and contract language. www.sustainablefoodpolicy.org

FINDING GREENER PRODUCTS AND SERVICES

General

Environmental Specialty Catalog (General Services Administration). Extensive online directory of greener products and services. Although only government agencies can purchase products directly from the site, it is a valuable information resource for businesses. www.gsaadvantage.gov

Environmentally Preferable Purchasing (EPA). Tools and resources to help purchasing professionals find and evaluate green products and services, calculate costs and benefits of purchasing choices, and implement green procurement practices. www.epa.gov/epp

Responsible Purchasing Network Guides. Purchasing Guides for a range of products and services, including: bottled water, carbon offsets, cleaners, computers, copy paper, fleets, food services, green power, light-duty tires and wheel weights, lighting, office electronics, paint, and toner cartridges. www.responsiblepurchasing.org

Green Pages Online (Co-op America). Guide to socially and environmentally responsible businesses. Most helpful to small businesses looking to advertise or find local suppliers. www.greenamericatoday.org

Green Seal Products Directory. The Green Seal product label is reserved for products that have undergone stringent evaluations to ensure lower impact on the environment and human health. www.greenseal.org

Office Supplies

The Green Office. Comprehensive selection of greener office products including technology, lighting, paper, furniture, cleaning and janitorial supplies, and more. www.thegreenoffice.com

Wood and Paper Products

"Sustainable Procurement of Wood and Paper-Based Products: Guide and Resource Kit" (World Resources Institute and World Business Council on Sustainable Development). Comprehensive resource to help purchasers develop sustainable procurement strategies around wood and paper-based products. Helps purchasers define requirements for procurement policies, engage in dialogue with stakeholders, assess suppliers, and find specialized tools and resources. www.sustainableforestprods.org

Environmental Papers (Conservatree). A one-stop source for information on environmental papers. Includes lists of products and where to buy. www.conservatree.org

Forest Certification Resource Center (Metafore). Clearinghouse site for locating certified wood and paper manufacturers, wholesalers, and distributors around the world. www.metafore.org

Electronics

EPEAT—Electronic Product Environmental Assessment Tool. Helps institutional purchasers evaluate, compare, and select desktop computers, notebooks, and monitors based on environmental attributes. www.epeat.net

Buildings

GreenSpec Product Database (Building Green). Product descriptions for over 2,000 environmentally preferable products in the buildings industry. www.buildinggreen.com

Chemicals

Green Chemical Alternatives Purchasing Wizard. A web-based tool that allows the user to search from a select list of solvents commonly used in the laboratory and associated processes. www.mit.edu

ECO-LABELS AND CERTIFICATIONS

Ecolabel Index and "Global Ecolabel Monitor." Definitive, searchable online guide to ecolabels across all industry sectors. www.ecolabelindex.com

"**Global Ecolabel Monitor**" (Ecolabel Index and World Resources Institute, 2010). A report on the performance and organizational structure of eco-labels around the world. www.wri.org

Big Room Inc. is working to set up a .eco domain that would provide an open platform for product-level eco-information. www.bigroom.ca

Chapter 13 Manufacturing and Processing

Toyota Motor Company began as a subsidiary of a loom manufacturing company in 1933 and quickly established itself as a premier automaker in Japan.[1] However, World War II and the accompanying economic depression in Japan hit the young company hard. By 1949, Toyota was spending more money producing cars than it was selling them. Payrolls were suspended, workers went on strike, and the company nearly collapsed. The CEO and all of his executive staff resigned.

Shaw Industries, the flooring manufacturer, saved $623,000 in energy costs during 2008 by converting 9.5 million pounds of carpet and 12 million pounds of wood waste into energy and using it to run a manufacturing plant in Georgia.[2]

ArcelorMittal's specialty rolling mill plant in Pennsylvania has saved $200,000 in annual energy bills thanks to improvements in efficiency, particularly systems that automatically idle machinery during production delays.[3]

Hewlett Packard is designing printer cartridges to be recycled and reused. Between 50 and 70 percent of the plastic in recycled cartridges (about 10 million pounds annually) is reused by HP to create new cartridges.[4]

3M's 3P (Pollution Prevention Pays) program, which focuses on preventing pollution at the source in products and manufacturing processes, has saved the company nearly $1.4 billion since its inception in 1975.[5]

Intel saved millions of dollars annually by creating lighter-weight plastic trays to move microprocessor units through the fabrication process.[6]

Sonoco conducted waste audits in 34 North American plants and found more than 70,000 tons of recyclable scrap, opening up a revenue stream of $770,000 in 2008.[7]

Seeking to rebuild Toyota's broken manufacturing and reputation, new CEO Eiji Toyoda sought inspiration from Ford Motor Company's automobile factories. At the time, Ford's assembly line was considered the most advanced manufacturing process in the world. However, Toyota didn't simply copy Ford's model, it adapted it and improved on it continuously. Unlike Ford at the time, Toyota recognized that in order to drive innovation, a company needs to develop its employees. Toyota empowers its employees to make suggestions for improvement and take ownership of their part of the production process. This engagement drives employee morale and loyalty, which often translates to higher quality products. Innovation at Toyota has led to the creation of just-in-time manufacturing, total production maintenance, and other lean manufacturing techniques that are now well known.

Today, Toyota is one of the top-three-selling car companies in the world. While it has faced recent market challenges, the company continues to add value for its customers by creating alternative fuel vehicles, adopting greener manufacturing processes, and contributing to corporate sustainability efforts.

Toyota shows how a culture of innovation led a company from crisis to global competitive advantage. Today the "Toyota Way" of manufacturing is copied all over the world as the model of lean manufacturing. But companies, including Toyota, shouldn't stop there. Today, environmental concerns offer companies new manufacturing risks to manage and opportunities to add value. Everyone with a hand in the manufacturing process—engineers, plant managers, line workers, and more—stands to benefit from using a green lens to uncover new ways to save costs, head off risks, raise product quality, and generate other business benefits. This chapter introduces a series of "green manufacturing" plays designed to help companies:

- Cut manufacturing costs.
- Improve manufacturing process flow.
- Lower operational risks, including compliance-related issues.
- Better meet customer needs.

BASIC PLAYS: USE A GREEN LENS TO IMPROVE ENERGY EFFICIENCY IN OPERATIONS

Greener manufacturing is ultimately about doing more with less. Like the principles behind lean manufacturing, it's about efficiency and common sense. Why leave money on the table in the form of waste? It's about quality—produce better products that delight customers. And it's about innovation—employ cost-effective production processes that require fewer inputs from the natural world and generate less (or no) waste that harms people or ecosystems.

As we argue in "Building a Winning Eco-Advantage Strategy" (Chapter 3), the companies that adopt a hard-nosed, strategic *mindset* about sustainability will reap the biggest benefits. Leading-edge companies adopt a company-wide "ecosystem" approach that connects the dots among all the critical parts of the value chain—product design, procurement, manufacturing, logistics, marketing, and more. They make design and planning decisions early in the value chain, opening up a world of new possibilities in cost savings, risk reduction, revenue creation, and other business benefits. For instance, eco-minded engineers imagine ways to make better products without toxic chemicals so that plant managers don't even have to buy and manage them in the first place, *or* lose sleep over potential spills that could harm workers. High-performance companies plan from the outset how to make products easier to assemble and disassemble, which can speed up manufacturing processes, reduce defect rates, improve product reliability, lower service costs—and facilitate the recovery of valuable materials that can be reused or sold for profit.

Companies that are just starting to explore green manufacturing opportunities can find plenty of low-hanging fruit—some of it even lying on the ground—available to *every* business that manufactures any type of product. We recommend you start by focusing on opportunities connected to saving *energy*. Every operations group we've worked with saw the business value of cutting energy costs. An energy-focused eco-efficiency push usually pays quick dividends.

1. Involve Employees in the Search for Energy Savings

Companies that have excelled in seizing business advantages from greener manufacturing share a secret weapon: they tap into the talent, expertise, and energy of front-line employees—the people who are best positioned to spot opportunities to cut energy, pollution, and waste. 3M's Pollution Prevention Pays (3P) program, which rewards and recognizes employees for seizing eco-efficiency and pollution prevention opportunities, offers a shining example.[8] Between 2000 and 2005, 3M not only achieved a reduction in volatile organic compound (VOC) emissions indexed to net sales of 58 percent (compared to a goal of 25 percent), it also saw a rise in employee-initiated 3P projects of over 550 percent (compared to a goal of a little more than 100 percent).[9]

Eventually, you will want all your employees to use a green lens to spot costs, problems, and business opportunities they otherwise would not see. One way to get started is to involve employees in facility-wide "treasure hunts" designed to find waste and inefficiency. GE enlisted thousands of employees in just such a series of searches for energy-saving opportunities.[10] The resulting hunts identified more than 5,000 projects with the opportunity to eliminate 700,000 metric tons of greenhouse gas emissions and $111 million in operational cost. More important, the treasure hunts initiated a cultural change by getting thousands of employees to view their jobs through a green lens.

A three-day treasure hunt at a GE manufacturing plant in Wisconsin set a goal of identifying ways to reduce the plant's carbon footprint and find at least $700,000 in energy savings.[11] Teams walked through the facility over the weekend when equipment was in sleep mode to see how energy was being used when nothing was actually being produced. After inspecting everything from water use and ventilation to lightbulbs and computer monitors, the teams identified opportunities for $3 million in savings and a reduction of nearly 24,000 metric tons of CO_2.

2. Do a Systematic Energy Audit and Measure Energy Use from Individual Processes

Use comprehensive energy audits to benchmark a plant's energy use against industry averages and reveal energy-saving opportunities that walk-through exercises can miss. Audits involve simple techniques, like reviewing utility bills, to complex ones—such as analyzing historical energy use and energy-efficiency investment options. Local utilities and non-profit organizations sometimes offer free or low-cost energy audit services. In addition, measuring the energy use of individual production and support processes provides invaluable information on where to focus your efforts. Process heating systems and motor-driven equipment are two of the best places to look first for substantial energy savings. The Additional Resources Section at the end of this chapter provides recommendations for other excellent resources and tools to help—including a guide to programs that offer free audit assistance to small and medium-sized manufacturers.

MAKE GREEN ROUTINE AND VISUAL

Consider the following steps to build green best practices into standard work:

- Build best practices into training materials and standard work for equipment operation and maintenance.
- Include tips in internal communications.
- Use visuals to reinforce best practice or flag problems (e.g., color-coded ties on pipes to report leaks, signs over power switches to remind operators to turn off equipment when not in use, or floor markings and placards to identify containers for collecting hazardous and non-hazardous wastes).

Source: Adapted from U.S. EPA, *Lean and Environment Toolkit,* EPA, October 2007; U.S. EPA, *Lean and Energy Toolkit,* EPA, October 2007; and U.S. EPA, *Lean and Chemicals Toolkit,* EPA, August 2009. www.epa.gov/lean/ (accessed August 22, 2010).

INTERMEDIATE PLAYS: GET LEANER BY GOING GREEN

3. Eliminate Waste

"Lean and Green" manufacturing builds on the same concept: rooting out waste and inefficiency. The only difference is that applying a green lens reveals new forms of waste, beyond just lost product, that are often missed by traditional lean manufacturing initiatives. In particular, look for:

- **Wasted energy,** which drives up companies' energy bills and results in air, land, and water pollution. For example, Steelcase Inc., a global leader in the office furniture industry, reduced its energy use by 60 percent and water use by 80 percent by using a greener washer in its manufacturing process.[12]

- **Scrap,** which raises waste management and disposal costs, signals that companies are throwing away valuable inputs (from precious metals to fresh water). Baxter Healthcare Corporation, a worldwide manufacturer of global medical products, saved 170,000 gallons of water per day and $17,000 with little or no capital investment within 3 months of implementing a green manufacturing action plan.[13] In today's cost-conscious world, "resource productivity"—getting the most out of all inputs—must be a priority for every manufacturer.

- **Chemical discharges,** which carry high compliance-related costs, often mean that expensive inputs are going to waste. Beyond the regulatory burden of tracking hazardous waste and paying exorbitant fees for its disposal, toxic materials impose an ecological burden on humans and our natural environment. Sometimes as much as 40 percent of a company's chemical supplies become hazardous waste before they are even taken off the shelves.[14]

A GREEN LENS ON WASTE

Lean manufacturing principles build on these fundamental notions of waste, extending them into seven categories:

1. Overproduction
2. Excess inventory
3. Inefficient transportation or conveyance
4. Unnecessary motion
5. Defects
6. Overprocessing
7. Waiting

Each of these 7 "deadly" areas of waste that lean manufacturing tries to eliminate can be put under a "green" spotlight to further extend the search to root out inefficiency.

Source: Ron Wince, "The 7 "Deadly" Wastes That Could Cost Your Company," *Six Sigma & Process Excellence,* June 1, 2007, www.sixsigmaiq.com/ (accessed August 22, 2010).

You can find environmental wastes in almost any process. A good place to start looking is any process that requires environmental permits—such as painting, metal finishing, and hazardous waste management. The EPA identifies 10 common manufacturing processes with the biggest environmental opportunities:

1. Metal casting
2. Materials treatment
3. Metal fabrication and machining

4. Cleaning and surface preparation
5. Bonding and sealing
6. Welding
7. Metal finishing and plating
8. Painting and coating
9. Chemical and hazardous materials management
10. Waste management[15]

A company's Environmental Health and Safety department often has the clues to key environmental impacts associated with a company's processes.

4. Integrate Energy and Environment Factors into Value Stream Mapping

What goes in has to come out. Value Stream Mapping (VSM), a lean manufacturing technique, produces a visual representation of what goes in and out of the production process. The maps help managers uncover the largest sources of waste in the value stream so they can prioritize opportunities for process improvements. Conventional value stream maps track production processes but can overlook environmental considerations such as raw materials used in products and processes; pollution and other environmental wastes in the value stream; and flows of information to environmental regulatory agencies.[16] By adding energy and environmental considerations into VSM, companies can identify new opportunities to cut energy costs and raise productivity. Figure 13.1 is a sample value stream map with inputs and outputs and opportunities for Environmental Health and Safety improvements in the boxes labeled with the "EHS" oval.

The U.S. EPA recommends the following key steps for integrating green into value stream mapping:

- Use icons to identify energy-efficiency environmental opportunities in each process.
- Record the primary resource "inputs" for each process (e.g., raw materials, energy, and water use) and the key nonproduct "outputs" resulting from each process (e.g., scrap, air emissions, hazardous waste, etc.) directly onto value stream maps. Use different colors to show resource flows and waste flows out of each process data box on the value stream map.
- Record the amount of waste generated by each process. Be sure to include purchasing costs of the raw materials, time spent managing the wastes, and costs of disposal.
- Analyze materials used by each process versus materials that actually end up in the product, and summarize this information on value stream maps.
- Add energy and water inputs and emitted greenhouse gases and other pollutants.[17]

Figure 13.1   **Value Stream Map with Environmental Data**

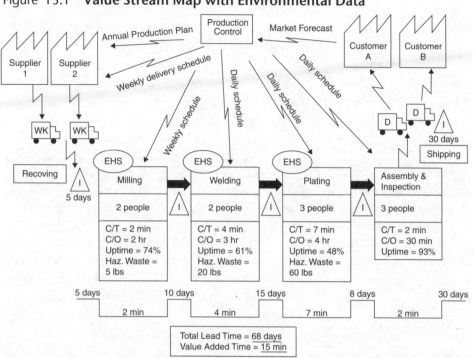

Source: U.S. EPA, *Lean and the Environmental Toolkit*, October 2007, www.epa.gov/lean/toolkit/ch3.htm (accessed August 23, 2010).

TO BE "LEAN AND GREEN" THE EPA RECOMMENDS:

- **Adding environmental metrics** to better understand the environmental performance of production areas.
- **Showing management commitment and support** by providing resources and recognition.
- **Integrating environment into Lean training programs.**
- **Making environmental wastes visible and simple to eliminate** by using signs and other visual controls in the workplace.
- **Recognizing and rewarding environmental success** accomplished through Lean.

Source: U.S. EPA, *Lean and the Environment Toolkit, Chapter* 3: *Value Stream Mapping*, October 2007, www.epa.gov/lean/toolkit/ch3.htm (accessed August 22, 2010).

5. Use Green Six Sigma

Six Sigma uses statistical analysis to improve performance and reduce defects in manufacturing processes. Six Sigma was developed by Motorola in the 1990s using established quality control techniques and data analysis methods. The term sigma is a Greek alphabet letter (σ) used to describe variability. A sigma quality level describes how often defects are likely to occur in processes, parts, or products. A Six Sigma quality level indicates high quality and minimal process variability, or approximately 3.4 defects per million opportunities.

THE IMPORTANCE OF GOOD METRICS

The right metrics can help accelerate progress and fuel continuous improvement. Companies focused on green manufacturing track the following basic metrics:

- Scrap/Nonproduct output
- Air emissions
- Materials use
- Solid waste
- Hazardous materials use
- Hazardous waste
- Energy use
- Water pollution/Wastewater
- Water use

3M tracks many environmental indicators including greenhouse gas emissions, volatile organic compound emissions, and waste by-products—then **indexes these factors to net sales**, which gives employees a set of readily understandable ratios that they can track from year to year.[18]

DuPont devised a simple metric to track its progress in reducing waste: **shareholder value added (SVA) per pound of product produced**.[19] The company calculates the weight of everything it produces and indexes that figure to financial performance, which pushes employees to strive to find ways to produce more with fewer environmental resources.

SolFocus uses **"Greenhouse Gas Return on Investment (GROI)."**[20] The company takes information from a life cycle analysis of current manufacturing GHG emissions then divides this amount by GHG emissions prevented per year by new technology. The resulting "GROI" figure provides a metric for how quickly an investment in new technology can be "paid back" in terms of emissions saved.

See Chapters 6 (Assess and Measure), 7 (Benchmark), and 22 (Communicate and Report) for recommendations and tools to help choose metrics and build evaluation systems.

Source: U.S. EPA, *Lean and the Environment Toolkit,* October 2007, www.epa.gov/lean/toolkit/ (accessed August 22, 2010).

Lean Six Sigma helped 3M reduce energy use by 27 percent and reduce toxic wastes by 64 percent (when indexed to net sales) from 2000 to 2005.[21] 3M launched a corporate-wide Lean Six Sigma initiative in February 2001. By 2006, more than 55,000 salaried employees at 3M were trained in Lean Six Sigma processes and methodologies and more than 45,000 Lean Six Sigma projects had been initiated. All Environmental Health and Safety workers at 3M are required to receive two weeks of Lean Six Sigma training and to lead one Six Sigma project. In addition, Six Sigma is being used as a focus for company operations and viewed as a basic component of 3M's corporate culture.

IBM has developed a comprehensive system called Green Sigma, which employs sophisticated sensors to monitor energy, GHG emissions, waste, and water throughout company operations.[22] Data from these sensors feeds into software applications such as dashboards, which can be used by manufacturing managers to monitor processes for unwanted emissions and waste. IBM formed a coalition of partners to build out its Green Sigma initiative, including industry leaders Johnson Controls, Honeywell Building Solutions, ABB Group, Eaton Corp., Environmental Support Solutions, Cisco Systems, Siemens Building Technologies Division, and Schneider Electric.

6. Add an Energy Efficiency Focus to Total Productive Maintenance

Applying a green lens to maintenance offers another way to sharpen operational efficiency. One "easy win" derives from incorporating energy reduction best practices into a total productive maintenance (TPM) program. Traditionally, many companies delegate equipment maintenance to a maintenance department, while those who operate the machines do not know how to repair them. In many cases, maintenance only happens when equipment breaks down, which causes delays and difficulties in repair. Under TPM, workers in all departments and levels are involved to ensure optimal equipment performance.[23] TPM strives to incorporate maintenance into day-to-day operations in order to prevent breakdowns. Under autonomous maintenance, a key component of TPM, workers who operate equipment take charge of routine maintenance and repairs, leaving more challenging maintenance issues to professional maintenance staff. TPM seeks to prevent equipment failure, decrease the incidence of defects, and cut down on worker accidents—and, in doing so, cuts down on scrap and waste. Adding green considerations to a TPM program can drive additional benefits such as increasing equipment life, which translates into avoided costs in buying new equipment as well as less waste and pollution.

To integrate energy-reduction efforts into TPM,[24] companies should:

- Explore reduction opportunities in autonomous maintenance activities.
- Train employees on how to identify energy inefficiencies and how to maintain equipment.
- Build energy-efficiency best practices into day-to-day operations.[25]

Eastman Kodak encourages TPM at its facilities through coordinated visibility efforts. Each month the company produces a kaizen newsletter and posts it in hallways where managers are sure to see it. The newsletter lists actions taken and what follow-up is required. A TPM checklist is prominently displayed on the plant floor for the operators of each shift. Employees are encouraged to share what they have learned and are acknowledged at team meetings for achieving good results. Kodak also trains TPM coordinators to act as "catalysts within a local area to keep the action moving."[26] Since instituting these practices, Kodak attributes a $16 million increase in profits to a $5 million investment in TPM.[27]

Other companies have also reported cost savings and efficiency gains as a result of TPM. One appliance manufacturer reported a decrease in the amount of time required to change dies on a forming press from several hours to twenty minutes. Texas Instruments reported increased production figures of up to 80 percent in some areas using TPM. Ford, Kodak, Dana Corp, and Harley-Davidson all reported 50 percent or greater reductions in downtime, spare parts inventory, and increased on-time deliveries.[28] These translate into huge environmental benefits as well.

ADVANCED PLAYS: TAKE EFFICIENCY TO NEW HEIGHTS

7. Use Cellular Manufacturing and Right-Sized Equipment

Cellular manufacturing streamlines production by breaking down large unit processes into right-sized and highly flexible "cells." In the traditional "batch and queue" process, a large quantity of materials goes through a single production stage before it is transported and processed by the next stage. This sometimes results in overproduction and delays, because production must complete one process before moving on to the next one. In cellular manufacturing, right-sized equipment processes one piece (or smaller quantities of material), which is then transferred quickly from stage to stage. Production processes are located in close proximity to each other to minimize transfer time. The process allows a single product to move quickly through the production process in response to customer demand. A single product can be changed without creating a large batch of the same product.[29]

Cellular manufacturing often utilizes the following innovations:

- **Single-minute exchange of die (SMED)** means that workers can quickly convert a machine or process to produce a different variation of the product without the time-consuming alterations required in batch and queue processes.
- **Autonomation** or the ability of machines to stop, start, load, and unload automatically so that a product flows smoothly through the production process without constant supervision.
- **Right-sized equipment** or equipment designed to efficiently process products one at a time or in small quantities allowing for more flexibility in response to customer demand.

Cellular manufacturing has the potential to eliminate overproduction—and thus to promote sustainability—by reducing the amount of raw materials, energy, and labor used in production. By putting production processes in closer and more logical configurations, transfers waste less time and energy, and production can be supervised more efficiently.[30] An aerospace foundry in the United States (which does not want to be named) successfully used this approach to reduce waste and increase productivity in its manufacturing process.[31]

Before the implementation of cellular manufacturing, the company used a batch and queue process with production centers located in several different buildings. Dozens of people would make a four-to-eight block trip several times a day to transfer products from the processing center to the nondestructive testing center. Additionally, workers had to transport parts via carts, trucks, and forklifts each time, a process that used huge amounts of energy and led to many unnecessary complications. Guided by cellular manufacturing, the managers at the foundry consolidated production and testing into a centrally located space. They also incorporated a lab and the packing and shipping dock adjacent to the central facility. After considerable streamlining and workflow improvements, the new process cut down on thousands of hours of labor and reduced defects. The company estimates that the improvements save them more than $2 million annually.

8. Switch to Just-in-Time Manufacturing and Delivery

Just-in-time (JIT) manufacturing and delivery can help companies cut down on waste, lower energy consumption with reduced warehouse space and avoid overproduction. In basic terms, just-in-time manufacturing means inputs arrive just when they are needed rather than waiting in inventory.

Adding green considerations to JIT can translate into benefits such as an increase in materials and energy efficiency by eliminating (or greatly reducing) overproduction; a reduction in defects and all of the waste associated with them; a reduction in energy due to lower factory and warehouse floor-space requirements; and a reduction in energy (and emissions) from unnecessary transportation of materials from suppliers and of products to customers. For example, applying JIT to chemical management can lead to fewer chemicals stored on-site. Having chemicals delivered when you need them, and in the amounts that you need, supports lean goals while reducing risks and wastes. As Hubbard Hal, a Waterbay, Connecticut, chemical distributor has shown, manufacturers may get multiple "wins" from outsourcing chemical management services to a company that specializes in managing chemical inventories, preventing spills, and fulfilling regulatory burdens.

Dell has been using JIT to get ahead of its competition in the computer technology industry since 2000. Dell eliminates overproduction and streamlines distribution by taking custom orders directly from customers. The company keeps only five days of inventory on hand while other companies in the industry hold between 20 and 30 days worth of inventory.[32] Dell's small inventory allows it to have maximum flexibility when it comes to fulfilling customer's orders and shortens the amount of time it takes to deliver products to customers. Dell's use of JIT manufacturing results in cost savings, greater customer satisfaction, and reduced waste and pollution. Dell can manufacture "what their customers ask them to make, when they ask them."[33]

Not everyone can implement JIT manufacturing, and doing so requires a high degree of organization in the company. A larger inventory buffers companies from sudden changes in the market such as strikes, demand fluctuations, interrupted supplies, communication outages, and other unforeseen interruptions. Because JIT minimizes the amount of inventory, a breakdown in the supply chain can cause the company to run out of components and hold up the rest of the production process. JIT is more suited to mass-produced and highly automated production systems that rely on frequent updates in inventory. JIT manufacturers also need reliable suppliers and excellent communications with suppliers so that inventories can be restocked at the pace demanded by JIT.[34]

9. Green Your Kaizen Events

Coming from a Japanese word that means "continual improvement," kaizen events aim to enhance operational efficiency by identifying process improvement opportunities. Kaizen events center on getting production teams to make rapid changes to targeted areas of the workplace.[35] During a kaizen event, workers from multiple functions and levels get together to identify ways to quickly eliminate waste in a targeted process or production area. Strategies are typically implemented within 72 hours and do not involve large capital outlays. Using a green lens at kaizen events can reveal new forms of "defects" and waste—including energy waste and costly and dangerous pollution.

A green kaizen event requires a cross-functional team of employees, including environmental staff experts, that can quickly identify the process areas with the biggest eco-related impacts and help spot the biggest opportunities for improved production. Some kaizen events focus exclusively on energy inefficiency, others on chemical use, and yet others cast a wider net. Helpful tools for planning and implementing kaizen events include:

1. Value stream maps to identify potential focus areas.
2. Questions to help employees identify lean-environment opportunities.
3. Hierarchical process mapping, which goes deeper than value stream maps to reveal specific sources of waste from a single process.
4. Process-specific pollution prevention resources.

Goodrich Corporation, a supplier of products and services to the aerospace industry, uses kaizen events to drive waste elimination.[36] Team members of an event assess hazardous waste streams; identify and implement pollution prevention techniques; and target environmental, health, and safety (EHS) issues. Since 1995 Goodrich has conducted over 350 kaizen events. Staff identify EHS objectives at all kaizen events and make efforts to involve EHS personnel. Converting to cellular manufacturing and shifting to lean point-of-use chemical management systems also helped Goodrich to eliminate labor and reduce chemical use.

Baxter International, a global medical products and services company, used kaizen events to manage energy use at its facility in Spain. The facility recorded daily energy use for one year. Each time energy use exceeded average use by 15 percent, the facility held a kaizen event to address the root causes of the peak. The facility saved approximately $300,000 in one year.[37]

10. Integrate Green Issues into "5S" Programs

5S is a lean manufacturing tool designed to lead to a clean and orderly workplace as well as create efficient processes. The 5S's are: sort, set in order, shine, standardize, and sustain. Some companies add "safety" as a sixth. 5S practitioners apply all the S's to workplace layout and manufacturing processes. Integrating environmental management procedures into standard work procedures can further reduce workplace errors, such as spills, lead to fewer product defects, and generate higher productivity due to more efficient placement and use of tools—which, in turn, can lead to more efficient use of materials. For example, using a simple color-coded tagging process during the "Sort" phase (such as with sticky notes) to identify hazardous chemicals can prevent mistakes later in the process and help avoid accidents. Identifying hazardous materials can also help managers keep track of how much is being used in the manufacturing process and find ways to reduce the use of such materials.

Many companies have radically reengineered their use of chemicals in manufacturing to lessen their environmental impact. IBM, as part of its design for environment initiative, recently eliminated the use of perfluorooctane sulfonate (PFOS) and perfluorooctanoic acid (PFOA) compounds from some of its chip-making processes.[38] It used these chemicals to etch circuits onto microchips, a common industry practice, but it worked with its chemical suppliers to develop more environmentally friendly alternatives. U.S. and EU regulatory authorities severely restricted the use of PFOS and PFOA in 2010. By eliminating its use of these bioaccumulative chemicals entirely, IBM got ahead of regulations and avoided costly efforts to handle them.

11. Use Energy from Less-Polluting Fuel Sources

Depending on your region's utility, electricity is generated from polluting sources such as coal or fuel oil, or cleaner sources such as hydro and nuclear. Utility bills often tell only part of the energy story. Understanding the *energy end uses*—what work the energy does—reveals more useful information that can be used to identify opportunities for improving efficiency and reducing costs.

Switching to a cleaner fuel can result in huge reductions in greenhouse gases and toxic air emissions. For example, switching from electricity to natural gas heating can reduce heating costs by as much as 75 percent.[39] Some companies can use waste products from their own manufacturing processes to produce energy. Spoetzl Brewery in Shiner, Texas, anticipates reducing the facility's carbon emissions by more than 500 metric tons by installing a biogas generation and wastewater treatment facility. The new facility will convert Spoetzl's waste products from its brewing processes into methane gas, which it will use to fuel the boilers for beer production. In addition to reducing carbon emissions, the facility will reduce Spoetzl's natural gas consumption by more than 95,000 therms per year.[40] Companies that use their own waste products for fuel won't need to purchase as much fuel, which also cuts down on their disposal costs.

Companies can also utilize alternative energy through purchasing agreements or via on-site installation of renewable energy sources. These options range from small to large operations. Phoenix Press, a tiny printing company in New Haven, Connecticut, installed a 100-kilowatt wind turbine in 2010 to cut its reliance on traditional power companies and get a green "image" edge in the competitive local market. Phoenix estimated a payback time of four years.[41] Other companies, particularly ones producing green-certified products, purchase Renewable Energy Certificates (RECs), which are now widely available. For example, paper products giant Cascades, Inc. committed to purchasing 20,000 megawatt hours of wind-generated RECs to produce its North River tissue and towel products.[42] Many energy utilities also provide their customers with the option to purchase a percentage of their electricity as "green power." The premiums that utilities charge for green power are invested into the development of new renewable energy sources. Between 2000 and 2009 the average net price premium for utility green power has decreased from 3.48 cents per kilowatt hour to 1.75 cents per kilowatt hour.[43] See EPA's Green Power Partnership website (www.epa.gov/greenpower) for more information on purchasing renewable energy from utilities.

12. Introduce Advanced Manufacturing Technologies

Many technologies today allow manufacturers to lean and green their products and processes. These technologies combine equipment with software interfaces that can be used as stand-alone units or integrated into the manufacturing process. Examples of some of the new technologies available to help "green" processes such as design, fabrication, handling, and inspection include:

- **Computer-aided design and manufacturing** (CAD/CAM) including electronic design automation.
- **Rapid prototyping** technology.
- **Computer numerically controlled machines**, including laser and waterjet cutting.
- **Robotics and automation** including welding, pick-and-place information communication technologies, and electronics-based systems including control, tracking, intelligent inspection, and predictive maintenance.
- **Digital manufacturing**, a technique using integrated software that assists in product design, planning, resource management, and supply chain management. The software helps to test structural properties and visualization of designs, workspace, workflow, and scheduling before manufacture, which avoids costly rework and redesign.[44]

Digital manufacturing assists Norwegian pleasure boat builder Hydrolift in many stages of design and manufacturing. The software provides 3-D models that allow engineers to perform aerodynamic analyses, precise visualizations, and full mechanical systems modeling. Bard Eker, managing director and owner of Hydrolift says, "[Digital manufacturing] is an important backbone in our design house philosophy, in which we go from ideas through design, tool production, prototyping, and mass production as one complete delivery."[45]

Many companies combine IT capabilities with energy efficiency metrics to manage energy consumption in manufacturing operations. Called "energy intelligence," these initiatives allow managers to closely track energy usage and identify inefficiencies. A report from the Aberdeen Group, commissioned by software provider EPS, found that companies deploying this IT-based energy management strategy achieved an average reduction in energy use of 15 percent.[46]

Steel giant ArcelorMittal created a software-based energy intelligence system that allows its Conshohocken plant to idle powerful water pumps during a process called descaling.[47] Prior to implementation of this system, the Pennsylvania facility constantly ran the motors required to pump water over rolled steel to remove impurities, even though the water pumping process only occurred in 2 percent of the rolling operations. ArcelorMittal invested $300,000 in installing a system to idle the pumps during downtime. The investment saves them $200,000 annually with only a year and a half payback period.

13. Get Environmentally Strategic about Location

In real estate, location is everything. The same can be said about green manufacturing. Where a product is manufactured, how far supplies travel to the factory, and how far finished products travel to customers play a big role in a company's overall environmental footprint. A product's environmental impact is contained in its "embodied energy," or the amount of energy used in every phase of its production, from resource extraction to transportation. Green manufacturing guru David Dornfeld, relying on data from the Ford Motor Company, notes that manufacturing a car in France, which derives most of its power from nuclear energy, creates about one seventh the amount of greenhouse gas emissions as manufacturing the same car in the United States, which relies much more on coal and natural gas-fired power plants.[48] Manufacturing the same car in China, which overwhelmingly relies on coal-fired plants, will produce 10 times the amount of greenhouse gas emissions as manufacturing it in France. The differences can even be seen on the state level. Dornfeld notes that a car manufactured in California, which uses a mix of renewable energy sources such as wind and solar, results in three times fewer GHG emissions than a car manufactured in Kentucky, which relies predominately on coal-fired plants.[49]

The distance that parts and finished products must travel also plays a role. Using suppliers and distributors closer to manufacturing operations may result in less fuel consumption, which saves money and prevents unnecessary greenhouse gas emissions. Consider the following when thinking about where manufacturing should take place:

- **Supply chains:** Choose suppliers that are located closest to your manufacturing plant or produce supplies using the least amount of embodied energy.
- **Manufacturing/assembly:** Whenever economically and logistically possible, establish manufacturing operations in locations with the lowest possible embodied energy.
- **Distribution:** Locate manufacturing closer to centers of distribution.

Taking all three factors into account can be tricky, but arriving at the right mix can be cost effective and environmentally beneficial.

14. "Close the Loops" and Innovate toward Zero Impact

Leading-edge companies have gone beyond thinking about "reducing" waste and are working to eliminate it altogether. Their work builds on two foundational concepts: "industrial ecology" and "industrial symbiosis." *Industrial ecology* attempts to optimize the use of resources by viewing production processes in the context of surrounding industrial and ecological systems.[50] *Industrial symbiosis*, a subset of industrial ecology, pushes us to think of processes as "closed-loop" systems, with outputs, including waste, to be recycled or reused again as inputs.

The Danish town of Kalundborg offers the most famous example of industrial symbiosis.[51] The entire process starts with water from a local reservoir, which the town uses as its municipal water source. Treated water goes to a local oil refinery, a power plant, and a chemical enzyme producer. The chemical producer feeds enzymes to a pharmaceutical plant, which then sends industrial alcohol by-product to the municipal wastewater treatment plant, which uses the alcohol to feed the biological processes used to purify wastewater. The treatment plant feeds sludge to a waste recycling plant, which converts it to soil and feeds it to a local materials recycler. The recycler then combines the soil with recycled plasterboard and feeds it to a gypsum plant, which creates new plasterboard. It gets even more complicated when the power plant and oil refinery get factored in, but you get the idea. One company/operation receives a waste output from another, which it uses as an input. It then feeds its waste output to another company, which in turn uses it as an input, and so on.[52]

Not many companies will have Kalundborg-like opportunities for industrial symbiosis, but even limited systems integration can pay dividends. In manufacturing, closed-loop thinking can drive innovation. Bissell, a manufacturer of floor cleaners, such as vacuum sweepers, has implemented a closed-loop manufacturing process for the plastic bottles it manufactures for its machines.[53] Bissell takes cuttings from its bottle blowing operation and combines them with post-consumer recycled plastic, such as milk jugs. It then takes this material and creates new plastic resin, which it uses to blow new bottles for its sweepers. The company estimates that this closed-loop process allowed it to save 1 million pounds of polyethylene plastic in 2009, a 470 percent increase over 2005. This industrial ecology approach saved Bissell the expense of buying new, virgin resin, and also prevented the disposal of waste product associated with the creation of virgin resin and disposal of the finished product, where it might have entered the environment.

General Mills, the cereal producer, found an environmentally friendly way to use oat hulls discarded during the production of Cheerios and other foods at its Fridley, Minnesota, plant. Rather than send them to landfills, General Mills uses them as feedstock for a biomass power plant. The power plant supplies 90 percent of the energy necessary to produce steam used in flour production and plant heating. This move saves General Mills $500,000 per year and reduces this particular plant's annual GHG emissions by 21 percent.[54]

Riviera, an Australian company that makes about 450 luxury boats annually, installed a water recycling system that filters stormwater runoff and graywater that is used in pressure cleaning and testing boats for leaks.[55] With boats being tested and pressure cleaned five nights a week, the water recycling system saves the company roughly $18,000 and 4 million gallons of water per year.

Ideal Recycling, a Michigan-based start-up, has found a way to recapture old asphalt shingles and turn them into an aggregate that can be used in paving. Ideal's charge of about $20/ton for taking away the old roofing materials represents a nice cost savings for the contractors who've been paying tipping fees of twice that amount.[56]

Leaders at disposal giant Waste Management recognize a tremendous market opportunity in closed-loop services. They see a huge growth in what they describe as the emerging "organics" market, which includes food scraps, lawn cuttings, and the like. As CEO David Steiner notes, "Organics is very fragmented; nobody has a national network of organics processing facilities." Yet Waste Management, with its national network of disposal and recycling facilities, is hoping it has the scale required to consolidate the market, separate organics from its waste stream, and create an entirely new business in biomass and biofuels.

A company once known for trash could transform its core product—the contents of dumpsters—separate it into its components, and use these components to create environmentally friendly, low carbon fuels. "Today's organics business is where gasoline was in the 1880s," Steiner says. "Back then, gasoline replaced whale fat as lamp oil. It [the fat] was an inefficient way to use oil and it created a lot of waste. Over time, more value was extracted from gasoline through different technologies and applications. Organics has similar potential. We believe that when we break organics into its constituent parts, and extract 100 percent of its energy content, it will be extremely valuable. We want to own that waste stream."[57]

SUMMARY

Key Plays

1.. Involve employees in the search for energy savings.
2. Do a systematic energy audit and measure energy use from individual processes.
3. Eliminate waste.
4. Integrate energy and environment factors into value stream mapping.
5. Use Green Six Sigma.
6. Add an energy-efficiency focus to total productive maintenance.
7. Use cellular manufacturing and right-sized equipment.
8. Switch to just-in-time manufacturing and delivery.
9. Green your kaizen events.
10. Integrate green issues into "5S" programs.
11. Produce energy from less-polluting fuel sources.
12. Introduce advanced manufacturing technologies.
13. Get environmentally strategic about location.
14. "Close the loops" and innovate toward zero impact.

Figure 13.2   **Key Steps to Leaner and Greener Manufacturing**

BASIC PRINCIPLES
• **Invest in high-quality, ongoing maintenance and optimization** to extend life and maximize efficiency of systems and equipment. • **Design plant layout and flow to maximize the efficiency of** *systems*, **not just components** (e.g., laying out a system with big pipes that need small pumps, not using many small pipes requiring big pumps). • **Choose the right size equipment for the job.** (e.g., "rather than relying on one large paint booth or parts cleaning tank station to service all painting and degreasing needs for a facility, shift to right-sized paint and degreasing stations that are embedded in manufacturing cells"). • **Replace old inefficient equipment** with new high-efficiency equipment that will deliver payback and ROI in energy savings over its life span. • **Make green routine and visual** by putting best practices into standardized training and work procedures, using visual signals, and by making it easy or "mistake-proofing." • **Look for opportunities to "close loops"** where you or others can turn outputs back into inputs.

Facilities (lighting, HVAC, cleaning, grounds, and more)	• Use "**Eco-smart Buildings Checklist**" in Chapter 9, "Buildings and Facilities."
Insulate and Repair Leaks	• **Insulate hot pipes and surfaces** to cut heat loss up to 90 percent. • **Check for leaks** by shutting off other equipment and listening or using an ultrasonic leak detector. • **Repair compressed air leaks** (100 psig) to save $30–$90 per leak per shift per year. • **Repair high-pressure steam leaks** (125 pounds per square inch gauge [psig]) can save $150–$500 per leak per shift per year. • **Repair low-pressure steam leaks** (15 psig) can save $30–$110 per leak per shift per year.
Use Compressed Air Efficiently	• **Regularly service and maintain compressor systems.** • **Make sure compressed air systems are properly sized.** Replace large compressors operating at part load with smaller systems that can operate at full load. For large multi-compressor systems, consider an electronic control system that can match supply with demand. • **Don't use high-pressure air for cleaning, cooling, or drying** when low-pressure air from blowers or fans would work as well. • **Consider a variable speed drive** if the compressor operates under a range of loads. • **Match air pressure to the system demand.** Reducing average load by 7.5 kW can save $391/year, and reducing by 110 kW can save $5,597/year.

(*continued*)

Figure 13.2 (*Continued*)

	• Ensure that the temperature of the intake air is as low as possible (e.g., ducted air from a cool, shaded area outside). • Shut down unnecessary compressors, using timers after production is finished.
Combustion Systems	• Operate furnaces and boilers at or close to design capacity. • Reduce excess air used for combustion. • Clean heat transfer surfaces. • Reduce radiation losses from openings. • Use proper furnace or boiler insulation to reduce wall heat losses. • Adequately insulate air- or water-cooled surfaces exposed to the furnace environment and steam lines leaving the boiler. • Install air preheat or other heat-recovery equipment.
Steam Generation Systems	• Improve water treatment to minimize boiler blowdown. • Optimize deaerator vent rate. • Repair steam leaks. • Minimize vented steam. • Implement effective steam trap maintenance program.
Process Heating Systems	• Minimize air leakage into the furnace by sealing openings. • Maintain proper, slightly positive furnace pressure. • Reduce weight of or eliminate material handling fixtures. • Recover furnace exhaust gas heat by modifying the furnace system or using a separate heating system. • Recover part of the furnace exhaust heat for use in lower-temperature processes.
Mechanical Systems and Motor-Driven Equipment	• Lower process heating temperatures if they are set unnecessarily high. • Run equipment during nonpeak hours when possible to save money and reduce demand on utilities. • Make sure motors, pumps, and equipment are properly sized to match actual loads. • Install energy-efficient motors, pumps, and equipment. • Install energy-efficient flat and conveyer belts (e.g., replace standard V-belts with cogged or synchronous belt drives). • Fine-tune settings of all electric motor-driven systems (air compressors, pumps, fans) to minimize installed horsepower and maximize motor efficiency.

Figure 13.2   (*Continued*)

	• **Install right-sized, high-efficiency, adjustable-speed fans and motors** (EPA). Right-size fan systems by using larger pulleys or using only static pressure adjustment variable air volume (VAV) systems.
	• **Install multiple small motors** to handle varying volumes rather than one big motor.
	• **Make sure systems are not left running when not in operation. "Mistake-proof" equipment** to ensure it gets shut down manually or automatically.
	• **Move operating shift to off-peak times** to save $75 per hp per year.
	• **Move other electric equipment to off-peak** to save $120 per kW per year.
	• **Use variable speed machines**—rather than running at a constant rpm, the machine can decelerate and even idle between use, saving energy and preventing GHG emissions.
	• **Use multi-purpose or multi-spindle machines.** A dual-spindle machine from STAMA America, for example, uses only 20 percent more energy to finish two, rather than one part, reducing finishing costs per part by 40 percent.
	• **Reduce cycle time for finishing.** Although this requires higher rpm machines, the energy required for higher rpms can be offset by the reduction in finishing time combined with the use of variable speed machines.
	• **Recycle energy using Kinetic Energy Recovery Systems (KERS)**—energy saved can be fed back into floor operations, reducing your energy bill, or sold back to the power grid.
Use Submetering Devices	• **Consider submetering for evaporative cooling towers,** which can be installed on most cooling towers for less than $1,000* and can result in sewage treatment savings of $9 per ton per shift per year.
Chemicals Management	• **Eliminate hazardous chemicals** from products and processes or replace with less toxic alternatives.
	• **Right-size equipment and containers for tasks** to limit unnecessary use of chemicals and increase process efficiency.
	• **Consider "kitting"**—gathering all necessary parts and materials for a process step and issuing the kit to the manufacturing line at the right time and in the right quantity.

(*continued*)

Figure 13.2   *(Continued)*

	• Consider point-of-use storage (POUS) where small amounts of inventory are stored in right-sized containers at the point in a manufacturing process where the materials are used—such as in or near a manufacturing cell. • Use drip trays for solvent transfer, paint mixing, and equipment cleaning. • Clean up spills promptly with absorbent materials. • Use dedicated facilities and measures like drop sheets to contain all painting and sanding materials.
Water and Wastewater	• Repair any water leaks in hoses, pumps, and valves. Fixing a 1 mm hole under pressure of about 400 kPa can save 3,000 L each day—worth $1,300 annually. • Conduct all activities that generate wastewater on impervious surfaces such as concrete, with diversion drains or bunds to direct water to a collection pit via a silt trap. • Vacuum or sweep work areas instead of hosing them down unless absolutely necessary. • Consider filtering and recycling washdown water through a closed-loop system.

*Water Management, Inc., "Cooling Tower System Design," www.watermgt.com/Coolingtower design.html (accessed June 21, 2010).

This list consolidates recommendations from the following sources:

U.S. EPA, *The Lean and Energy Toolkit*, www.epa.gov/lean/toolkit/LeanEnergyToolkit.pdf (accessed August 9, 2010).

U.S. EPA, *The Lean and Chemicals Toolkit*,www.epa.gov/lean/chemicalstoolkit/resources/Lean-and-Chemicals-Toolkit.pdf (accessed August 9, 2010).

U.S. DOE, Energy Efficiency and Renewable Energy, "20 Ways to Save Energy Now," www.p2pays.org/ref/40/39977.pdf (accessed August 21, 2010).

U.S. EPA, *The Lean and Environment Toolkit*, www.epa.gov/lean/toolkit/LeanEnviroToolkit.pdf (accessed August 9, 2010).

Ray C. Anderson, *Mid-Course Correction: Toward a Sustainable Enterprise: The Interface Model* 2005.

EnergyStar, *Building Upgrade Manual*, www.energystar.gov/ia/business/BUM.pdf (accessed August 9, 2010).

Eco-efficiency for Queensland Manufacturers website, www.ecoefficiency.com.au/(accessed August 9, 2010).

Alan Richter, "Power Down," in *Cutting Tool Engineering* 61 (2009).

Amory B. Lovins, "Energy End Use Efficiency," Rocky Mountain Institute, September 2005, pp. 16–17.

ADDITIONAL RESOURCES

GENERAL

Sustainable Manufacturing and Eco-Innovation Website

(Organisation for Economic Co-operation and Development). Guides users to major sustainable manufacturing research and related tools. www.oecd.org

Lean Manufacturing and the Environment Website (EPA). Features free, comprehensive reports and tools drawing on multiple business case studies.

Major reports include:

- *Lean Manufacturing and the Environment* (2003)—includes details on advanced manufacturing systems and the environment.
- *The Lean and Energy Toolkit* (2007)—focuses on reducing energy waste in manufacturing.
- *The Lean and Chemicals Toolkit* (2009)—provides recommendations related to chemical management and use in manufacturing.
- *The Environmental Professional's Guide to Lean & Six Sigma* (2009)—offers guidance on how environmental professionals can use Lean and Six Sigma approaches to generate better environmental and operational results.
- *Total Productive Maintenance (TPM)*—online guide to using the TPM method for greener results.

  www.epa.gov/lean/leanenvironment.htm

Energy Efficiency Toolkit for Manufacturers: Eight Proven Ways to Reduce Your Costs (National Association of Manufacturers). Provides manufacturers energy conservation strategies, case studies, and resources to help reduce energy use and costs. www.fypower.org

Lean to Green Sustainability Tech Group Website (Society of Manufacturing Engineers). Features a wealth of resources and tools on lean and green manufacturing. www.sme.org/leantogreen

DOE Industrial Technologies Program (Department of Energy). Offers free industry-specific and technology-specific tools to help industry cut energy costs, raise productivity, and reduce carbon emissions.
www1.eere.energy.gov/industry

ITP Best Practices Website. Features a wealth of free tools, including software, to help identify and analyze energy-savings opportunities at plants and industrial facilities. Provides training opportunities for plant personnel.
www1.eere.energy.gov/industry/bestpractices/

ENERGY STAR Industries in Focus. Offers free industry-specific energy management tools and resources. www.energystar.gov

AUDITS AND ASSESSMENTS

Industrial Audit Guidebook (Bonneville Power Administration). Practical tips for performing walk-through energy audits of industrial facilities to identify energy-saving opportunities. For technical and non-technical audiences. www.bpa.gov

Resource Efficiency Management (Washington State University). Offers workbooks, checklists, commercial and industrial user fact sheets, and other guidance for conducting energy audits. www.energy.wsu.edu

Quick Plant Energy Profiler (PEP). Online software tool to help industrial plants personnel understand how energy is being used at plants and how to cut energy and costs. www.eere.energy.gov

U.S. DOE Save Energy Now Energy Savings Assessments. Conducts assessments for U.S. manufacturing facilities that focus on immediate opportunities to save energy and money through altering heating, steam, pumps, fans, and compressed air systems. Prioritizes "LEADER" companies that pledge to reduce their facilities' energy intensity by 25 percent in 10 years. www.eere.energy.gov

Environmental Management Systems: Process Mapping Approach (EPA). How to use process mapping to improve efficiency and enhance environmental performance. www.epa.gov

For Small and Medium-Sized Manufacturers

Self-Assessment Workbook for Small Manufacturers (IAC). Step-by-step methodology for small manufacturers to identify opportunities to save energy, improve operations, and cut costs. http://iac.rutgers.edu

Green Suppliers Network (EPA and National Institute of Standards and Technology Manufacturing Extension Partnership). Collaborative involving large companies that provides low-cost "Lean and Clean" facility assessments to small and medium-sized businesses. www.greensuppliers.gov

U.S. DOE Industrial Assessment Centers (IACs). Offer free energy and waste assessments to eligible small and medium-sized manufacturers. www.eere.energy.gov

Chapter 14 Logistics and Transport

When FedEx set out to deliver packages "absolutely, positively overnight" in the 1970s, few of its customers asked it to meet its promises with an eye on environmental effects as well. Times have changed. With heightened understanding of the heavy toll transportation-related activities can take on the planet. FedEx customers increasingly expect more than on-time performance at a competitive price. A growing segment also want options for lower-emissions shipping, more eco-friendly packaging, data on individual shipments, and strong sustainability performance from FedEx itself. FedEx has responded not only with serious eco-initiatives but also a new motto: "We understand. You want to ship your package today but not at the expense of tomorrow."

FedEx takes the new agenda very seriously. In January 2007, the company went so far as to be the first transportation logistics group to call on Congress to set fuel efficiency and greenhouse gas standards for commercial vehicles. As Mitch Jackson, vice president for FedEx Environmental Affairs and Sustainability, says, "Companies want to do business with other responsible companies."[1]

For many logistics professionals, adding environmental variables to the complex mix of factors already being juggled in supply chain management can be daunting. It's hard enough to make sure things end up precisely *where* they should, *when* they should, in the right quantities and condition, *and* at the right price. One major misstep can cause a chain reaction that wreaks havoc on budgets, quality, safety, customer satisfaction, or reputation. The good news—many of the companies, including FedEx, that have embraced the challenge to "green up" their logistics and transportation strategies, are achieving a solid ROI alongside eco-results. More generally, according to a recent survey by Eye For Transport, a British logistics consultancy, three-quarters of shipping professionals say they've achieved either "very" or "fairly" successful returns on their green initiatives, while only 3 percent report no cost savings.

This chapter focuses on the eco-related challenges and opportunities within supply chain management connected to the *storage* and *movement* of goods and services needed or produced—including raw materials for manufacturing, products and services needed by a business to operate, finished goods, services to customers, and product returns and waste. Specifically, this chapter will help you better understand distribution-related issues and opportunities and highlight ways to achieve cost and emissions reductions in the following areas:

- **Transportation** of the goods and services a company uses or sells to and from manufacturing plants, warehouses, distribution facilities, customers, intermediaries, offices, or anywhere else in the value chain—whether using your company's own resources or outsourcing to a third-party provider.

- **Storage** and inventory management of purchases, product components, or finished goods.

- **Reverse logistics** activities, which involve managing the flows of product returns or unsold goods for refunds, service, reuse, resale, or disposal.

GETTING A RETURN ON GREENER LOGISTICS

Cisco generated $24 million in annual savings by cutting 4.5 million pounds from its packaging and increasing transportation load utilization.[2]

Walmart reduced its transportation costs by 30 percent from 2005 by increasing the efficiency of its fleet by 25 percent, saving $35 to $50 million a year.[3]

UPS streamlined its pickup schedule for small and medium-sized business shipping customers and expects to save about 800,000 gallons of fuel a year.[4]

McKesson Corp. ramped up the fuel efficiency of the vehicles its pharmaceutical sales reps use, saving $300,000 in 2010 in the process.[5]

AT&T purchase 105 renewable-energy vehicles saving the company more than 34,000 gallons of fuels and cut emissions by more than 300 metric tons in 2008.[6]

JC Penney increased its backhauling by 208 percent, resulting in a net reduction of 14.7 million pounds of CO_2 emissions, with a savings of $5.6 million.[7]

3M saved well over $1 million per year by eliminating the use of pallets and filling all of the available space in some of their trailer-loading processes. These changes have allowed more cartons to be loaded into the trailer and ultimately reduced the number of trucks required to ship 3M products.[8]

Poland Spring saved $20,000 per year by eliminating idling by its trucking fleet.[9]

Clorox converted its fleet of company cars to hybrids, which cut fuel consumption in half and reduced greenhouse gas emissions by 700 metric tons per year.[10]

FedEx saved 45 million gallons of fuel (and almost half a million metric tons of CO_2 emissions) between 2005 and 2009 by rebalancing its fleet with more fuel-efficient Sprinter vans and optimizing its routes and the size of its vehicles.[11]

BASIC PLAYS: SEIZE LOW-COST, HIGH-RETURN OPPORTUNITIES

These Basic Plays outline a number of general recommendations designed to help companies spot win-win opportunities that save money and the environment. We give particular focus to greenhouse gas emissions, which represent the biggest overall eco-impact from logistics and transportation.

1. Improve Fleet Efficiency through Better Maintenance, Driver Training, and Low-Cost Upgrades

Any company that depends heavily on transportation wants to keep fuel costs as low as possible, extend the useful life of assets, and keep drivers safe. Applying a green lens to transportation and fleet management strategies—or choosing third-party providers that do—can help companies save money on fuel, improve safety records, *and* reduce greenhouse gas emissions and other harmful environmental impacts. We've identified a range of cost-effective measures companies are using to get results:

- **Improve vehicle maintenance.** Rigorous and comprehensive maintenance schedules and procedures can significantly improve fuel efficiency and extend vehicle life. Does your company have an effective program in place to ensure regular fleet maintenance and inspections? Are drivers trained and incentivized to perform daily preventive maintenance activities, such as inspecting and inflating tires?

- **Reduce idling.** According to the Environmental Defense Fund, idling for over 10 seconds uses more gas and emits more global warming pollution than restarting a vehicle.[12] Companies can reduce idling by adopting no-idling policies, creating "no-idling zones" in places like loading zones where idling is commonplace, and by installing idling reduction devices that provide heat, air-conditioning, and electricity when the engine isn't running.

- **Promote fuel-efficient driving habits.** Drivers have the power to cut a vehicle's average fuel costs by up to 33 percent simply through the way that they drive.[13] Many of the techniques that improve safety and reduce crash-related costs are the most important ones in achieving those fuel cost savings: obeying speed limits, reducing hard acceleration, and anticipating stops so as not to slam on the brakes. Progressive shifting (shifting gears upward as early as possible when accelerating) can save fuel and reduce wear on transmissions.[14] Use cruise control to cut fuel costs. Use air-conditioning only when it's really needed. *Slow Down.* Con-way Truckload cut its cruising truck speed from 70 mph to 66 mph and saved 2.8 million gallons of fuel per year—and reduced annual carbon emissions by 32,000 tons.[15]

Many technologies are available today to help drivers optimize their fuel efficiency while driving. Navigation systems such as GPS not only help drivers find their destinations but also reduce fuel use on trips. A study performed in NuStats in 2008 tracked fuel usage from a group of drivers who didn't have a navigation device, a group of drivers who had one, and a group of drivers provided with navigation supplemented with real-time traffic data. The results show that drivers who had navigation devices improved their fuel efficiency by 12 percent, which translates to a 24 percent decrease in carbon dioxide emissions.[16] The ability to steer clear of traffic jams further improves results. Green driving systems powered by GPS technology can "look down the road" to warn drivers of speed changes ahead and guide them on accelerating or decelerating safely and economically. Many hybrid car models also contain fuel-efficiency monitors that alert drivers to the fuel intensity of their driving.

USE DRIVING SIMULATORS TO REDUCE FUEL EMISSIONS

Training drivers can put a lot of miles on the company's transportation footprint. Driving simulator software allows drivers to practice driving without getting on the road. Driving simulators are an important training tool at **Schneider National**, a leading provider of logistics, truckload, and intermodal services, where they not only enable more, and better, driver training, but also conserve fuel by reducing the miles training trucks must drive on the road. According to Don Osterberg, senior vice president of safety, driver training, and security at Schneider, using simulators saves the company about 1 million gallons of fuel a year by replacing as many as 300 training trucks on the road at any given time. Each driver spends about 15 hours in a simulator, which saves approximately 33.5 gallons of fuel per student per year. Osterberg notes that the drivers that achieve the most miles per gallon are also the safest drivers. In a study of the company's top and bottom performers in terms of miles per gallon, the top 100 drivers had a 37 percent lower accident rate than the bottom 100 drivers in terms of miles per gallon.

Source: Wendy Leavitt, "2010 Green Fleet of the Year: Schneider National," *Fleet Owner* magazine, April 1, 2010.

---

2. Drive Energy Savings at Warehouse and Distribution Centers

Warehouses and distribution centers often have high energy bills. The biggest culprits are usually HVAC, lighting, and equipment like conveyors and forklifts used for picking and put-away.[17] We urge facilities managers to consider the general recommendations and checklists for driving energy savings in "Buildings and Facilities" in Chapter 9, including undergoing a building "commissioning" process to ensure that building systems are operating as efficiently as possible.

After seizing low-hanging fruit from no- or low-cost efficiency improvements, consider investing in energy-saving technologies that may cost more up front and require patience for payback, but lead to dramatic ROI over time. A system like Digital Lumens' Intelligent Lighting System can reduce lighting-related energy use up to 90 percent.[18]

3. Improve Hazardous Material Storage and Transportation Practices

Greener logistics is not just about driving upside benefits like energy and fuel savings; it is also about reducing the downside risk from handling danger-ous materials—including paints, fuels, solvents, and chemicals used in routine operations.[19] Improper handling or transportation can temporarily suspend operations, drive up regulatory compliance costs and insurance premiums, and make it harder to obtain a license to operate. One little mistake can lead to disastrous consequences that can have a crippling effect on a company's bottom line and brand. Eco-Advantage companies take every step possible to ensure safe handling and disposal of hazardous materials, including:

- **Thorough knowledge of and compliance with all relevant regulations** relating to the storage, transportation, and disposal of hazardous materials.
- **Rigorous employee training programs and procedures** to ensure proper implementation of the regulations—including routine safety and inspection procedures, security protocols, and emergency procedures.
- **The use of planning and tracking software** that factors hazardous materials issues into recommendations and alerts employees to potentially dangerous situations.[20]

INTERMEDIATE PLAYS: DRIVE BIGGER RETURNS THROUGH MORE EFFICIENT SYSTEMS

4. Boost Fleet Performance and Fuel Efficiency with Technology Upgrades

Relatively simple upgrades can cut fuel use and emissions by improving vehicle aerodynamics, preventing the need for idling and making engines run more smoothly. Start by checking out the "Upgrade Kits" offered by EPA's SmartWay program, which can be customized to the needs of particular businesses. The kits include idling reduction devices, emissions control devices, tractor and/or trailer aerodynamics (fairings added to trailers to reduce drag), automatic tire inflation, and low-rolling resistance dual- or single-wide tires—all of which can improve fuel economy up to 15 percent, reduce oxides of nitrogen (NO_x) up to 15 percent, and reduce particulate matter (PM) up to 90 percent. The EPA offers low-interest financing to qualified businesses that may not be able to cover the upfront investment cost.[21]

5. Optimize Route Planning, and Match the Right Vehicles to the Right Routes

As Illinois-based EA Logistics discovered, "the shortest distance between two points may not be the best route."[22] We all know this from our daily lives, having suffered the consequences of choosing routes prone to traffic jams or red lights timed to force frustrating starts and stops. New eco-routing technologies enable drivers to plan not only the fastest route but also the most fuel-efficient routes as well. These systems take into account factors such as severity of slopes, start-and-stop sequences, and speed limit changes in order to come up with the "greenest route." In a test comparing the fastest route with the greenest route using such technology, experimenters found that the greenest routes used at least 5 percent less fuel per trip than the fastest route, sometimes much less. Moreover, the greenest routes were only a few minutes slower than the fastest routes.[23] UPS, using smart-routing techniques, saved 3 million gallons of fuel and cut about 29 million miles by eliminating most left-hand turns from delivery drivers' routes.[24]

A key part of route optimization is matching the right vehicles to the right routes. For instance, lower-capacity vehicles with high fuel economy are generally better suited for high-mileage routes—whereas higher-capacity vehicles with low fuel economy are better for low-mileage routes.

6. Pack Lighter and Tighter

How products get packaged and loaded for transport can significantly alter logistics-related costs and environmental impacts. Excessive packaging and shipping materials weigh down vehicles and force them to work harder, resulting in higher fuel costs and emissions. Likewise, ineffective load planning leads to empty vehicles that waste time and money. A truck shipping only 25 percent of its capacity burns two-and-a-half times more fuel per ton-mile as one that is 75 percent full.[25]

BUSINESS BENEFITS OF ECO-SMART PACKAGING		
Less packaging	→	Lower per unit costs
Less storage space used	→	Improved asset utilization and postponed capital outlays
Improved load factor on trucks	→	Better asset utilization, fuel and energy savings, and lower emissions
Less product damage	→	Less waste

Source: Greater Vancouver Regional District, "Sustainable Supply Chain Logistics Guide," 2009.

Eco-smart companies have found that eliminating unnecessary packaging and increasing "load factor"—the percentage of a vehicle or container's capacity being used—cuts fuel costs, lowers shipping costs per unit, improves asset utilization, and reduces emissions.[26] For instance, a modest redesign of cereal maker Nature's Path's product boxes enabled it to stack six more boxes per pallet, which led to an 8 percent improvement in load factor on trucks. Dell's switch from wooden pallets to lighter, recycled plastic "slip sheets" saved over $30 million in packaging expenses in the first year and boosted load factor in shipping containers by 25 percent.[27] Walmart boosted its U.S. fleet efficiency by 60 percent between 2005 and 2010 in large part by consolidating deliveries and loading trailers more effectively.[28]

Best-practice companies focus on the following areas to cut costs and reduce eco-impacts from logistics-related activities:

- **Eliminate unnecessary items from shipments.** Does your customer really need or want everything that accompanies your product—manuals, duplicate cables or chargers, fancy boxes within boxes—or will they just end up in the trash or recycling bin? Cisco, for instance, recently replaced lengthy paper documentation for its IP phone with concise 3×5 cards, and now the company ships three phones in the same space that previously held only two.[29]

- **Root out excess packaging and shipping materials wherever possible.** Puma, after trying for 21 months to reduce the size of its shoe boxes, decided in 2010 to eliminate boxes altogether and replace them with a "clever little bag"—a packaging innovation that is expected to save the company 500,000 liters of diesel annually on top of cutting many other eco-impacts.[30] Sometimes a lot of packaging is required to protect especially fragile or hazardous materials—something that Amazon.com's "Frustration-Free Packaging" initiative learned the hard way when its scaled-down packages failed to protect computer hard drives.[31] When product protection is an issue, explore air cellular products and inflatable packaging systems, which create air-filled cushions that can provide better protection in smaller, lighter packages.[32] Reducing packaging is also better for consumers who must deal with recycling or discarding it.

- **Switch to reusable (and recyclable) packaging, containers, and pallets.** Use collapsible, nestable, and stackable containers. CAPTIN, which makes aluminum wheel products for Toyota and ships 6,000 wheels a day, replaced cardboard cartons and wooden pallets (which customers threw away or recycled) with reusable plastic pallets and dividers that are returned to the company after each use—an investment that drove down per unit costs, raised productivity in packaging, was paid back within two years, and is preferred by employees and customers.[33]

- **Use load-planning software.** "Loading a truck may seem simple, but making sure that a truck is truly 'full' is a science," says Pat Penman, Director of Global Environmental and Safety Actions at SC Johnson.[34] A truck that appears completely full may only be 90 percent full, and reorganizing to use that extra 10 percent will translate into bottom-line and environmental results. Load planning software with simulation capabilities can help determine the most efficient ways to pack trucks, railcars, and air or sea containers. Look for software that factors in variables like trailer size, unit load sizes, package size, stackability, weight, safety, and regulatory requirements.[35]

- **Consolidate loads.** As IBM supply chain experts Paul Brody and Mondher Ben-Hamida have pointed out, "there's a reason Amazon charges you less for shipping if you consolidate your order and have all items shipped at once—it saves them money." Consolidating shipments may take more time and sorting, but the returns can be significant. CVS Pharmacy eliminated 6,541 routes across its carrier network by consolidating its deliveries, a move which saved

218,730 gallons of fuel and 2,260 metric tons of CO_2 emissions.[36] In addition to loading as many items on a truck as possible, paying attention to the weight of loads also has a significant impact. A truck filled to maximum weight *and* volume capacity will be more fuel-efficient than a truck simply filled to maximum volume capacity. SC Johnson cut fuel usage by 168,000 gallons in a year by strategically loading multiple orders and multiple products on the same truck to optimize both volume and weight capacity.[37]

- **Fill empty backhauls.** If your trucks come back empty, then you are wasting half of the cost of delivery. The Voluntary Inter-Industry Commerce Solutions Association runs a program called "Empty Miles Service" that matches one company's empty trucks with another company's cargo needs. Macy's reports annualized transportation cost reductions in the hundreds of thousands of dollars. Schneider National, one of the shippers that participates in the Empty Miles program, reports an increase in annual backhaul revenue of 25 percent and fuel savings of over 5,000 gallons.[38]

7. Switch to Less-Polluting Modes of Transportation

Air transport may get goods to destinations fast, but it can come at a steep cost—both to the bottom line and the environment. Ask whether lower-impact ground transportation would suffice—or better yet, even lower-impact rail or marine. Timex, for instance, the maker of watches that "take a licking and keep on ticking," saved millions of dollars and many tons of emissions by switching from air freight to ocean shipping.[39]

Likewise, Catalyst, a Vancouver-based paper producer, now bypasses "time-consuming and fuel-burning road congestion" by moving paper from the mill to warehouse by barge and from the warehouse to distribution centers by rail. Shipping by rail versus truck translates into a 30 to 40 percent cost reduction, along with happier customers who have obtained efficiency gains in receiving and handling due to larger rail shipments.[40]

When it comes to fuel savings and eco-results, the old adage "patience is a virtue" generally applies. Routinely shifting from next-day to two- or three-day service when possible can mean the difference between using air or ground, which adds up to big benefits over time. Companies that previously rushed to ship temperature-sensitive items, like food and drugs, can buy themselves time by using better insulation such as efficient polyurethane foam. This switch has a side-benefit of reducing the amount of necessary cooling materials like dry ice, thereby cutting packaging weight and associated shipping costs.[41]

And for the shippers themselves, literally "slowing it down" can seriously pay off. By lowering cruising speeds to match port entry slots, shipping behemoth Maersk saved about 30 percent in fuel costs between 2008 and 2010, which more than compensated for the added labor costs of having crews at sea for longer periods.[42] The same idea applies on the roads. Driving at 55 mph instead of 65 mph cuts carbon dioxide emissions by about 20 percent.[43] So if speed is *not* of the essence, slow down and let the environment win.

ADVANCED PLAYS: OPTIMIZE AND INNOVATE

8. Choose Cleaner, High-Efficiency Vehicles and Fuels

When choosing vehicles to purchase or lease, Eco-Advantage companies are always on the lookout for best-in-class, fuel-efficient options that fit their budget and performance needs—including alternative-fuel vehicles. They explore all options and are not automatically deterred by higher up-front expense. Instead, they evaluate total life cycle costs and benefits including fuel, maintenance, tax incentives, potential resale value, emissions reductions, and reputational benefits. UPS Chief Financial Officer Kurt Kuehn, for instance, says he "signs the checks" for his company's investments in alternative-fuel vehicles not to save money but because "we have to hedge against high costs—like a potential $200 barrel of oil—and we want to be part of the solution that creates a green vehicle that works for our industry."[44]

Which vehicles and fuels are the best choices? The answers, of course, vary greatly in light of businesses' diverse objectives and needs. In general, we recommend buying or leasing the most fuel-efficient, lowest-emissions vehicles available that are only as large or powerful as you really need them to be—otherwise you'll waste fuel and generate unnecessary emissions. Beyond that, choosing the right make, model, specs, and fuel requires that you consider your company's unique fleet-related needs in the context of rapidly changing technologies, costs, regulations, and available fueling infrastructure. The key is finding the right vehicle and configuration that will be both effective and efficient—and in most cases, that means a balanced portfolio of solutions. As UPS's head of sustainability Bob Stoffel warns, "A more efficient technology not being used efficiently is a waste of time and money for your business."[45]

Fleet management is an area where experimentation can really pay off. AT&T, for instance, tested a variety of "clean fuel" vehicles before making a decision on how best to "green" its fleet of 77,000 cars and trucks. After evaluating the different vehicles' performance firsthand and assessing their impact on employees' daily routines, AT&T chose to spend $565 million in 2009 to convert 8,000 service vehicles to compressed natural gas (CNG) and to replace all passenger cars with alternative-fuel vehicles within ten years.[46] Walmart is building a wealth of experience in this area, constantly testing alternative technologies from commercial trucks that run on reclaimed cooking grease generated from its stores to heavy-duty hybrids to yard trucks that run on liquid natural gas.[47]

EPA's SmartWay Transport Partnership offers another resource for companies considering a switch to cleaner vehicles. SmartWay certifies vehicles that are in the cleanest 20 percent in terms of combined air pollution and greenhouse gas emissions. Companies can display the SmartWay logo if their transportation carrier network uses 100 percent SmartWay compliant carriers. HP and other consumer-facing companies have begun to display the SmartWay logo on their packaging as a signal to the public of their focus on green logistics.[48]

We offer in the following pages a brief overview of major categories of commercially available alternative-fuel vehicles, followed by recommended resources at the end of the chapter to help you track and evaluate choices in this rapidly evolving area.

NATURAL GAS VEHICLES (NGVs)

Natural gas, the cleanest burning of all fossil fuels, is a high-octane fuel comprised mostly of methane. When used as a transportation fuel, it emits 30 to 40 percent less smog-producing pollutants than gasoline.[49] It is nontoxic and doesn't contaminate land or water ecosystems if released.[50] Vehicles can use it as fuel in the form of compressed natural gas (CNG) or liquefied natural gas (LNG)—and, at least at the present moment, it is cheaper than gasoline or diesel fuel. Conventional gasoline and diesel vehicles can be retrofitted to use natural gas, and over 50 different manufacturers produce around 150 models of light, medium, and heavy-duty vehicles and engines that are either dedicated natural gas vehicles or *"dual-fuel"* vehicles that have separate tanks for gasoline, diesel, or ethanol when natural gas is not readily available.[51]

Higher up-front costs and limited fueling infrastructure, especially for liquefied natural gas, have emerged as the main stumbling blocks to a broad-based switch to natural gas powered vehicles. LNG-powered trucks can cost up to twice as much as diesel-powered counterparts, and building an LNG refueling station can cost between $350,000 and $1 million.[52] Government incentives, however, can still make the overall investment attractive in some circumstances. Generous federal and state tax credits are available in the United States for commercial truck operators who switch their fleets over to natural gas, including a tax credit up to $30,000 for refueling infrastructure and a 50 cent per gallon tax rebate.[53]

The market is responding. Republic Services, a waste and recycling hauler that operates in California, Washington, and Idaho, deploys more than 459 compressed natural gas and liquefied natural gas vehicles.[54] To support its fleet, the company is building compressed natural gas fueling stations in all of its operating states. As it invests in new compressed natural gas taxis, Yellow Cab Chicago also builds fueling stations to go along with the shift.

PROPANE VEHICLES

Propane, also known as liquefied petroleum gas (LPG), is a fossil fuel with high energy density that can be compressed into a liquid for use as a vehicle fuel. A by-product of natural gas processing and crude oil refining, propane is the third most-used vehicle fuel in the United States after gasoline and diesel.[55] Propane is one of the cleanest burning of all alternative fuels. LPG is nontoxic and burns clearer than gasoline—though not as cleanly as natural gas—and produces about 16 percent less carbon dioxide than gasoline.[56] According to the U.S. Department of Energy, propane has been popular with delivery trucks, taxis, and buses especially because of lower maintenance costs, as documented engine life is up to two times that of a gasoline engine.[57] The price of propane is typically two-thirds that of gasoline.[58] It also has the advantage of having the most developed fueling infrastructure of all alternative vehicle fuels in the United States.[59]

Relatively few propane vehicles are commercially available, so most propane vehicles on the road are vehicles that have been converted to run on LPG—either as dedicated propane or bifuel vehicles.[60] Propane conversions are performed by specialized outfitters on light-duty vehicles, full-size pickups, vans and chassis cabs, step vans, and both medium- and heavy-duty vocational trucks.[61] Conversion costs are often offset by lower operating and maintenance costs over vehicles' life spans.[62] UPS and the U.S. Postal Service are among the fleets that use propane-powered vehicles as part of their multi-pronged efforts to reduce GHG emissions.[63] The airport shuttle company, Prime Time Shuttle, announced in 2010 it would convert its 200-van fleet to propane-powered Ford E350's to save 1.5 million gallons of gasoline each year.[64]

ETHANOL VEHICLES

Ethyl alcohol, or "ethanol," is known as a renewable "biofuel" because it can be made from organic material including corn, sugarcane, potatoes, grains, switchgrass, and more. Henry Ford, who designed his Model T to run on either gasoline or ethanol, predicted in 1925 that ethanol would be the "fuel of the future"—and today it is widely used in some countries, notably Brazil.[65] Ethanol is approved by all U.S. car manufacturers for use in any modern car when blended into gasoline at low levels of up to 10 percent.[66] "Flexible-fuel" or "flex-fuel" vehicles can run on pure ethanol or gasoline but perform best on a blend of 85 percent ethanol and 15 percent gasoline known as "E85," which overcomes the challenge of starting engines in cold weather with pure alcohol. E85 ethanol-powered vehicles have 20 to 25 percent less fuel economy than conventional gasoline, but the price of E85 ethanol is about 10 to 30 percent less than gasoline.[67] As of June 2010, there are 6,602 ethanol fueling stations in the United States and the number is increasing rapidly.[68]

In terms of environmental benefits, gasoline ethanol emits 21 percent less greenhouse gas emissions when burned than conventional gasoline.[69] Unfortunately, the benefits from "life cycle" perspective may be much lower, depending on how the ethanol is made.[70] Corn-based ethanol, for instance, provides far less net emissions benefit than ethanol from sugarcane because it requires much more fossil-based energy to produce. Sugarcane ethanol, used widely in Brazil, offers about six times the net environmental benefit over corn-based ethanol—and next-generation ethanol made from switchgrass or even algae promises to deliver even greater benefits.[71] And some studies show lower fuel efficiency with ethanol-blended gasoline.[72]

DIESEL AND BIODIESEL VEHICLES

Until recently, most diesel fuels were made from petroleum (aka "petrodiesel," or "fossil diesel") and caused major soot and smog problems—but today's ultra-low sulfur diesel (ULSD) burns far cleaner. As of 2010, all diesel sold in the United States will be ULSD. Diesel engines are 20 to 40 percent more fuel efficient than their gasoline counterparts and are generally the fuel of choice for large trucks and equipment that carry heavy loads at low speeds.[73] Ultra-low sulfur diesel has 15 parts per million or lower sulfur content than petrodiesel. In addition to higher fuel efficiency, ultra-low sulfur diesel makes it possible to put advanced emissions control equipment on trucks and other heavy-duty vehicles. The U.S. Department of Energy estimates that replacing current heavy-duty fleets with ULSD vehicles combined with advanced emission control technologies has the potential to remove pollution from more than 90 percent of today's trucks and buses. Most diesel engines last longer than gasoline engines, and diesel fuel is widely available (about 40 percent of U.S. service stations carry it). Diesel costs about 18 cents more than gasoline, but because it is more fuel efficient, its energy equivalent cost is actually 13 cents less than gasoline.[74]

Biodiesel burns even cleaner than ultra-low sulfur diesel. Typically made from soybeans or canola oil, although animal fats and recycled cooking oils are also used, biodiesel can be blended with petroleum diesel in any percentage. B20 (20 percent biodiesel, 80 percent petroleum diesel) is the most common blend, and it avoids issues such as deteriorated cold-weather performance associated with B100 percent biodiesel.[75] Biodiesel improves engine operation because of its lubricating properties and is far less combustible than petroleum diesel, although biodiesel can break down the fuel lines in older trucks.[76] Using a B20 biodiesel blended fuel costs slightly more per gallon and causes a 1 to 2 percent loss in fuel economy. But blends of B20 or higher qualify for federal alternative fuel credits—which can make up the cost difference.

Biodiesel generates substantially less pollution than petroleum-based diesel. B20 biodiesel reduces total hydrocarbons by up to 30 percent, carbon monoxide up to 20 percent, and total particulate matter up to 15 percent.[77] The U.S. Department of Energy also found that biodiesel produces 78 percent less CO_2 emissions.[78] In addition, biodiesel is biodegradable and nontoxic, and can be used by all modern diesel engines—including standard pickups and heavy-duty commercial trucks.[79] However, as with ethanol, the net environmental benefits of biodiesel depend on how and where fuels are made. Locally sourced biodiesel made from waste cooking oil, for instance, offers significant net benefits—whereas imported biodiesel from soybeans or palm oil produced by destroying natural forests probably ends up doing more harm than good.

Maine-based clothing retailer L.L.Bean has a growing fleet of heavy-duty vehicles that operate exclusively on B20 with no problems even during intense winter weather.[80] In 2007, Tennessee-based Eastman Chemical

Company decided to power its entire diesel vehicle fleet—including dump trucks, tractor trailers, and cranes—with B30 after a pilot program showed that drivers were pleased with equipment performance and decreased odor and smoke.[81]

HYBRID-ELECTRIC VEHICLES

Hybrid-electric vehicles (HEVs) combine traditional internal combustion engines with battery-powered electric motors and are growing rapidly in popularity, availability, and affordability. A key benefit of hybrid-electric vehicles is being able to tap into electricity from car batteries while vehicles aren't running for other critical vehicle functions such as hydraulic lifts on bucket trucks or heating and cooling. Traditional HEVs recharge themselves automatically by capturing extra energy from the engine or brakes, though they can be retrofitted or manufactured to have a "plug-in" feature. Hybrids are ideal for vehicles that require multiple stops and have varying payloads (such as for pickup and delivery), particularly on low-mileage city or nonhighway routes. In addition, fleets can move to hybrid engines without having to change fuels or fueling infrastructure.

While passenger and light-truck HEVs are most familiar to consumers, dozens of medium- and heavy-duty hybrid trucks (including diesel-electric heavy-duty, long-haul trucks) are now commercially available too—thanks to a pioneering partnership between FedEx and the Environmental Defense Fund (EDF) that developed the first hybrid delivery truck in 2000. According to EDF, hybrid trucks can reduce greenhouse emissions by 30 to 50 percent, decrease particulate matter by 96 percent, and improve fuel economy 30 to 50 percent.[82] Combining hybrids with alternative fuels such as biodiesel can improve energy efficiency and environmental benefits even more.[83]

Companies considering a shift to hybrids must be prepared to pay an upfront price premium, which can take several years to recoup in fuel savings. Government incentives often sweeten the deal. Hybrid engine prices are expected to fall in the next few years as worldwide demand rises. Pike Research projects worldwide sales of medium- and heavy-duty hybrids and electric trucks will grow at a compound annual growth rate of 63 percent between 2010 and 2015.[84]

Today, over 100 companies have hybrid trucks in their fleets including Coca-Cola, Duke Energy, Pepsi, AT&T, NextEra Energy, PG&E, UPS, Kraft, and Walmart.[85] Purolator, a North American courier company, is replacing its entire 3,000-unit in-city pickup and delivery fleet with hybrid-electric vehicles after a highly successful pilot program showed three-year payback on hybrids through a 50 percent fuel savings and 20 percent reduction in maintenance costs.[86] Likewise, Kraft Foods began using diesel-electric hybrid delivery trucks in March 2009, which it projects will save the company 30 percent in fuel usage compared with traditional diesel powered trucks. Figure 14.1 provides some basic fuel source comparisons.[87]

Figure 14.1   **Fuel Comparison**

Fuel	Cost (per gallon*)	Gasoline (per gallon equivalent cost**)	Environmental Benefits	Fuel Economy	Drawbacks
Gasoline	$2.84	$2.84			
Natural gas	$1.90	$1.90	Reduces (CO_2) emissions by 20%–30% Reduces (CO) emissions by 70%–90% Reduces (NO_x) emissions by 75%–95% Reduction of up to 90% of particle matter (PM) Reduces (VOCs) by 89%	Equivalent to gasoline	Limited distribution infrastructure
Propane	$2.89	$3.99	Produces 16% fewer greenhouse gas emissions		Requires vehicle conversions
Ethanol (E85)	$2.42	$3.42	Reduces tailpipe carbon monoxide emissions by as much as 30% Reduces exhaust volatile organic compounds (VOC) emissions by 12% Reduces toxic emissions by 30% Reduces particulate matter (PM) emissions by more than 25%	20% less fuel economy	Controversies regarding using food for fuel or replacing rainforests with agriculture
Biodiesel (B20)	$3.12	$2.85	Reduces total hydrocarbons by up to 30%, carbon monoxide up to 20%, and total particulate matter up to 15% compared with petrodiesel. Produces 78% less CO2 emissions.	1%–2% less fuel economy	Better in trucks and large vehicles than cars
Hybrid-electric			Reduces greenhouse gas emissions by 30%–50%	30%–40% higher fuel economy	Better in urban environments

*Overall average prices from U.S. Department of Energy's Clean Cities Alternative Fuel Price Report, April 2010.
**Overall average prices adjusted for fuel economy compared to gasoline.
Sources:
CNG Now, "CNG Is a Clean Alternative to Gasoline and Other Fuels," www.cngnow.com (accessed August 4, 1010).
Carbon Trust, Energy and Carbon Conversions, 2009.
EthanolFacts.com, www.ethanolfacts.com (accessed August 4, 2010).
National Biodiesel Board, "Environmental Benefits," www.biodiesel.org (accessed August 4, 2010).
Environmental Defense Fund, "Hybrids Are a Win-Win for the Environment," http://innovation.edf.org (accessed July 16, 2010).

CHOOSING THE RIGHT VEHICLE SPECIFICATION

The right vehicle specs can dramatically boost fuel economy and reduce emissions. Here are a few of the important things to look for:

- **Power train:** According to Robert Johnson, director of fleet relations for the National Truck Equipment Association, a properly spec'd power train ensures a truck's engine operates within its peak efficiency power band at all times. "Truck dealers are equipped with computer software programs that can match engine ratings, transmission gear ratios, and final drive [rear end] gear ratios to achieve the desired performance," he says.[88] Vehicles outfitted with automated mechanical transmissions (AMT), for instance, shift at exactly the right moment for the best possible fuel economy, generating fuel savings within 18 months that recoup the higher up-front price.[89]

- **Weight:** The frame, suspension, and wheels are areas to look for in weight savings. According to Johnson, "wide-base tires on a tractor's drive axles and trailer can save 1,000 pounds, boosting fuel economy by as much as 0.2 mpg." He adds: "Newer engine cooling systems and oil filters are more efficient than those of even a few years ago. Eliminating an unneeded bypass oil filter will save close to 100 pounds. An oversized fuel tank will also add unnecessary weight."[90]

- **Aerodynamics:** Attention to the airflow over a truck's cab, bumpers, and other features can push up fuel efficiency a couple of percent points at typical highway speeds.[91] You can achieve further efficiency gains by eliminating exterior features that catch the wind such as frame-mounted battery boxes, bypass oil filters, and vertical exhaust stacks with perforated stainless steel heat shields. Low-rolling resistance tires offer another way to push up fuel efficiency.[92]

- **Auxiliary power generation:** Providing auxiliary power generation is another fuel-saving strategy. "If an application requires a limited amount of hydraulic or electric power, a small auxiliary engine generator set may provide sufficient energy to eliminate the need for idling the truck engine for extended periods of time," observes Johnson, "or if electricity is only needed for relatively short periods of time, a static inverter may do the trick."[93]

9. Organize Warehouses and Distribution Centers for Peak Efficiency

Eco-Advantage companies know that bringing a green lens to operations at warehouses and distribution centers can both help the environment and translate into productivity gains, improved asset utilization, better customer service, and lower operating costs.

Consider the opportunities in the following areas:

- **Put-away methods:** As with optimizing load factors in vehicles, it pays to maximize storage capacity in your existing space—which requires both efficient processes for moving items from receipt to storage space, and for organizing the storage space itself. More efficient use of space means less building space needed, which helps companies avoid costs (e.g., leasing or new construction) and to save on energy (less lighting and HVAC needed). Look for new ways to configure cartons, pallets, and racking to maximize use of space. London Drugs, for instance, trains workers not to put less-than-full pallets on to warehouse racking, but rather to remove cartons and put them in a special area so they can be slotted into smaller shelves—which makes sure the entire height of pallet racks is used.[94] Use standardized and modular pallets or containers that can be stacked more efficiently. Consider investing in a Warehouse Management System to map the best routes and using product and pallet ID labels (e.g., bar codes or radio frequency identification (RFID) labels) to track and manage inventory and flows as efficiently as possible.[95]

- **Picking methods:** Order picking can be responsible for 60 percent of warehouse operating costs.[96] Warehouse management expert Kevin Collins of Smartturn argues that because average warehouses and distribution centers have many more shipments than receipts, picking optimization deserves priority attention.[97] The goal, Collins says, is to minimize walk time and product handling. For instance, he urges companies to store products by pick frequency, stocking the "fastest moving SKUs as close to the pick point as possible and at easily accessible heights."[98] London Drugs avoided having to build new warehouses and distribution centers in part by redesigning its picking strategy, including installing multilevel work platforms connected to its network of conveyors and storing thousands of small items in compact carousel racks (like those at dry cleaners) that rotate via computerized sequence instructions.[99] Tools and techniques are constantly evolving—for instance, voice-recognition technology now exists for voice-directed picking that can boost productivity and accuracy—so Collins recommends viewing picking optimization as a never-ending process.[100]

- **Clean energy-powered equipment and facilities:** While payback periods may be long, some companies have chosen to invest in clean-powered buildings and mechanical-handling equipment. Sysco's food distribution facility in Houston, Texas, uses numerous hydrogen fuel cell forklifts and pallet trucks, with two indoor H_2 refueling stations that can fuel a forklift or pallet truck in two minutes. The fuel cells are expected to last 10 years and have eliminated the costs and risks associated with charging, changing, and disposing of toxic lead acid batteries used in similar vehicles.[101] Walmart Canada's refrigerated distribution center in Alberta became 60 percent more energy efficient when it leveraged a variety of green technologies, including hydrogen forklifts, solar-heated hot water, low-energy LED lighting, and a wind turbine.[102]

Smucker Natural Foods' new LEED gold status warehouse in California generates 94 percent of its own energy needs and includes solar arrays that offset energy costs by 56 percent and a solar water heater that provides 53 percent of the building's hot water.[103] The payback from these investments comes partly in the form of credit for environmental leadership and customer goodwill.

- **Automation:** Automated operations can save energy costs by running in the dark or in nonheated environments.[104] Automated conveyor systems, which use sorters and diverters to move products to the right storage areas, can dramatically boost efficiency for companies that receive many case-sized shipments or have significant transit times from receiving to storage.[105] Similarly, automated storage and retrieval systems can cut needed storage space by 40 percent[106] while also reducing product damage, picking errors, and associated waste.[107] Zappos.com, an online shoe retailer, began using "robots" at its warehouse in Louisville, Kentucky, in 2008 after learning that office suppliers merchant Staples had been using them for more than two years. The automation system, made by Kiva Systems, combines robotics, software, wireless technology, and special warehouse infrastructure to pick items from shelves with consistent accuracy. Zappos says since the system has been installed, the amount of time it takes to fulfill an order has been drastically reduced. "It now takes about 45 minutes from the point where a customer clicks her mouse to the order getting onto the truck, and it can be as short as 10 minutes," says Craig Adkins, vice president of services and operations. The amount of labor has also been reduced 40 percent.[108]

10. Relocate Warehouses and Distribution Centers Closer to the Action

Companies can reduce fuel use by shortening distances between suppliers, warehouses, and customers. Kimberly Clark's decision to put its key distribution centers near major cities in 2007 helped the company reduce its usage of diesel fuel by 1.7 million gallons and cut carbon dioxide emissions by 113,728 tons, the equivalent of removing over 15,000 cars from the road.[109] Nature's Path cut delivery lead time in half by building a new distribution center near Chicago that serves as a hub to a majority of its customers. Instead of shipping products by truck from British Columbia, the company sends bulk shipments by rail to the Chicago facility and efficiently routes products to customers from there.[110]

"CLUSTERING" FOR LOGISTICS EFFICIENCY

Air Products had a fleet of 645 heavy-duty trucks that traveled about 50 million miles in 2009. To cut fuel costs and environmental impacts, it organized into approximately 60 Logical Business Units (LBUs) globally—small clusters of plants and customers—to help keep product deliveries within a 150-mile radius of facilities. The company uses proprietary tools to optimize distribution routes and payload, along with driver training and standardized measures for speed traveled, engine idling time, hard braking, and other efficiencies.[111]

Companies can also choose suppliers located close to major markets. Logistics optimization software can help support decisionmaking about locations by factoring in multiple variables including distance, weight, and cube volume, asset mix, location, customer requirements, fuel energy consumption, and emissions.[112]

11. Turn Reverse Logistics into a Profit Center

Reverse logistics (or "reverse supply chain") refers to all the activities involved in retrieving and managing goods after their sale, including handling customer returns and disposing of excess inventory. Traditionally, companies have thought of reverse logistics in terms of cost and compliance—keeping costs down and disposing of waste properly—especially in light of rising expectations and regulatory requirements around "product take-back." But where others see cost as hassle, Eco-Advantage companies see dollar signs and opportunity. They know that getting reverse logistics right can translate into happier customers, bottom-line savings, and even profit.

At the heart of greener reverse logistics is a closed-loop system that can help you spot value where others see junk. Before throwing anything into the trash or recycling bin, ask: "Can we reuse this product or any of its parts—or sell it to someone who will?" Rodney Moore, a principal at UPS Supply Chain Solutions, outlines the full suite of options that every company should consider for reclaimed products—"refurbish (improve product beyond original specs), recondition (return product to original specs), salvage (separate components for reuse), repair (prepare for sale as a used product), sell to third party, recycle, or discard/liquidation (landfill)."[113] U-Haul International reuses the detached bodies from retired trucks as self-storage units, eliminating 17.3 tons of greenhouse gas emissions from every thousand square feet of reused truck body.[114]

For Cisco, the payoff of a changed mindset has been dramatic. In 2005, reverse logistics cost the company over $8 million a year. According to then VP of Supply Chain Field Operations Dan Gilbert, "we were missing a trick by making 'recycle' our default setting. . . . While it was green to recycle, it was actually better and greener to reuse products as much as possible."[115] Today, Cisco recovers and reuses or recycles over 99 percent of its returned electronic equipment worldwide—a feat that by 2008 was making a net contribution of over $100 million a year to Cisco's shareholders.[116] Best Buy, too, has fast become a leader in this area. According to the company's VP of Secondary Markets Kevin Winneroski, Best Buy is "maximizing profit in the reverse logistics business" through partnerships with customers, manufacturers, and third-party service providers and moving towards providing customers "full life cycle management" for products. The strategy presently involves reselling returned product on eBay and other online channels, providing an online trade-in program that gives customers a fast-and-easy way to sell online themselves, integrating refurbished products into its warranty replacement program, and offering free recycling to customers.[117]

At Eco-Advantage-minded companies, reverse logistics professionals are at the table helping redesign products and improve customer service strategies to reduce the amount of returns in the first place. Continued reverse logistics efforts involves improving the efficiency of the returns and servicing process, and improving the chances of converting returned products and packaging into assets that can be reused or resold.[118]

SUMMARY

Key Plays

1. Improve fleet efficiency through better maintenance, driver training, and low-cost upgrades.
2. Drive energy savings at warehouse and distribution centers.
3. Improve hazardous material storage and transportation practices.
4. Boost fleet performance and fuel efficiency with technology upgrades.
5. Optimize route planning, and match the right vehicles to the right routes.
6. Pack lighter and tighter.
7. Switch to less-polluting modes of transportation.
8. Choose cleaner, high-efficiency vehicles and fuels.
9. Organize warehouses and distribution centers for peak efficiency.
10. Relocate warehouses and distribution centers closer to the action.
11. Turn reverse logistics into a profit center.

ADDITIONAL RESOURCES

GENERAL/STRATEGY DEVELOPMENT

"Forging New Links: Enhancing Supply Chain Value through Environmental Excellence" (Global Environmental Management Initiative, 2004). Outlines strategies for using supply chain initiatives to boost overall supply chain performance and enhance shareholder value. www.gemi.org

"Business Guide to a Sustainable Supply Chain—A Practical Guide" (New Zealand Business Council for Sustainable Development). A website with guidance for implementing a sustainable supply chain, including online self-diagnostic tools. www.nzbcsd.org.nz/supplychain

"Sustainable Supply Chain Logistics Guide" (Metro Vancouver). Guide to implementing sustainable supply chain logistics, including storage, transport and reverse logistics. www.metrovancouver.org

"The Good Haul: Freight Innovations for the 21st Century" (Environmental Defense Fund). Guide that highlights case studies of innovative technologies and practices that improve freight transportation and reduce environmental impacts. www.edf.org

SmartWay (EPA). Programs to help companies reduce transportation-related emissions, including:

SmartWay Certification: Certification for fuel efficient and low polluting vehicles.

Green Vehicle Guide: How to find and purchase clean vehicles.

SmartWay Financing Options: Grants and loans to help finance cleaner vehicles.

SmartWay Transport Partnership: An EPA-freight sector collaboration to improve energy efficiency, reduce greenhouse gas and air pollutant emissions.

SmartWay Tractors and Trailers: How to certify or purchase energy efficient tractors and trailers. www.epa.gov/smartway

"Choosing and Developing a Multi-modal Transport Solution" (UK Department for Transport). Guide to evaluating possible shift to rail or water transportation options. www.freightbestpractice.org

IMPROVING NAVIGATION AND DRIVER HABITS

Fleet Drivers and Fuel-Smart Driving Handbook (Environmental Defense Fund). Recommendations, tips, and resources for developing a customized driver education program that results in better fuel economy, improvements in driving safety, lower maintenance costs, and reduced emissions. www.edf.org

Idle Reduction Related Links (DOE). Tools and resources to help reduce idling. www.afdc.energy.gov

BOOSTING FLEET PERFORMANCE AND FUEL EFFICIENCY

The Five Step Green Fleet Framework (Environmental Defense Fund). Easy, cost-effective ways for fleets to "go green" and reduce their environmental impacts and operating costs. http://innovation.edf.org

Upgrade Kits (EPA). Provides a list of the types of technologies available to reduce fuel consumption and/or emissions when added to trucks. www.epa.gov

Greenhouse Gas Management for Medium-Duty Truck Fleets (Environmental Defense Fund). Recommendations to raise fuel efficiency and lower emissions. www.edf.org

SmartWay calculator (EPA). Helps truck owners compare costs and estimate fuel savings associated with various efficiency technologies. www.epa.gov/smartway

"Diesel Tuning" by David Kolman (*Fleet Maintenance*, December 2009). Short article with how-to advice for reprogramming diesel engines for better fuel efficiency. www.fleetmag.com

CHOOSING GREENER VEHICLES AND FUELS

Alternative Fuels and Advanced Vehicles Data Center (U.S. Department of Energy). Comprehensive website on alternative fuels and advanced vehicles with information on U.S. laws and regulations, vehicle and fuel specifications, financial opportunities, station locations, fleet applications, technical assistance, and more. www.afdc.energy.gov

Fueleconomy.gov (DOE). The official government source for information on fuel economy ratings, electric vehicles, hybrids, alternative fuels, tax incentives, and gas prices. http://fueleconomy.gov

Green Vehicle Guide (EPA). Guide to choosing alternative fuel vehicles. www.epa.gov/greenvehicles

SmartWay Vehicles (EPA). Outlines benefits of SmartWay-certified vehicles and how to find them. www.epa.gov/smartway

ACEEE's Green Book (American Council for an Energy-Efficient Economy). Online subscription website with interactive database enabling users to build custom lists for comparing vehicles. www.greenercars.org

Clean Cities 2010 Vehicle Buyer's Guide (DOE). Buyers guide for natural gas, propane, hybrid electric, ethanol, and biodiesel vehicles. Includes vehicle-specific information on fuel economy, emissions, vehicle specifications, estimated cost, and warranty. www.afdc.energy.gov

Cool Fleets (Sierra Club). Interactive tool allowing vehicle comparisons according to cost, fuel efficiency, and greenhouse gas pollutants. www.coolfleets.com

Available Models of Medium- to Heavy-Duty Hybrid and Electric Trucks (Environmental Defense Fund). Compares medium- to heavy-duty hybrid and electric trucks in terms of their power train, body type/application, engine, fuel, GVW, and class. http://innovation.edf.org

Find Alternative Fueling Stations (DOE). Resources for finding fueling stations for biodiesel, compressed natural gas (CNG), electric, ethanol, hydrogen, liquefied natural gas (LNG), and liquefied petroleum gas (propane). www.eere.energy.gov

LAWS, FINANCING, AND INCENTIVES

The Tax Incentives Assistance Project. Clearinghouse site with information on federal income tax incentives for energy efficient products and technologies. www.energytaxincentives.org

Federal and State Incentives and Laws (DOE). Contains a database of federal and state laws and incentives related to alternative fuels and vehicles, air quality, fuel efficiency, and other transportation-related topics. www.afdc.energy.gov

SmartWay Finance Center. Information on financing alternative fuel vehicles. www.smartwayfinancecenter.com

Hybrid Trucks Financial Incentives Guide (Environmental Defense Fund). Guide to financial incentives for purchasing hybrid trucks, including federal funding and state and local tax credit programs. EDF also offers customized incentive funding assessments for companies considering hybrid truck fleet purchases. http://innovation.edf.org

REDUCING GREENHOUSE GAS EMISSIONS FROM TRANSPORTATION

Greenhouse Gas Inventory Protocol for Calculating Direct Emissions from Mobile Combustion Sources (EPA). Guidance for calculating direct greenhouse gas emissions resulting from the operation of owned or leased mobile sources. www.epa.gov

Fleet Greenhouse Gas Emissions Calculator (Environmental Defense Fund). Tool to calculate fleet greenhouse gas emissions using aggregate fuel use data. http://innovation.edf.org

EcoTransIT. Web-based software tool for assessing direct and indirect energy consumption and emissions of freight by various transport modes. Calculates energy consumption, carbon dioxide, and other emissions. www.ecotransit.org

Fuel and Energy Source Codes and Emission Coefficients (U.S. Energy Information Administration). Lists CO_2 emission coefficients for commonly used fuels to help calculate greenhouse gas emissions from vehicle fuel use. www.eia.doe.gov

WAREHOUSING

"Warehousing/Wholesaling Guide" (Greater Vancouver Regional District). Recommendations, case studies, links, and resources on improving the efficiency and reducing environmental impacts from warehousing and wholesaling. www.metrovancouver.org

Chapter 15 Marketing and Sales

People respect trusted brands, but true loyalty happens when companies "reach your heart as well as your mind, creating an intimate, emotional connection that you just can't live without," proclaims Kevin Roberts, CEO of global advertising giant Saatchi & Saatchi.[1] Beyond brand value, such "lovemarks" transcend traditional brand-based guarantees such as quality, safety, and prestige. They inspire our passions, affirm our values, and give our dreams content. "To be a lovemark today," says Roberts, "you've got to be sustainable or you will be rejected and judged harshly."[2] Even those who don't aspire to high-end green marketing must pay attention to sustainability as a sales factor. As Bob Lipp, President of the Marcomm Group notes, the paradigm for business-to-business marketing today has become: "Cheaper, Faster, Better, Greener."[3]

Marketing executives ignore the sustainability megatrend at their peril. Consumer demand for green products has exploded in the last decade. The organic food and beverages business grew from a niche market of $1 billion in 1990 to a $25 billion industry in 2009.[4] Demand for green household cleaning products jumped 400 percent from 2003 to 2008, and sustainability-oriented products will most likely to represent 30 percent of the market by 2013.[5] You can see similar trends in personal care products, interior furnishings, cars, appliances, and more. A 2010 report by EcoFocus Worldwide found that 69 percent of American mothers consider themselves "EcoAware Moms," and have a preference for chemical-free, organic, and sustainable products. This group alone represents $1.45 trillion worth of buying power.[6] This trend isn't limited to the United States. According to GlobeScan's "2009 Greendex," in Brazil, India, and China, the percentage of consumers planning to increase their spending on green products ranged from an astounding 73 to 78 percent.[7]

While the opportunity is clear, companies need to tread carefully. Surveys haven't always translated into sales. Large numbers of consumers may choose a greener product when all other things are equal, but the majority refuse to pay much (if any) of a price premium for their environmental or sustainability values. As *Green to Gold* made clear, environmental attributes generally only work as a "third button" marketers can push—once they've met price and quality/performance expectations. And most consumers, even those who say they want to purchase sustainable goods, will not invest time trying to figure out which products are greener. Many consumers explain they don't buy green because they lack information or are confused by seemingly contradictory information. "I heard the Prius has a battery that is a big environmental problem!" you might hear them say. Many consumers are overwhelmed by choices ("who knows whether paper or plastic is the right answer for shopping bags?"). Others distrust product eco-claims or are skeptical that their purchase will make a difference. In some quarters, doubts linger over the quality of eco-marketed products because of early inferior green goods—such as the first-generation flickering greenish fluorescent lights.

But things are changing. The green marketplace is maturing. Companies that make an effort to show consumers the way to a greener future will be increasingly rewarded. After all, who wants toxics-laced, greenhouse gas-emitting, rainforest-destroying products that harm the planet if there is a good alternative available?

This chapter helps anyone in marketing or sales roles to:

- Identify the relevant green attributes of products or services.
- Ensure that glaring environmental or sustainability shortcomings don't trip up a green marketing initiative.
- Design and execute a green marketing strategy.
- Avoid greenwashing.
- Expand the demand for green products and services.

BASIC PLAYS: LEARN BEFORE YOU LEAP

1. Identify Your Sustainability Opportunities

The best green marketing and sales efforts are not just "add-ons" to existing corporate marketing efforts; instead, they emerge from careful analysis of how sustainability fits into a company's overall sales and growth strategy. So before moving forward with a green marketing campaign, think about why your company wants to go green. Or more precisely: Why do your customers want you to go green? What is your sustainability-oriented value proposition? Clorox's Green Works line of safer and more natural cleaning products turned out to be a big hit because it: (1) addressed pressing consumer concerns about chemicals in their homes; and (2) aligned with a broader repositioning of the company. Indeed, the push to "green" the company's cleaning products was reinforced by the purchase of Burt's Bees, a natural line of personal care products.

GE's wildly successful ecomagination brand repositioning initiative offers a case in point. According to GE's Executive Director of Advertising and Branding,

Judy Hu, the marketing team viewed the ecomagination thrust as "a business initiative first and foremost"—not just an ad campaign. The strategy grew out of a clear and compelling corporate vision aimed at positioning GE as an environmental solutions provider and using green as a platform for business growth. According to Hu, the strategy worked because it tapped into the GE culture's core qualities of curiosity, relentless drive, innovation, and an optimistic belief that "the future can be better because you can make it better."[8] And GE ran the whole effort in a very businesslike manner, backed by a commitment to track and report results—both in terms of revenue (about $20 billion a year by 2010) and reduction of environmental impacts.[9]

Sometimes a product or service offered by a company already has green attributes but is not being marketed as such. Getting a clear picture of how your products and services stack up relative to your competitors' products on critical pollution control, natural resource consumption, or sustainability parameters is the place to start. If you've got a leadership position—especially products or services that could help your customers solve their environmental problems—you may be able to use that attribute to distinguish yourself from the competition.

Brita, the California-based water filter manufacturer, saw its annual sales jump 23 percent when it began advertising its water filters as the eco-friendly alternative to bottled water.[10] There were, however, some initial bumps along the way. Notably, watchdog groups gave the company a lot of heat for claiming a green alternative when filters were nonrecyclable. The company took this criticism to heart and responded quickly by launching a partnership with Preserve, a manufacturer of 100 percent recycled household consumer goods, to collect and recycle Brita pitcher filters.[11] Brita's success relied on the fact that it highlighted the green attributes of its product but did not oversell its Eco-Advantage. The company was honest about what the product could do and did not claim to be a green company merely by virtue of the product. A company that pitches its environmental elements too hard is in danger of being criticized for "greenwashing," especially if the company isn't squeaky clean across the board.

To find your sustainability opportunities, systematically review the environmental or sustainability strengths, weaknesses, opportunities, and threats facing your industry. Assess your own position on each issue vis-à-vis your competition—and potential competition. This scan may require a SWOT (strengths, weaknesses, opportunities, and threats) analysis by product line (see Figure 15.1).

Strengths can be opportunities for green marketing. If you cannot identify ways that your products or services stand out (or could be made to stand out) from a sustainability perspective, you're not well-positioned to market on this agenda. But remember that weaknesses or threats can be turned into opportunities with a product or service innovation that overcomes the issue in questions. (See Chapter 11 for guidance on eco-minded redesign.)

Figure 15.1   **Green Marketing Baseline Analysis**

Environmental	Industry	Your Product	Competitor's Products	Potential Competitor's Products
Strengths				
Weaknesses				
Opportunities				
Threats				

2. Solidify Your "Defense" before Going on the "Offense"

Companies trying to be sustainability leaders cannot succeed if they have glaring gaps in their own environmental practices or product portfolios. The fact that you've got a leading product in one category is not enough to be a green leader. In fact, companies that try to claim a green mantle will be subject to extra scrutiny by environmental groups, consumer watchdogs, and other NGOs, not to mention the ever-growing list of self-appointed corporate critics.

Just ask Bill Ford, Chairman (and former CEO) of the Ford Motor Company. His attempts to "green" his company in the mid-2000s with an environmentally cutting-edge retrofit of the company's historic River Rouge factory and commitments to produce more hybrid vehicles generated scorn and derision because the company continued to produce millions of gas-guzzling SUVs and trucks. So before going on a green marketing offensive, make sure your "ducks are in a row." Often this means answering tough questions about the spectrum of eco-issues and being clear on your sustainability strategy. If you identify gaps, we've provided some guidance on where to turn to address them:

- What are the company's biggest environmental and sustainability challenges? Are there plans in place to address these issues? (Chapters 3 and 5)
- What are your company's major environmental-related risks, exposures, and impacts? (Chapter 5 and 6)
- What environment or sustainability policies and programs are in place? How do accomplishments to date compare to best practice and competitors' accomplishments? What goals have been announced? Have they been reached? (Chapter 7)
- Has the company assessed the eco-footprint of its products? How green are they relative to competitors' products? (Chapter 6 and 11)
- What (and how) has the company reported on its sustainability strategy and performance? (Chapter 22)

- Are there any green-related skeletons in the closet that the company fears "getting out" if it takes a more active approach in communicating its green accomplishments? (Chapter 3)

3. Build on Current Green Strengths

Sometimes companies develop a leading-edge environmental position in the marketplace by highlighting existing (but perhaps underappreciating) green attributes of a product. GE's ecomagination campaign initially involved no product innovation. It simply focused marketing dollars on the energy efficiency and other environmental attributes of the company's jet engines, locomotives, and appliances.

In other cases, companies launch a greener version of an existing product as the centerpiece of a green marketing campaign. Honda, for instance, has had great success with the hybrid version of its popular Civic, launched in 2002. Kimberly Clark has driven growth with a Green Seal-certified, 100 percent recycled-fiber line of SCOTT towels and bathroom tissues. Backed by the trusted Clorox name, the company's Green Works products grabbed 42 percent of the market share for natural household cleaning products within their first three years[12]—and helped the company to a top position in the 2009 Green Brands Survey.[13]

As you reflect on your company's sustainability opportunities, consider how these strengths can contribute to the company's broader business goals. Or if sustainability is your main value, think about how to integrate that with other things that consumers care about, such as quality, health, and affordability. And if your existing sustainability strengths are not known or appreciated by your customers, ask yourself why. What information, if communicated effectively, might help bolster corporate or brand image, strengthen customer loyalty, or attract new customers?

4. Deepen Understanding of Customers' Needs, Attitudes, and Buying Behaviors

As with any marketing and sales initiative, effective green-related initiatives require solid intelligence about customer attitudes, values, and willingness to pay. A 2009 IBM study found that while over two-thirds of executives surveyed said their companies were using sustainability to create new sources of revenue, only 35 percent believed they knew their customers' sustainability motivations and expectations "well."[14]

Listening to customers can lead to breakthrough solutions and green marketing opportunities. With more and more customers wanting to recycle their beverage containers, Alcoa has dedicated a top executive to "innovation," including sustainability opportunities. By using better alloys and other technology improvements, the company developed ways to make cans lighter and more re-cyclable while cutting emissions and lowering costs. The innovation team has also found ways to convert unwanted by-products into valuable assets. For example, the company now makes construction fill material and soil fertiliz-ers out of the "red mud" that long burdened aluminum smelters.[15] Similarly, Bloom Energy CEO K.R. Sridhar says interviewing his customers to uncover their sustainability perspectives and needs—including plug-and-play energy technol-ogy that was accessible anywhere in the world and immune to wildly volatile energy prices—provided the impetus for creating the company's pioneering "Bloom Box," a brick-sized fuel cell that can power an average European home.[16]

HOW GREEN ARE CONSUMERS REALLY?

Market research on consumer attitudes and behaviors related to sustainability has exploded in recent years. Analysts have sliced and diced consumers into various segments using their own catchy (but sometimes confusing) terminology. As an introduction to the latest in "green marketing" research, we've highlighted some frequently referenced consumer segments and their interest in sustainable products:

- **LOHAS (lifestyles of health and sustainability):** According to the National Marketing Institute, as of 2009, 19 percent of U.S. consumers have all or part of their purchasing shaped by their belief in sustainability as a core value and their commitment to a more healthy and natural lifestyle.

- **Naturalites:** Represent a segment of the market (perhaps 15 percent) that chooses green or organic products mainly to reduce chemical exposures and to improve their own and their families' health. Their focus is generally narrower than LOHAS consumers and centers on buying natural or organic consumer packaged goods, especially food and beverages, as well as personal care and cleaning products.

- **Conventionals:** Pragmatic consumers who don't have strong environmental attitudes or motivations but buy "green" if it saves money. They would, for instance, buy a hybrid car to get better mileage or install a compact fluorescent lightbulb to trim their electric bill.

- **Drifters:** Have green "intentions" but their shopping behavior is influenced by many other factors, including being trendy. So they buy green only occasionally.

- **Dream Greens:** Represent a market segment that claims to want to buy green but then says they don't have enough information. They rarely pick the greener product.

- **Apathetics/Unconcerned:** They show little interest in the environment and are definitely not focused on buying green products.

- **"Mean Greens":** Define themselves as being *against* environmentalists and environmentalism. They are cynical or apprehensive about the green agenda.

Sources: GfK Roper Consulting (2007); Natural Marketing Institute (2010); The Hartman Group (2010).[17]

As you assess the opportunities to turn green to gold in the marketplace, work to understand not only *what* target customers think, but also about *how* they think—and how that translates into real-world *behaviors* that affect purchasing decisions. Which sustainability issues matter most to your customers? What are the values and motivations behind their interest? How important are sustainability attributes? Will your customer pay a price premium for a greener product? Do customers say one thing in surveys but another when actual dollars are on the line? What's getting in the way of greener purchases—quality, price, access, convenience, mistrust, misperceptions, a sense of powerlessness, a belief that someone else is responsible for solving the problem (like government or business), or something else? As you gather feedback from customers, focus on how you can provide solutions to your customers' sustainability problems and drive revenue for your company.

Consumer product companies that make it a priority to learn about their retailers' perspective on sustainability have the opportunity to increase exposure and become favored suppliers. According to a 2009 survey by the Retail Systems Research Association and the Retail Industry Leaders Association, 48 percent of retailers believe sustainability is strategically important to them given their customers growing interest in energy and fuel savings and other environmental concerns.[18] Walmart and Tesco are among the retailers making a big commitment to market their green credentials. They've launched big sustainability initiatives and put eco-labels on products. But they're not alone. Walgreen's New York City–based subsidiary Duane Reade launched a new line of organic and eco-friendly private-label products in 2010, along with a loyalty program called the "EcoClub," which gives members double points in the regular Duane Reade rewards program when they buy designated green products.[19]

INTERMEDIATE PLAYS: SEIZE THE OPPORTUNITIES

5. Step Ahead of the Pack

Real marketing magic happens when companies anticipate what customers will think and get ahead of green trends before an energy-efficiency feature or eco-attribute becomes standard. To seize an eco-marketing opportunity, a sales team must work in lockstep with sustainability experts. Working together to analyze consumer behavior and to share insights, they will be better positioned to spot emerging trends and shifting attitudes and thus to dodge new business risks and capture opportunities. (See Chapter 5, "Spot the Eco-Issues that Could Impact Your Bottom Line," for more guidance on issue spotting.) Honda and Toyota did this famously in the auto market in the early 2000s, leaping ahead of competitors in innovating and marketing around green technology. GE also got a first-mover advantage in the marketplace by launching its ecomagination initiative ahead of the pack, although Honeywell, Johnson Controls, United Technologies, and Siemens all now market the eco-efficiency of their products.

CONNECTING WITH CUSTOMER VALUES

In 2007, 29-year-old entrepreneur Carolyn Coquillette took a gamble and opened the first U.S. auto repair shop specializing in hybrids, **"Luscious Garage"** (www. lusciousgarage.com). An expert in regular auto repair, Coquillette sensed a booming business opportunity in hybrids. She also believed that hybrid drivers would be "open to a shift in the paradigm of the repair experience"—one that valued sustainability at the core.

Coquillette offered a very green experience, in part by putting the garage "in the cloud." Many of her peers have raised eyebrows, thinking green was a passing fad, and simply said "good luck." By 2010, however, Luscious Garage had become a resounding success. Customers rave on YELP. What's accounted for the success? "The biggest key has been authenticity," Coquillette told us. "People can sense a poser a mile away. Customers know that we don't just fix hybrids, we also really care about people and the environment. We want people to walk into the shop and feel like they belong—like we have the same priorities they do. For us, marketing and branding success is about talking on an equal level."[20]

---

6. Take it Public

There's no magic recipe for successful green marketing, brand building, or public relations. But there are several ingredients that the companies we've worked with point to when we asked them about the lessons they've learned in this sphere.

QUALITY AND PRICE

First and foremost, products and services that have sustainability attributes don't sell on green alone. They will only succeed in the marketplace if they perform as well as their competitors and deliver good value. Mainstream customers will always put quality and price first. Green attributes can tip the balance in purchasing decisions, but not if they come with trade-offs in value or performance. This "green as the third button" marketing principle is true in both the business-to-business (B2B) and consumer markets. As Walmart's former Chief Sustainability Officer, Matt Kistler explained, "we pay more for a product that's better for the environment." In the same breath, however, he noted "but it's got to work, it's got to perform, or else I really don't consider it green."[21]

There will always be niche exceptions. A small segment of "green pioneers" will pay a premium and take a risk on new "super-green" products with higher up-front costs so long as they promise to deliver real environmental gains or long-term savings. So Tesla is selling $100,000 electric cars to a small market segment (including Brad Pitt, George Clooney, and Arnold Schwarzenegger) willing to pay a huge premium to put their environmental commitment on display and help to create a new industry. On a smaller scale, coffee filter maker Melitta found a niche market willing to pay a bit of a premium for unbleached brown paper filters—and, more recently, ones made of bamboo.

RELEVANCE

For green claims to resonate, they need to connect to what the customer cares about. It sounds obvious, but many green marketing efforts fail this test. So you'll need to target your sustainability-oriented sales pitch carefully. Will the product help save money? Improve health? Save time and add convenience? Boost productivity? Cut operational and maintenance costs? Make buyers feel good for supporting a cause that's close to their heart? Highlight what's most important to *your* audience.

The experience of Greenhouse Strategies (GHS), a lighting solutions company offering high-efficiency LEDs, shows how assumptions about customers' priorities may be off the mark and need adjustment. Initially, GHS thought it could convince corporate customers to pay the higher up-front costs for their product by stressing that LEDs are 75 percent more efficient than industry-standard metal halide bulbs and would thus cut energy bills over time. The company suspected that municipalities would respond more to the cost savings argument and less to the pollution-prevention characteristics of LEDs. But the actual marketplace experience proved to be somewhat different. For many companies, the most effective selling point was that LEDs promised to save them waste management fees and government fines that can be imposed for improper disposal of broken metal halide lamps. And it also turned out that many municipalities cared a great deal about the bottom-line savings from lower energy costs.[22]

When it comes to tapping into consumers' emotional desire to make a difference on environmental issues, one major retailer we spoke with found that a key to their green marketing success centered on framing messages to consumers around *their own* environment rather than the *general* environment. This isn't because people don't care about anything beyond their local communities; rather, it's because consumers are more apt to think their choices will actually make an impact locally, whereas they'd be meaningless when it comes to overwhelming issues like climate change. Likewise, it's important to remember that most people care about "green" because they want to preserve or improve the quality of life for people and their children today, not to protect nature in the abstract (even in the form of polar bears or other charismatic animals). Thus, Brand Strategist Russ Meyer of Landor Associates recommends crafting stories around tangible, local benefits not abstract "save the world" visions.[23] The emphasis on "tangible" is critical. Many consumers *will* respond to practical calls to action that go beyond their "local" sphere of influence *if* they believe doing so will add up to real, measurable results.

AUTHENTICITY

We can't stress enough the need to be authentic. Green-related sales, PR, marketing, or communications efforts must be grounded in the truth, the whole truth, and nothing but the truth—or they are likely to do more harm than good to a company or brand. Be guided at all times by Warren Buffett's cautionary bit of wisdom: "It takes 20 years to build a reputation and five minutes to ruin it."[24] Stretching green claims invites trouble as does overpromising and underdelivering. In today's world of hyperconnectivity, companies must expect "attack dogs" to be ready to pounce if they misstate, understate, overstate, or otherwise mislead—using every means available from social networks such as Facebook, YouTube, and Twitter.

Some market segments are especially skeptical about corporate claims in general and environmental promises in particular. "Millennials" (also known as "Generation Y") tend to be highly suspicious of corporate PR and advertising. They look for authenticity, transparency, and verification before purchasing. A recent Havas Media survey of over 20,000 consumers worldwide found that 64 percent viewed sustainability merely as "marketing tool" and were distrustful of claims.[25]

GREENWASHING WON'T SELL

Environmentalist Jay Westerveld coined the term "greenwashing" in a 1986 essay criticizing hotels for saying they were "green" just because they offered guests the option of reusing towels.[26] Today, communication that misleads consumers about a company's environmental record or the eco-benefits of products or services usually gets tagged as "greenwashing."[27] So those seeking to sell based on sustainability must steer clear of the top 10 sins of green marketing (based on TerraChoice's Seven Sins of Greenwashing work):

- **Vague wording and claims:** Words like "eco-friendly" and "all-natural" mean nothing unless backed by specifics. Even products containing hazardous substances such as mercury and arsenic can technically be called 100 percent natural because those substances are derived from natural elements.

- **Misleading images:** Just because a company's new automobile gets better-than-average gas mileage doesn't give it the right to show pictures of butterflies coming out of tailpipes. The UK's Advertising Standards Authority censured Shell in 2007 for a print ad featuring an oil refinery's chimney's emitting flowers.[28]

- **Greener products from "dirty" companies:** If a company wants rewards in the marketplace for a green clothing line, it better be sure its factories (or those of its suppliers) aren't dumping nasty chemicals into local waterways or subjecting workers to unhealthy conditions.

- **Green claims in isolation:** No product is eco-perfect. But one eco-friendly attribute (say, high energy efficiency) does not justify green hype and cannot compensate for other negative qualities (such as the presence of highly toxic materials). Selective reporting or glossing over inconvenient facts can get companies into hot water. The French cement maker, Lafarge, learned this lesson the hard way in 2007. While claiming to have a "proactive and radical" greenhouse gas emissions control strategy, the company was busted by the eco-website Treehugger and *Business-*

(continued)

(Continued)

Week, which uncovered the inconvenient truth that the Lafarge emissions had gone up 11 percent over two years.[29]

- **Exaggerated benefits:** A hybrid SUV that gets 31 miles a gallon instead of the industry average of 20 represents a step forward, but not a big one. Getting 31 miles per gallon hardly qualifies for green bragging rights. Companies that claim their products are "greener" than competitors' should expect extra scrutiny. If you are going to make environmental claims, do your homework first. Life cycle analysis (discussed in Chapter 6) and other analytic tools can provide the proper foundation for green marketing.

- **Irrelevant claims:** Companies can't use green as a differentiator when their products merely comply with regulations. For example, a claim that a product is "CFC-free" won't wash because ozone-layer-damaging CFCs were banned 20 years ago. Likewise, you can't legitimately boast that a product's packaging is "biodegradable" or "compostable" if it takes 10 years to degrade or only breaks down in specialized settings.[30]

- **No proof or made-up labels:** A company can't boast its product is "certified organic" or made with "50 percent recycled content" without having evidence to back the claim posted online for all to see and scrutinize. In the United States, the Federal Trade Commission has begun to crack down on "self-certifications" and misleading environmental claims. Companies that slap made-up green labels onto products or imply third-party certification are at risk of both governmental sanction and consumer watchdog backlash.

- **Outright lies:** While increasingly rare, companies that make false environmental claims, such as suggesting that their products are certified when they are not, will almost certainly be caught—and suffer significant legal and marketplace consequences.

REAL DIFFERENTIATION

As we've mentioned before, "green" can be the tie-breaking element for customers when other things are equal. But the green attributes that help you stand out from the pack today may not be the ones that work tomorrow as green continues to go mainstream. Take product packaging, for instance. A few years ago, packaging boasting recycled content might have stood out as exceptional. But today customers see eco-packaging as "standard." So recycled content in packaging has become "table stakes." To really differentiate a product now, you'll have to do more.

CONSISTENCY WITH BRAND IDENTITY

Unless you're launching an entirely new brand, green-related marketing works best when the message aligns with the existing corporate or brand identity. Shaklee's "Get Clean" line of cleaning supplies sold as "safe for you, your home, and your planet" worked because it built on the company's 50-year history of selling healthy and natural products. Companies whose communications seem to depart from their basic identity—either in substance or tone—risk being perceived as inauthentic in a consumer culture that has grown discerning. So a company with a history of getting fined for environmental noncompliance would fail miserably if it launched an ad campaign around the "intergenerational responsibility" theme. It might, however, get traction if it soberly addressed how it planned to tackle its past environmental deficiencies. In this regard, Northeast Utilities won awards for its straightforward environmental report after pleading guilty to several environmental violations.

CREATIVITY AND DELIGHT—NOT GLOOM AND DOOM

Companies are finding what environmental advocacy groups have learned the hard way when it comes to reaching mainstream audiences on "green" issues: People don't like communications that make them feel guilty or overwhelm them with fear.[31] What they do respond to, as Yahoo!'s climate and energy director Christina Page told us, are "interesting, delightful, catchy stories." Walmart's upbeat sustainability ads are a great example. One 2010 TV ad that aired during Earth Month, "It's Rollback Time at Walmart," featured a truck driver who explains how the company's green efforts help customers "save money" and "live better" while improving the company's environmental performance:

> Just by driving smarter routes and making sure our tractors are packed fuller, we save millions of dollars on fuel costs. And when costs go down, prices go down. We're talking about thousands of rollbacks on the things you need every day. It's a beautiful thing. My name is Mike, and I save people money so they can live better.[32]

Consumers also appreciate a sense of humor. Timberland's highly successful, laugh-out-loud "Earthkeepers" TV ad features a hiker relentlessly assaulted by angry bees and trees with a tagline that warns: "Wear new Earthkeepers™ . . . or nature might get you back." Hanes took a similar approach with its hilarious "Future Generations" ad in which sinister-looking children shoot evil glances at a shopper who is not wearing Hanes "EcoSmart"™ clothing. The spot received over 40,000 views (with mainly gushing comments) on YouTube within months of its first airing in 2010.

BEYOND "GREEN": PRAGMATISM AND INNOVATION

Many green-related marketing and branding efforts have succeeded by tapping into the pragmatic, can-do spirit of mainstream audiences instead of relying on narrower eco-themes such as "saving the earth." IBM's 2010 eco-ad campaign, for instance, calls for a "smarter planet" not a "greener one."

GOOD MESSENGERS

Getting green messaging to resonate requires a credible messenger. When conducting a green marketing strategy for consumers, be sure to consider *who* can deliver the message best. The answer can vary wildly depending on your product and target audience. One Global 500 company discovered that its customers tuned out celebrity endorsements preferring ordinary people with real stories to which they could relate. Employees can sometimes be the most effective messengers of all. Aveda, a leading retailer of natural and organic personal care products, enlists employees at retail stores to communicate in ways that reinforce its brand identity and build customer loyalty. Salespeople are encouraged to ask customers "Would you like to help *support our mission* to protect the environment by using your own bag for your purchases today?" One of us (P.J.) saw this in action and overheard a customer gleefully respond, "Yes, and thank you so much for asking!"

Don't expect employees to use salient messages from dense sustainability reports or jargon-filled corporate communications. Find easy, fun ways to communicate what's notable about your company's environmental efforts and the green attributes of products. For example, Motorola, which sells most of its hardware through third-party channels, felt its strong sustainability story wasn't reaching consumers. To fix this, they distributed easy-to-use sustainability information to channel partners, giving them the tools to sell green to their customers.[33] The more employees know, and the more they feel ownership and pride in the company's accomplishments, the better ambassadors they'll be.

THE RIGHT COMMUNICATIONS CHANNELS

Choices about communications channels can make or break a strategy. As you weigh the possibilities appropriate for your intended audience—print and broadcast ads, websites, viral marketing and social media, press releases, point-of-sale advertising, packaging, stunts, or other means—use the green lens to think outside the box.

At Stonyfield Farm, CE-Yo Gary Hirshberg has been a master of clever eco-marketing. On his way to building a brand that is now the world's top-selling organic yogurt, he once challenged a radio host who claimed his yogurt tasted worse than camel dung to a taste-off—getting thousands of dollars for free airtime. More recently, he came up with the idea of setting up a roadside tire inflation station to get out the message that properly inflated tires means better gas mileage, fuel savings, and lower greenhouse gas emissions.[34] What does tire inflation possibly have to do with Stonyfield Farm and yogurt? Drivers quickly got the connection: the company is reducing its own greenhouse gas emissions, educating consumers about climate change, *and* producing top-quality yogurt—all from something aimed at what is good for the land and people's health. On top of that, drivers who stopped to get their tires inflated got a free sample of Stonyfield Farm yogurt. The creative effort grabbed millions of dollars of "earned" media as TV coverage took the stunt far beyond the consumers who got their tires inflated.

Ricoh, a leading technology company, similarly attracted lots of publicity for launching Times Square's first 100 percent solar- and wind-powered billboard—using the story to reach consumers with its message of environmental leadership. Corporate Communications Director Jason Dizzine said, "Most billboards deliver a message, but this billboard is itself the message."[35]

Finally, do your best to minimize environment impacts when choosing your communications vehicles. One consumer we spoke with who considers himself a "core green" told us how dismayed he was that a well-known company that loudly trumpets its Earth-friendly credentials sent a shipment that included two free gifts he considered useless: "They never asked if I wanted the stuff, wasted materials and plastic in the process, and the extra shipping weight caused more carbon emissions. It left a really bad taste in my mouth."

VALIDATION

Getting a stamp of approval from reputable third-party sources can insulate companies from accusations of greenwashing, raise visibility, and help bolster customers' confidence that choosing a particular product is the right way to go. While a dizzying array of eco-certification schemes and green labels exist, some such seals of approval deliver real marketing value. The Forest Stewardship Council, for example, has achieved real traction as a guide to sustainable lumber and wood products. Although getting approval can take considerable time and resources, the payoff in the marketplace can be significant because green-conscious consumers are desperate for credible information shortcuts to make better purchasing decisions. The EU's "Energy" labels for major appliances, which rates products from A (best) to G (worst) in terms of energy efficiency, shows the power of a good scheme. The label bumped up the market share of "A-rated" products from nearly zero in 1996 to about 80 percent in 2006.[36] The most practical, comprehensive guide to existing certifications and labels is available at www.ecolabelindex.com.

PARTNERSHIPS

Another way to earn credibility is to partner with highly credible groups that are willing to publicly vouch for your efforts. Strategic partnerships have been at the heart of success of several green marketing and communications efforts. Clorox's success in rebranding its Brita water filter products as a "green" purchase (no need to buy all that bottled water in plastic) can be attributed in part to its collaboration with reusable bottle manufacturer Nalgene and the nonprofit Surfrider Foundation. Together, they launched a "Filter for Good" campaign (www.filterforgood.com) that helped shoppers understand the multiple environmental benefits of choosing Brita water in Nalgene bottles.[37] FilterForGood has since launched other effective strategic partnerships, including one with "The Biggest Loser" trainer Bob Harper. Computer giant HP entered a valuable partnership with Walmart based on the retailers' "Home Entertainment Design Challenge," a contest to develop eco-friendly products. HP's repackaging design, which cut 97 percent of the waste packaging required for its Pavilion notebook computer by replacing boxes with stylish bags, garnered HP a tremendous amount of earned media and premium shelf placement at stores.[38]

When developing your plan, consider all the possible partnerships that could add value to your efforts and seize those opportunities. Put retailers at the top of the list; eco-savvy retailers will welcome a conversation about a good marketing idea that could both help the environment and generate more sales.

ADVANCED PLAYS: TRANSFORM THE MARKETPLACE

7. Change Customer Attitudes and Behaviors

As we've already mentioned, a lot of barriers stand in the way of turning latent customer interest in green into active purchasing—confusion, skepticism of green claims, resistance to changing routine behaviors, and more. Companies committed to building an Eco-Advantage don't let this slow them down. They develop strategies to educate and engage customers in ways that help overcome barriers. In so doing, they accelerate the growth of markets for greener products and services. And they know that being seen as part of a movement that's solving environmental problems will bolster their brand value and build customer loyalty. Tod Arbogast, Vice President of Sustainability at Avon Cosmetics, told us shaping environmental attitudes represents the "new wave of business sustainability leadership: empowering, educating, engaging, and helping create a catalytic movement among consumers."

Many companies are helping their customers go green by using media to influence attitudes and perceptions. Procter & Gamble launched an uplifting media campaign in 2010 to educate consumers on energy, water, and waste-related problems alongside promoting specific products to help consumers reduce their energy and water use and become "future friendly."[39] Avon, a global company with 43,000 employees and $12 billion in sales, makes sustainability education and engagement a core element of its business strategy. The company uses its woman-to-woman network of 6.2 million Avon Representatives and 300 million customers to create "a global women's environmental movement to nurture nature." Levis changed the labels on its jeans to encourage consumers to wash jeans in cold water, dry on low heat or a clothesline, and donate after they are finished with them.

8. Create Product Infrastructure

Some green marketing efforts will only succeed if accompanied by a changed context for the product, meaning evolution in lifestyles, technology, or infrastructure. For example, many dot-com companies of the 1990s failed because there were not enough Internet users for them to be viable. Once wireless technology became widely deployed, however, the next generation of online businesses found ready customers. Electric cars cannot flourish in an environment in the absence of "plug-in" stations. In the same way, renewable energy systems are impractical if they cannot be connected to the electricity grid.

Companies with new green products or services need to think about the context in which people will use their product—and invest in the supporting infrastructure if it does not already exist. Almost overnight, Apple's iPod transformed the music industry—getting the public to buy mp3 files rather than physical CDs, cassettes, or records. In other cases, a company with vision and great marketing skill may be able to transform consumer habits on its own. The success of eco-entrepreneur Shai Agassi's vision of battery swapping as a way to make electric cars more convenient and affordable requires big societal investment in "swapping stations." But Agassi has been a brilliant salesperson when it comes to creating a vision of a brighter future—and he now has governments all over the world as well as Renault and Nissan working with his company, Better Place, to test his business model. This may require PR efforts to get governments to build the requisite infrastructure or create policy incentives that induce the necessary investment by the private sector.

SUMMARY

Key Plays

1. Identify your sustainability opportunities.
2. Solidify your "defense" before going on the "offense."
3. Build on current green strengths.
4. Deepen understanding of customers' needs, attitudes, and buying behaviors.
5. Step ahead of the pack.
6. Take it public.
7. Change customer attitudes and behaviors.
8. Create product infrastructure.

ADDITIONAL RESOURCES

GENERAL

The New Rules of Green Marketing: Strategies, Tools, and Inspiration for Sustainable Branding by Jacqueline Ottman (Berrett-Koehler, 2011). Reviews consumer research, gives case examples of successful sustainable products and green campaigns, and outlines time-tested recommendations. www.greenmarketing.com

Green Marketing Manifesto by John Grant (John Wiley & Sons, 2008). Recommendations for marketers with examples from companies and brands making headway in green marketing.

"From Greenwash to Great: A Practical Guide to Great Green Marketing (without the Greenwash)" (Ogilvy Earth). Recommendations and real-world examples on effective green marketing. www.ogilvyearth.com/greenwash

"Eco-promising: Communicating the Environmental Credentials of Your Products and Services" by Ryan Schuchard, Tom Berry, Claire Skinner, Emma Stewart, and Sally Uren (Forum for the Future/Business for Social Responsibility, 2008) www.bsr.org

CONSUMER AND MARKET RESEARCH

Mintel Green Living Report. Examines size, scope, and growth of the green consumer marketplace, as well as driving forces that will shape its future. Focuses on six sectors: food and beverage; personal care products; building and home improvement supplies; electronics; automobiles; and restaurants and lodging. http://oxygen.mintel.com

Green Confidence Index (GreenBiz). Monthly index of consumers' environmental beliefs and behaviors, identifying shifts in marketplace perceptions. www.greenbiz.com

ImagePower Green Brands Survey (Landor). Explores consumer attitudes towards green issues by surveying people in eight countries—Australia, Brazil, China, France, Germany, India, United States, and UK—and ranking nearly 350 brands. http://landor.com

BBMG Conscious Consumer Report. Explores the attitudes, preferences, values, and experiences that shape consumer purchasing behavior, brand loyalty and peer-to-peer influence. Combines ethnographic research in two U.S. markets with a national survey of 2,000 adults. www.bbmg.com

LOHAS Consumer Trends Database (Natural Marketing Institute). Data on U.S. attitudes, behaviors, product usage rates, lifestyle patterns, and demographics in the LOHAS (Lifestyles of Health and Sustainability) marketplace. www.nmisolutions.com

Green Gauge Report—U.S. and Global editions (GfK Group). Studies of environmental attitudes and buying behavior drawing on face-to-face interviews with a broad cross-section of consumers. "Green Gauge Global" covers 25 countries. www.gfkamerica.com

Greendex (National Geographic and GlobeScan, 2009). Measures and monitors consumer behaviors that have an impact on the environment. www.globescan.com

BRAND EVALUATION

Havas Media's Sustainable Futures 09. Framework that helps companies measure, track, and connect sustainability to brand value. Includes a Sustainability Futures Quotient (SFQ), a proprietary cross-sector measurement tool that can track and compare companies' performances sustainability over time. www.havasmedia.com

Interbrand is developing a methodology to analyze the link between a company's corporate social responsibility (CSR) performance and its brand value. www.interbrand.com

Harris Interactive Annual RQ (Reputation Quotient). Captures perceptions from stakeholders surveyed in six categories: products and services; financial performance; workplace environment; social responsibility; vision and leadership; and emotional appeal. www.harrisinteractive.com

The Boston College—Reputation Institute's CSR Index (CSRI). Measures the public's perceptions of a company's citizenship, governance, and workplace practices from a representative sample of at least 100 local respondents familiar with the company. www.reputationinstitute.com

ECO-LABELS AND PRODUCT DECLARATIONS

Ecolabel Index and "Global Ecolabel Monitor." Definitive, searchable online guide to eco-labels across all industry sectors. www.ecolabelindex.com

"Global Ecolabel Monitor" (Ecolabel Index and World Resources Institute, 2010). A report on the performance and organizational structure of eco-labels around the world. www.wri.org

Environmental Product Declarations. Website with guidelines and resources to help companies prepare Environmental Product Declaration. www.environmentalproductdeclarations.com

AVOIDING GREENWASHING

Understanding and Preventing Greenwash: A Business Guide (BSR and Futerra). www.bsr.org

"The Seven Sins of Greenwashing" (TerraChoice). A study of environmental claims made on retail products that identifies environmental marketing trends. www.sinsofgreenwashing.org/findings

The Greenwashing Index (EnviroMedia Social Marketing and the University of Oregon). A website that allows people to upload, rate, and discuss green advertisements. www.greenwashingindex.com

Stop Greenwash (Greenpeace). A watchdog/advocacy project to identify and stop corporate greenwashing. www.stopgreenwash.org

GREEN MARKETING GUIDELINES AND STANDARDS

Guides for the Use of Environmental Marketing Claims (U.S. Federal Trade Commission). Reviews laws on environmental claims made in labeling, advertising, promotional materials, and all other forms of marketing found in Section 5 of the FTC Act developed by the U.S. Federal Trade Commission. www.ftc.gov

ISO Standard 14021. Standards developed by the International Organization for Standardization on self-declared environmental claims. www.iso.org

Environmental Claims: A Guide for Industry and Advertisers (Canadian Standards Association). Helps Canadian businesses adhere to ISO 14021 and comply with relevant provisions of the *Competition Act*, the *Consumer Packaging and Labelling Act*, and the *Textile Labelling Act*, administered and enforced by the Competition Bureau of Canada. www.competitionbureau.gc.ca

Green Claims—Practical Guidance (Department for Environment Food and Rural Affairs, UK). Principles and case studies for businesses seeking to make legitimate environmental claims consistent with ISO14021. www.defra.gov.uk

Chapter 16 Legal and Regulatory Affairs

Once dubbed "the black hole of Europe," the city of Hamburg has been pressuring its industries to clean up with tough environmental regulations since the 1980s. Aurubis AG, the largest copper producer and processor in Europe, had one of the dirtiest factories in the city and was faced with the options of shutting down or moving elsewhere. But instead of fighting the regulations, Aurubis embraced them. Over the past 30 years, the company invested $410 million—a third of its total capital expenditure—in a sweeping initiative to turn its aging factory into a state-of-the-art facility. The new plant and equipment offered high-end energy efficiency and eliminated up to 95 percent of air and water pollutants. The Hamburg site has become a world leader in copper recycling technology. As CEO Bernd Drouven observed, "The pressure from regulations and society forced us to be creative in finding technological solutions and ideas in order to cope."[1] And Hamburg has benefitted too—having been designated the 2011 Green Capital of Europe by the European Commission.[2]

As the Aurubis story demonstrates, strict environmental regulations do not have to spell doom even for the most resource-intensive companies. And this example is not all that unusual. Harvard Business School professor and corporate strategy guru Mike Porter has shown (in what is known as the "Porter Hypothesis")[3] that, in many cases, strict regulatory standards can spur innovation and help both companies and countries get ahead of the competition.

Businesses tend to evolve over time in their attitudes toward environmental regulation (see Figure 16.1). We've seen a pattern that (1) begins with "resistance," (2) moves to "compliance," (3) then goes beyond compliance to embrace eco-efficiency, and finally (4) sees law and regulation as an element of strategy.

This chapter introduces plays to help companies:

- Comply with environmental regulations and avoid the fines and damages of incurring violations.
- Go beyond compliance to set environmental standards that meet market expectations rather than mere legal minimums.
- Use regulations to structure the competitive playing field.

Figure 16.1   **Environmental Compliance**

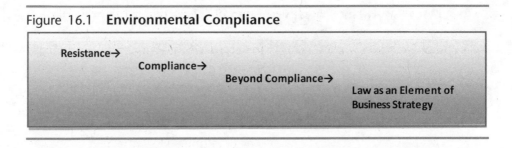

BASIC PLAYS: COMPLY WITH ENVIRONMENTAL REGULATIONS

Both big and small companies need to be sure that they are in compliance with the law at all times. This strict commitment to compliance may sound straightforward, but it can often be challenging to carry out in practice. It is essential that companies ensure that they are in full compliance with the law before moving to any of the more advanced "green to gold" plays discussed in this book. In short, it is important to "be clean before you go green." In fact, companies that make a big push toward raising their environmental profile but do not address basic environmental compliance issues will often find themselves in trouble.

BP learned this lesson in the aftermath of the Gulf of Mexico oil spill. In the early 2000s, CEO Lord John Browne focused on marketing BP as serious about climate change and environmental protection. He touted the company's commitment to renewable energy and even rebranded the company as "beyond petroleum." But the Gulf oil spill wiped out any goodwill these efforts may have generated. The world now knows that in its rush to go green, BP forgot to prioritize safe oil drilling and basic environmental protection. The price for this lapse has been high. CEO Tony Hayward lost his job. And the market capitalization of the company has fallen by $60 billion.

BP is not alone in paying dearly for environmental noncompliance. Irika Shipping suffered a $4 million penalty and five years of probation for illegally dumping 140 barrels of waste oil and bilge waste. Aside from the hefty fine, it is now subject to an Enhanced Environmental Compliance Program and external audits.[4] Another shipping company, Trafigura, paid $250 million to Côte d'Ivoire and its citizens for improper disposal of toxic sludge that resulted in 16 deaths and thousands more getting sick. It is still facing criminal charges for what has become a tragic disaster.[5]

It is not just big businesses that face consequences for failures to abide by environmental law. Small companies are prosecuted every week across the country for noncompliance with one or another element of the complex structure of federal, state, and local environmental law. And the consequences for violating these laws have become much more severe. Fines and penalties can run to millions of dollars. Every year, dozens of executives across the United States go to jail for environmental violations—some for the actual harm they've caused but even more for falsifying reports.

The Internet makes violations easy for all to see and raises the penalty paid in the marketplace for infractions that sour customers, investors, and other stakeholders on a company. The EPA's online "Annual Noncompliance Report" provides a portal for viewing violations of the Clean Air Act, Clean Water Act, and other laws. Anyone can go to the EPA website and search by state or company name to find a list of violators. Even in the developing world, there is a growing emphasis on holding companies to account for environmental performance. As a result, companies all over the world are investing significant resources to comply with environmental regulations.

1. Know Relevant Laws and Regulations

Trying to keep up with all the environmental rules that apply to businesses in America can seem like a daunting task. And the process is not much simpler in other countries. In the United States, the structure of environmental law has three distinct layers: federal, state, and local. The basic architecture of environmental law is drawn from a series of federal statutes that mandate emissions limits, pollutions control equipment, or procedures for handling problems such as toxic waste. Many of the federal laws are implemented by state authorities. For many companies, their interaction with regulatory authorities will be with a state department of environmental protection or some similarly named state agency. In addition, companies will need to deal with local authorities for concerns related to siting facilities or other matters that fall under the jurisdiction of local planning and zoning commissions.

Companies of any significant size will probably need to have a legal team manage environmental compliance. Large companies often have environmental specialists in their general counsel's office as well as outside lawyers who provide more detailed advice on pollution control requirements and natural resource management rules. Middle-sized companies often have a mix of inside expertise and outside advice—sometimes provided through trade associations as well as through law firms and others who specialize in legal affairs. For small businesses, much of the advice comes through trade associations or business and industry associations that specialize in helping small businesses.

For example, the Connecticut Business and Industry Association (CBIA) created a notebook on "Environmental Compliance in Connecticut," which provides details on all of the laws that a small business needs to be aware of and comply with. In addition, CBIA provides a subscription service that includes a monthly newsletter on environmental law in Connecticut and bimonthly updates for the compliance notebook. Other states have similar business or industry associations that provide detailed guidance to small and medium-sized businesses.

No matter how you approach environmental compliance, it is important to note that the specific requirements will vary from company to company and from industry to industry depending on production activities and products. It is important for all companies to be clear on the legal rules that apply in their own industry related to air or water emissions, waste generation, and chemicals use in either the production processes or the products themselves.

While keeping up with all of the legal requirements can seem complex, there are a wide range of resources available to help companies, particularly small businesses, to understand and meet their obligations. In many states, business or industry associations have environmental compliance support systems in place. The previously mentioned Connecticut Business and Industry Association (CBIA) has an entire online library of resources to help small businesses meet environmental obligations. These resources include a CD-ROM with a compendium of all environmental laws applicable to companies doing business in Connecticut, a binder kept up to date with monthly new materials for environmental managers, and other guidance documents. Examine the Department of Environmental Protection website for the state in which your company is located for guidelines on complying with state environmental laws and regulations.

More generically, the U.S. Environmental Protection Agency supports a Small Business Environmental Home Page (www.smallbiz-enviroweb.org), which provides checklists and other resources to help small businesses figure out exactly what they need to do to meet obligations under each of the major statutes. With regard to the Clean Air Act, for example, the web page provides details on how to maintain operating records, emissions monitoring rules, hazardous air pollutants requirements (maximum available control technology), prevention of serious deterioration (PSD) rules, new source review (NSR), and permitting through state agencies. Figure 16.2 provides a quick summary of the major environmental laws in the United States.

2. Build an Environmental Compliance Management System

Most companies will find it valuable to systematize their compliance with environmental laws and regulations through a computer-based tracking system. Making sure that everyone in the company who needs to know is aware of all of the permits required and compliance deadlines is quite easy through software programs that are widely available. For example, EPOCH Environmental Compliance and Task Management Software enables companies to track, report, and comply with a range of environmental issues, including toxic chemical release, air and water emissions, hazardous waste storage and disposal, and health and safety. The software enables you to track your company's performance in all areas and match them against standards set by local and federal regulatory agencies. The software also has task management abilities that enable you to stay on top of deadlines, notifications, and events.

Figure 16.2   **U.S. Environmental Law in Brief**

Air Pollution   The Clean Air Act (CAA) regulates air emissions including: carbon monoxide, sulfur dioxide, oxides of nitrogen, volatile organic compounds (VOCs), particulates, and lead. The Supreme Court has also ruled that the CAA gives the federal government authority to regulate greenhouse gas emissions, but it has not yet done so.

Water Pollution   The Clean Water Act (CWA) controls the discharge of hazardous and nonhazardous water pollutants into streams, rivers, lakes, and wetlands.

The Safe Drinking Water Act (SDWA) protects drinking water from specified contaminants.

Waste   The Resource Conservation Recovery Act (RCRA) sets out strict rules for the treatment, storage, and disposal of hazardous waste and somewhat less strict rules for nonhazardous (or "solid") waste.

The Comprehensive Environmental Response Compensation and Liability Act (CERCLA) governs the clean up of abandoned toxic waste sites and imposes liability on current and past owners and operators of contaminated waste dumps.

Chemicals   The Toxic Substances Control Act (TSCA) authorizes the EPA to regulate chemicals and to restrict or ban those deemed to pose unreasonable risks to the environment and human health.

The Federal Insecticide, Fungicide, and Rodenticide Act (FIFRA) regulates the sale, distribution, and use of insecticides and pesticides.

Land Use   The National Environmental Policy Act (NEPA) requires federal agencies to consider the environmental impacts of their proposed actions and analyze reasonable alternatives that might be less environmentally harmful.

The Coastal Zone Management Act (CZMA) provides federal assistance to states to establish programs to protect, restore, and enhance valuable natural coastal resources such as wetlands, floodplains, beaches, and barrier islands.

The Endangered Species Act (ESA) prohibits killing or harming endangered species or the destruction of their habitats.

Source: Based on Robert Percival, et al., *Environmental Regulation: Law, Science, and Policy,* 6th ed. (2009).

In developing an environmental law and regulatory compliance system, it may seem that the challenge is largely a legal one. But, in many cases, the issues are best understood as engineering problems. Thus, many small- and mid-sized companies find that rather than hiring lawyers to help them build a compliance management system, it makes more sense to hire an engineering consulting firm specializing in their industry's issues.

INTERMEDIATE PLAYS: BE PROACTIVE

3. Reduce Compliance Burdens

Once company leaders understand their company's environmental compliance obligations, they should verify whether any of these obligations could be eliminated by re-engineering either products or manufacturing processes. In particular, if a production process currently uses hazardous materials that are not absolutely necessary and require complicated regulatory tracking, then it makes great sense to consider a new process to eliminate the use of those chemicals. Compliance with hazardous waste laws is often the most complex and time consuming of all environmental regulations. Likewise, any product containing toxic or hazardous materials might also be a candidate for redesign, which could eliminate the materials in question and thereby reduce your company's regulatory burden.

A practical first step for most companies is to map out all the elements used in each of their products so they know what sensitive materials they are using. SC Johnson has taken this exercise to a particularly sophisticated level. The company's "green list" clarifies exactly what materials go into each product the company makes. They rate each raw material used in one of their products on a scale of 0 to 3, with 0 being the worst in terms of its health and environmental impacts and 3 being the best. When SC Johnson scientists make a new product or reformulate an old one, they strive to use only materials rated 3 or 2. Only when alternatives are not viable or the material is used on a limited basis do scientists use materials rated 1 or 0.[6]

Sometimes companies must respond to regulatory heterogeneity with reorganization. Scotts Miracle-Gro, an Ohio-based maker of lawn and garden products, found that its biggest challenge came from divergent standards across states and sometimes even municipalities. In response, CEO Jim Hagedorn decentralized his regulatory compliance group and put government affairs experts into the company's regional offices across the country. This reorganization allows Scotts Miracle-Gro to track issues in a much more granular fashion and to stay ahead of regulatory pressures.[7]

4. Use Over-the-Horizon Issue Spotting

Environmental regulations are not static. As the science of pollution and chemical exposures evolves, so do the legal standards. Companies need to be constantly vigilant for emerging concerns and regulatory responses. For example, recent science revealed that phthalates, a class of chemicals used to harden plastics used in water bottles and storage containers, interfere with the development of fetuses and young children. Canada and a number of U.S. states have thus banned phthalates. Water bottle makers and others using these plastic hardeners have therefore had to reformulate some of the basic products they sell. Companies that were prepared for this change in the law had the advantage. Those who had not been tracking the prospect of legal change were caught off guard.

There are a number of legal changes emerging in the United States that companies need to be watching carefully. In particular, the prospect looks strong for new chemical and toxic substance regulations. In Europe, the REACH Directive (Registration, Evaluation, Authorisation and Restriction of Chemicals) shifts the burden of proving that a new chemical is safe from the government to the company that produces the chemical. A similar shift in the "burden of proof" is likely to emerge as the Toxic Substances Control Act (TSCA) is amended in the United States.

5. Track Regulatory Compliance Up and Downstream

Companies are now held accountable not just for their own behavior but for the compliance of their suppliers and their customers. In particular, big brands will find that they are held responsible for the misdeeds of their suppliers. As we discussed in an earlier chapter, Mattel was forced to recall millions of Barbie dolls and Fisher-Price toys in 2007 because its supplier in China used unacceptable amounts of lead paint on these products. This recall cost the company hundreds of millions of dollars and resulted in a $2.3 million fine being levied by the Consumer Product Safety Commission.[8] The company is still paying for this failure to attend carefully to the legal compliance of its suppliers as it faces a series of class action lawsuits.

We discussed supply chain management in more detail in Chapter 12, but please recall that any company with an extensive supply chain, particularly one that extends overseas, should be tracking the legal compliance and regulatory filings of each one of its suppliers. Indeed, for companies who have invested in serious environmental management, the greatest legal exposure is likely to be upstream—related to suppliers. Supply chain audits are thus an essential way to ensure that suppliers have met the requirements of all relevant laws and regulations.

ADVANCED PLAYS: GET AHEAD OF THE CURVE

6. Use Regulations as a Sword

If your company exceeds existing legal standards with regard to various aspects of environmental law and regulation, then you might consider pushing for higher standards. Such a strategy aims to "level the playing field" so that your low-standard competitors do not have a cost advantage in the marketplace. While a few companies we've worked with recognize the opportunity to use law and regulations as an element of strategy, most companies are not familiar with using the law as a competitiveness tool.

In fact, most companies have a knee-jerk reaction to resist all new rules or regulations. But there are a growing number of examples of companies that have found Eco-Advantage by pushing for higher standards. Most famously, DuPont realized in 1990 that it should stop fighting regulations to phase out chlorofluorocarbons (CFCs) that were thinning the ozone layer. Once the company realized that it had substitutes for CFCs that would work in many applications, it pushed the U.S. government to agree to a phaseout of CFCs, leaving the company as one of just a few suppliers of the substitutes. In the marketplace that emerged, DuPont's share of CFC substitutes was bigger and its profits greater.

Climate change is another area where some businesses are demanding tougher regulation—perhaps because they expect to thrive in a carbon-constrained world. The U.S. Climate Action Partnership (USCAP), which includes GE, Dow, and DuPont, has called on the federal government to "quickly enact strong national legislation to require significant reductions of greenhouse gas emissions." Of course, GE, Dow, and DuPont all have climate change "solutions" that might realize rising demand in the face of new carbon constraints or a price on greenhouse gas emissions.

7. Work with Others to Raise Industry Standards ahead of Legislation

All companies have a critical strategic choice to make—does a particular environmental challenge represent an opportunity to step out in front of the pack by using the issue as a point of competitive differentiation? Or would it be better to work with others in the industry on a common approach to the problem (giving up any prospect of competitive advantage)? If a company is likely to suffer negative consequences because of the sub-par environmental performance of others in the industry, then a common, industry-wide approach is likely to be preferable. The leading companies in the chemical industry realized, in the wake of the Bhopal disaster, for example, that they could not separate themselves from weak performers in the eyes of the public. As a result, they led the charge on an industry-wide initiative called "responsible care" that sought to elevate standards for everyone and ensure that nobody was producing risks that might blow back on the industry as a whole. Likewise, when many companies use the same small set of suppliers, it often makes sense to work on an industry-wide basis to improve the performance of those upstream. As we discussed in Chapter 12, the major players in the U.S. home entertainment industry realized that the same six factories in China produced all the videos and DVDs sold across the United States. Thus, the industry worked on a common set of supplier standards, which was a much more cost-effective way to go for Disney, 20th Century Fox, Warner Brothers, and the other industry participants. The same principle—favoring an industry-wide approach—applies when a company is small (and less powerful) than its suppliers.

SUMMARY

Key Plays

1. Know the relevant laws and regulations.
2. Build an environmental compliance management system.
3. Reduce compliance burdens.
4. Use over-the-horizon issue spotting.
5. Track regulatory compliance up and downstream.
6. Use regulations as a sword.
7. Work with others to raise industry standards ahead of legislation.

ADDITIONAL RESOURCES

ENVIRONMENTAL LAW PRIMERS

Environmental Law in a Nut Shell, 8th edition, by Daniel A. Farber and Robert W. Findley (West Group, 2010). Primer for understanding environmental law, including statutory and common-law regulations.

Environmental Law & Policy, 3rd edition, by James Salzman and Barton Thompson (West, 2010). Comprehensive overview of environmental law, including climate change and energy legislation.

International Environmental Law in a Nutshell, 3rd edition, by Lakshman D. Guruswamy and Brent R. Hendricks (West Group, June 2007). Introduction to international environmental laws regarding climate change, ozone depletion, toxic and hazardous wastes, population, biodiversity, water, land pollution, and desertification.

COMPLIANCE RESOURCES

Regulatory Information by Business Sector (EPA). Features comprehensive information on federal and state regulations by sector. Includes regulations' text, history, statutory authority, supporting analyses, compliance information, and related guidance. www.epa.gov

Business.gov Environmental Regulations Site (Business.gov). Clearinghouse of federal government resources to help businesses understand their legal responsibilities. www.business.gov

Small Business Environmental Home Page. EPA-funded clearinghouse site for small businesses with resources on a wide range of environmental topics, including compliance and best practices. www.smallbiz-enviroweb.org

Enviro.BLR.com. Subscription website with access to federal and state environmental regulations, forms, tools, and training materials on compliance. www.enviro.blr.com

Chapter 17 Accounting and Finance

If you are a CFO or responsible for your company's financial situation, you may be skeptical of grand promises that "going green" will improve your bottom line. You should be. As we've argued elsewhere in the book, any claim that going green *always* pays off is nonsense. Turning *green* to *gold* requires the same analytic rigor and tough-minded approach that undergirds any other successful business initiative.

Getting bottom-line results from an environmental strategy does, however, sometimes require moving beyond the "business as usual" mindset and assumptions. Nowhere is that more true than when it comes to accounting and finance. Strict adherence to prevailing wisdom and traditional approaches can actually blind decision makers to environmental-related risks and opportunities. As a study by CFO Research Services and Jones Lang LaSalle concluded in 2008, "CFOs usually pride themselves on their ability to see the road ahead and help drive their companies to success; however, when it comes to sustainability, many CFOs seem to be using the rear-view mirror."[1]

The same study observed that building sustainability into the finance function remains a "work in progress," but also found that many finance departments "have advanced their work to a very high level."[2] At UPS, for instance, CFO Kurt Kuehn calls sustainability a "strategic imperative," noting that environmental issues increasingly connect with his top mandate: "using resources wisely and ensuring that an enterprise can thrive for decades to come."[3] Kuehn is not alone. According to Rice University management professor Marc Epstein, senior finance executives no longer question *whether* to undertake sustainability efforts, but rather they want to know *how* to.[4] Cutting-edge financial executives know that sustainability thinking and tools can help:

- **Reveal hidden risks.** One of the CFO's chief responsibilities is to assess and reduce long-term risks. As UPS's Kuehn highlights: "a sustainability lens presents a new way of looking at forecasts and risks."[5] Weyerhaeuser VP of Investor Relations Kathy McAuley agrees, warning that companies "that don't get it from the sustainability point of view could be subject to adverse market conditions [and] . . . penalties levied on them because of their practices."[6] A 2010 study by Verdantix, a London-based market research firm, argues that energy and carbon issues, in particular, have become a "new imperative for the CFO" given rising energy prices, the hidden costs of carbon, energy supply volatility, and board-level climate change compliance issues. The Verdantix analysts urge CFOs to create financial plans that ensure robust management of energy and carbon, and thereby avoid any unfortunate surprises in the future.[7]

- **Identify untapped cost-savings opportunities.** New reports come out every day from companies large and small whose environmental initiatives have produced impressive cost savings—especially from operational efficiency measures designed to root out excess energy use and other forms of waste (see the "Real-World ROI Success Stories" in Chapter 4 for examples). But many businesses are missing the "eco-efficiency" boat, sometimes because cost/benefit and ROI analyses fail to include all the factors they should. Other companies can't get past high up-front investment costs or payback periods that don't meet their traditional investment criteria. In fact, McKinsey estimated in 2007 that only 25 percent of companies would invest in efficiency measures with paybacks longer than two years. In practice, this means companies may be turning down some energy efficiency investments with an internal rate of return of up to 40 percent.[8]

- **Increase revenue and long-term value creation.** Jones Lang LaSalle CFO Lauralee Martin says: "my number one job when I get up in the morning is to help the CEO make shareholder value decisions." She credits the company's carbon reduction efforts for generating a whole range of new value-creating results, including the $100 million in savings the company helped clients achieve in 2009 from carbon-reduction efforts.[9] Herman Miller CFO Curt Pullen has likewise seen firsthand the financial rewards that come from his company's sustainability initiatives. He knows that seizing opportunities sometimes requires giving a green light to projects that don't meet typical financial "hurdles."[10] These forward-looking CFOs see smart environmental expenditures as *investments* (not merely costs) that contribute to long-term shareholder value.

- **Attract capital.** CFO Research Services notes that "study after study points to a correlation between companies focused on sustainability and higher investor yields over time."[11] This fact has not been lost on money managers, who each year are paying greater attention to corporate sustainability performance—and putting their money where their mouths are. One measure of this trend can be found in the growth of the Ceres Network on Climate Risk, which now includes investors representing over $13 trillion in assets.

- **Venture capitalists around the world are now betting in a big way on green technology (see Figure 17.1).** Major banking institutions like Bank of America are increasingly factoring the environment into lending decisions. New "green" banks, such as Pennsylvania-based e3Bank, have begun to crop up with a mission that centers on extending credit to triple-bottom-line projects. Herman

Figure 17.1   **Venture Capital Investment into North American Cleantech Companies ($USm)**

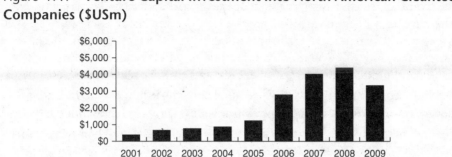

Source: Cleantech Group (www.cleantech.com). Reprinted with permission.

Miller's Curt Pullen sees sustainability becoming a key differentiator for certain investors: "I think it's clearly going to grow in prominence . . . and ultimately affect a company's ability to attract capital at a reasonable rate."[12]

- **Meet new reporting and disclosure expectations.** In what the April 2010 *Harvard Business Review* cover story calls our "Age of Transparency," companies are under more and more pressure from investors, regulators, customers, and watchdog groups to report on their environmental impacts and risks, as well as their efforts to reduce their eco-footprint. Indeed, the U.S. Securities and Exchange Commission (SEC) has introduced new environmental disclosure rules. All signs point to environmental issues spilling over more frequently into financial reporting.

- **Tap into green tax benefits and incentives.** Eco-Advantage-minded companies may be able to gain access to a variety of federal, state, and local economic incentives, including tax breaks, subsidized loans, and grants designed to support investments in energy efficiency and other clean energy projects (see Additional Resources at the end of the chapter for examples). As societies across the world step up their efforts to limit greenhouse gas emissions, these incentive programs will expand. Look for them!

- **Stay ahead of regulation.** Companies that wait until new regulations are imposed often find themselves at a disadvantage compared to those who stepped up to new environmental standards in advance of legal requirements. Global forest products firm Weyerhaeuser, for instance, has a long-term commitment to going "beyond compliance." Investing in more efficient equipment and cutting-edge facilities that exceed current legal mandates—such as its $1 million capital expenditure on pollution prevention technology at a plant in Uruguay—has helped the company stay ahead of the curve and prepare itself for future regulations.[13] Factoring in future regulatory costs has become standard procedure in many industries. American Electric Power (AEP), like many other power producers, knows that a price on carbon is coming, so its finance team routinely factors a "shadow price" for carbon into analyses.[14]

We designed this chapter to help people with accounting or finance responsibilities to bring an environmental lens to their work. Specifically, the plays laid out here will show you how to:

- Incorporate environmental-related factors into financial analysis, decision making, and reporting.
- Facilitate communications between financial and nonfinancial executives—especially promoting a dialogue among accountants and sustainability experts.
- Understand the financial implications of the emerging sustainability agenda.

BASIC PLAYS: LOOK AT FINANCIAL ANALYSES THROUGH A SUSTAINABILITY LENS

1. Understand Why Traditional Accounting Tools Miss Important Environmental Costs and Benefits

Traditional accounting and financial practices often overlook or understate environmental costs and benefits. As a result, companies may make business decisions on the basis of incomplete or distorted information. For example, many eco-related costs are buried in overhead. You can't manage what you don't measure. And you certainly can't measure what you can't see. Yet this is precisely what happens when environmental costs get lumped into broad accounting categories such as "general and administrative" (G&A) expenses. In many cases, companies assign their total energy and waste bills to overhead and then allocate a portion of these costs to individual units based on their headcount or revenue—not on how much energy they actually used or waste they created. This practice dulls the incentive for energy conservation and waste reduction. What's more, the true financial picture needed for smart decision making gets lost. It's hard work to track down who's responsible for what portion of environmental costs. So many companies simply don't bother. But this "shortcut" comes at a price in terms of lost opportunities to advance eco-efficiency. See Figure 17.2.

Traditional accounting practices also tend to obscure the real cost of materials. A comprehensive, accurate assessment of a company's environmental costs requires good data on the real costs of materials—which, in turn, relies on non-monetary data on the use, flows, and final destination of energy, water, materials, and wastes. As the International Federation of Accountants reports, such information is important because: "(1) the use of energy, water and materials, as well as the generation of waste and emissions, are directly related to many of the environmental impacts of organizational operations; and (2) materials purchase costs are a major cost driver in many organizations."[15] With conventional accounting, however, such data is inconsistent, incomplete, scattered, and imprecise.

Finally, traditional ROI and cost-benefit analyses often fail to account for hard-to-quantify costs and benefits that can be real and significant. For instance,

Figure 17.2 **Allocating Eco-Costs to Overhead Can Distort the True Financial Picture**

	'Clean' Process A	'Dirty' Process B
Revenues	$200	$200
Production costs	$100	$100
Environmental costs	$0	$50
True profit	$100	$50
If environmental costs are overhead	$75	$25
Then the book profit is	$75	$75
Which is incorrect by	−25%	−33%

Process A (Clean) does not cause any environment-driven costs for the company, whereas Process B (Dirty) causes $50 of extra eco-costs. When the bill for eco-costs is charged to general overhead and allocated equally, both processes appear to create a profit of $75. In reality, Process A had $100 profit while Process B only contributed $50 profit.

Source: Müller Schahegger, "Example of Correct and Incorrect Cost Allocation," cited in *UN Environmental Management and Accounting Procedures* (1997), p. 74. Reprinted with permission.

many companies have trouble tracking items such as: avoided compliance costs (including the savings, for instance, from eliminating a toxic chemical from a production process), the value of retaining an employee or keeping a customer who values environmental goals, or the benefit of improved stakeholder perceptions of a company's reputation (see Figure 4.2, "Eco-Related Costs and Benefits," in Chapter 4 for many other examples). If tracked and measured, such factors could lead to entirely different analytic outcomes—and thus strategy decisions. The best executives have an intuitive feel for these sorts of "intangibles," but the rest of us need systematic ways to bring the full spectrum of environmental issues and sustainability factors into our decision-making processes.

INTERMEDIATE PLAYS: EXPLORE NEW SUSTAINABILITY TOOLS

An ever-expanding toolkit exists to address the shortcomings in traditional finance systems. But translating eco-related costs and benefits into dollars and cents isn't easy. No simple, one-size-fits-all method can meet the diverse requirements of every executive reading this book. If your company is at an intermediate stage on the path to Eco-Advantage, you will have to invest time examining the available methods and tools so you can determine how best to meet the needs and cultures of your company.

WHY DO ECO-FACTORS GET LEFT OUT?

In trying to fold sustainability thinking into accounting, a number of challenges emerge:

- **Time horizons:** Eco-related costs and benefits can be enormous, but their effects often fall outside the narrow time horizons used in most accounting and investment frameworks. As a recent Boston Consulting Sustainability study observes, the time frame problem is "further exacerbated by the short-term performance expectations of investors and analysts."

- **Complexity:** Financial analysts find it difficult enough to identify and track all of the standard, tangible elements of their business. Given time pressure and methodological complexity, they often don't even attempt to capture intangible impacts or externalized costs and benefits.

- **Uncertainty:** Many environmental costs are contingent and will only arise if certain future conditions or scenarios play out. Some of the factors contributing to eco-uncertainty include changes in regulatory requirements, customer preferences, and changed natural resource prices. Likewise traditional strategic planning is deductive—and highly dependent on assumptions about the future. But when companies draw on past experience or standard gauges to predict where assumptions about the market are heading—and then design strategies on the basis of those forecast calculations—they may miss many sustainability drivers that don't follow historic patterns.

- **Boundaries:** Many sustainability-related costs and potential benefits fall not only outside the time frame of traditional accounting systems, but they may also go beyond the physical boundaries of standard analysis. So upstream impacts (affecting suppliers) and downstream ones (affecting customers) often get overlooked.

Source: Esty and Winston, *Green to Gold* (2009); Boston Consulting Group, *The Business of Sustainability* (2009).

2. Use Activity-Based Accounting to Reveal Eco-Costs Hidden in Overhead

Activity-based costing (ABC) helps company leaders better understand their cost structures and thus make better management decisions based on a more granular accounting and allocation of overhead. ABC provides a sleuthing technique that makes it easier to track particular elements of overhead or indirect costs to their source. ABC determines which activities are responsible for what share of costs, and then allocates costs appropriately to products, processes, systems, facilities, or units based on their level of responsibility or use. For instance, a company might put a microscope on its total energy bill (costs normally assigned to "General and Administrative" or overhead) to find out which activities are responsible for what share of the bill. With more refined energy use data in hand, executive teams can take appropriate actions to control costs. eBay has taken this kind of approach to manage its data center costs. In particular, the company has assigned data center facility energy bills to the CIO's budget—not overhead.

This accounting allocation incentivizes the entire IT organization to make the data centers as energy efficient as possible.[16]

ABC is no easy feat: It requires drawing on knowledge from many people to identify all relevant costs associated with a given activity. But strategically applied it can produce valuable information that empowers decision makers to make smarter decisions about budgets, product or process design, pricing, and investments. When used to lift the veil on hidden environment-related costs, ABC can help eliminate unintentional but costly "cross-subsidization of dirty or environmentally damaging products, processes, sites, and departments."[17]

3. Evaluate How Other "Environmental Accounting" Tools Could Help Your Business

Activity-based costing methods address a subset of often-neglected eco-related costs and benefits, but they fail to account for many other intangible, hard-to-quantify or contingent factors that can make or break business results. In response, practitioners have experimented with a range of "environmental accounting" methods to track and quantify eco-related costs and benefits more comprehensively. Environmental accounting is an umbrella term for a variety of relatively new and emerging methods of measuring, analyzing, and reporting environmental costs and benefits. In the corporate sphere, environmental accounting tools exist to complement traditional accounting approaches in two main areas:[18]

1. **Financial accounting** is the field of accounting focused on helping companies prepare financial reports for *external* audiences like investors, lenders, and regulatory agencies. Environmental accounting tools in this sphere are designed to help companies analyze and report on environment-related costs, liabilities, and risks. Pharmaceutical giant Baxter, for instance, pioneered the practice of publishing an annual "Environmental Financial Statement"—essentially a restated profit and loss (P&L) statement—that summarizes total annual environmental expenditures and the financial savings (including avoided costs) that accrue as a result.[19] With this analysis, Baxter has estimated that it has received an average return of approximately $3 for every $1 invested in its environmental initiatives over the past decade.[20]
   In a similar vein, the UK's Wessex Water has experimented with extending its balance sheets to take a fuller account of its eco-related assets and liabilities.[21] And many other companies have begun to practice some form of environmental accounting.

2. **Management accounting** is the field of accounting focused on identifying, collecting, and analyzing information to help companies with internal planning, decision making, and management. In this realm, "Environmental management accounting (EMA)" has emerged as a subfield with a burgeoning set of tools designed to help managers with strategic planning, budgeting,

purchasing, capital investment, product and process design, product pricing, and any number of other business decisions.[22] Environmental management accounting requires an interdisciplinary approach. On the one hand, you need the people who can identify the full range of potential costs and benefits that should be analyzed—scientists, engineers, product designers, purchasers, and others. On the other hand, to do the analysis properly requires creative and motivated accountants who can apply their expertise in allocating costs within both traditional and emerging accounting frameworks.[23]

REALITY CHECK

Environmental management accounting tools can shed new light on old assumptions. For years, an Ohio-based manufacturer of machine parts didn't worry much about excess metalworking fluids that ended up as oil mist on its equipment and factory floor. It assumed the problem was only costing about $8,000 a year in disposal fees. The picture changed entirely once a careful accounting revealed that the actual cost was:

$8,000	Disposal costs
+$25,570	Cost of actual metalworking fluid lost, plus filters and absorbent materials purchased to capture the mist
+$11,020	Labor costs to mop the floor, change the filters, and manage the absorbent materials
+$2,000	Time spent on regulatory compliance and filing of forms
$46,590	

Source: Adapted from Ohio EPA, Office of Pollution Prevention, "Waste: What Is It Really Costing You?" Number 72, August 1999. web.epa.state.oh.us/opp/planning/fact72.pdf (accessed August 21, 2010).

Behind all the diverse environmental accounting tools lies a simple idea: Leaders can make better decisions if they *account for real costs and benefits that usually get ignored.* Examples abound of how the analysis changes when cost managers fully factor in environmental information. Say, for instance, a line manager wants to replace a hazardous chemical in a manufacturing process with a nontoxic but more expensive alternative. Under traditional accounting, the CFO may reject the substitution as too expensive. But a comprehensive accounting of all the cost implications could produce a different outcome. Costs that companies should factor into this big-picture analysis include: the elimination of environmental permits and paperwork for the EH&S department, the no longer needed protective equipment for plant operations, and the hazmat training that won't be required.[24] For a comprehensive list of types of environmental costs and benefits that environmental accounting seeks to include, see Figure 4.2, "Eco-Related Costs and Benefits," in Chapter 4.

The thorny question at the heart of the matter involves *scope*. How deep or broad should you make the analysis? Where do you draw the lines on what gets included and what is left out? The broader the scope, the tougher the task (See Figure 17.3 below). It's easy, for instance, to account for the direct cost of a "cleantech" capital investment. It's tougher to estimate all the costs avoided from an environmental initiative, or the resulting bottom-line value of retaining a customer or employee. And it gets very tricky to put numbers on the costs or benefits to a local community from a firm's environmental negligence or good deeds.

Figure 17.3   **Which Costs and Benefits to Factor In?**

A key distinction is between *"internal"* (aka "private") costs directly borne by a firm versus *"external"* (aka "societal") costs paid for by society.

Internal					External
Conventional and Direct	Overhead/ Administrative/ Indirect	Contingent/ Future	Internal Intangible	Relationship/ Image	Societal/ Externalities
Easier to Measure				Harder to Measure	

Source: Adapted from "The Spectrum of Environmental Costs," U.S. EPA. "An Introduction to Environmental Accounting as a Business Management Tool: Key Concepts and Terms," www.epa.gov/opptintr/library/pubs/archive/acct-archive/pubs/busmgt.pdf, June 1995, p. 14.

The good news is that the dynamic field of environmental accounting boasts a diverse array of tools for different objectives. The bad news is that this field is filled with a dizzying array of terms and definitions that are sometimes contradictory, given the lack of standardization and relative newness of the field. For instance, some people use the following terms interchangeably—"full cost accounting," "total cost accounting," "true cost accounting," or "life cycle accounting." Others have tried to develop tight definitions around each separate concept. The variations occasionally stem from differences in professional background. For example, environmental experts use "full cost accounting" usually to refer to frameworks that accommodate "external" (societal) costs and benefits, while professional accountants use "full costing" to mean "the allocation of all direct and indirect costs to a product or product line for the purposes of inventory valuation, profitability analysis, and pricing decisions."[25] To complicate matters, a variety of "sustainability accounting" frameworks and tools are cropping up that add social costs and benefits into the mix. Some of the tools we think worth considering include:

- **Life cycle costing.** This tool assesses costs related to a product or asset over its entire life cycle, from production to use, maintenance, and disposal. The idea is to help managers better evaluate options during a product design or asset acquisition phase by looking beyond a product's purchase price, which usually reflects only a tiny portion of the costs a product/asset will ultimately cause. This tool ensures that costs such as installation, electricity or fuel, service and maintenance, compliance, replacement, and disposal get factored into the analysis. The U.S. military began using life cycle costing in the 1960s to better assess the total expense of tanks, tractors, and other long-lived equipment. Since then, many different industry sectors have also applied this methodology.[26]

- **Material flow cost accounting.** This system helps companies spot opportunities for cost savings relating to resource use, waste, and emissions. It tracks all physical inputs (including raw materials, energy, and water) and outputs (waste, scrap, and emissions) during production processes to determine their effect on costs (including materials, labor, systems, energy, and waste management.[27] The essential idea is that all physical inputs eventually become outputs, either as products or as waste and emissions—and inputs and outputs must balance.[28] Some companies calculate "energy balances" and "water balances" separately from other materials balances. This methodology is currently being standardized through ISO and is expected to be published as ISO 14051 in 2011.[29]

Environmental accounting tools can help companies of all shapes and sizes from just about any industry. They can be applied systematically and company-wide or on a pilot or ad hoc basis. If you are a financial professional, consider knocking on the door of sustainability counterparts in your organization to explore opportunities to collaborate on building your company's capacity in this area.

ADVANCED PLAYS: APPLY THE SUSTAINABILITY LENS

Once you've become familiar with the range of sustainability accounting tools, the next step is to conduct analyses to reflect pollution, waste, and natural resource use. The goal really is to make better management decisions over time.

4. Work with Your Sustainability Team to Put the Best Tools into Practice

Leading-edge companies routinely build environmental factors into cost accounting, financial, and operating decisions. They systematically consider the environment and social factors in their performance management and reward systems, purchasing, risk management, and reporting.[30] As Rice University's Marc Epstein puts it, "when the CFO's office is partnering with the environmental and social responsibility folks to make better decisions, when they're measuring the impact on brand value and reputation—that is, I think, the next step in best practice."[31] Best-practice companies do this by systematically applying the kinds of methods we reviewed in the previous section, but usually with custom-built and proprietary tools to meet their particular needs and circumstances.

PUTTING A PRICE TAG ON EXTERNAL COSTS AND BENEFITS

Putting a price on environmental harms can be hard to do—especially if there is no "market" to offer a guide. To provide a starting point, the British Standards Institution partnered with two UK sustainability-oriented consultancies, Forum for the Future and AccountAbility, to develop "Sustainability Integrated Guidelines for Management." The effort identified the following two methods for assigning value to external environmental costs:

1. **Demand-side methods** based on estimating stakeholders' "willingness to pay" to obtain environmental benefits (e.g., improvement in local air quality) or "willingness to accept" compensation to suffer an environmental loss (e.g., degradation in local air quality) including:

   - *Hedonic Pricing:* Uses information from a surrogate market to estimate the implicit value of an environmental good or service (e.g., differential housing prices used to estimate how much extra people are willing to pay for residential property in areas free from pollution).

   - *Travel Cost Method:* Uses surveys and surrogate markets to estimate willingness to pay for environmental goods and services based on the time and expense involved in traveling to them. Used mainly to derive values for recreational sites.

   - *Contingent Valuation Method:* Uses surveys, questionnaires, or experimental techniques to obtain environmental preference information directly from individuals. Based on hypothetical behavior inferred from surveys or experiments rather than on actual observed behavior (and therefore the most unreliable of the three demand-side methods because it is subject to inherent bias).

2. **Supply-side methods** based on the costs of supplying resources or services to prevent environmental damage, restore a place to its original state, or replace something lost, including:

   - *Preventive Expenditure (also known as Avoidance Cost) Method*: Based on actual expenditure incurred to prevent, eradicate, or reduce adverse environmental effects.

   - *Replacement (also known as Restoration) Cost Method:* Estimates costs once environmental damage has taken place (e.g., expenses needed to neutralize soil and water acidity from agricultural runoff).

   - *Productivity Approach:* Based on costs to productivity and production due to environmental damage (e.g., costs of soil erosion connected to lost agricultural yields).

Source: Adapted from Sigma Project. *The Sigma Guidelines—Toolkit: Sustainability Accounting Guide* (London: Sigma Project, September 2003), www.projectsigma.co.uk/Toolkit/SIGMASustainabilityAccounting.pdf.

Making the right choices about which tools to use—and applying them effectively—requires teams with diverse backgrounds and skills sets. That's because environmental accounting, as a pioneering EPA study on the topic pointed out years ago, is "not solely an accounting issue." Success in bringing an eco-lens to the finance world must center on new ways of looking at a company's environment-related risks as well as costs and benefits, which ultimately involves financial and nonfinancial executives learning to speak each others' language and finding common ground.

5. Triangulate to Overcome Uncertainties and Narrow Perspectives

Herman Miller CFO Curt Pullen, whose company has reaped substantial financial rewards from their "green finance" efforts says his team believes that they "get to the ultimate financial answer" when they draw on multiple reference points and factor in "all the nonfinancial things that also matter." American Electric Power's SVP of Corporate Planning and Budgeting, Rich Munczinski, shares the outlook that drawing on multiple perspectives for complex environmental analyses can make all the difference in getting the numbers right. Munczinski has built a finance group with high-level expertise on technical, operational, and financial matters that includes engineers, accountants, and finance people. For him, the key is "to get the best information into these models, and then get the best information out of the models and get it shared with the functional groups . . . to help them understand how their actions are affecting the company's bottom line."[32]

Remember the goal: to systematically factor environmental and social considerations into accounting systems and finance—without *excessive* emphasis on sustainability issues.

SUMMARY

Key Plays

1. Understand why traditional accounting tools miss important environmental costs and benefits.
2. Use activity-based accounting to reveal eco-costs hidden in overhead.
3. Evaluate how other "environmental accounting" tools could help your business.
4. Work with your sustainability team to put the best tools into practice.
5. Triangulate to overcome uncertainties and narrow perspectives.

ADDITIONAL RESOURCES

GENERAL

"The Role of Finance in Environmental Sustainability Efforts" (CFO Publishing, 2008). www.cfo.com

ENVIRONMENTAL ACCOUNTING OVERVIEWS

An Introduction to Environmental Accounting as a Business Management Tool: Key Concepts and Terms. (June 1995) Outstanding overview of environmental accounting principles and definitions for financial and nonfinancial executives alike. www.epa.gov

International Guidance Document: Environmental Management Accounting (EMA). International Federation of Accountants (IFAC) issued this 2005 guidance document for accountants and financial professionals to give "a general framework and set of definitions for EMA that is fairly comprehensive and as consistent as possible with other existing, widely used environmental accounting frameworks with which EMA must coexist." www.ifac.org. It reviews:

- Management accounting techniques designed to help identify and quantify the full range of internal and external environmental and social costs.
- In-depth review of material flow cost accounting.
- Cost categories that represent "international practice to the best extent possible" to help "provide a common language for future discussion."
- Real-world examples of EMA applications for internal management including EMA approaches for supply chain management, logistics management, investment appraisal, and tracking annual environment-related costs.

GENERAL COST ASSESSMENT AND VALUATION TOOLS

American Institute of Chemical Engineers' Total Cost Assessment (TCA) Methodology. Developed in 2000 with manual, spreadsheets, and software to identify and monetize many hard-to-quantify internal and external environmental and health-related costs and benefits. Designed to complement, not replace, existing capital project and product development cost-estimating practices. Sylvatica, a consulting firm, developed the TCAce supporting software. www.earthshift.com

Sieglinde Fuller, "Life Cycle Cost Analysis," Whole Building Design Guide. Overview of method for assessing the total cost of facility ownership. www.wbdg.org

LCCLight. A general tool developed by ABB Corporate Research that allows users to enter cost data for different life cycle phases and evaluate the total cost of different alternatives. www.dantes.info

Applying Total Cost of Ownership to Sustainability Purchasing—Workbook.
Sustainability Purchasing Network's guide to using Total Cost of Ownership
(TCO) to assess which everyday purchasing decisions are most cost-effective
and sustainable. www.buysmartbc.com

MONETIZING POTENTIAL LIABILITY COSTS AND RISKS

*Valuing Potential Environmental Liabilities for Managerial Decision-Making:
A Review of Available Techniques.* Describes publicly available tools for
estimating the monetary value of potential, preventable environmental
liability costs. www.epa.gov

Making Sustainability Work by Marc J. Epstein (Sheffield, UK: Greenleaf, 2008).
Method with accompanying worksheets to factor eco-related risks into ROI
calculations. See pp. 156–162 and 183–190. For an abridged version, see
"Measuring and Managing Social and Political Risk" by Tamara Bekefi and
Mark J. Epstein, *Strategic Finance*, February 2008.

UPDATING THE P&L STATEMENT AND BALANCE SHEET

The Sustainability Accounting Guide (Project Sigma) provides recommendations and tools for incorporating sustainability-related costs and benefits
into traditional financial statements. www.projectsigma.co.uk

The Sustainability Handbook by William R. Blackburn (London: EarthScan,
2007). Appendix 5 details the "Method for Calculating Savings and Cost
Avoidance for Baxter's Environmental Financial Statement," pp. 709–712.

MONETIZING EXTERNAL/SOCIETAL COSTS

Sustainability Accounting Guide (Project Sigma). See previous entry. Summarizes various approaches to valuation of external costs.

MONETIZING VALUE OF INNOVATION

"Innovation Killers: How Financial Tools Destroy Your Capacity to Do New
Things" by Clayton M. Christensen, Stephen P. Kaufman, and Willy Shih.
Harvard Business Review, January 2008.

MONETIZING VALUE TO BRAND

Interbrand has a brand valuation methodology that calculates the future earnings value attributable to a company's brand overall. It draws on analysts' projections, company financial documents, and its own qualitative and
quantitative analysis to arrive at a net present value of future earnings. Interbrand is developing a new methodology to analyze the link between a
company's corporate social responsibility (CSR) performance and its brand
value. www.interbrand.com

Harris Interactive Annual RQ (Reputation Quotient) captures perceptions from
stakeholders surveyed in six categories: products and services; financial performance; workplace environment; social responsibility; vision and leadership; and emotional appeal. www.harrisinteractive.com

The Boston College-Reputation Institute's CSR Index (CSRI) measures the public's perceptions of a company's citizenship, governance, and workplace practices from a representative sample of at least 100 local respondents familiar with the company. www.reputationinstitute.com

ROI AND COST/BENEFIT ANALYSIS MODELS

See Additional Resources in Chapter 4, "Making the Internal Business Case for Going Greener."

SUSTAINABLE INVESTING

Sustainable Investing: The Art of Long-Term Performance by Cary Krosinsky and Nick Robins (EarthScan, 2008).

See also **"Major Investment Indices and Reports"** *in Additional Resources at end of Chapter 7 ("Benchmark Your Performance").*

GREEN TAX BENEFITS AND INCENTIVES

"Are Your Green Initiatives Tax Efficient?" (Deloitte). www.deloitte.com

BNA Green Incentives Navigator Library. Subscription service providing guidance on federal and state tax (and nontax) incentives that encourage the development and use of renewable energy and conservation. www.bnatax.com/green

ENERGY EFFICIENCY AND RENEWABLE ENERGY INCENTIVES

Database of State Incentives for Renewables & Efficiency (DOE). Free, comprehensive source of information on U.S. state, local, utility, and federal incentives and policies. www.dsireusa.org

Environmental Grants, Loans, and Incentives (Business.gov). List of financial and technical assistance for developers of greener technologies. www.business.gov

FLEET EFFICIENCY AND ALTERNATIVE VEHICLES INCENTIVES

"Hybrid Vehicles Financial Incentives Guide" (Environmental Defense Fund). Environmental Defense Fund list of U.S. state and federal incentives for alternative vehicles and hybrid trucks. http://innovation.edf.org

EPA SmartWay Incentive Programs. www.epa.gov/smartway

Part Five **Mobilize: Execute and Engage**

Chapter 18 Create an Action Plan—and Execute

Getting your "green to gold" strategy to pay off depends fundamentally on execution. Plans only carry you so far. You must translate strategy into action that delivers on-the-ground results to reduce risks, lower costs, increase revenue, and build intangible value through stronger brands and corporate reputation. We have seen companies with well-thought-out sustainability plans falter because they failed to invest equal effort in their execution strategies. Even the best laid plans may crash and burn as a result of unanticipated market realities or changed circumstances. Companies that launched green initiatives as the world economy sagged in 2008 might well have found themselves falling short of anticipated results. You cannot anticipate every crisis; however, good execution can dramatically increase the odds that your environment or sustainability strategy will lead you to Eco-Advantage in the marketplace.

You must bring the same discipline and businesslike approach that you would use to execute any other initiative to the delivery of "green to gold" action plans. Before launching any sustainability initiative, executives must do their homework, sharply define the business case for action, understand clearly the parameters that will determine success, assess the capabilities and resources needed for a positive outcome, and spell out a well-conceived execution plan.

In this chapter, we offer suggestions designed to support your successful execution of sustainability strategies including recommendations on how to:

- Create an environment or sustainability action plan.
- Build the necessary management infrastructure.
- Undertake the appropriate communications and reporting.
- Engage all necessary stakeholders in the sustainability endeavor.
- Transform a business by positioning it to succeed in the face of the emerging sustainability megatrend.

BASIC: BUILD THE EXECUTION PLAN

1. Prioritize Sustainability Options

If you have read this far, then you already know that many elements go into a successful sustainability strategy. The options and opportunities as well as the risks and challenges are almost endless. It can be daunting to figure out where to begin.

KEY PRIORITIZATION CRITERIA

1. **Legal requirements:** Before turning to any other sustainability initiatives, you should ensure that your company is in full compliance with all applicable laws and regulations at the local, state, and federal levels.

2. **Market imperatives:** To be successful in the marketplace, companies must deliver value to their customers. What the buying public perceives to be "value" is in constant flux. Benchmark your company's products and services against your competitors' products and services to continually reassess the expectations and requirements of the market.

3. **Cost effectiveness:** Assess initiatives based on how much they will cost to carry out as well as their probability of success. You should also evaluate the potential for a sustainability initiative to expand revenues or increase margins. While some of these factors can be hard to pin down precisely, some quantitative analysis is helpful even if it simply involves a range of potential outcomes.

4. **Intangible value impacts:** As we have stressed throughout this *Playbook*, leading companies recognize that the payback for some of their sustainability efforts will come in hard-to-see forms such as enhanced brand value, improved corporate reputation, increased customer loyalty, easier recruitment and retention of employees, and higher productivity from a more engaged workforce. Although all of these value elements may be hard to assess quantitatively, smart members of management with a focus on Eco-Advantage know to factor these issues into their company's prioritization calculus.

5. **Evolving expectations and changed marketplace circumstances:** Markets are dynamic. The factors that lead to success today may not be the critical elements for continued success tomorrow. If you understand how key stakeholders prioritize issues and examine other factors that might change how competition takes place—potential technology developments, recent scientific understanding about risks and harms, shifts in the market prices of critical production materials, or the emergence of new competitors—then you hold the keys to a systematic prioritization analysis.

You must view any effort to bring sustainability or environmental thinking into your company's strategy not as a project to be accomplished but rather as a journey—requiring long-term commitment and continuous renewal. With this reality in mind, it makes sense to identify a top-tier set of priorities, followed by a second tier, and beyond that a third tier. In prior Chapters (notably Chapter 4, "Making the Internal Business Case for Going Greener" and Chapter 7, "Benchmark Your Performance against Competitors and Best Practices"), we provided frameworks to help you with the prioritization process. You will find many of those same tools useful as you move from strategy development to execution, particularly, when deciding what to focus on initially. Keep in mind the critical issues that your company faces (by using the AUDIO framework or other issue spotting tools as a guide), a sense of which issues create risk and which might create opportunities, a picture of the externally derived issues of concern (based on stakeholder mapping), some sense of how your marketplace might be evolving (based on trend tracking), and an appreciation for the cost-effectiveness of possible interventions. In the chart presented next, we provide a distilled set of evaluation criteria that you can use for the prioritization process.

With so many sustainability initiatives to choose from, which should your company undertake first? With any other business decision, it makes sense to focus on the net present value of each potential action item. As we noted earlier, traditional cost-benefit analysis may be inadequate in understanding which items are truly going to deliver the best returns. Sustainability-minded executives consider elements that are not usually factored into the traditional accounting processes, including the costs and benefits that are harder to see, emerge over time, or can only be captured in cooperation with suppliers or customers across the value chain.

2. Create Short-, Medium-, and Long-Term Action Plans

Because the push to integrate sustainability into strategy requires a long-term perspective, your company cannot do everything at once. We suggest creating a one-year action plan, a three-year action plan, and a five-year action plan. In the one-year plan, focus on the sustainability agenda items that your company can achieve most quickly and easily. For you to identify potential "quick wins," you need some sense of your company's core capabilities and the difficulty of carrying out particular sustainability initiatives. As Mary Armstrong, vice president of Environment, Health and Safety at Boeing, told us, getting foam cups out of the cafeteria might not register as the highest return-on-investment (ROI) item, but it is relatively easy to do and provides a clear signal of commitment to employees who are looking for evidence that their company is serious about its environmental efforts.

We agree that "putting points on the board" is important. Demonstrating that sustainability can be folded into business strategy without great burden or cost will often be critical to buy-in across the company. To show the practicality of his action agenda, Jeff Seabright, Vice President for Water and the Environment at the Coca-Cola Company, led the charge to improve the water efficiency of the company's production process. Building on a commitment to operational efficiency, Coca-Cola reduced its water use ratio from 2.61 liters per liter of product produced to 2.43 from 2005 to 2008. This success allowed the company to show real progress on an issue of critical concern to a large number of stakeholders, including the many communities within which it (and its partner bottlers) operates. Seabright knew that bolder initiatives, such as a commitment to make the company "water neutral" would take more time and had to be put on the three-year action plan.

Because some of the initiatives that might be launched have a high potential ROI, but also a significant degree of uncertainty, it makes sense to undertake pilot projects first as a way to gauge whether to commit more resources. Hannaford, a Maine-based grocery chain, tested out a variety of eco-efficiency ideas in a model "eco-store" before rolling out the successful elements chainwide. The pilot effort, resulting in a LEED platinum-rated "supermarket of the future" in Augusta, Maine, revealed payoffs from a number of sustainability-motivated ideas but simultaneously showed that others would be harder to execute in practice than had been foreseen.

With a three-year action plan, you can incorporate more elements that require building capacity or greater investment. It makes good sense, for example, to expand pilot projects that have proven their worth by taking these initiatives company-wide. You will also need to put redesigned manufacturing processes or the greening of buildings on your multi-year action agenda. Likewise, operational efficiency gains often require a degree of planning and investment that makes them unsuitable for the short-term action plan.

Give systematic attention to all of the various aspects of Eco-Advantage in your three-year action plan. Make a careful examination of the full spectrum of opportunities for risk reduction, cost control, enhanced revenues, and brand building outlined in Part III. The best way to do this is to have each job function (as outlined in Chapters 8–17) responsible for developing its own sustainability agenda. As suggested by the previous chapters, there are opportunities (and risks) that relate to every function of a company. On a three-year time horizon, there is no excuse for leaving any of these aspects of sustainability out of the picture.

A three-year action plan should also ensure that sustainability initiatives align with the broader corporate business strategy. If operational efficiency is a priority for your business as a whole, then put it at the center of your sustainability program. If your company wants to spur innovation and drive revenues, then assign high priorities to these activities when it comes to the sustainability agenda.

As your company develops its one-year and three-year action plans, it also makes sense to think about your longer-term sustainability program. Opportunities to transform an industry or a line of business will emerge over this longer time horizon. Fundamentally rethinking or redesigning a product often requires years of design work and planning (see Chapter 11 for more thoughts on how to bring a green focus to product design). Although it may take real work to deeply integrate a sustainability focus into every aspect of business and to use this commitment as leverage for transforming strategy, it is just such an audacious action agenda that may separate the winners from the losers as the pressures related to the environment and sustainability emerge with ever greater force over the coming years.

Already we can see signs of winners and losers as some companies have figured out how to ride the Green Wave that is sweeping across society while others are being taken under by it. Alan Mulally has brought transportation into the twenty-first century (first at Boeing and now at Ford) with his push for advanced materials and smart systems that dramatically improve fuel efficiency and performance. Having taken over the Ford Motor Company at a time when it was in steep decline, he has now reversed that trend and positioned his company as the strongest U.S. automaker, showing substantial profits by the end of 2010.

3. Establish a Clear Vision and Framework for Action

Exactly what frame a company wants to bring to its environment or sustainability efforts is a matter of corporate culture, industry, and other factors. In some settings, a focus on "sustainability" makes great sense. In other circumstances, the word "environment" may be more evocative. Coca-Cola, for a number of years, centered its efforts on "stewardship." A number of other companies have focused on "corporate social responsibility." The precise frame does not matter as long as there is a clear vision about the direction the company is going and everyone in the enterprise understands that direction. In a small business, this may not be difficult because there may be only a few employees. But in a big company, establishing a clear direction for the sustainability agenda requires real leadership.

In our research, we have found very few examples where a company has succeeded with a sustainability initiative that emerged entirely from the bottom up. In almost every case, sustainability becomes a serious part of corporate strategy as a result of leadership from the top down. In fact, in the companies that have the most success with a "green to gold" thrust, CEO leadership is almost always behind the effort. One of the first things a company should do is establish a clear vision (and perhaps mission statement)—articulated by the CEO and disseminated to all employees. At an early stage, the vision and mission need not be complicated. It might simply say that the company seeks to be an environmental leader and will apply a sustainability focus to how it does business.

Company leaders who have been thinking about sustainability for some time may be able to take the emphasis on vision to a higher level. As David

Lubin and Dan Esty argue in their 2010 *Harvard Business Review* article, "The Sustainability Imperative," mastering sustainability as an element of corporate strategy requires an iterative approach. Companies often begin with a focus on risk and cost reduction, shifting over time to strategies designed to increase value creation beginning with growth opportunities and moving on to intangibles such as brand building and corporate culture. We lay out below the Lubin-Esty four-stage model for sustainability value creation.

STAGES OF SUSTAINABILITY VALUE CREATION

Stage 1: **Do Old Things in New Ways.** In this initial phase, firms focus on out-performing competitors on regulatory compliance and environment-related cost and risk management. In doing so, they prove the value of eco-efficiency. At its inception 35 years ago, the 3M Pollution Prevention Pays (3P) program was just this kind of initiative. Through 2010, 3P projects have resulted in the elimination of more than 3 billion pounds of pollution and saved the company more than $1.4 billion. It also laid the foundation for 3M to establish public environmental goals, first initiated way back in 1990 and continuing today. The company's 2010 Environmental Targets have led to further reductions in energy usage, emissions, and waste.

Stage 2: **Do New Things in New Ways.** In this phase, firms redesign products, processes, and whole systems to optimize natural resource efficiencies and risk management across their value chains. DuPont's "zero waste" commitment, for instance, made vivid the company's prioritization of eco-efficiency across all oper-ations. Its decision to shed divisions with big eco-footprints, such as carpets and nylon, was based on an analysis that the emerging business and environmental risks in these lines of business would outweigh their potential contribution to future earnings.

Stage 3: **Transform the Core Business.** As the vision expands further, sustainability innovations become the source of new revenues and growth. Dow's sweeping 2015 Sustainability Goals, designed to drive innovation across its many lines of business, have generated new products and technology breakthroughs in areas from solar roof shingles to hybrid batteries. Dow's core business, which had tra-ditionally relied on commodity chemicals, has shifted toward advanced materials and high-tech energy opportunities.

Stage 4: **Create a New Business Model.** At the highest level, firms exploit the sus-tainability megatrend as a source of differentiation in their business model, brand, employee engagement, and other intangibles. They reposition the company and redefine its strategy to obtain an Eco-Advantage. GE's ecomagination initiative, which delivered more than $20 billion in revenues in 2010, enabled CEO Jeff Im-melt not just to reposition the company as an energy and environmental solutions provider but to build a green aura into the GE brand.

Source: David Lubin and Daniel Esty, "The Sustainability Imperative," *Harvard Business Review* (May 2010). Reprinted with permission.

INTERMEDIATE PLAYS: EXPAND EXECUTION CAPABILITIES

Bringing a focus on sustainability and the environment into business strategy depends on broad-gauge effort across an entire enterprise. Nevertheless, executing on this agenda requires a dedicated leader who works systematically over time to improve the company's capacity to address sustainability issues. In many large companies, we see a trend toward having a "Chief Sustainability Officer" (or CSO). Yet a recent survey revealed that only 12 percent of companies have a senior-level executive responsible for green initiatives.[1] In smaller companies, a dedicated official of this sort may not be possible. Having someone who has the CSO role (among other responsibilities) and clear accountability for their company's sustainability agenda makes sense in every scale of enterprise.

Better execution on sustainability initiatives also depends on the professionalization of the field of sustainability management. Business schools across the country are taking up this challenge and spelling out what is needed in the way of sustainability methods, models, and management systems. While not every school has a "business and the environment" program that dates back thirty years (as Yale does)[2], almost every business school now has some program or curriculum devoted to corporate environment or sustainability management. Management scholarship and research to support this professionalization is expanding rapidly. For example, the Alliance for Research on Corporate Sustainability (ARCS)[3]—a consortium of a dozen major business schools across North America—has rapidly expanded and is helping to provide rigor and structure to the emerging field of sustainability management.

ORGANIZING FOR SUSTAINABILITY SUCCESS

General Mills appointed a new Chief Sustainability Officer in 2010, Jerry Lynch, with a strong business credentials within the organization. A former General Manager who ran the Progresso business unit, Lynch told us his "personal mission over the next five years is to get the organization as fluent in sustainability as it is now in quality or productivity." The strategy is to have only a small full-time sustainability team and create structures that encourage all business leaders to consider sustainability part of their job. For instance, Lynch chairs a cross-functional team with leaders from every one of the company's business units to continually evaluate and refine business strategy in light of sustainability issues and trends. In parallel, the company set up a "Technical Community Team," chaired by the company's vice president for engineering, comprised of R&D and supply chain leaders who Lynch says "act as innovation agents within the organization to seize opportunities to apply the sustainability lens to product design and manufacturing." According to Lynch, the spirit cultivated by General Mills CEO is: "Let's keep pushing innovative sustainability ideas into the market and our business, no matter how small they are, and learn as we go."[4]

4. Build the Necessary Data-Gathering System

"What gets measured gets done" may be the oldest business maxim in the book, but it is still true. To execute effectively, companies need systems to capture key quantitative data tied to their material issues and stated goals—including metrics for daily implementation needs (such as real-time energy use statistics and the prices paid for energy in different markets) and measures for performance evaluation over time (such as annual reductions in total water consumption by facility). In Chapter 6 ("Assess and Measure Your Environmental Impacts"), we give examples of common metrics used to evaluate business environmental impacts, but these are only illustrative. Each company must decide exactly what information it needs to track to deliver on its own sustainability game plan—and build the systems to get it.

Don't waste time and money trying to track everything. Getting solid data on a handful of key metrics is more valuable than getting spotty information on a long list of potentially interesting items. Focus on what matters most. Start with compliance requirements and the material issues, impacts, and risks you identified during your initial assessments (Chapters 5 through 7). In addition, consider the following as you prioritize:

- **What data do you need to track progress on your company's eco-strategy goals?** Consider particular needs across the organization—R&D, product development, manufacturing, procurement, logistics, fulfillment, real estate, remediation, services delivery, and so on. Who needs what? How granular should this information be? With what frequency should data be collected and aggregated? Who determines what targets to set?

- **Which metrics do you need to assess the return on your company's eco-investments?** What data is needed to quantify business value from eco-related initiatives and expenditures? How should costs and benefits be calculated? What must be tracked to assess avoided costs? How does intangible value such as a stronger brand or enhanced reputation get factored into the analysis?

- **Which environmental issues and impacts should you track and on what basis?** Every company needs data on air and water emissions, energy consumption, and waste. But exactly what metrics needs to be reported? Absolute levels? Percentages? Does the data need to be normalized (perhaps to show impacts per unit sold)? Are other "intensity" measures important? What data disclosure is required by law? Are there voluntary reporting venues with which the company wants to engage such as the Carbon Disclosure Project or *Newsweek*'s Green Ratings? What data do these entities require?

- **What additional data do you need for external communications objectives?** What do key stakeholders expect in the way of reporting? Are there industry norms that should be met? Does the data need to be broken out in certain ways to respond to specific constituencies? For example, facility by facility information may be needed to meet the demands of the communities where a factory is located. Chapter 22 "Communicate and Report Results" offers more detailed guidance on this challenge.

5. Construct an Environmental Management System

Good data provides the essential starting point for execution, but companies also need to develop an environmental (or sustainability) management system (EMS) to clarify priorities, establish clear lines of accountability, track progress, and provide a mechanism for feedback. Everyone needs to know who's responsible for what. As Lynn Jean, owner of Best Impressions Environmental Management Systems, says, "What you monitor and what you measure is what you control and what you improve."[5] Companies at the cutting edge use a variety of tools to collect and manage their enterprise-wide environment, health, and sustainability data, from simple spreadsheets to complex relational databases. Software providers are competing fiercely and constantly innovating to develop improved solutions to meet rising EMS demands.

Some companies have found that they want a more granular or tailored approach to environmental management and have designed their own systems. While Vice President for Environment, Health, and Safety at GE, Steve Ramsey helped create the company's "PowerSuite," an EMS program that provides everything from a regulatory calendar that updates executives on when reports are due and permit renewals must be filed, to detailed information on energy consumption, emissions, safety violations, and compliance. GE's PowerSuite provides a real-time "digital cockpit" that allows managers to analyze data at every scale—from company-wide to a particular production line within a facility.

IBM continually refines a Lotus Notes-based environmental database it created in the late 1980s to cope with the ever-expanding data needs across its global operations as a strategic element of its EMS. According to the company's top environmental executive, Wayne Balta, the system works in part because the company is filled with tens of thousands of "type A personalities and the culture drives measurement, performance, inspection, and data." Valerie Patrick, the executive responsible for sustainability strategy at Bayer North America, told us that her company built its own EMS structure for cultural reasons: "We have a historically very strong culture of environmental responsibility going back to the start of the company. . . . For us, ownership of this data in all of its forms is very important to us emotionally from a cultural standpoint."

For companies that need help in designing an environmental performance tracking system without great expense, ISO 14000 offers a very useful place to start. This structure for "Environmental Management Systems," designed by the International Organization for Standardization (ISO), lays out a basic EMS template that can be modified to meet individual company needs. For some companies, ISO 14000 provides more than a model EMS structure. They follow the ISO framework because their customers demand "certification" that their EMS is ISO 14000 compliant.

Creating the EMS needed to guide your company's implementation of sustainability initiatives cannot be treated as a "one-time" activity. Metrics need to be constantly reevaluated and refined. Similarly, targets and goals need to be regularly updated and realigned with changing norms and expectations.

6. Establish Accountability with Appropriate Incentives

No matter what management system is chosen, a company should design it to hold managers accountable for environmental and sustainability performance. In large and sophisticated companies, the CEO (and perhaps the CSO) will need information about company-wide results and more disaggregated sustainability performance. In small businesses, the entire management team will need to focus on the big picture. Good EMS systems provide quantitative targets that are explicitly connected to various sustainability strategy elements thereby creating sharp incentives for managers to deliver on their assigned action items. Any accountability system should make it easy for senior management to evaluate their managers in an objective fashion—rewarding those who hit their goals with stronger annual performance reviews, higher bonuses, and promotions.

The evidence is now clear: companies that write sustainability objectives into the executive evaluation systems get better results in terms of execution. At Alcoa, for example, the top 200 managers in the company all have environment-related KPIs, reflecting CEO Klaus Kleinfeld's commitment to make the company a sustainability leader.[6] And as AkzoNobel's CEO Hans Wijers told us, sustainability factors now make up a full 20 percent of the rating for all senior managers at his company.[7]

The best accountability systems also work more generally as mechanisms for highlighting successes as well as shortfalls. Companies that are serious about their sustainability strategies know that every employee needs to feel some responsibility for the agenda—and pride in their company's accomplishments. So company leaders regularly review progress toward their established targets in staff meetings and post results on company websites. To sharpen the incentives for line employees, who don't have specific environmental elements in their performance evaluations, to take action when they see an opportunity (or risk), many companies give out annual environmental awards honoring notable contributions to the company's sustainability program.

7. Invest in Sustainability Training

Employee training represents a critical pathway to better sustainability results. People can't do what they don't know how to do. With this in mind, most of the large companies that we have worked with have now structured environment or sustainability modules as part of their internal human resource development programs. Specific training, of course, is required for some roles. People who are handling toxic materials, for example, must be made aware of the tracking rules and other legal requirements they must follow. The best of these training programs do more than simply alert employees to the relevant rules and regulations. They also create an understanding of the opportunities available for Eco-Advantage. If everyone is looking for ways to reduce costs, manage risks, drive revenues, and build a reputation for environmental concern, it is much easier for a company to achieve its sustainability goals.

We provide a deeper discussion on how to use sustainability as an element of employee engagement in Chapter 20 ("Mobilize Employees and Build an Eco-Advantage Culture"). So we will not go into a great deal of detail here on the various ways that you can bring employees into corporate sustainability efforts. Success in delivering on a "green to gold" agenda requires that everyone step up his or her game—from the mailroom to the c-suite.

8. Refine Communications and Reporting

We live in an era of transparency, so reporting on environmental and sustainability results has become an expectation for companies of almost any scale. As we spell out in Chapter 19 ("Build Your Climate Change Plan"), some reporting, such as disclosure of greenhouse gas emissions, is no longer voluntary but rather required by EPA regulations (at least for larger companies). More generally, we review best practices in sustainability reporting and communications in Chapter 22 ("Communicate and Report Results"). From an execution perspective, reporting on environment and sustainability performance reinforces a company's commitment to action.

In motivating successful sustainability initiative implementation, the reporting that matters most is that aimed at employees rather than external audiences. As we noted in the accountability discussion earlier, clear targets and regular results reporting can help keep managers responsible for delivering on initiatives focused. Broader sustainability reporting, aimed at all employees, is important to creating an Eco-Advantage corporate culture that prizes sustainability and inspires action. Celebrating success (and acknowledging ongoing challenges) helps everyone feel a part of the company's environment and sustainability commitment. Transparency about targets, what has been accomplished, who has contributed, and what remains to be done all serve to make this commitment more authentic and likely to inspire employee action.

The successful execution of a corporate environmental or sustainability strategy also requires that companies communicate about shortcomings and failures. In particular, it is important to openly discuss problems that have occurred, such as accidents or spills, or any other activities that compromise environmental, health, or safety standards. It is good practice, after a serious environmental incident, to undertake a "root cause" analysis and to publish the results so that the lessons learned from the problem get disseminated across the company.

ADVANCED PLAYS: SUSTAINABILITY TRANSFORMATION

9. Expand Work across the Value Chain

Sustainability is a fluid and dynamic concept. Expectations constantly change—and the goalposts shift regularly. As a result, many companies find it useful to develop their environmental strategies in conjunction with critical stakeholders. Opening up the strategy development process changes the focus from entirely internal execution to one of "co-creation" with partners including suppliers, customers, government officials, and sometimes even NGO critics.

As one of the leaders in sustainability execution, the Coca-Cola Company regularly refines its environmental targets and other sustainability goals, in part, based on feedback from critical stakeholders including its bottling partners, suppliers, and the general public. In addition to a public advisory committee that meets twice a year with top executives to discuss the company's performance and to "peer review" the company's strategies and scientific analyses, the company has undertaken a series of "NGO Roundtables" in which top executives engage in an open conversation with thought leaders from environmental groups, nutrition advocacy organizations, and academic institutions. While the criticisms can sometimes be hard-hitting, it is much better to hear bad news privately before it goes public. These open dialogues have helped the company refine its water use commitments and its response to criticisms related to the obesity concerns arising from the caloric content of its drinks. We expect others to follow Coca-Cola's lead and use a "co-creation" process to refine their sustainability strategies and execution plans.

10. Innovate and Transform Markets

Those companies with a clear sustainability vision, a well-developed strategy for advancing their established goals, and an execution action plan that delivers steady progress will be best positioned to take advantage of the Green Wave that is sweeping across society. As Lubin and Esty argue in the *Harvard Business Review* article mentioned earlier, sustainability is an "emerging megatrend." As with prior business megatrends, such as the emergence of information technology as a core competitive factor, and the emphasis on quality as a critical business focus, the result will be fundamental shifts in how companies compete and who "wins" in the marketplace.

Companies that take their execution efforts to the highest level and focus on innovation as a way to transform their core lines of business will be best positioned to introduce the new products or technology breakthroughs that deliver new lines of revenue and profits. The very best of these companies may even develop entirely new business models and "Blue Ocean" strategies that allow them to differentiate their goods and services in consumers' minds in ways that eliminate all real competition. As Chan Kim and Renee Mauborgne explain in their best-selling book of the same title, it is this sort of "value innovation" that delivers the biggest competitive advantages.

SUMMARY

Key Plays

1. Prioritize sustainability options.
2. Create short-, middle-, and long-term action plans.
3. Establish a clear vision and framework for action.
4. Build the necessary data gathering system.
5. Construct an environmental management system.
6. Establish accountability with appropriate incentives.
7. Invest in sustainability training.
8. Refine communications and reporting.
9. Expand work across the value chain.
10. Innovate and transform markets.

ADDITIONAL RESOURCES

"ISO 14000 Essentials." Web pages with background on the two major international standards covering environmental management systems (EMS): *ISO 14001*, which outlines requirements for an EMS, and *ISO 14004*, which gives guidelines for setting up an EMS. www.iso.org/iso/iso_14000_essentials

Making Sustainability Work: Best Practices in Managing and Measuring Corporate Social, Environmental, and Economic Impacts by Marc J. Epstein (Greenleaf, 2008).

Practical Guide to Environmental Management, 10th edition, by Frank Friedman (Environmental Law Institute, 2006).

The Business Guide to Sustainability: Practical Strategies and Tools for Organizations by Darcy E. Hitchcock and Marsha L. Willard (EarthScan, 2008).

"The Secrets to Successful Strategy Execution," by Gary L. Neilson, Karla L. Martin, and Elizabeth Powers (*Harvard Business Review*, 2008).

The Sustainability Handbook: The Complete Management Guide to Achieving Social, Economic, and Environmental Responsibility by William R. Blackburn (Environmental Law Institute, 2007).

Chapter 19 Build Your Climate Change Plan

In 2007, the airline industry became a target for climate change activists. As a leader in business aviation, NetJets Europe found itself with a bull's-eye on its back because of the sector's extensive and rapidly growing greenhouse gas emissions. Environmentalists demanded action. Some protestors even chained themselves to a private plane at a London airport. And as European regulators geared up their emissions trading system, aviation looked likely to bear a much heavier burden from the new carbon controls than other industries. Then-CEO Mark Booth concluded that he needed a carbon offset program to allow his customers to contribute to the climate change solution and not just be part of the problem.[1] He soon realized, however, that a voluntary offset program would not be sufficient. In fact, a number of airlines had introduced similar carbon offset programs but had "uptake" rates of only about 1 percent of their passengers.

So Booth decided to go on offense. He committed NetJets Europe to a broad-gauge climate change action plan that started with an acceptance of the company's responsibility for the issue—and a promise to reduce NetJet Europe's own emissions by 10 percent while growing the business substantially. In addition, he purchased carbon offsets for all of the emissions generated by the company's operations and made customer offsets mandatory in all new flight contracts. His investment in a carbon-free "jet fuel of the future" development project signaled an interest in a long-term solution to the emissions problem. Saying that he wanted to hold his company's "feet to the fire," Booth also launched outreach efforts to the environmental community and formed an environmental advisory board of outside experts to review the NetJets Europe climate change agenda.[2] And he committed the company to regular progress updates on a very engaging website as well as to issuing an annual sustainability report.

Not every company needs to do as much as NetJets Europe. But every company needs to keep an eye on climate change as an issue and track its potential to lead to game-changing impacts that fundamentally restructure the competitive landscape.[3] Given the scope and scale of greenhouse gas emissions built up in the atmosphere, implicating every business as well as every person in the world, climate change represents a megachallenge from the corporate strategy point of view. As energy prices rise due to carbon regulations or indirect constraints on emissions, market conditions will evolve. Carbon-intensive companies and industries will see demand slacken. Competitive advantage will shift toward companies that have reduced their carbon exposure.

At a macroscale, there will be winners and losers. Some products and even whole industries will suffer. The demise of GM's Hummer looks like an early casualty of this megatrend. But other companies will profit as they ride this element of the Green Wave. For example, Tesla Motors, with its sporty electric car, saw the price of its stock rise 60 percent on the day of its 2010 initial public offering, reflecting investor enthusiasm for a new generation of vehicles that don't pollute.

Despite the economic downtown in some sectors, Ernst & Young estimated a 64 percent increase in venture capital investment in clean technology companies in 2010.[4] While government regulations may drive much of this change in the business landscape, other factors are also in play. Given diminishing supplies of relatively accessible oil and steadily rising energy consumption, especially in emerging economies such as China and India, energy demand is likely to outstrip supply for some time to come, driving prices up. Shifting rainfall patterns and rising temperatures will disrupt farming, forestry, fishing, and other industries dependent on weather conditions. Rising sea levels and the increased intensity of windstorms threaten both existing real estate and future coastal property development.

Simply put, climate change represents a strategic imperative to which companies must respond. Your company stands to benefit if it has already reduced its exposure to the changes that are likely to unfold. Companies positioned to help their customers and society meet the challenge of climate change will thrive. Others will fall by the wayside as the requirements for success in firm strategy, structure, and competitive positioning shift. In this chapter we will help you:

- Assess your company's carbon footprint.
- Set targets for reducing emissions.
- Identify and implement emissions reductions strategies.
- Incorporate carbon offsets into your climate action plan.

BASIC AND INTERMEDIATE PLAYS: REDUCE GREENHOUSE GAS EMISSIONS FROM COMPANY OPERATIONS

1. Assess Your Company's Carbon Footprint

Every company needs to understand its "carbon exposure" and identify the sources of its carbon footprint (using the tools laid out in Chapters 5 and 6). Indeed, companies now face demands from a range of stakeholders looking for information on greenhouse gas emissions—and expecting progress to reduce these emissions over time. As we mentioned earlier, a London-based NGO called the Carbon Disclosure Project (CDP) has invited more than 3,000 companies across the globe to report on emissions voluntarily as a way to help sharpen focus on climate change as an important issue of corporate strategy. More than 1,500 companies now produce greenhouse gas inventories following the CDP methodology, which builds on work done by the World Resources Institute and the World Business Council for Sustainable Development.

CLIMATE CHANGE SCIENCE AND POLICY

In late 2009, the science behind climate change came under scrutiny—and even attack. A handful of scientists involved in the UN-backed process of establishing the analytic framework for climate change policymaking (the Intergovernmental Panel on Climate Change or IPCC) had been inattentive to the elements of the scientific method. These scientists, representing just a few of the thousands involved in the IPCC process, failed to put forward the data on which they based their analysis, inviting intense scrutiny of their work. Publishing all underlying data so that others can replicate (or not) results is a fundamental tenet of the scientific method. In addition, the most recent IPCC Scientific Assessment included reference to some studies that were not fully peer reviewed. These shortcomings in scientific practices were real. But these problems were not significant enough to change the consensus that the buildup of greenhouse gas emissions in the atmosphere poses a real risk to our planet.

In addition, a number of political leaders and some scientists have not been careful about how they describe the state of climate science. To suggest, for example, that the science of climate change is "settled" isn't quite right. Science is never *settled*. The essence of the scientific process is ongoing review, rethinking, and refinement. There are, moreover, significant uncertainties about the pace, scale, and distribution of potential climate change impacts. It would be more appropriate for thought leaders to say that the science of climate change is "settled enough" for us to know that there is a potentially serious problem that justifies policy action.

Dispute continues over the best policy response to climate change. Europe has adopted a "cap and trade" program—the EU Emissions Trading System (ETS)—where companies must either reduce their emissions to meet their targets or buy additional offsets in the emerging carbon market. Questions about the validity of some of these offsets and other hiccups have arisen as the new ETS unfolded. But the kinks have now been worked out, and the carbon market has begun to induce energy efficiency and investment in carbon-free alternative energy.

In the United States, substantial doubt exists over whether a cap and trade approach offers the right policy path to a clean energy future. Most observers agree that the centerpiece of any climate change policy should be a "price signal" that creates incentives for innovation. The most straightforward approach would be to put a price on greenhouse gas emissions. Such a "harm charge" would ensure that everyone consuming fossil fuel energy would have an incentive to look for ways to conserve—and create a demand for energy efficiency and alternative energy sources free of greenhouse gas emissions.

Note that most big companies are now required by government regulations to disclose their greenhouse gas emissions. Reporting is also mandatory in Europe. The U.S. Environmental Protection Agency has launched reporting rules for the 10,000 largest emitters across the United States, representing about 88 percent of the nation's greenhouse gas emissions.[5] The facilities that must comply include coal mines, waste water treatment systems, industrial landfills, and many factories. In addition, the Securities and Exchange Commission (SEC) is also ramping up environmental reporting requirements, including specific greenhouse gas disclosures,[6] and the White House Council on Environmental Quality recently issued requirements for emissions monitoring of all operations associated with the Federal government.[7]

Many tools are now available to help companies of all sizes measure and understand their contribution to greenhouse gas emissions—or what has come to be known as their "carbon footprint." The Greenhouse Gas Protocol developed by the World Resources Institute and the World Business Council for Sustainable Development provides the best practice in terms of methodology—and is fast becoming the only accepted standard.[8] This methodology breaks reporting into three "scopes," separating emissions from: (1) a company's own operations including fossil fuel combustion in industrial activities and fuel use, (2) purchased electricity, and (3) indirect activities such as business travel, commuting by employees, and supplier or contractor activities. Over sixty major corporations recently completed a "road test" of these standards and found them practical and effective.[9] Chapter 6 "Assess and Measure Your Environmental Impacts" discusses in detail what you need to know to compile a greenhouse gas inventory and provides recommended tools and resources.

2. Set Reduction Targets

Once a company identifies where its emissions come from, the next step is to set a target for reducing those emissions. Appropriate goals will vary widely depending on a company's industry, capacity, and market position. For example, USG, a Chicago-based building materials supplier, has committed to reduce its greenhouse gas emissions by 20 percent by 2020 using 2005 as its base year.[10] MillerCoors, the brewing giant, set a target of reducing total energy use by 15 percent by 2015 from its 2009 baseline[11] Panasonic sought to reduce its EU emissions for 2009 by 10 percent. The Japanese electronics leader dramatically exceeded this goal, achieving a reduction of 34 percent in its European manufacturing operations.[12] Intel exceeded its initial target by reducing emissions 45 percent below 2007 levels in 2009.[13]

In setting a target, it is important to stretch but also to be realistic. Set your short-term and publicly announced targets with an eye toward success. Missing a target does not need to produce a crisis but does require some explanation. It is critical to be forthright about the shortfall and explain what went wrong. Longer-term and more ambitious targets can inspire more transformational thinking—but may be best kept within the company.

3. Draft a Climate Action Plan

A climate action plan should address both impacts and opportunities. It should spell out how a company intends to reduce its own greenhouse gas emissions—and how it might help its customers address theirs. Good action plans build on a solid company-wide greenhouse gas inventory. They define the scope of the problem at hand, set reduction targets, and spell out strategies for reaching those targets across business departments and functions. If a company can operate as a solutions provider, then its action plan should indicate how it can develop this opportunity. To execute the strategy, break out individual initiatives and implementation plans.

Creating a climate action plan usually requires a team effort. Involve employees from every department and operation in the essential data gathering, strategy development, and implementation. Employees who work directly in emissions-intensive departments or functions often have the best idea about what could reduce energy consumption and otherwise improve efficiency in their particular operations. Early involvement of the company's senior leaders increases the odds that the emerging climate action plan will align with the company business objectives and get the management and financial support necessary for successful implementation.

While some companies have all the expertise needed to pull together a strong climate change action plan in house, others find it useful to get help from climate change experts including consultants and environmental groups that offer advice. An outsider's perspective can often strengthen a climate action plan by ensuring that a company considers "best practices" and addresses sometimes-overlooked issues.

4. Identify and Implement Emissions Reduction Strategies

Throughout this book, we have offered recommendations, tools, and resources for reducing greenhouse gas emissions in various business functions. Specific strategies for critical business activities can be found in the following chapters:

- Office activities (Chapter 8)
- Buildings and facilities (Chapter 9)
- Information technology (Chapter 10)
- Product design (Chapter 11)
- Manufacturing and process (Chapter 13)
- Logistics and transport (Chapter 14)

In most cases, improved eco-efficiency lies at the heart of a climate change strategy. Many companies find that investments in operational efficiencies and energy savings are relatively easy to find and implement—and result in quick paybacks. Bigger picture initiatives like restructuring supply chains or redesigning production processes are more complicated to implement and generally deliver slower paybacks. When looking for opportunities, focus on your company's facilities or operations that produce the most emissions. Looking for relatively easy interventions that produce "quick wins" is also quite valuable. Performing a life-cycle analysis, which is discussed in detail in Chapter 6, often reveals such opportunities and is a good first step towards greater efficiency.

As we have stressed in all efforts to bring a sustainability focus to strategy, the key to success is analytic rigor. Deciding which emissions reduction investments to take on requires systematic review and careful consideration. A variety of factors should come into play:

- Potential GHG emissions reduction (defined in tons, often as a range).
- Cost to implement the initiative (including capital costs, installation, operating and maintenance, and any other staffing requirements).
- Robustness of the assumptions on which the analysis is based.
- Cost effectiveness (measured in tons of CO_2e eliminated per dollar invested).
- Expected net return on the investment (ROI) reflecting all costs and benefits.
- Payback schedule (estimating how many years it will take to recoup the investment).
- Time to implement.
- Skills needed to deliver a good outcome (and an assessment of the existing internal capacity to deliver).
- Leadership (notably, is there a committed internal "champion" to lead the effort?).
- Anticipated internal obstacles to success (and plans to overcome them).
- Momentum from existing complementary initiatives.
- Degree of cooperation required from company departments or offices.
- Opportunities to have external support or collaboration.
- Visibility and contribution to brand worth.
- Collateral benefits to the company, the environment, and the community.
- Potential external barriers to success.[14]

Every company has a different way of prioritizing initiatives based on these factors. Most companies find it pays to prioritize strategies that offer fast paybacks in terms of both cost and emissions reductions. As noted earlier, we'd argue as well for doing some relatively easy things up front as a way to build momentum if their impact is not huge. For more difficult areas, it is probably best to launch pilot projects and replicate those which work out well. For example,

Jones Apparel Group, the clothing retailer, tested a lighting retrofit that promised substantial reductions in electricity (and lower greenhouse gas emissions) in one store before rolling the game plan out company-wide.

ADVANCED PLAYS: LOOK BEYOND YOUR OWN OPERATIONS

5. Seek Reductions across the Supply Chain

Many companies understand that while their own carbon footprints may be relatively small, they cannot say the same for their suppliers. And those are the impacts for which they will increasingly be held accountable. For instance, Stonyfield Farm, the organic yogurt maker, found that cows produced the largest portion—43 percent—of its value-chain-wide carbon footprint.[15] As a result, the company began to invest in more carbon-efficient milk production. It recently launched an initiative to get the farmers they buy milk from to adjust the feed they give their cows to reduce the amount they burp and fart. Seems crazy? In fact, this intervention reduced the cow's methane emissions (a greenhouse gas 23 times more potent than carbon dioxide) by an impressive 12 percent.[16]

In Chapter 6, we discussed how to do a life cycle analysis, which can help you determine whether a focus on greenhouse gas emissions coming from the supply chain makes sense. As a starting point, companies that depend on agriculture or resource extraction for critical inputs to their products are most likely to find big opportunities upstream.

To get a supplier not directly under a company's control to change his or her production practices to reduce emissions often takes some finesse. Work with—not against—your key suppliers. It may be sensible to start with a limited focus. Ford Motor Company, for example, announced in 2010 that it will initially work with its top 35 global suppliers on their energy use and estimated greenhouse gas emissions.[17] We offer more detail on how companies can manage the risks and opportunities of their supply chain in Chapter 12 ("Sourcing and Procurement").

In some cases, the real opportunities lie not upstream but downstream with the user of the product. Companies selling consumer products that entail substantial energy use on the part of the buyers of these items are prime candidates for carbon strategies that concentrate on downstream impacts. In this regard, Chapter 11 ("Product Design") discusses how companies can shape the behavior and environmental impact of their customers through practices such as design for recycling and product stewardship.

6. Buy Carbon Offsets

Some companies are unable to identify cost-effective options to reduce emissions within their business. Others have promised to be "carbon neutral" as a way to differentiate themselves in the marketplace. In either case, companies can supplement internal emissions reduction strategies with "carbon offsets" to neutralize emissions that they cannot prevent. Of course, carbon offsets—which entail paying for others to reduce emissions—are seen by some as too easy a way out. Some critics have suggested that carbon offsets are like the old Catholic Church tradition of selling "indulgences" to absolve sins. We see offsets as a useful element of a broader climate change strategy but no substitute for a company reducing its own emissions.

When a company buys a carbon offset, it invests money in reducing someone else's emissions—and then gets credit for those reductions. For example, when a company buys a carbon offset in Chicago, the money may go toward installing a wind turbine outside Beijing, which reduces the demand in China for coal-based power. The company that bought the offset gets credited with this reduction, although its own emissions have not gone down.

Conversely, a company that generates renewable energy may be able to show that its power production reduced greenhouse gas emissions by displacing electricity that would have come from a fossil energy facility. Any such reduction has the potential to be sold as a carbon offset to someone else.

CARBON OFFSET PROVIDERS

- The Climate Action Reserve (www.climateactionreserve.org)
- Carbonfund.org (www.carbonfund.org)
- Myclimate (www.myclimate.org)
- The Carbon Neutral Company (www.carbonneutral.com)
- Renewable Choice Energy (www.renewablechoice.com)
- EcoSecurities (www.ecosecurities.com)
- e-BlueHorizons (www.e-bluehorizons.net)
- 3Degrees Group, Inc. (www.3degreesinc.com)
- TerraPass (www.terrapass.com)
- BeGreenNow (www.begreennow.com)
- Sustainable Travel International (http://carbonoffsets.org)
- Conservation Fund (www.convervationfund.org/gozero)

Because carbon offsets are an easy way to get credit for emissions reductions, some companies rely heavily on them in their climate strategies. Buying offsets or related renewable energy credits (RECs) represents a good beginning, but any company serious about climate change must work to reduce its own emissions or those in its value chain. Thus, while PepsiCo became the world's leading purchaser of RECs in 2007 in order to position itself as a climate change leader, CEO Indra Nooyi quickly realized that the company needed instead to focus on reducing emissions internally. As a result, she has recently pushed Pepsi toward on-property alternative energy projects including a co-generation plant at Frito-Lay's (a division of PepsiCo) manufacturing facility in Killingly, Connecticut, which will generate almost 100 percent of the site's electrical requirements.[18]

Shaklee Corporation, with a 50-year track record of selling natural and healthy nutritional supplements, green cleaning products, and personal care products, went carbon neutral by combining an ambitious goal of reducing its own emissions by 30 percent from a year 2000 baseline with a substantial purchase of carbon credits to offset the rest of the company's emissions. In addition to investing in renewable energy projects in Asia, Africa, and the United States, Shaklee also launched a partnership with Nobel Peace Prize winner Wangari Maathai in Kenya to plant trees and prevent deforestation in African villages—boosting the world's natural carbon sinks.[19]

7. Solve Your Customer's Climate Change Problems

Companies can have a huge impact by reducing their own emissions, but working to solve a customer's climate change problems or to reduce societal emissions more generally can generate even more significant results. Unilever calculates, for example, that its laundry products are used worldwide for more than 125 billion washes per year. As the Sustainable Consumption Institute notes, a single innovation, multiplied billions of times, results in far a greater impact than anything a company can accomplish in regard to its own footprint.[20] Solving a customer's climate change problem not only represents a way to get leverage on greenhouse gas emissions, but can also add value from a customer's perspective and generate brand loyalty. This reality—both in terms of scope of impact and potential upside opportunity—explains why Unilever CEO Paul Polman has committed his company to addressing climate change on a value-chain-wide basis.

We've seen enormous creativity in how companies, big and small, tap into the power of consumers to reduce emissions. Eileen Fisher, a women's clothing company, makes timelessly designed skirts, pants, and blouses using high-quality materials. The company's emphasis on durability and fashions that don't go out of style enables its customers to wear their Eco Collection clothes longer, reducing their need to buy new—and the emissions that inevitably accompany new production. And every farmers market across the country, of which hundreds have sprung up in the past few years, taps into customer interest in more local and fresh products, but also reduces "food miles" and cuts emissions.

8. Join a Climate Change Leaders Group

As we discuss in Chapter 21 ("Engaging Stakeholders"), partnering with NGOs or government entities can be a powerful way to improve your company's own climate impacts and change the landscape of an industry. To give just one example, the Climate Savers Initiative, led by the World Wildlife Fund, helps large companies cut carbon emissions and gain recognition as corporate leaders on climate change. As of 2010, the 20+ companies in the Climate Savers program have collectively reduced greenhouse gas emissions by some 50 million tons per year—equal to taking more than 3 million cars off the road.[21] Dozens of other partnership opportunities exist with NGOs such as the Environmental Defense Fund, The Nature Conservancy, Natural Resources Defense Council, and government bodies from the local to the global scale.

9. Shape Climate Change Policy

More and more, companies are taking an active role in shaping climate change policy, especially in the United States where the debate over how best to address the problem remains intense. The U.S. Climate Action Partnership (USCAP) formed by dozens of major corporations in partnership with major environmental NGOs has been out in front of efforts to get a "cap and trade" program adopted in the United States. Members of the USCAP include companies such as GE, Duke Energy, Dupont, Honeywell, Johnson & Johnson, and Alcoa as well as NGOs such as NRDC, World Resources Institute, The Nature Conservancy, Environmental Defense Fund, and the Pew Center on Global Climate Change. Similarly, Nike, Starbucks, Timberland, Johnson & Johnson, and Stonyfield Farm have banded together with other businesses to form the Business for Innovative Climate and Energy Policy (or BICEP). This group has called for even stronger measures to control greenhouse gas emissions including adapting a national renewable energy portfolio standard and federal assistance for developing countries in reducing their emissions.

SUMMARY

Key Plays

1. Assess your company's carbon footprint.
2. Set reduction targets.
3. Draft a climate action plan.
4. Identify and implement emissions reduction strategies.
5. Seek reductions across the supply chain.
6. Buy carbon offsets.
7. Solve your customer's climate change problems.
8. Join a climate change leaders group.
9. Shape climate change policy.

ADDITIONAL RESOURCES

GENERAL

Climate Change: What's Your Business Strategy? by Andrew Hoffman and John Woody (Harvard Business Press, 2008). Drawing from their extensive experience working with organizations to address issues of environmental sustainability, the authors explain the impact of climate change on businesses and present a three-step process for developing an effective climate-change strategy.

Climate Change Deskbook by Tom Mounteer (Environmental Law Institute, 2009).

Getting to Zero: Defining Corporate Carbon Neutrality (Clean Air Cool Planet and Forum for the Future). Explores corporate claims on carbon neutrality and makes recommendations about what should lie behind any declaration of neutrality. www.cleanair-coolplanet.org

World Resources Institute (WRI) Website. Research and tools to help business practitioners develop and implement climate strategies. www.wri.orgclimate

ClimateBiz.com. Online clearinghouse designed to help companies of all sizes and sectors understand and address climate change in a way that aligns with business success. www.climatebiz.com

Pew Center on Global Climate Change. Nonprofit organization dedicated to facilitating dialogue among business leaders, policy makers, and scientists. Website tracks developments in international and U.S. policy and offers business-focused research and analysis. www.pewclimate.org

Climate Corps (Environmental Defense Fund and NetImpact). Matches students from leading business schools with corporations seeking to improve efficiency and environmental performance. http://edfclimatecorps.org

Clinton Climate Initiative. The William J. Clinton Foundation partners with governments, NGOs, and businesses to make cities more efficient, ramp up green power generation, and preserve the world's forests. www.clintonfoundation.org

Climate Savers Program (WWF). Partners with companies to cut carbon dioxide emissions through efficiency improvements. www.worldwildlife.org

Carbon Trust. Created by the UK government, this nonprofit helps the business community move toward a low carbon economy by creating climate change strategies and helping implement energy efficient equipment by providing no interest loans. www.carbontrust.co.uk

Intergovernmental Panel on Climate Change (IPCC). International body charged with assessing the science and potential socioeconomic and environmental consequences of climate change, established by the United Nations Environment Programme (UNEP) and the World Meteorological Organization (WMO). www.ipcc.ch

RealClimate.org. A moderated discussion forum among climate scientists tracking new findings and debates in climate-related research. www.realclimate.org

MEASURING ORGANIZATIONAL AND PRODUCT CARBON FOOTPRINT

See Additional Resources at the end of Chapter 6 ("Assess and Measure Your Environmental Impacts").

BENCHMARKING AND SELF-ASSESSMENT

See Additional Resources at the end of Chapter 7 ("Benchmark Your Performance").

CARBON LABELS AND CERTIFICATIONS

Ecolabel Index. Definitive, searchable online guide to eco-labels across all industry sectors. www.ecolabelindex.com

"Global Ecolabel Monitor" (Ecolabel Index and World Resources Institute, 2010). A report on the performance and organizational structure of eco-labels around the world. www.wri.org

CARBON OFFSETS

A Consumer's Guide to Retail Carbon Offset Providers (Clean Air Cool Planet). Practical overview of the carbon offset market. www.cleanair-coolplanet.org

CarbonFund.org. Partners with businesses and provides carbon offsets from third-party validated renewable energy, energy efficiency and reforestation projects globally. www.carbonfund.org

Climate Action Reserve. Issues regulatory-quality carbon offsets from emissions reduction projects in North America. www.climateactionreserve.org

Chapter 20 Mobilize Employees and Build an Eco-Advantage Culture

John Matthews, Senior Vice President for Global Corporate Affairs at Diversey, a Wisconsin-based cleaning supplies company with annual sales of over $3 billion, joined the company in part because of its ethic of environmental stewardship passed down over generations by the company's founder, Sam Johnson. But in recent years, Matthews has seen that environmental commitment translate into bottom-line value—especially when it comes to attracting and retaining employees. In fact, he told us that a leading candidate for a top job recently put it bluntly: "I wouldn't be sitting in this chair right now if it weren't for the commitment Diversey has made to the environment. I don't even take an interview with a company that hasn't demonstrated a measurable, long-term commitment to improving the planet." As Matthews looks at the Diversey leadership team worldwide, he pushes the point further, declaring that many wouldn't be on the payroll if it weren't for the company's culture-defining sustainability commitment.

EMPLOYEE ENGAGEMENT

Dow Chemical's Waste Reduction Always Pays (WRAP) program has engaged thousands of employees—and generated projects with a net value of $20 billion.[1] The company's EVERGREEN website lets employees access and share sustainability information, case studies, and recommendations for inside and outside the office. Worldwide, these projects have reduced waste by 230,000 tons and wastewater by 13 million tons, as well as saving 8 trillion BTUs of energy.

Blue Coat, a global software company, mobilized employee teams from all functional areas to develop and implement its BluePlanet initiative reducing waste and use of resources and fuel. The company expects to generate $4 million in operational cost savings within 18 months.[2]

While some see a sustainability payoff in the form of enhanced employee recruiting and retention as "soft," analysts are getting better at showing the bottom-line impact of such intangible sources of value. In fact, recent studies show that losing and replacing a good employee costs a company between 70 and 200 percent of that employee's annual salary.[3] As more workers—especially high-end "knowledge workers"—insist on "bringing their values to work," which include a commitment to a healthier planet, the human resources payoff to corporate sustainability efforts is likely to multiply.

Companies with strong sustainability records will have an advantage over environmental laggards in attracting top talent in the years ahead, but those that find ways to use this agenda to energize and engage all their employees will reap even bigger gains. So while we've emphasized the need for CEO leadership, without the value of a dedicated Chief Sustainability Officer and the gains from a motivated "green team," no individual or small group can create a sustainable enterprise. Companies must engage employees from top to bottom in the process. Whether driving a truck, on the shop floor, or in sales, employees know the business intimately and are in the best position to uncover new ways to generate Eco-Advantage.

Given the diversity of company sizes, workforces, and corporate cultures, we cannot provide one single road map to effective employee engagement. This chapter does, however, offer a variety of tools and guideposts to support mobilization of the workforce around a sustainability theme. In particular, it will help you:

- Engage your entire workforce in defining, aligning, and executing sustainability initiatives.
- Move beyond informal, ad hoc sustainability efforts to build a more deeply rooted and strategically rewarding sustainability structure.
- Create a culture in which every employee actively participates in the sustainability mission.

BASIC PLAYS: LAY THE GROUNDWORK

1. Bringing Sustainability to Life

A critical first step is to make sustainability "real" and relevant to audiences. As we've noted, the word "sustainability" means very little to most people. And even if you talk about the "environment," many employees still will not be clear on what it has to do with them. We've seen corporate leaders bring the issue to life in a variety of ways.

One *Fortune* 500 company invited a much-admired head of a business unit to speak to first-round trainees. The speaker—a tough-minded, no-nonsense executive with a track record of success—disarmed skeptics in the room by sharing personal details about how he "got religion" on environmental issues. Other companies invite an executive from a nearby company with more of an established sustainability track record to discuss their company's successes (and failures!). Still others bring in compelling outside speakers who can lay out in simple terms the "green to gold" opportunity. Some executives find that using case studies or "what if?" scenario exercises help their employees see the risks and opportunities inherent in the sustainability agenda.

We've seen CEOs stress the risks inherent in failing to apply a green lens to strategy. Others believe that they get more traction with a focus on upside opportunities. A video that showcases diverse green success stories can be a good way to jump-start a sustainability dialogue. (We suggest some videos and clips in the "Additional Resources" section at the end of the chapter.) You might even consider giving portable video recorders to some of your employees and asking them to interview co-workers about their thoughts on sustainability. Don't look for answers at this early stage. Your goal is simply to get people talking.

2. Engage Key Internal Stakeholders in Building the Employee Engagement Strategy

No executive, not even the CEO, can command people to think differently and embrace change. And when the push is to bring an environmental or sustainability focus to every aspect of business activity, some employees will take up this charge with relish. Others will not. The best way to build support for a new sustainability strategy is to invite key internal stakeholders to be *part of* the process of refining the vision and shaping the plan. Bring middle managers, in particular, into the development of the strategy; don't just present them with a precooked plan. Investing the time up front in genuine consultation and dialogue dramatically raises the odds of long-term success—and helps you avoid missteps that lead to confusion or costly delays.

As we highlighted in prior chapters (see Chapter 3 "Building a Winning Eco-Advantage Strategy" and Chapter 18 "Create an Action Plan—and Execute"), a collaborative process will strengthen your overarching strategy and up the odds for your company's successful execution. The same logic for "co-creation" applies in the context of employee engagement.[4] Many companies we've worked with—from small businesses to Walmart—found it useful to create a cross-functional team charged with developing and overseeing the employee engagement strategy. Consider organizing special meetings, such as off-site retreats, at which diverse sets of employees react to initial thinking and help refine the strategy. Aim to find common ground, not to convince everyone to be an environmental enthusiast. Bring in external perspectives to enrich the conversation and thinking. Harrah's Entertainment, for instance, consulted more than a dozen NGOs, outside advisors, and consultants in forming their award-winning employee engagement strategy.[5]

3. Understand Employee Attitudes

One of the most common missteps in employee engagement efforts is for leaders—especially in the executive suite—to assume that they know how employees think. One human resources executive we spoke with learned that just because their culture had a hierarchical management style didn't mean people simply wanted to be "told what to do." Another company discovered that their pragmatic, results-oriented employees, particularly those who were parents or grandparents, were in fact deeply motivated by a sense of environmental responsibility to their communities and a desire to be good stewards for future generations.

Before making final decisions about your employee engagement strategy, we recommend doing a careful assessment of attitudes across your company about the environment and sustainability. Using interviews, walk-throughs, anonymous surveys, small-group meetings, town hall gatherings, or any other means appropriate to your organization, gather information from employees on the following topics:

- What are people's reactions to words like "green," "environmental," and "sustainability?"
- Are there skeptics about climate change or environmental protection more generally?
- How do employees envision environmental and sustainability issues connecting to their day-to-day work? How do these issues connect to their values and the things they care about in their own lives?
- What does the broad workforce know about the company's environmental and sustainability efforts? Would they like the company to do more? Or less?

KNOWING WHEN TO SLOW DOWN

Kathrin Winkler, Chief Sustainability Officer at the **EMC Corporation**, says that one of the hardest lessons she's had to learn is about restraint. "I tend to be a systems thinker—and like many of us working on sustainability, our strength in seeing the big picture. But there have been times I've tried to draw the big picture for others and gotten the response, 'Kathrin, you overwhelm me.' I've learned to look for 'wedge issues' where addressing the sliver of an issue provides an opening for broader thinking and action over time." For instance, Winkler learned that if she tried to tackle every aspect of her company's e-waste initiatives all at once, it would make people run in the other direction. Instead, she got traction by focusing on a couple of key areas, which created a climate where it became more natural for cross-functional conversations about comprehensive strategies. "Now it's routine," Winkler says, "for people to work together across various units on sustainability— and for ideas to spread across the enterprise. Today we see adoption of eco-innovations like adaptive cooling and virtual provisioning implemented across our entire portfolio of hardware enterprise storage products—not just in individual 'green' products."[6]

- How many people would be personally interested in helping the company become more sustainable? What would motivate them to get more involved?
- What aspects of other employee engagement initiatives such as TQM, health, or diversity worked? Which aspects didn't? And why?

This information will provide a useful foundation for successful employee engagement on the environment or sustainability. Look, in particular, for groups or individuals who might take a leadership role, pockets of apathy or outright resistance, and issues or initiatives that will resonate broadly.

4. Get Clear on the Goals and Strategic Choices

After gauging employees' attitudes and perceptions, you are ready to set employee engagement goals and determine the outreach strategy. As we've stressed, it's important to do this in a collaborative way. Some of the important decisions you should address in an employee engagement strategy include:

- **What are your goals and objectives?** What will be the focus of the effort? What are the realistic goals for the next 12 to 18 months? Where do you want to be in five years?
- **Will you use "new" or existing channels?** Should you introduce the employee sustainability effort as a new initiative, perhaps with distinctive branding? Or should you integrate it into existing initiatives, perhaps a popular health and wellness program, or a successful lean manufacturing initiative?
- **What is the task?** What specifically will you ask employees to do? Make changes in how they do their jobs? Bring a dimension of sustainability to their personal lives? Participate in a company-organized community service event? Volunteer to spend time with a community group of their choice? Implement a specific new sustainability-oriented procedure? Or something even bigger, such as a detailed plan to advance specific corporate-wide sustainability goals? Will the task differ among employees?
- **Is participation optional or mandatory?** Will you invite employees to participate in efforts on a volunteer basis, strongly urge them to take part, or require them to do so? Will it be mandatory for some but optional for others?
- **Who calls the shots?** Will there be a formal decision-making body or informal consultative process? Will employees have an opportunity to participate in decision making? If people are encouraged to be entrepreneurial, from whom do they need permission to implement their initiatives?
- **How will you track and evaluate progress?** Which metrics, quantitative and qualitative, will you use to evaluate progress? What system will you use to collect and evaluate information? Options include:
  - Conducting before-and-after surveys to evaluate initiatives.
  - Using web-based applications to track goals and results. For example, AngelPoints (www.angelpoints.com) offers a customizable software program

designed to help companies track "Personal Sustainability Projects" and add them into corporate-wide metrics, such as total water saved or carbon emissions prevented.

- Charging green team leaders with the responsibility of gathering and reporting on results—and explaining which metrics they chose and why.
- Adapting a set of publicly available metrics to the company's own needs. Harrah's Entertainment, for instance, created "sustainability scorecards" that green team leaders complete.
- Surveying customers on the environmental knowledge of customer service representatives.
- Gathering anecdotal evidence obtained through in-person interviews (including exit interviews), unsolicited feedback, and other means.

ASK EMPLOYEES TO "DO ONE THING"

An effective first step in getting employees to engage on sustainability is to ask them to take one simple action in their work or at home. In 2007, **Walmart** asked its 1.3 million U.S. associates to choose a "Personal Sustainability Project (PSP)"—to advance sustainability in their lives, communities, or workplace.[7] Some employees promised to lose weight, which translates not only into better health but substantial energy savings. Others replaced their incandescent lights with compact florescent bulbs. And still others signed up to do beach clean ups, tree planting, or other neighborhood environmental activities.

Many benefits have been intangible. Surveys of employees show that those with PSPs feel strongly that their morale has improved and that they have an opportunity to help the company achieve its goals.[8] But the program has also generated clear business results. One thoughtful employee recommended turning off unnecessary lights inside the break room vending machines. This inspired idea has since saved the company about $1 million a year.[9]

In 2009, **Kimberly-Clark** launched a similar "Small Steps" program. Nearly 2,000 employees have signed up since the program launch in June 2009.[10] Remember that the action of each individual employee, multiplied many times, has the potential to generate significant results over time.

5. Build Capacity

Almost every company that has successfully embedded a commitment to sustainability into its day-to-day strategy has developed training programs to deepen its employees' knowledge base and capacity to act. Companies can build employee understanding and skills in formal classroom-style training, informal learn-by-doing initiatives, or web-based self-directed sustainability modules. Here are some options to consider as you choose the best tools for your particular corporate culture and goals.

FORMAL TRAINING AND LEADERSHIP DEVELOPMENT

Formal training (whether done in person or online) often provides a powerful way to engage employees. It sends the message that management is serious about having people understand the initiative and getting everyone on the same page. Consider whether it's best in your culture to launch a stand-alone training on sustainability or to incorporate a sustainability module into existing training programs such as new employee orientation.

Many companies develop different levels of sustainability training for different groups of employees. IKEA trains all employees on corporate sustainability, global environmental issues, the company's sustainability committee structure, recycling, and environmental management. Specialists receive training on topics such as procurement standards, regulatory rules, the company's approach to forestry, and environmental partnerships. Leaders go through an even more detailed series of sustainability training exercises.[11] Many companies insist that all candidates for top management roles go through environmental or sustainability training.

At Nokia, CEO Olli-Pekka Kallasvuo personally participated in the sustainability sessions of his company's global leadership training program. Other CEOs target middle managers, recognizing that they are the ones who often scramble to reconcile sustainability goals with demands for top-line growth, lower costs, and better margins. Northeast Utilities, for example, created a program tailored to those with line responsibilities centered on "hard choices" such as managing competing pressures for profit and sustainability.[12]

INFORMAL EDUCATION

Many companies combine formal training programs with informal educational approaches, such as periodic brown-bag lunches, special seminars, movie screenings, field trips, or special sustainability events. By offering a variety of possibilities, employers can truly "meet people where they are" and allow employees to opt into whichever topics and types of events appeal to them most. Calling a gathering "training," might send the wrong message when the real intention is to start a conversation, elicit ideas, or inspire action. Microsoft holds regular brown-bag lunch talks, inviting sustainability leaders from around the nation and the world to present their latest thinking. HP has organized "how to" lunchtime seminars on topics such as how to install solar panels on a roof and where to look for government tax breaks and other incentives to subsidize home energy-efficiency investments.[13] Interface Carpet couples job-specific training and online learning modules with a diverse array of other activities—including outdoor experiences and storytelling—to support employee learning and development. A major goal, according to Senior Vice President Joyce LaValle, is to "open people up to expressing ideas and thoughts" and to "provide room for anybody to question anything."[14] If you're at the early stages of getting people on board, a "nontraining" event may help you get off on the right foot.

LEARNING BY DOING

Sometimes rolling up your sleeves and getting your hands dirty is the best way to change mindsets and build employee capacity. GE has had great success with "Treasure Hunts" during which employees come together to evaluate opportunities for energy-efficiency improvements in targeted areas of the workplace. (See Chapter 13, "Manufacturing and Processing," for ideas on organizing similar events based on "kaizen" principles.) Since 2005, more than 200 Treasure Hunts have identified energy savings exceeding $130 million.[15]

The opportunities for sustainability training are truly endless. What matters is finding an approach that meshes with your own company's traditions and your employees' interests.

6. Outline a Compelling Communications Strategy

In addition to *what* to include in an employee engagement strategy, companies need to plan carefully *how* to communicate the strategy. We discuss some key considerations in communicating an employee engagement strategy next.

AGREEING ON THE BIG IDEAS AND "NARRATIVE"

First, get clear on the big, overarching concepts you want to convey. What is the story you want to tell about sustainability? How does this narrative differ from the "external" story—or what employees already know? What are the values and beliefs that support your sustainability strategy? Your job will be far easier if your company has already developed a clear, compelling corporate vision and mission statement around sustainability that enjoys deep support among senior executives. If that's not the case then work with your peers to get buy-in for an overarching sustainability vision. Having a clear set of priority principles and programs provides the foundation for authentic and consistent communications both internally and externally.

FRAMING THE MESSAGE

Having a clear story is one thing, but getting people to hear it is something else entirely. In a small business with a single location, the challenge may not be so great. But for big businesses, the same message that resonates with call center employees in Chicago may fall on deaf ears at a manufacturing plant in Michigan. The images or text that inspire an employee in South America may have unintended negative connotations in China. You may need to frame your story differently depending on target audiences' backgrounds, priorities, and belief systems.

By "framing differently" we mean tailoring communications in authentic ways that allow you to get your points across effectively to particular audiences, not "spinning" the message in ways that stray from the core elements of your corporate sustainability strategy. Effective framing involves choosing the right words, tone, visuals, and trusted messengers. Nike, for instance, learned that framing its company's sustainability message to product designers around the concept of "innovation" was far more inspiring than making communications about "eco-efficiency."[16] As we stressed earlier, do not assume that you know what will work for your audience. Find ways to involve target audiences in the development of communications strategies and be sure to test assumptions in the field.

SPREADING MESSAGES AND FACILITATING INFORMATION FLOWS

Most companies find that a mixed-media strategy is the most effective way to galvanize the troops. Common tactics include using physical collateral such as posters, table tents, buttons, and stickers as well as virtual outreach. Internet-based communications, including e-newsletters, intranet sites, wikis, blogs, webcasts, and video are also useful. Other forms of communication include teleconference and videoconference, small group meetings, and town hall events. Regardless of the venues used, communications should be viewed as a two-way street. Don't simply "broadcast" your message. Set up ways to listen as well. Companies with successful employee engagement programs say that creating the means for employees to have back-and-forth exchanges of information, tips, success stories, tools, and lessons learned is vitally important to getting results over the long-term.

Cisco, for instance, uses Web 2.0 technologies including a dedicated intranet site with video and discussion forums to engage employees. Its "Let's Talk Cisco Green" discussion forum quickly became the company's top-visited forum, with over 60,000 views and 91 conversation threads within the first six months. Employees have used the discussion forum to share tips—such as where to recycle electronic waste—and to offer suggestions for how Cisco can reduce its environmental footprint.[17] HP organizes a popular "Live Green" program that involves posting articles on the company's Internet portal, hosting guest speakers and broadcasting the recorded videos.[18] Other companies have gotten the best results through face-to-face communications. After PepsiCo manager Andrei Aroneanu's attempts to woo green volunteers through posters and emails flopped, he resorted to simply talking up green issues at regular meetings with co-workers. He says the "face-to-face enthusiasm" rubbed off on people in way that didn't come through in email.[19]

Companies are also turning to social networking tools such as Facebook to reach out to employees. Online travel company Sabre created a "Good Network" that includes both a public facing blog and an employee-only area for internal social networking. Employees can record their sustainability goals and actions, track their progress, post ideas or questions, and find individuals with similar interests. Some employees even use the site to find carpools. The system is also set up to assign actual metrics to employee actions, enabling Sabre to add up the total benefits of employee activities by city and by country.

INTERMEDIATE PLAYS: BUILD A TRACK RECORD OF SUCCESS

7. Roll Out the Strategy with Pilot Efforts

After building internal support and weighing the options, it's time to execute. We strongly recommend using pilot projects to test your ideas and assumptions and work out any kinks before launching any company-wide initiatives. Gwen Migita, Director of Corporate Sustainability at Harrah's Entertainment, said that the company's biggest mistake was to ask employees to take on too much too soon. Once the company switched to a one-new-initiative-a-month strategy, employees began to respond favorably. Moreover, small, careful, initial steps are a great way to build a track record of success that boosts credibility and attracts internal support. Prioritize quick-win opportunities that demonstrate business value. Steer people initially toward eco-efficiency opportunities where low-cost (or zero cost) activities could quickly produce bottom-line results. Seek out the employees who are passionate about environmental issues and ask for their help. Give them tools and space to run, and you'll get results.

8. Align Your Employee Engagement Efforts with Broader Strategy

Employees will quickly notice any disconnect between an employee engagement initiative and your company's broader sustainability strategy or business priorities. Here are our **top 10 recommendations** to improve your odds of proper alignment, successful employee mobilization, and ultimately creation of an Eco-Advantage culture.

#1. **Be "Urgently Patient."** As a 34-year IBM veteran, Bob Willard has seen countless successful (and failed) experiments in employee engagement and culture change. With this base of experience in mind, he urges companies to "go slow to go fast" when it comes to sustainability engagement. If you push the wrong messages or projects, you risk undermining the initiative's effectiveness. Accelerating too quickly or pushing at the wrong time can lead to a backlash and burned bridges. Invest the time up front to consult with others. Know that changing a culture takes time, usually years, so don't try to do everything at once.

#2. **Make It Personal and Upbeat.** Employees are motivated to invest time and energy when they believe that what they're being asked to do matters to the business (doing the "smart and pragmatic" thing) *and* advances a cause they believe in (doing the "right" thing). At Duke Energy, CEO Jim Rogers frequently says he wants his grandchildren to be able to look back and say, "My granddaddy made a good decision, and it's still a good decision."[20] Who can disagree with that sentiment? We're also convinced that positive messages are much more inspiring than gloom-and-doom ones. Look for ways to make people feel good about what they're doing—and make it fun.

#3. **Connect to Core Business Objectives and Company-Wide Sustainability Goals.** Employees need to know why being sustainable matters. They'll want clarity on where the company is headed on sustainability and why. Be careful not to overload everyone with a long list of detailed sustainability objectives—leave the details to managers accountable for performing against specific objectives. But *do* help everyone understand the company's sustainability vision, mission, *and* big goals. Ray Anderson, the dynamic founder of Interface Carpets, famously galvanized his company's employees with a radical "Mission Zero" plan aimed to "convert Interface to a restorative enterprise" and have the company return more than it takes from the earth—a bold sustainability goal aligned with a big business vision.[21]

#4. **Demonstrate High-Level Support and "Walk the Talk."** Unless senior management genuinely sees sustainability as integral to the business, employee engagement efforts will not thrive or take root. One important step CEOs and chairmen can take is to issue a comprehensive letter detailing the company's commitment to sustainability. But leadership by example can be even more powerful. Sustainability advisors Marsha Willard and Darcy Hitchcock suggest steps like designating prime parking spots for carpoolers, cycling to work, using teleconferences to avoid business travel, and using the most fuel-efficient cars.[22] These small steps will go miles in preventing a perception that sustainability is yet another "flavor of the month."

#5. **Choose Leaders and Messengers Carefully.** At the end of the day, getting people engaged and changing the culture is about leadership. It's about helping employees see things differently and inspiring them to act differently—which not only requires sustainability knowledge, but also soft skills including intuition, judgment, empathy, patience, and charisma. At GE, CEO Jeff Immelt asked Lorraine Bolsinger to head up ecomagination efforts not because she was an environmental expert, but because she had spent years building trust and credibility throughout the organization as a tough, get-it-done business leader. The best sustainability advocates are generally leaders with proven line management experience. Be sure that the individuals chosen to introduce employees to new concepts create a great first impression. One nurse at a New York City hospital told us about a failed environmental training effort she attended that had been designed and led by an outside contractor with no connection to the hospital and little knowledge of medical practices. Because of its disconnect from hospital reality, the suggested eco-approach produced more eye rolling and resistance than learning. That unfortunate result could have been easily avoided if a well-respected hospital authority had co-developed and co-led the training effort.

#6. **Make the Agenda Clear and Actionable—and Consistent with Existing Workloads.** Be clear about what you are asking people to do, and what you expect of them. One of IKEA's big lessons learned about sustainability training was that only when employees walked away with clear action steps could they make sense of what they learned.[23] Be sure that what you're asking people to do is realistic given what employees already have on their plates. Otherwise they (or their managers and co-workers) will become frustrated or resentful. JCPenney, for instance, told the recruits for its volunteer "energy captain" program that they shouldn't spend more than an hour every couple weeks on their work.[24] If the "ask" of a particular employee requires a substantial time commitment, be sure his or her manager (and everyone else affected) is aligned and that the employee's job description reflects the new priority. Finally, be crystal clear about accountability mechanisms: Who needs to ask whom for approval before taking action? Who reports what to whom, and how?

#7. **Create Tools to Set People Up for Success.** Whether simple checklists or sophisticated online databases, be sure employees have what they need to hit the ground running. For example, Darden Restaurants, the parent company of Red Lobster and Olive Garden restaurants, worked with the New England Aquarium to develop a Sustainable Seafood Dashboard that helps its seafood buyers make environmentally sound choices. Darden's seafood buyers attend a daylong workshop with the Aquarium's conservation specialists to learn how to use the tool, which summarizes the top environmental issues associated with various seafood species.[25] The most effective tools you can build, however, will come through a process of co-creation with the people you want to use them. Never assume what will work for you will work for others, or that "if we build it they will come." The best-constructed website or database that you spend big money on may not appeal to those you've designed it for. Ask people what they think they will need to succeed. Use pilot projects to test ideas, giving people templates and drafts to react to and being prepared for them to help re-create them.

#8. **Provide Sufficient Flexibility and Autonomy.** The most successful engagement and change management efforts balance clear direction from the top with considerable autonomy. They offer broad vision and direction, but let employees figure out the best ways to get there. Nike has embraced this approach with its "Power of One" program, which sets an ambitious goal of requiring designers to deliver one sustainable design element per season without specifying any particular objective—inspiring employees to think without mental boundaries about how to generate new solutions by fundamentally challenging assumptions about materials and processes.[26]

Similarly, Google encourages its engineers to spend 20 percent of their time on projects that interest them, regardless of their relevance to the individual's job description. This time allowance has resulted in an estimated 50 percent of new products launched, many of which focus on sustainability solutions.[27]

#9. **Use a Personal Touch.** Kevin Moss, the head of sustainability for BT Americas, has presided over scores of successful engagement efforts—from using more recycled paper to building solar installations and electric bike recharging stations. He has found that "nothing can replace reaching out to people on a one to one basis and asking them if they will champion an initiative . . . [personal outreach can] make the critical difference that moves someone from thinking of helping (which most people do when they see a corporate communication) to taking action."[28]

#10. **Follow Through Visibly and Consistently—and Acknowledge Mistakes.** Programs with great ideas may draw participants initially, but only those with a strong follow-through can keep them involved and generate sustained results. Use a variety of methods—posters, stickers, events, e-communications, videos and more—to build a steady presence across facilities and offices. Publicize success to keep building trust, credibility and momentum. Most important, keep a steady communications flow with and among the leaders you've asked to take on special roles. Use meetings, phone calls, and web platforms to give them regular opportunities to share what they're learning and what they need.

9. Incentivize, Recognize, and Reward

Creating the right mix of rewards and incentives is key to getting results. Explore these six common approaches when considering what the right formula is for your particular culture and circumstances: (1) public recognition and awards, (2) contests and competitions, (3) transparency, (4) eco-related employee benefits, (5) linking environmental performance to budgeting, and (6) tying compensation and bonuses to environmental performance.

PUBLIC RECOGNITION AND AWARDS

Whether a simple pat on the back or a prestigious award, acknowledgment by superiors and peers is often all it takes to fuel meaningful green contributions. At the PepsiCo R&D plant in Valhalla, New York, the management team discovered that *publicly* thanking employees who'd taken leadership roles at its "Good Morning Valhalla" meetings proved to be far more meaningful and effective than *privately* giving tokens of appreciation.[29] Davis & Warshow, Inc., a New York-based plumbing supply wholesaler, runs a cash lottery to encourage its staff to choose greener commuting options. Employees can enter the lottery every 10 times they carpool, take mass transit, ride their bikes, or walk to work.

The lottery awards $1,000, $500, and $100 cash prizes every quarter to three winners, and even bigger cash rewards and other prizes, including flat-screen TVs, at the end of the year.[30] Sainsbury's, the UK-supermarket chain, organizes an annual "Local Heroes" award ceremony to honor exceptional employees. Local Heroes winners have been invited to visit overseas Fairtrade suppliers in places like the Winward Islands, from which Sainsbury's sources most of its Fairtrade bananas. The company found that giving employees the opportunity to see sustainability in action solidifies their commitment to the issues and makes them exceptional ambassadors of Sainsbury's sustainability vision.[31]

CONTESTS AND COMPETITIONS

Many companies now use contests and competitions to motivate employees on sustainability goals. Food giant ConAgra's employee-led contest for environmental innovation collectively achieved big reductions in carbon emissions, solid waste, packaging waste, and water use that altogether saved the company over $28 million.[32] Electricité de France (EDF) holds a global competition every two years that awards winners with "Sustainable Development Trophies" and up to 10,000 euros to implement innovations. In 2010, a panel reviewed 538 entries before selecting 23 winners. Many of the "losing" projects still get completed—and the competition energizes employees around the world while underscoring the company's commitment to sustainable development.[33]

ECO-RELATED EMPLOYEE BENEFITS

Some companies offer benefits that encourage employees to live sustainably in their daily lives. Bank of America, Google, and Timberland are among the companies that offer employees cash incentives for buying hybrid electric vehicles.[34] HP, as part of its agreement with SunPower when it installed a 1.1 megawatt solar energy system at its San Diego facility, started a program offering joint rebates to install solar electricity for employee's residences.[35] NRG Systems, a manufacturer of wind energy assessment equipment, gives employees $300 annually to implement energy-efficiency measures in their households.[36] The company also offers its employees $1,000 per year toward replacing their cars with Toyota Priuses and an additional $1,000 to install a wind turbine, solar PV panels, solar hot water system, or a wood furnace. NRG estimates that in 2006 76 percent of its employees utilized these energy-efficiency benefits.

For those who are cost conscious, it makes sense to focus as well as on eliminating environmentally harmful perks. Start by getting rid of free parking. If this can't be done, then subsidize those who take mass transit.

TRANSPARENCY

Simply disseminating the company's environmental impact and performance data can engage and motivate employees, sometimes spurring healthy competition to improve performance. Yahoo!, for example, set up a "green screen" at its corporate headquarters to show employees campus energy use in real time.[37]

Other companies use "smart metering" to give employees detailed, real-time information on facilities' electricity, gas, and water consumption. JCPenney created a web-based Energy Center and named "energy captains" for each of its stores. These captains have access to energy consumption data for their sites as well as data for other stores, facilitating comparative analysis. In addition, captains can obtain energy consumption information from the previous day in 15-minute increments, which enables them to spot spikes in energy use, look for causes, and find solutions.[38]

Holding managers accountable in public settings for green results can have a similar effect. GE organizes a series of Session E annual meetings, which are an offshoot of the company's famous Session C meetings. Managers get praised for outstanding performance but also get direct feedback regarding failures. The resulting peer pressure drives results and continuous improvement.[39]

LINKING ENVIRONMENTAL PERFORMANCE TO BUDGETING

Some companies reward employees for eco-efficiency by giving them part or all of the savings. JCPenney, for example, occasionally recognizes outstanding energy-efficiency efforts by paying the utility bills of high-performing stores to improve their revenue picture at the end of the year.[40] STMicroelectronics, one of the world's largest semiconductor companies, offers an increased monthly automobile allowance to North America-based employees who drive fuel-efficient vehicles. Automobiles with fuel consumption ratings of 39.2 mpg to 46.9 mpg are given an additional $83.34 in monthly allowance, while those with 47 mpg or higher receive an additional $166.67 per month.[41]

Other companies have learned that simply reallocating budget responsibility can be a powerful incentive for change. Notably, making departments responsible for their own energy and waste bills—instead of the typical practice of charging a fixed percentage of the overhead—turns out to be a serious motivator. Microsoft realized it had created a perverse incentive for individual business units to be inefficient by calculating energy bills based on how much space their servers took up. Users were overloading individual servers to save physical space which jacked up air-conditioning costs. Bills went down as soon as the company started charging units for energy based on actual power use.[42]

LINKING COMPENSATION AND BONUSES TO SUSTAINABILITY PERFORMANCE

The boldest incentive is to link environmental performance to pay. Defense industry giant Northrop Grumman now ties its executive compensation to the company's greenhouse gas reduction goals. "If we can do it as a security

company," says the company's GreeNG Director David Hitchings, "anyone can." DSM, the Dutch life sciences group, ties half the bonuses for its
management board to sustainability targets including the reduction of greenhouse gas emissions and energy use and the introduction of new environmentally friendly products. "Sustainability is the key driver of our whole strategy . . . and remuneration is one of the ultimate expressions of your values,"
says DSM CEO Feike Sijbesma.[43] Shell uses a scorecard to appraise business
performance and bases 20 percent of the score on environmental and social
metrics.[44] This scorecard directly affects the level of annual bonuses of nearly
all Shell staff and rewards employees and teams for contributions to sustainability goals. The company also links senior staff rewards to their sustainability
contributions.

TYING SUSTAINABILITY TO CORPORATE PERFORMANCE EVALUATION

Like most companies, Dutch multinational **AkzoNobel** started out its sustainability
journey focused on risk management and eco-efficiency plays. By 1995, it had shaved
20 percent off its energy bill—representing serious cost savings that inspired employees across the company to ask, "What next?" A decade later, the company had
embraced sustainability as a key driver of its growth and innovation strategy. Today,
half of the long-term compensation of its top executives is tied to the company's performance on the Dow Jones Sustainability Index. "We evaluate our corporate strategy
and performance using not just lagging indicators based on our past, but also *leading*
indicators about our future—such as growth in emerging markets and in new products," explained Azko's top sustainability officer Andre Veneman. "It would be very
silly not to include sustainability in long-term renumeration if you really believe this
is your growth agenda," Veneman told us.[45]

ADVANCED PLAYS: EXPAND THE NETWORK

10. Keep Building on what Works and Share Lessons Learned

Successfully engaged employees don't view sustainability as "someone else's
job," but rather as an automatic, routine part of what they do every day.
These employees keep expanding the ranks of sustainability leaders, all of whom
are constantly looking for fresh ways to inspire others and deepen sustainability commitment within the culture. These leaders continue to refine systems,
human and electronic, that enable ever-expanding networks of committed individuals in their companies to spread knowledge and best practices, and to
share ideas and collaborate. We recommend that companies at this stage document their practices and lessons learned, share them widely, and exchange ideas
and experiences with other companies at all stages of building a sustainable
culture.

SUMMARY

Key Plays

1. Bring sustainability to life.
2. Engage key internal stakeholders in building the employee engagement strategy.
3. Understand employee attitudes.
4. Get clear on the goals and strategic choices.
5. Build capacity.
6. Outline a compelling communications strategy.
7. Roll out the strategy with pilot efforts.
8. Align the employee engagement efforts with broader strategy.
9. Incentivize, recognize, and reward.
10. Keep building on what works and share lessons learned.

ADDITIONAL RESOURCES

AFFECTING CHANGE IN YOUR ORGANIZATION

The Sustainability Champion's Guidebook: How to Transform Your Company by Bob Willard (New Society, 2009). Crisp, must-read for anyone working on green engagement within their companies—from multinational CEOs to green team leaders and employee champions.

Point B: A Short Guide to Leading a Big Change by Peter Bregman (Space for Change, 2007). Outlines effective strategies for changing organizational mindsets and behaviors based on real-world failures and successes.

BRINGING SUSTAINABILITY TO LIFE (VIDEOS)

Walmart "Sustainability 2.0" videos http://walmartstores.com/

Ray Anderson, CEO of Interface, 2009 TED talk on the "Business Logic of Sustainability" www.ted.com

GE "Hunt for CO_2"—Treasure Hunts in action www.youtube.com

"What Is Garbage/How Terracycle Works" video, Tom Szaky, CEO www.terracycle.net

LESSONS LEARNED FROM EMPLOYEE ENGAGEMENT INITIATIVES

"Generating Sustainable Value: Moving Beyond Green Teams to Transformation Collaboratives" (Sabre Holdings Group, 2010). Outlines findings and best practices from an in-depth study of 14 companies "Green Teams." www.sabre-holdings.com

"Green Teams: Engaging Employees in Sustainability" by Deborah Fleischer (GreenBiz Reports). Recommendations for building a company's sustainability mission into all employees' daily activities. www.greenbiz.com

"Collective "Green" Wisdom: Environmental Initiatives Evoke Unprecedented Power of Multifunctional Collaboration" (TFI Environment). How cross-functional collaboration can generate powerful results. www.eetimes.com

Engaged Organization: Corporate Employee Environmental Education Survey and Case Study Findings (National Environmental Education Foundation). www.neefusa.org

Chapter 21 Engaging Stakeholders

Until recently, Chiquita, the Ohio-based company best known for its bananas, might have been a candidate for the Corporate Irresponsibility Hall of Shame. From the mid-1800s through most of the twentieth century, Chiquita (formerly known as United Fruit) took part in deforesting thousands of acres of rainforests, exposed workers to dangerous pesticides, and even conspired with the CIA to overthrow the democratically elected government of Guatemala. In the 1990s, NGOs and European customers demanded a better banana. Chiquita executives realized that they had to make some real changes and found an unlikely partner in Rainforest Alliance.

With a range of other stakeholders, Chiquita and Rainforest Alliance designed a set of guidelines for producing bananas in an environmentally and socially responsible way. Pesticide use went down, worker satisfaction went up, and farm productivity increased 27 percent in the first decade.[1] According to Raul Gomez, a farm manager who has worked for Chiquita in Costa Rica for over 15 years, "Chiquita's adoption of the standards has brought about far-reaching changes not just in our farming practices, but in the minds and attitudes of our people as well."[2]

As we noted in Chapter 5, it is critical for companies to map the full spectrum of stakeholders whose interests and concerns factor into the construction of a comprehensive sustainability strategy. Engaging NGOs, governments, and industry peers can bring a sharper focus to sustainability efforts and build a capacity for seeing "over the horizon." It can also help the company leverage skills and perspectives not available internally, build respect and credibility, influence market dynamics, and shape public policy to ensure that sustainability enhances competitiveness.

This chapter will show you how to:

- Open a dialogue with NGOs and other stakeholders.
- Better anticipate emerging sustainability issues.
- Engage communities and create outreach programs.

- Form strategic partnerships with key stakeholders.
- Formalize and expand partnerships across industries in your value chain.

BASIC PLAYS: INITIAL STEPS

A company interested in adding environmental credentials but not ready to "sleep with the enemy" or overhaul its operations can take small steps to engage external stakeholders. It can support the work of another organization, join an environmental business or corporate responsibility network, or initiate an outreach effort within its own community. Doing so signals a business's interest in being a good corporate citizen. Many organizations make it easy for businesses to partner with them. In return, those companies receive positive brand association, community goodwill, and access to external perspectives and resources.

1. Open a Dialogue

Many companies have viewed environmental groups and other NGOs as enemies for so long that they don't know where to start when attempting to engage these organizations. The answer is simple: Start a conversation.

Understanding what your stakeholders want is the first step toward a constructive relationship with them. So call up the leaders of active groups in your area and invite them over for lunch. Here's a straightforward formula for success:

- Don't come with an agenda.
- Be prepared to listen.
- Ask questions—invite your guests to explain their current and future priority issues.
- Try not to be defensive.
- Take their views seriously.
- Look for points of agreement.
- Recognize that, on some issues, no convergence of views will be possible.
- Build trust—and personal relationships.

2. Support a Cause

You can ally your company with an organization very simply by supporting one of its causes. The Chesapeake Bay Foundation, a Maryland-based environmental organization, holds an annual golf tournament to raise awareness about sustainable lawn care and raise funds for the organization. For $1,000 to $50,000, companies can sponsor the event and get their logo on the event's items, recognition on the foundation's website and promotional materials, and the chance to promote the company's products or services at the event.

Larger organizations can afford to make bigger contributions and generate more media attention. These types of contributions are most effective if the cause that the company is supporting relates to one of its core environmental impacts. For example, Waste Management in 2005 gave $130,000 to Freecycle, the grassroots network that allows members to give and take unwanted items from each other for free. Through this sponsorship, Waste Management shows its support for reducing waste—one of the company's core environmental concerns.[3]

Other companies add to their environmental credentials by donating a portion of profits to a worthy cause. For example, Endangered Species Chocolate donates 10 percent of its proceeds to organizations like the African Wildlife Foundation or the Ocean Conservancy. In the past few years, L.L. Bean has given away a total of $6 million to environmental NGOs like the National Park Foundation, which shows that conservation is one of its core values. Some corporations make their giving a core element of their business model. Patagonia has pledged to support environmental activism with 1 percent of its annual sales or 10 percent of pretax profits, whichever is more. Since this program's inception in 1985, Patagonia has given over $38 million in grants to more than 1,000 organizations.[4]

Small businesses can play this game too. Blue State Coffee in New Haven, Connecticut, lets customers vote each day for one of four nonprofit entities they like and then donates 5 percent of their profits to the winner. The "voting" list of NGOs changes each month—but you can be sure that the groups involved encourage their friends and supporters to buy Blue State Coffee.

3. Join an Environmental Corporate Social Responsibility Organization

Many organizations work with the private sector to help companies advance their sustainability initiatives. Ceres, a Boston-based organization committed to "sustainable prosperity," works with companies and investors to integrate environmental results and social concerns into capital market assessments of corporate performance and valuations. Companies can join Ceres to receive expert advice on sustainability reporting; participate in sustainability dialogues; and access the Investor Network on Climate Risk, a group of more than 80 leading investors with more than $7 trillion of assets working on climate change issues. As we discuss later in detail, many of the major environmental groups—Environmental Defense Fund (EDF), Natural Resource Defense Council (NRDC), The Nature Conservancy (TNC), Conservation International (CI), and the World Wildlife Fund (WWF)—have dedicated teams to work with the private sector. For a more complete list of these groups as well as other resources, see Additional Resources at the end of this chapter.

4. Conduct Community Outreach

One of the essential stakeholder groups for almost every company will be the leaders of the communities in which it operates. Everyone has probably heard of a company that got crosswise with its neighbors or broader community to bad effect. Community-scale issues can sometimes grow to become market-threatening problems. Coca-Cola experienced this when its bottling operation in the South Indian state of Kerala was shut down in 2007 after a protracted dispute with local leaders and farmers over water rights.

Partnering with well-respected community groups can be an effective way to learn about local concerns and then work to address them. For example, PT Aqua Gölden Mississippi, a major distributor of bottled water in Indonesia, faced harsh criticism from local NGOs for allowing large quantities of used water bottles to clog the waste stream. It turned to Dana Mitra Lingkungan (DML), a local NGO headed by environmentally conscious businessmen, to bridge the gap between the company's needs and the local government's environmental concerns. PT Aqua and DML partnered to develop a project focused on bottle recycling. By rejecting the conventional adversity between NGOs and businesses, PT Aqua managed to work toward a goal that was mutually beneficial for external stakeholders and the company itself.

Reaching out to local communities through jointly sponsored projects can be an especially effective way to gain exposure and customer loyalty for businesses that interface with the public. REI, the national sports and outdoor clothing and equipment retailer, supports a host of community-oriented programs and partnerships. Each year, REI's employees nominate hundreds of local nonprofit organizations that share REI's commitment to conservation and recreation to receive company grants. REI focuses on projects that help youth participate in outdoor activities. The company also supports local organizations and recreation clubs by donating meeting space and allowing them to advertise their events and opportunities on store Outdoor Resource Center bulletin boards and the store event calendars on its website.[5] In addition, REI runs educational programs that take local children and youth on nature outings and to outdoor sport activities.[6] For those who don't own equipment, REI operates a gear bank to rent equipment to local participants. REI's outreach programs not only generate community goodwill but also create new outdoor enthusiasts who may purchase their products.

INTERMEDIATE PLAYS: ENGAGE IN STRATEGIC PARTNERSHIPS

If your company wants to advance its sustainability goals beyond its own communities, engage in strategic partnerships with governments, NGOs, industry peers, or consultants. Companies in the intermediate stage of stakeholder partnerships form strategic alliances that will help them most in achieving their sustainability goals. Knowing the issues and environmental impacts that are most relevant to your company should be the first step.

5. Identify and Evaluate Potential Partners

Before engaging in a significant partnership that goes beyond donations, it is important for companies to find the right partner, define the goals and parameters of their initiatives, and clarify who will bring what resources and capabilities to the joint efforts. From a business perspective, it makes sense to team up with others when facing a critical issue in which the company lacks expertise. Any strategic partnership requires a degree of "due diligence."

The Environmental Defense Fund recommends asking the following sets of questions when evaluating a potential partnership:

- **Environmental impacts:** Will the project address significant environmental impacts from the company? Will it result in measurable long-term benefits to the environment?
- **Business benefits:** Will the project add business value? Will the benefits be significant, long lasting, and measurable? Is the project aligned with the mission and goals of the company and of the partner?
- **Project scope:** Is it possible to develop a project that is both aggressive and manageable? Is the project feasible, given available financial and staff resources?
- **Leverage potential:** Can other parts of the company, other industry players, government agencies, NGOs, or the community at large replicate the results of the project? Does the partner have a national or international presence that will maximize the visibility and impact of the project?
- **Fit with company/partner capabilities:** Does the project fit well with the current capabilities of the company and the partner? Is it an area where the partner's capabilities add value to the company and vice versa? Are both organizations excited about the project?[7]

THE VALUE OF STRATEGIC PARTNERSHIPS

Kraft Foods believes partnerships are an "absolute necessity," according to Vice President of Sustainability Steve Yucknut. "We've found them to be more important in the sustainability space than any other area of business success," he told us. "There has been someone else behind the curtain for every one of our successes, like Rainforest Alliance contributing to our work in coffee and cocoa, or Terracycle's contribution to our waste reduction. There isn't a single area where we've reached our goals by ourselves."[8]

Focusing on the right issues is critical. Ford Motor Company in the early 2000s gave $12 million to Conservation International to establish CI's Center for Environmental Leadership in Business. However, CI's focus is biodiversity, which is hardly a core issue for an automaker. In the meantime, Toyota was partnering with alternative fuel companies to develop better cars and improve the energy efficiency of its manufacturing plants.

Companies should find a partner whose initiatives match with their own objectives. Nike understood that its sustainability challenge went beyond environmental concerns and included a range of social issues including labor and human rights issues. As a result, it launched a partnership with Ashoka—an organization focused on driving change through investment in innovative social projects. With Ashoka support, Nike launched a "sports for a better world" competition aimed at identifying innovative individuals and organizations using sports to address societal challenges. Nike identified the "change makers" it would support, including an organization that educates young people in South Africa about AIDS as part of their soccer league and a "Sports 4 Kids" initiative designed to get U.S. schoolchildren to become more active to reduce obesity and other health issues that arise in our modern sedentary society. This partnership played to Nike's strength as well as to Ashoka's leadership position.

6. Reach Out to Potential NGO Partners

Many large national environmental NGOs work in strategic partnerships with businesses to improve their sustainability. The World Wildlife Fund, led by former McKinsey consultant Carter Roberts, has mobilized companies to cut carbon dioxide through its highly regarded Climate Savers Initiative.[9] WWF works with a wide range of companies, including IBM and Coca Cola, to develop climate emissions reduction plans. Those who can meet WWF's strict guidelines for voluntary emissions reductions get to associate their brands with the iconic WWF panda—as a certification of responsible action for the environment.

The Natural Resource Defense Council's E2 (Environmental Entrepreneurs) program recruits and mobilizes the business community to act on important environmental issues. With more than 850 members from the business community in over 20 states, E2 provides timely and accurate information about pressing environmental issues to its members, enabling them to take rapid and forceful action. It offers an especially effective way for small and medium-sized companies to stay abreast of environmental policy developments. As a result, E2 members have pushed for political progress on climate change—writing letters, issuing position statements, and visiting legislators. Many observers say that E2 played an essential role in the passage of the California Global Warming Solutions Act.[10]

The Environmental Defense Fund (EDF), another national environmental group, reaches out to companies in a variety of ways. Its Corporate Partnership

Program, run by the highly regarded Gwen Ruta, has helped dozens of companies think through their sustainability opportunities. EDF's high-profile efforts to "green" investor groups like KKR, have been especially notable. EDF's Climate Corps program, developed in partnership with NetImpact, places students from leading business schools in companies interested in reducing their energy use. Students spend the summer identifying opportunities to save energy and reduce climate change impacts. Climate Corps fellows have identified almost $90 million in potential savings for the companies in which they have worked. In return, the students receive training and experience implementing energy-efficiency strategies with a real company.[11]

For small and medium-sized companies, it may be easier to partner with local NGOs or the local chapters of the large national groups. The Nature Conservancy, the Sierra Club, and the Audubon Society, for instance, all have local chapters in many states.

7. Build a Bridge to the Government

Most companies of any significant size recognize that they must deal continually with governments, officials, and regulatory agencies. Legal compliance is a starting point for any sustainability program. But the law has gray areas that require interpretation, so it is important for companies to maintain good relations with those officials who will decide when to pursue a borderline violation—and when to let it drop. It is important for companies to be forthcoming in their dealings with regulatory authorities. Developing a reputation for integrity and straight answers is critical to winning the benefit of the doubt from government entities and public officials.

The federal government and many state governments run environment-related initiatives aimed at encouraging companies to step up their environmental performance. For many years, the EPA's Climate Leaders program helped hundreds of companies reduce their impact on the environment with comprehensive climate change strategies—and many achieved extraordinary results. For example, 3M reduced its greenhouse gas emissions 54 percent in 2006 from a 1990 baseline.[12] Although the Climate Leaders program was phased out in 2010, the U.S. government offers businesses many other partnership opportunities. For instance, the U.S. Department of Energy's Industrial Technologies Program offers free industry-specific and technology-specific tools to help industry cut energy costs, raise productivity, and reduce carbon emissions. And EPA's SmartWay Transport Partnership fosters collaboration between the U.S. EPA and major freight shippers, trucking companies, railroads, logistics companies, and trade/professional associations to drive improvements and cost savings.

On a smaller scale, state and local governments often have programs to help businesses comply with regulations and become more sustainable. Maryland's Department of the Environment provides technical assistance, informational resources, and recognition to businesses striving to improve their environmental performance. Businesses can take advantage of a free, confidential assessment of their facility by engineers at the University of Maryland Manufacturing Assistance Program and receive a report listing waste reduction and energy conservation opportunities. The program will also place engineering students to research and implement cost-saving waste reduction opportunities. Businesses that achieve excellence in sustainability can receive recognition in the form of certificates and endorsements from the Maryland Department of the Environment.[13]

8. Explore "Co-Opetition" through Industry Partnerships

Rather than competing with others in the industry on environmental issues, sometimes it makes sense for companies to work with competitors in a shared initiative to address common concerns. The chemical industry found itself pressed to improve environment and safety concerns in the wake of the Bhopal disaster in 1986. This led DuPont, Dow, and other leading chemical companies to launch the "Responsible Care" initiative designed to lift standards across the industry for the manufacturer related to storage, transportation, and tracking of potentially hazardous chemicals. Organized by the industry association, Responsible Care has become a model of industry-wide cooperation aimed at improving performance and putting pressure on companies whose standards have been subpar.

The cement industry has long been seen as one of the dirtiest businesses in the world. With this reputation becoming a source of strain, a number of leading companies including Lafarge, Holcim, and Cemex launched a sectorwide initiative under the auspices of the World Business Council for Sustainable Development (www.wbcsdcement.org) to reduce carbon dioxide emissions and address other environmental challenges related to the production of cement. With 23 major cement producers representing 40 percent of the world's cement production, this initiative has helped the member companies transform their practices and shift public perception about the cement industry.

ADVANCED PLAYS: FORMALIZE ENGAGEMENT EFFORTS AND EXPAND PARTNERSHIPS

9. Form a Sustainability Advisory Board

A number of leading companies have found that their ability to manage sustainability issues can be enhanced by retaining an advisory board of external experts. Dow Chemical Company has had an Environmental Advisory Council in place since 1996. The council includes former government officials, leading NGO representatives, environmental researchers and academics, as well as community leaders. The group has two main purposes. First, the council serves as a feedback mechanism for Dow's own environmental initiatives. By providing in effect a "peer review," the company gets honest reactions and guidance to its planned sustainability efforts. Second, the council serves to provide Dow with a look at upcoming issues. With experts that represent a range of perspectives and political viewpoints, the company is able to use the council's debate as a way to clarify critical emerging issues and determine which concerns will become priorities.

HOW TO WORK EFFECTIVELY WITH YOUR PARTNER

Sign a written agreement defining goals and ground rules. To clarify expectations of both parties, be explicit about what you want to accomplish. Understand that your goals can be set as a "test run" if you are considering a more developed partnership in the future.

Lay out a timeline. Create a detailed project timeline for both parties to coordinate working paces.

Establish a baseline. A baseline will help you benchmark environmental and business progress. Include initial and projected future revenues and costs in your baseline. Conduct this and future business analyses concurrently with environmental analyses. Doing so will make it easier to identify the most cost effective ways to enhance environmental performance.

Maintain your independence. Do not establish a partnership that compromises your broader stances. Additionally, you must convince your stakeholders of your integrity. Sustain public transparency of financial support (including funding arrangements with your partner), the decision-making process, and results.

Set up a team. Establish a *cross-functional* team from different branches of your organization. Some areas could include: operations, marketing, engineering, purchasing, legal, public relations, and government relations. A cross-functional team will tap the strength of all areas within your partnership and make it easier to bring in new people.

Run your team. Make sure your team members are ready and excited to promote the project internally. Have a lead person oversee the implementation and completion of specific tasks to reach your goals.

Coordinate effectively. Plan routine meetings with your partner. Be flexible: reevaluate the project goals and timeline if milestones are not met. It is often best to start off with picking low-hanging fruit. Early, measurable victories add momentum and generate enthusiasm, making future coordination smoother.

Share your success. Make sure you establish your right to disseminate information in your initial agreement. To make your project replicable among others groups, consider sharing information, tools, and methodologies. Before marketing your project, however, make sure results have already been achieved to avoid being labeled as a "greenwasher."

Source: GEMI and EDF "Guide to Successful Corporate-NGO Partnerships" GEMI, 2008. www.gemi.org (accessed August 6, 2010).

Outreach resources, especially time from top executives, will always be limited, but the greater a company's commitment to engage critical stakeholders, the better it is likely to fare in the marketplace. Business results today are not just a function of delivering a superior product at a competitive price. Success also depends on managing societal expectations and mastering the policy domain, both of which shape the business landscape and define the opportunities available. Next, we identify a variety of tools and strategies to make this sort of concerted and sustained outreach possible.

10. Create Value Chain Partnerships

In 2008, Walmart convened a group of experts to determine how the corporation could advance its sustainability agenda. Recognizing that much of the Walmart footprint arises "upstream" in its supply chain, the company and its advisors settled on the idea of quantifying product sustainability and establishing a sustainability "best practices" database. Developing such a benchmarking tool, especially on a global scale, was not easy. To tackle this colossal challenge, the group recommended that Walmart create a consortium of companies, NGOs, and academic thought leaders to develop a multidisciplinary approach based on product life cycle analysis.[14] Walmart's Sustainability Consortium now includes big names like Waste Management, Disney, Kellogg's, Best Buy, and even the EPA. Arizona State University and the University of Arkansas administer the project, which has made substantial progress toward a standardized product scorecard.[15]

Others have come to the same conclusion that managing their sustainability issues requires an effort across their value chain. Unilever learned from a careful environmental footprint analysis that the vast majority of the environmental impacts of its products arose upstream with the agricultural practices of the farmers who supply ingredients in the food the company sells—or downstream with the consumers who use their personal care products. As a result, the company has launched a series of sustainability projects up and down its value chain. As early as the 1990s, Unilever brought a sustainable agriculture initiative to its thousands of farmers. Unilever's leadership has generated other breakthroughs such as the Marine Stewardship Council, which brings together fishermen, environmental leaders, and the companies that sell fish to establish standards for sustainable fisheries.

More recently, Unilever has taken the same approach to addressing the challenge of palm oil. Palm oil's production was expanding at the cost of increased deforestation, particularly in Southeast Asia. Based on prior experience, Unilever knew that to undertake a major commitment to sustainability on its own would subject the company to cost burdens that their competitors might not face. As a result, Unilever launched the Roundtable on Sustainable Palm Oil (RSPO), an NGO that brings together palm oil producers, processors, traders, consumer goods manufacturers, retailers, bankers, and investors to develop and implement global standards for sustainable palm oil. The RSPO has allowed Unilever to maintain its commitment to sustainability without facing significant competitive disadvantages. Unilever has now committed to purchase only sustainably produced palm oil in all of its products from margarine to cooking oils.[16] Going above and beyond legal requirements to create multistakeholder organizations and develop standards and procedures to promote sustainability represents the cutting edge of partnerships.

MAKING PARTNERSHIPS WORK

Rosabeth Kanter of the Harvard Business School has developed a set of guidelines for companies seeking to build alliances. She identifies the "Eight I's That Make We"—principles to build successful business alliances (and she says they also work for marriages):

- **Individual excellence:** Both parties must have strengths on their own because weak players cannot prop each other up.
- **Importance:** The relationship must have strategic significance. If it is just casual, don't bother.
- **Interdependence:** The strongest and most enduring alliances occur when the parties are different in some respects and need each other to carry out an activity they would not otherwise do.
- **Investment:** One sign of commitment is a willingness to invest something in the partner's success, such as equities or personnel swaps (business "hostages for peace").
- **Information:** Transparency aids relationship formation. If you don't want a partner to know too much about you, why are you in the alliance?
- **Integration:** There must be many points of contact that tie the organizations together in joint activities.
- **Institutionalization:** A formal structure and governing board ensures objectivity, and that the alliance's interests are considered, not just each company's interests.
- **Integrity:** Trust is essential. Alliances fall apart in conflict and lawsuits when partners do not act ethically toward one another or strive to contribute to each other's success.

Source: Rosabeth Kanter, "15 Steps for Successful Strategic Alliances (and Marriages)." *Harvard Business Review* Blogs, http://blogs.hbr.org/kanter (accessed August 09, 2010); and Rosabeth Moss Kanter, *World Class: Thriving Locally in the Global Economy* (1995).

Other companies have targeted the suppliers of their products' critical inputs for special attention. Starbucks, most notably, launched a program designed to support coffee farmers who sell to Starbucks. The company partnered with

Conservation International to develop ethical buying guidelines and works with wholesalers to ensure that farmers are paid fairly. Starbucks established Farm Support Centers in Costa Rica and Rwanda to provide coffee farmers with resources and expertise to implement sustainability and quality improvement practices. Starbucks also provides funding to organizations that make loans to coffee growers that enable them to invest in their farms and make capital improvements.[17]

11. Create Policy Coalitions

In some cases, companies find that it makes sense not just to work with others in their industry but rather with a broad range of companies. Perhaps the best example of recent activities in this regard is the U.S. Climate Action Partnership (USCAP). Tired of waiting for the federal government to pass climate change legislation, dozens of major corporations in partnership with major environmental NGOs decided to work together to move climate change policy forward in the United States. Much of the climate legislation that has been under debate in the United States came out of the background work done by USCAP members. Members of the USCAP include companies such as Chrysler, Duke Energy, Honeywell, Johnson & Johnson, Shell, and NGOs such as NRDC, World Resources Institute, The Nature Conservancy, Environmental Defense Fund, and the Pew Center on Global Climate Change. There have been strains within the coalition, and a number of members have now withdrawn, but no one can deny the policy impact of this group.

SUMMARY

Key Plays

1. Open a dialogue.
2. Support a cause.
3. Join an environmental corporate social responsibility organization.
4. Conduct community outreach.
5. Identify and evaluate potential partners.
6. Reach out to potential partners.
7. Build a bridge to the government.
8. Explore "co-opetition" through industry partnerships.
9. Form a sustainability advisory board.
10. Create value chain partnerships.
11. Join policy coalitions.

ADDITIONAL RESOURCES

GENERAL

"Stakeholder Engagement: A Good Practice Handbook for Companies Doing Business in Emerging Markets" (International Finance Corporation, 2008). www.ifc.org

"Ceres Roadmap for Sustainability" (Ceres). Outlines 20 sustainability criteria Ceres believes companies must meet to stay competitive in the twenty-first century, with special attention to stakeholder engagement. www.ceres.org

AA1000 Stakeholder Engagement Standard. A standard developed by the non-profit organization AccountAbility to help organizations "ensure stakeholder engagement processes are purpose driven, robust and deliver results." www.accountability.org

ISO 26000. A new international standard developed by the International Organization for Standardization covering corporate social responsibility and stakeholder involvement. www.iso.org

CORPORATE-NGO PARTNERSHIPS

"Guide to Successful Corporate-NGO Partnerships" (Global Environmental Management Initiative and Environmental Defense Fund). www.gemi.org

KEY NONPROFITS FOCUSED ON BUSINESS AND ENVIRONMENT

See Additional Resources in other chapters for other key nonprofits specializing in particular issues such as climate change.

Business for Social Responsibility (BSR). Through consulting, research, and cross-sector collaboration, BSR works to improve corporate social responsibility globally. www.bsr.org

Ceres. Network of investors, environmental organizations, and public interest groups aiming to integrate sustainability into capital markets. www.ceres.org

Center for Environmental Leadership in Business (Conservation International). CI works strategically with businesses to achieve investments that improve ecological footprints, discover conservation opportunities, and develop communications campaigns to engage consumers and employees. www.conservation.org/sites/celb

EarthShare. Helps businesses establish workplace-giving programs to support environmental charities. www.earthshare.org

The Nature Conservancy's International Leadership Council: Corporate Forum. Devoted to cross-industry networking, benchmarking, and best-practice sharing to generate conservation results. www.nature.org

Corporate Partnerships Program and "Innovation Exchange" (Environmental Defense Fund). Partners with business to find practical solutions to environmental problems. Hosts an online "Innovation Exchange" featuring practical tools to improve the health of business and the planet. www.innovation.edf.org

Rainforest Alliance. Works with corporations to improve global environmental conditions, with special attention to sustainable farming, forestry, and tourism. www.rainforest-alliance.org

Rocky Mountain Institute. Self-described "think and do tank" that helps companies achieve new heights in energy efficiency, green transportation, buildings, and clean energy. www.rmi.org

World Business Council on Sustainable Development (WBCSD). Global association of over 200 companies dedicated to promoting sustainable solutions.

Part Six **Optimize: Evaluate, Report, and Reassess**

Chapter 22 Communicate and Report Results

Sidney Falken, SVP at Hanesbrands, got a call in early 2009 from Rich Noll, her CEO. Noll told Falken that it was time for the company to start telling its sustainability story better. Hanesbrands, a trusted name in the apparel industry since 1901, had quietly pursued a number of green initiatives over the previous several years. And while the company has a notable environmental leader, Jessica Mathews, President of the Carnegie Endowment, on its board, the Hanesbrands management had launched its sustainability agenda because it felt it was the right thing to do and a smart way to control costs. Noll also knew that his customers increasingly wanted more information about how Hanesbrands made underwear.

Falken hung up the phone and moved to follow through on her boss's request. She assembled a team that included not just communications experts, but also the manufacturing and supply chain folks who were doing the heavy lifting every day to deliver on the company's eco-commitments. Together, their team built a strategy that stands as a model for doing sustainability communications right. And the recognition has begun to pour in. In 2010, Hanesbrands won the prestigious EPA Energy Star Partner of the Year Award for the company's advances in energy efficiency across all aspects of the business.

Hanesbrands also launched a "Future Generations" environmental marketing campaign, which included eye-catching TV spots, outdoor billboards, an Earth Day consumer promotion, and editorial space in their catalogs. These outreach efforts attracted 90,000 unique visitors to a new consumer-oriented green website (hanesgreen.com), which highlights key facts about the company's sustainability goals and achievements in an engaging and consumer-friendly manner. The communications strategy has helped to reposition Hanesbrands in the eyes of the public—but it has done much more. According to Falken, potential employees are coming to Hanes because they are impressed by what they've learned. And B2B customers have called to explore possible partnerships, saying simply, "we want to do something with you guys."[1]

When companies have a genuinely good story to tell about green efforts, they ought to tell it—both to the world outside their companies' walls and to all the employees within them. The best internal and external communications and reporting strategies help:

- Make employees feel even better about the company they work for—strengthening workforce motivation as well as recruitment and retention.
- Give employees a common language with which to discuss the company's sustainability agenda.
- Strengthen internal support for sustainability objectives and ensure that all employees know what they can do to help achieve the established goals.
- Generate information that helps managers and employees better execute against sustainability goals, including making better daily decisions.
- Reveal sustainability risks and opportunities.
- Facilitate benchmarking and comparative analysis—not only between companies but also internally between facilities and factories, which spotlights best practices.
- Disseminate lessons learned from successes and failures, enabling people to build on what works and avoid repeating mistakes.
- Boost company brands and reputations in the marketplace by demonstrating attentiveness to material risks and showing progress on reducing eco-impacts.
- Improve company reputations in the eyes of regulators.

As we've stressed throughout this *Playbook*, all groups are holding companies to ever-higher standards when it comes to reporting on their eco-performance. Investors, regulators, customers, and watchdog groups are applying more and more pressure on companies to publish data on their environmental impacts and liabilities as well as their efforts to reduce their eco-footprints. Perhaps the most insistent demands come from the marketplace. Walmart led the way with supplier sustainability scorecards, but many companies now insist that their suppliers provide them with environmental performance data and assurances that upstream activities will not create environmental exposure that could come back to bite a consumer-facing brand.

Mandatory reporting rules are also on the rise. The U.S. Securities and Exchange Commission (SEC) has introduced new environmental disclosure requirements for all public companies. Large corporations operating in Europe must report on their greenhouse gas emissions as part of the EU's Emissions Trading System. The U.S. Environmental Protection Agency has also issued greenhouse gas reporting regulations for large emitters.

When it comes to eco-reporting, there is little room for error. The facts and figures must be right both for legal reasons and to avoid serious market backlash. And how companies talk about their sustainability agendas has a growing impact on their corporate reputations *and* the attitudes of regulators, NGOs, and consumers.

But figuring out *how* to do effective eco-reporting and communications requires a lot more than ticking a series of boxes on a checklist. The patchwork of expectations and demands has created a situation that can easily overwhelm companies trying to do the right thing. This chapter sheds light on how best to address the conflicting pressures and requirements. It provides a framework that will help you:

- Identify best practices for good internal and external reporting.
- Build an appropriate system to collect and analyze the data you need.
- Generate effective communications and reporting.
- Maximize your chances for a positive market response to the information you release.

BASIC PLAYS: PRIORITIZE INFORMATION NEEDS

1. Build Communications on the Same Data That Drives Strategy Execution

Corporate sustainability data collection and reporting should be designed to meet both management and communications needs. The key to good sustainability communications is to have a good substantive story to tell. Often the data and information required to drive effective execution of an eco-strategy is exactly what key stakeholders want to see as well. In practice, companies must be strategic and disciplined—not tactical or reactive—when making choices about what metrics to track, how to analyze performance data, and what to report to whom. Above all, communications and reporting, consistent with sustainability strategy more generally, should focus on top priorities, expanding over time to include a broader set of metrics.

First, as we stressed in Chapter 18 ("Create an Action Plan—and Execute"), you must construct a data collection and evaluation system that meets your company's *internal* information needs for effective management and execution of your stated sustainability goals. This exercise must build, of course, on systematic identification of your company's eco-issues, stakeholder priorities, marketplace trends, and the prioritization of those elements with the greatest potential for business impact (as spelled out in Chapter 5). The precise issues and impacts to track will vary from company to company but should be driven by the strategy agenda.

2. Clarify What Information External Stakeholders Care About

As we noted in Chapter 3's Top 10 Action Items, it is no longer best practice to simply put out an environmental or sustainability report that features the information *you* want to communicate. Companies must respond to a variety of stakeholders including customers, regulators, community leaders, and capital markets. The requests for information flowing in from various directions seem to be multiplying beyond control—not to mention being duplicative and inconsistent in their methodologies and requirements. Who should you pay attention to? Regulators and mandatory reporting requirements must get top priority. Most companies put some effort into sustainability information requests from stock market analysts such as Innovest and KLD (now both part of Risk Metrics, which has been subsumed by MSCI), Sustainable Asset Management, and Trucost. Failing to be responsive to these inquiries can lead to bad ratings. Additionally, few companies think it wise to stiff their customers' requests for environmental performance data.

Who else gets a share of the limited time and effort that can go into reporting? Beyond deciding whose surveys to fill out, there is still the question about what data to collect. Some core categories—green house gas emissions, other air emissions, water pollution and use, and waste—are common to most requests. But some reporting frameworks go much further. For instance, early versions of the Global Reporting Initiative (GRI) asked for pages and pages of information but did nothing to tailor the request to the nature of the company filling out the form or its industry. In the face of such exhaustive requests, many companies simply gave up trying to gather all the information and declined to follow the GRI model. The most recent GRI templates, as we discuss next in this chapter, offer a much more tightly focused structure for sustainability reporting—and may, in fact, be a useful way to get a picture of the issues that your company should consider.

In the end, you won't be able to respond to all of the requests or please all of your stakeholders all of the time. But there's no getting around the fact that companies need to up their game when preparing communications and reporting for external audiences. Here's our framework for deciding what is most important to include in a sustainability data system—and ultimately to put into environment or sustainability reports.

GET CLEAR ON INDUSTRY NORMS

If you haven't already done this sort of benchmarking (as recommended in Chapter 7), it makes sense to figure out what information your industry peers are reporting. Their websites and sustainability reports will provide everything you need to know about larger companies. For small businesses, industry associations and government resources may provide the best starting point.

REVIEW ESTABLISHED TEMPLATES LIKE THE GLOBAL REPORTING
INITIATIVE GUIDELINES

Years of consultation with diverse stakeholders built the Global Reporting Initiative (GRI) Guidelines for sustainability reporting (see Additional Resources at the end of the chapter). Because of its extensive consultative process, the GRI has become the most commonly accepted global sustainability reporting framework. Many companies, however, find the Guidelines impractical because they can lead to reporting that covers too much ground. So view the GRI Guidelines as a "menu" from which you select key items relevant for your company and industry. GRI also offers specialized reporting guidance and recommended indicators for a growing set of specific industry sectors.[2] When it comes to preparing an environment or sustainability report, the prevailing best practice is to report on the issues in a way that makes sense within your company's own context and then add an appendix to the report that explains how you addressed the GRI issue checklist.

Other entities, such as the Global Environmental Management Institute (GEMI) and the World Business Council for Sustainable Development (WBCSD) have also produced useful issues lists to track metrics that companies need to develop.

CONSULT WITH STAKEHOLDERS

As we discuss in Chapters 5 and 21, reaching out to key stakeholders to understand their priority concerns and expectations has great value. To be blunt, no company can set its own reporting agenda in isolation. Stakeholder expectations cannot be ignored. Listen carefully and distill from your company's stakeholder consultations a list of items that your company will report, not because they matter to the company itself but because the world in which your company operates prioritizes them. Of course, it makes no sense to report on every stakeholder's pet concern. Sometimes you can ignore issues with limited backing. In other cases, a one-on-one conversation with the interested party will suffice.

BE FAMILIAR WITH INDUSTRY GUIDELINES AND HIGH-PROFILE SCORECARDS

Many groups have created specialized guidance and tools to help standardize reporting within particular sectors on certain hot-button issues like climate change. The American Chemistry Council's Responsible Care Initiative, for instance, provides reporting and stakeholder engagement guidance for chemical companies. Various other industries—including cement, financial services, mining, and electronics recycling—have also developed industry-based reporting standards. Small and mid-sized businesses, in particular, will find that industry norms are their best guide to reporting.

In some instances, NGO-based sustainability guidelines or standards have gotten enough market traction that they must be seen as an important baseline for corporate reporting. The Forest Stewardship Council (www.fsc.org) and the Marine Stewardship Council (www.msc.org) offer two such examples. And, as noted in Chapter 19, "Build Your Climate Change Plan," the Carbon Disclosure Project (CDP) offers a widely accepted framework for reporting carbon emissions (www.cdproject.net) and has now launched a Global Water Disclosure Project that is likely to become an established reporting standard. Likewise, the scorecard developed by Climate Counts (www.climatecounts.org), a New Hampshire-based NGO that rates companies based on their commitment to address climate change, has gotten a good deal of publicity and provides another important list of reporting criteria for companies.

INTERMEDIATE PLAYS: REPORT ON RESULTS

3. Communicate Results to External Audiences

Companies must undertake external communications and reporting with considerable care because the stories told and promises made represent the company's public face to the world. In particular, remember that published internal sustainability goals go from targets to obligations. There are a growing number of self-appointed watchdog groups (and individuals) tracking corporate environmental and social performance and issuing their commentaries, scorecards, and blog critiques of what they find.

For most businesses operating in our Internet era, the outside world's picture of the business comes largely from your corporate website. Some companies still find it useful to publish an environment or sustainability report. We believe, however, that the "best practice" today is to have a sustainability or environment "button" on the website providing access to a regularly updated set of metrics, stories, and explanations of the company's vision and plans.

Your company has many options about when and how to report—and what to communicate about environmental or sustainability strategy. Next, we provide our sense of the best practices when it comes to external reporting and communications.

PRIORITIZE WEB-BASED REPORTING

Your corporate website needs to be your number one sustainability communications tool. Some companies still put together comprehensive annual environment or sustainability reports. Others publish sustainability results as part of their annual reports. But the paper consumed by these documents is at odds with the spirit of reduced environmental impact. We suggest assembling a sustainability report, but "publishing" it online. In some cases, printing a few hundred hard copies to hand out to office visitors or others who want the old-fashioned document may make sense.

We prefer the virtual report not only for its lighter footprint, but also because you can update it whenever new data become available. The best websites, we might add, work hard to be user friendly. They provide relevant and accurate information—and provide easy ways for people with specific interests to click on key topics and drill down to more detailed information.

People will scrutinize *everything* on a corporate website, so the importance of accuracy and completeness cannot be overstated. Triple check any sustainability information. Any claims that might be disputed should include justifications or citations.

Authenticity is a virtue of rapidly growing importance. Thus, attention must be paid to the image and tone of company websites. Priorities must be clear. Pictures or images need to align with the sustainability "story" that you are telling. And the alignment of the environmental and social agenda with the company's broader business strategy and positioning should be obvious to all who visit your site.

SHARE THE GOOD, THE BAD, AND THE UGLY

As we have stressed, sharing both good and bad news is fundamental to credibility. Trying to hide missed targets or subpar performance doesn't wash in our transparent world. Even problems in the most distant facility on the other side of the world will eventually leak out. So it is far better for the company to tell the story first.

The key to communications success in the face of a problem is openness and honesty—and a willingness to take responsibility. Johnson & Johnson's swift handling of its 1982 Tylenol incident remains the gold standard for how to respond to a crisis and keep a corporate reputation intact. In contrast, BP's perceived dissembling about how much oil spilled in the course of the 2010 Gulf of Mexico disaster and attempts to shift responsibility to its drilling partners severely hurt the company. James Donnelly, senior vice president for crisis management at public relations firm Ketchum, notes that we never hear about companies that handle crises well. "There's not a lot of news when the company takes responsibility and moves on," he says. "The good crisis-management examples rarely end waving the flag of victory. They end with a whisper, and it's over in a day or two.[3]

PUT FORWARD TARGETS—WITH CARE

Publishing your company's sustainability performance metrics is no longer sufficient. Key stakeholders also want a sense of a company's plans to address critical impacts. This interest puts pressure on companies to report their goals and targets for the future. Of course, once made public, a goal is really no longer voluntary. NGOs and other critics will come down hard on companies that fall short of their targets. Nevertheless, companies that explain shortcomings with candor and honesty will have an advantage as opposed to those that either hide bad results or don't put forward targets at all.

SPECIALIZE COMMUNICATIONS FOR PARTICULAR AUDIENCES

Put some effort into tailoring reports for specific audiences. Some companies prepare reports on each of their lines of business. Other companies find it useful to prepare sustainability reports for each country in which they operate. Yet others do detailed reports on each facility as part of their outreach to the communities in which they operate. Your intended audience should help determine the level of generality of a report. While NGOs will want to see lots of data and detail, reports going to busy politicians probably need to be in summary style. Figure 22.1 offers a structure for assessing the various types of communications and their functions.

Figure 22.1   Think About What Is Right for Your Business

Function	Types of Communications
Sales and marketing communications	• Advertisements, company brochures and other sales material may include messages on CR performance, position statements on specific issues or CR policies • Product information may include performance data relating to social or environmental attributes of the product (e.g. CO_2 emissions from product use)
Corporate communications	• Annual reports and accounts may include CR performance data. Some companies go a step further and fully integrate their CR reporting into these reports • Public relations may issue position statements or respond to particular issues or events with CR performance data or company views
Procurement	• Supplier communications may include details of the companies performance indicating their aspirations for future product specifications
Public affairs	• Lobbying with Regional, National and International Government agencies may involve disclosure of CR performance (e.g. demonstrating performance beyond compliance to shape future regulations) • Responding to concerns or issues raised by Government(s)
Human resources	• CR reporting may be used to enhance perception amongst potential recruits. For example, recruitment material and events may include information on the companies' position on specific issues to build empathy with prospective candidates
Investor relations	• Responding to questionnaires and surveys received from investors or their representatives • Responding to CR issues raised at AGMs or Investor relations meetings

Source: Arthur D. Little, et al., "Director's Guide to CR Reporting," www.bitc.org.uk/document. Reprinted with permission.

USE CLEAR METHODOLOGY AND CRITERIA

Companies need to be clear on what reporting methodologies they are following—including their choice of a baseline year for trend data, how data has been normalized to ensure appropriate comparisons can be made, and whether numbers are absolute or intensity based. Specify the assumptions on which your company's analyses depend. On topics where law determines reporting requirements or established methodologies have taken root, self-defined metrics based on idiosyncratic methodologies will not be acceptable. Thus, for example, companies reporting on their greenhouse gas emissions need to follow the protocol established by the World Business Council for Sustainable Development and the World Resources Institute.

PUT DATA INTO MEANINGFUL CONTEXTS

Information means little when companies offer it without the necessary context. A statement such as, "We recycled 564 tons of paper last year" means nothing to readers without a basis for comparison. Companies must put numbers into meaningful context such as, "We recycled 564 tons of paper last year, which reduced our solid waste stream 10 percent by weight." For nonexpert audiences, it's important to go a step further by eliminating jargon and translating numbers into something people can relate to. For instance, instead of talking about tons of CO_2 avoided, give readers a sense of context by putting the reduction in terms of "cars taken off the road."

LINK TO FINANCIAL REPORTING

There is growing marketplace interest in the link between sustainability results and financial performance. In response, some companies have begun to align their sustainability reporting with their financial reporting. SAP's environmental team deliberately timed the release of their 2009 sustainability results to coincide with the announcement of the company's financial results, according to the company's Executive Director for Sustainability, Energy & Carbon Impact Jim Davis. Moreover, they monetized the value of their sustainability activities and came up with an estimated € 90 million contribution to the company's reported earnings. This link grabbed the attention of several investors.

To facilitate the link from sustainability to financial performance, Prince Charles has pioneered an approach called "Connected Reporting" that provides guidance for connecting financial and nonfinancial information (see Additional Resources). We see the relationship between sustainability and financial results as an area of growing interest because more companies want to demonstrate that their investments in Eco-Advantage are delivering superior performance, and they would like for that performance to be recognized with an eco-premium in the stock market.

DO NOT GREENWASH

As we discussed at length in Chapter 15 "Marketing and Sales," companies that stretch the truth about their sustainability performance in general or the environmental attributes of their products in particular expose themselves to considerable peril. Credibility is hard to establish and easy to destroy. Consumer loyalty depends on trust—and should never be put in jeopardy.

GET EXTERNAL VALIDATION

As mentioned earlier in the *Playbook*, getting third-party validation of reported results or environmental attributes of a specific product from reputable sources can boost a company's credibility. However, many companies cannot justify the cost of getting such validation (which can be considerable). Big companies may be able to spread the expense widely enough to make such validation worthwhile. Most small and even mid-sized companies will not find a sufficient payoff from external certification to justify the cost, except in unusual circumstances.

Some companies only pay to validate a subset of their data—say, for carbon emissions in sectors where climate change scrutiny is particularly intense. Others have found that getting a well-regarded NGO leader to comment on the company's performance or an environmental group to give its stamp of approval to a product is more meaningful than a letter from a major accounting firm. Thus, Shell uses an external review committee with notables from around the world, such as David Runnalls of the International Institute for Sustainable Development in Canada, to lend credibility to its reports. And Clorox got special validation for its Green Works line of products through an endorsement from the Sierra Club.

SOLICIT FEEDBACK

Whether through surveys, comment boxes on a website, or other means, ask audiences: What did you find useful? What wasn't? What was missing? The responses will help you sharpen your strategy. Consider publishing critiques online as a way to build your company's reputation for seriousness about its sustainability agenda—and authenticity about your company's commitment. Shell's invitation to sustainability report readers to "Tell Shell" what they thought about the information presented and about Shell's efforts more generally offers a best practice for other companies to examine.

4. Connect with the Internal Audience on Their Terms

Don't expect your employees to read long annual sustainability reports. Not a single company we've worked with relies on these reports to communicate internally. Instead, find creative ways to keep employees abreast of your company's environmental and social initiatives and results. Whether this takes the form of newsletters, three-page foldouts, online web resources, or "blast" emails, companies have much to gain by disseminating sustainability information so that everyone in the enterprise can be part of the program.

In companies where employees perform work on the factory floor, in vehicles, or otherwise away from computers, it is a mistake to rely on online communications tools alone. Find creative ways (including talking to people in person) to get your word out. Duke Energy, which has a long tradition of holding "safety moments," recently decided to adopt a "sustainability moment" across its organization, giving managers and employees opportunities to highlight both corporate-wide information and to share locally relevant news. As with external audiences, invite feedback from employees to find out which types of information and communications modes they value. See Chapter 20 "Mobilize Employees and Build an Eco-Advantage Culture" for additional ideas and recommendations.

ADVANCED PLAYS: FORGE NEW GROUND

5. Create a Dialogue

You should gear all sustainability communications to create a dialogue. Your goal should be to engage both internal and external audiences in a sufficiently robust way that they feel connected to the company and "authorized" to come back with suggestions, comments, and criticism—even when they have not been specifically asked. The key to success is to create a relationship with key stakeholders. Employees are a critical target audience because you can dramatically enhance their commitment to the company's sustainability efforts if you make them feel personally connected to the agenda. But try as well to build sustained links with key external stakeholders—even groups and individuals who seem hostile. Remember that it will be much harder for them to level stinging criticisms against your company if they have a connection and ongoing relationship with you.

6. Advance Best Practices as a Market Differentiator

Leading companies help advance best practices in sustainability communications and reporting—some by pioneering new approaches and others by joining collaborative efforts to raise the overall quality of reporting within a defined sector or on a particular issue. While these efforts take resources and create risk by putting your company out in front of the market, sustainability leaders know that their company's image depends in part on being willing to run ahead of the pack.

Timberland, for instance, has begun to provide product-specific information on the environmental impacts of its hiking boots and other products with an eco-label that breaks new ground in providing consumer information. Similarly, Patagonia has launched an interactive website called the "Footprint Chronicles," which allows users to trace the impacts associated with Patagonia products from design to delivery and learn how the company is working to reduce its impacts across its value chain.

Green cleaning product leader Seventh Generation is practicing (and advocating) what CEO Jeffrey Hollender calls "radical transparency." As Hollender explains: "Publicly sharing all our activities preempts our critics, and more eyes on our behavior means more advocates and friends. Radical transparency also creates new partnerships and in this way becomes the first step towards overcoming the deficiencies that ultimately harm our profitability."[4] There are endless leadership opportunities to explore in sustainability communications, *and* those efforts that connect with consumers and other key stakeholders offer the promise of Eco-Advantage in the marketplace.

SUMMARY

Key Plays

1. Build communications on the same data that drives strategy execution.
2. Clarify what information external stakeholders care about.
3. Communicate results to external audiences.
4. Connect with the internal audience on their terms.
5. Create a dialogue.
6. Advance best practices as a market differentiator.

ADDITIONAL RESOURCES

REPORTING AND COMMUNICATIONS STRATEGY

"From Transparency to Performance: Industry-Based Sustainability Reporting on Key Issues" (Steve Lydenberg, Jean Rogers, and David Wood—Hauser Center and Initiative for Responsible Investment, 2010). Outlines a materiality-based approach to corporate reporting, with recommendations for choosing key performance indicators on sustainability impacts of US corporations in specific industries. www.hausercenter.org

Global Reporting Initiative (GRI). The GRI's mission is to "create conditions for the transparent and reliable exchange of sustainability information" and issues guidelines for sustainability reporting along with lists of sustainability indicators—environmental, social, and economic. www.globalreporting.org

GRI Guidelines for Small and Medium Enterprise. Features reporting examples from small and medium-sized businesses. www.globalreporting.org

"**Connected Reporting: A Practical Guide with Worked Examples**" (Accounting for Sustainability). How to implement "connected reporting"—an approach designed to produce a more balanced and comprehensive picture of an organization's overall performance to satisfy the long-term needs of investors and executive management.
www.connectedreporting.accountingforsustainability.org/

"**Communicating Corporate Responsibility**" (Ogilvy). Practical recommendations for communicating corporate social responsibility. www.ogilvypr.com

International Integrated Reporting Committee (IIRC). A collaborative effort of the Prince's Accounting for Sustainability Project and the GRI to standardize corporate reporting internationally. Aims to create a globally accepted framework that "provides an integrated picture of an organization and the impact of environmental and social factors on its performance."
www.integratedreporting.org

Corporate Register. UK-based clearinghouse site with extensive library of corporate responsibility reports. www.corporateregister.com

ISSUE-SPECIFIC RESOURCES

The Greenhouse Gas Protocol (GHG) Initiative (WRI and WBCSD). The most widely used standard for accounting and reporting greenhouse gas emissions. www.ghgprotocol.org

Carbon Disclosure Project (CDP). Nonprofit effort that collects data on corporate carbon and greenhouse gas emissions and climate change strategies. Top scorers demonstrate strong internal data management systems and a good understanding of the risks and opportunities climate change poses to their business. www.cdproject.net/

Water Disclosure Project. A CDP effort that collects increasingly important data from companies on their water consumption, means of conservation, and reporting initiatives. www.cdproject.net/

Forest Footprint Disclosure Project. A UK government initiative modeled after the CDP to help companies monitor and report their impacts on the world's forests. www.forestdisclosure.com

See also Additional Resources at the end of Chapter 6, "Assess and Measure Your Environmental Impacts."

Chapter 23 Celebrate Success and Promote Continuous Improvement

Sustainability should not be seen as an endpoint. In fact, no company that we have studied is anywhere close to being fully sustainable. Nor is any country. As we have stressed, sustainability is better understood as a journey. As a society, we need to find ways to reduce the harm our activities cause to the planet and to consume natural resources only as fast as they can be renewed. Businesses of all sizes and shapes have a role to play in this quest. Indeed, long-term economic success—call it *sustainable* prosperity—depends on better managing the natural capital on which all life and all commerce depends.

As a practical matter, companies moving toward products and practices that are more sustainable will need to constantly reassess their strategies and refine their game plans. We hope that companies will work their way through this entire book and fold a focus on sustainability into each and every aspect of their operations. Any business that completes this process should go back to the beginning of the book and start over—stepping up its efforts to the next level. The push to make a business more sustainable never ends.

In fact, what people mean by sustainability constantly evolves. As a result, societal expectations about pollution control, natural resource management, and other aspects of sustainability are also constantly changing. As the old football metaphor goes, the goalposts are continually being moved. What might have counted as sustainable leadership last year is almost certainly not going to be seen as cutting-edge next year. Only companies that make sustainability a priority and understand that they must continually improve their efforts to examine all aspects of their business through a sustainability lens will stay at the forefront of the rising expectations that define this realm.

Multiple drivers of change must be tracked. New harms will emerge. For example, just as we were all being told to move away from disposable plastic drink bottles and use refillable plastic bottles, concerns emerged about phthalates, a family of chemicals (esters of phthalic acid) used to improve the flexibility, durability, and clarity of plastic. It now appears that these "plasticizers" may be responsible for significant health risks including potential disruption of endocrine production and other hormone levels. As a result, aluminum and glass reusable bottles have become popular substitutes.

New scientific discoveries that change our assumptions about the best environmental path forward are a near certainty. We have seen the same pattern unfold many times before. For example, the 1990 Clean Air Act promoted the use of MTBE (methyl tertiary butyl ether) as a way to oxygenate gasoline and improve air quality. But within a few years, the Environmental Protection Agency concluded that MTBE posed a threat to drinking water. By 1997, the EPA reversed direction and withdrew its endorsement of MTBE as a pathway to better air quality based on the substantial evidence that MTBE was leaking into the environment from various places where gasoline was being stored—and contaminating water supplies.

We are certain to see scientific advances in the coming years as new tools, particularly superpowered information management systems and other advanced computer-based technologies, reshape our view of the environmental landscape. Additional chemicals will be found harmful, resulting in demands for tougher regulatory standards, reformulated products, and changed production practices. Companies large and small will need to monitor these scientific advances to stay ahead of changing public expectations and policy requirements.

> **Technologies will also evolve in ways that redefine the environmental baseline from which companies must operate—and compete.**

Examples abound. Until very recently, dry cleaners believed that clothes could not be adequately cleaned without chemical solvents, most typically perchloroethylene (often abbreviated "PERC"). Concerns about the potential carcinogenicity of PERC and other cleaning solvents have led to a dramatic shift in the technology of dry cleaning. Today, many cleaners advertise alternative methods of removing stains and cleaning clothes that do not involve the use of toxic chemicals. As Junior's Cleaners of Cheshire, Connecticut, promises, "Our nontoxic cleaning method provides safer and cleaner garments for our customers."[1] Junior isn't alone. All across the country, "environmentally friendly" cleaners are popping up. More broadly, "greener" versions of every sort of business can be found entering the marketplace.

The agenda will also change based on shifting stakeholder expectations. Government regulations will become more strict. In the United States, plans are moving forward to rewrite the Toxic Substances Control Act (TSCA). In Europe, the parallel Registration, Evaluation, Authorisation, and Restriction of Chemicals regulation (known as the REACH Directive) is already transforming how companies manage the chemicals in their products and production processes. The United States and Europe, and rapidly industrializing countries like China and India, have implemented higher standards for air quality. Many countries are adopting new rules on packaging, waste, food safety, and other issues.

Other stakeholders are also reshaping the environmental playing field. Nongovernmental organizations are becoming more numerous, diverse, and active. This means that companies have more tracking to do and an ever-broader set of NGO expectations to follow, if not meet. As we noted earlier, the pressure to achieve higher standards is also coming from employees, customers, insurance companies, and investors. With the growing emphasis on transparency and more focus on environmental performance metrics, the ability of these stakeholders to reward those companies that meet the sustainability challenge and punish those that do not is rapidly rising.

What is a corporate leader committed to sustainability to make of all this? The answer is simple. Understand sustainability for what it is—a *business megatrend*. As Dan Esty and David Lubin observed in their May 2010 *Harvard Business Review* article, "The Sustainability Imperative," business megatrends "force fundamental and persistent shifts in how companies compete."[2] We reiterate this conclusion: "Managers can no longer afford to ignore sustainability as a central factor in their company's long-term competitiveness." We are confident, however, that business leaders who deploy the ideas and frameworks in this book will be able to position themselves for success in the changing world that lies ahead. Of course, executives must continue to analyze, strategize, and mobilize their companies to deal with the emerging requirements of the sustainability imperative. But they can meet the challenge.

> **Success will require not only a clear vision of what needs to be done to establish an Eco-Advantage in the marketplace but also a carefully structured action plan. For many companies, *execution* of the sustainability strategy represents the next big challenge.**

Success requires not just clarity about the pollution control and natural resource management issues and trends that are reshaping the business world, but also hard-nosed analysis of how to manage these pressures in a way that yields competitive advantage. As we have stressed in the preceding chapters, companies that apply a sustainability lens to their business strategies will find ways to lessen environment-related risks; improve their eco-efficiency so that they can reduce their energy expenses and cut other costs; drive revenues through innovation tied to changing sustainability expectations; and build their corporate reputations, contributing in multiple ways to the intangible value of their companies.

Successful execution requires an elevated sustainability focus by top executives, new methods and models to bring this focus systematically into business planning and strategy, concerted efforts to align success incentives on the sustainability agenda with the core business strategy, new accountability and management commitment approaches to the sustainability goals, and more engaging communication and rigorous reporting about progress on the sustainability journey.

This process will not be easy. Not every environment or sustainability initiative will succeed. Progress will often be slower than top executives would like. Some companies will have to overhaul traditional strategies that have delivered great profitability in the past. Some top executives are already reaching for the opportunities that a sustainability-minded future presents. Dave Steiner, CEO of Waste Management, for example, has committed his company to a quite radical shift in its business model—moving away from being a company that collects garbage and dumps it in landfills to being one that truly "manages" a variety of waste streams. The challenge of transformation is particularly great in circumstances like Waste Management's because their existing lines of business remain highly profitable. But any time your customers want to see less of you and are seeking to minimize the amount of product or services they acquire from you, it is a signal that your company needs to rethink its strategy. As Steiner told us, "We can't stand still. We've got to re-gear our business as the markets we operate in evolve."

> **To be successful in meeting the demands of the sustainability imperative, companies must accept the complexity of the path forward and stay committed to a process of continuous improvement.**

Corporate executives should have high aspirations and audacious goals for transformative change over time. But they also need day-to-day and quarter-to-quarter operational targets for which they hold managers accountable, as well as a commitment to celebrating success along their sustainability journey. They will be committed to professionalizing the management of pollution control and natural resource management issues and a broader set of sustainability concerns. They will adapt along with society to meet changing expectations and realities that unfold as the implications of the sustainability megatrend become clearer.

We hope *The Green to Gold Business Playbook* provides some guideposts for this journey. In the spirit of continuous improvement, we invite you to share stories of your successes (and shortfalls) with us at *The Green to Gold Business Playbook* website: www.greentogoldplaybook.com. We are eager to hear what works and what doesn't as you bring a sustainability focus to your work and your life.

Notes

PART ONE. INTRODUCTION

CHAPTER 1. WHY EVERY BUSINESS NEEDS AN ECO-STRATEGY

1. General Electric, "Ecomagination." www.ecomagination.com (accessed August 4, 2010).

2. General Electric, "GEnx Aircraft Engine." www.ecomagination.com/technologies (accessed August 15, 2010).

3. General Electric, "Ecomagination Fact Sheet." www.ecomagination.com/about/fact-sheet (accessed August 15, 2010).

4. Curtis Packaging, *Curtis Packaging Sustainability Report 2007*. www.curtispackaging.com/CurtisSustainabilityReport.pdf (accessed August 15, 2010).

5. *Sky Canaves*, "Steep Fine for Mattel over Lead Paint in Chinese-Made Toys," *Wall Street Journal*, June 8, 2009. http://blogs.wsj.com/chinarealtime/2009/06/08/steep-fine-for-mattel-over-lead-paint-in-chinese-made-toys/ (accessed August 15, 2010).

6. Author Interview with Jeff Seabright, Vice President for Water and Environment, The Coca Cola Company (September 2010).

7. "Red Bull Runs Afoul of U.K. Recycling Laws," *GreenBiz*, July 21, 2009. http://greenbiz.com/news/2009/07/31/red-bull-runs-afoul-uk-recycling-laws (accessed August 15, 2010).

8. Adobe, "Adobe's Road to Platinum Video." www.adobe.com/corporateresponsibility (accessed August 15, 2010).

9. Bruce Buckbee, Managing Partner at Leisure Green Inc., phone interview, July 30, 2010.

10. Bruce Buckbee, Managing Partner at Leisure Green Inc., phone interview, July 30, 2010.

11. Maersk Line, "Constant Care for the Environment." www.maerskline.com/globalfile/?path=/pdf/environmental_brochure (accessed August 15, 2010).

12. U.S. Environmental Protection Agency, "3M Lean Six Sigma and Sustainability." www.epa.gov/lean/studies/3m.htm (accessed August 15, 2010).

13. Esther Durkalski Hertzfeld, "Cardpak Sustains Its Future Growth," *Packaging-Online*, August 1, 2008. www.packaging-online.com/paperboard-packaging-content/cardpak-sustains-its-future-growth (accessed August 15, 2010).

14. "Green Products Are the 'Sweet Spot' for Spending During Downtown: Report," *GreenBiz*, January 25, 2009. www.greenbiz.com/news/2009/01/25/green-products-are-sweet-spot-spending-during-downtown-report (accessed August 15, 2010).

15. Cohn & Wolfe, "Despite Global Economic Meltdown, Consumers Have Increased Appetite for Green," July 21, 2009. http://3blmedia.com/theCSRfeed/Despite-Global-Economic-Meltdown-Consumers-Have-Increased-Appetite-Green (accessed August 15, 2010).

16. Michael E. Porter, *The Competitive Advantage of Nations* (Free Press, 1985).

17. Michael E. Porter, "America's Green Strategy," *Scientific American* (April 1991); Michael E. Porter and Claas vander Linde, "Green and Competitive: Ending the Stalemate," *Harvard Business Review*, September 1, 1995.

18. Barbara Kessler, "Clorox Is Leading the Green Cleaning Charge," *ABC7.com Green Right Now,* June 11, 2009. www.greenrightnow.com/kabc/2009/06/11/ (accessed August 15, 2010).

19. AZcentral.com, "Clorox Takes Top Share of Natural Cleaners Market," January 11, 2009. www.azcentral.com/business/consumer/articles/2009/01/11/20090111clorox-ON. html?&wired (accessed August 15, 2010).

20. Straus Communications, "Public Relations and Marketing for Agriculture, Environment, and Community." www.strauscom.com/about_us.php?id=sp5d.inc (accessed August 15, 2010).

21. Starwood Hotels & Resorts, "Element Makes a Difference." www.starwoodhotels. com/element (accessed August 15, 2010).

22. Accenture, "A New Era of Sustainability," UN Global Compact-Accenture CEO study 2010. http://unglobalcompact.org/docs/news_events/8.1/UNGC_Accenture_CEO_Study_2010.pdf (accessed October 15, 2010).

23. Glenn Hasek, "2010 TourBooks Will Note Green Properties with 'Eco' Icon," *Green Lodging News,* July 7, 2010. www.greenlodgingnews.com/Content.aspx?id=3617 (accessed August 15, 2010).

24. Clean Air Lawn Care, "Leading Sustainable, Organic, Lawn Care Service." www. cleanairlawncare.com (accessed August 15, 2010).

25. Andrew L. Shapiro, "Coca Cola Goes Green" Forbes.com, January 29, 2010. www.forbes .com/2010/01/29/muhtar-kent-coca-cola-leadership-citizenship-sustainability.html (accessed December 21, 2010).

26. Robert Kaplan and David Norton, *The Balanced Scorecard* (Harvard Business Publishing, 1996).

27. Paula Oliveira and Andrea Sullivan, "Sustainability and Its Impact on Brand Value," *Environmental Leader,* September 28, 2008. www.environmentalleader.com/2008/09/28/ (accessed August 15, 2010).

28. Bob Willard, *The Sustainability Advantage: Seven Business Case Benefits of a Triple Bottom Line* (Gabriola Island, B.C.: New Society Publishers, 2002), p. 51.

29. New Belgium Brewing Company, "2007 Sustainability Report." www.newbelgium. com/sustainability (accessed August 4, 2010).

PART TWO. GEAR UP: WHAT LEADERS NEED TO KNOW

CHAPTER 3. BUILDING A WINNING ECO-ADVANTAGE STRATEGY: TOP 10 ACTION ITEMS

1. Author interview, October 2010.

2. This list draws on many actual company dialogues and Catherine Greener and Marc Major, "Top 10 Sustainability Myths in the Supplier Community," September 11, 2009, published on *GreenBiz.com* (accessed August 16, 2010).

3. David A. Lubin and Daniel C. Esty, "The Sustainability Imperative," *Harvard Business Review,* May 2010.

CHAPTER 4. MAKING THE INTERNAL BUSINESS CASE FOR GOING GREENER

1. Darcy Hitchcock and Marsha Willard. The Business Guide to Sustainability: Practical Strategies and Tools for Organizations (Earthscan, 2007), p. 217.

2. Greater Vancouver Regional District, Sustainable Supply Chain Logistics Guide, 2009, p. 39. www.metrovancouver.org/about/publications/Publications/sustainablesclguide final-june23.pdf (accessed August 22, 2010).

3. Carbon Trust, *Making the Business Case for a Carbon Reduction Project: How to Win Over the Board and Influence People,* March 2009, p. 11. www.britishchambers.org.uk/

business_services/carbon/carbon%20reduction%20project.pdf (accessed August 22, 2010).

4. This box draws on P.J. Simmons and M.R. Rangaswami, "Show Me the Money: Demonstrating Green Business Value to Skeptics," Corporate Eco Forum, 2009, p. 21.

5. Gil Friend, "Key Sustainability KPIs: The Simple, the Sobering, the Significant," *New Bottom Line*, Volume 13.1. www.natlogic.com/resources/publications/new-bottom-line/vol13/ (accessed August 15, 2010).

6. See an example at www.steppingforward.org.uk/rf/emissions.htm.

7. Gil Friend, "Key Sustainability KPIs."

8. Author interview, October 2010.

9. Adapted from a list included in Carbon Trust, Making the Business Case for a Carbon Reduction Project, p. 23.

10. Daniel C. Esty and Andrew S. Winston, *Green to Gold: How Smart Companies Use Environmental Strategy to Innovate, Create Value, and Build Competitive Advantage* (Hoboken, NJ: John Wiley & Sons, 2009), p. 214.

11. Esty and Winston, p. 212.

12. Esty and Winston, p. 212.

13. Esty and Winston, p. 213.

14. Clayton M. Christensen, Stephen p. Kaufman, and Willy Shih, "Innovation Killers: How Financial Tools Destroy Your Capacity to Do New Things," *Harvard Business Review*, January 2008.

15. "Dell Cuts Power Use by 48M KWH, Saves $5.8M," *Environmental Leader*, August 13, 2009. www.environmentalleader.com/2009/08/13 (accessed August 18, 2010).

16. "ROI Success Stories: Mack Molding," *Corporate Eco Forum* Weekly Briefing, March 16, 2009. http://corporateecoforum.com/newsletter_archive/20090316.htm (accessed August 18, 2010).

17. "EPA Unveils Top 25 U.S. Cities with the Most Energy Star Buildings," U.S. EPA, March 3, 2009. www.epa.gov/agingepa/press/epanews/2009/2009_0303_1.htm (accessed August 18, 2010).

18. Adobe, "Adobe's Road to Platinum," July 14, 2009. www.adobe.com/corporateresponsibility/environmental.html (accessed August 18, 2010).

19. Northrop Grumman, "2008 Corporate Social Responsibility Report," April 14, 2010, p. 23. www.northropgrumman.com/pdf/2008-noc-csr-report.pdf (accessed August 18, 2010).

20. NEEF, *The Engaged Organization: Corporate Employee Environmental Education Survey and Case Study Findings*, March 2009, p. 32.

21. "Toyota USA's Data Center Efficiencies Reduce Energy Use 10 Percent," *Environmental Leader*, October 13, 2009. www.environmentalleader.com/2009/10/13 (accessed August 18, 2010).

22. GreenerComputing, "IBM's Data Center Remodel Saves 98% of Costs, Boosts Capacity 8x," *GreenBiz*, October 1, 2009. www.greenbiz.com/news/2009/10/01/ibms-data-center-remodel-saves-98-percent-costs-boosts-capacity-8x (accessed August 18, 2010).

23. "Citi Announces First LEED Platinum Data Center," *SustainableBusiness.com*, April 28, 2009. www.sustainablebusiness.com/index.cfm/go/news.display/id/18084 (accessed August 18, 2010).

24. Don Atwood and John G. Miner, "Reducing Data Center Cost with an Air Economizer," Intel IT@IntelBrief, August 2008. www.intel.com (accessed August 18, 2010).

25. Ram Nidumolu, C.K. Prahalad, and M.R. Rangaswami, "Why Sustainability Is Now the Key Driver of Innovation," *Harvard Business Review*, September, 2009, p. 9.

26. Nidumolu, Prahalad, Rangaswami, "Why Sustainability."

27. "Agilent to Save $3.5M over 10 Years with Solar," *Environmental Leader*, November 20, 2009. www.environmentalleader.com/2009/11/20 (accessed August 18, 2010).

28. "Verdegaal Bros. Offsets 99% of Energy Bill with Solar," *Environmental Leader*, October 22, 2009. www.environmentalleader.com/2009/10/22 (accessed August 18, 2010).

29. Emily Reyna, "Climate Corps: 54 Million Reasons to Celebrate Energy Efficiency," *ClimateBiz*, October 14, 2009. www.greenbiz.com/blog/2009/10/14/2009-climate-corps-fellows-find-54m-energy-savings (accessed August 18, 2010).

30. Thomas Miner, "Holiday Inn Saves $4 Million with LED Signage," September 8, 2009. www.sustainablelifemedia.com/content/story/strategy/holidayinn_saves_millions_with_led (accessed August 18, 2010).

31. David McCann, "Staples CFO: Going Green Means Saving Green," *CFO Magazine*. www.cfo.com/article.cfm/13402881 (accessed August 18, 2010).

32. Hosea Sanders and Sylvia Jones, "Pepsico Goes Green in Chicago," ABC7News, March 9, 2009. http://abclocal.go.com/wls/index (accessed August 18, 2010).

33. 3M, "3P—Pollution Prevention Pays," 2010. http://solutions.3m.com/wps/portal/3M/en_US/3M-Sustainability/Global/Environment/3P/ (accessed August 18, 2010).

34. Dow, *Setting the Standard for Sustainability*, 2008. www.dow.com/commitments/pdf/setting_standard_sustainability.pdf (accessed August 18, 2010).

35. Baxter International, *2008 Environmental Financial Statement*, 2008. http://sustainability.baxter.com/EHS/2008_environmental_financial_statement.html (accessed August 18, 2010).

36. Lockheed Martin, "Lockheed Martin Reduces Water Usage by 275 Million Gallons," March 23, 2009. www.lockheedmartin.com/news/press_releases/2009/0323hq-esh.html (accessed August 18, 2010).

37. U.S. EPA, *The Lean and Energy Toolkit, Chapter 3: Energy Assessment Strategies*, December 2, 2009. www.epa.gov/lean/energytoolkit/ch3.htm (accessed August 18, 2010).

38. U.S. EPA, *Lean and Chemicals Toolkit, Chapter 3: Driving Out Chemical Waste with Lean Events*, December 2, 2009. www.epa.gov/lean/chemicalstoolkit/ch3.htm (accessed August 18, 2010).

39. U.S. EPA, *The Lean and Energy Toolkit, Chapter 3*.

40. "GE Makes $17 Billion with Ecomagination," *GE Reports*, October 22, 2008. www.gereports.com/ge-makes-17-billion-with-ecomagination (accessed August 18, 2010).

41. "Jones Lang LaSalle Reports Carbon Footprint Data for Global Operations," *PRNewswire-FirstCall*, April 27, 2009. www.prnewswire.com/ (accessed August 18, 2010).

42. The Climate Group, *Low Carbon Leader*, February 1, 2007. p. 11. www.theclimategroup.org/publications/2007/2/1/carbon-down-profits-up–new-edition/ (accessed November 10, 2010).

43. The Climate Group, *Low Carbon Leader*, p. 5.

44. U.S. EPA, *Lean Manufacturing and the Environment: Case Studies & Best Practices*, 2010. www.epa.gov/lean/studies/index.htm (accessed August 18, 2010).

45. "Cadbury and Sprint to Save Tons of Waste with New Greener Packaging," *GreenBiz*, November 4, 2009. www.greenbiz.com/news/2009/11/04/cadbury-and-sprint-save-tons-waste-new-greener-packaging (accessed August 18, 2010).

46. "Cadbury and Sprint to Save Tons of Waste . . ."

47. Andrew L. Shapiro and Noam Ross, "Four Lean, Green Strategies for an Uncertain Economy," *Harvard Business Review Blog*, October 29, 2008. http://blogs.hbr.org/leadinggreen/2008/10/4-lean-green-strategies-for-an.html (accessed August 18, 2010).

48. Thomas Miner, "Wal-Mart Saves $3.5 Million with Slim Packaging," *Sustainable Life Media*, September 25, 2009. www.sustainablelifemedia.com/content/story/strategy/walmart_saves_3.5million_slim_packaging (accessed August 18, 2010).

49. Lillian Laurence, "100% Recycled and Recyclable Clamshells from Earthbound Farms," *Sustainable Life Media*, July 28, 2009. http://sustainablelifemedia.com/%20content/story/design/100_percent_recycled_and_recyclable_earthbound_farms (accessed August 18, 2010).

50. "ArcelorMittal Saves $200,000 Annually by Idling Machinery during Production Delays," *Environmental Leader*, March 29, 2010. www.environmentalleader.com/2010/03/29 (accessed August 18, 2010).

51. "Recycled Carpets and Energy from Trash: Shaw Industries Releases First Sustainability Report," *GreenBiz*, October 15, 2009. www.greenbiz.com/news/2009/10/15/recycled-carpets-and-energy-trash-shaw-industries-releases-first-sustainability-repo (accessed August 18, 2010).

52. "Waste Audits to Save Sonoco $1M Annually," *Greenbiz*, August 3, 2009. www.greenbiz.com/news/2009/08/03/waste-audits-save-sonoco-1m-annually (accessed August 18, 2010).

53. Lisa Manley, Director of Sustainability Communications at The Coca-Cola Company, email correspondence, October 1, 2010.

54. "Hospitals Saved $138M in 2008 by Reprocessing Medical Waste," *Environmental Leader*, February 26, 2010. www.environmentalleader.com/2010/02/26 (accessed August 18, 2010).

55. UPS, "Right Turn at the Right Time," *UPS Pressroom*, June 12, 2010. www.pressroom.ups.com/About+UPS/UPS+Leadership/Speeches (accessed August 21, 2010).

56. Kathryn Siranosian, "UPS Announces Smart Pickup, a New Green Shipping Option for Businesses," Triplepundit.com, March 24, 2010. www.triplepundit.com/2010/03/24/ (accessed August 21, 2010).

57. Werbach, Adam, *Strategy for Sustainability: A Business Manifesto* (Boston: Harvard Business Press, 2009), p. 19.

58. "McKesson to Save $300K Via Fuel-Efficient Vehicles," *Environmental Leader*, November 5, 2009. www.environmentalleader.com/2009/11/05 (accessed August 21, 2010).

59. "Macy's Cuts GHG Emissions, Transportation Costs," *Environmental Leader*, October 13, 2009. www.environmentalleader.com/2009/10/13 (accessed August 21, 2010).

60. "AT&T California Cuts Fleet Emissions by 300+ Metric Tons," *Environmental Leader*, August 14, 2009. www.environmentalleader.com/2009/08/14 (accessed August 21, 2010).

61. Procter & Gamble, *Designed to Matter: 2009 Sustainability Report*. www.pg.com/en_US/downloads/sustainability/reports/PG_2009_Sustainability_Report.pdf (accessed August 21, 2010).

62. Claudia Girrbach, "How Cisco's Packaging Diet Saves $24 Million a Year," *Greenbiz*, March 10, 2010. www.greenbiz.com/blog/2010/03/10/how-ciscos-packaging-diet-saves-24-million-year (accessed August 21, 2010).

63. Kevin Wilhelm, *Return to Sustainability* (Indianapolis, IN: Dog Ear Publishing, 2009), p. 141.

64. Kevin Wilhelm, *Return to Sustainability*, p. 141.

65. Kevin Wilhelm, *Return to Sustainability*, p. 141.

66. Environmental Defense Fund, *Norvo Nordisk Drivers Help Cut Fuel Cost*. www.edf.org/documents/10637_EDFCasestudy_NovoNordisk.pdf (accessed August 21, 2010).

67. Environmental Defense Fund, *Carrier Cuts Emissions with Telematics*. www.edf. org/documents/10638_EDFCasestudy_Carrier.pdf (accessed August 21, 2010).

68. Environmental Defense Fund, *Poland Springs Reduces Idling to Curb Emissions*. www.edf.org/documents/10639_EDFCasestudy_PolandSpring.pdf (accessed August 21, 2010).

69. Environmental Defense Fund, *Abbot Laboratories—GreenFleet Participant*. www.edf. org/page.cfm?tagID=1462 (accessed August 21, 2010).

70. Environmental Defense Fund, *Infinity—GreenFleet Participant*. www.edf.org/page. cfm?tagID=1461 (accessed August 21, 2010).

71. Martin Murray, *Intro to Green Supply Chain*, About.com. http://logistics.about. com/od/greensupplychain/a/green_intro.htm (accessed August 21, 2010).

72. LMI Government Consulting, *Best Practices in Implementing Green Supply Chains*, 2005, p. 5.

73. Kevin Wilhelm, *Return to Sustainability*, p. 143.

74. Kevin Wilhelm, *Return to Sustainability*, p. 144.

75. Procter & Gamble. "Procter & Gamble Deepens Corporate Commitment to Sustainability," *CSR Wire*, March 26, 2009. www.csrwire.com/press_releases (accessed August 21, 2010).

76. "One Year On, Clorox's Green Works Dominates Market," *Sustainable Life Media*, January 15, 2009. www.sustainablelifemedia.com/content/story/strategy/one_year_on_cloroxs_green_works_dominates_market (accessed August 21, 2010).

77. "Chemical Management Industry Grows Revenue with Waste, Chemical Reduction Services," *GreenBiz*, October 29, 2009. www.greenbiz.com/news/2009/10/29/chemical-management-industry-grows-revenue-waste-chemical-reduction-services (accessed August 21, 2010).

78. "Boeing Tailored Arrivals ATM Concept Cuts Fuel, Emissions in Initial Deployment," *Reuters News*, July 11, 2008. www.reuters.com/article/idUS140926+11-Jul-2008+PRN20080711 (accessed August 21, 2010).

79. DuPont, "DuPont Expands Sustainability Commitments to Include R&D, Revenue Goals," October 10, 2006. http://vocuspr.vocus.com/VocusPR30 (accessed August 21, 2010).

80. "GE: Ecomagination Revenues Reach $18 Billion in 2009," *Environmental Leader*, July 24, 2010. www.environmentalleader.com/2010/06/24 (accessed August 21, 2010).

81. Mitsubishi, "Mitsubishi Electric to Extend Sustainable Growth in Global Warming-Related Business," November 6, 2008. http://global.mitsubishielectric.com/news/news_releases/2008/mel0720.pdf (accessed August 21, 2010).

82. *Terry Waghorn*, "Sustainability-Based Performance Drives Innovation," *Forbes*, March 2, 2009. www.forbes.com/2009/03/02/sustainability-performance-innovation-leadership_waghorn.html (accessed August 21, 2010).

83. Philips, "Sustainability Performance Highlights." www.philips.com/about/sustainability/sustainabilityupdates/performancehighlights.page (accessed August 21, 2010).

84. Werbach, Adam, *Strategy for Sustainability*, p. 23.

85. Esther Durkalski Hertzfeld, "CardPak Sustains Its Future Growth," August 1, 2008. www.packaging-online.com/paperboard-packaging-content/cardpak-sustains-its-future-growth (accessed August 21, 2010).

86. Curtis Packaging, *Curtis Packaging Sustainability Report 2007*. www.curtispackaging. com/CurtisSustainabilityReport.pdf (accessed August 21, 2010).

87. Kevin Wilhelm, Return to Sustainability, p. 144.

PART THREE. ANALYZE: IDENTIFY YOUR ECO-RISKS AND OPPORTUNITIES

CHAPTER 5. SPOT THE ECO-ISSUES THAT COULD IMPACT YOUR BOTTOM LINE

1. WRI and A. T. Kearney, *Rattling Supply Chains*, November 2008. http://pdf.wri.org/rattling_supply_chains.pdf (accessed August 5, 2010), pp. 18–20.

2. Nike, Inc., "Nike Outlines Global Strategy for Creating a More Sustainable Business," January 22, 2010. www.nikebiz.com/media (accessed August 1, 2010).

3. Tom Graedel (Professor of Industrial Ecology, Yale University), in discussion with the authors, August 25, 2010.

4. AccountAbility, BT, and LRQA, *The Materiality Report: Aligning Strategy, Performance, and Reporting*, November 1, 2006. www.accountability21.net/uploadedFiles/publications/The%20Materiality%20Report%20-%20Briefing.pdf (accessed August 15, 2010).

5. Michael E. Porter, *Competitive Advantage: Creating and Sustaining Superior Performance* (New York: Free Press, 1985).

6. Royal Dutch Shell, *Scenarios: An Explorer's Guide*, last updated 2008. www.static.shell.com/static/public/downloads/brochures/corporate_pkg/scenarios/explorers_guide.pdf (accessed August 15, 2010).

CHAPTER 6. ASSESS AND MEASURE YOUR ENVIRONMENTAL IMPACTS

1. Paul Baier, "10 Things I've Learned about Carbon Footprinting," June 21, 2010. www.greenbiz.com/blog/2010/06/21/10-things-ive-learned-about-carbon-footprinting (accessed August 3, 2010).

2. Leslie Kaufman, "Car Crashes to Please Mother Nature," *New York Times*, March 1, 2009. www.nytimes.com/2009/03/02/arts/television/02twen.html (accessed August 18, 2010).

3. Christopher Meyer and Julia Kirby, "The Big Idea: Leadership in the Age of Transparency," *Harvard Business Review*, April 2010. http://hbr.org/2010/04/the-big-idea-leadership-in-the-age-of-transparency (accessed August 3, 2010).

4. DANTES project, "Environmental Performance Indicators EPI." www.dantes.info/Tools&Methods/Environmentalinformation/enviro_info_spi_epi.html (accessed August 3, 2010).

5. Paul Baier, "10 Things I've Learned about Carbon Footprinting."

6. Paul Baier, "10 Things I've Learned about Carbon Footprinting."

7. The Greenhouse Gas Protocol Initiative. www.ghgprotocol.org (accessed October 22, 2010).

8. World Business Council for Sustainable Development and World Resources Institute, *The Greenhouse Gas Protocol: A Corporate Accounting and Reporting Standard.* www.ghgprotocol.org/files/ghg-protocol-revised.pdf (accessed August 4, 2010).

9. Paul Lingl, Deborah Carlson, and the David Suzuki Foundation, *Doing Business in a New Climate: A Guide to Measuring, Reducing and Offsetting Greenhouse Gas Emissions*, (Washington, DC: Earthscan, 2010), p. 14.

10. Lingl, Carlson, Suzuki Foundation, *Doing Business in a New Climate*, p. 13.

11. Lingl, Carlson, Suzuki Foundation, *Doing Business in a New Climate*, p. 12.

12. Tilde Herrera, "PG&E Claims Industry First with Supply Chain Footprint Project," June 20, 2010. www.greenbiz.com/news/2010/06/30/pge-claims-industry-first-supply-chain-carbon-footprint-project (accessed August 3, 2010).

13. Gil Friend, Natural Logic, *The Truth about Green Business* (Upper Saddle River, NJ: FT Press, 2009), p. 60.

14. Tilde Herrera, "PG&E Claims Industry First with Supply Chain Footprint Project."

15. Paul Baier, "10 Things I've Learned about Carbon Footprinting."

16. Paul Baier, ""10 Things I've Learned about Carbon Footprinting."

17. Preston, Holly H, "Mysteries of Water and the Future of a Scarce Resource," *New York Times*, April 25, 2008. www.nytimes.com/2008/04/25/your-money/25iht-mwater26.1.12339292.html?_r=2 (accessed August 5, 2010).

18. Water Environment Federation, *The Water Quality People*. www.wef.org (accessed August 4, 2010).

19. Alexandra Alter, "Yet Another 'Footprint' to Worry About: Water," *Wall Street Journal*, February 17, 2009, A11. http://online.wsj.com/article/SB123483638138996305.html (accessed August 21, 2010); Brian Merchant, "How Many Gallons of Water Does It Take to Make . . ." *Treehugger.com*, June 24, 2009. www.treehugger.com/files/2009/06/how-many-gallons-of-water.php (accessed August 21, 2010); James Owen, "Will Water Footprints Be the Next 'Energy Star'?" February 26, 2010, *National Geographic News*. http://news.nationalgeographic.com/news/2009/11/091127-virtual-water-footprints.html (accessed August 4, 2010).

20. Waterfootprint.org, "Water Footprint and Virtual Water." www.waterfootprint.org/?page=files/home (accessed August 3, 2010).

21. "New Tool Takes a Deeper Dive into Assessing Water Impacts," *GreenBiz*, July 21, 2010. www.greenbiz.com/news/2010/07/21/new-tool-takes-deeper-dive-assessing-water-impacts (accessed August 3, 2010).

22. CDProject, "CDP Water Disclosure." https://www.cdproject.net/ (accessed August 4, 2010).

23. Walmart, "Supplier Sustainability Assessment." walmartstores.com/download/4055.pdf (accessed August 4, 2010).

24. Tilde Herrera, "Exploring the Forgotten Water Footprint," February 26, 2010. www.greenbiz.com/blog/2010/02/26/forgotten-water-footprint#ixzzouQ4etOmw (accessed August 3, 2010).

25. Tilde Herrera, "Exploring the Forgotten Water Footprint."

26. SAB Miller, "Water Footprinting: Identifying & Addressing Water Risks in the Value Chain." www.sabmiller.com/files/reports/water_footprinting_report.pdf (accessed August 4, 2010).

27. World Resources Institute, UNEP, UNPD, and World Bank, "Valuing Ecosystem Services," in World Resources 1998–99, May 1998. http://earthtrends.wri.org (accessed August 3, 2010).

28. EarthLab, "The Carbon Footprint." www.earthlab.com/articles/thecarbonfootprint.aspx (accessed August 3, 2010).

29. Stonyfield Farm, "Life Cycle Assessment of the Stonyfield Farm Product Delivery System." www.stonyfield.com/healthy_planet/what_we_do (accessed August 3, 2010).

30. Myoo Create, "Care to Air Design Challenge." http://myoocreate.com/challenges/care-to-air-design-challenge#overview (accessed August 4, 2010).

31. Andrew Martin. "How Green Is My Orange?" *New York Times*, January 21, 2009. www.nytimes.com/2009/01/22/business/22pepsi.html (accessed August 4, 2010).

32. Eric Corey Freed, "Coca Cola's Life Cycle Assessment (LCA) Dilemma." www.ecomii.com/building/coca-cola-dilemma (accessed August 3, 2010).

33. "Life Cycle Assessment," Wikipedia, the free encyclopedia. http://en.wikipedia.org/wiki/Life_cycle_assessment (accessed August 3, 2010).

34. Carnegie Mellon University, "Approaches to LCA." www.eiolca.net/Method/ LCAapproaches.html (accessed August 3, 2010).

35. Deloitte Development LLC, "Lifecycle Assessment: Where Is It on Your Sustainability Agenda?" 2009. www.deloitte.com (accessed August 4, 2010).

36. Timothy Allan, "Life Cycle Tools and Approaches—Implementing Change," *Pro/Design* 96, 2008, p. 54.

PART FOUR. STRATEGIZE: HOW EACH BUSINESS FUNCTION CAN BENEFIT AND CONTRIBUTE

CHAPTER 8. OFFICE ACTIVITIES

1. Sun Light & Power, "A Company Culture that Believes in Solar—and Working Green." http://sunlightandpower.com/leadership/ (accessed August 31, 2010).

2. Jessica Heffner, "Brewery Hits 'Zero Waste' Target," BNET, April 22, 2010. http://findarticles.com/p/news-articles/dayton-daily-news/mi_8035/is_20100422/brewery-hits-waste-target/ai_n53259517/ (accessed September 1, 2010).

3. "Cox Cuts Paper Use by More than 3 Tons with Oracle Software," *Environmental Leader*, August 2, 2010. www.environmentalleader.com/2010/08/02 (accessed August 31, 2010).

4. Adobe Corporation, "Adobe Corporate Social Responsibility Summary 2009," p. 12.

5. "Online Banking: The Pros and Cons of Going Paperless." Credit Loan. www.creditloan.com/blog/2010/07/08/ (accessed September 01, 2010).

6. Daniel Lyons, "The Paper Chasers," *Newsweek*, November 21, 2008. www.newsweek.com/2008/11/20/the-paper-chasers.print.html (accessed November 10, 2010).

7. "Copy Paper: Hidden Costs, Real Opportunities," Environmental Paper. www.environmentalpaper.com/documents/citigroup-update.pdf (accessed August 31, 2010).

8. "Office Paper Reduction," Green and Save. www.greenandsave.com/greenoffice/paper/office_paper_reduction (accessed September 1, 2010).

9. "Tips and Tools," Shrink. www.shrinkpaper.org/pages/tips-and-tools/shrink-for-businesses.shtml (accessed November 10, 2010).

10. Patty Calkins, global vice president of Environment, Health and Safety at Xerox. Personal interview, October 2010.

11. "Build a Greener Operation—Starting in Your Office," Nexus, July 7, 2010. www.nexusboston.org/blog/2010/07/build-greener-operation-starting-your-office (accessed November 10, 2010).

12. "Ricoh Offers @Remote Green Reports," *Recharger Magazine*, May 7, 2010. http://rechargermag.com/articles/2010/05/07/ricoh-fleet-based-remote-green-reports.aspx (accessed November 10, 2010).

13. Activeion Cleaning Solutions. www.activeion.com.

14. Ed Lonergan, President & CEO at Diversey Inc. Personal interview. Sturtevant, WI, April 2007.

15. Tom Lutzenberger, "Styrofoam Life Cycle in Landfills," eHow, June 4, 2010. www.ehow.com/about_6586836_styrofoam-life-cycle-landfills.html (accessed November 10, 2010).

16. Joel Makower, "How to Green Your Company's Cafeteria," *Grist*, September 6, 2005. www.grist.org/article/cafeteria/ (accessed November 10, 2010).

17. Joel Makower, "How to Green Your Company's Cafeteria."

18. Erin Lyons, Saatchi & Saatchi Blue Team coordinator. Personal interview, October 2010.

19. Tim Ferguson, "BT Cuts Carbon with Videoconferencing," *Bloomberg Businessweek*, May 21, 2007. www.businessweek.com/globalbiz/content/may2007 (accessed August 31, 2010); Steve Lohr, "As Travel Costs Rise, More Meetings Go Virtual," *New York Times*, July 22, 2008. www.nytimes.com/2008/07/22/technology/22meet.html (accessed August 31, 2010).

20. "Why RouteRANK?" RouteRANK. www.routerank.com/en-ch/motivation/ (accessed September 1, 2010).

21. "Telecommuting: Is Working from Home Really All It's Cracked Up to Be?" *Aspen Organizational Development Blog,* August 9, 2008. http://aspenod.com/blog/2008/08/09/ (accessed September 1, 2010).

22. Dawn Foster, "Telecommuting + Flextime = More Productive Corporate Workforce," Giga Om. http://gigaom.com/collaboration/ (accessed August 31, 2010).

23. "Congress Wants More Gov't Workers Telecommuting," CBS News, July 14, 2010. www.cbsnews.com/stories/2010/07/14/business/main6678365.shtml (accessed September 1, 2010).

24. "The Benefits of Telework," developed collaboratively by the U.S. General Services Administration (GSA) and the Telework Exchange. www.teleworkexchange.com/pdfs/The-Benefits-of-Telework.pdf (accessed August 31, 2010), p. 2.

25. "Best Benefits: Telecommuting," *CNNMoney,* February 8, 2010. http://money.cnn.com/magazines/fortune/bestcompanies/2010/benefits/telecommuting.html (accessed September 1, 2010).

26. "Green Metrics and Key Performance Indicator Examples for Reducing Paper Consumption," *SmartKPIs Blog,* January 27, 2010. www.smartkpis.com/blog/2010/01/27/ (accessed September 1, 2010).

27. Dave Lindorff, "General Electric and Real Time," *CIO Insight,* November 11, 2002. www.cioinsight.com/c/a/Past-News/ (accessed September 1, 2010).

28. "Cox Cuts Paper Use by More than 3 Tons with Oracle Software," *Environmental Leader,* August 2, 2010. www.environmentalleader.com/2010/08/02 (accessed August 31, 2010).

29. "Enterprise Case Study: Insurance Goes Paperless," Developers Net. www.developers.net/intelisdshowcase/view/2530 (accessed September 1, 2010).

30. "Western Forest Products," Xerox Case Studies. http://docushare.xerox.com/pdf/cs/cs_westernForest.pdf (accessed November 10, 2010).

31. Adobe Corporation, "Adobe Corporate Social Responsibility Summary 2009," p. 12. www.adobe.com/corporateresponsibility/pdfs/csr_summary.pdf (accessed November 10, 2010).

32. "PBD Goes Paperless on International Shipments," Connect Ship. www.connectship.com/CaseStudies/PDF/PBD.pdf (accessed August 31, 2010).

33. Allison Heinrichs, "New Children's Is a Pioneer in Paperless," Pittsburgh Live. www.pittsburghlive.com (accessed August 31, 2010).

34. "Who Has the Largest Hybrid Fleet? Enterprise Does!" Hybrid Rental Car. www.hybrid-rental-car.com (accessed August 31, 2010).

35. Jessie Cacciola, "Whole Foods Introduces Pizza 'GreenBox,'" July 19, 2010. www.slashfood.com/2010/07/19/whole-foods-introduces-pizza-greenbox/ (accessed August 31, 2010).

CHAPTER 9. BUILDINGS AND FACILITIES

1. PRWeb, "Bank of America Tower at One Bryant Park Is First Commercial Skyscraper in U.S. to Achieve LEED Platinum," *Earth Times,* May 20, 2010. www.earthtimes.org/ (accessed August 3, 2010).

2. IBM, in discussion with Dan Esty, October 7, 2010.

3. "Mack Molding Works with Efficiency Vermont to Install 2,100 Energy Efficient Fixtures," *Vermont Business* magazine, February 27, 2009. www.vermontbiz.com/news/february/mack-molding-works-efficiency-vermont-install-2100-energy-efficient-fixtures (accessed August 5, 2010).

4. Dow, in discussion with Dan Esty, September 2010.

5. "Northrop Grumman Saves $2M in Energy at One CA," *Environmental Leader,* August 6, 2009. www.environmentalleader.com/2009/08/06 (accessed August 5, 2010).

6. Sari Krieger, "Half of Non-Residential Buildings Will Be Green by 2015—Study," U.S. Green Building Council, January 6, 2010. www.usgbc.org/News (accessed June 30, 2010).

7. Ceres, *Energy Efficiency and Real Estate: Opportunities for Investors,* 2010. www.ceres.org/realestatereport (accessed August 4, 2010).

8. Nadine Lihach, "Meticulous Study Makes the Case for Cost-Effective Commercial-Building Commissioning," BetterBricks, 2002. http://cx.lbl.gov/documents/bb-commissioning.pdf (accessed August 5, 2010).

9. WBCSD, *Energy Efficiency in Buildings.* www.wbcsd.org/web/eeb/Energyefficiencyinbuilding.pdf (accessed August 4, 2010).

10. WBCSD, *Energy Efficiency in Buildings.*

11. Oak Ridge National Laboratory, "Radiant Barrier Fact Sheet," last revised June 27, 2001. www.ornl.gov/sci/roofs walls/radiant/rb_02.html (accessed August 3, 2010).

12. "Con Edison 'Cool' Roofs Reduce Energy Costs," *Environmental Leader,* May 5, 2010. www.environmentalleader.com/2010/05/05 (accessed June 30, 2010).

13. Raymond Evans et al., *The Long Term Costs of Owning and Using Buildings* (London: The Royal Academy of Engineering, 1998).

14. Wendy Koch, "Light bulb war? New LEDs by GE, Home Depot compete," *USA Today. com, GreenHouse Blog,* May 10, 2010. http://content.usatoday.com/communities/greenhouse/post/2010/05/light-bulb-war-new-leds-by-ge-home-depot-compete/1 (accessed June 30, 2010).

15. EnergyStar, "Light Bulbs (CFL)." www.energystar.gov (accessed August 15, 2010).

16. PG&E Energy Efficiency Information, "Occupancy Controls for Lighting," last revised April 25, 2007. www.lightingassociates.org (accessed August 17, 2010).

17. The Lighting Research Center at Rensselaer Polytechnic Institute, "Photosensor Dimming: Solutions." www.lrc.rpi.edu/researchAreas/reducingbarriers/photosensorSolutions.asp (accessed August 17, 2010).

18. FacilitiesNet, "Lighting Upgrades Bring Energy Savings," August 2010. www.facilitiesnet.com/lighting (accessed August 31, 2010).

19. EnerNOC, "EnerNOC University Customers Win Energy Efficiency Best Practice Awards," *Wall Street Journal MarketWatch,* July 14, 2010. www.marketwatch.com (accessed August 31, 2010).

20. ALSI, "Pennsylvania Manufacturer Selected in Innovative Energy Saving Relighting Project at Pittsburgh International Airport," *Wall Street Journal MarketWatch,* July 9, 2010. www.marketwatch.com (accessed August 31, 2010).

21. ReGreen Corporation, "Westwood Gateway Reduces Annual Energy Costs by $160,000,", July 22, 2010. www.regreencorp.com/show-article?id=17.

22. WBCSD, *Energy Efficiency in Buildings.*

23. Wendy Koch, "Light bulb war?"

24. Wendy Koch, "Light bulb war?"

25. U.S. DOE Energy Efficiency and Renewable Energy, "Lower Water Heating Temperature for Energy Savings." www.energysavers.gov/your_home/water_heating (accessed August 15, 2010).

26. U.S. EPA's Water Sense, "Fix a Leak Week, March 15–21, 2010." www.epa.gov/WaterSense/pubs/fixleak.html (accessed August 15, 2010).

27. Green Building Encyclopedia, "Water Conservation in Buildings." http://whygreenbuildings.com/water_conservation.php (accessed August 3, 2010).

28. Energy Savers, "The Economics of a Solar Water Heater." www.energysavers.gov/your_home/water_heating (accessed August 3, 2010).

29. Candace Lombardi, "Minnesota Twins Stadium to Recycle Rainwater." *CNET*, January13, 2010. http://news.cnet.com/8301-11128_3-10433834-54.html (accessed June 29, 2010).

30. Wendy Koch, "Light bulb war?"

31. Severson, Kim, "The Rise of Company Gardens," *New York Times*, May 11, 2010. www.nytimes.com/2010/05/12/dining/12gardens.html (accessed August 4, 2010).

32. U.S. Green Building Council, "Newly Released Studies Confirm Energy Savings Significant in LEED, ENERGY STAR Buildings," April 3, 2008. www.usgbc.org (accessed August 5, 2010).

33. "Lake Champlain Chocolates Opens LEED-Certified Packaging and Distribution Facility." Efficient Energy. http://myefficientenergy.com/26908 (accessed November 8, 2010).

34. Tennessee Valley Authority, "Generation Partners." www.tva.gov/greenpowerswitch/partners/index.htm (accessed December 22, 2010).

35. World Energy, "Adventist HealthCare Goes Greener, Reduces Future Energy Costs with Help of World Energy," March 9, 2010. www.worldenergy.com (accessed June 30, 2010).

36. "Sam's Club Installs On-Site Wind Power," *Environmental Leader,* April 30, 2010. www.environmentalleader.com/2010/04/30/ (accessed August 3, 2010).

37. "New Cogeneration System Enables Wastewater Treatment Plant to Use Treatment Byproducts as Fuel," *PR Newswire*, May 3, 2010. www. prnewswire.com/news-releases (accessed August 3, 2010).

38. "Cow Manure Project to Produce 38,000 mWh of Power Annually," *Environmental Leader*, May 6, 2010. www.environmentalleader.com/2010/05/06/ (accessed August 3, 2010).

39. Author interview with Development Committee members and architects, March 2000.

40. Andrea Caruthers, "Negotiating Green Leases: Top Issues for Tenants," *Environmental Leader*, August 9, 2010. www.environmentalleader.com/2010/08/09 (accessed August 31, 2010).

CHAPTER 10. INFORMATION TECHNOLOGY

1. Jeff Hinkle, "Interview: Green Initiatives and Energy Conservation in a Modern Atlanta Datacenter," *GNAX*. www.gnax.net/pdf/GNAX_Green_Initiatives.pdf (accessed August 4, 2010).

2. GreenerComputing, "IBM's Data Center Remodel Saves 98% of Costs, Boosts Capacity 8x," *GreenBiz*, October 1, 2009. www.greenbiz.com/news/2009/10/01/ibms-data-center-remodel-saves-98-percent-costs-boosts-capacity-8x (accessed August 18, 2010).

3. "China Mobile's Low Carbon Solutions Cut Emissions," *Environmental Leader,* May 17, 2010. www.environmentalleader.com/2010/05/17/ (accessed August 3, 2010).

4. "Ricoh Unveils Carbon Tracking Tool for Printers," *Environmental Leader,* May 7, 2010. www.environmentalleader.com/2010/05/07/ (accessed August 3, 2010); www.xerox.com and http://rechargermag.com/articles/2010/05/07/ricoh-fleet-based-remote-green-reports.aspx (accessed November 13, 2010).

5. John Lamb, *The Greening of IT: How Companies Can Make a Difference for the Environment* (IBM Press, 2009).

6. Joab Jackson, "IT Should Pay the Power Bill, Reasons EBay Exec," *PCWorld*, May 18, 2010. www.pcworld.com/businesscenter/article/196614/ (accessed August 3, 2010).

7. Adapted from Marty Poniatowski, *Foundations of Green IT: Consolidation, Virtualization, Efficiency, and ROI in the Data Center* (Prentice Hall, 2009), pp. 277–282.

8. "PC Power Management Saves California School District $350,000 per Year," *Faronics*, June 15, 2010. www.faronics.com/Faronics/Documents/PressReleases/PR_Chaffey_EN.pdf (accessed August 3, 2010).

9. "Save Thousands by Switching Printer Fonts," *Environmental Leader*, April 7, 2010. www.environmentalleader.com/2010/04/07/ (accessed August 3, 2010).

10. Energy Star, "Computers." www.energystar.gov/index.cfm?fuseaction=find_a_product. ShowProductGroup&pgw_code=CO (accessed August 3, 2010).

11. Alan Hedge, *Ergonomics Considerations of LCD versus CRT Displays*, May 2003. http://ergo.human.cornell.edu/Pub/LCD_vs_CRT_AH.pdf (accessed August 4, 2010).

12. Greenpeace, "Guide to Greener Electronics," May 26, 2010. www.greenpeace.org/international/en/campaigns/toxics/electronics/ (accessed August 3, 2010).

13. "Manufacturers to Pay for E-Waste under New Wisconsin Law," *Environmental Leader*, September 2, 2010. www.environmentalleader.com/2010/09/02/manufacturers-to-pay-for-e-waste-under-new-wisconsin-law/ (accessed November 17, 2010).

14. U.S. EPA, *Municipal Solid Waste in the United States 2007 Facts and Figures*, November 2008. www.epa.gov/osw/nonhaz/municipal/pubs/msw07-rpt.pdf (accessed August 4, 2010).

15. PR Log, "Global E-Waste Market Is Forecast to Reach 53 Million Tonnes by 2012 Says New Report," December 15, 2009. www.prlog.org/10453267-global-ewaste-market-is-forecast-to-reach-53-million-tonnes-by-2012-says-new-report.html (accessed August 3, 2010).

16. Dan Esty serves on TechTurn Board of Directors.

17. Cara Garretson, "Tech Recycling: Big IT Shops Get Serious about Asset Disposal," *Computerworld*, May 11, 2010. www.computerworld.com/s/article/9176378/ (accessed August 3, 2010).

18. Cara Garretson, "Tech Recycling."

19. "Carbon Footprint: Global Greenhouse Gas Emissions," Motorola. http://responsibility.motorola.com/index.php/environment/climate/opcrbnftpt/ (accessed August 17, 2010).

20. Anamika Singh, "Green Technology Companies Opting for Videoconferencing to Cut Cost on Business Travel," *TMCnet*, January 30, 2009. http://green.tmcnet.com/topics/green/articles/49767-companies-opting-videoconferencing-cut-cost-business-travel.htm (accessed August 3, 2010).

21. Hyoun Park, "Being in Two Places at Once: Telepresence versus Videoconferencing in the Enterprise," *Aberdeen Group Blog*, December 31, 2008. http://research.aberdeen.com/index.php/communications-blog/ (accessed August 3, 2010).

22. "CDP Offers the Business Case for Telepresence," *GreenBiz*, June 16, 2010. www.greenbiz.com/news/2010/06/16/early-telepresence-adopters-enjoy-fast-roi-smaller-carbon-footprint-cdp (accessed August 3, 2010).

23. Uses an estimate of 5.5 metric tons of carbon dioxide emitted annually per passenger vehicle, per U.S. EPA recommendation. www.epa.gov/oms/climate/420f05004.htm.

24. Undress4Success, "Telework Pros and Cons." http://undress4success.com/telework-pros-cons (accessed August 3, 2010).

25. Author conversation with IBM, October 2010.

26. U.S. EPA, "EPA Reports Significant Energy Efficiency Opportunities for U.S. Servers and Data Centers," August 3, 2007. http://yosemite.epa.gov/opa/admpress.nsf/ (accessed August 3, 2010).

27. "Networking Providers Tout the Virtues of Virtualization," *Environmental Leader*, April 28, 2010. www.environmentalleader.com/2010/04/28/ (accessed August 3, 2010);

1e, *Server Energy and Efficiency Report 2009*. www.1e.com/energycampaign/down loads/Server_Energy_and_Efficiency_Report_2009.pdf (accessed August 4, 2010).

28. Forrester Consulting, "The Business Value of Virtualization," July 2009. www.vmware. com/files/pdf/solutions/Business-Value-Virtualization.pdf (accessed August 4, 2010).

29. Google, "Going Green at Google: Data Center Efficiency Measures." www.google. com/corporate/green/datacenters/measuring.html (accessed August 3, 2010); Christian Belady, *Green Grind Data Center Power Efficiency Metrics: PUE and DCIE*, October 23, 2007. The Green Grid, 2008. www.thegreengrid.org/Global/Content/white-papers/The-Green-Grid-Data-Center-Power-Efficiency-Metrics-PUE-and-DCiE (accessed August 5, 2010).

30. "PGS Data Center Delivers Cost Savings of Nearly $1M," *Environmental Leader*, June 15, 2010. www.environmentalleader.com/2010/06/15/ (accessed August 3, 2010).

31. Ken Brill, "Uptime Institute Inc. Presentation," National Data Center Energy Efficiency Strategy Workshop. http://events.energetics.com/datacenters08/pdfs/Short_Take_Brill.pdf (accessed August 4, 2010).

32. Lucas Mearian, "A Waste of Space: Bulk of Drive Capacity Still Underutilized," July 28, 2010. www.computerworld.com/s/article/9179751 (accessed August 20, 2010).

33. Ted Samson, "7 Green Technologies Poised for Success," *InfoWorld*, June 18, 2009. www.infoworld.com/d/green-it/ (accessed August 3, 2010).

34. "Intel ITs Role in Sustainability," YouTube.com (accessed August 3, 2010).

35. Johanna Ambrosio, "Green IT: Popularity Due to Savings or Morals?" *Computerworld*, September 13, 2007. www.pcworld.com/businesscenter/article/137171/green_it_popu larity_due_to_savings_or_morals.html (accessed August 3, 2010).

36. Google, "Going Green at Google: Data Center Best Practices." www.google.com/corporate/green/datacenters/best-practices.html (accessed August 3, 2010).

37. Hewlett-Packard, "Green Data Centre," February 2, 2009. www.greendatacenternews. org/ (accessed August 3, 2010).

38. "Yahoo Unveils 'Chicken Coop' Data Center," *Environmental Leader*, September 20, 2010. www.environmentalleader.com/2010/09/20/yahoo-unveils-chicken-coop-data-center/ (accessed November 17, 2010).

39. Martin LaMonica, "IBM Liquid-Cooled Supercomputer Heats Building," *CNET News*, May 10, 2010. http://news.cnet.com/8301-11128_3-20004543-54.html (accessed August 3, 2010).

40. "EPA Launches Energy Star Label for Data Centers," *Environmental Leader*, June 8, 2010. www.environmentalleader.com/2010/06/08/ (accessed August 3, 2010).

41. For a good introduction to cloud computing, see Eric Knorr and Galen Gruman, "What Cloud Computing Really Means," *InfoWorld*. www.infoworld.com/d/cloud-computing.

42. "Cloud Computing Can Cut Carbon Emissions per User by 30% to 90%," *Environmental Leader*, November 5, 2010. www.environmentalleader.com/2010/11/05/cloud-computing-can-cut-carbon-emissions-per-user-by-30/ (accessed November 17, 2010).

43. NetSuite, "Research Shows NetSuite Cloud Computing Platform Saves the Equivalent of 423,000 Metric Tons of Carbon Dioxide per Year," July 15, 2009. www.netsuite.com/portal/press/releases/nlpr07-15-09.shtml (accessed August 3, 2010).

44. Economist Intelligence Unit, *IT and Sustainability: Bringing Best Practices to the Business*, 2009. www.oracle.com/green/economist-intellgence-unit-it-sustainability-bringing-best-practices.pdf (accessed August 4, 2010).

45. IBM, *Leading a Sustainable Enterprise*, 2009. ftp://ftp.software.ibm.com/common/ssi/pm/xb/n/gbe03226usen/GBE03226USEN.PDF (accessed August 4, 2010).

46. GreenerDesign, "Online Directory Links Plastic Waste Buyers and Sellers," *GreenBiz*, January 28, 2010. www.greenbiz.com/news/2010/01/28/online-directory-links-plastic-waste-buyers-and-sellers (accessed August 3, 2010).

47. Rebecca Henderson, Richard M. Locke, Christopher Lyddy, and Cate Reavis, "Nike Considered: Getting Traction on Sustainability," MIT Sloan Management, January 21, 2009. https://mitsloan.mit.edu/MSTIR/sustainability/NikeConsidered/Documents/ (accessed August 4, 2010).

48. Microsoft, "Seventh Generation ERP Solution Helps Global Distributor Manage Environmental Performance," December 29, 2008. www.microsoft.com/casestudies/Case_Study_Detail.aspx?CaseStudyID=4000003409 (accessed August 4, 2010).

49. Preston Gralla, "Get Ready for Green IT 2.0," GreenBiz, September 8, 2009. www. greenercomputing.com/blog/2009/09/08/get-ready-green-it-20 (accessed August 3, 2010).

50. CA Technologies, "Tesco Explains How They Use CA ecoSoftware from CA Technologies," June 21, 2010. www.youtube.com/watch?v=2TBM-Qs167k (accessed November 3, 2010).

51. "Safeway Inks Deal with Hara to Further Reduce Energy Use and Carbon Footprint," Mother Nature Network, February 17, 2010. www.mnn.com/food/healthy-eating-recipes/stories/safeway-inks-deal-with-hara-to-further-reduce-energy-use-and-car# (accessed November 17, 2010).

52. "Role of Social Media in Sustainability Evolves," Environmental Leader, July 15, 2009. www.environmentalleader.com/2009/07/15/ (accessed August 3, 2010).

53. Celestial Seasonings Herbal Tea, "Celestial Seasonings' Ethical Trade and Charity Donations." www.celestialseasonings.com/about/community/social_responsibility/goodness.html (accessed August 3, 2010).

54. "Travelocity Uses Facebook to Promote Travel Carbon Offsetting," Environmental Leader, November 20, 2009. www.environmentalleader.com/2009/11/30/ (accessed August 3, 2010).

55. "Role of Social Media..." Environmental Leader, July 15, 2009. www.environmentalleader.com/2009/07/15/ (accessed November 10, 2010).

56. "Role of Social Media..." Environmental Leader, July 15, 2009. www.environmentalleader.com/2009/07/15/ (accessed November 10, 2010).

57. Author interview with David Struhs, C3 Carbon, November 2011.

58. IBM Institute for Business Value, Green and Beyond: Getting Smarter about the Environment, 2009. ftp://public.dhe.ibm.com/common/ssi/ecm/en/gbe03246usen/GBE03246USEN.PDF (accessed August 4, 2010).

59. Katrice R. Jalbuena, "Stockholm Becomes Testing Ground for Smarter Transport Systems" Ecoseed, April 20, 2010. www.ecoseed.org/en/general-green-news/green-topics/green-transportation/alternative-transport/6936 (accessed August 4, 2010).

CHAPTER 11. PRODUCT DESIGN

1. Sto Corp, "StoCoat Lotusan: The Exterior Coating with Lotus-Effect." http://stodistributor.com/allweb.nsf/lotusanpage (accessed November 9, 2010).

2. Daniel C. Esty and Andrew S. Winston, Green to Gold (Hoboken, NJ: John Wiley & Sons, 2009), p. 196.

3. "P&G Ups 2012 Green Product Sales Target to $50 Billion," Environmental Leader, March 26, 2009. www.environmentalleader.com/2009/03/26/pg-expands-sustainability-targets-by-2012/ (accessed November 9, 2010).

4. DuPont, "DuPont Expands Sustainability Commitments to Include R&D, Revenue Goals." www.prnewswire.com/news-releases/dupont- expands-sustainability-commitments-to-include-rd-revenue-goals-56395492.html (accessed November 9, 2010).

5. Heidi Siegelbaum, "99% Natural and 42% Market Share, Green Works Flexes Its Muscle," Greenwash Brigade, January 23, 2009. www.publicradio.org/columns/sustain

ability/greenwash/2009/01/99_natural_and_42_market_share.html (accessed August 6, 2010).

6. "GE: Ecomagination Revenues Reach $18 Billion in 2009," *Environmental Leader*, June 24, 2010. www.environmentalleader.com/2010/06/24/ge-ecomagination-revenue-reach-18-billion-in-2009/ (accessed November 9, 2010).

7. "Industry Survey Shows Chemical Suppliers Realize Significant Business Growth by Reducing Chemical Use and Costs for Their Customers," *Reuters*, October 21, 2009. www.reuters.com/article/idUS107428+21-Oct-2009+BW20091021 (accessed August 6, 2010).

8. P.J. Simmons and M.R. Rangaswami, "Show Me the Money: Demonstrating Green Business Value to Skeptics," *Corporate Eco Forum*, November 2009. http://corporateeco forum.com/ecoinnovator/?p=4821 (accessed August 6, 2010).

9. Philips, "Sustainability Updates." www.philips.com/about/sustainability/sustainability updates (accessed August 6, 2010).

10. Esmé E. Deprez, "Wal-Mart Spurs Sustainable Toy Animals into $1 Billion Market," *Bloomberg Business Week*, March 26, 2010.

11. Joel Makower, "Packaging Companies Rethink the Box: The State of Green Business 2010," *GreenBiz*, February 15, 2010. www.greenbiz.com/news/2010/02/15/packaging-companies-rethink-box-state-green-business-2010 (accessed August 6, 2010).

12. Ray C. Anderson, "Toward a More Sustainable Way of Business." www.interface global.com/Sustainability.aspx (accessed November 9, 2010).

13. "TerraCycle," Wikipedia, the free encyclopedia. http://en.wikipedia.org/wiki/TerraCycle (accessed April 7, 2010).

14. Chad White with Emma Stewart (BSR's Environmental R&D team), and Ted Howes with Bob Adams (IDEO), *Aligned for Sustainable Design: An A-B-C-D Approach to Making Better Products*, Business for Social Responsibility, May 2008. www.bsr. org/reports/BSR_Sustainable_Design_Report_0508.pdf (accessed August 22, 2010).

15. Gil Friend, *The Truth about Green Business* (FT Press: 2009), p. 88.

16. Chad White and others, *Aligned for Sustainable Design*, p. 37.

17. A substantial "industrial ecology" literature has been developed. See, for example, Thomas E. Graedel and Braden R. Allenby, *Industrial Ecology*, 2nd edition, (Prentice Hall, 2002) and Thomas E. Graedel and Braden R. Allenby, *Industrial Ecology and Sustainable Engineering* (Prentice Hall, 2009).

18. William A. McDonough and Michael Braungart, *Cradle to Cradle: Remaking the Way We Make Things* (North Point Press, 2002).

19. William A. McDonough, "From Inspiration to Innovation," FAIA. www.mcdonough. com/writings/inspiration_innovation.htm (accessed June 23, 2010).

20. Chad White and others, *Aligned for Sustainable Design*, p. 13.

21. Author interview, October 2010, and www.investor.jnj.com.

22. Chad White and others, *Aligned for Sustainable Design*, p. 32. See this source for other data cited in the paragraph.

23. "Environmental Product Summary: Aeron Chair," Herman Miller. 2009. www. hermanmiller.com/MarketFacingTech/hmc/products/Aeron_Chairs/EPS_AER.pdf (accessed August 4, 2010).

24. Chad White and others, *Aligned for Sustainable Design*, p. 28.

25. Nick Aster, "Cold Water Tide: Provoking the Ah-Ha Moment at Procter & Gamble," *Triple Pundit*. November 13, 2009. www.triplepundit.com/2009/11/coldwater-tide-provoking-the-ah-ha-moment-at-proctor-gamble/ (accessed August 4, 2010); "Tide Coldwater® Is First Detergent to Receive Green Good Housekeeping Seal," *PR Newswire*, March 24, 2009. www.tradingmarkets.com/adv.php?ref=%2Fnews%2

Fpress-release%2Fpg_tide-coldwater-r-is-first-detergent-to-receive-green-good-house keeping-seal-869171.html (accessed November 9, 2010).

26. "HP Wins Walmart Design Challenge with Innovative Notebook Packaging," Hewlett-Packard, September 3, 2008. www.hp.com/hpinfo/newsroom/press/2008/080903a.html (accessed June 23, 2010).

27. Nestlé, "Easier to Hold, Easier to Live With." www.nestlepurelife.us/flavors/ecoshape.asp. (accessed November 4, 2010).

28. For a full list, see www.epa.gov/greenchemistry/pubs/principles.html.

29. SC Johnson, "Our Greenlist™ Process." www.scjohnson.com/en/commitment/focus-on/greener-products/greenlist.aspx (accessed August 23, 2010).

30. U.S. EPA, "Design for the Environment," last updated August 17, 2010. www.epa.gov/dfe/ (accessed August 22, 2010).

31. Clorox, "Green Works Cleaners: Powerful, Naturally," January 14, 2008. http://investors.thecloroxcompany.com/releasedetail.cfm?ReleaseID=286938 (accessed August 6, 2010).

32. Esty and Winston, *Green to Gold*, p. 199.

33. European Commission, "EU Targets." http://ec.europa.eu/research/leaflets/recycling/en/page2.html (accessed August 22, 2010).

34. Sebastian Blanco, ""KBA likes VW's Early Adoption of Vehicle Recycling Laws," *GreenAutoblog*, June 18, 2007. http://green.autoblog.com/2007/06/18/kba-likes-vws-early-adoption-of-vehicle-recycling-laws/ (accessed August 22, 2010).

35. L.L. Bean, "Return and Exchange Information," 2010. www.llbean.com/ customerService/FAQs/returnsExchanges.html (accessed August 22, 2010).

36. Interface, "Interface Flor," 2010. www.interfaceflor.com (accessed August 22, 2010).

37. European Commission Environment, "Recast of the WEEE and RoHS Directives Proposed," last updated March 6, 2010. http://ec.europa.eu/environment/waste/weee/index_en.htm (accessed August 22, 2010).

38. Cal Recycle, "Electronic Waste Recyling Act of 2003: Covered Electronic Waste Payment System," last updated February 9, 2010. www.calrecycle.ca.gov/electronics/act2003/ (accessed August 22, 2010).

39. William McDonough and Michael Braungart. "The Promise of Nylon 6—BASF." www.mcdonough.com/writings/promise_nylon.htm (accessed June 23, 2010).

40. Author interview, October 2010.

41. MBDC Cradle to Cradle, "Certification Overview." www.mbdc.com/detail.aspx?linkid=2&sublink=8 (accessed August 22, 2010).

42. Richard Conniff, "In the Name of the Law," *Smithsonian.com*, October 2007. www.smithsonianmag.com/arts-culture/last-oct07.html (accessed August 22, 2010).

43. Author interview, November 2010.

44. William Bostwick, "Starbucks Sponsors Coffee-Cup Redesign Contest," *FastCompany*, March 16, 2010. www.fastcompany.com/1585666/starbucks-sponsors-coffee-cup-redesign-contest (accessed June 23, 2010).

45. Agnes Mazur, "Green Xchange: Creating a Meta-Map of Sustainability," *Worldchanging*, May 5, 2009. www.worldchanging.com/archives/009822.html (accessed June 23, 2010).

46. Kelly Lauber, Director of Sustainable Business & Innovation at Nike, Inc. Personal interview. Davos, Switzerland, 2010.

47. Janine M. Benyus, *Biomimicry: Innovation Inspired by Nature*. (New York: Perennial, 1998). Others have extended this concept with focus on "biophilic" design. See Stephen R. Kellert, et al., *Biophilic Design: The Theory, Science, and Practice of Bringing Buildings to Life* (Hoboken, NJ: John Wiley & Sons, 2009).

48. This is drawn from Janine Benyus and the Biomimicry Guild, "What Is Biomimicry?" and "The Challenge to Biology Design Spiral." www.biomimicryguild.com/guild_biomimicry.html and www.biomimicryinstitute.org/about-us/biomimicry-a-tool-for-innovation.html (accessed June 23, 2010).

49. Claire Cain Miller, "Mixing in Some Carbon," *New York Times,* March 21, 2010. www.nytimes.com/2010/03/22/business/energy-environment/22cement.html?_r=1&ref=science (accessed August 21, 2010).

50. Boeing Corp., "Benefits from Operators' Using Blended Winglets." www.boeing.com/commercial/aeromagazine/articles/qtr_03_09/article_03_1.html (accessed August 15, 2010).

51. FedEx, "FedEx Office Print Online." https://printonline.fedex.com/nextgen/ (accessed August 15, 2010).

52. Zipcar, "Green Benefits." www.zipcar.com/is-it/greenbenefits (accessed June 23, 2010).

53. Chegg, "Jobs." http://newton.newtonsoftware.com/career/CareerHome.action?clientId=4028f88c27c011540127cfd85f3809bc (accessed August 4, 2010).

54. Christopher Weber, "The Energy and Climate Change Impacts of Different Music Delivery Methods," August 17, 2009. http://download.intel.com/pressroom/pdf/ CDsvsdownloadsrelease.pdf (accessed August 4, 2010).

CHAPTER 12. SOURCING AND PROCUREMENT

1. Frank Blake, chairman and CEO, The Home Depot. Conversation with Dan Esty, August 4, 2010.

2. Home Depot, "Supplier Reference Guidelines and Terms & Conditions." http:// suppliercenter.homedepot.com/wps/portal/SBA (accessed August 21, 2010).

3. LMI Government Consulting, *Best Practices in Implementing Green Supply Chains*, April 5, 2005. http://postconflict.unep.ch/humanitarianaction/documents/02_08-04_05-25.pdf (accessed August 11, 2010).

4. "Wal-Mart Switches to Local Fruit, Veggies," *CBS News*, July 2, 2008. www.cbsnews.com/stories/2008/07/02/business/main4227280.shtml (accessed August 11, 2010).

5. GEMI, "Reel-Less Cable Packaging at Duke Power." www.gemi.org/supplychain/G1F.htm (accessed August 11, 2010).

6. Ariel Schwartz, "Mars Promises Candy from Sustainable Cocoa," *FastCompany Blog,* April 10, 2009. www.fastcompany.com/blog/ariel-schwartz/sustainability/mars-promises-candy-sustainable-cocoa (accessed August 21, 2010).

7. GEMI, *Forging New Links,* June 2004, p. 32.

8. GEMI, *New Paths to Business Value*, March 2001. www.gemi.org/resources/newpath.pdf.

9. "Green Procurement," *GreenBiz*, January 20, 2004. www.greenbiz.com/business/research/report/2004/01/20/green-procurement (accessed August 11, 2010).

10. CarbonFund.Org, "Carbonfund.org Announces CarbonFree™ Certified Product Label," *CSRWire.com*, July 6, 2007. www.csrwire.com/press_releases/19573-Carbonfund-org-Announces-CarbonFree-TM-Certified-Product-Label (accessed August 24, 2010).

11. Darcy Hitchcock and Marsha Willard, *The Business Guide to Sustainability* (Earthscan, 2006), pp. 190–191.

12. Hitchcock and Willard, *The Business Guide to Sustainability*, pp. 188–189.

13. Apple, "Apple Supplier Code of Conduct." http://images.apple.com/supplierresponsibility/pdf/Supplier_Code_of_Conduct_V3_1.pdf (accessed August 11, 2010).

14. HP, "HP Global Citizenship Report: Supply Chain Responsibility." www.hp.com/hpinfo/globalcitizenship/07gcreport/supplychain.html (accessed August 11, 2010).

15. M.R. Rangaswami and Ram Nidumolu, *Achieving Sustainable Supply Chains: Insight and Practices from Global 500 Enterprises*, Corporate Ecoforum, December 2008, p. 12.

16. Devendra Mishra, Green Media Summit, "Welcome to the Green Media Summit." www.entertainmentsupplychain.com/portal/greenmediasummit/downloads/program.pdf (accessed August 22, 2010).

17. Electric Utility Industry Sustainable Supply Chain Alliance. www.euissca.org/default.aspx (accessed August 11, 2010).

18. GEMI, *Forging New Links*, p. 30; GEMI, *New Paths to Business Value*, p. 20.

19. GEMI, *New Paths to Business Value*, p. 41.

20. GEMI, *New Paths to Business Value*, p. 48.

21. "Patagonia Is First to Track Environmental and Social Impact of Its Products," *CSRwire*, March 24, 2008. www.csrwire.com/press/press_release/18935 (accessed August 11, 2010).

22. Daniel C. Esty and Andrew S. Winston, *Green to Gold* (Hoboken, NJ: John Wiley & Sons, 2009), p. 203.

23. Kanal Consulting, *Best Practices in Sustainability: Supply Chain*, September 2009. www.kanalconsulting.com/Sustainability_SupplyChain_KanalConsulting.pdf (accessed August 11, 2010).

24. Aberdeen Group, "Building a Green Supply Chain: Social Responsibility for Fun and Profit." March 6, 2008. www.aberdeen.com/Aberdeen-Library/4966/RP-green-supply-chain.aspx (accessed October 29, 2010).

25. Hitchcock and Willard, *The Business Guide to Sustainability*, p. 195.

26. AIM, "Responsible Sourcing." www.aim.be/responsible_sourcing.htm (accessed August 11, 2010).

CHAPTER 13. MANUFACTURING AND PROCESSING

1. Pete Abilla, "Toyota Motor Corporation: Company History," Shmula, January 5, 2007. www.shmula.com/291/toyota-motor-corporation-company-history (accessed August 4, 2010). Further discussion of Toyota history based on the same source.

2. "Recycled Carpets and Energy from Trash: Shaw Industries Releases First Sustainability Report," *GreenBiz,* October 15, 2009. www.greenbiz.com/news/2009/10/15/recycled-carpets-and-energy-trash-shaw-industries-releases-first-sustainability-repo (accessed August 6, 2010).

3. "ArcelorMittal Saves $200,000 Annually by Idling Machinery during Production Delays," *Environmental Leader,* March 29, 2010. www.environmentalleader.com/2010/03/29/ (accessed August 6, 2010).

4. HP, "HP Ecosolutions: Use of Recycled Content in Original HP Ink Cartridges," March 2010. www.hp.com/hpinfo/globalcitizenship/environment/productdata/recycledcontentink.pdf (accessed August 23, 2010).

5. "3P." 3M. http://solutions.3m.com/wps/portal/3M/en_US/3M-Sustainability/Global/Environment/3P (accessed October 22, 2010).

6. GEMI, "Case Study: Packaging Innovation at Intel Corporation," 2004. www.gemi.org/supplychain/G1G.htm (accessed August 6, 2010).

7. P.J. Simmons and M.R. Rangaswami, "Show Me the Money: Demonstrating Green Business Value."

8. U.S. EPA, "3M Lean Six Sigma and Sustainability," December 2, 2009. http://epa.gov/lean/studies/3m.htm (accessed June 21, 2010). See this source for other data cited in the paragraph.

9. 3M, in conversation with Dan Esty, October 22, 2010.

10. Gretchen Hancock, "How GE's 'Treasure Hunts' Discovered More than $110M in Energy Savings," *GreenBiz*, May 13, 2009. www.greenbiz.com/blog/2009/05/13/how-ges-treasure-hunts-discovered-more-110m-energy-savings (accessed June 21, 2010). See this source for other GE information provided in the paragraph.

11. GE, "On the Hunt for Sunken Treasure at GE," May 15, 2009. www.gereports.com/on-the-hunt-for-sunken-treasure-at-ge/ (accessed June 21, 2010). Other GE data provided in this paragraph from this source.

12. U.S. EPA, "Steelcase and DuBois-JohnsonDiversey," December 2, 2009. www.epa.gov/lean/studies/steelcase.html (accessed June 21, 2010).

13. U.S. EPA, "Baxter Healthcare Corporation." www.epa.gov/ lean/studies/baxter.htm (accessed June 21, 2010).

14. U.S. EPA, *Lean Manufacturing and the Environment: Research on Advanced Manufacturing Systems and the Environment*, October 2003, p. 25. www.epa.gov/lean/leanreport.pdf (accessed August 4, 2010).

15. U.S. EPA, *Lean and the Environment Toolkit*, October 2007, p. 24. www.epa.gov/lean/toolkit/ (accessed August 4, 2010).

16. U.S. EPA, *Lean and the Environment Toolkit*.

17. U.S. EPA, *Lean and the Environment Toolkit*; U.S. EPA, *The Lean and Chemicals Toolkit*, August 2009. www.epa.gov/lean/chemicalstoolkit/resources/Lean-and-Chemicals-Toolkit.pdf (accessed August 4, 2010).

18. 3M, "3P: Goals and Progress," 2010. http://solutions.3m.com/wps/portal/3M/en_US/3M-Sustainability/Global/Environment/GoalsProgress/ (accessed on August 23, 2010).

19. Joseph Fiksel and Diane Guyse Fiksel, *From Here to Sustainability: A Global* Perspective," Chemistry Business, April 2001, p. 3. www.eco-nomics.com/images/From%20Here%20to%20Sustainability.pdf (accessed on August 23, 2010). See this source for other data on DuPont mentioned in the paragraph.

20. David Dornfeld, "Greening the Supply Chain, Part 4," *Green Manufacturing Blog,* April 10, 2010. http://green-manufacturing.blogspot.com/2010/04/greening-supply-chain-part-4.html (accessed on August 23, 2010). See this source for other data cited in the paragraph.

21. U.S. EPA, "3M Lean Six Sigma and Sustainability." www.epa.gov/lean/studies/3m.htm (accessed August 9, 2010). Further 3M data in the paragraph from this source.

22. "IBM's Green Sigma Coalition Lines Up Industry Leaders," *Environmental Leader,* June 23, 2009. www.environmentalleader.com/2009/06/23/ibms-green-sigma-coalition-lines-up-industry-leaders/ (accessed June 21, 2010). See this source for other data on IBM mentioned in the paragraph.

23. U.S. EPA, "Total Productive Maintenance (TPM)," December 2, 2009. www.epa.gov/lean/thinking/tpm.htm (accessed June 21, 2010). See this source for other data on TPM cited in the paragraph.

24. U.S. EPA, "Total Productive Maintenance (TPM)."

25. U.S. EPA, "Lean Manufacturing and the Environment," May 20, 2010. www.epa.gov/lean/energytoolkit/ch4.htm (accessed June 21, 2010).

26. Productivity Press, *TPM. Collected Practices & Cases: Insights on Implementation* (New York: Productivity Press, 2005).

27. Jack Roberts, "Total Productive Maintenance," *Technology Interface*, Fall 1997. http://et.nmsu.edu/~etti/fall97/manufacturing/tpm2.html (accessed June 21, 2010).

28. Jack Roberts, "Total Productive Maintenance."

29. U.S. EPA, "Cellular Manufacturing," December 2, 2009. www.epa.gov/lean/thinking/cellular.htm (accessed June 21, 2010).

30. U.S. EPA, "Cellular Manufacturing."

31. ThroughPut Solutions "Results & Case Studies. Foundry: Aerospace/Commercial." www.tpslean.com/resultsall.htm (accessed June 21, 2010). See this source for data relevant to this case study cited in the paragraph.

32. David Broyles et al., "Just-In-Time Inventory Management & Lean Manufacturing," *Academic Mind,* April 2005. www.academicmind.com/unpublishedpapers/business/operationsmanagement/2005-04-000aaf-just-in-time-inventory-management.html (accessed June 21, 2010). See this source for data on Dell cited in the paragraph.

33. David Broyles et al., "Just-In-Time Inventory Management & Lean Manufacturing."

34. David Broyles et al., "Just-In-Time Inventory Management & Lean Manufacturing."

35. U.S. EPA, *Lean and the Environment Toolkit,* October 2007. www.epa.gov/lean/toolkit/app-a.htm (accessed June 21, 2010). See this source for other data relevant to kaizen event cited in the paragraph.

36. U.S. EPA, *Lean and the Environment Toolkit.* See this source for other data cited in the paragraph.

37. U.S. EPA, *Lean and Energy Toolkit,* October 2007. www.epa.gov/lean/toolkit/LeanEnergyToolkit.pdf (accessed August 9, 2010). See this source for other data cited in the paragraph.

38. "IBM First to Eliminate PFOS and PFOA in Chip Processes," *Environmental Leader.* www.environmentalleader.com/2010/03/02/ (accessed August 9, 2010). See this source for other data cited in the paragraph.

39. Center for Energy Efficiency & Renewable Energy. www.ceere.org/iac/assessment%20tool/ARC2140.html (accessed November 10, 2010).

40. U.S. EPA, *Lean and Energy Toolkit,* October 2007, 39; "Spoetzl Brewery to Add $3 Million Biogas Facility," *Environmental Leader,* May 14, 2010. www. environmental-leader.com/2010/05/14/ (accessed June 21, 2010). See this source for other data cited in the paragraph.

41. Eric Gershon, "New Haven Printing Company Readies Wind Turbine," *CT Now.com,* February 18, 2010. www.ctnow.com/business/hc-windpower.artfeb18,0,1783341.story (accessed August 21, 2010).

42. North American Windpower, "Cascades Tissue Group Purchases Additional Wind Power," April 14, 2010. www.csrwire.com/press_releases/29328-Cascades-Tissue-Group-Doubles-Commitment-to-Wind-Energy-Based-Manufacturing- (accessed August 4, 2010).

43. "Pricing for Utility Green Power Continues to Fall," *Environmental Leader,* May 4, 2010. www.environmentalleader.com/2010/05/04/ (accessed June 21, 2010).

44. Queensland Government, "Digital Manufacturing." http://203.210.126.185/dsdweb/v4/apps/web/secure/docs/2508.pdf (accessed August 4, 2010).

45. Dassault Systèmes, "Hydrolift Boats Fly without Wings with PLM Solutions from IBM and Dassault Systèmes," June 9, 2005. www.3ds.com/fileadmin/COMPANY/PRESS/PR/PDF/2005-06-09-889-Hydrolift_Boats_Fly_Without.pdf (accessed August 21, 2010). See this source for other data cited in the paragraph.

46. "Energy Intelligence Results in 15% Efficiency Boost for Manufacturers," *Environmental Leader,* January 15, 2010. www.environmentalleader.com/2010/01/15/ (accessed June 21, 2010).

47. Andrew Maykuth, "ArcelorMittal Plant Cited for Energy Efficiency," *Philly.com,* March 28, 2010. www.philly.com/philly/business/89343432.html (accessed August 3, 2010). See this source for other data cited in the paragraph.

48. David Dornfeld, "Why Green Manufacturing? Part 2," *Green Manufacturing Blog,* July 23, 2009. http://green-manufacturing.blogspot.com/2009/07/why-green-manufacturing-part-2.html (accessed June 21, 2010).

49. David Dornfeld, "Greening the Supply Chain, Part 3," *Environmental Leader*, May 10, 2010. www.environmentalleader.com/2010/05/10/ (accessed June 21, 2010).

50. Yale Center for Industrial Ecology, "Welcome to the Center for Industrial Ecology." http://cie.research.yale.edu/ (accessed June 21, 2010).

51. John R. Ehrenfeld and Marian Chertow, "Industrial Symbiosis: The Legacy of Kalundborg," In *A Handbook of Industrial Ecology*, edited by Robert U. Ayres and Leslie Ayres (Edward Elgar, 2002), p. 334. See this source for data on Kalundborg case cited in this text.

52. To get a sense of the complexity of the arrangement, visit www.symbiosis.dk/industrial-symbiosis.aspx.

53. BISSELL, "Processes." www.bissell.com/Detail.aspx?id=61 (accessed June 21, 2010). See this source for other data cited in this paragraph.

54. ClimateBiz, "General Mills Product Shifts Lead to Climate Goal Challenges," *GreenBiz*, April 14, 2010. www.greenbiz.com/news/2010/04/14/general-mills-product-changes-climate-goal-challenges#ixzzolTSr4GEB (accessed June 21, 2010).

55. Queensland Government, "Water Efficiency." http://203.210.126.185/dsdweb/v4/apps/web/secure/docs/2500.pdf (accessed August 4, 2010). See this source for other data relevant to this paragraph.

56. "Shingle Recycling Business Allows Roofers, Haulers to Go Green." WebWire. www.webwire.com/ViewPressRel.asp?aId=119793 (accessed October 14, 2010).

57. Heather King, "The View from the C-Suite: Waste Management CEO David Steiner," *GreenBiz*, April 19, 2010. www.greenbiz.com/blog/2010/04/19/view-csuite-waste-management-david-steiner?page=0,1 (accessed June 21, 2010). See this source for other relevant data cited in this paragraph.

CHAPTER 14. LOGISTICS AND TRANSPORT

1. See http://citizenshipblog.fedex.designcdt.com/node/810; and NYSE Magazine. www.nysemagazine.com/the-power-of-green?page=3).

2. Claudia Girrbach, "How Cisco's Packaging Diet Saves $24 Million a Year," *GreenBiz*, March 12, 2010. www.greenbiz.com/blog/2010/03/10/how-ciscos-packaging-diet-saves-24-million-year (accessed July 16, 2010).

3. Walmart, "Walmart Tests New Hybrid Trucks, Alternative Fuels," February 2, 2010. http://walmartstores.com/FactsNews/NewsRoom/8949.aspx (accessed July 16, 2010).

4. "UPS Streamlining Business Pickup Schedule to Trim Fuel, Emissions," *Environmental Leader*, March 24, 2010. www.environmentalleader.com/2010/03/24/ (accessed July 16, 2010).

5. "McKesson to Save $300K via Fuel-Efficient Vehicles," *Environmental Leader*, November 5, 2009. www.environmentalleader.com/2009/11/05/ (accessed July 16, 2010).

6. AT&T, "AT&T Public Policy." www.att.com/gen/public-affairs?pid=12907 (accessed August 21, 2010).

7. "JCPenney to Reduce Energy Use 20% by 2015," *Environmental Leader*, May 4, 2010. www.environmentalleader.com/2010/05/04 (accessed July 16, 2010).

8. 3M, "Sustainability at 3M." http://solutions.3m.com/wps/portal/3M/en_US/3M-Sustainability/Global/ (accessed November 9, 2010).

9. Environmental Defense Fund, "Fleet Vehicles." http://innovation.edf.org/page.cfm?tagID=30617&redirect=greenfleet (accessed July 16, 2010).

10. Clorox, "Operational Footprint." www.cloroxcsr.com/op-footprint/ (accessed July 16, 2010).

11. "FedEx Expands Hybrid-Electric Fleet by 50%," *Environmental Leader,* July 23, 2009. www.environmentalleader.com/2009/07/23/ (accessed July 16, 2010).

12. Environmental Defense Fund, *Fleet Drivers and Fuel-Smart Driving.* www.edf.org/documents/10406_EDF_Fuel-Smart-Driving-Handbook.pdf (accessed August 4, 2010).

13. U.S. DoE, Energy Efficiency and Renewable Energy, "Driving More Efficiently." www.fueleconomy.gov/feg/drivehabits.shtml (accessed August 21, 2010).

14. "Progressive Shifting," Wikipedia, the free encyclopedia. http://en.wikipedia.org/wiki/Progressive_shifting (accessed July 16, 2010).

15. Sean Kilcarr, "Good for the Long Haul," *Fleet Owner* magazine, November 13, 2008. http://fleetowner.com/green/good_long_haul_1108/ (accessed July 16, 2010).

16. Bob Denaro, "Five Ways Technology Can Boost Green Driving Practices," *GreenBiz,* May 21, 2010. www.greenbiz.com/blog/2010/05/21/five-ways-technology-can-boost-green-driving-practices (accessed July 16, 2010).

17. Greater Vancouver Regional District, *Sustainable Supply Chain Logistics Guide,* 2009, p. 18.

18. Digital Lumens, "Industrial Lighting and Commercial Lighting." www.digitallumens.com/products/ (accessed July 16, 2010).

19. Greater Vancouver Regional District, *Sustainable Supply Chain Logistics Guide,* p. 19.

20. Greater Vancouver Regional District, *Sustainable Supply Chain Logistics Guide,* pp. 19–20, 26.

21. U.S. EPA, SmartWay Transport Partnership, "Technologies-Upgrade Kits." www. epa.gov/smartwaylogistics/transport/what-smartway/upgrade-kits-tech.htm (accessed July 16, 2010); SmartWay Partnership, "SmartWay Technology Upgrade Kits for Trucking Companies. Concept Proposal," September 2005. www.marama.org/diesel/frieght/Wachovia_%20SmartWay_Concept_%20Document.pdf (accessed August 21, 2010).

22. EA Logistics, *Get It There Green,* June 2009. www.ealogistics.com/docs/get_it_there_green.pdf (accessed August 4, 2010).

23. Bob Denaro, "Five Ways Technology Can Boost..."

24. Paul Brody and Mondher Ben-Hamida, "12 Steps to a 'Greener' Supply Chain," *Environmental Leader,* November 30, 2008. www.environmentalleader.com/2008/11/30 (accessed July 16, 2010).

25. Greater Vancouver Regional District, *Sustainable Supply Chain Logistics Guide,* p. 24.

26. Greater Vancouver Regional District, *Sustainable Supply Chain Logistics Guide,* p. 24.

27. Fresh Pak Corp., "Case Studies." www.freshpakcorp.com/case-studies/case-studies.html (accessed July 16, 2010).

28. Walmart, *Walmart Sustainability Report 2010.* http://walmartstores.com/sites/ sustainabilityreport/2010/commitments_energy.aspx (accessed July 16, 2010).

29. Claudia Girrbach, "How Cisco's Packaging Diet Saves $24 Million a Year."

30. Lovely Package, "Puma—Clever Little Bag," April 14, 2010. http://lovelypackage.com/pumas-clever-little-bag/ (accessed July 16, 2010).

31. John Brownlee, "Amazon's 'frustration-free' packaging ruins customers' hard drives," *Geek.com,* March 31, 2010. www.geek.com/articles/news/amazons-frustration-free-packaging-ruins-customers-hard-drives-20100331/ (accessed July 16, 2010).

32. Bill Armstrong and Arnold Barlow, "Hold Everything: Adopting Protective Packaging Practices," *Inbound Logistics,* March 2010. www.inboundlogistics.com/ articles/green/green0310.shtml (accessed July 16, 2010).

33. Greater Vancouver Regional District, *Sustainable Supply Chain Logistics Guide*, p. 26.

34. David Blanchard, "SC Johnson Finds a 'Greener' Way to Load Trucks," *Industry-Week*, February 1, 2008. www.industryweek.com/articles/sc_johnson_finds_a_greener_way_to_load_trucks_15608.aspx?ShowAll=1 (accessed July 16, 2010).

35. Pradeep Chaudhary, "Green Landscape," *Inbound Logistics*, November 2009. www.inboundlogistics.com/articles/green/green1109.shtml (accessed July 16, 2010).

36. "New Stores Increase CVS' CO_2 Emissions Nearly 10% in 2009," *Environmental Leader,* May 14, 2010. www.environmentalleader.com/2010/05/14/ (accessed July 16, 2010).

37. David Blanchard, "SC Johnson Finds a 'Greener' Way."

38. "Macy's Cuts GHG Emissions, Transportation Costs," *Environmental Leader*, October 13, 2009. www.environmentalleader.com/2009/10/13/ (accessed July 16, 2010).

39. Esty Environmental Partners worked with Timex on this project.

40. Greater Vancouver Regional District, *Sustainable Supply Chain Logistics Guide*, p. 23.

41. Bill Armstrong and Arnold Barlow. "Green Landscape," *Inbound Logistics*, March 2010. www.inboundlogistics.com/articles/green/green0310.shtml (accessed July 16, 2010).

42. Elisabeth Rosenthal, "Slow Trip across Sea Aids Profit and Environment," *New York Times*, February 16, 2010. www.nytimes.com/2010/02/17/business/energy-environment/17speed.html (accessed August 4, 2010).

43. Rosenthal, Elisabeth. "Slow Trip across Sea."

44. Kurt Kuehn, "Five Ways to Convince Your CFO that Sustainability Pays," *Green-Biz,* April 13, 2010 www.greenbiz.com/blog/2010/04/13/five-ways-convince-your-cfo-sustainability-pays (accessed July 16, 2010).

45. "UPS Expands Hybrid EV Fleet to NYC, DC, Chicago, Other Major Cities," *Environmental Leader,* April 6, 2010. www.environmentalleader.com/2010/04/06/ (accessed July 16, 2010).

46. AT&T, "News Room: AT&T to Deploy More than 15,000 Alternative-Fuel Vehicles," March 11, 2009. www.att.com/gen/press-room?pid=4800&cdvn=news&newsarticleid=26598 (accessed July 16, 2010).

47. "Wal-Mart Tests New Trucks, Surpasses Fuel Efficiency Goals," *Environmental Leader,* February 3, 2009. www.environmentalleader.com/2009/02/03/ (accessed July 16, 2010).

48. "HP Packaging to Carry EPA SmartWay Logos," *Environmental Leader*, April 20, 2008. www.environmentalleader.com/2008/04/20/ (accessed July 16, 2010).

49. Fuel Economy.gov, "Natural Gas—CNG & LNG." www.fueleconomy.gov/feg/bifueltech.shtml (accessed July 16, 2010); Sean Kilcarr, "All-Natural Power," *Fleet Owner* magazine, November 13, 2008. http://fleetowner.com/green/allnatural_power_1108/ (accessed July 16, 2010).

50. U.S. DoE, Energy Efficiency and Renewable Energy, "What Is Natural Gas?" www.afdc.energy.gov/afdc/fuels/natural_gas_what_is.html (accessed July 16, 2010).

51. David Cullen, "Alternative Power Choices," *Fleet Owner* magazine, April 1, 2010. http://fleetowner.com/green/alternative-power-choices-0401/ (accessed July 16, 2010).

52. Sean Kilcarr, "All-Natural Power."

53. "Cleaning Up Refuse Trucks," *Fleet Owner* magazine; November 13, 2008. http://fleetowner.com/green/cleaning_refuse_trucks_1108/ (accessed July 16, 2010); "Clean Transportation Funding Opportunities," North Carolina Solar Center—Home page. www.ncsc.ncsu.edu/cleantransportation/funding.htm (accessed July 16, 2010).

54. "Republic Services Adds 226 Natural Gas Trucks," *Environmental Leader*, April 5, 2010. www.environmentalleader.com/2010/04/05/ (accessed July 16, 2010).

55. U.S. DoE, Energy Efficiency and Renewable Energy, "Propane as an Alternative Fuel." www.afdc.energy.gov/afdc/fuels/propane_alternative.html (accessed July 16, 2010);

U.S. DoE, Energy Efficiency and Renewable Energy, "What Is Propane?" www. afdc.energy.gov/afdc/fuels/propane_what_is.html (accessed July 16, 2010).

56. Carbon Trust, *Energy and Carbon Conversions*, July 16, 2009. www.minus3.org/ dokumenti/Final_Report_16_July_2009/Appendix_7_-_Carbon_Conversion_Factors_-_ Carbon_Trust.pdf (accessed August 4, 2010).

57. U.S. DoE, Energy Efficiency and Renewable Energy, "What Is a Propane Vehicle?" www.afdc.energy.gov/afdc/vehicles/propane_what_is.html (accessed July 16, 2010).

58. U.S. DoE, Energy Efficiency and Renewable Energy, *Clean Cities 2010 Vehicle Buyer's Guide*, December 2009, p. 7. www.afdc.energy.gov/afdc/pdfs/46432.pdf (accessed August 4, 2010).

59. "Propane," Wikipedia, the free encyclopedia. http://en.wikipedia.org/wiki/Propane (accessed July 16, 2010).

60. U.S. DoE, Energy Efficiency and Renewable Energy, "Propane Emissions." www.afdc. energy.gov/afdc/vehicles/emissions_propane.html (accessed July 16, 2010).

61. David Cullen, "Alternative Power Choices."

62. U.S. DoE, Energy Efficiency and Renewable Energy, "Propane Vehicle Availability." www.afdc.energy.gov/afdc/vehicles/propane_availability.html#conversions (accessed July 16, 2010).

63. "New Ford Propane Conversion Systems," *Environmental Leader,* June 17, 2010. www.environmentalleader.com/2010/06/17/ (accessed July 16, 2010).

64. PrimeTime Shuttle, "Prime Time Shuttle to Save 1.5 Million…" *Business Wire*, June 23, 2010. www.businesswire.com/portal/site/home/permalink (accessed July 16, 2010).

65. David Sandalow, *Freedom from Oil: How the Next President Can End the United States' Oil Addiction* (New York: McGraw-Hill, 2008), p. 83.

66. American Coalition for Ethanol, "Ethanol & Your Vehicle." www.ethanol.org/ index.php?id=50&parentid=8 (accessed July 16, 2010).

67. U.S. DoE, Energy Efficiency and Renewable Energy, *Clean Cities 2010 Vehicle Buyer's Guide*, p. 14.

68. U.S. DoE, Energy Efficiency and Renewable Energy, "Alternative Fueling Station Total Counts by State and Fuel Type." www.afdc.energy.gov/afdc/fuels/stations_counts.html (accessed July 16, 2010).

69. U.S. EPA, "Greenhouse Gas Impacts of Expanded Renewable and Alternative Fuels Use," April 2007. www.epa.gov/oms/renewablefuels/420f07035.htm (accessed August 21, 2010).

70. American Coalition for Ethanol, "Environment & Clean Air." www.ethanol.org/ index.php?id=34&parentid=8#Environment (accessed July 16, 2010).

71. Jeff Cox, "Sugar Cane Ethanol's Not-So-Sweet Future," *CNNMoney.com*, August 7, 2007. http://money.cnn.com/2007/08/06/news/economy/sugarcane_ethanol/index.htm (accessed July 16, 2010).

72. National Renewable Energy Laboratory and Oak Ridge National Laboratory, "Effects of Intermediate Ethanol Blends on Legacy Vehicles and Small Non-Road Engines" (October 2008).

73. U.S. DoE, Energy Efficiency and Renewable Energy, "Ultra-Low Sulfur Diesel Benefits." www.afdc.energy.gov/afdc/fuels/emerging_sulfur_diesel_benefits.html (accessed July 16, 2010).

74. U.S. DoE, Energy Efficiency and Renewable Energy, *Clean Cities Alternative Fuel Price Report*, April 2010. www.afdc.energy.gov/afdc/pdfs/afpr_apr_10.pdf (accessed August 4, 2010), p. 5.

75. U.S. DoE, Energy Efficiency and Renewable Energy, "B20 and B100: Alternative Fuels." www.afdc.energy.gov/afdc/fuels/biodiesel_alternative.html (accessed July 16, 2010).

76. Sean Kilcarr, "All-Natural Power."

77. Biodiesel Sustainability, "The Economics of Biodiesel Production and the Effect on Food Prices." www.biodieselsustainability.com/faq.html (accessed August 9, 2010).

78. National Biodiesel Board, "Environmental Benefits." www.biodiesel.org/pdf_files/fuelfactsheets/Enviro_Benefits.PDF (accessed August 4, 2010).

79. U.S. EPA, "Fuel Options." www.epa.gov/smartway/vehicles/smartway-fuels.htm (accessed July 16, 2010); U.S. DoE, Energy Efficiency and Renewable Energy, "What Is Biodiesel?" www.afdc.energy.gov/afdc/fuels/biodiesel_what_is.html (accessed July 16, 2010).

80. U.S. DoE, Energy Efficiency and Renewable Energy, "Biodiesel Fleet Experiences: L.L. Bean Delivers with Biodiesel," June 19, 2010. www.afdc.energy.gov/afdc/progs/fleet_exp_fuel.php/BD (accessed July 16, 2010).

81. U.S. DoE, Energy Efficiency and Renewable Energy, "Biodiesel Fleet Experiences." www.afdc.energy.gov/afdc/progs/fleet_exp_fuel.php/BD (accessed July 16, 2010).

82. Environmental Defense Fund, "Hybrids Are a Win-Win for the Environment," August 8, 2008. http://innovation.edf.org/page.cfm?tagID=24156 (accessed July 16, 2010).

83. Sean Kilcarr, "Medium-Duty Hybrids Projected to Be Strongest Sellers," *Fleet Owner* magazine, May 20, 2010. http://fleetowner.com/green/archive/medium-duty-hybrids-strongest-sellers-0520/ (accessed July 16, 2010).

84. Green Car Congress, "Pike Research Forecasts 300,000 Medium- and Heavy-Duty Hybrid Trucks and Buses Worldwide by 2015; 63% CAGR," June 2, 2010. www.greencarcongress.com/hydraulic_hybrid/ (accessed July 16, 2010).

85. Environmental Defense Fund, *Greenhouse Gas Management for Medium-Duty Truck Fleets*, December 2009, p. 4. http://edf.org/documents/10860_fleets-med-ghg-management.pdf (accessed August 4, 2010).

86. Greater Vancouver Regional District, *Sustainable Supply Chain Logistics Guide*, 2009, p. 21.

87. "Kraft Foods Rolls Out "Green" Truck," *Environmental Leader,* March 5, 2009. www.environmentalleader.com/2009/03/05/ (accessed July 16, 2010).

88. Robert Johnson, "Specing Trucks for Fuel Efficiency," *Government Engineering*, January–February 2009, p. 22. www.govengr.com/ArticlesJan09/fuel.pdf (accessed July 16, 2010).

89. Sean Kilcarr, "Good for the Long Haul."

90. Sean Kilcarr, "Good for the Long Haul."

91. Sean Kilcarr, "Good for the Long Haul."

92. "Getting Green in the Dirt," *Fleet Owner* magazine. http://fleetowner.com/green/getting_green_dirt_1108/ (accessed July 16, 2010).

93. "Getting Green in the Dirt."

94. Greater Vancouver Regional District, *Sustainable Supply Chain Logistics Guide*, 2009, p. 15.

95. Kevin Collins, "Best Practices for Putaway," *SmartTurn*, October 23, 2008. www.smartturn.com/forums/blogs/kevin-collins/10-best-practices-putaway.html (accessed July 16, 2010).

96. Kevin Collins, "Best Practices for Picking in Warehouses and Distribution Centers," *SmartTurn*, October 23, 2008. www.smartturn.com/forums/blogs/kevin-collins/11-best-practices-picking-warehouses-distribution-centers.html (accessed July 16, 2010).

97. Kevin Collins, "Best Practices for Picking in Warehouses and Distribution Centers."

98. Kevin Collins, "Best Practices for Picking in Warehouses and Distribution Centers."

99. Greater Vancouver Regional District, *Sustainable Supply Chain Logistics Guide*, 2009, p. 15.

100. Kevin Collins, "Best Practices for Picking in Warehouses and Distribution Centers."

101. "Sysco Warehouse Opens with Fuel Cell Forklifts, Palette Trucks," Hydrogen Fuel Cars Now website, *Hydrogen Car Blog,* June 21, 2010. www.hydrogencarsnow.com/blog2/index.php/hydrogenforklifts (accessed July 16, 2010).

102. Nicole Mordant, "Walmart Canada to Build Green Distribution Hub," *Reuters.com,* February 10, 2010. www.reuters.com/article/idUSN1018851220100210 (accessed July 16, 2010).

103. "Smucker DC Generates 94% of Own Energy," *Environmental Leader,* February 3, 2010. www.environmentalleader.com/2010/02/03/ (accessed July 16, 2010).

104. Asian Productivity Organization, *Green Productivity and Green Supply Chain Manual* (Tokyo: APO, 2008), p. 61.

105. Kevin Collins, "Best Practices for Putaway."

106. Westfalia, "Automated Storage & Retrieval Systems." www.westfaliausa.com/ (accessed July 16, 2010);
Laura Worker, "Green Landscape," *Inbound Logistics,* June 2010. www.inbound logistics.com/articles/green/green0610.shtml (accessed July 16, 2010).

107. Laura Worker, "Green Landscape."

108. Patrick Barnard, "Zappos DC Does the Robot," *Multichannel Merchant,* July 22, 2008. http://multichannelmerchant.com/opsandfulfillment/advisor/0722-zappos-warehouse-robots/ (accessed July 16, 2010).

109. Kimberly-Clark, "Kimberly-Clark Wins U.S. EPA SmartWay Environmental Excellence Award," October 7, 2008. http://investor.kimberly-clark.com/releasedetail.cfm?ReleaseID=338773 (accessed July 16, 2010).

110. Greater Vancouver Regional District, *Sustainable Supply Chain Logistics Guide,* 2009, p. 11.

111. Air Products, *2010 Sustainability Report,* p. 37. www.airproducts.com/ Responsibility/2010AnnualReport.htm (accessed November 10, 2010).

112. Greater Vancouver Regional District, *Sustainable Supply Chain Logistics Guide,* 2009, p. 13.

113. UPS, *Reverse Logistics—the Least Used Differentiator,* 2005. www.ups-scs.com/ solutions/white_papers/wp_reverse_logistics.pdf (accessed August 5, 2010).

114. "U-Haul, OPOWER Win Alliance Awards," *Environmental Leader,* June 14, 2010. www.environmentalleader.com/2010/06/14/ (accessed July 16, 2010).

115. Maryann Jones Thompson, "Turning 'Scrap' into Profit," *Corporate Eco Forum,* November 19, 2008. http://corporateecoforum.com/ecoinnovator/?p=936 (accessed July 16, 2010).

116. "Cisco Reduces Net GHG Emissions by 40%," *Environmental Leader,* December 8, 2009. www.environmentalleader.com/2009/12/08/ (accessed July 16, 2010).

117. RLM, "Best Buy Turning Returns Processing into Profit Center," *Reverse Logistics Magazine,* Edition 15, p. 28. www.rlmagazine.com/edition15p28.php (accessed July 16, 2010).

118. RLM, "Best Buy Turning Returns Processing into Profit Center."

CHAPTER 15. MARKETING AND SALES

1. Lovemarks, "Lovemarks: The Future Beyond Brands." www.lovemarks.com/index.php?pageID=20020 (accessed August 11, 2010).

2. "Interview with Kevin Roberts, CEO Worldwide of Saatchi & Saatchi," IESE website, June 17, 2010. www.iese.edu/aplicaciones/news/view.asp?id=2380&lan=en (accessed August 11, 2010); Kevin Roberts, "Turning a Green Apple Blue," *KR Connect Blog,*

June 21, 2010. http://krconnect.blogspot.com/2010/06/turning-green-apple-blue.html (accessed August 11, 2010).

3. Bob Lipp, "Impact of B2B Green Marketing in an Increasingly Environmentally Conscious World," *Environmental Leader*, June 14, 2010. www.environmentalleader.com/2010/06/14/impact-of-b2b-green-marketing-in-an-increasingly-environmentally-conscious-world/(accessed August 11, 2010).

4. Organic Trade Association, "Industry Statistics and Projected Growth," June 2010. www.ota.com/organic/mt/business.html (accessed August 18, 2010).

5. Becky Ebenkamp, "Mintel: Households Embracing Eco-Friendly Cleaning Products," *Brandweek*, February 10, 2009.

6. EcoFocus Worldwide, "EcoFocus Report Identifies Opportunities for Companies to Target $1.45 Trillion Market for EcoAware Moms," September 8, 2010. http://ecofocusworldwide.com/?p=855 (accessed November 5, 2010).

7. Cohn and Wolfe and others, "2010 ImagePower Green Brands Survey." www.wpp.com/wpp/press/press/default.htm?guid={b983b1a9-ab92-4427-b75f-ab35f2565dad} (accessed August 18, 2010).

8. "GE's Judy Hu: 'We're Reinventing a Brand and a Company.'" *Knowledge@Wharton*, December 19, 2007. www.knowledgeatwharton.com.cn/index.cfm?fa=viewfeature&articleid=1759&languageid=1 (accessed August 18, 2010); Laura Petrecca and Theresa Howard. "Eco-Marketing a Hot Topic for Advertisers at Cannes," *USAToday.com*, June 22, 2007. www.usatoday.com/money/advertising/2007-06-22-cannes-green-usat_N.htm (accessed August 11, 2010).

9. "GE to Invest $10B More in Ecomagination R&D by 2015," *GreenBiz*, June 24, 2010. www.greenbiz.com/news/2010/06/24/ge-invest-10b-more-ecomagination-rd-2015 (accessed August 11, 2010).

10. Gregory Unruh and Richard Ettenson. "Growing Green," *Harvard Business Review,* June 2010. http://hbr.org/2010/06/growing-green/ar/1 (accessed June 23, 2010).

11. Brita, "Recycle Your Brita Filter." www.brita.com/support/filter-recycling/ (accessed August 21, 2010).

12. "One Year On, Clorox's Green Works Dominates Market," *Sustainable Life Media*, January 15, 2009. www.sustainablelifemedia.com/content/story/strategy/one_year_on_cloroxs_green_works_dominates_market (accessed August 11, 2010).

13. "Clorox Green Works, Burt's Bees, Tom's of Maine—Top U.S. Green Brands," *Environmental Leader,* July 21, 2009. www.environmentalleader.com/2009/07/21/clorox-green-works-burts-bees-toms-of-maine-top-us-green-brands/ (accessed August 18, 2010; reviewed August 16, 2010).

14. Jeffrey Hittner and Eric Riddleberger, *Leading a Sustainable Enterprise: Leveraging Insight and Information to Act*, IBM Institute for Business Value, 2009; IBM, "Leading a Sustainable Enterprise." www.935.ibm.com/services/us/gbs/bus/html/csr-study-2009.html (accessed August 11, 2010).

15. Kevin Kramer, "Remarks on Sustainability: The Next Growth Engine Video," *Corporate Eco Forum*, June 7, 2010. http://corporateecoforum.com/conference/videos_2010.php (accessed August 11, 2010).

16. KR Sridhar, "Remarks on Sustainability as Key Driver of Innovation Video," *Corporate Eco Forum,* June 8, 2010. http://corporateecoforum.com/conference/videos_2010.php (accessed August 11, 2010).

17. GfK Roper Consulting, "Study: Americans Reach Environmental Turning Point, Companies Must Catch Up," *Marketing Charts*, August 24, 2007. www.marketingcharts.com/topics/demographics/study-americans-reach-environmental-turning-point-companies-must-catch-up-1369/ (accessed August 18, 2010); GfK Roper Consulting,

"Green Gets Real ... Current Economic Environment Subduing Green Enthusiasm but Driving Practical Action," GfK Roper website, 2008. www.gfkamerica. com/newsroom/press_releases/single_sites/003698/index.en.html (accessed August 18, 2010); "The LOHAS Consumer Trends Database," *Natural Marketing Institute.* www.nmisolutions.com/lohasd_segment.html (accessed August 18, 2010); Kaoru Kunita, "LOHAS Takes Japan," LOHAS Online. www.lohas.com/journal/japan.html (accessed August 18, 2010); Hartman Group, "State of the Organic Consumer Webinar," April, 2010. www.authorstream.com/Presentation/larrycouch-366444-beyond-natural-organic-2010-bon-webinar-apr2010-news-reports-ppt-powerpoint/ (accessed August 18, 2010).

18. Russ Meyer, "Five Reasons Not to Have a Green Brand (And Why Those Reasons Are Wrong)," *Landor Associates*, September 2009, p. 3.

19. "Duane Reade launches new eco-friendly products," *Organic-Market,* April 21, 2010. www.organic-market.info/web/News_in_brief/Regional_Marketing/New_York/176/194/20/7623.html (accessed August 11, 2010); "Duane Reade: Your City. Your Drugstore," Duane Reade website. https://secure.duanereade.com/EcoClub.aspx (accessed August 11, 2010).

20. Author interview, August 2010.

21. Matt Kistler, "Remarks on Progress Towards Measuring Sustainability Video," *Corporate Eco Forum*, June 7, 2010. http://corporateecoforum.com/conference/videos_2010.php (accessed August 11, 2010).

22. Bob Lipp, "Tailoring Green Messages for Your Target Market," *Environmental Leader*, August 4, 2010. www.environmentalleader.com/ 2010/08/04/tailoring-green-messages-for-your-target-market/ (accessed August 11, 2010).

23. Russ Meyer, "Five Reasons Not to Have a Green Brand (And Why Those Reasons Are Wrong)."

24. "Quotations for Public Relations Consultants," Parker Wayne & Kent Ltd. www.pwkpr.com/public_relations_quotations/Reputations.htm (accessed August 11, 2010).

25. "New Research Shows that Despite the Economic Recession, Consumers Still Place Considerable Value on Sustainability," *Havas Media.com*, April 29, 2009. www.havasmedia. com/dynfiles/SF09Global%20release.pdf (accessed August 18, 2010).

26. "Greenwashing," Wikipedia, the free encyclopedia. http://en.wikipedia.org/wiki/Greenwash (accessed August 11, 2010).

27. "The Seven Sins of Greenwashing," TerraChoice Environmental Marketing. http://sinsofgreenwashing.org/ (accessed August 11, 2010).

28. Chris Tryhorn, "No Bouquets for Shell Press Ad," *Guardian.co.uk*, November 7, 2007. www.guardian.co.uk/media/2007/nov/07/asa.advertising (accessed August 11, 2010).

29. "The Fuzzy Math of Eco-Accolades," *BusinessWeek,* October 29, 2007. www.businessweek.com/magazine/content/07_44/b4056003.htm (accessed November 9, 2010).

30. Rory Harrington, "Report Outlines Compostable Packaging Challenges," *Food Ingredients*, June 7, 2010. www.foodnavigator-usa.com/Financial-Industry/Report-outlines-compostable-packaging-challenges (accessed August 11, 2010).

31. "U.S. in the World: Talking Global Issues with Americans—A Practical Guide." www.usintheworld.org (accessed August 18, 2010).

32. Walmart, "It's Rollback Time at Walmart, Video," 2010. www.youtube.com/watch?v=s5CyX8043Pc (accessed August 18, 2010).

33. Motorola, "Greener by Design." http://responsibility.motorola.com/index.php/environment/casestudies/ (accessed November 9, 2010).

34. Gil Friend, *The Truth about Green Business* (FT Press, 2009), p. 69.

35. Ricoh USA, "Ricoh Completes Times Square's First 100 Percent Solar Powered Billboard." www.ricoh-usa.com/about/press/releases.asp?id=627 (accessed August 11, 2010).

36. Fabio Forfori, *Evaluation of the British Energy Efficiency Commitment*, AID-EE, August 2006. www.aid-ee.org/documents/004EEC-UnitedKingdom.PDF (accessed August 18, 2010), p. 13.

37. "Brita, Nalgene Take Advantage of Bottled Water Backlash," *Environmental Leader*, August 15, 2007. www.environmentalleader.com/2007/08/15/brita-nalgene-take-advantage-of-bottled-water-backlash/ (accessed August 11, 2010).

38. HP, "HP Wins Walmart's Design Challenge." http://h71036.www7.hp.com/hho/cache/605859-0-0-225-121.html (accessed August 11, 2010); Walmart, "HP Wins Walmart Design Challenge with Innovative Notebook Packaging," September 3, 2008. http://walmartstores.com/pressroom/news/8565.aspx (accessed August 11, 2010).

39. "P&G "Future Friendly" Green Crayon Commercial," *Homadge Blog*, May 28, 2010. http://homadge.blogspot.com/2010/04/pg-future-friendly-green-crayon.html (accessed August 11, 2010).

CHAPTER 16. LEGAL AND REGULATORY AFFAIRS

1. Stacy Perman, "Radical Green," *Time* 175, no. 15, April 12, 2010.

2. Stacy Perman, "Radical Green."

3. Michael Porter, "America's Green Strategy," *Scientific American* 264, no. 4, April 1991.

4. "Irika Shipping to Pay $4M Penalty for Violating Maritime Pollution Law." Environmental Leader. www.environmentalleader.com/2010/07/12/ (accessed November 10, 2010).

5. Simons, Marlise, "Netherlands: Oil Trading Company Fined in Dumping of Toxic Sludge," *New York Times*, July 23, 2010.

6. SC Johnson, "Our GreenList™ Process." www.scjohnson.com/en/commitment/focus-on/greener-products/greenlist.aspx (accessed August 3, 2010).

7. EEp. Personal interview, October 2010.

8. Jennifer C. Kerr, "Mattel Fined $2.3M for Lead Paint on Toys," *USA Today.com*, June 5, 2009. www.usatoday.com/money/industries/retail/2009-06-05-mattel-fine_N.htm (accessed August 3, 2010).

CHAPTER 17. ACCOUNTING AND FINANCE

1. CFO Research Services and Jones Lang LaSalle, *The Role of Finance in Environmental Sustainability Efforts* (Boston: CFO Publishing Corp, 2008), p. 20.

2. CFO Research Services and Jones Lang LaSalle, *The Role of Finance*, p. 2.

3. Kurt Kuehn, "Five Ways to Convince Your CFO that Sustainability Pays," April 13 2010, *GreenBiz*. www.greenbiz.com/print/34193 (accessed August 21, 2010).

4. CFO Research Services and Jones Lang LaSalle, *The Role of Finance*, p. 2.

5. Kurt Kuehn, "Five Ways to Convince Your CFO."

6. CFO Research Services and Jones Lang LaSalle, *The Role of Finance*, p. 17.

7. Aysu Katun, "Why CFOs Need a Financial Strategy for Energy and Carbon," *The Green Economy Post*, April 12, 2010. http://greeneconomypost.com/cfos-financial-strategy-energy-carbon-9444.htm (accessed August 21, 2010).

8. Maria Harris, Millie Chu Baird, Jeff Crystal, *Climate Corps Handbook*, Environmental Defense Fund, 2008, p. 7. www.edf.org/documents/7865_climatecorps_handbook.pdf (accessed August 21, 2010).

9. Lauralee Martin remarks at *Corporate Eco Forum* Annual Meeting, San Francisco, June 6, 2010. http://corporateecoforum.com/conference/videos_2010.php.

10. CFO Research Services and Jones Lang LaSalle, *The Role of Finance,* p. 17.
11. CFO Research Services and Jones Lang LaSalle, *The Role of Finance,* p. 7.
12. CFO Research Services and Jones Lang LaSalle, *The Role of Finance,* p. 17.
13. CFO Research Services and Jones Lang LaSalle, *The Role of Finance,* p. 11.
14. CFO Research Services and Jones Lang LaSalle, *The Role of Finance,* p. 13.
15. International Federation of Accountants (IFAC), *Environmental Management Accounting, International Guidance Document,* August 2005, p. 30.
16. "IT Should Pay the Power Bill, Reasons EBay Exec," *CIO.com,* May 18, 2010. www.cio.com/article/594116/IT_Should_Pay_the_Power_Bill_Reasons_EBay_Exec (accessed August 21, 2010).
17. "Environmental Accounting—an Activity Based Costing (ABC) Approach," *FSN,* November 27, 2006. www.fsn.co.uk/channel_kpi_environment/environmental_accounting_an_activity_based_costing_abc_approach / (accessed August 4, 2010).
18. U.S. EPA. "An Introduction to Environmental Accounting as a Business Management Tool: Key Concepts and Terms," U.S. EPA 742-R-95-001, June 1995, pp. 4–5, 28–29; Robert J.p. Gale and Peter K. Stokoe, "Environmental Cost Accounting and Business Strategy," in Chris Madu (ed.), *Handbook of Environmentally Conscious Manufacturing* (Kluwer Academic Publishers, 2001).
19. Baxter, *2009 Sustainability Report.* http://sustainability.baxter.com/EHS/2008_environmental_financial_statement.html (accessed August 4, 2010).
20. Baxter, *2009 Sustainability Report.*
21. The Sigma Project, *The Sigma Guidelines—Toolkit: Sustainability Accounting Guide.* (London: Yachnin & Associates; Sustainable Investment Group, 2003), pp. 23–24.
22. U.S. EPA, "An Introduction to Environmental Accounting," pp. 4–5, 28–29.
23. Robert J.p. Gale and Peter K. Stokoe, "Environmental Cost Accounting and Business Strategy," p. 121.
24. Darcy Hitchcock and Marsha Willard, *The Business Guide to Sustainability: Practical Strategies and Tools for Organizations* (Earthscan, 2007), p. 217.
25. U.S. EPA, "An Introduction to Environmental Accounting," p. 7.
26. UNEP, *Guidelines for Social Life Cycle Assessment of Products,* 2009, p. 35. www.unep.org/publications/search/pub_details_s.asp?ID=4102 (accessed August 21, 2010).
27. IFAC, *Environmental Management Accounting,* pp. 30, 66; Motiva, "Development of the Material Flow Cost Accounting Standard (ISO 14051)." www.motiva.fi/en/areas_of_operation/material_efficiency/development_of_the_material_flow_cost_accounting_standard_(iso_14051) (accessed August 4, 2010).
28. IFAC, *Environmental Management Accounting,* pp. 30–31.
29. "Motiva—Development of the Material Flow Cost Accounting Standard (ISO 14051)."
30. CFO Research Services and Jones Lang LaSalle, *The Role of Finance,* p. 8.
31. CFO Research Services and Jones Lang LaSalle, *The Role of Finance,* p. 19.
32. CFO Research Services and Jones Lang LaSalle, *The Role of Finance,* p. 13.

PART FIVE. MOBILIZE: EXECUTE AND ENGAGE

CHAPTER 18. CREATE AN ACTION PLAN—AND EXECUTE

1. "U.S. Consumers, Executives Skeptical about Corporate Sustainability Commitment," *Environmental Leader,* August 12, 2010. www.environmentalleader.com/2010/08/12/u-s-consumers-executives-skeptical-about-corporate-sustainability-commitment/ (accessed November 9, 2010).
2. See the Yale Center for Business and the Environment (www.yale.edu/cbey).
3. See www.corporate-sustainability.org.

4. Author interview, October 2010.

5. Lynn Jean, "How to Conduct Internal Audits of Your Environmental Management System," *Environmental Leader*. www.environmentalleader.com/2010/08/13/how-to-conduct-internal-audits-of-your-environmental-management-system/ (accessed November 9, 2010).

6. Klaus Kleinfeld, CEO of Alcoa Inc. and the Alcoa Sustainability Leadership team, in discussion with Dan Esty, June 21, 2010.

7. Hans Wijers, CEO of AkzoNobel, personal interview. Davos, Switzerland, 2010.

CHAPTER 19. BUILD YOUR CLIMATE CHANGE PLAN

1. Dan Esty and Esty Environmental Partners worked with NetJets Europe on their climate action strategy.

2. Mark Booth statement to Dan Esty and other NetJets Europe Environmental Advisory Board members in London, September 11, 2008.

3. Daniel C. Esty and David A. Lubin, "The Sustainability Imperative: Lessons for Leaders from Previous Game-Changing Megatrends," *Harvard Business Review*, May 2010.

4. BusinessGreen, "Fresh Report Confirms Soaring Clean Tech VC Investment," August 4, 2010. www.businessgreen.com/business-green/news/2267613/fresh-report-confirms-soaring (accessed August 21, 2010).

5. U.S. EPA, "EPA Finalizes Nation's First Greenhouse Gas Reporting System," September 9, 2009. http://yosemite.epa.gov/opa/admpress.nsf/docf6618525a9efb85257359003fb69d/194e412153fcffea8525763900530d75!OpenDocument (accessed November 10, 2010).

6. U.S. SEC, "SEC Issues Interpretive Guidance on Disclosure Related to Business or Legal Developments Regarding Climate Change," January 27, 2010. www.sec.gov/news/press/2010/2010-15.htm (accessed November 10, 2010).

7. C.E.Q., "Guidance for Federal Greenhouse Gas Accounting and Reporting." www.whitehouse.gov/administration/eop/ceq/sustainability/fed-ghg (accessed November 10, 2010).

8. Greenhouse Gas Protocol, "The Greenhouse Gas Protocol Initiative." www.ghgprotocol.org (accessed November 10, 2010).

9. "Testing Completed for New GHG Protocol Standards," *Environmental Leader*, August 18, 2010. www.environmentalleader.com/2010/08/18/testing-completed-for-new-ghg-protocol-standards/ (accessed November 10, 2010).

10. "USG Corporate Sustainability Report: Sets Target to Reduce GHG Emissions 20% by 2020," *Environmental Leader*, August 5, 2010. www.environmentalleader.com/2010/08/05/usg-corporate-sustainability-report-sets-target-to-reduce-ghg-emissions-20-by-2020/ (accessed August 21, 2010).

11. "Molson Coors Sustainability Report: Water Use Up 3%, GHG Emissions Down 15%," *Environmental Leader*, July 7, 2010. www.environmentalleader.com/2010/07/07/molson-coors-corporate-sustainability-report-water-use-up-3-ghg-emissions-down-15/ (accessed August 21, 2010).

12. "Panasonic Exceeds CO_2 Reduction Targets," *Environmental Leader*, June 17, 2010. www.environmentalleader.com/2010/06/17/panasonic-exceeds-co2-reduction-targets/ (accessed August 21, 2010).

13. "Intel Cuts Emissions by 45%, Water Use Rises 3%," *Environmental Leader*, May 20, 2010. www.environmentalleader.com/2010/05/20/intel-cuts-emissions-by-45-water-use-rises-3/ (accessed August 21, 2010).

14. List based on authors' refinement of information presented in: Paul Lingl, Deborah Carlson, and the David Suzuki Foundation, *Doing Business in a New Climate: A Guide*

to Measuring, Reducing and Offsetting Greenhouse Gas Emissions (Washington DC: Earthscan, 2010).

15. Gary Hirshberg. *Stirring It Up: How to Make Money and Save the World* (Hyperion, 2008).

16. "Stonyfield Targets Cow Burps for Emissions Reductions," *Environmental Leader,* June 9, 2009. www.environmentalleader.com/2009/06/09/stonyfield-targets-cow-burps-for-emissions-reductions/ (accessed August 21, 2010).

17. "Ford to Measure Supply Chain Emissions," *Environmental Leader,* May 21, 2010. www.environmentalleader.com/2010/05/21/ford-to-measure-supply-chain-emissions/ (accessed August 21, 2010).

18. PepsiCo, "Climate Change." www.pepsico.com/Purpose/Environmental-Sustainability/Climate-Change.html (accessed August 21, 2010).

19. Author discussions with Shaklee CEO Roger Barnett and CSO Jil Zilligen in January 2010; "Climate Change," Shaklee website. www.shaklee.com/causes_climatechange.shtml (accessed August 21, 2010).

20. M. Munasinghe and others, *Consumers, Business and Climate Change.* Sustainable Consumption Institute, The University of Manchester, October 2009. www.ciesnet.com/pfiles/publications/copenhagenpaper.pdf (accessed August 21, 2010).

21. World Wildlife Fund, "Climate Savers—Mobilizing Companies to Cut Carbon Dioxide." www.worldwildlife.org/climate/climatesavers2.html (accessed July 7, 2010).

CHAPTER 20. MOBILIZE EMPLOYEES AND BUILD AND ECO-ADVANTAGE CULTURE

1. Dow Chemicals, "Dow Sustainability—Waste Reduction Always Pays (WRAP)." www.dow.com/commitments/studies/wrap.htm (accessed August 21, 2010). Further information in the paragraph based on the same source.

2. Kimberly Allen and Pamela J. Gordon, Collective "Green" Wisdom, TFI Environment, 2009. www.techforecasters.com/whitepapers/wp_gordon_Collective_Wisdom.pdf (accessed August 21, 2010), p. 4.

3. NEEF, *The Business Case for Environmental and Sustainability Employee Education,* February 2010. www.neefusa.org/BusinessEnv/white_paper_feb2010.pdf (accessed August 21, 2010), p. 9. Other citations in the paragraph based on the same source.

4. For more on "co-creation," see Venkat Ramaswamy and Francis Gouillart, *The Power of Co-Creation* (New York: Simon & Schuster, 2010).

5. Gwen Migita, Director of Sustainability & Corporate Social Responsibility, Harrah's Entertainment, in discussion with the authors, August 12, 2010.

6. Author interview, October 2010.

7. Walmart, "Wal-Mart Announces Expansion of Associate-Driven Personal Sustainability Projects," April 5, 2007. http://walmartstores.com/pressroom/news/6379.aspx (accessed August 21, 2010).

8. NEEF, *The Business Case for Environmental and Sustainability,* p. 11.

9. NEEF, *The Engaged Organization,* March 2009, p. 32.

10. NEEF, *The Business Case for Environmental and Sustainability,* p. 11.

11. NEEF, *The Engaged Organization,* p. 10.

12. Esty and Winston, *Green to Gold,* p. 232.

13. NEEF, *The Engaged Organization,* p. 30.

14. NEEF, *The Engaged Organization,* p. 33.

15. "GE Discovers Demand for Its Energy Efficiency Treasure Hunts," *GreenBiz,* July 29, 2010. www.greenbiz.com/news/2010/07/29/ge-discovers-demand-energy-efficiency-treasure-hunts (accessed August 21, 2010).

16. William McDonough and Michael Braungart, "From Inspiration to Innovation," 2002. www.mcdonough.com/writings/inspiration_innovation.htm (accessed June 23, 2010).

17. NEEF, *The Engaged Organization*, pp. 16–17, 26.

18. NEEF, *The Engaged Organization*, p. 20

19. Judith Nemes, "Leading from the Middle: The Power of the Green Champion," *GreenBiz*, October 12, 2008. www.greenbiz.com/news/2008/10/12/leading-middle-power-green-champion (accessed August 21, 2010).

20. Clive Thompson, "A Green Coal Baron?" *New York Times*, June 22, 2008.

21. InterfaceFLOR, "Toward a More Sustainable Way of Business." www.interfaceglobal.com/Sustainability.aspx (accessed August 20, 2010).

22. Darcy Hitchcock and Marsha Willard, *The Business Guide to Sustainability* (London: Earthscan, 2009), pp. 143–144.

23. Natural Step, "The Natural Step: Organizational Case Summary." www.naturalstep.it/learn/docs/cs/case_ikea.pdf (accessed August 21, 2010).

24. Judith Nemes, "Leading from the Middle."

25. NEEF, *The Business Case for Environmental and Sustainability*, p. 9.

26. Esty and Winston, *Green to Gold*, p. 222.

27. Deloitte and Kyoto Publishing, *The Sustainable Enterprise Report: Turning Awareness into Action*, April 22, 2008, p. 26.

28. Judith Nemes, "Leading from the Middle."

29. Judith Nemes, "Leading from the Middle."

30. Judith Nemes, "Leading from the Middle."

31. Stephanie Draper, Lena Staafgård, and Sally Uren, *Leader Business 2.0. Hallmarks of Sustainable Performance*, Forum for the Future, May 2008, p. 23.

32. Thomas Mine, "ConAgra Awards Sustainability-Focused Intrapreneurs," Sustainable *Life Media*, April 29, 2010. www.sustainablelifemedia.com/content/story/brands/ (accessed August 21, 2010).

33. GVEP, "EDF Sustainable Development Trophies Awards 23 Projects," August 2, 2010. www.gvepinternational.org/news/232 (accessed August 21, 2010); WBCSD, "Employee Involvement Brings Company-Wide Benefits: Electricité de France (EDF)," May 17, 2005. www.wbcsd.org (accessed August 21, 2010).

34. "Bank of America Is Offering $3000 to Employees," *Hybridautoreview,* April 18, 2010. www.hybridautoreview.net/bank-of-america-is-offering-3000-to-employees.html (accessed August 21, 2010).

35. NEEF, *The Business Case for Environmental and Sustainability*, p. 11.

36. Dawn E. Dzurilla, "Renewable Energy Firms Strike Gold with Green Employee Benefits," *EarthToys.* www.earthtoys.com/emagazine.php?issue_number=08.02.01&article=benefits (accessed August 21, 2010). See this source for other facts cited in the paragraph.

37. Richard Goode, "Employee Engagement: How IT Can Help," *Sustainable Life Media.* www.sustainablelifemedia.com/content/column/greenIT/employee_engagement_how_it_can_help (accessed August 21, 2010).

38. Judith Nemes, "Leading from the Middle."

39. Esty and Winston, *Green to Gold*, p. 220.

40. Judith Nemes, "Leading from the Middle."

41. "Corporate Incentives for Hybrids and Alternative Cars," *HybridCars*, June 8, 2008. www.hybridcars.com/corporate-incentives.html (accessed August 21, 2010).

42. Emily, "Microsoft Targets Datacenter 'Behaviors,' Not Technologies," *Sustainable Life Media*, July 10, 2008. www.sustainablelifemedia.com/content/story/greenIT/microsoft_targets_datacenter_behaviors_not_technologies (accessed August 21, 2010).

43. Richard Milne and Michael Steen, "Executive Bonuses Tied to Green Targets," *BusinessWeek*, February 24, 2010. http://bx.businessweek.com (accessed August 21, 2010).

44. Stratos Consulting, *Royal Dutch Shell—Sustainability Integration Case Study*. www.stratos-sts.com/documents/SI_Report_Case_Study_Royal_Dutch_Shell.pdf (accessed August 21, 2010). See this source for further facts cited in the paragraph.

45. Author interview, October 2010.

CHAPTER 21. ENGAGING STAKEHOLDERS

1. Daniel C. Esty and Andrew S. Winston, *Green to Gold: How Smart Companies Use Environmental Strategy to Innovate, Create Value, and Build Competitive Advantage*. (New Haven, CT: Yale University Press, 2006), p. 185.

2. Rainforest Alliance, "Profiles in Sustainable Agriculture. Chiquita Reaps a Better Banana." www.rainforest-alliance.org/profiles/documents/chiquita_profile.pdf (accessed July 7, 2010).

3. Matt Weiser, "As Freecycle Grows, Idealism and Reality Collide," Grist, May 19, 2005. www.grist.org/article/weiser-freecycle/ (accessed July 7, 2010).

4. Patagonia, "Patagonia Environmental Grants Program." www.patagonia.com/web/us/patagonia.go?assetid=2927 (accessed August 9, 2010).

5. REI, "2008 REI Stewardship Report: Community-Based Grants and National Partnerships." www.rei.com/aboutrei/csr/2008/community-based-grants-national-partnerships-recreation.html (accessed July 7, 2010); GEMI and EDF. *Guide to Successful Corporate-NGO Partnerships*. GEMI, 2008. www.gemi.org/resources/GEMI-EDF%20Guide.pdf (accessed August 6, 2010).

6. REI, "2008 REI Stewardship Report: REI Passport to Adventure." www.rei.com/aboutrei/csr/2008/rei-kids-passport-to-adventures.html (accessed July 7, 2010).

7. GEMI and EDF. *Guide to Successful Corporate-NGO Partnerships*, p. 5.

8. Author interview, October 2010.

9. World Wildlife Fund, "Mobilizing Companies to Cut Carbon Dioxide." www.worldwildlife.org/climate/climatesavers2.html (accessed July 7, 2010).

10. E2 Environmental Entrepreneurs, "About E2." www.e2.org/jsp/controller?cmd=liqabout (accessed July 7, 2010).

11. Environmental Defense Fund, "EDF Climate Corps." http://edfclimatecorps.org/page.cfm?tagID=54008 (accessed July 7, 2010).

12. Heather Tansey, "3M's Energy Management Program Presentation," *EPA*, December 2007. www.epa.gov/stateply/documents/events/dec2007/Heather_Tansey.pdf (accessed August 4, 2010).

13. Maryland Department of the Environment, "Pollution Prevention Home." www.mde.state.md.us/programs/BusinessInfoCenter/Greening%20Your%20Business%20Facility/Pages/BusinessInfoCenter/PollutionPrevention/index.aspx (accessed July 7, 2010).

14. Joel Makower, "Inside Walmart's Sustainability Consortium," Joel Makower Blog, August 16, 2009. http://makower.typepad.com/joel_makower/2009/08/inside-walmarts-sustainability-consortium.html (accessed July 7, 2010).

15. The Sustainability Consortium. www.sustainabilityconsortium.org (accessed July 7, 2010).

16. Unilever, "Sustainable Palm Oil: Unilever Takes the Lead." www.unilever.com/images/es_Unilever_PalmOil_v71_tcm13-126357.pdf (accessed July 7, 2010).

17. Starbucks Corporation, "Supporting Farmers and Their Communities." www.starbucks.com/responsibility/sourcing/farmer-support (accessed July 7, 2010).

PART SIX. OPTIMIZE: EVALUATE, REPORT, AND REASSESS

CHAPTER 22. COMMUNICATE AND REPORT RESULTS

1. Author interviews, September 2010. Esty Environmental Partners assisted Hanesbrands with its sustainability, strategy, and communications plan.
2. Steve Lydenberg, Jean Rogers, and David Wood, *From Transparency to Performance*, Hauser Center for Nonprofit Organizations, Harvard University, June 2010, p. 11.
3. Peter S. Goodman, "In Case of Emergency: What Not to Do," *New York Times*, August 21, 2010. www.nytimes.com/2010/08/22/business/22crisis.html?_r=2&hp (accessed August 22, 2010).
4. Jeffrey Hollender, "10 Things I've Learned about Building a Revolutionary Responsible Company," *GreenBiz*, June 21, 2010. www.greenbiz.com/blog/2010/06/21/10-things-ive-learned-about-building-revolutionary-responsible-company (accessed August 22, 2010).

CHAPTER 23. CELEBRATE SUCCESS AND PROMOTE CONTINUOUS IMPROVEMENT

1. Junior's Cleaners. "What We Offer." http://juniorscleaners.com/aboutjuniorscleaners.html (accessed August 6, 2010).
2. David A. Lubin and Daniel C. Esty, "The Sustainability Imperative: Lessons for Leaders from Previous Game-Changing Megatrends," *Harvard Business Review*, May 2010.

Index